WILLIAM KALUSH has been a dedicated student of the art of magic for more than twenty-five years. Founder of the Conjuring Arts Research Center and publisher of *Gibecière*, an esteemed magic history journal, he has helped create several world-famous magic stunts and prime-time network television specials.

LARRY SLOMAN is an award-winning author best known for his collaborations with radio personality Howard Stern on *Private Parts* and *Miss America*. He became interested in magic history after working with David Blaine on his best-selling memoir *Mysterious Stranger*.

The Secret Life of Houdini

THE MAKING OF AMERICA'S FIRST SUPERHERO

WILLIAM KALUSH

and

LARRY SLOMAN

POCKET BOOKS

LONDON • SYDNEY • NEW YORK • TORONTO

First published in the USA by Simon & Schuster Inc., 2006
First published in Great Britain by Pocket Books, 2007
An imprint of Simon & Schuster UK Ltd
A CBS COMPANY

1 3 5 7 9 10 8 6 4 2

Simon & Schuster UK Ltd
Africa House
64–78 Kingsway
London WC2B 6AH

www.simonsays.co.uk

Simon & Schuster Australia
Sydney

A CIP catalogue for this book is available from the British Library.

ISBN 978-1-84739-082-0

Printed and bound in Great Britain by
Cox & Wyman Ltd, Reading, Berks

For three wonderful mothers—
Cecilia Weiss, Lilyan Sloman, and Jean Kalush

From the collection of Dr. Bruce Averbook

Table of Contents

Foreword

As an amateur magician, I frequently ask members of an audience to just think of a famous magician. When I ask people to raise their hands if they happen to be thinking of Houdini, inevitably about three-quarters of the hands go up—this despite the fact that Harry Houdini died eighty years ago.

No one would be more pleased with this than Houdini himself, who, as this book illustrates, sought throughout his life to imbed his image in the world's consciousness. He did this with strenuous feats of daring that fully justify the appellation the authors apply—America's first superhero.

My own interest in magic ignited when as a child I saw the 1953 movie biography of Houdini, starring Tony Curtis and Janet Leigh. I ran immediately to my local public library and checked out what was then the only full-length biography, *Houdini: His Life Story*. It was written by Harold Kellock two years after Houdini's death, with the "recollections and documents" of the magician's wife, Beatrice. It was remarkably thorough for an authorized biography and is still a good read, but it was told, of course, from the perspective of a devoted spouse.

There have been many subsequent biographies, and the better ones have each penetrated a bit deeper below the surface of the Houdini legend. But it is hard to imagine a more difficult subject for biographers than a man who was in his time one of the world's foremost exponents of secrecy and who was determined to tell the public only those things that burnished his legend. Getting to the essence of the man—what made him tick—has been an extraordinary and almost always controversial task.

The book you now hold breaks new ground. The evidence the authors have amassed is rich in new detail about many previously charted facets of Houdini's life. More important, though, it opens a tantalizing new possibility: that

Houdini might have used his expertise—along with the access his escapes and fame gave him around the world—to advise intelligence and security services in the United Kingdom and the United States, particularly in the years just before World War I. Working with fragmentary new evidence, the authors have put together a plausible case that, as the world headed toward war, there would have been high-level interest in some of what Houdini learned while escaping from various police and security service constraints in places like Germany and Russia and dealing with many of their officials.

Houdini would undoubtedly love the fact that people will now have another set of clues to debate about his mysterious life—clues that will keep us talking about the "Master Mystifier" long into the future. In fact, I suspect that a hundred years from now the same large proportion of hands will go up for Houdini when some performer asks the audience to think of a famous magician.

Houdini always said he would do his best to come back from the dead. As far as we know, he has never succeeded. But he would probably regard the endless fascination with his life and legend as the next best thing.

John McLaughlin

Former deputy director and acting director
of the Central Intelligence Agency (2000–2004)

Introduction

HOUDINI DIDN'T DIE IN THE WATER torture cell. He didn't have a mother fixation. And he wasn't just a great showman. Eventually, all legends get cluttered by apocryphal stories, and the legend of the greatest professional master of deception is no exception. Much of what has become his story is fabrication. Ironically, the real story is better.

Seven years ago, one of us had an epiphany. It was on April 6, 1999, Houdini's 125th birthday. Bill Kalush was outside of David Blaine's first stunt, "Buried Alive." Blaine had been buried for a couple of days and since Kalush had planned the stunt with him, he felt it was only right to stand by him all day and night. At about four A.M., he noticed that some of the same people were coming back each night. They weren't friends of the magician or even acquaintances. They were strangers who were somehow compelled to come at all hours to visit a man they didn't know, concerned with his well-being. Somehow they had become emotionally attached to him. In that moment, Bill Kalush understood why we are all interested in Houdini. He, like Blaine after him, compelled us to feel for him and root for him.

A few years later Kalush met writer Larry Sloman. Sloman, a professional writer for most of his life, wrote books on topics as varied as Bob Dylan and ice hockey, and he wrote a major biography of the sixties radical Abbie Hoffman that relied on more than two hundred interviews and years of relentless digging through archival sources. As it happened, Sloman had read all of the major books about Houdini. What struck both of us was that there were huge gaps in Houdini's life story and some puzzling inconsistencies. So we embarked on a journey to discover the real man.

Early on, we discovered an important connection that most biographers had seemed to miss. The young Houdini, though stunningly creative and clever, couldn't make enough money to succeed at magic. Hungry and crestfallen, he was ready to give up his dream, until he walked into a Chicago police station and met a detective who would change his life. Immediately after this fateful encounter, his picture graced the front page of a Chicago newspaper. That picture catapulted him to renown. Within months, he had gone from cheap beer halls and dime museums to the big-time—vaudeville. In one year's time, he had gone from literally eating rabbits for survival to making what today would equal $45,000 a week. (Throughout the book, for the purposes of comparison, we have converted dollars in Houdini's time to today's values. This is a highly contentious endeavor, but we have relied on the unskilled wage conversion rate provided by www.eh.net, operated by Miami University and Wake Forest University.)

Now came the next mystery. Why would someone who had finally made it big risk everything and leave behind lucrative contracts to go to England with no real prospects in sight? Perhaps what happened to Houdini next answers the question. Within days of arriving in England, Houdini met with a prominent Scotland Yard inspector and once again, his career took off. What was going on, and why hadn't it come to light? In hindsight, Houdini made all the right moves, but at the time, they were wildly risky, even for a man who would come to be known for his death-defying stunts. Did Houdini know something that made sense of these seemingly suicidal career moves?

Before we could even begin to answer these questions, we read and reread all the books about Houdini, as well as many from the magic field in general. Cognizant that we needed primary source material, we started to gather massive piles of photocopied documents. Houdini's personal scrapbooks alone amounted to more than 17,000 pages. He was an astounding letter writer, perhaps writing as many as 150,000 letters in his life and receiving just as many. In our quest, we found thousands of pages of correspondence, but most letters have been lost to history. Oftentimes we found only one letter from an otherwise unknown intimate, knowing full well that there must have been hundreds more.

Early on, we discovered an interesting letter from a man in Scotland who was reporting to Houdini that there were rumors circulating that he was a spy. Dots started to connect, and as we answered some questions, new ones began presenting themselves.

When we looked back at why Houdini suddenly succeeded in Chicago after having done substantially the same act for years in anonymity, we found some stunning connections. The particular Chicago detective who boosted Houdini's career at a most critical point was a member of an exclusive private club. Another club member was the chief of the U.S. Secret Service. We dug and dug and discovered that the chief was also a magician, and he admitted to using magicians as operatives. Perhaps this was the opportunity Houdini had needed.

Then we found some startling new evidence about Houdini's first visit to Scotland Yard. It turned out that the inspector who he had met with was actually England's leading foreign intelligence officer, a spymaster who would go on to start England's famed MI-5.

We gathered more and more documents and found ourselves overwhelmed with data. Then we made a breakthrough in the form of Alexander, our fully text-searchable database, designed by computer genius Mike Friedman. We fed Alexander our photocopies and original books, then, in agreement with the Conjuring Arts Research Center, we scanned and digitized enormous swaths of magic history—whole runs of magazines, some of which were in circulation for more than one hundred years, and thousands of books. Alexander now contains more than 700,000 pages of magic material, with tens of thousands of references to Houdini.

Once Alexander was operational, we started to break down Houdini's life day by day, creating a timeline of every moment we could account for. Then we discovered Andrew Cook, one of the world's leading espionage experts. Cook filled in our knowledge about MI-5 and then dropped a bombshell: He had in his possession a diary of Houdini's spymaster friend from Scotland Yard. What's more, Houdini was mentioned in the diary entries.

There was, however, a fly in the ointment. Early spy records are notoriously incomplete. Spy agencies were miniscule by today's standards and relied on coopting all sorts of amateurs to ferret out information in foreign countries. These special agents were very often only given oral directions and filed oral reports. Anything that had been recorded on paper was often destroyed.

A year into our research, we were spun in a whole new direction. Through a chance meeting at an annual Houdini séance, we met a lovely young lady who happened to be the great-granddaughter of Margery, the famous Boston medium, and Houdini's nemesis. When we asked if she happened to have any of her relative's papers lying around, we were stunned that she invited us to her home and opened up a closet filled from top to bottom with scrapbooks, letters, and photographs documenting Margery's life as a medium. For more than eighty years, this material had gone unseen by any researcher. We pored over the thousands of documents and discovered the most amazing story of what really happened when Houdini took on the fraudulent Spiritualists. As a by-product, we learned a great deal about Sir Arthur Conan Doyle. Suffice it to say that he's not the genial old duffer of popular portrayals.

Now we intensified our research. We electronically searched through as many as two hundred million articles in all of the major newspapers and many minor ones. We searched through millions of census and government records that a few years ago would have required years to digest. We like to think that this is the first Houdini biography of the new digital age.

What you'll read in this text is what we surmise the story to be after reading tens of thousands of documents, chasing down thousands of leads, and making all sorts of connections. To make certain stories come alive for the reader, we've dramatized scenes using composite material, but although we occasionally shift what people said in time, we've always remained faithful to what the players said and thought. When we give you Houdini's thoughts, they are based on interviews or letters in which he's revealed them. We've made nothing up; in some cases, we've just turned the facts into dialogue.[1]

Finally, we've spent countless hours discussing with each other and the world's experts what it all means. We are happy to finally present you with the results of all our research, study, and pondering on not only what Houdini did but also who he was. We realized that the trajectory of Houdini's life was influenced by forces that lay well below the surface. All of our lives are. Did these motivations include pride? Greed? Machismo? Lust? Vanity? Love? Whatever he was seeking, did he ultimately find it?

We leave this for you to discover in the pages of *The Secret Life of Houdini*.

[1] Every fact in this book has been substantiated, but the notes are so extensive, that we have decided to publish them online instead, at www.conjuringarts.org.

The Secret Life of

Houdini

1

The Oath

THE FIRST SHOVEL-LOAD MISSED HIS TORSO and struck his neck, sending soil flying up his nostrils and into his mouth. He started choking and coughing.

"Sorry, boss," Collins said, looking down into the hole. "I guess the wind took it."

Stay calm. Conserve energy. Keep the heart rate down.

Collins and Vickery continued to fill the cavity with moist Santa Ana soil. They had been at this since a little past dawn and their arms were beginning to ache with fatigue. They could only imagine how he must feel. Subconsciously, they moved into a rhythm, one scraping his shovel into the mounds of dirt piled high around them, the other sending his payload straight down into the dank hole. Vickery thought of how his friends would react when he told them of Harry's latest stunt. Of course, that would have to wait until after it was performed. He'd never forget that oath of secrecy that he'd sworn and how seriously Harry seemed to take it.

Am I pushing myself too hard? I'm forty-one but I look fifty. I'm so gray.

Vickery began to admit to himself his concern. He had expected his boss to have no problem with the one- and even the two-foot "plantings," as he called them, and he didn't. But the four- and five-foot escapes seemed to really have taken something out of him. What if he hurt himself now, like the time he did in Buffalo? Ever since Harry had burst that blood vessel getting out of those chains, he was in such intense chronic pain he'd had to sleep with a pillow under his left kidney. Vickery never forgave himself for allowing those bastards to pull the chains so tight.

It's so much hotter down here. How can a few feet make such a difference? I'm starting to feel faint. Stay calm.

By now the dirt had almost completely covered Houdini's body. The shackles that held his ankles together were completely buried, and the content of two or three more shovelfuls would obscure the last traces of the handcuffs. He knew that his head would be covered next so he braced for the assault of the heavy soil, so as not to eat some again.

This would be so much easier if I did it in a coffin. We could gimmick a plank. I'd be able to disperse so much more soil using that instead of my bare hands. I'd be out in half the time.

As soon as he was completely covered by the soil, he began to go to work. Even though his assistants were still filling in the last of the grave, he swiftly slipped out of the cuffs, crouched into a fetal position, and began working on the leg irons. Within seconds, he was free of them too. Now all he had to do was work his way up against the loose earth, slowly, methodically, timing it so that he would be just below the ground when they had finished filling in the hole. Then he'd claw through the loose topsoil and literally escape the grave. But he didn't figure on panicking.

It wasn't the eerie darkness or the complete silence down there that horrified him; he had grown accustomed to that. It was the sudden realization that he was six feet underground—the legal requirement for corpses—that sent a chill up his spine.

What if I die here? What a field day they'd have in the papers. Houdini Digs His Own Grave. I'd be a laughingstock.

He gasped involuntarily. Now he began to claw and knee the soil without any concern that he'd get out before they had finished filling in the hole. But that momentary scare—the irretrievable mistake of all daredevils—had wasted a fraction of his breath, when every last fraction was needed to get out of the hole. Up above, Collins and Vickery and the others in the party had no idea of the drama that was unfolding four feet below them.

No! This can't be! Out! Get out! GET OUT!

All of a sudden the weight of the earth above him felt like a thousand tons. His body stiffened and for one quick second he smelled the acrid odor of death. And then, for the first time in his life, he screamed for help. But that just made it worse. There was no way they could hear him, and now he was squandering what little air and energy he had left. He started pawing at the dirt above him like a wild animal, scratching his hands and arms on the coarse soil. He had long abandoned his slow, steady rhythmic breathing and now he was operating on pure instinct, swallowing and inhaling as much soil as air in one last desperate attempt to escape.

On the ground, Collins put down his shovel and took out his watch. When it passed the ten-minute mark, he looked at Vickery with concern.

"If he's not up in thirty seconds, we better go get him," he said. Vickery nodded grimly. The clock slowly ticked off the requisite seconds, and then, just as Collins and Vickery grabbed their shovels and started to frantically dig, the earth suddenly burst open and expelled a bloody, battered, and filthy Houdini, grateful for that measure of fresh, cool, California air.

"Come, come. Push, push. It's almost over."

Anne Fleischmann was urging Cecilia Weisz on, alternately wiping her brow and giving her some ice chips to suck on. On March 24, 1874, the small room at Rákosárok utca 1. sz. had been emptied, the three young boys sent out to play. Only a few neighbors were there as Anne expertly cradled the baby's head and turned it slightly to allow the shoulders to emerge. She gently grabbed the baby's chest as the rest of the bloody body was expelled from the womb.

"Another boy!" Anne said, expertly clipping the umbilical cord and swathing the child in a clean sheet. Then she presented little Erik to his mother, who immediately nestled him to her bosom, where her heartbeat seemed to have a soothing effect on the newborn. It was a sanctuary to which he would often return, that steady heartbeat and her warm caress, a place where the woes of the world could be forgotten.

Of course, a newborn meant another mouth to feed, and another warm body to share this typically small "room-and-kitchen" flat in the predominately Jewish section of Pest, part of the newly consolidated town of Budapest, Hungary. That made four sons now for Mayer Samuel Weisz, who had recently graduated law school. One could only assume that Mayer Samuel would make a very eloquent solicitor if the story of the courtship of his future wife was any indication.

Weisz had been a recent widower, his first wife having died during or shortly after giving birth to their son Armin. Perhaps to escape the memories, he moved from the Hungarian countryside to Budapest, a thriving, tolerant, cosmopolitan city destined to become one of the great showpieces of Europe. In Pest a friend of his, in obvious homage to his charisma, asked him to intervene for him in an affair of the heart. His friend was in love with a pretty young maiden, Cecilia Steiner, but he was too shy to make his intentions known to her. Mayer Samuel, who knew Cecilia's mother and her three daughters well, took on this assignment and called upon Cecilia at the small apartment that she shared with her family. Somewhere in

Rabbi Mayer Samuel Weisz, Houdini's father. *From the collection of Tom Boldt*

A young Erik Weisz poses with baby brother Dezso in Hungary before the family migrated to the United States. *From the collection of Roger Dreyer*

the middle of his loquacious address, he realized that he was no proxy; he was expressing his own heartfelt sentiments. And Cecilia, moved, reciprocated. This verbal expression was followed with a formal written marriage proposal, a letter in which, according to family legend, Mayer Samuel documented his whole life history, "telling Her everything, so no one could ever come to Her and relate things."

They married in 1863 and by 1876 Mayer Samuel Weisz had set off for a new life in America. With Weisz already overseas, Cecilia and the five children sailed from Hamburg for New York on June 19, 1878. They traveled on the *Frisia*, a six-year-old 364-foot, three-and-a-half-thousand-ton steamship that was powered by a single screw propeller with its one smokestack supplemented by two masts. One could only imagine what memories the young boys had of this fateful trip to America. Armin, fifteen by now, was charged to help Cecilia mind the other boys for she had her hands full with little four-year-old Erik and the two-year-old Dezso. The family traveled in steerage. Cecilia's ticket cost $30 and that afforded her and her sons the privilege of being packed like cattle below the deck in a fetid, poorly lit and ventilated dormitory that held 620 people. Luckily, on this particular voyage the ship was less than half full, which allowed Cecilia to spread out over several cots instead of just one.

They arrived in New York on July 3 and were processed at the Castle Garden immigration building, where each of them received a new name. Since Cecilia didn't speak English, her responses to the officials were in German. So their names became English variants of German names. Armin became Herman, eight-year-old Natan just had an "h" added, six-year-old Gottfried Vilmos was dubbed William, Erik turned into Ehrich, and Ferencz Dezso was officially named Theo—later to be nicknamed Dash—and the family name became Weiss. Cecilia was reunited in New York with her mother and two sisters, who had emigrated earlier, but by September, the entire Weiss family was together again in Appleton, Wisconsin.

Appleton was a stark contrast to the cramped tenement buildings of New York. Only in existence for twenty-five years, it still had the feel in some ways of a frontier outpost. For the first three years of the Weisses' residence there, livestock were allowed to run free in the streets of the city. It took an additional year for a sewer system to be built and another year to get municipal water flowing (although the system was too primitive to be used above the ground floor of buildings). On the other hand, with a long established college, Lawrence University, a soon-to-open Opera House, and as a regular stop on the lecture circuit, there was a sense of culture that set Appleton apart from its sleepy farm-based small Midwestern town counterparts.

And for Mayer Samuel Weiss, it had one advantage. He was a friend of one of the town's most prominent businessmen. David Hammel was a clear example of the assimilationist spirit of many Eastern European Jews. He ran several businesses, including a lumberyard, a mill, and a wheat farm. But most of all, he was connected in local politics. Mayer Samuel Weiss came to Appleton with no knowledge of English but with a craving for respectability. Back home he had been a soap maker, but by the time they left the country he had taken law courses and was a practicing solicitor. But this was a different world, and when his friend Hammel told him that the town needed a rabbi, he didn't hesitate.

"Okay, that's me," said Mayer Samuel.

So he donned his robes and began conducting services in a makeshift temple, earning $750 a year. At first "the Hebrews of this city," as a local newspaper called them, seemed pleased with the services of their "able" rabbi and hoped that he would "remain permanently among us." His particular forte seemed to be wise words of counsel at milestone events like weddings and funerals. Even though he conducted all his ceremonies and homilies in German, his addresses commanded "the most profound respect."

Morality lessons weren't just reserved for the pulpit. When Ehrich was only five years old, his father noticed his son playing with some large iron spikes. Further inquiries disclosed that Ehrich had taken them from a local construction site where a bridge was being built.

"This is theft!" the rabbi thundered. "Theft cannot be tolerated, especially in this household, especially by the son of a rabbi."

Ehrich was ushered back to the scene of the crime, where he was forced to replace the spikes and confess his guilt to the foreman. He was a decent child, ready to learn from his mistakes and to accept the wisdom of his elders. And he certainly had a winning personality. When Ehrich was about seven, he happened upon his teacher on the streets of Appleton. She smiled and wished him

Ehrich's schoolhouse in Appleton. *From the collection of Dr. Bruce Averbook*

"good morning," but the boy just mumbled in embarrassment. The teacher looked him square in his steel-blue eyes. "When a gentleman meets a lady, Ehrich, he should take off his hat and bow." With that he took off, sprinted around the block, timing it so he would meet her at the next corner, where, to her astonishment, he doffed his cap and bowed reverentially.

With its open spaces, parks, and woods, Appleton was the ideal playground for a young child, and it was here that Ehrich began to display an athletic prowess that would blossom later in his life. It started when he was barely seven and went to see a traveling street circus that was passing through Appleton. He tolerated the clowns and the acrobats, but he was positively enthralled by a man in tights who climbed twenty feet up into the air to a small platform, where he was about to walk across a taut wire that had been stretched between two poles. Keeping his center of gravity low by using a long curved pole, Jean Weitzman, Ehrich's instant hero, began to slowly walk across that wire. Ehrich held his breath as he realized that just one small misstep would send Weitzman to an almost certain death. The fact that a performer was risking his life right in front of him was both inconceivable and thrilling. Step by step, Weitzman navigated that wire, and when he made it to the far pole, the whole crowd cheered. But Ehrich was even more amazed when he saw Weitzman perform a routine where he suspended himself from the high wire by his teeth.

That afternoon Ehrich rushed home, scrounged up some rope, and tied it between two trees an appropriate distance apart. The first time he tried to balance on the rope, he fell to the ground so violently that he could barely get up again. But he persevered and soon was adept at walking the tightrope. His replication of hanging by the teeth was not quite as successful. He hadn't realized that Weitzman used a mouthpiece for that feat. "Out came a couple of front teeth," Houdini remembered, "but luckily they grew back again."

These early years in Appleton were, in retrospect, idyllic years for the Weisses. There were two new additions to the family, a boy Leopold, and finally, a girl named Gladys. In June of 1882, Mayer Samuel and his children embraced their new country by becoming citizens of the United States. Then disaster struck. Rabbi Weiss's congregation revolted, with a faction believing that he was too old and too antiquated in his ways for their tastes.

"One morning my father awoke to find himself thrown upon the world, his long locks of hair having silvered in service, with seven children to feed, without a position, and without any visible means of support," Houdini said. "We thereon moved to Milwaukee, Wis., where such hardships and hunger became our lot that the less said on the subject the better."

Settling in Milwaukee in December of 1882, the Weisses became almost nomadic; at least four addresses in four years suggested that they were keeping one step ahead of the rent collector. The boys were all put to work; Ehrich sold newspapers in front of the Plankington House and shined shoes. Some days his younger brother Theo would assist him. One day, the two boys accumulated more than $2, which Theo deposited in the pocket of his overcoat. They caught a ride home on a sled and on arrival discovered that Theo had lost the change. Cecilia was near tears, but Ehrich quickly conceived a plan to remedy the damage. He grabbed Theo and with his last nickel in hand, they went to a nearby florist shop. He bought a flower, went outside, and quickly sold it for a dime. They marched back to the florist shop and bought two flowers and this time both boys sold theirs for a dime. A few hours later they were back home with a fresh $2 in change, the fruits of the nine-year-old's resourcefulness.

Ehrich Weiss hadn't even made a dent in the heavy handcuffs when the hacksaw blade snapped in two—for the sixth time—which did not amuse the unusually large, repellently ugly man who had the misfortune of currently being fettered by those resilient manacles.

"You're lucky that blade didn't cut me up," the man snarled ominously.

Ehrich swallowed hard. He didn't want to show that he was scared, never wanted to do that, but he was. He didn't even know if it was possible to saw through the cuffs and he certainly didn't want to disappoint his boss, Mr. Hanauer. Ehrich had been a fixture at Hanauer's shop on Appleton Street since he was a little kid living around the corner. It wasn't the guns that Hanauer sold; those didn't really interest him. Ehrich was fascinated by the locks. He had always been intrigued by all types of locks and fasteners and hardware, practicing at home by opening the drawers, closets, and pantries of his house at will, using a small buttonhook. He had become notorious in Appleton as the boy who had unlocked all the doors to the shops on College Avenue one night. Now that he had turned eleven, and since things were so hard in Milwaukee, his parents had decided to send Ehrich back to Appleton to start a formal apprenticeship with Hanauer.

But this was baptism by fire. The sheriff had come into the shop one day, with a behemoth of a prisoner in tow. He was the scariest and ugliest person Ehrich had ever seen—sporting a bristly beard punctuated by a long, ominous-looking blue-white scar.

"John, for some unknown reason, the justice found this here feller innocent as charged, but my damn key broke off in the lock," the sheriff explained. "Think you can saw through this?"

Just as Hanauer started examining the cuffs, he realized it was lunch time. He called Ehrich aside.

"Ehrie, get a hacksaw and cut that handcuff off. I'm going out for a drink with the sheriff."

Hanauer was known to throw back a few beers at lunch, a daily ritual that usually took him fifty-five minutes, but with ten minutes left Ehrich still hadn't gotten the bracelets off.

The hacksaw was out of the question. He couldn't smash the cuffs off. In fact, he wasn't too comfortable about being in a store alone with this guy and a case full of handguns and derringers, even if he was handcuffed. Then, suddenly, he remembered his buttonhook. Ehrich had customized it over the years, and it had proved infallible in opening the occasional door or desk drawer. Why not use it on a handcuff lock? They were more sophisticated but maybe, just maybe . . .

But no, it was too big. Unperturbed, he fashioned another one out of piano wire. The giant man eyed him with suspicion.

He slowly inserted the pick into one of the cuff locks.

"Can you just look away for a second?" Ehrich asked politely. The last thing he wanted was for this guy to see how he was going to open the cuffs.

"Like hell I can," the giant said. And he almost stared a hole in the cuffs.

Ehrich had no choice. Fumbling from nerves, he awkwardly stuck his pick in the mechanism of the cuff. And, to both his and the prisoner's amazement, after about a minute, the cuff clicked open. It took him half the time to get the other cuff open.

To Ehrich's great relief, the sheriff and Hanauer entered the shop just then.

"Well, you're free to go. But if I was you, I'd put a little distance between myself and the great municipality of Appleton," the sheriff said.

The giant was too stunned to move. He picked up the cuffs and examined them. It was then that the other men realized that Ehrich hadn't sawed through them. He had figured out a way to defeat them.

Hanauer took the cuffs from the prisoner and gave them the once-over. He turned to his apprentice.

"That is good work, Ehrich," he said. "That is damned good work."

This trivial incident would change the whole course of Ehrich's life. "The very manner in which I then picked the lock of the handcuff contained the basic principle which I employed in opening handcuffs all over the world. *Not with a duplicate key*, which seems to have been the only way others had of duplicating my performance." But in doing so, Houdini gave his secret away to the prisoner. "He is the only person in the world beside my wife who knows how I open locks, and I have never heard from him since," he remembered.

Working in a locksmith's shop wasn't really in Ehrich's blood. He still idolized Weitzman, the high-wire wizard. So when Jack Hoeffler, an Appleton friend who was a few years older than him, decided to put on a five-cent circus, Ehrich convinced his mother to darn him long red woolen stockings to simulate the proper tights that professional acrobats wore. He was billed as "Ehrich, the Prince of the Air," and his act probably consisted of swinging from ropes and doing contortionist feats and acrobatic tumbling on an old field in the Sixth Ward that Hoeffler had located.

Houdini always marked the October 28, 1883 Jack Hoeffler 5-Cent Circus performance as his legitimate entrance into show business. He earned thirty-five cents. But more important, he was continuing to develop the skill sets that would serve him well in the future. By 1919, Houdini could look back on this sandlot performance as another turning point. "My training as a contortionist was, of course, the first step toward my present occupation of escaping from strait-jackets and chains, for it is chiefly through my ability to twist my body and dislocate my joints, together with abnormal expansion and contraction powers, which renders me independent of the tightest bonds. Thus, to any young man who has in mind a career similar to mine, I would say: 'First try bending over backward and picking up a pin with your teeth from the floor.' . . . That was *my* first stunt."

With the show business bug running through his veins, Ehrich "made a bolt for the door" and returned to his family in Milwaukee. It wasn't a far stretch for his interests to widen from gymnastics and acrobatics to magic. Young Ehrich was a voracious reader, thanks largely to the influence of his father, who had a most impressive library of theology books. He began by devouring the biblical tales and the Talmudic legends in the rabbi's collection, but the first book that he purchased himself was a ten-cent pamphlet, "pilfered from the pages of a magician named Hoffma[n]," that he found in a small bookshop in Appleton. Now back in Milwaukee, he began to frequent the public library, reading books at random, exploring the boundaries of his inquisitive mind.

Dr. Lynn was a magician and a good one. His thrice-daily shows at London's famous Egyptian Hall had captured the imagination of the British public. Lynn performed many of the then-standard effects—decapitation and restoration of a pigeon, spiritualistic table-rappings, rope ties, and aerial suspensions—but what set Dr. Lynn apart from his contemporaries was his marvelous stage patter. Lynn would crack deadpan jokes, tell long shaggy dog anecdotes, slyly insult volunteers from the audience, all the time diverting the audience's attention from the effect he was performing. After thus mystifying the crowd, he'd solemnly pronounce, "That's how it's done," which had become an instant catchphrase in England.

So when Dr. Lynn came to Milwaukee during a U.S. tour, Rabbi Weiss, cognizant of Ehrich's budding interest in magic, brought his twelve-year-old to the show. The effect that forever changed the young boy had the grandiose title of "Palingenesia."

Dr. Lynn solemnly announced that he was going to "cut somebody into pieces." At this, a somber-looking young man appeared onstage, carrying a large scimitar in his right hand and a black cloth over his left arm. He could have easily been mistaken for an executioner.

Dr. Lynn kept up a steady stream of patter, maintaining that he was working "strictly in the interests of science to expand our knowledge and to show that a man might be decapitated and then be as good as new, once his head is restored."

He turned and gestured to an assistant near the rear of the stage.

"Here is a young man who came with me from England. He isn't of much use, so I might as well cut him up."

An upright board with two thick cords hanging from hooks was set up at the back of the stage. A screen was pulled in front of the board and Dr. Lynn invited two volunteers to go behind the screen and watch him tie up his assistant. They did and then the screen was pulled aside and the audience saw the assistant facing them, standing with his back to the board, the two cords tied around his body. The two volunteers, at Lynn's urging, confirmed to the audience that they saw the man being tied up. And to suggest that this was no illusion, the trussed-up assistant stroked his mustache, moved his foot, and briefly spoke to the audience.

Then Dr. Lynn went into action. "What will you have?" he asked one young volunteer. "A wing, eh?" He poised his scimitar over the hapless assistant's left arm, and, as the ladies in the audience covered their eyes with their handkerchiefs, he lopped the whole arm off and carried it over to the seated young volunteer and placed it on his lap.

"And you?" He turned to the other volunteer. "What will you have? A leg, eh?" And he severed his assistant's left leg, again bloodlessly, and handed it to that volunteer.

"Now I'll cut off his head," he screamed and, throwing the black cloth over the victim's head, he slashed at the neck with his scimitar, and bundled it up into his black cloth. Now he advanced on the footlights.

"What lady desires the head?" he said mournfully.

There were no takers. He waited a second and then shrugged.

"Well then, I'll throw it away," he said and opened the cloth. It was empty. Back at the board, the headless torso, with his one good arm, pointed toward the doctor and then toward the vacant spot where his head had once resided.

Dr. Lynn moved back in front of the half-man. "He wants his head," the doctor said calmly and threw the black cloth over the torso. When he pulled it away, his assistant's head had been restored, and the man rubbed at his eyes as if he had been asleep.

Lynn tossed the arm and the leg into the enclosure and pulled the curtain back over it. "There, put yourself together."

He had just gotten the words out of his mouth when the man stepped out from behind the screen, wholly restored. And then the theater's curtain dropped.

Ehrich sat there, too numb to talk. Rabbi Weiss smiled at him.

"Did you enjoy that?" the rabbi wondered.

The two of them got up and started walking out of the theater. Ehrich had read about magic and even fantasized about what a real wizard could do, but this was different. This was real.

"I *really* thought that the man's arm, leg, and head were being cut off," he told his father, and he kept walking in silence, visions of magic dancing through his head.

It wasn't out of character for Rabbi Weiss to take his son to see a magician perform. He would often regale young Ehrich with stories of another great conjurer, whose elegant demeanor and brilliant showmanship had propelled him to such wealth and fame that his portrait still hangs on the wall of a national museum in Austria. The rabbi described his wondrous magic, but he also was able to relate to his son intimate details of the magician's life off the stage. And why not? His first marriage had made him the great Compars Herrmann's first cousin. Compars was the most famous magician of his time. He had performed at the White House, and presented his illusions before the royalty of almost every country in Europe. The idea of becoming a professional magician had not crystallized in young Ehrich's mind, although he did begin to perform simple

Compars Herrmann. *Conjuring Arts Research Center*

magic on amateur nights at the old Litt Museum on Grand Avenue in Milwaukee. Developing his magical skills had to take a back- seat to helping his family through very difficult times. Rabbi Weiss could never get a full-time position with a congregation in Milwaukee, and his private "Hebrew school," which operated out of his home and probably consisted of tutoring a few youngsters, was a dismal failure. Cecilia was forced to repeatedly apply to the Hebrew Relief Society for such bare necessities as coal and cash for provisions.

Ehrich was always ready to help the family. His industriousness and maturity beyond his years were evidence of the strong work ethic that his parents had instilled in him. Years later, he would write to his friend Jim Bard and proudly recall a school song that had become a credo to him:

Keep working, tis wiser then waiting aside,
Or crying, or wailing and awaiting the tide.
In Lifes earnest battle those only prevail
Who daily march onward, and NEVER SAY FAIL

In December of 1885, the family suffered a horrific blow when Herman, Mayer Samuel's son from his first marriage, died in New York from tuberculosis at the age of twenty-two. Herman's death sent the rabbi into a tailspin. He became bedridden, sick with grief, but he was profoundly impressed when his eleven-year-old son Ehrich offered up his life savings of $10 to pay for his half brother's funeral.

The rabbi remained disconsolate for months. Ehrich was about to turn twelve and he felt that there were no opportunities for him in Milwaukee. He wanted to strike out in the world to seek his fortune, and then, of course, share it with his family. On the boy's birthday, his father called him to his bedside.

"My boy, I am poor in this world's goods, but rich in the wonderful woman God gave as my wife and your mother—rich also in the children we have brought into the world and raised to sturdy manhood," he said gently. He took a well-worn book of the Torah from his bed stand and handed it to Ehrich.

"Promise me, my boy, that after I am gone your dear Mother will never want for anything. Promise that you will make her declining days as carefree and comfortable as I have tried to make them."

Ehrich bowed his head and placed his hand on the holy book.

"I promise. With all my heart and soul," he said.

And with that promise on his twelfth birthday, a year before his Bar Mitzvah, Ehrich became a man.

He was gone before dawn, making sure not to wake anyone in the house. He had a small bag packed with the essential accoutrements of a twelve-year-old boy—some books, his lockpick, a deck of playing cards. He also carried his shoeshine kit to finance his trip into the wider world. Ehrich had heard the U.S. Cavalry was on their way westward, and it was a perfect opportunity for him to strike out from home and follow real-live soldiers, shining their black leather boots for spare change.

When the cavalry got to Delavan, Wisconsin, they encamped at the town armory. Curious to see "army life" firsthand, a young local boy named Al Flitcroft tiptoed up the steps of the armory building but was shocked when he got to the top of the stairs and found a bushy-haired, disheveled ragamuffin fast asleep on a pile of old burlap bags. Soon, the young hobo was awake and regaling Al with his tales of travel. When he mentioned that he was starving, Al suggested that they go back to his South Sixth Street house, where his mom could feed them.

The visitor introduced himself as "Harry White" (an indication that at least one Weiss knew how to assimilate in this country). Hannah Flitcroft, who had

Houdini poses with the Flitcrofts, a Delavan, Wisconsin, couple who took him in when he ran away from home at age twelve. *Library of Congress*

two sons of her own, was captivated by this charming, curly-headed little urchin, and she immediately began a makeover. He was fed, bathed, and his filthy, ragged trousers were washed and patched. The guest was shrewd enough to claim that the warm, soft bed that Mrs. Flitcroft tucked him into was the first one he could ever remember occupying.

The cavalry left town but at Mrs. Flitcroft's insistence, Harry (which was a logical variant of his nickname "Ehrie") stayed with the family and looked for work. Pickings were slim for a twelve-year-old then, so she suggested he try nearby Beloit. She packed a bag full of sandwiches and slipped him some money, and Harry hopped a freight train for the bigger city. After a few days of fruitless searching, and without funds, he walked the twenty-five miles back to Delavan. When Mrs. Flitcroft asked him if he had received a letter of encouragement that she had mailed to him care of General Delivery in Beloit, Harry left the next day, again on foot, and walked to Beloit and back, just to retrieve the first letter that anyone had ever sent him.

Harry would never forget the kindness that "old" Mrs. Flitcroft (to the young boy, the forty-five-year-old mother was ancient) had tendered to him. When he settled in New York about a year later and held down a paying job, he sent her a blouse that had a dollar bill tucked into each of its four pockets, with another single pinned to the front. He'd often send her beautiful presents from around the world and when, years later, he had returned from Europe and received word from Al that his mother was gravely ill, Harry and his wife rushed to Delavan to see Mrs. Flitcroft, who died shortly after his visit. Harry's love for his own mother spurred him to embrace motherhood in all its varieties.

While Harry set out to seek his fortune, Rabbi Weiss left his family behind and traveled east, looking for work. His dutiful heir apparent joined him there sometime in 1887. Ehrich and his father shared a room in Mrs. Leffler's boardinghouse at 244 East Seventy-ninth Street in Manhattan. The rabbi's meager income from tutoring Hebrew students was far from sufficient to bring his family to New York so Ehrich was compelled to get a job as a messenger boy. Apparently Harry believed that his oath to provide for his family wouldn't have to wait until Mayer Samuel's demise. By 1888 they had saved enough to rent their own second-floor cold-water flat in a tenement building at 227 East Seventy-fifth Street and reunite the family. Ehrich met them at Grand Central Station and escorted them to their new home.

Even though both Mayer Samuel and Cecilia were more comfortable in a large city, life was anything but easy. The first winter was a harsh one. They not only ran out of coal but the landlord was threatening eviction also, if the rent wasn't paid in a few days. Rabbi Weiss was distraught but helpless, pacing up and down the room, reduced to murmuring, "The Lord will provide. The Lord will provide." Not content to rely on divine intervention, Harry, realizing that the Christmas season had already put people in the holiday spirit, went to his messenger job the next day with a neatly printed sign pinned on his hat:

Christmas is coming,
Turkeys are fat,
Please drop a quarter
In the messenger boy's hat.

All day long, passersby read the message and laughed and deposited their silver into his hat. Before he got home, he hid the coins up his sleeves, behind his ears, in his shirt collar, everywhere he could find. When he walked in the door, he marched up to his mother.

"Shake me, I'm magic," he said.

She was dubious, but she complied, and the coins cascaded down from all parts of his body. The more she shook, the more money showered down, and the better her spirits. When the coins were all counted, there was almost enough to pay the rent.

Harry Weiss, prior to becoming Houdini, was a track star and amateur boxer in New York.
Library of Congress

Harry showed the same ingenuity when he temporarily found himself unemployed. Applying for a job at Richter's necktie company on Broadway, he saw a long line of hopefuls behind a sign that read: "Assistant Necktie Cutter Wanted." With brash confidence, he walked up and removed the sign.

"Thank you for coming, but I regret to inform you that this position has been filled," he said in his most officious manner.

After the applicants dispersed, Harry entered the building, sign in hand, and was immediately hired.

In New York, Harry expanded his athletic interests. Besides gymnastics, he began to box, and by the time he was seventeen, he was tough enough to compete for the 115-pound boxing championship of the Amateur Athletic Union, oftentimes a segue to a professional boxing career. Illness intervened and knocked him out of the finals, but he had already defeated the boy who would go on to win the medal. He also took up long-distance running, and when he was eighteen, he set a record for the run around Central Park. Around the same time, he defeated Sidney Thomas, an English champion, in a twenty-mile race. Thomas would later set world records for ten-, fifteen-, and twenty-mile races.

By 1890, thanks to the income from Harry and his brothers, the family was able to move to a larger apartment at 305 East Sixty-ninth Street. Harry continued to maintain an interest in magic in New York, but its practice, beyond card or coin magic, was severely limited by his lack of funds. He learned some coin effects from his brother Theo, who in turn had learned them from his boss, a photographer. In the spring of 1889, Jacob Hyman, a coworker at Richter's, discovered their shared enthusiasm for magic, and they began to practice together. Harry's technical knowledge was growing; his friends would be irritated at him when they would attend a magic performance and at the end of every effect, Harry would blurt out, "I know how he does that." They challenged him to go onstage and do them himself and he did, performing card and coin effects at neighborhood venues like Schillerbund Hall and for the Literary Society of the Young Men's Hebrew Association, where he billed himself as either "Ehrich Weiss" or "Eric the Great."

Then he found the book that changed his life and the entire art of magic, *Memoirs of Robert-Houdin, Ambassador, Author and Conjurer, Written by Himself.*

He bought the book and that evening, after dinner, sat by his bed and read the life story of the man who had elevated magic to an art form.

Harry read on late into the night, identifying with this picaresque chronicle of a life in magic. Much like Harry would, Robert-Houdin became obsessed with reading about magic, and constantly worked on coin and card manipulations, even during his meals when he'd practice with one hand while eating soup with the other. Then after jumping off a train, delirious from a bout of food poisoning, Robert-Houdin was rescued by an old conjurer named Torrini, who initiated him into the magical arts. Harry soaked in Robert-Houdin's account of his wonderful exhibitions called the "Soirées Fantastiques" held at his own theater in Paris in 1845. Wine bottles poured any drink the audience would desire and in inexhaustible amounts. Orange trees grew and blossomed before the audience's eyes. A small, mechanical automaton of a baker would dart inside his store to fetch actual pastries. Robert-Houdin's son would be blindfolded yet still be able to identify objects in the possession of audience members, then, thanks to his father's discovery of a new property of ether, a quantity of the anesthetic would be inhaled by him until he was rendered so light-headed that he could actually be suspended horizontally in midair supported by only a cane.

Then there were the accounts of the royal entertainments. Harry was particularly taken with a demonstration before King Louis Philippe and his family at his palace at St. Cloud. Robert-Houdin began by borrowing several handkerchiefs from his audience. He bundled them into a small packet and placed them on the table in front of him. He then asked the royal assemblage to write on a slip of paper a destination where they would desire these handkerchiefs to be magically transported. The king would pick three of these slips at random and then choose the final destination for the bundle. He selected the three. The first locale was under one of the candelabras on the mantelpiece, which he rejected because it was too obvious a hiding place. The second was the dome of the Invalides, which was also rejected because it was much too far away for the entire group to go. The last slip suggested that the handkerchiefs be transported into the planter of the last orange tree on the right of the road leading to the chateau.

The king picked that last option and immediately dispatched guards to secure the spot. But it was too late. Robert-Houdin took the parcel containing the handkerchiefs and placed it under a bell of opaque glass. Then, waving his wand, he implored that the parcel should go directly where the king desired. He then raised the glass bell and the package was gone, replaced by a white turtledove. Louis Philippe then ordered one of his servants to open that last planter and bring back whatever might be there. The man returned shortly with a small rusted iron coffer. The king then mockingly inquired whether the handkerchiefs were in the box. Robert-Houdin replied that not only were they in the box but also had been there for sixty years.

When asked for proof of that wild assertion, Louis-Phillipe was told to open the box using the key, which was on a string affixed to the neck of the turtledove. When the box was opened, the first thing the monarch saw was a yellowed parchment. He read it aloud:

This day, the 6th of June, 1786, this iron box, containing six handkerchiefs, was placed among the roots of an orange tree by me, Balsamo, Count of Cagliostro, to serve in performing an act of magic, which will be executed on the same day sixty years hence before Louis Philippe of Orleans and his family.

Of course, when he opened the parcel within, it contained the handkerchiefs.

Cecilia woke up the next morning to a startling sight. Harry was sitting in the same position as the previous night, with his clothes still on, lost in the pages of that book he had brought home. "My interest in conjuring and magic and my enthusiasm for Robert-Houdin came into existence simultaneously. From the moment that I began to study the art, he became my guide and hero," he wrote later. "I accepted his writings as my text-book and my gospel. . . . To my unsophisticated mind, his 'Memoirs' gave to the profession a dignity worth attaining at the cost of earnest, life-long effort."

Harry began amassing what eventually would become one of the greatest libraries of magic ever assembled. In that library were Robert-Houdin's other books, where he presented his theories on the art of magic, theories that would have a great impact on Houdini. Robert-Houdin believed that a magician is not merely a juggler, or someone who does tricks. For him, a magician is an actor playing the part of a man who has supernatural powers. Further, that even though fundamentally what a performer says during his performance is a "tissue of lies," he has to believe it himself for it to be successful. Is it a coincidence that around this time, Harry began to study acting and debate at the Edwin Forrest Amateur Dramatic Association on Columbia Street?

It was certainly no coincidence how he chose his stage name. His friend and sometime partner in amateur performances, Jacob Hyman, told Harry that adding the letter "i" to a person's name in the French language means "like" that person. And since "I asked nothing more of life than to become in my profession 'like Robert-Houdin,'" the transformation was complete. Ehrich Weiss was now Harry Houdini.

On April 3, 1891, he gave notice at Richter's, but on the advice of his friend and fellow runner Joe Rinn, he got a letter from H. Richter, commending his two-and-a-half-year service, "cheerfully recommend[ing] him as an honest, industrious young man."

Harry and Jacob Hyman joined forces at first as "The Brothers Houdini." Their first show was in the fall of 1891, doing inexpensive magic effects (disappearing silks, appearing flowers) as well as card work and a trunk escape. The bookings were scarce. At times, Harry would play solo engagements. In the spring, Harry talked his way into a job at Huber's Museum on Fourteenth Street. Surrounded by circus sideshow acts, he did some card magic, but more important, he met George Dexter, an Australian magician who was managing Huber's. Dexter was what was known as an "inside talker," and his wonderful patter was displayed through his role of master of ceremonies. Just as important for Houdini, he was a master of rope-tie escapes, and he taught Harry the rudiments of the art.

The original Brothers Houdini didn't last. Harry and Jacob argued, and Hyman decided to dissolve the partnership. Jacob's brother Joe filled in for the few bookings that had already been contracted. Now Harry brought his brother Theo into the act. Theo had been working for Johnson and Co. and had saved $26 at the Citizen Savings Bank on the Bowery and was only too willing to invest that princely sum into the act.

With bookings few and far between, Harry took any available work. In October of 1892, he was performing at a downtown dime museum doing twenty shows a day. The admission, which included seeing all the other acts on the bill, was five cents. That particular day, he was on the barker's platform, pulling people into the show, when a little boy came rushing up to him.

"Hey, magician, go on home. Your father's dying," he yelled.

Rabbi Weiss had recently undergone an operation for cancer. He had returned home from the hospital, but his prognosis was grim. This was the news that Harry had dreaded to hear.

Dressed in his stage costume, he ran inside the building to the dressing room, threw on a robe, borrowed every penny he could to add to what change he had, and rushed out. He hailed a passing cab. The sound of the horse's hooves on the pavement paralleled the beating of his heart. It seemed like it took forever to travel the sixty blocks. Now he was running up the five floors to his apartment, three steps to a stride.

He burst through the door and went straight to his parents' room. His father was lying in bed, head propped up by a pillow, but his eyes were closed. He was emaciated and his skin had the pallor of impending death. Cecilia was sitting next to the bed, rocking and muttering in German. Every few seconds, she would look at her husband and start sobbing. Harry's brothers Nat, William, Theo, and Leopold were clustered around the bed, along with his little sister, Gladys, but they all looked helpless and lost.

It was clear to Rabbi Weiss that his son Ehrich, while not the eldest, was by far the most responsible, creative, and compassionate of his brood. It was Ehrich who he would charge with the responsibility of providing for the family and becoming the head of household.

Harry went straight to his father's side.

"Papa, Papa, it's Ehrich," he said.

His father slowly opened his eyes. He smiled wanly.

"My Ehrich," he said, his voice a weak, hoarse rasp.

Ehrich leaned over and kissed him. Underneath his beard, the rabbi's skin was cold and clammy.

A thousand thoughts cascaded through Harry's brain. He remembered seeing his father for the first time in the United States, realizing how much he had missed him those two years. And he remembered Appleton and his parents laughing and drinking coffee in the park and watching him and his brothers playing. Then he remembered his father's sudden dismissal and the toll it took on him. Papa never recovered from that incident, and in the eyes of the world, his father was a man out of time and place, but he knew better. No, Mayer Samuel never attained worldly goods, but he was never interested in them. He was a man of God, and he lived his life in strict accordance with the books that lined his cluttered bookshelves, filled with the sayings of the fathers. Ehrich sat for hours upon hours with his father, listening to him read the tales from the Talmud, and it was there that they both had attained a world of good. They learned about compassion and justice and charity and of the importance of doing the correct thing, even if it meant self-sacrifice. But these thoughts were eclipsed when his father leaned toward him and implored, "You must never forget your promise."

Ehrich nodded. And then Rabbi Mayer Samuel Weiss turned to his wife of twenty-eight years and held out his hand. Cecilia softly cradled his hand in hers, massaging it with small, delicate circular motions.

"Don't worry, Mamma," the rabbi said in a whisper that was almost inaudible. "Ehrie will pour gold in your apron someday."

From the collection of Kenneth M. Trombly

2

Starving for a Living

THE CROWD, PART OF THE THRONG attending the nearby world's fair, the Columbian Exposition of 1893, surrounded the small, dark-skinned yogi wearing the flowing robes of his native land. He had just sat down on a mat, carrying a bag stuffed with the tools of his mystic trade and a pot containing some earth.

Sitting cross-legged, he spread the earth on the mat. Then he reached into the bag and brought out what looked like the forearm of a girl, charred at one end. He began to fondle it with a strange devotion.

"In order to have power to manipulate the natural stages of life, one must possess the arm that directs such processes. In the East, we would be helpless to conjure up what we desire without this talisman," he said.

Then he reached into his bag and removed an odd-shaped bottle containing water and a perforated box.

"The elementary ingredients of life—water in the bottle, and the mango tree powder which will cause our seed to grow into a beautiful tree."

He pulled some seeds out of the bag and spread them into the earth. Then he handed the empty bag to the audience for examination, who confirmed that there was nothing in the bag.

The yogi carefully sprinkled some of the powder and then doused it with a few drops of water. Then he passed his hands over the soil and began a strange chant.

"Goly, goly, chelly gol," he sang.

At that moment, another dark-complexioned man dressed in a white burnoose, who had been standing off to the side, began to twang on his small lyre.

The yogi covered the earth with a red cloth as he continued chanting. Peeking under the cloth, he frowned.

"Please, please, plant. Blossom into your beautiful splendor," he said and resumed his chant.

But nothing happened. Now he chanted louder and with some annoyance.

"Goly, goly, chelly job, chelly job," he intoned and then started chirping like a bird.

The audience looked mystified. The lyre player started strumming with more intensity. The yogi reached under the cloth and sprinkled more powder on the earth. Again he sang, chanting in time to the sonorous sound of the lyre.

"It's coming, it's coming!" he said and made quick passes with his hand over the cloth. A smile suddenly crossed his face and he threw back the red cloth with childish delight. There were two separate sprouts, each five inches in height. The crowd gasped.

The yogi invited the audience members to feel the sprouts, to ascertain that they were real. A few spectators stepped up and confirmed this.

Again he covered the sprouts and resumed his singing. And after more applications of powder and more hand passing and more lyre playing, and some more frowns, finally he cackled with delight and threw the cloth to the side, revealing two mature mango trees, thirty inches high.

The crowd applauded and threw change into the hat of the lyre player, who made the rounds. And when the throng dispersed, Harry Houdini and his brother Theo went into their tent to divvy up the proceeds.

Houdini was desperate to make a living as an entertainer, and if that meant dressing up as a Hindu conjurer and charming a snake or performing the Indian basket (where the yogi puts a small boy into a basket that barely contains him, closes the lid, and then pierces the basket repeatedly with his sword), then so be it.

The Houdinis wouldn't have made the pilgrimage to Chicago if it hadn't been for a twenty-two-year-old native son named Sol Bloom. Initially the plans for the fairgrounds next to the world's fair were quite tasteful. Conceived by a Harvard professor, the intent was that a leisurely stroll down the grounds would be a reenactment of the evolution of mankind—beginning in Africa, spanning the Near and Far East, and culminating in Europe.

But then Bloom got involved. He had a P. T. Barnum–like sense for the bizarre and the spectacular and had made a name for himself by managing a theater in San Francisco. When the Harvard professor faltered, Bloom was brought in. Exhibitions of peasant cheese production went by the wayside, and acrobats, fire-eaters, and belly dancers were hired. Lots of belly dancers. Bloom

The Midway Plaisance at the Columbian Exposition of 1893, as viewed from the giant Ferris wheel. *From the collection of Jim Steinmeyer*

even wrote a song for them, a ditty that became a standard for the suggestive dance craze that would be known as "Hoochy-Koochy."

Bloom was also a magician, so the word got out in the magic community that if you got to Chicago that summer, you might get to pocket some of the change that the millions of tourists would leave behind. The Brothers Houdini stayed on the fairgrounds for about a month, until Harry dispatched his younger brother home and moved across town to take some solo work at Kohl and Middleton's Dime Museum. Dime museums were among the lowest rungs of show business, usually large rooms where long stages had been partitioned off to exhibit several entertainers at once. Often the most popular of these entertainers were the freaks and other curious aberrations of the human form.

Houdini had worked at Kohl and Middleton's before, and he could count on periodic work from Mr. Hedges, the manager. Now that Theo had gone, Houdini's turn consisted of simple magic effects and some card work. It was routine work, a chance to earn some shekels before returning to New York, but his return to Kohl's reminded him of an invaluable lesson he had learned on that same stage.

During his last appearance there, Houdini had been on the bill with a woman named Mattie Lee Price. Mattie was only twenty-two years old, barely ninety pounds, and had the sickly appearance of a "consumptive." Yet this weakling was able to perform feats requiring such superhuman strength and endurance that most of the people who witnessed them were convinced that she had assistance from either good spirits or the devil himself. As wondrous as these feats appeared, Houdini, who knew they were done using subtle leverage techniques, attributed her sensational notices to the management of her husband, Mr. White, who was a brilliant salesman and showman and whose verbal eloquence "'sold' the act as no other man has sold an act before or since." During the engagement, Miss Price's affections were alienated by a circus grifter who had come between the symbiotic pair. By the next stop, Milwaukee, White was gone and the grifter was now Mattie's new lecturer. He was a far better womanizer than a showman, and by the time Houdini had returned to Kohl's, Mattie's star had permanently dimmed in the celestial sky of show business.

Houdini learned an important lesson here. For variety artists to win over an audience, the performance itself must be amplified by other variables like presentation. The audience comes to the show essentially unprepared. What's different about this performance? Is this the first time it's ever been done? Is it particularly hard to do? Showmanship is the element that provides the context for the audience to understand what they're seeing. It's a way of making a performance exceptional. That was Mr. White's genius—the ability to contextualize his wife's performance in a grandiose way.

"This was one of the most positive demonstrations I have ever seen of the fact that showmanship is the largest factor in putting an act over. Miss Price was a marvelous performer, but without her husband-lecturer she was no longer a drawing card, and . . . her act was no longer even entertaining," Houdini realized.

You couldn't walk ten steps down the Bowery without hearing about it.

"Da Houdinis are putting Risey in the box tonight at Vacca's. You goin'?"

Risey was a local fixture around the Bowery section of Coney Island, the magical place where New Yorkers escaped the drudgery of their everyday lives to swim in the surf and go to the amusement parks. He was a wizened old showman who had worked the circuses, the beer halls, and even some legitimate theaters for some "thirty-seven year," as he said. No one really knew what he *did* at Vacca's Theater, only that he was the "High Mighty Muck." But they all knew that tonight he was going in the box.

The Houdinis' box was actually a steamer trunk that could be thoroughly and completely examined by audience members. Harry would then be bound and placed into a cloth sack that was tied shut. He was then locked into the trunk, which was roped and then enclosed from view by what was called a cabinet—actually a frame with fabric draped around it on three sides and a curtain in the front. Theo would then stand inside the cabinet and announce, "Behold, a miracle!" He would then close the curtain and clap his hands three times. The curtain immediately was pulled open to reveal Harry, liberated, standing in front of the box. After Harry unlocked the trunk and untied the sack, his brother emerged. The transformation was remarkable. A version of the trunk substitution had just been performed locally the previous winter by the Jewel Brothers, but the Houdinis put it over spectacularly, and both the audiences and the employees of Vacca's were mystified by the effect.

Except for Risey. He started bad-mouthing the brothers and their box. He claimed that a duo known as the Davenport Brothers had done a better box trick twenty years before, and he had showed them up then. Risey shot his mouth off so long and so loud about "fakers" and "fake box tricks" that when he ran into Harry, who was taking a stroll with one of the Floral Sisters, a song-and-dance act also appearing in Coney Island, a crowd gathered around.

"In de presence of me ladyfren', I'll say notin'," Houdini snarled, reverting back to the language of the New York streets, "but I'll do youse dirt when I get back."

It was then that Vacca, the owner of the theater, stepped in to mediate a truce. Risey, it was announced, would go into the box and try to get out of it and expose the whole effect. And Houdini would pay him the princely sum of $100 if he was able to back up his words with action.

So the stage was set for that evening. The joint was filled, with the two private boxes packed with local politicians, actors, newspapermen, and Brooklyn power brokers. The Houdinis went onstage first, and the crowd gave them a polite greeting, but when the audience saw the grizzled head of old Risey, they erupted in a torrent of cheers and a chorus of "Speech, speech, speech." Risey was forced to step up to center stage.

"I have been a showman for thirty-seven year, and I know what's what. I have exposed the Davenport Brothers and called down the great Herrmann. I know fakers when I sees them, so these Hunyadi Brothers don't scare me none. This is a fake box and I'm going to show this thing up or die trying," the old veteran said.

The audience cheered louder.

Then it was time. Not even bothering to tie his hands behind his back, Harry and Theo assisted Risey into the silken bag and tied it at the top. Then they lifted him into the trunk and pushed it into the cabinet. And everyone waited.

For five minutes the audience seemed to hold its breath. Then there was the faint muffled sound of "Help!" followed by some serious pounding on the inside of the box. Harry and his brother immediately leapt up, tore aside the curtain of the cabinet, and pulled the trunk out. They whipped out knives and frantically began cutting the ropes. Harry opened the lock, pulled the bag out of the trunk, cut the cord, and yanked the limp form of old Risey from the bag. He was perspiring heavily and trying to catch his breath.

This was a crucial moment in the early career of Houdini. Risey, the old-timer, was likely a confederate. A mock rivalry was generated; harsh words were uttered casting doubts on the ability of The Brothers Houdini, and the ensuing publicity packed the house for the first time. Harry was beginning to learn the value of controversy and publicity.

Houdini had also learned a tactic from the Spiritualists—the monetary or "prize" challenge. Or at least what seemed to be a challenge. It was loudly proclaimed that if Risey could get out of that box, Houdini would pay him $100, a substantial amount of money back in 1894. Of course, Houdini worked the odds so that there was very little chance that his money would ever be in jeopardy.

There is one other interesting aspect of this Risey story. It was reported in the papers of June 22, 1894, which means that it probably took place the previous night. The fact that Bess Raymond of the Floral Sisters was in the wings cheerleading for Houdini was no accident. On the next day, after knowing each other a little more than a week, they would get married.

Bess, whose real name was Wilhelmina Beatrice Rahner, was a Brooklyn girl from a strict German Roman Catholic family. Her father had died at an early age, and she was consigned to working at a brother-in-law's tailor shop. But she had wanderlust in her blood and a natural inclination toward singing and dancing, so when she was sixteen, she got a job as a seamstress in a traveling circus. Soon afterward, she made friends with two girls, the Floral Sisters, who had a song-and-dance act. Within weeks, she had persuaded them to let her join the group.

Harry's brother Theo had arranged a blind date with two of the sisters for Harry and himself. Love-at-first-sight ensued, and soon Harry and Bess were inseparable. Houdini didn't have the money to properly woo his love (Bess would later crack that she had "sold her virginity to Houdini for an orange") and according to her account, not only did she have to contribute the lion's share for her wedding ring but also had to loan Harry the $2 needed for the marriage license. Besides the civil ceremony, Bess claimed that they were married twice more, once by a rabbi and once by a Roman Catholic priest.

Cecilia welcomed Bess into the family, but it was quite a different story for Bess's people. "Though the matter had not been mentioned, I gathered from Ehrich's appearance that he was a Jew," Bess wrote, "and in our simple Catholic upbringing, a Jew was a person of doubtful human attributes." In fact, Bess's mother shunned her daughter for twelve years after her marriage, relenting only when Houdini and one of his brothers traveled to her home in 1906 and refused to leave until Mrs. Rahner would agree to pay a visit to her then seriously ill daughter.

Houdini was gaining not only a wife but a partner too. He had decided that Bess would replace his brother Theo in the act. For one, she was much smaller, less than five feet tall and weighing in at under ninety pounds. She'd have a lot less trouble making the switch in the trunk than Theo, who was much larger than his diminutive older brother. Besides, Harry had been upset with Theo when they were first starting out. Theo had botched the substitution trunk bit by forgetting to bring his gimmick into the trunk, making him a prisoner. The act had to be stopped as a red-faced Theo was freed. That gaffe cost them the rest of their booking at the Imperial Music Hall in Manhattan and from that time on, it was Harry who was bound and locked in the trunk.

That night, Houdini led his brother and Bess on a walk toward the roaring ocean. There was a strange feeling in the salt air, the crescent moon peeking in and out from behind rapidly moving clouds. They walked over an old bridge that traversed some fast-running brackish water. Suddenly, in the middle of the bridge, Houdini stopped and stood in silent contemplation. Somewhere in the distance, a church bell rang out twelve peals.

As soon as that last ring faded, Houdini took his brother's hand and clasped it with Bess's. Then he slowly raised both their hands aloft.

"Beatrice and Theo, raise your hands to Heaven and swear you will both be true to me," Houdini intoned. "Never betray me in any way, so help you God."

Theo and Bess repeated the vow after him. Then Houdini kissed Bess and shook Dash's hand.

"I know you will keep that sacred vow," he said with satisfaction, having done everything in his power to protect his magic secrets.

But this was too much for the constitutionally frail Bess.

"By this time I was in a state of panicky terror," she remembered. "The eerie sky, the lonely bridge in a waste of marshland, the black water—and then this dramatic and terrible vow—these things seemed wholly abnormal and strange. It was apparent that this Houdini whom I had known less than two weeks was . . . probably a madman, and his brother was no better. I glanced at the black water and wondered what those two strangers intended to do to me next in that lonely place. . . . Houdini sensed my fears and immediately began to lead me away and reassure me. By the time we reached the lighted streets his gentleness and tenderness had restored my tranquillity."

The next morning, Theo began initiating Bess into the mysteries of the trunk effect, which they called "Metamorphosis," resigned to the fact that the meager income generated by the act would preclude his further participation. And from the perspective of pure showmanship, the substitution trunk would be transformed and enhanced with Bess in the act. Now it would be a true metamorphosis, with a cuffed, bound magician being magically transformed into a cuffed, bound, beautiful female.

"Your attention toward this end of the hall! Here you will find a clever young man. He will mystify you if he can, a great magician, it's no bunk. Houdini, look at him; there he goes into the trunk." Professor Hudson Langdon, the barker at Huber's Fourteenth Street Museum, would steer the audience drifting by to Houdini's slice of the stage in the Curio Hall. Competing for the attention of the crowd with Unthan, the Legless Wonder; Big Alice, a fat lady; and Blue Eagle, who would break boards over his head to show the strength of his skull, Houdini and Bess began doing as many as twenty shows a day.

Those were the good venues. One time, while they were on their honeymoon, the newlyweds were booked at a wine room, which was basically a low-class bordello that featured entertainment. "We opened and when I found out what kind of a theatre it was, good night and good bye," Houdini wrote. More often than not The Great Houdinis, as Harry billed them, would play raucous beer halls where the alcoholic audience took great delight in calling for the "hook" for acts that didn't please them. Bess's petite figure didn't help. The fashion in those days was for "generously curved amazons" and Bess felt that most managers "looked askance at my uncompromising flatness." One time they couldn't get a booking at a dime museum or even a beer hall, so they tried to break into a burlesque show. "What the hell do you think I'm running?" the manager said, after eyeing Bess over. "A kindergarten?"

By the end of 1894, the Houdinis were playing small theaters in the South. On the road, they had established a rhythm of sorts. Harry never slept more than four hours a night and he used the additional waking hours to their fullest. He was always up at five, shopping for whatever meager provisions their current income would allow. Then he'd pick up some coffee and bring it back to their

An early poster for the Houdinis depicting their celebrated Metamorphosis.
Library of Congress

furnished room while Bess would sleep in. Houdini would then go out and hustle, visiting barrooms, buying playing cards, and doing some card effects to raise extra cash. In January they were thrilled to get an engagement in New York at Tony Pastor's, a prestigious, legitimate vaudeville theater. Despite their taking ads out in the theatrical papers, the booking did little for their career, as they were buried way down at the bottom of the bill. After that it was back to the lowly dime museums. Bess got so discouraged that she actually left the act when they were playing Huber's, leaving Houdini to finish the engagement solo.

It was one of those early spring rains that chilled to the bone. The darkness was so thick that Harry and Bess began to think they were hopelessly lost. Still they plodded on through the mud, each carrying one end of the trunk that doubled as both their stage prop and their luggage. They walked for what seemed like miles, until they heard a voice from out of the darkness calling them.

"Is that the Houdinis?"

"Yes, sir," Harry answered back.

A hand swooped down out of the dark and pulled them into what looked like the entrance of a cave. Peering into the dark, they could barely make out that it was an old railroad freight car that had been transformed into living quarters. A lantern flashed in front of their faces.

"Well, what do you do?" a man with a walrus mustache asked them. He was Mike Welsh, one of the proprietors of the Welsh Brothers Circus.

"Anything," Houdini blurted out. They were desperate to make this potential twenty-six-week gig stick.

"Well, the first thing that you do with this outfit is to work in the sideshow," Welsh said. "You do Punch and Judy—the wife, mind-reading. In the concert, Houdini to do magic, wife to sing and dance—then your trunk trick. And, of course, you are in the parade. Twenty-five a week and cakes."

They understood the money part, and later they would discover that cakes meant meals. For the rest of his life, Houdini would rave about the wonderful food that was served up by the circus chef.

Clear on their commitments, Welsh then escorted Harry and Bess down the narrow corridor of the train car.

"Here are the Houdinis," he shouted.

"Hello," "Welcome to our city," "Good evening," a chorus of voices came at them from behind the partitioned-off makeshift rooms. Welsh stopped at one of these miniscule compartments and pulled the flimsy curtain to one side.

Harry and Bess pose for their first professional pictures in 1894. *Library of Congress*

"This is your lodging," he said. They looked in and saw a single cot, which was taking up almost all of the available space. The partitions between rooms were made of cardboard. After Welsh left, Bess, soaking wet and upset at the bizarre cramped quarters, fell onto the cot, crying hysterically. Houdini comforted her at first, but then he set down to work and began to scribble some little rhymes for her song turn.

The next morning when Houdini signed his contract, he didn't bother to ask what the words "AND FOUND," which were inserted after his salary, meant. He found out a few nights later when the audience began clambering for "Projea, the Wild Man of Mexico," an advertised attraction. It seems that the regular "wild man" was ill and wasn't on this run. Backstage, the managers conferred, and John Welsh approached Houdini.

"Put some paint on your face and get in the cage. They want the wild man," he said. And then he explained that "AND FOUND" meant whatever other work for him they could find. So Houdini cheerfully rumpled up his hair, painted some red stripes on his cheeks, made his chin blue, dabbed black paint around his eyes, improvised a caveman outfit out of a burlap sack, and climbed into the cage as Projea. Then they pushed the cage onstage and Clint Newton, the show's direc-

Welsh Brothers Circus Troupe, 1896. Harry and Bess are in the front row; in the back marked "6" is Houdini's close friend Jim Bard. *From the collection of Kevin Connolly*

tor, approached with some raw meat. He tore off a piece and threw it into the cage. Projea pounced on it and tore at it with his teeth, growling and shaking the bars from time to time.

Houdini's willingness to try anything was a function of his insatiable thirst for knowledge of every aspect of show business—and his shrewd ability to take unrelated skills and use them to his own advantage. By treating the dime museum freaks with dignity and respect, he befriended them and soaked up skills that would later be useful. A. Lutes, an armless man, so impressed him with his ability to use his toes as fingers that Houdini practiced and practiced until his own toes developed prehensile abilities, which would be invaluable to him in later escape work. He learned the techniques of circus strongmen, fire-resisters, and sword-swallowers. On the Welsh Brothers Tour, he befriended a member of the San Kitchi Akimoti, a Japanese balancing act, who taught him how to seemingly swallow objects and then regurgitate them at will by hiding them in his gullet.

Somewhere during those early years, he learned an astounding effect where he would swallow a large number of needles, ingest a long piece of thread, and, after an examination of his mouth, pull out the long thread with the needles dangling from it. The "needles" would become a mainstay of his act for his entire life.

One particularly alluring performer was the beautiful Evatima Tardo, who would allow herself to be bitten on her bare shoulder by a rattlesnake, be impaled on a makeshift cross, and have her face and neck used as a cushion for dozens of pins. Her amazing tolerance for pain and resistance to poison came from an incident in her childhood in Cuba when she was bitten by a fer-de-lance, the most poisonous snake in the hemisphere. Houdini was smitten both by her beauty and her showmanship; while undergoing some of these tortures, she would blithely laugh and sing. Her end was grisly, however. Although immune to pain and poison, she fell victim to love and bullets, dying in a double-murder-suicide love triangle.

Financially, the stint with the circus was a godsend. Houdini made extra money selling soap and toiletries to the other performers, and Bess pulled in two extra dollars by singing the songs from the official circus songbook that was for sale. Since they didn't have expenses to speak of, Houdini was able to bank their entire income (minus the $12 he'd religiously send to Cecilia each week). But on this tour they had one of their first major flare-ups. Houdini had "forbidden" Bess to go see a show in the town that the troupe was currently playing. She was adamant, and Harry told her that if she "disobeyed" him, he would "send her home." She ignored him, so he burst into the theater, carried her out, and "spanked" her. Dividing their savings, he took her to the train station and bought her a ticket to Bridgeport, where her sister lived.

As the train was about to pull out, he handed her their small dog.

"I always keep my word. Good-by, Mrs. Houdini," he said, mockingly tipping his hat.

Bess was hysterical the whole ride to Bridgeport. When she got to her sister's, she was fawned over and Houdini was cursed, but she just wanted to beg his forgiveness and go back to him. At two A.M. the doorbell rang and Bess got her chance.

She rushed to the door where Houdini stood and fell into his arms.

"See, darling, I told you I would send you away if you disobeyed, but I didn't say I wouldn't fly after you and bring you back."

The chastened couple returned to the circus and vowed not to let their private disputes impinge on their professional responsibilities again.

With the circus season over, Houdini had managed to save some money, so when Henry Newman, his cousin on his mother's side, approached him with an opportunity to buy a partnership in a touring burlesque company for which he was doing the advance work, Harry became an entrepreneur, part owner of the American Gaiety Girls.

Although the Houdinis got good notices for their Metamorphosis, the burlesque segments of the show got mixed reviews. They toured the Northeast until the end of January and resumed a swing through New England in March. During the February hiatus, Houdini managed to join up with another burlesque company and perform a turn as "Professor Morat," a European hypnotist, who put a man in a trance and then demonstrated that he was impervious to pain by allowing the audience to jab pins and needles into the soft parts of the man's anatomy. Morat also hypnotized several subjects from the audience and had them do ridiculous things under the influence, much to the delight of the rest of the crowd. Back with the Gaiety Girls in March, and desperate to pull in larger box offices, Houdini and his partners even brought in a female wrestler who would wrangle with local male volunteers (up to 122 pounds) in a very surrealistic performance. But by the end of April, the Gaiety Girls came to an ugly end with the manager of the troupe arrested for fraud and the performers stranded in Woonsocket, Rhode Island. It was a blow to the entrepreneurial dreams of Harry, but, in some ways, it was just as much a blow to his younger brother Leopold, who would routinely escape from his medical school studies to tag along with the traveling troupe until "that illustrious Prof Morat gave him a kick in the pants and sent him home, because he had to go to college and preferred to look at the nice padded shapes of those beautiful burlesquers."

Desperate for work and with debts to pay off, the Houdinis traveled to Boston at the end of May to work with Marco the Magician for a tour of the Maritime Provinces in Canada. Marco was in reality the mild-mannered Edward J. Dooley, a church organist from Connecticut who had saved for years to take out a large magic show patterned after his idol, Alexander Herrmann, Compars's younger brother, the most famous living magician at that time. He was, in some ways, the first of a succession of father figures to Harry. Houdini was even introduced to the audience as Marco's son-in-law and "successor," and his Metamorphosis with Bess was a showstopper. But business lagged because a performer named "Markos" had traveled this route the previous summer and had ruined the audience with a night of horrid, amateurish magic. By the beginning of July, the Marco show went bust.

The only real memorable thing about this half-year was that, desperate to make his mark in show business, Houdini started to perform handcuff escapes, first as a refinement of Metamorphosis, then as a vehicle to promote the shows, and eventually as the beginning of a pure escape act. At the end of September 1895, Houdini had bought a handcuff escape act (basically a ring of handcuff keys) from W. D. LeRoy, a Boston-based magician turned magic dealer. The act itself had been created by a brilliant inventor named (ironically) B. B. Keyes. Determined to improve Metamorphosis, Houdini began to fetter his hands with handcuffs instead of rope or braid. On November 8, 1895, he even offered to use a pair of borrowed handcuffs from an audience member for the effect, much as he would sometimes borrow a jacket from the audience and put it on right before he entered the trunk, the jacket magically being worn by Bess when she was brought out.

Cognizant of the fact that most people not only didn't own their own pair of handcuffs but also probably had never even handled a pair and certainly didn't know much about cuffs, chains, or shackles, Houdini came up with the brilliant idea of promoting his shows by challenging the unassailable authorities in the field of restraint—the police. Unlike his previous monetary "prize" challenges, here Houdini was not challenging others to prove themselves, now he was defying the authorities to keep him subjugated. On November 22, Houdini walked into the police station in Gloucester, Massachusetts, and offered to escape from any handcuffs they could place on him. And he did, freeing himself from both the modern and "old-time" police bracelets. This dramatic challenge and escape naturally got much attention in the newspapers. He repeated this publicity stunt in every city for the rest of the tour.

By March of 1896, the ante had been raised. After an exhibition of escaping from handcuffs in the New Britain police station, Houdini announced that he would "release himself" from any pair of handcuffs that were brought to the show. Houdini had hit on a surefire way of demonstrating his prowess. If the audience couldn't come with him to his exhibitions in the police stations, he would bring the authorities onstage.

On June 10, responding to announcements that Houdini would test "anything in St. John [New Brunswick] that could bind him," Officer Baxter and private citizens Arthur McGinley and John McCafferty strode onstage laden with heavy chains, handcuffs, and leg irons. They wrapped the chains around his body and handcuffed Houdini with his hands behind his back. At the same time they shackled his feet. Helped into his small curtained cabinet that he called his "ghost box," he took only minutes to emerge a free man. It was such a marvelous performance that many in the audience were convinced that he was "in league with the spirits."

A few weeks later, at the Academy of Music in Halifax, after an announcement had been made that Houdini could release himself from any handcuffs that might be brought onstage, Sergeant Collins came forward with police handcuffs and with the assistance of Mr. Urnan, the chef at the Halifax Hotel, trussed the magician into an impossible-looking contorted position. It took him a little more than a minute to free himself. The performance was billed as "Escape from Dorchester." The seeds of Houdini's world-famous challenge handcuff act had been sown.

Houdini's police challenges never failed to generate press, but he knew from his experience with circus parades that outdoor spectacles were instrumental in generating word-of-mouth publicity for those who might not read a daily newspaper. On a pleasant summer day in Halifax, Houdini invited the press, local dignitaries, and any curious bystanders to convene on a highway outside of town to see him make an escape that had never been attempted before. All of the local reporters showed up, one even accompanied by the owner of his paper. After all, who would want to miss seeing this young magician free himself after he had been tied onto the back of a horse like some Wild West desperado? After exchanging pleasantries with the group, Houdini mounted his steed. First his hands were tied behind his back and then the horse's trainer bound Houdini's feet together under the horse's belly.

From then on things began to go downhill fast. Houdini had specified that he wanted the most docile beast they had in the stable, but whether by accident or malicious design, the trainer had brought a frisky, young, barely broken colt. Not used to having someone tied to its back, the horse began to buck furiously. There was no danger that Houdini would be thrown by the animal, but the very real possibility existed that the creature would just drop to the ground and try to roll its burden off, which would have crushed its human cargo.

Then the horse switched tactics altogether. To the dismay of Houdini, and the assembled press and local luminaries, the colt just took off at a breakneck pace down the road. Now there was no way that Houdini could effect his escape, not until the horse had been thoroughly tired out. It wasn't until they rode for a few more miles that Houdini was able to work at the ropes and free himself. The only problem was that nobody was there to see it—the newsmen were halfway back to their offices by then, joking about the ridiculous stunt.

Houdini had made a rare miscalculation by not trying out the escape beforehand, but he learned a valuable lesson: You don't practice in public. Plan ahead and be prepared for all contingencies.

Houdini started the straitjacket escape in 1899. This is a movie still taken twenty years later.
From the collection of Roger Dreyer

The insane asylum patient lay still for a few seconds, his sweat pouring onto the canvas-padded floor. The only sound you could hear in the small cell was his staccato panting. If not for the fury in his eyes, you might have thought that he was finished. But he wasn't.

Suddenly he started rolling over and over and over again, like a crazed dervish, kicking the floor as he twirled, every muscle in his body straining against the restraint. It looked like he was trying to lift his arms over his head, but it was all in vain. But still he struggled.

"It's really much better than the restraint muffs we formerly used," Dr. Steeves said, peering at the man through the small, barred window. "By criss-crossing the arms in front and strapping them securely in the back, the poor fellow has no chance of hurting others. Or himself. It's really the most modern device we have. We call it the straitjacket."

Dr. Steeves turned away from the small window.

"Now if we proceed down this corridor . . ."

Houdini really hadn't heard a word the doctor said. He was still staring through that little window, entranced. Not because he was empathizing with the patient, although he had a soft spot in his heart for the weak and infirm. No, he was fascinated with the mechanics of the restraint device.

Now if he were only able to dislocate one arm at the shoulder joint, I bet that would give him enough slack to eventually get his arms free. But he'd need some solid foundation to place the elbow. . . .

That night Houdini hardly slept at all. During the few moments that he managed to doze off, all he dreamt of were straitjackets, maniacs, and padded cells. The rest of the time he wondered how the audience would react to seeing a man bound into a straitjacket effect his freedom.

The very next morning Houdini called Dr. Steeves and borrowed one of the canvas jackets. By the end of the week, Houdini was escaping from a straitjacket onstage.

As creative as Houdini was, he still hadn't really learned how to sell his escapes, except for the Metamorphosis, of course. When he retreated into his ghost box, and managed to writhe and twist until he could get that infernal straitjacket off, the audience didn't know what to think, and they certainly missed all the drama. It wasn't until 1904 that his brother Theo hit upon the idea of performing the straitjacket escape in full view of the audience, a simple but brilliant conception that Houdini immediately embraced.

After the Marco show folded, Houdini convinced the old magician to loan him the props, and Harry mounted his own full-on magic show in Canada. Despite very favorable reviews, he couldn't make it go. So with magic bookings still few and far between, the Houdinis tried anything to stay in show business. From the summer of 1896 until the fall of 1897, they wandered up and down the coast and ventured out to the Midwest, taking any work they could. Houdini appeared as Cardo, the King of Cards. They did a comedy routine, and they acted in melodramas. They wrote to prominent magicians like Alexander Herrmann and Harry Kellar, applying for work as assistants. Herrmann never responded to his brother's distant cousin, but at least they got a nice rejection letter from Kellar.

Even when they were working, getting paid was sometimes harder than getting out of restraints. In Toledo, Harry arrived for a job at a vaudeville hall only to learn that salaries were not being issued. He marched into the box office, waited until enough cash had come in to cover his salary, and paid himself on the spot. The next day he quit. In Newark, a manager decided to lay him off for his Sunday show, which would have paid him $15, and wrote him a letter to that effect. Houdini read it, calmly tore it up, showed up at the theater on Sunday, and denied ever having received a letter. Negotiating on the spot, he did the date for $8.

All of this strain took a toll on the frail Bess. She fell ill numerous times those first three years. By July of 1897, they were back in New York, where a depressed and dispirited Houdini went to four of the largest newspapers and offered to sell all his secrets, including those of his handcuff act, for twenty-five dollars. There were no takers. He tried to open a magic school, but except for one older man in Chicago, he had no pupils. Making a deal with his friend Gus

It was Houdini's brother Theo who, later performing as Hardeen, came up with the idea of doing the straitjacket escape in full view of the audience. *New York Public Library*

Roterberg, a magic dealer in Chicago, he tried to sell magic effects, even publishing a catalog entitled *Magic Made Easy*. The orders were few and far between.

In the fall, when their season resumed, they were back on the road. They finished their first booking at a music hall in Milwaukee only to learn that the theater manager had swindled them out of their salary. Their next show was at Kohl and Middleton's in Chicago, but in an attempt to make back their losses, Houdini dropped $60 in a craps game. Could their luck get any worse?

Nobody had seen anything like it in all their lives. They gathered around the front of the locomotive and watched as the railroad officials tried to pry the young man off the tracks so that the journey could continue. But pull as they might, there seemed to be no way that the brakemen could get the stubborn man off the rails. He was holding on with such force that his hands were bruised and bleeding.

By now a third railroad man had joined the struggle—to no avail. Houdini had dug his fingers around one rail and clamped his toes on the other. His muscles were like steel, but he was also using leveraging techniques so that a hundred railmen couldn't get him off.

Finally the conductor walked over.

"Say, your damned trunks are onboard. How about letting us start?" he said.

Houdini immediately sprang off the track and walked over to Bess, who was standing among the crowd, fretting.

"I told you it would work," he whispered to her as he hugged her. And then they both climbed on board for their trip to the Indian Territory.

Houdini had just gotten a solid fifteen-week booking to work with Dr. Hill's California Concert Company, an old-time medicine show, and they were en route to join the troupe. In his mind, this could be their ticket to the big-time. They were to change trains at three A.M., but their train pulled in late and the express was ready to roll. To Harry's horror, there were no porters around to help him move his four heavy trunks from the old train to the new one, and even with the help of a few fellow passengers, they had only gotten two of the trunks transferred when the order to disembark was given. If they missed this train, they would miss their first performance and jeopardize their future. So he hatched his little dramatic plan. That experience "has always seemed to me to be the turning point in my career," he wrote. But not because he got to the engagement on time.

"That was the first time I realised the public wanted drama. Give 'em a hint of danger, perhaps of death—and you'll have 'em packing in to see you!"

Houdini immediately adapted to life with a traveling medicine show. Dr. Hill was a young man with long flowing hair, a silky brown beard, and a remarkable ability to produce silver-tongued oratory praising the virtues of his homemade patent medicine, an ability that was definitely enhanced by his generous consumption of store-bought alcohol. His partner, Dr. Pratt, was a benign-looking white-haired old man.

The troupe would pull into a town in a carriage that was large enough to transport Dr. Pratt's organ. Stopping at a congested corner, Dr. Pratt would play while Houdini banged a tambourine and Bessie sang. After a crowd gathered, Dr. Hill would give a grandiose pitch for his wonderful medicine that could cure every illness imaginable. Houdini collected the coins from the eager crowd as Bess and the others dispensed the bottles. Then they'd announce their evening show at the local town hall, a show that cost only ten, fifteen, or twenty-five cents.

Within a short time, Houdini and his wonderful escapes became the focal point of the Dr. Hill show. Maybe all the struggle was finally starting to pay off. For six years now, Houdini had been leading a nomadic existence, soaking up technique and skills like a sponge, enduring hunger (he and Bess once subsisted for a few weeks on two rabbits they bought with a borrowed quarter), pain, and humiliation in his quest to make a name for himself. The responsibility that he had been given by his father was his constant companion—no matter how much he and Bess made, he was sure to send the biggest chunk of it back home to his mother. But that pledge transcended mere financial aid. Houdini was on a quest for respectability, for the legitimacy that had always evaded his noble and worthy father.

In Lima, Ohio, a young reporter named H. M. Walker saw a performance. He was impressed to see Houdini escape from handcuffs, transform water into ink, and do wonderful card manipulations. After the show, he went backstage to interview Harry. Perhaps because they were both young and both neophytes in their chosen profession, Houdini seemed to relate to Walker, and his stage mask slipped a bit.

"I haven't learned to coin my thrill in publicity," Houdini said frankly. "I think no one can beat me at magic—but I'm still obscure."

And then he looked Walker straight in the eye and smiled. "It doesn't bother me, however. I know I am going to be famous."

Fashionable Spiritualistic Event of the Season.

TO-NIGHT

Sunday, Feb. 27

AT

A. O. U. W. LODGE ROOM

Rock Island Building, Sixth and Edmond

Grand, Brilliant, Bewildering and Startling Spiritualistic Seance, given by

..Prof. Harry Houdini..

The Great Mystifier,

ASSISTED BY

Mlle. Beatrice Houdini

The Celebrated Psycrometic Clairvoyant

Spiritual forms materialized, tables and musical instruments float in midair when conditions are favorable: messages received from dead and departed friends.

$100 Reward!

Which amount has been placed in the hands of

MAYOR L. A. VORIES,

Money to be given to any SHERIFF, CONSTABLE, OFFICER, or private individual who can bring Prof. Houdini any Handcuffs or Leg Fetters from which he cannot escape.

INDEPENDENT SPIRIT SLATE WRITING...

Skeptics cordially invited up as a committee

BRING YOUR OWN HANDCUFFS AND ROPES!

General Admission, 25c.

One lady's ticket FREE with every paid admission. Doors open 7:30. Carriages 10:45.

3

The Celebrated Clairvoyants

"WE HAVE JUST RECENTLY BECOME AWARE of a tragic situation in this good town of Garnett, Kansas," the Great Houdini said.

The audience, which had filled the old opera house to the rafters that November night in 1897, held its breath. This was what they had been waiting for all night. Houdini, who along with his wife had the *power*, was going to reveal just who had killed Sadie Timmins. Sadie's murder had been brutal, they knew that much. Sheriff Keeney had scoured the hills and the hollows of town for the murderer—to no avail. Now this outsider, this charismatic wonder-worker was going to contact the spirit world and get the inside dope. Well, maybe he could, the townsfolk thought. After all, he had already escaped from the old stone jail just minutes after the sheriff had locked him in there, and he was able to find all those items that had been hidden around town by the councilmen, while he was blindfolded. So naming an unknown killer might be a cakewalk for the likes of him.

"A lovely young lady, Miss Sadie Timmins, was discovered brutally murdered," Houdini said. "Now, the sheriff, Mr. Keeney, is a good and a great man, and he has done everything that is earthly possible to bring the killer to justice."

A buzz went through the crowd. Not everyone there believed that Sheriff Keeney was, in fact, so diligent.

"*Earthly* possible. We propose to contact the spirit world, our ancestors who lovingly and with great concern watch over our every movement on this sphere. You cannot hide a nefarious deed from the spirits!" Houdini thundered.

Then he signaled and Mlle. Beatrice Houdini, the celebrated "Psychometric Clairvoyant," walked onto the stage. Bess was resplendent in an antique lace dress and a beautifully embroidered vest. Houdini sat her in a chair and tied a blindfold around her head.

Standing with his arm on Bess's shoulder, he signaled backstage. A man walked out with a large sheet.

"In order to facilitate communication with the spirits, I will now have Mlle. Houdini covered by this shroud, concentrating her energy and filtering out extraneous vibrations that might interfere with our communication."

The man covered Bess with the sheet.

"Before we begin, please join me in a few choruses of 'Nearer My God to Thee.'"

The band began to play, and the entire assemblage sang the hymn together, until Houdini dramatically cut them off with a sweeping gesture of his hand.

Bess, who had been sitting upright, suddenly slumped to one side in her chair.

"Mlle. Houdini is in a trance state," Houdini announced. "She is ready and receptive to answer questions about this tragedy."

Houdini began to pace back and forth on the stage.

"Was Sadie Timmons murdered on her property?" he began.

"Yes," Bess answered in a quavering voice.

"Can you tell us where?"

"In her kitchen," Bess replied.

"With what instrumentality?"

"She was stabbed seventeen times with a butcher knife," Bess said in a slow, robotic voice.

"Was the killer an intruder?"

"No."

"So he was known to her?" Houdini stopped dramatically.

"Yes."

Several women in the audience gasped audibly. The killer was an acquaintance, which meant that the killer might even be right there in the auditorium.

"Can you describe the killer for us?" Houdini asked.

Bess began to breathe rapidly.

"He's tall. With a black moustache and goatee."

"More!" Houdini cried.

"I see lizard boots. And an old gold handwatch that's got some sort of inscription."

Bess was straining under the sheet.

"Go on!"

"A long brown suede duster. And I see the blood. Her blood is splattering against the coat. It's getting on the coat and the boots. And the gloves. Black leather gloves with the fingers cut off. Now she's struggling back. She's hitting him and scratching him on his neck."

The audience was transfixed, watching the frail, shrouded woman relive the horrific crime.

Houdini walked beside his wife.

"What is the murderer's name?" he whispered. It was so quiet you could hear his utterance at the back of the hall.

Bess just sat there.

"His name," Houdini repeated, louder this time. "What is the murderer's name?"

Again, no response. He strode a few paces from his wife and then turned and faced her.

"Quick. Answer. What is his name?" he screamed.

Bess shivered and shrank down in the chair.

"Answer!" he screamed.

"It . . . it . . ." Bess stammered. The audience leaned forward as one.

"Answer!"

The medium started shaking.

"His name . . ." she said in a shaky tone. "His name is . . . is . . . is . . ."

Suddenly Bess threw up both arms and, with a sickening cry, slumped back into her chair.

Houdini rushed to his wife's side and pulled the shroud off of her.

"Is there a doctor in the house? My wife has fainted!"

The audience was in an uproar. Women were crying; men were arguing; the sheriff was surrounded by an angry crowd.

Of course, Bess recovered. She never did reveal the name of the murderer; it didn't really matter. What mattered was that the California Concert Company now had plenty of cash to pay for their rooms that night and to continue on their Kansas tour. Dr. Hill had come to Houdini in desperation. The regular shows just weren't drawing, and he had heard that there were traveling mediums in the territories who were raking in the dough doing their séances.

"Houdini, can't you do something on a Sunday night of a religious nature so we can get a house?" Dr. Hill asked him.

"There is one thing I can do of a religious nature and that is make a collection," Houdini cracked.

But when the California Concert Company needed a medium, Harry, like his father before him, just shrugged and said, "Okay, that's me."

The notion that a medium could communicate with dead spirits was still a fairly new one. Spiritualism, the religion that held that fact as its central tenet, was conceived on March 31, 1848, in a modest farmhouse in the upstate hamlet of Hydesville, New York, when two teenage sisters, Katie and Margaret Fox, began hearing mysterious raps. Within days the girls found they had the ability to not only elicit these noises but also communicate with the alleged spirit entity that was producing them. Devising a simple "yes" or "no" code, the Fox Sisters became the first mediums in modern history. Suddenly the floodgates were open. Within years the movement had spread across the planet, and a vast number of people found that they too had an innate ability to channel messages from a spirit world that just seemed bursting with the desire to communicate with loved ones back on Earth.

As a grassroots, populist religious revival, Spiritualism adherents were often at the forefront of other reform movements, championing the cause of women's rights, child labor concerns, and the temperance and antismut crusades. By the Civil War, one Spiritualist leader claimed eleven million converts in the United States alone.

It was a natural progression to the concert stage. The Fox Sisters themselves were the first Spiritualist "performers," and they were soon followed by others, including Henry Slade, Minnie Williams, Madame Diss Debar, and Anna Eva Fay. Then the magicians climbed on the bandwagon. The Spiritualists soon expanded their repertoire from eliciting raps to making tables tilt, instruments float, and producing slates that had words chalked on them from communicative spirits. At first, magicians like Robert Heller and John Henry Anderson, and even Dr. Lynn, merely replicated the Spiritualist phenomenon in their own shows. Then the most eminent magicians like Alexander Herrmann and Harry Kellar began to expose what they considered the tricks of the mediums.

The idea that the dead could communicate with the living had an allure for a young Houdini. Being the son of a rabbi had predisposed Harry to a belief in both God and a hereafter. It was not such a radical jump to embrace Spiritualism, but from the very beginning, Houdini's experiences with mediums were frustratingly disappointing. While still a teen, Harry attended a series of séances at the home of a tailor in Beloit, Wisconsin. The tailor/medium was noted for his ability to put his sitters in touch with the spirits of great historical figures like Washington, Napoleon, and Columbus by using a small trumpet, which was placed on a table in front of the sitters who encircled it. Under the protective

The Fox Sisters, patron saints of the worldwide Spiritualist movement.
From the collection of Roger Dreyer

cover of darkness, eerie disembodied voices would issue from the trumpet, the voices of the dead.

Getting in touch with Lincoln was a big mistake, though. The great emancipator was Harry's childhood hero, and he knew every last detail of his life. Vaguely uneasy that something fishy was going on, he decided to confront the spirit.

"Mr. Lincoln, what was the first thing you did after your mother was buried?" Harry asked.

"I felt very bad," Lincoln responded. "I went to my room and I wouldn't speak to anyone for days."

Harry knew that Lincoln's first act was to get a preacher to say a proper service over her grave, which Lincoln's father had neglected.

This led Harry to pay closer attention to what was happening in the séance room. He realized that all of the celestial notables who visited spoke with one of three voices. He also kept hearing an odd hissing sound emanating from the trumpet when the spirits talked. One day, after a séance, Harry asked the medium why this was so.

"Well, you've caught me," the medium laughed. "But you've got to admit that I do more good than harm by consoling sorrowing people who long for a message from their loved ones."

The Davenport Brothers sitting in their spirit cabinet. *From the collection of Ricky Jay*

Harry was stunned.

"Caught him! I had no intention of catching him! . . . I had been innocently seeking information about what I regarded as my religion," Houdini wrote. "It came as a painful shock to me that one whom I had trusted and believed in completely should so readily confess himself a fraud."

Still Harry tried to cling to his faith.

"But surely all mediums are not like you? There must be some genuine ones?" he asked.

The tailor chuckled. "None that I know of. They're tricksters—every one of them."

Houdini's interest in Spiritualism seemed to wane until he discovered the marvelous feats of the Davenport Brothers. The two smallish, long-haired, walrus-mustachioed Americans, had created a worldwide sensation by their feat of producing a marvelous cacophony of sounds from tambourines, guitars, violins, and bells, all while they sat with their hands securely bound by rope in a seven-foot-long cabinet. Even though they never publicly claimed supernatural powers or assistance from the spirits, their presentation was ambiguous enough for the Spiritualists to consider them legitimate mediums. Their concept of Spiritualism—bound hand and foot in a cabinet—is a direct precursor to what Houdini would develop as an escape show.

Early in 1891, Houdini found another book that impacted his life, a slim volume called *The Revelations of a Spirit Medium* by A. Medium. Houdini was enthralled, because within these covers lay the secret of every trick in the medium's repertoire. The one revelation that particularly struck both Houdini and his friend Joseph Rinn was the fact that a medium, although seemingly securely bound with ropes, could release himself, produce phenomena, and then get back into his bonds, which, on inspection, seemed never to have been breached. Harry and Joe followed the book's explicit directions, and in a few months they were both experts in escape from bondage with ropes.

The wooden post had been securely fastened to the boards, which had previously been nailed to the floor of the bedroom. A large metal ring was then bolted to the center of the post. Now the Russian pulled a stool up in front of the column and sat down. He ran his fingers through his large mustache and nodded that he was ready.

The first thing the young man did was to nail the Russian's coat to the stool. Then he tied the older man's wrists together with some bandages. Pulling out a needle and some thread, he then sewed the knots together. On top of that, he slathered on some thick layers of surgeon's plaster. With the hands immobilized, he began to work on the neck. He ran the bandages around the Russian's neck and then ran them through the ring that was affixed to the post. He then nailed the ends of the cloth to the post. The last step was to secure the man's ankles to the legs of the stool. Content that the older man was completely immobilized, the young man made one last sweep of the room, looking for trapdoors or false walls or panels. Then he placed a cup and saucer and spoon on a nearby chair. When he drew the curtains, the room was pitch black. He sat down and he waited.

Within seconds, a tambourine began to beat out a slow, sad tune. Suddenly, he heard the sound of nails being driven into wood. The carnival of noise pierced the darkness and a chill ran down Houdini's back.

Maybe I was wrong. Maybe there are *people with the power. I can actually feel spirits in this room!*

"You may ask any question that comes into your mind," Dr. Josef Gregorowitsch said. "The spirits will answer. One rap for yes, two for no."

Houdini peppered the man with questions, and each time the spirits rapped the answer out by banging the spoon against the cup.

"Open the curtains," Dr. Gregorowitsch commanded, and Houdini went to the window and drew the curtains back. When he turned around, he was amazed to see that the Russian was tied exactly as he had been before the manifestations began.

Houdini had met Gregorowitsch a few weeks earlier, when he had begun his run at a dime museum in Milwaukee in 1892. A dapper, top-hatted gentleman had continuously come to Harry's shows and when they struck up an acquaintance, Gregorowitsch told the magician that he was a Spiritualist, faith healer, and hypnotist. Houdini taught him some sleight of hand. Gregorowitsch, in return, invited him to witness some of his séances. The first one was a circle convened around the sickbed of a woman who the doctors had predicted was near death. A glass was held in the air; Gregorowitsch invoked the spirits, and when the gaslights were turned up, the glass was filled to the brim with the healing potion. The subsequent séances were interesting, but the private demonstration in Gregorowitsch's bedroom (which was nearly adjacent to a Milwaukee police station, further testament to the medium's honesty in Houdini's eyes) had convinced him that perhaps he had been too hasty to write off all spirit mediums as frauds. When Houdini asked Gregorowitsch for an explanation that night, the Russian just smiled paternally and said, "My boy, you are much too young to understand this. Perhaps some day the spirits may help you duplicate these weird tests."

So when Houdini's father died later that year, it was not out of the question that he would attempt to communicate with him by seeking out mediums, especially after his Milwaukee experience. Although Mayer Samuel had an insurance policy, the trying economic conditions prior to his death had forced him to miss some premium payments. Houdini pawned his watch, a treasured gift from his father, and used the money to visit a few mediums to try to get in touch with his father and ascertain what to do about the insurance snafu. Houdini brought his mother to the séances, and Rabbi Weiss was contacted. Instead of advice, he was far more interested in telling his wife and son how happy he was in the afterlife. "It seemed strange to me that my father, knowing our pinched circumstances, would say any such thing," Houdini wrote.

The old German's heart was beating with anticipation as he knocked on the door of the stately house on Michigan Avenue on Chicago's north side. For most people in May of 1893, the place to be was on the *south* side of town, where twenty-seven million visitors from around the world were flocking to the amazing Columbian Exposition. But this old man had no interest in riding the massive Ferris wheel or taking in an astonishing demonstration of electricity by Nicola Tesla, the inventor of alternating current.

No, this German was intent on having sexual relations with his dead wife, and Professor Slater, the thin, handsome man who opened the door, was the person who could make that possible. Why not? Slater had already cured him of his eye problem, giving him a pail filled with a thick brown substance that had been magically infused with healing powers. In gratitude, the man had sent Slater a check for a thousand dollars, double the agreed-upon fee. And when he was informed that the spirits had been the means of his cure, he had asked Slater to see if those same spirits could bring his dearly departed wife back.

On his second visit he was ushered into a small room that was heavily draped in black velvet. He was shown to a seat, and then Slater sat down opposite him. The lights were turned off, throwing the room into total darkness. A soft ethereal melody began playing from the Victrola.

"O spirits from the other side, I call upon you to make your presence felt," Slater intoned. "Reunite poor Mr. Schiller with his wife of twenty-five years. Shatter that baleful veil that separates us from our loved ones. Return, return, return." The medium began palpably shaking and a cold breeze swept into the room.

Suddenly, a faint white glow was visible on the far side of the room. A chill went down Mr. Schiller's spine. Slowly the glow began to take on the shape of a human, the features becoming more and more distinct. It was her! It was Mrs. Schiller!

"My wife!" Schiller stammered, "My darling, you're here!" He rushed over to her, sobbing, grabbed her, and began kissing her. Slater and an assistant had to pull him away, and he watched in pain as his wife's form slowly dematerialized, and the room was pitch black again.

The next day Schiller called Slater, wondering if a conjugal visit could be arranged, for the appropriate fee, of course. Slater seemed reluctant, afraid to violate the sanctity of the separation between the spheres, but when the already generous offer was doubled, he agreed. So now Schiller had returned to spend one more hour of bliss with his dead wife.

Of course, the tryst would not be with his wife. Waiting for him in a large room that had been decorated like a bridal chamber was a local prostitute who had been expertly made up to look like Schiller's wife, a photograph of whom had been obtained by one of the detectives that Slater had hired to dig up information about his clients. Another woman, with a bit more virtue, had been similarly made up to impersonate his wife on that second visit and "materialized" in the velvet room through the manipulations of two black-clad assistants who were invisible in the dark. And that miracle cauldron full of the spirit-infused preparation that had cured his sight? That was common gutter mud. In fact, Professor Slater wasn't even Professor Slater. He was Zanzic, an itinerant magician.

Who Zanzic was is another question. His real name might have been Harry Robenstein, although some people knew him as Brenner, others as Henry Tourpie, and he also used the name Henry Andre. He was said to be from New Orleans, the product of a Jewish father and a Creole fortune-telling mother. Others swore that he was a French-Canadian. But everyone agreed that Zanzic enjoyed fine wine, beautiful women, and the green-felt gaming tables to excess. Drawn to Chicago by the lure of a fast buck, he devised an elaborate spiritual scam. But his greatest coup was in convincing his old pal Billy Robinson, one of the most brilliant magic mechanists, to design a Spiritualist parlor that would put the common garden-variety phony mediums to shame.

Bankrolled to the tune of $5,000 by Jack Curry, Zanzic's New Orleans manager, Robinson began by installing a trapdoor under the table in the main séance room that opened to a state-of-the-art workshop below, where Robinson and Sam Bailey, a Boston-based magician, could open sealed letters, read their contents, and replace the seals without detection. In this way, Zanzic could satisfactorily reply to any secret message or question. The materialization room operated on the old black art principle. The double-lined black velvet curtains would allow the black-clad assistant to manipulate gauzy fabric coated with phosphorescent paint (which was obtainable in any magic supply store) and create ghosts.

Robinson also had the brilliant idea to use trained carrier pigeons that would be introduced into the darkened séance room with a specific message tied around their neck. When the lights came up, the pigeons were trained to circle the room and then land on the shoulder of the chosen sitter, conveying to him a message that nine out of ten times would answer the client's question satisfactorily. And those chills that descended down the backs of the marks were often produced by solid rubber hands that were affixed to a fishing rod and placed on ice for six hours at a time. In the dark, it was the spirits doing the touching.

The scam had been wildly successful, but Zanzic and Robinson had taken it a little too far with Mr. Schiller. The old man had been told that he could spend only an hour with his wife, because after that time she would dematerialize and if he was near her when that happened, his health could be at risk. But Schiller hadn't been in the "bridal chamber" for fifteen minutes when they heard a bloodcurdling scream.

"Mrs. Schiller" ran out, clutching a sheet over her nude body.

Zanzic, magician and fake Spiritualist. *Conjuring Arts Research Center*

"He croaked," the prostitute said. "He's dead."

And he was. Apparently Schiller had worse health problems than his eyes, and the excitement of consummating relations with his dead wife had taxed his heart. With the assistance of the prostitute, they dressed poor Schiller, and then Zanzic and Robinson carried him outside and leaned the body against the building, hoping that it would be discovered the next morning and chalked up as a passer-by who had had a heart attack. What they didn't reckon on was Schiller's driver, who was sitting outside in the car. He notified the police, and Chicago's finest came right over and interrogated Zanzic and Robinson. It's not known how much of that exorbitant fee changed hands, but the two magicians were told to get out of town promptly, which is what they did.

Zanzic would return to the stage, where he would shoot his finger off, gouge his eye out, and then trail off into obscurity. Robinson returned to New York and gained the respect of the magic world as assistant to Alexander Herrmann and then Harry Kellar, two of the greatest magicians of all time. Then, virtually overnight, he changed his name and his appearance, left the country, and broke many of his connections. Years later, his only brother wouldn't even be able to find him.

Billy Robinson, brilliant magic mechanist. *From the collection of Todd Karr*

Harry may have been dubious, but he certainly could admire the wonderful theatrical performances that were being created in the name of Spiritualism. After Harry married Bess and gained a new partner, there was no reason why the young couple couldn't add a mind reading routine to their repertoire—except for the fact that Bess came from a highly superstitious family that believed in ghosts and the supernatural. When her sister Stella's fiancé died right before their wedding, both sisters were convinced that a witch had cast an evil eye upon him.

Harry realized that he had to disabuse Bess of these notions. One night early in their marriage, the solution came to him. They were home and Harry innocuously remarked that Bess had never told him her late father's first name. He then asked her to write the name on a piece of paper, crumple it in her hand, and burn it over the stove without showing it to him. Bess complied.

"Now give me the ashes," Houdini requested.

He pulled his sleeve up and rubbed the ashes on his bare forearm, and, as if by magic, her father's name, Gebhardt, mysteriously was emblazoned on his skin in bloodred letters. What Houdini didn't tell her was that he had learned that effect within the pages of *The Revelations of a Spirit Medium.*

"I was paralyzed with fear," Bess remembered. "Then, slowly, a full realization of the significance of this diabolical thing dawned on me. In my early folklore, the devil, disguised as a handsome young man, lured girls to destruction. It was clear to me that I had married the devil. Stealthily, my eyes on Houdini, I backed toward the door, and then turned suddenly and ran, screaming frantically, from . . . the house."

Houdini caught up to her and pulled her into his arms.

"Silly kid, it was only a trick," he said, laughing.

Bess kept screaming and started biting and kicking Houdini. She finally calmed down, they returned to their room, and he showed her how the simple effect was done.

"By such demonstrations he gradually drove away my superstitions," Bess wrote. "Among other things he taught me the secret of mind-reading and all the arts of legerdemain, including how to go into trances and tell fortunes. My inside view of the mechanism of such phenomena did more than anything else to exorcise the ghosts and hobgoblins that had peopled my world."

Before six months had elapsed, Houdini was integrating these new skills into the act. On January 1, 1895, they were touring the Wonderland circuit as "Professor and Mlle. Houdini, the Occult Expositors," and critics were raving that their act "borders on the supernatural." By June of 1896, Houdini had even incorporated Bess's mind reading effects into his jailhouse publicity stunts. While at the station, he would have the police chief think of a card. A messenger was then sent back to the hotel where "Mme. Marco" waited with the question "What card was thought of?" Bess would send back the answer, which invariably was the correct card.

Despite Bess's swoon to avoid naming the murderer that November night in Garnett, Kansas, Harry and Bess were such a hit that their Spiritualist séances became a regular part of Dr. Hill's show, usually performed on Sunday nights. Some nights Bess played the medium, others Harry enacted the communication with the spirits. The spirits were conveniently obliging, telling them the most intimate details of the personal lives of the astonished audience members who jammed the hall. When the spirits failed them, there was always the visit to the local cemetery with the sexton and old Uncle Rufus, the town gossip. Houdini would carry a notebook, and they'd go from grave to grave talking family history and family scandal. At the end of the day, the two locals would be tipped properly for their cooperation. What gossip Houdini didn't get at the graveyard, he could usually pick up around the boardinghouse dining table.

Houdini instinctively realized the power that was generated by these small, intimate biographical details. Audiences tolerated the song-and-dance numbers and the other routines, but they were starved to hear what Houdini and his spirits had to say about their lives. The reason that the séance act resonated so well was because it was presented as if it was real, down to Bess's swooning. Although he would later remove the Spiritualist context, Houdini would take this energy that was generated by the audience implicitly believing in the reality of what they were experiencing and skillfully use it for the rest of his career.

Sometimes the information that Professor Harry Houdini imparted was too much for the audience to bear. During the first week with Dr. Hill, on a cemetery reconnaissance mission, Houdini had found the fresh grave of six-year-old Joe Osbourne. At the next séance in Garnett, which broke the record for admissions at the opera house, Bess was in a trance when she suddenly said she had a message from "little Joe" for his parents. Someone rushed out and brought back a white-faced Mr. and Mrs. Harry Osbourne.

"Joe says he's in a happy place. And he says, 'Don't cry, Momma. There'll be another one soon to take my place,'" Bess relayed.

The fact was Mrs. Osbourne *was* pregnant, a shrewd guess by Houdini since they were a young, grief-stricken couple. After the séance, an irate Harry Osbourne came backstage to give Houdini a thrashing.

"How could we know of your family circumstances if the medium was not clairvoyant?" Houdini asked him. Then he had Bess rattle off a number of other family secrets that had Osbourne mystified as he left the opera house. This incident made an indelible mark on Houdini. Twenty-six years later, Hallie Nichols, who had been in the opera house that night, went to see Houdini give a lecture on Spiritualism in Kansas City. Receiving a note that she had been in his audience in Garnett years earlier, Houdini asked her to come backstage after the show. She dined with Bess and Harry, and Houdini asked her if she was still in contact with the Osbournes. She said she was and gave Houdini their new California address. He eventually sent the Osbournes a long letter of abject apology for trifling with their emotions.

By the end of Dr. Hill's engagement in Garnett, two local businessmen actually came to Houdini's dressing room and offered him $25 if he would promise not to give any more séances in town. Perhaps they feared the skeletons in their closets might be rattled next.

It was the same at every stop for the rest of the tour. In Galena, before another packed audience at the local opera hall on January 9, 1898, Harry played the role of the medium. Prior to the show, a local tipster had told Houdini that a black man named Benny Carter had been murdered recently, and two of his associates, who were suspects in the killing, were actually in attendance. Later, during the séance, Houdini seized on the information.

"I'm getting a message now. I see coming before me, uh, it's a man. A black man," Houdini said, then paused dramatically, pawing at the air in front of him.

"He's lame—and his throat is cut from ear to ear. Who can this be?"

He was almost screaming now.

"He says his name is Benny. Benny Carter."

There was the sound of commotion from the gallery.

"He says that he has a message for Bill Doakes and Jim Saunders. He says, 'Yo' boys bettah put yo' razors away, or yo' is sho' goin' ter be where Ah is now.' Are Bill Doakes and Jim Saunders present?" Houdini asked.

The hall was deathly silent. Then two men jumped up in the gallery and knocked some chairs over in their haste to make it to the exit.

"Yes, dey is here, but they ain't staying," someone yelled out.

By the beginning of February the Dr. Hill show had finished, and now Bess and Harry barnstormed the Midwest on their own. Houdini had made some good coin doing the Spiritualist séances, enough to buy himself a nice overcoat for $10, to spend $15 on a "fine red dress" for Bess, and to write in his diary that he "lived like a king." There was even enough to deposit $100 cash on February 23, 1898 with L.A. Vories, the mayor of St. Joseph, Missouri, who was instructed to deliver said sum to "any person who can furnish or place upon him handcuffs from which he is unable to extricate himself or to so fasten him to a chair that he cannot release himself therefrom." Bess was aghast—for one, she had no idea that he had saved up such a large sum of money. Then she felt it was reckless and rash to risk their nest egg on a challenge like that. She needn't have worried. No one could defeat him, even though the mayor did hold the bankroll two extra weeks to see if there were any late challengers.

Houdini's newfound affluence was solely due to his séance work. His legitimate shows weren't setting the box offices on fire. So for the next few months he decided that he and Bess would set up in the medium business. For the blueprint he had only to consult his well-used copy of *The Revelations of a Spirit Medium*. From that book he learned of the existence of what was called "The Blue Book," a central clearinghouse of personal information about clients that mediums shared. Houdini got into the mediums' network and was able to get information on the local séance attendees in the town they had just arrived in. He also learned the Bible trick. A peek into a family Bible was sometimes better than hours of scavenging in cemeteries in terms of information and births and deaths in a family. So Harry and Bess became reps for a company that sold musical Bibles door-to-door. Of course, they would compare their musical Bible with the old-fashioned Good Book the family currently owned, allowing them to gather the much-needed data.

Going all out as phony mediums certainly paid the bills, but the moral implications must have weighed heavily on the rabbi's son's mind. While he could rationalize doing a séance act with Bess as a way to save her from "objectionable" contacts in the poorer class of concert halls, the bottom line was he was preying on people who were grief-stricken and vulnerable. What was more absurd to him was that when the actual data that they had dug up was fully mined, Houdini could tell the most outrageous lies imaginable and at least one of these credulous believers would claim it as a direct message to them.

The Houdinis' Spiritualist career sputtered to an end in Canada. One night, Houdini looked out over the audience and recognized a woman he had seen earlier on the street of the same town they were playing. She had been scolding her young son for riding recklessly on his bicycle. During the séance, Houdini called her out and told her that the spirits had prophesied that her young son would break his arm in a fall from his bicycle. As he later discovered, by the time the woman had returned home, the prediction had been fulfilled. The irony of his lucky guess turning out true was the final straw.

"When it was all over I saw and felt that the audience believed in me . . . they believed that my tricks were true communications from those dear dead. The beautiful simplicity of their faith—it appealed to me as a religion—

suddenly gripped me . . . from that day to this I have never posed as a genuine medium," Houdini wrote. "I was brought to a realization of the seriousness of trifling with the hallowed reverence which the average human being bestows on the departed . . . I was chagrined that I should ever have been guilty of such frivolity and for the first time realized that it bordered on crime."

Giving up the Spiritualist buck put the Houdinis right back where they were before they joined up with Dr. Hill. Now they were forced to join a traveling repertoire group that specialized in corny melodramas. According to Bess, Houdini was so mortified to be in this production that he appeared under an assumed name and stuffed his cheeks with wads of paper so no one would recognize him.

It was a mercifully short interlude as Houdini had previously signed up for a second tour with the Welsh Brothers Circus. In the intervening three years since they had last performed with the circus, the brothers had honed their troupe into the best and largest ten-cent show in the country. This time around, Houdini refused to go for the AND FOUND clause in his contract, so his salary was fixed at $25 a week for him to work as "King of Cards" and for the two of them to perform their Metamorphosis. The act went so well and garnered such rave reviews, that pretty soon they closed the show with it.

Shortly after rejoining the circus, the Bard Brothers, an acrobatic act, came on board. Houdini struck up a fast friendship with them, and pretty soon he was seriously training as an acrobat. He started long distance running again, played baseball, and even worked one night as a clown on the horizontal bars. By the summer, he had mastered double and back somersaults and had perfected a routine where he would boomerang a playing card out into the audience, then do a back somersault and land in time to catch the incoming card.

In the fall, the circus came to an end, and now Harry and Bess found themselves back in New York with no real prospects. Clearly discouraged, he paid a visit to his friend Joe Rinn. Rinn was now a leading figure in Spiritualist circles in New York. Through his father, the manager of New York's largest hotel, he had met many of the leading Spiritualists, including Margaret Fox Kane, one of the founders of the movement. Rinn's faith in Spiritualism had been shaken when his parallel interest in magic brought him to Martinka's Magic Shop, then located on New York City's Sixth Avenue. After establishing a friendship with Francis Martinka, one of the proprietors, Rinn discovered that many of the most famous mediums were Martinka's customers, buying magic props that were essential to put over their séances.

"I don't know what to make of our business, Joe," he said. "I feel that my handcuff and trunk escape act should make a hit with the public but it doesn't seem to get across."

"Well, why not proclaim that you are released from your bonds by spirits?" Rinn suggested. "Let them prove otherwise."

"No, I can't do that," Houdini countered. "I got disgusted with myself when Bessie and I were doing our psychic act . . . The poor fools wept and believed we were in touch with the spirit world."

It was more than that though. Houdini would rather fail than dishonor his oath to his father by supporting his mother with the proceeds of a morally bankrupt enterprise.

Rinn, as usual, offered to front Houdini some money, and Houdini, as usual, had too much pride to take him up on the offer. Around that time, Bess's brother-in-law, who had good contacts at the Yale Lock factory, offered to get Houdini a job there. Houdini must have seriously considered it, because he later wrote that things had become so bad at the end of 1898 that, "I contemplated quitting the show business, and retire to private life, meaning to work by day at one of my trades . . . and open a school of magic."

He published an expanded version of *Magic Made Easy*, sixteen pages now, that included a full back-page ad for Professor Harry Houdini's School of Magic at 221 East Sixty-ninth Street, which was his mother's address. A perusal of that catalog made it clear that Houdini was about to call it quits because nestled in those ads for gypsy fortune-teller books and talking skulls and vanishing handkerchiefs and instructions detailing *How to Hypnotize any Animal* was a small ad on page ten. It read:

57 HANDCUFF ACT.

The only complete act of its kind. You defy the police authorities and sheriffs to place handcuffs or leg shackles on you, and you can easily escape. Price on application. If interested, write.

No one was interested.

4

Quid Pro Quo

THE ROTUND, REDHEADED LIEUTENANT HAD JUST finished placing a pair of handcuffs on Houdini's wrists, double-locking them to insure their security. He wasn't through yet. Now he bent down, not an easy job for a man of his immense girth, and fastened a brand-spanking-new set of leg irons around Houdini's ankles. With some effort, he straightened up and surveyed his work.

"Hey, Andy," Frank Corbus, one of his fellow detectives, yelled, "you're going easy on the lad unless you use the newest jewelry."

Andy Rohan nodded. Corbus would know—he was legendary around the central station as one of the best sleight-of-hand men in the area. In fact, many of his colleagues had placed side bets that he could equal, if not excel, this Houdini fellow as a magician.

"A capital idea," Rohan said, and walked over to his desk. From the bottom drawer he removed a state-of-the-art set of handcuffs.

"Get out of these handcuffs and leg irons and I'll think that I'm walking in my sleep sure enough," Rohan quipped as he snapped one end of the cuffs to the leg irons. Then he maneuvered Houdini into a crouching position and fastened the other end to the first pair of handcuffs. The magician was so trussed-up that it was impossible for him to even walk.

"I don't think you're going anywhere without the aid of these," Rohan said, as he dangled the keys in front of Houdini's face.

Houdini just smiled.

"I guess you'll need some assistance to get to your cabinet," said Rohan, gesturing to two detectives who were watching the demonstration. Detectives Duffy and Fitzgerald lifted Houdini up and carried him over to the makeshift cabinet that had been set up in the middle of the large room.

Lieutenant Andrew Rohan of the Chicago Police Department. *Library of Congress*

Houdini began laughing.

They deposited him in the cabinet and then closed the curtain. The room was still for a couple of minutes, and then the silence was shattered by the thud of steel hitting the floor. A minute later, the curtain was pushed back, and Houdini emerged, holding the irons and cuffs in his hand.

"Here are your handcuffs, Mr. Rohan. Please remember that good scrap steel is going for a quarter of a cent per pound," Houdini said.

The crowd in the roll-call room buzzed with excitement.

"I'm having a nightmare, sure enough," Rohan said, as he took the irons from Houdini. The detectives circled Rohan and examined the cuffs. They were amazed to see that they were securely locked and undamaged in any way.

The year 1899 was getting off to a good start for Houdini. He had come to the Midwest on December 5, merely to fulfill some earlier bookings, still pessimistic about his future as a magician. Toledo went poorly, and he was laid off halfway through his engagement. Grand Rapids didn't go much better, but he could always rely on Middleton's in Chicago, where he'd make some extra money by selling his small pitch book between shows. Then he could go back to New York with a little bit of a financial cushion before he had to make the decision that he was dreading.

This time in Chicago something different happened. It's not known who made the initial contact, but for two days before this exhibition at Central Station on the evening of January 4, Houdini conferred with Lieutenant Andrew Rohan, a fixture on the Chicago police force since "Twenty-second Street was a swamp," the papers wrote. After these meetings, Rohan had arranged for Houdini to give a demonstration of his escape artistry right in the middle of the roll-call room, before an audience of more than two hundred people that included a good number of the police brass, all of the city detectives, a "miscellaneous assortment of experts," and, of course, the press. The only person missing that night was one of the deans of the Chicago press corps, a friend of Rohan's, who had coauthored a massive history of the Chicago police in 1887. No, John E. Wilkie couldn't be present that night in Chicago. He was busy in Washington, D.C., serving as the new chief of the U.S. Secret Service.

President William McKinley had taken office in 1897 in the midst of one of the most debilitating economic depressions in U.S. history. Charged with the task of turning the economy around was Treasury Secretary Lyman Gage, the former president of the First National Bank of Chicago. His undersecretary, Frank

Vanderlip, was a former newspaperman who had served under Wilkie at *The Chicago Tribune*. Gage and Vanderlip had been running Treasury for almost a year when they decided that a change in leadership at the Secret Service was needed.

"We want a man who is not an old-fashioned detective, who is a gentleman, who has administrative ability, who is diplomatic, a good 'mixer,' and will be at home with Prince or pauper, whose honesty is unquestioned, who has, above all, sticktoitiveness," Gage said. What he didn't say was that the McKinley administration was contemplating a major realignment of the duties of the Secret Service. No longer would Secret Service merely be the agency that officially tracked down counterfeiters and, at that time, unofficially protected the president. They were about to charge the Secret Service with the responsibility for the vast majority of the intelligence and counterintelligence gathering for the United States. And John Wilkie was going to be their spymaster.

They couldn't have chosen a better candidate. Born in Elgin, Illinois, Wilkie followed in the footsteps of his father, Franc Wilkie, a famous Civil War correspondent, and at eighteen was a night reporter at the same paper, *The Chicago Times*. Journeying with his father to London, he immediately made a name for himself by sending back a dispatch that ridiculed the published reports in London papers of great preparations for war against Russia. Wilkie traveled around England, visiting many major ports, and found no signs of preparedness evident. Returning to Chicago, he became a police reporter in 1881 for *The Chicago Tribune*, the *Times*' great rival.

Wilkie was sworn in as chief of the U.S. Secret Service, at an annual salary of $3,500, on February 28, 1898, two weeks after an explosion rocked the battleship *Maine*, killing 260 sailors. By then, it was clear that the United States was about to go to war with Spain, which had been blamed for the carnage. With no CIA or FBI in existence, Wilkie was charged with coordinating both counterintelligence and foreign espionage. Going outside the ranks of his agency, Wilkie brought in fresh blood, and less than two months later had a special task force assembled and was trailing Spanish spies in the United States.

When the trail led to Montreal, where the Spanish attaché who headed the ring was quartered, Wilkie used two actors from the Bob Fitzsimmons Theatrical Company to accompany his Secret Service agent, who, under the guise of looking for housing, gained entry into the attaché's rented quarters, where the agent stole a letter destined for Spain that outlined the ongoing espionage against the United States. Leaked to the papers, the letter provoked outrage, and Canada was forced to expel the Spaniards, effectively breaking the back of the spy ring.

It was forward-thinking for the chief of America's only intelligence operation to be using entertainers for covert activities in 1898. There was something

John E. Wilkie, chief of the U.S. Secret Service. *Library of Congress*

else intriguing about using this particular troupe. Bob Fitzsimmons wasn't just a theatrical impresario. He was the then-reigning heavyweight champion of the world. He was also a magician.

There was precedent for the Secret Service recruiting magicians.

Even before it was called the Secret Service, Horatio G. Cooke, an eighteen-year-old magician, dazzled President Abraham Lincoln with his skills at escaping rope ties, and was appointed by Lincoln as a scout, the then-current term for spies who infiltrated Confederate lines during the Civil War. He utilized his skills as an escape artist to free his scouting party and save them from execution after they had been ambushed and tied up by the Confederates.

Cooke became close with Lincoln. He was in the theater when the president was shot and was one of the few people to be at his bedside when he died. After the war, he became a professional magician and spent forty-one years exposing fraudulent spirit mediums. Near the end of his life, he became close friends with Houdini.

On May 15, 1886, *The New York Times* ran a small article about some counterfeiters who had been arrested near Detroit. Ezekiel Wellington Jones, a "colored" man, had been taken into custody after his home was raided. During the raid, the sheriff, accompanied by a Deputy United States Marshall also arrested "one 'Professor' Louis S. Leon, a reputed magician and sleight of hand performer." Leon provided information leading to a seizure at a nearby underground cellar of large quantities of dies, and finished and unfinished coins. The article went on to note that while the "professor" was currently being held in jail at Cassopolis, "it is suspected there that Leon is really a detective." In fact, it had always been Secret Service policy that undercover agents would take an arrest and maintain their cover until Washington could contact the local authorities and gain their release. It seems to have worked in this case, because two months later, Professor Leon was back in the newspapers, this time for ropewalking 1,440 feet over the chasm at Tallulah Falls, Georgia. In the early 1900s the Secret Service also reached out to an escape artist named R. G. Herrmann, who retired from the stage and went to work for the service, and probably utilized his skills as a safe expert.

There was one other compelling reason why Wilkie would have the mindset to think to utilize a magician as a Secret Service operative—Chief Wilkie was an adept magician himself. Wilkie was circumspect about his skills at legerdemain, yet by 1902 a newspaper reporter had revealed that the head of the Secret Service was not only a magician but a "disciple of the illustrious Herrmann." His utilization of associates in the course of doing mind reading to unsuspecting visitors to his office was documented in newspapers and magic magazines. While still a reporter in Chicago, he single-handedly created the most enduring myth in the field of magic—the Indian rope trick. In 1908 Wilkie revealed to a reporter that "sleight of hand is figuring more and more in the operations of the secret service." Even though a respected magic magazine maintained that he was one of the best amateurs in the country, Wilkie told the reporter that he had "several men" at the bureau who were much better at magic than him.

The ability to perform sleight of hand would be indispensable to a Secret Service field operative charged with breaking up counterfeit currency rings. Wilkie himself in that 1908 *Washington Post* article recounts one such incident. "One of our men who is pretty handy with his fingers was trying to land a gang of counterfeiters and succeeded in establishing friendly relations with the bunch. Every newcomer is naturally looked upon with suspicion until he commits some overt act, and in this instance the gang determined to have a showdown. In floating bad money each man is given so much of it and keeps half of the good money he gets hold of, turning the remainder in to the makers. The operator was given a lot of $1 imitations and told to get rid of them, another of the gang going along to see that he made good. Each time that he entered a store to make a small purchase, as the real crook thought, he came out with the proper change. But for some reason his companion was not satisfied and adopted the policy of entering the places with him, watching him closely as he bought. It was a pretty trying situation, but our man managed to do the sleight of hand trick so well that good American dollars found their way to the cash drawer while the 'phony' ones disappeared somewhere on his person, as evidence against the counterfeiters."

With his early success in smashing Spain's spy ring in the short-lived Spanish-American War, Wilkie knew that the purview of his agency had changed. Faced with more than six hundred suspected threats to national security, which had been winnowed down from more than a thousand tips, he also knew that he was seriously understaffed for the task at hand.

There were about 1,300 protestors at the workers' rally in Haymarket Square in Chicago on May 4, 1886, when the rains came. Apparently, for most of the people there, their indignation over the murder of four unarmed strikers at the McCormick Reaper Works factory by members of the Chicago Police Department the previous day was not as strong as their fear of getting wet, because 1,000 of the dissidents promptly left the square. So it seemed a little like overkill for 180 of Chicago's finest to march in and demand that the 300 remaining diehards disperse immediately. It was shortly after that the bomb exploded in the center of the police ranks. One policeman died on the spot, seven died later, and many were injured. The police responded with wild gunfire. At the end of the night, at least seven protestors were dead and a hundred were wounded, half civilians and half policemen.

The reaction was swift. A wave of fear convulsed the nation. Politicians, civic leaders, prominent businessmen, even some renegade union leaders pointed fingers at the foreign-born anarchists who were fomenting a wave of terror, not only in the United States but across the planet. Four nights later there was a knock on the door of the rooming house on 229 West Lake Street. Andy Rohan, not yet a lieutenant on the detective squad, was directed to the room of a Thomas Brown, an Irish immigrant who was an active socialist and had been at a meeting of the American Group of the International Workingmen's Association just minutes before the Haymarket rally commenced. Even though Brown claimed that he had only attended the rally for a few minutes that evening and had sought refuge at Zeph's Saloon for a beer or two when the deluge began, Rohan arrested him for conspiracy to commit murder in connection with the deadly bombing at Haymarket Square.

The notion of an international anarchist conspiracy to create disorder and topple the established world order gained strength among all sectors of society as the 1880s progressed—with good reason. The years from 1892 until 1901 would be noted as the Decade of Regicide, a time when more kings, prime ministers, and even presidents met their fate at the hands of assassins than in any other period in recorded history. Even in cases like the assassination of Alexander II of Russia in 1881, or the attempted assassinations of Kaiser Wilhelm I in 1878 and King Humbert of Italy in 1878 and Alexander III in 1887, where the assailants were revolutionary socialists or just plain lone nuts, the violence was attributed to anarchists. The only man in America who had both the raw data and the ability to analyze it within the context of an international problem was Chief Wilkie. With the Secret Service serving as both the de facto national police force and the only federal counterintelligence agency, Wilkie knew that reports like the ones that had been generated during that conflict were essential to safeguard both the president (which was his unofficial responsibility) and the public order. Tracking anarchists in the United States wouldn't really present such a problem, but to gain information in Europe, where that "tribe" originated, was another story. What little information we obtained overseas was generated by our naval attachés. Wilkie instinctively knew this was not enough. When the Spanish-American War broke out, our intelligence with respect to the capability and even location of the Spanish fleet was woefully inadequate. Rather than waiting for meager intelligence to filter in, Wilkie dispatched a Secret Service operative to Madrid a few weeks after hostilities commenced. With the dispatch of that agent, Wilkie had broadened the powers of the Secret Service from counterintelligence to active intelligence-gathering overseas.

Back stateside, Wilkie was hamstrung by the small number of agents that the Secret Service employed. Because of our unique system of federalism, America never had a national police force, but he could look to one other place, a private club, for cooperation in coordinating responses against criminal activity. The International Association of Chiefs of Police was founded in 1893 (and originally named the National Chiefs of Police Union) when police chiefs from all over America assembled in Chicago to form a cooperative network to apprehend and return wanted criminals who had fled their local jurisdictions. Within a few years, the IACP (which now included members from Canada and Latin America) founded the National Bureau of Identification—a repository of both photographs and measurements (done according to the Bertillon system of classification, which measured parts of the body and skull to positively identify criminals since fingerprinting had not yet been perfected) of known criminals in the United States. Located in Chicago, the bureau amassed a large database and lobbied to get the Bertillon system adopted by federal agencies. Detective Andy Rohan became one of the acknowledged U.S. experts in the Bertillon system of criminal identification. Wilkie would later funnel police requests from other countries to the IACP, unofficially sanctioning it as a national police organization.

In early May of 1898, just a few weeks into the Spanish-American War, the IACP convened their sixth annual convention in Milwaukee. Joining the chiefs of police from almost every major city in the country were two old friends from Chicago, John Wilkie and Andy Rohan.

"Let's see your hands," Detective McCarthy ordered Houdini, after the magician had escaped from another pair of handcuffs that night at the central station.

McCarthy was astounded to note that Houdini's hands weren't in the least bit cut or chafed.

"He's got wooden legs," Detective Cudmore interjected, as he examined the magician's muscular limbs. For the next forty-five minutes the police officers tried more handcuffs, rope, cords, whatever they could think of to bind Houdini. Every time, he'd retreat to his cabinet and emerge a free man.

None of the detectives could even come up with a theory on how Houdini was liberating himself. They were in total awe of him. Houdini laughed at their amazement and then sat down and showed them some card magic.

It fell to Rohan to give the newspaper reporters the lines that would be quoted in the next day's accounts.

"I cannot explain how that fellow got out of those handcuffs," Lieutenant Rohan marveled. "It was simply impossible to either pick the lock or slip them off. I would have banked my life that a prisoner bound as he was could never have regained his freedom. It is miraculous. These cuffs are the best made, and the prisoner they will not hold cannot be kept in custody by the strongest bars or the best locks. No wonder the Lima bank, with its modern and complicated locks, was robbed."

Just a week before, a seemingly impregnable time lock on a bank in Lima, Ohio, had been compromised and $18,170 was stolen.

"I'll go through your time locks on your banks and open your combinations as the Lima robbers did without any trouble," Houdini bluffed. "It is all trickery."

Then he collected his cards, signaled to Bess, and said his good-byes to Lieutenant Rohan and the assembled reporters.

Just as Houdini was disappearing through the doorway, Rohan, as if to punctuate the story, shouted after him, "Stay away from here! We don't want to have you locked up in this station. You'd give these coppers the cold shivers so badly that they couldn't work."

Leaving the precinct, Houdini knew the constant work was finally beginning to pay off. By now, he had already mastered almost all of the skills he would rely upon for the rest of his life. Through his knowledge of showmanship, he could make a mountain out of a molehill. He understood a great deal about mental misdirection—how to plant ideas, how to get an audience to think what—not just look where—he wanted. Although he would never rate with the top handful of masters, his sleight of hand was well practiced. He knew the fundamentals of locks, and building upon that base, he would become the master. He understood what it meant to be in the public eye, to tell a good story, and to get the newsmen to write an even better one—and most important, to get them to love him. He not only comprehended the methods of the fraudulent mediums, he knew why they worked, the psychology of what the sitter was there to see. Houdini had learned a great lesson from the Spiritualists—his escape had to be perceived as real. Not in the supernatural sense, but in the sense that he was always capable, at all times, of escaping from anything. Every act he'd ever crossed paths with had rubbed off on him. He did backflips he'd learned from his friend Jim Bard and watched Evatima Tardo so closely, he knew she would only let the snakes bite after her stomach was full of milk and nothing but milk. He'd graduated magna cum laude from the university of deception. He had the tools, and he knew it.

Now the sun, the moon, and the stars came into alignment. For the only time in the history of the United States, a magician ran the Secret Service. This same magician understood that special tasks took special people. The next morning, after his early morning coffee run, Houdini burst into his hotel room, waving the papers. He was holding a copy of *The Chicago Journal* and there, on the front page, under a headline of "Amazes the Detectives" was a large, splendid drawing of Houdini. He woke Bess up.

"Bess! Bess! I'm famous! Look at my picture in the papers!"

Harry Houdini
PHOTO - TAKEN - 1903
July 9 - 1909 Brighton Eng.
BIOGRAPH

Library of Congress

5

The King of Handcuffs

THEY'RE PLUGGED! THE SON OF A bitch plugged these cuffs. What am I going to do? There's no way I can get out unless I saw these off.

Houdini's mind raced. He couldn't comprehend how things could have gone so wrong. He had been packing the audiences into the Clark Street Museum in Chicago since his much-heralded escape from Rohan's handcuffs at the central station. All week long various police officers had come by, handcuffs in tow, to challenge him and to pick up the $50 reward that Houdini offered if he couldn't free himself from the restraints. Of course, no one left with any cash.

So Houdini didn't have second thoughts as a Sergeant Waldron slipped his cuffs around the magician's wrists and clicked them shut, but as soon as he retreated into his curtained-off cabinet, he knew that something was dreadfully wrong.

Maybe I should just go out and denounce him. No, it's probably better to wait. If I'm lucky, most of the audience will be gone. I just hope there are no reporters around. They'd write that it was my Waterloo.

Outside, Waldron waited patiently. The audience didn't share his equanimity.

"What's the matter, Houdini? You forgot your key?" someone shouted. The crowd laughed. After a half hour, the chuckles had turned to jeers. When Houdini finally emerged from his cabinet a full hour later, he had managed to get only one cuff off. It hardly mattered by then; the only people left were Waldron and Bess, who was bitterly weeping.

"So, do you give up, Houdini?" the sergeant asked.

"No," Houdini spat. "But you rigged these cuffs. They're impossible to get out of."

The policeman laughed. "You got me there. You can work on these till kingdom come and you won't get 'em open. I fixed a slug in it so it won't unlock."

Houdini was furious. He was even angrier after he had to saw through the metal to get the cuff off. That whole night, he replayed the humiliation over and over in his mind. And he vowed that never again would he accept a handcuff from a challenger without making them open the lock to prove that they were in working order. Not that it would matter. Not that he had a career left.

"Well, Bess, I'm done for. The whole world will know that I failed to get out of a cuff. We may as well quit," Houdini said, pacing their rented room. "I'll take that job your brother-in-law offered to get me at the Yale Lock factory."

His words had a hollow ring. This turn of events was inconceivable. Just a week earlier, Houdini had worked out a quid pro quo with Rohan. The arrangement had even been spelled out in *The National Detective Police Review*, billed as "American's Only Detective and Police Newspaper." Houdini would give the police the "benefit of his skill." In return, the police were supposed to boost his career, not destroy it.

The next day a glum Houdini went back to the museum to pick up his props.

"Well, two minutes late, are we?" Manager Hedges observed.

"You mean I'm still working here? After I had to be sawed loose from those cuffs?" Houdini said.

"Didn't you get out of that cuff? That's the first I knew about it," Hedges said.

"I couldn't. They were plugged," Houdini said.

"Well if they were fixed, what's the difference?" Hedges said. "Now get up on that platform and go to work."

Back to work he went. Waldron's "exposure" of Houdini received virtually no publicity, about a column inch in *The Chicago Journal*. Even then the paper took Houdini's side, noting that "they were not practicable handcuffs at all, having no lock whatever," and that "the affair was simply a joke on the part of the officer."

From this point on, for the next year and a half, Houdini would traverse the country with a set game plan to establish his name. He would arrive in town and immediately arrange a visit to the local precinct. A large number of police officers and brass (and press, of course) would marvel as he escaped from any restraint the police would throw at him. The police chief would then comment, as if reading from a script, that he hoped it would never be his misfortune to have a prisoner like Houdini, and that the magician had helped the police improve their security for the future. Houdini would then get a commendation letter signed by the officers and patrolmen in attendance, and it would go into his burgeoning scrapbook.

The point man for this arrangement was Lieutenant Andy Rohan in Chicago. In return for boosting Houdini, the police received tangible benefits. His expertise in the mechanics of police restraints was second to none. He began to expose cardsharping techniques, writing bylined newspaper articles exposing mechanical devices that literally secreted cards up the sleeves of the crooked card player, and spending hours demonstrating for reporters the secrets behind the three-card monte hustle. After revealing their techniques, Houdini sounded like a public service announcement: "All of which should warn an amateur not to wager money on cards when they are manipulated . . . A clever man can do everything but make them talk."

His prowess at card cheating sometimes reaped unwanted dividends, as it had a few years earlier in Coffeeville, Kansas, with the Dr. Hill medicine show. One night after his performance, he had been approached by two gamblers to break into the rear door of a gambling house after it had closed for the night. They didn't want to steal anything, they just wanted to fix some decks of cards and clean up the next day. They offered Houdini $100 for the job. "Morally, I had no compunctions. It is dog eat dog with gamblers, and the hundred looked good to me," Houdini wrote. "But so did life—and I knew that if we got caught I'd be strung up for my pains. I declined with thanks."

The gamblers wouldn't take no for an answer. Houdini had gone back to his hotel and had fallen asleep, when he was roused to go to the local telegram office to pick up an urgent message from New York. It was just a ruse. On the way to the office, he felt the cold sensation of a gun muzzle right behind his ear. The gamblers marched him to the opera house, where he got his "pickers," and right to the back door of that gambling joint. As soon as he picked the lock, he jerked the door open, knocking down the two ruffians in the process. He dashed inside, locked the door behind him, and waited for the men to leave. He didn't figure on one of the gamblers spying him through the grating of the cellar window and firing off a shot. Houdini had raised his hand to shield himself. To the end of his days, Houdini carried that bullet in his hand.

Houdini and Bess had just settled into their hotel in St. Paul, Minnesota, when the magician read the newspaper reports. A handcuffed criminal had escaped from the police, who were now combing the city in an attempt to find him. Then, oddly enough, over the next few days, every time that he left his room, whether it was to go dine or to travel to the Palm Garden, where he was

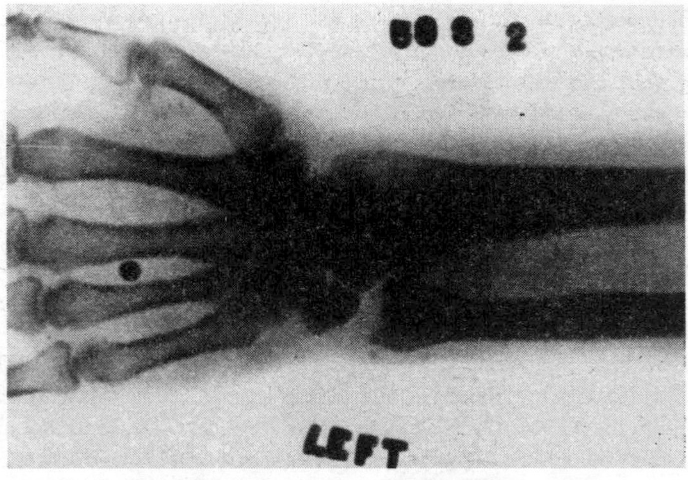

X-ray showing the bullet in Houdini's hand. *From the collection of Kevin Connolly*

performing, Houdini noticed that the doors to the two rooms that were directly adjacent to his also opened, and each time, the same two men walked into the corridor at precisely the same time he had.

One afternoon at about three-thirty, Houdini heard a scuffle in the hallway outside his room. He stepped outside to investigate, and he saw his two mysterious neighbors fighting with a man who was wearing a long opera cloak. The two men finally managed to subdue their lone victim. And then he saw that underneath that long cloak, the man's hands were handcuffed.

"It's all right, Houdini," one of the detectives said. "We knew he'd come to you." They were so confident, they hadn't even bothered to inform the magician that he was being used as bait.

An escaped con with a hankering to shed his bracelets wasn't the only big fish that Houdini reeled in during that engagement in St. Paul. One night a party of theater managers came to see his show. One of them was Martin Beck, the powerful impresario who ran the Orpheum vaudeville circuit, which had a virtual monopoly on all the good theaters in the Midwest and on the West Coast. Beck, who was based in Chicago, had probably read about Houdini's escape from Rohan's cuffs. Now he wanted to see the magician do it firsthand. He returned the next night with three sets of cuffs that he'd purchased. Houdini defeated them all.

Back in Chicago, Beck sent Houdini a telegram offering him a tryout in his theater in Omaha at the end of March. He'd pay him sixty dollars a week, come see the show, and "probably make you proposition for all next season." From the beginning, Houdini's relationship with Beck was contentious. Beck advised Houdini to cut out all his magic effects and to present only handcuff escapes and the Metamorphosis. Houdini compromised by keeping his card work but omitting the silk handkerchief routine and shipping off the birds to a friend in Chicago, who promptly ate them.

When Houdini first set foot into the Creighton-Orpheum Theater in Omaha, he felt like he was entering another world. With its eight-hundred-plus plush seats and lavishly appointed dressing rooms, Harry had finally made the big time. Sharing the block with an equally impressive mansard-roofed mansion of a local mining magnate, Houdini was literally and figuratively in a new neighborhood. No more sharing a dime museum stage with the Marvelous Little Askenas Triplets or The Dog-Faced Boy.

Houdini was ready for prime time. "He gives a performance that rivals in almost every respect the showing made by any of the better known magicians," one critic wrote, comparing him favorably to Alexander Herrmann and Harry Kellar. One night, responding to Houdini's challenge, a committee of five local businessmen ambled onstage to challenge Houdini to escape the handcuff they produced, which featured a time lock mechanism that couldn't be opened in less than sixty minutes. The cuffs were fitted and locked; Houdini retreated to his cabinet and the wait began. After four minutes, there wasn't a sound to be heard anywhere in the auditorium. Then "thirteen seconds more and the professor stepped quietly from the tent. The handcuffs were dangling from the tip of his right forefinger, while a smile of triumph curled his lips. He was roundly cheered and the committee retired somewhat abashed," a local paper reported.

He was just as much a sensation in Kansas City, the next stop on the Orpheum tour. One night, he was challenged by a man with a pair of double-lock cuffs. Rather than having them fastened with his hands in front of him, Houdini suggested that they be locked while his arms were behind his back. The committee complied. Houdini stepped back into his cabinet, but for the first time ever, he didn't draw the curtain, so he was still standing in full view of the audience. For a full minute he stood there motionless and then he suddenly threw the handcuffs disdainfully to the floor. Houdini wrote in his diary: "1st time I took off Hcuffs with curtain open . . . was the hit of act."

Houdini's handcuff act created such a sensation that he began to be billed as "The Wizard of Shackles, A Man of Marvels." Sometimes it was merely "Man of Shackles," other times Bess got equal billing as half of "The Houdinis." By Joplin, Missouri, Houdini had finally decided on a billing commensurate to his ability. From then on, he was "The King of Handcuffs." The handcuff act became such a phenomenon that local merchants began featuring him in ads.

Not everybody appreciated the newly crowned Handcuff King's brash and boastful style of self-promotion. One critic, after admitting that his escape work was wonderful, felt that "Houdini wastes a lot of valuable time in telling the audience how good he is." And the Nebraska Clothing Company hinted at collusion with the police in its ad in *The Kansas City Star*. The ad must have rankled Houdini, because on his next stop through Kansas City, four months later, he visited the clothing store and confronted the employee who wrote the ad.

"I'm Houdini. You're from Missouri. I'll show you," he said, and then he escaped from cuffs, did some card effects, unlocked a door lock using a wooden toothpick, produced a fine cigar out of thin air, pulled a pristine match out of a black inkwell, and lit up. The next ad recounted all this and added, "Give Houdini a few more years and he'll have cigars to burn and money to burn as well." By the time they had finished lavishing praise on Houdini, there were barely a few lines left to tout the ties they had on sale that week.

The train was just about to leave the station in Albuquerque to make its run to San Francisco, and Houdini was missing. He had left the car over an hour ago, promising to bring back some ice cream to take the edge off the intense desert heat, and that was the last Bess had seen of him. Then, just as the starting whistle blew and the train's engine began to wheeze, she looked out the window and there he was, running like a madman with a huge can under his arm. George, the porter, had to literally haul him aboard the train.

"Come, folks, ice-cream for all," Houdini shouted gleefully as he walked down the aisle of the train. Bess sighed with relief.

"George, you're also in on this party, and here's a small present for your kindness," Houdini said, dropping five shiny new silver dollars into the porter's hand.

Bess was aghast. They had been down to their last five dollars, an amount that had to last them until they got paid in San Francisco. They had even shared a single cup of coffee each morning to economize. As soon as Houdini sat down, she interrogated him.

"Where did you get that money? Did you kill someone?"

"No, sweetheart," he laughed. "Let's eat the ice-cream first."

George produced dishes for all their fellow passengers, and everyone enjoyed the delicious treat. Everyone but Bess, who was too nervous to eat, especially after she caught a glimpse of her husband's pockets, which were near bursting from the weight of seventy-five silver dollars.

Later, Houdini explained that he had run into a crap game in town. He had secreted three of their five dollars in an inner pocket and tried his luck with the remaining two bucks. He described the game in detail, a description that was incomprehensible to Bess but left George the porter delirious with joy at Houdini's good luck. The $2 wager had been parlayed to eighty-five dollars. It was a fortuitous rest stop indeed.

This trip to the West Coast may also have been Houdini's first mission for the U. S. Secret Service. The counterfeiting of silver dollars in the Western portion of the country was a major problem for Wilkie in the spring of 1899. On the same day that Houdini was stepping off that train to San Francisco, his pockets bulging with silver dollars, there was an article in *The Los Angeles Times* warning that both California and the entire West Coast were being flooded with dangerous counterfeit coins manufactured using the hot-die process. Since the counterfeits were being generated from a mold of a legitimate silver dollar, the design and the weight of the fake coins were indistinguishable from the legitimate ones. "Secret Service officials are laboring earnestly to apprehend the offenders," Wilkie promised.

Houdini had been receiving orientation on counterfeiting techniques around the same time from police officers in Kansas City. On April 10, 1899 he paid a visit to police headquarters where he conferred with Chief Hayes, Inspector Halpin, Captain Branham, and the detective squad. After Houdini demonstrated his ability to escape from their cuffs and shackles, Chief Hayes took him to a back room and showed him a machine that had been employed to make counterfeit $20 pieces. According to the newspaper account, "Houdini was much pleased with the machine, and when shown how simple it was laughed heartily."

Houdini's first visit to California coincided perfectly with the anticounterfeiting operation launched by Wilkie. From June 2 to July 29, Houdini shuttled back and forth between San Francisco and Los Angeles, the two California cities where major counterfeiting rings had just been uncovered. Chief Wilkie also made a trip to California at exactly the same time, a trip "believed to have been connected with the attempt now being made to break up gangs of counterfeiters operating on the Pacific Coast," *The Washington Post* reported.

In San Francisco, Houdini insisted on renting a hotel room for six dollars a week, which included running water and a gas stove, luxuries they usually

Houdini being shackled in front of San Francisco policemen.

Conjuring Arts Research Center

eschewed. It also came with a flea infestation that kept Bess awake and scratching into the wee hours, while Houdini slept peacefully. He also slept through a minor earthquake that rolled both him and Bess out of bed and onto the floor. The next day, he was at the central police station. With the consent of Chief Lee, Houdini demonstrated his prowess in escaping restraints in front of four hundred officers, using a table set up in the center of the assembly room as a makeshift stage. At one point, he simultaneously escaped from four pairs of handcuffs and an Oregon Boot, a fifty-five-pound weight that encircled one leg and was secured by a combination lock. The ensuing publicity helped pack the Orpheum for his two-week run.

In Los Angeles, Houdini repeated his performance in Chief Glass's office at the central police station, much to the delight of an old policeman named Commodore Hill. Hill, an avowed Spiritualist who had previously been the laughingstock of the department, saw Houdini's escapes as confirmation of his religion. "I tell you, boys, it's the spirits," Hill said. "I have seen the same thing dozens of times at Spiritualist meetings, and there can't nobody do these things but spirits, I tell you." Comfortable with blurring the line, Houdini refused to confirm or deny Hill's assertion and told the policemen they should figure his method out for themselves. He did take umbrage with Hill's declaration that he could tie up Houdini with rope to the point where he couldn't escape. Houdini made a second trip to police headquarters and escaped Hill's ties with ease.

By now, Houdini was mastering the art of publicity. He became expert at bantering with reporters, giving them succinct, quotable answers to their queries. He began generating articles as well, big two-page spreads like "How I Effect My Rope Ties" that featured him posing for a seven-shot series of photos demonstrating his escape. "Any one can do the escape act if they only know how," he wrote. "This being aided by spirits in a dark cabinet is all bosh. Of course one must do the act out of sight of the audience, just as I do the escape from handcuffs at the Orpheum, or after people had seen how simple it is, they would not pay to see it again." Houdini's rope tie exposé article was the beginning of a cunning strategy to expose an act after he had stopped performing it, thereby making it much more difficult for his imitators to follow him. This salting the earth strategy would be implemented throughout his career.

With a full media blitz saturating the newspapers in San Francisco and Los Angeles, it seemed oddly timed that the first exposé of Houdini's act should be printed in San Francisco on the last day of Houdini's western engagement in

Los Angeles, but there it was—a full-page story by "Professor Benzon," an English card conjurer who had just moved to San Francisco, complete with photos of the magician unlocking handcuffs by means of a key in his mouth. *The Los Angeles Call* picked up the story the next day and prompted a curt response from Houdini. "Why I can do the trick stripped stark naked," he told the reporter. And that's exactly what he did, making an unscheduled return to the San Francisco police station, where he shed his clothes, was examined by a police surgeon, and proceeded to escape from ten pairs of police handcuffs that crisscrossed his arms and connected to leg shackles. Then, for good measure, he made an escape from a leather belt used to restrain the violently ill. At the conclusion of the demonstration, Houdini revealed that the Orpheum management had retained his services for the coming week, and that he had challenged Benzon to escape from his cuffs. If Benzon succeeded, Houdini would pay him $100. If he failed, all the magician wanted was "the privilege of cutting off his whiskers on the Orpheum stage."

Whether Benzon's exposé was a setup isn't known. If it wasn't, it showed Houdini's shrewd ability to turn a setback into a victory by going one step further than his opponent. The nude escape was conceptually brilliant—how could he be using keys or picks if he would consent to do the escape nude? In one fell swoop, Houdini had eclipsed all his rivals, whose acts consisted of buying keys, hiding them in a pocket, and using them to open the cuffs in the cabinet. The notion that Benzon was part of a choreographed feud must be considered, though. In Boston a few months later, the exact same article "exposing" Houdini was printed with the byline of "Professor Pooley" and timed to coincide with Houdini's first large engagement there. And years later, when Professor Benzon applied to the Society of American Magicians for membership, he was admitted despite the fact that the legendary grudge-holder Harry Houdini was then the president.

Taking his act from the dime museums to the considerably more prestigious Orpheum vaudeville circuit seemed to set Houdini's creative juices flowing. In September of 1899, while in St. Louis, he told a reporter that he would jump from the Eads Bridge into the river with handcuffs on his wrists and shackles on his ankles and come up unfettered. "I know I can do it, and I will . . . There is absolutely no question in my mind of my ability to free myself of the irons while I am underwater. That is an old trick of mine." Then he proposed another test—one in which he would be shackled, placed in a bag, then in a basket, which would then be closed and thrown into a deep tank. After a minute, the basket would be drawn up and found to contain only the bag and locks, while Houdini would be swimming freely around the tank. Both of these daring escapes would become major publicity stunts for him in the years to come.

In Buffalo, a few months later, Houdini refined his police station escape by allowing himself to be laced into a straitjacket, and then entwined three times with a long strap that was locked in the middle of his back. His mouth was plastered and bound with a handkerchief. It took the police fifteen minutes to restrain him in this fashion; he was free of everything in half that time, leaving the plaster and the handkerchief in place to show that he hadn't taken anything from his mouth.

By the end of 1899, Houdini had established himself as one of the new shining stars of vaudeville—at least of the Orpheum circuit. Now he was intent on breaking into the eastern houses, which were controlled by the Keith Brothers and their manager, E. F. Albee. Beck had arrangements with the eastern houses, so Houdini began his assault on the East Coast in early January 1900 in Boston. His first visit was to police headquarters, where Inspector William Watts was waiting. Watts was one of the prime movers in the IACP, the International Association of Chiefs of Police, a devotee of the Bertillon system, and a friend of Andy Rohan. And he certainly didn't deviate one iota from the script.

"I'm glad to see you, Houdini, but I guess I've got you up against the wall this time," Chief Watts said, holding a one-hundred-year-old pair of handcuffs that were handmade and featured a peculiar screw lock that could only be opened with a very odd-looking key.

"Well, Chief, I feel a little nervous because if I fail on these old cuffs, I am a ruined man in this business," Houdini said, anxiously looking over the cuffs. Then he turned to the crowd of detectives, officers, and newspapermen.

"I want you to see that I have no key about my person, so I will strip naked."

Once nude, he was examined by a police surgeon, and his mouth was covered with court plaster so he couldn't open it.

They began with an easy test, regulation police handcuffs. He was cuffed, his legs were fettered, and then he was led into a giant safe vault and the shackle on his left foot was secured around the bars on the inside of the safe. The safe was then locked. In exactly eleven minutes and twenty seconds, Houdini walked out and handed the irons to Chief Watts.

Then the real test began. He was handcuffed with the antique cuffs. A screw plug was inserted into the lock to prevent it from being picked. Again, he was locked in the vault. Nine minutes later, Houdini emerged. According to the news accounts, his hands were "red, swollen, sore, and bleeding" from the tight cuffs. But he was free. The crowd was "astounded." Watts congratulated Houdini and had the police brass and the reporters sign an official-looking proclamation on Bureau of Criminal Investigation stationery, attesting to Houdini's wonderful escape.

The press coverage drove the crowds to Keith's, and Houdini didn't disappoint.

"'The King of Handcuffs' is well named," *The Boston Herald* blared. "The man is like nothing or nobody in his line of performers, and one scarcely knows where to place him. What a splendid subject he would make for the old time spiritualistic business! How bells would ring and tambourines jingle and thump with Houdini tied up like a Christmas package in the cabinet!"

After the first week, Houdini's act had "scored a bigger hit" than Ching Ling Foo, the celebrated Chinese conjurer who was headlining the bill. By the second week, Houdini had been elevated to the star feature. Taking no chances, he began a second round of publicity. Accompanied by a *Boston Herald* reporter, Houdini visited the John Lovell Arms Company and escaped from their handcuffs right in the store, Houdini just turning his back and, "Presto! The handcuffs were unlocked and broken apart as though they were merely ropes of sand." Then they made a trip to visit with Captain Charles Bean, the venerated inventor of the Bean Giant handcuff that Houdini had defeated a few months earlier.

"I have spread your fame for making handcuffs all over the United States," Houdini said. "I take my hat off to your Yankee ingenuity."

Then Houdini slipped on a pair of the Bean Giants and within minutes had liberated himself.

"Well, that beats me how you get out of those handcuffs," Bean said. "I've probably fastened 10,000 prisoners in my time with those handcuffs, but you beat me."

Onstage, Houdini accepted all handcuff challenges, which led to some unique escapes and, of course, more publicity. On January 20, four officers from the Boston Police Department came onstage and placed leg irons and cuffs on his wrists. Then they conferred quietly with him. Houdini shook his head, as if in doubt.

"I don't know about that, let me see it," he said. One of the officers produced a small, nickel-plated object, which resembled a double Yale Lock.

"This is a thumb-cuff," Houdini told the audience. "I never saw one before in my life, but I will put it on, and see what I can do."

Within five minutes, he was free of everything.

The next day, a man walked down the aisle and came onstage with a large parcel under his arm. It was a straitjacket. It took them six minutes to lace it onto Houdini. In less than three minutes, he emerged from his cabinet with the jacket in his hand. The next day *The Boston Transcript* crowed, "Houdini . . . may now add to his titles that of 'emperor of strait-jackets.'"

In Providence, Rhode Island, Houdini's next stop, he took no chances. After releasing himself from four pairs of handcuffs and one set of leg irons at the police station on Friday morning, January 28, he accepted a challenge from a Boston dentist on the Keith's Theatre stage on Wednesday evening, January 31. Dr. Joseph E. Waitt brought a pair of handcuffs whose keyholes had been sealed in the presence of Detective Parker of the Providence police force and Superintendent Thornehill of the Pinkerton Agency in Boston. Onstage, Dr. Waitt sealed another pair of handcuffs that were placed on Houdini's ankles causing severe pain. Both seals were intact after Houdini made his escape, but what the newspaper reporters and the audience didn't know was that Houdini had met Dr. Waitt a week earlier when Waitt, who had been an avid magic fan since childhood, had been asked by the assistant theater manager to supervise Houdini's handcuff act at Keith's Theatre in Boston. In the intervening time, Houdini had turned a committee member whose job was to catch him in trickery into an accomplice in a sealed handcuff test. Waitt would become an intimate friend and confidant, even helping Houdini design a few of his later spectacular challenges.

"Let me out! Let me out!" Bess's screams echoed through the New York Theater. If they sounded a little muffled, it was because they were. She was screaming and pounding the sides of the Metamorphosis trunk; she was locked inside it. In fact, she'd been in there for five minutes by now. At first, the audience had laughed, thinking this was part of the act. Then the laughter turned to apprehension.

The effect had been progressing flawlessly, as usual. The transformation had startled the audience. It seemed like only a second after Bess had clapped her hands for the third time that Houdini emerged from the curtained cabinet and was bending down to open the trunk and reveal that his wife was now in the bag inside. Then something went very wrong.

Houdini called an assistant over as he knelt over the trunk, some whispered words were exchanged, and the assistant rushed away. Apparently Houdini had left the key to the trunk in the dressing room, which was five floors above the stage. The wait seemed interminable, but then the assistant returned empty-handed.

William McCormack, the theater manager, rushed onstage and conferred with Houdini. Another person was dispatched to find the key. By now Bess had begun to scream and pound at the sides of the trunk.

With Bess's oxygen supply rapidly dwindling, McCormack ran offstage and returned with a large ax. He had struck the trunk with one blow when the second assistant rushed up to him with the key. He unlocked the trunk and Bess, who had passed out, was lifted from the trunk and carried to the dressing room.

"So this is the way you try to kill me, is it?" she screamed at Houdini. She carried on for two solid hours, hysterical, then was taken to a hotel, where a doctor was consulted who reported that she was in serious condition. This had been some disaster of a homecoming for the Houdinis.

Or had it? If this was a real life-and-death situation, there's little chance that a world-class lock-pick expert would stand by and watch his wife suffocate. Houdini passively standing by is inconsistent with his nature. It's the manager who rushes to get an ax to free Bess, and the manager who receives the keys and opens the trunk. A reporter revealed that Houdini had informed him that the trunk was so airtight that Bess could only have survived seven minutes in it. Judging from the account, she was released just under the deadline. The truth is that a person could live for at least half an hour locked in that trunk. It's clear that Bess was merely emoting in a serio-comic scene written by her husband. Houdini instinctively realized the inherent drama of bringing the danger of death to the stage. Even so, her line, "So this is the way you try to kill me, is it?" is a bit overreaching.

The Houdinis' "fiasco" was reported in *The New York World*, then picked up and printed in a few other cities. The New York Theater was sold out for the rest of the run.

In some ways, Bess being locked in the trunk, keys forgotten, was an apt metaphor for the changing dynamics with respect to their act over the last year. Until Houdini began doing the vaudeville circuit, they were billed as The Houdinis, but as Harry transformed himself into Houdini, the King of Handcuffs, Bess was called his assistant, and by the time they reached Boston, Bess was completely omitted from the billing. According to Houdini, this was Bess's idea.

"Harry, I've never known an act billed as 'Mr. and Mrs.' to succeed. Suppose you bill yourself just as Houdini and leave me out of it," she told him one day.

"Won't you be jealous?" Harry asked.

"Why should I? Certainly not."

Bess might have been disingenuous, because there are later reports that she would bitterly listen to Harry's patter backstage and decry the frequency with which Houdini would use the word "I." Now, even though the petite soubrette was no longer singing and dancing, she was still performing the Metamorphosis. She threw the rest of her energies into collecting dolls and designing and sewing her costume.

A "little man with a thin, pale face" walked into detective headquarters in central station in Chicago just before six P.M. on Thursday, April 5, 1900.

"I would like to be locked up, please," he said.

Sergeant Kuebler, Detective Quinn, and Lieutenant Rohan looked up and "greeted the little man as an old friend."

"Aha, come back to fool us again, have you?" Kuebler, the lockup keeper, said. "Well, we'll fix you this time. No handcuffs, we'll just slip you in a cell, and if you get out without my permission, you're a beauty."

The little man was Houdini. Of course they would greet him as an old friend; Houdini had been back to the central station a dozen times since he escaped from Rohan's cuffs the first time.

This time Houdini bet Rohan a cigar that he could escape from a jail cell. It seemed like a daunting task. Each cell door had two locks. One was a standard lock, opened with a giant key, but over that keyhole there was a wide band of iron that looped over a staple placed a foot away from the door. That band was fastened by a padlock.

Rohan and Kuebler escorted Houdini to the cell and locked him in. They walked back around the corridor to the squad room. In three minutes, Houdini bounded out and asked Rohan for his cigar.

Houdini had certainly earned his smoke. Just hours before visiting Rohan that evening, Houdini had performed at a benefit for the Columbia Theatre employees, where he "created the sensation of the day" by freeing himself from handcuffs and manacles that were placed on him by an accredited member of the Secret Service.

The escape from a jail cell, a new twist, was repeated the next week in Kansas City. The jailer at the station, a man named Shavely, joked that they should lock him in a cell and see if he could get out.

"Getting out of a cell isn't in my contract and I don't guarantee it, but if you won't laugh too much if I fail, I'll try it," Houdini said.

"Better not try it," Chief Hayes warned. "We've got a new guaranteed lock on the cells down there that you can't always open even with the keys."

Houdini and the officers walked down the stairs to the cells. The jailer pointed out a cell door that was locked with one of those impenetrable locks.

Houdini took the lock into his hand and bent over it, with his back to the others, studying it closely. Thirty seconds later, he turned and faced them and held out the unlocked lock.

"We can use this one if you want," he said.

Sixteen months after that first Chicago police station escape that landed Houdini's picture on the front pages of the papers, he had become famous. His name was being used to sell clothing and meat, his exploits were being written up daily, and he was being compared to and even said to surpass the greatest magicians of his day. When they went to Toronto in February of 1900, *The Toronto World* heralded him as "one of the greatest living masters of mystery, the famous Houdini," but the recognition (and his increasing salary, which by now had escalated to $400 a week, an amount comparable to $45,000 today) hadn't really changed Houdini. He was still as hardworking and enthusiastic about his craft. H. J. Dillenback, a publicist with Keith's in Providence, wrote an unsolicited letter to a theater manager who had just booked Houdini. "You will find [him] to be the most appreciate [sic] man in the business, and more ready to cooperate in every way with you than any performer I have ever met. He is as square as a die, a thoroughly good fellow in every way, and one of the kind whom it is a decided pleasure to help along . . . I have found him such an exceptional man in every way that I feel desirous of doing anything in my humble power to 'boost' him."

Houdini didn't forget his humble origins either. He had maintained his membership in the tie cutters union and by the middle of 1900, he was regularly sending money to an old coworker at Richter's named L. Gorlitzer. Gorlitzer had worked at the tie factory for twenty-three years and had been promised a job for as long as he lived by old man Richter. Apparently the sons thought otherwise and Gorlitzer was "sent away" without even his $5-a-week pension. On hearing the news, Houdini was "thunderstruck" and started regularly sending Gorlitzer money, helping him to stave off eviction.

Houdini's newfound fame did have some drawbacks. By performing almost superhuman feats nightly, Houdini made himself vulnerable to exposure both on and off the stage. Onstage, the challenges got more difficult. In Philadelphia, two men challenged Houdini during the Metamorphosis effect. They tied Houdini's hands using their own braid, then substituted their own waterlogged string for the normal cord used to tie Houdini into the bag. As a final measure, they brought their own rope and used enough of it to tie twenty trunks. The audience protested what they thought was foul play, and after Houdini emerged from the trunk, they hissed the challengers off the stage.

Exposure could come anywhere, anytime. In Denver, Houdini was in the middle of a police station escape when he realized that some of Denver's "finest" had cut the eyes out of several of the paintings in the empty room where Houdini had gone to make his escape and were watching his every move. In Kansas City, E. P. Wilkins, a traveling salesman staying at the same hotel as Houdini, spied the magician using the lobby telephone box, procured a key from the front desk, quietly locked Houdini in, and sat back to watch the fun with a few friends. Houdini was not amused, especially when he read the next day's headline: "Houdini Locked In."

"The real Harry Houdini, who chats with his friends in the wings before and after his turn, is a serious sort of a chap. He has the physique of a young lion. His muscles are like steel. He has a nervous, artistic temperament. His hazel eyes are wonderfully eloquent and sympathetic. Before he makes his appearance at each performance, Houdini roams about the theater like a restless tiger. In his hands he carries a deck of cards with which he does a succession of wonderful tricks. He does this not to entertain the people with whom he is conversing, but to keep his fingers supple and agile . . . Before he goes on the stage he is all fire and excitement. When he comes off he is perfectly exhausted. Dark circles show around his eyes, and his face is pale under the rouge. He is glad it is over again. Why? Because Houdini says that someday a man will step upon that stage with a pair of handcuffs, whose lock he cannot unfasten. And when that time comes he will have to lay aside his scepter as King of Handcuffs. No circus performer enters the ring with the trepidation felt by Houdini when he steps toward the footlights. But he smiles and the audience remarks how confident he looks."

This was Houdini in Omaha in April of 1900, a snapshot in time courtesy of an anonymous reporter for *The Omaha Daily News*. Houdini's leonine physique was known to anyone who ever saw one of his beefcake publicity photos, but the intensity and nervous energy that he summoned up just to prepare for his performances were appreciated only by those who were privy to the backstages of the vaudeville circuit.

If you were backstage, you'd see that Bess shared all of Houdini's "nervous strain." Decked out in her Louis XIV costume, she'd anxiously wait in the wings as Harry entered his cabinet to defeat whatever cuffs were thrown his way. The magician would regularly talk to Bess while in his ghost box, sometimes just to alleviate her fears, other times in code if he had a potential problem. By 1900, Bess had been relegated to a lesser role in the performances. Still, the Omaha reporter thought it important enough to interview her too for his article.

"Madame Houdini has a singularly sun-shiny disposition. For days at a time her husband works on his tricks far away from her, in city and county jails, mastering locks, handcuffs, and shackles. His name is an open sesame at any jail in the country." In his very next sentence, the reporter revealed the next item on Houdini's agenda. "In September, he sails for England," he wrote, "where some severe tests await him in Scotland Yards."

Houdini had just finished his turn at the Orpheum, and now he was entering the parlor at 517 West Tenth Street, where Professor Paul Alexander Johnstone read palms. Johnstone, who was actually a magician, had been the most talked about palm reader in town and the local reporter, sensing a story, probably talked Houdini into letting his Herculean hands have the once-over. The enticement of a nice story with a reproduction of his palm probably sealed the deal.

"I feel nervous," Houdini said, as they walked over to West Tenth Street. "This constant fear of exposure is almost unbearable. I fully realize it is only a question of time until I am caught, and it is this suspense that causes my nerves to keep stirring."

Houdini settled into a large leather chair while the professor prepared the plaster of paris for the cast of his palm.

"To be stripped of clothing and then locked in the strongest steel cage the jail can afford, and this too, with a hundred pounds of iron on your forearms and ankles, to hear the bolts of the cell door scrape and crash as they pass into their sockets, and then to walk out into the corridor and hand the officers their handcuffs and shackles unlocked! It makes me nervous."

"You have been caught once or twice, have you not?" Professor Johnstone asked as he dipped Houdini's hand up to the wrist in the plaster.

"Yes, twice," Houdini replied, deliberately. "Once in Denver, and the man died the day after. Three months later, Nero, the great medium, detected how I performed these feats, and three days afterward he died. Rather a singular coincidence, don't you think?"

The palmist examined the cast of Houdini's palm.

"Unless you are exceedingly careful during your thirty-seventh year, a violent death is written in this line of life," he said. "Your moneymaking period began, I should judge, last year. Provided you save, you will attain great wealth."

"How about my work?" Houdini inquired.

"Your brains will protect you," the palmist replied. "I will trust to you getting out of anything put on you. You need not worry, Mr. Houdini. The safest way to keep you is to turn you loose on the prairie."

Johnstone was wrong about the prairie. On May 30, 1900, the man who two years earlier had been subsisting on potatoes and sleeping on benches under the stars was now willing to forsake a king's ransom in weekly salary to accompany his wife aboard the S.S. *Kensington* to set sail for England, where nothing awaited him. Except Scotland Yard.

From the collection of Kenneth M. Trombly

6

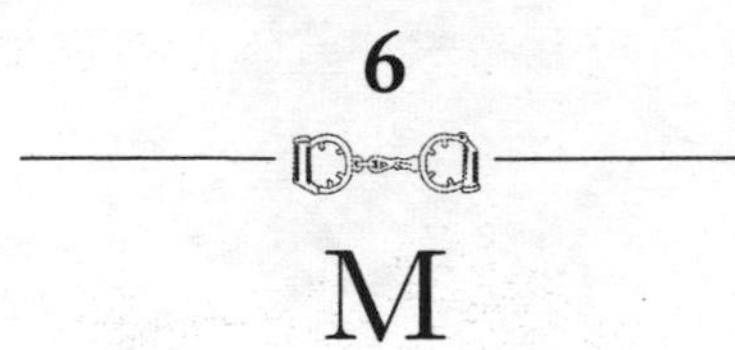

M

FINALLY HE SAW HIM. THE HUNCHBACK disguise didn't fool Police Inspector William Melville, who was in disguise himself as an anonymous businessman waiting for his train at Victoria Station in London. But the outline of a gun in the anarchist's pocket did dissuade the inspector from boarding the train and accosting Meunier in his small compartment. So Melville summoned a railroad official and identified himself.

"There's a hunchback in the fifth carriage from the engine. I want to get him out of the train without arousing his suspicions. Will you inspect his ticket and tell him that he is on the wrong train?" Melville suggested.

The official agreed and boarded the train. Shortly after, a concerned-looking Meunier leaped off the train. His feet hadn't even hit the ground before the forty-four-year-old Melville had executed a flying tackle and knocked him to the platform. Astonished passengers gathered around the two men as Meunier, "fighting like a mad dog," tried to escape Melville's grasp. The Frenchman, summoning up all his strength, almost succeeded in dragging Melville under the wheels of the train, which was just about to depart, until some railroad men came to Melville's aid. After a few more minutes, Meunier was finally subdued and, spewing oaths and threats, taken away. The next day's coverage of the arrest in the papers included a large drawing of Melville straddling Meunier entitled "Exciting Arrest of Anarchists in London." Melville had made sure that the press had been duly notified to be on hand at the station that night.

By the end of the century, William Melville was the highest-profile police officer in England. He had been head of Scotland Yard's Special Branch since

William Melville, England's most celebrated spymaster. *From the collection of Andrew Cook*

1893. Still hampered with a skeleton staff, he had a wide variety of informants in all strata of society, from foreign government agents to street prostitutes. Melville had developed particularly good contacts in the entertainment world. Most Londoners patronized music halls and theaters several times a week, so using showpeople as informants was vital in keeping track of the movements and associations of people of interest to Melville.

Melville was also charged with protecting the safety of the various visiting royalty, receiving decorations for his service from more than half the crowned heads of Europe. He had much contact, some of it back channel, with his counterespionage counterparts in France, Germany, and Russia. In 1899, without his government's knowledge, he had cooperated with the Okhrana, the Russian secret police, in arresting a Russian émigré who was publishing a newspaper that advocated the assassination of the czar. As a reward to one of his informants on this case, he had provided Sigmund Rosenblum with a new identity and a new passport so he could return to Russia. Melville's creation, Sidney Reilly, would go on to become one of the cleverest spies in history—and the real-life prototype for Ian Fleming's fictional character James Bond.

By June of 1900, Melville could look back on his twenty-eight-year career and marvel at how far the working-class Irish lad from County Kerry had come. He had consorted with kings and prostitutes, politicians and anarchists, celebrities and criminals. And right now, steaming through the ocean on his way from America was perhaps the most intriguing man that Melville would ever meet.

The Houdinis alighted in Southampton on June 9. They traveled up to London and took residence at 10 Keppel Street, a boardinghouse that catered to visiting American entertainers. The conventional wisdom was that Houdini spent weeks scouring the city for work, being turned down by manager after manager. The reality is that on June 14, a few days after their arrival, Harry Houdini, accompanied by London's most prestigious theater manager, C. Dundas Slater, and his assistant, Edward A. Pickering, was ushered into the office of England's most celebrated policeman and her majesty's chief counterterrorism official. Houdini's wife and assistant, Beatrice, was not privy to this meeting.

"I'll be happy to cuff him, Mr. Slater, but you must realize that Scotland Yard darbies are not stage handcuffs," Melville said. "These are the last word in scientific manacles."

"Well, the lad's game," Slater said. "If he can get out of your handcuffs, then he's got a job awaiting him at my theater."

Melville looked the young American over. He did seem confident. Opening a desk drawer, he pulled out a pair of handcuffs.

"Follow me," he said, and led the men out into a corridor of the building. He stopped next to a pillar.

"Well, here's how we fasten the Yankee criminals who come over here and get into trouble," Melville said, and, encircling Houdini's arms around the pillar, he snapped the handcuffs on.

"I'm going to leave you here while Mr. Slater and his colleague and I go out for lunch," Melville smiled. "We'll be back for you in a couple of hours."

They started toward the door.

"Wait!" he cried. "I'll go with you. Here's the way Yankees open the handcuffs."

He threw the cuffs on the ground and caught up with the three men. Melville was visibly shaken. He looked at Houdini and then smiled and held out his hand.

"Scotland Yard won't forget you, young man."

Houdini had passed his audition. Slater drove him back to his office and signed him to a two-week contract at the Alhambra Theater, London's most prestigious music hall.

In 2004, Andrew Cook, one of the world's leading experts on British espionage, published a book called *M—MI-5's First Spymaster*. Cook, who had spent years working for England as a foreign affairs and defense specialist, parlayed his contacts to gain access to classified intelligence services archives and, for the first time ever, document Melville's heretofore hidden life. In the course of that research, he obtained the only known copy of one of Melville's diaries—the rest were presumably sanitized by the agency, MI-5, that Melville ultimately worked for.

Given what Cook knows about Melville's disposition and responsibilities, he finds it highly unlikely to think that the inspector would entertain Slater, Pickering, and Houdini at his office and allow a fresh-off-the-boat unknown magician to escape from Scotland Yard handcuffs as an audition for a theater engagement.

The audition was for a job with Melville.

Like Rohan and Wilkie, Melville's counterparts in America, the Irishman perceived Houdini as a most valuable asset. Obviously, his ability to defeat any lock would come in handy to the Scotland Yard inspector, who often found himself in the position of breaking and entering premises where valuable information might be secreted. Melville saw Houdini as an ideal operative in another arena as well. As early as 1896, Melville had recognized the necessity for gathering information outside of Britain. At first happy to view the police of other nations as some sort of international brotherhood, Melville recognized that his counterparts in France, Russia, and Germany were spying on England during the normal course of their activities. While the idea of finding "suitable men to go abroad to obtain information" would not be part of his official duties until his work with what would eventually be designated MI-5, Melville began to groom operatives while still at Scotland Yard.

Houdini would be the ideal agent to relay information to Melville from abroad. He was nomadic, travel being a regular part of his work. He was also, of course, well-versed in techniques of secrecy and deception. Since his reputation hinged on his ability to escape from confinement and to produce other mystifying magical effects, it was natural for him to carry with him a large assortment of strange items, including lock-picking tools.

Unique to Houdini was his ability to interact with a country's police officials and do demonstrations inside their jails. No other operative could amass such a wealth of vital information with respect to the security, cells, locks, and prisoner conditions in a country's jails. As early as 1900, according to Cook, Melville was interested in gathering information in Germany, being prescient enough to see the Germans as Britain's future adversary. Houdini had the added bonus of being able to speak German fluently.

27th June 1900—Guest of HH at Alhambra
—FROM INSPECTOR MELVILLE'S DIARY

It was an odd sight, the British newshounds carrying ancient, rusted handcuffs and leg irons into the magnificently appointed Alhambra Theater in Leicester Square. With its Moorish facade, opulent private box tier, and dark and mysterious canteen, where many a well-heeled gentleman bought expensive champagne for the ballet girls after their performances, the Alhambra was the premier music hall in England. Dundas Slater, its manager, had summoned the press to a special private preview of his next great attraction, Harry Houdini, the young American Handcuff King. To pique their interest, Slater had encouraged them to bring their own restraints and challenge Houdini, intimating that if they could foil his escape, there might not be an opening night after all.

That was bait enough for *The London Evening Sun*'s representative, the same man who had earlier exposed Slater's last big sensation, the Georgia Magnet, a Mattie Lee Price–type leverage queen. He came onstage carrying a pair of antique irons and greeted Houdini, who was dressed in his best formal high white collar and tails, his normally unruly curly hair parted neatly in the center. Houdini's ghost house, which by now was actually a small waist-high enclosure consisting of metal piping and a black fabric that hid Houdini on three sides and could shield him totally by drawing the curtain on the front, had been set up on the stage.

The *Sun* reporter manacled Houdini with the antique slave iron. It was so rusty that it looked like it couldn't be opened even with a key, but Houdini cheerfully submitted to its bondage and then withdrew to his ghost house. In less than three minutes, he reappeared, the irons dangling in his hand.

"I don't know how you did it, but you did!" the reporter marveled and cordially shook Houdini's hand.

After a few more tests, Houdini allowed himself to be handcuffed behind his back and have his feet secured. Then, facing the audience and kneeling, he freed himself in full view of the spectators. He escaped from everything they threw at him, and then he mystified the group with his Metamorphosis trunk and some card effects.

Seated in the audience, Inspector Melville and some of his colleagues from Scotland Yard watched the proceedings with special interest.

The resultant press coverage was enormous. Houdini was universally praised and deemed worthy of his self-anointed titles. Many papers ran large drawings and engravings of him. "It was a remarkably clever exhibition by Mr. Harry Houdini, who describes himself as the World's Greatest Mystifier and King of Handcuffs," *The Morning Herald* reported. "Perhaps the highest tribute to Mr. Houdini's slipperiness is the fact that he has completely mystified the police of America, who have given him many testimonials." The would-be exposer from *The Evening Sun* even suggested, "if [Houdini] is wise, he will start an academy for the teaching of scientific lock-picking." Ironically enough, a few short years later, Melville would do exactly that, using Houdini's techniques as the core curriculum.

The mysterious Chinese conjurer walked onto the stage from the wings and was met there by his diminutive assistant, Suee Seen. She was standing next to a small table that held a large bowl filled with water. In her hands was a long fishing pole that she handed to the magician.

The Alhambra crowd stirred. This fishing effect had never been seen in London before Chung Ling Soo began performing it. They settled back expectantly in their seats to behold a miracle.

Soo pulled a small piece of bait out of his pocket and attached it to the hook that was dangling at the end of a five-foot line. Then he suddenly cast the line out over the heads of the audience, his long ornate Chinese robe flapping from the jerky motion. He paused for a few seconds and then slowly moved the bait from right to left, as if a mysterious school of invisible fish were swimming over the heads of the crowd. The mystery was heightened by focusing the spotlight directly on the dancing bait. Then, suddenly, Soo snapped his wrist, the line buckled, and a small goldfish miraculously appeared. Soo slowly withdrew the pole and unhooked the fish. He delicately dropped it into the waiting water, and it vigorously circled the bowl. He did this twice more, adding two more goldfish to the water. With that, Suee Seen appeared and carried the bowl to the wings, while Chung Ling Soo, the mysterious and Marvelous Chinese Conjuror, clasped his hands together, swirled them up and down, and graciously bowed to the audience.

Soo was concluding his engagement at the Alhambra, and his mysterious act had never failed to enthrall the audience, but tonight they were just as excited to see the debut of this new Yankee, this Handcuff King who was challenging the world to attempt to restrain him. Finally, the wait was over. Houdini, resplendent in his finest attire, strode confidently onto the stage in that marvelous, ornate theater. He stood bathed in the blue-white glow of the spotlight, took a deep breath, and began to address the audience.

"La-dies and gen-tle-men . . ." Houdini drew out the words like taffy, but before he could even complete his sentence, a stranger had leaped onto the stage.

"This man is a fraud," the mustachioed intruder bellowed. "He claims to be the King of Handcuffs, but that is a title that is reserved for me, The Great Cirnoc."

Ten seconds into the most important showing of his life, Houdini's performance had been hijacked by a competitor. This turn of events seemed to paralyze Houdini, and he was strangely mute as the interloper seized the center of the stage, denouncing him.

"I am the original Handcuff King. This man is an impostor. He claims to come from America and hold proclamations from the police chiefs of the major cities there, yet I declare that his man is not even an American. He has never even been in the United States!" Cirnoc thundered.

At that, a distinguished-looking man sitting in the front row stood up.

"That is not true," the man said calmly. "I know for a fact that that young man is an American. I also am an American, and I saw him several years ago doing his handcuff act."

Houdini's defender was none other than U.S. Senator Chauncey M. Depew, the junior senator from Houdini's home state of New York. Depew had long been prominent in New York politics and was a mentor to then Vice President Theodore Roosevelt. He also had connections to the world of magic through his nephew Ganson Depew, a practicing magician who later joined the Society of American Magicians.

Depew sat down to great applause. A testimonial from this distinguished guest seemed to bolster Houdini's confidence.

"Get me the Bean Giant," he whispered to Bess. "We'll fix this fellow now."

Bess supplied him with the cuffs, and Houdini advanced on Cirnoc, dangling the hardware from his fingertips.

"This is one of the finest handcuffs made in the United States," Houdini said. "I will give you 500 U.S. dollars if you can free yourself from these manacles."

Cirnoc frowned. "Let me see you get out of them first," he said.

"Lock me in," Houdini offered.

Cirnoc snapped the cuffs shut and Houdini retired to his cabinet. Minutes later, he emerged unfettered.

Then Houdini locked the cuffs on his rival. He even gave Cirnoc the key, but the humiliated intruder had to beg for Houdini to release him from his bonds. Houdini did, and a chagrined Cirnoc shook Houdini's hand and left the stage.

Houdini finished his act with great aplomb. Thanks to his years of experience, his showmanship had been finely honed. He knew exactly how to add the element of danger to magnify the effect and how to prolong the tension and emerge from his cabinet at the peak moment. Houdini's mastery even fooled his longtime friend Tommy Downs, who was sitting in the audience with William Hilliar, who would later migrate to America and become the founder and editor of the prestigious magic magazine *The Sphinx*.

"Downs and I both thought at one time during the progress of his act that Houdini would get 'stuck.' He stayed in the cabinet an inordinately long time, and we both noticed that his charming little wife and helpmate was very nervous. The tension had almost reached the 'snapping' point, when suddenly the cabinet burst open and Houdini rushed out—free. I shall never forget the storm of applause that greeted him. That one night was the foundation for his subsequent triumphs in Europe," Hilliar later wrote.

The critics agreed. They lavished praise both on Houdini's handcuff work and the Metamorphosis, calling him a "modern Jack Sheppard," after the legendary English convict who routinely escaped from his cells. More important was another endorsement. "Absolutely a miracle," gushed Superintendent Melville, London's most recognizable policeman. Melville's acknowledgment of Houdini's skills prompted the magician to jettison his newly printed advertising brochure and order a new one trumpeting the endorsement on the front cover. Quid pro quo. Houdini's stay at the Alhambra kept getting extended. He was the talk of the town and a visit to Houdini backstage at the Alhambra became de rigueur for London's most prominent people.

One of these was Alfred William Charles Harmsworth. Harmsworth was a self-made millionaire who started his publishing empire in 1888 at the age of

James William Elliot, Houdini's longtime enemy, and Tommy Downs, Houdini's longtime friend (l to r). *Conjuring Arts Research Center*

twenty-three by copying the format of *Tit-Bits*, a wildly successful monthly magazine that answered readers' questions. The success of Harmsworth's *Answers to Correspondents* enabled him to launch new children's and women's magazines. By 1894 he had branched out to newspapers, buying up the nearly bankrupt *Evening News*. Giving it a makeover and adding eye-catching headlines revived sales dramatically. Two years later, he founded *The Daily Mail*, the first newspaper in Britain that catered to an audience that wanted shorter, punchier, and more lifestyle-oriented articles. It was an immediate success and when—during the height of the Boer War with South Africa in 1899—Harmsworth identified the paper with "the power, the supremacy, and the greatness of the British Empire," patriotic readers sent the circulation skyrocketing to more than a million copies a day.

So it was a very prosperous, nattily dressed Harmsworth who was ushered into Houdini's dressing room by Dundas Slater one night at the beginning of his Alhambra run. Harmsworth's cherubic face belied the killer instinct that was necessary for survival in the highly competitive English newspaper racket. Hou-

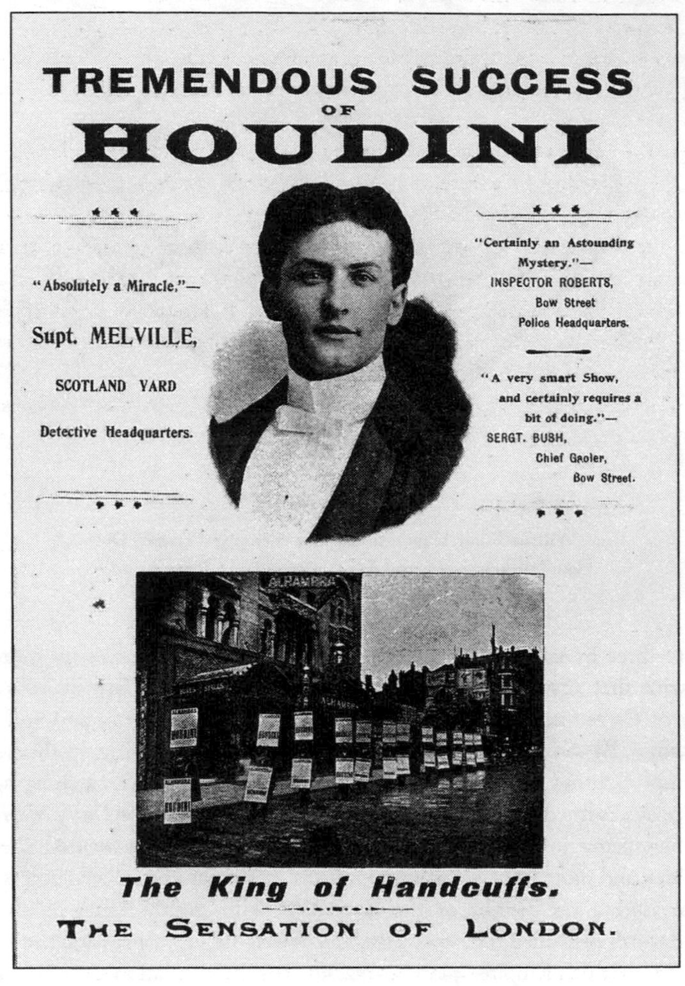

Superintendent Melville's ringing endorsement of Houdini.

From the collection of George and Sandy Daily

dini and Harmsworth immediately hit it off, and a friendship blossomed. Harmsworth took Houdini to long lunches, where the two men discussed Anglo-American relations for hours on end. "[Harmsworth] brought up a number of subjects on Americans [sic] views, which he was going to publish. I told him it was a grave error to do so, and eventually he decided to run them in spite of my advice to the contrary. But it appears he must have thought it over, for they never appeared."

For the next two months, Houdini was sitting on top of the world. He had conquered England in one fell swoop, selling out London's most prestigious music hall, receiving wild accolades from its normally cynical press, even influencing the opinions of its most powerful press lord. Houdini, a few months after his twenty-sixth birthday, was finally in a position where he could call his own shots. Yet, at the height of this triumph, he decided to ignore his London bookings, packed up his suitcases, bid farewell to Keppel Street, and set off on a journey to the land of the kaiser. Duty called.

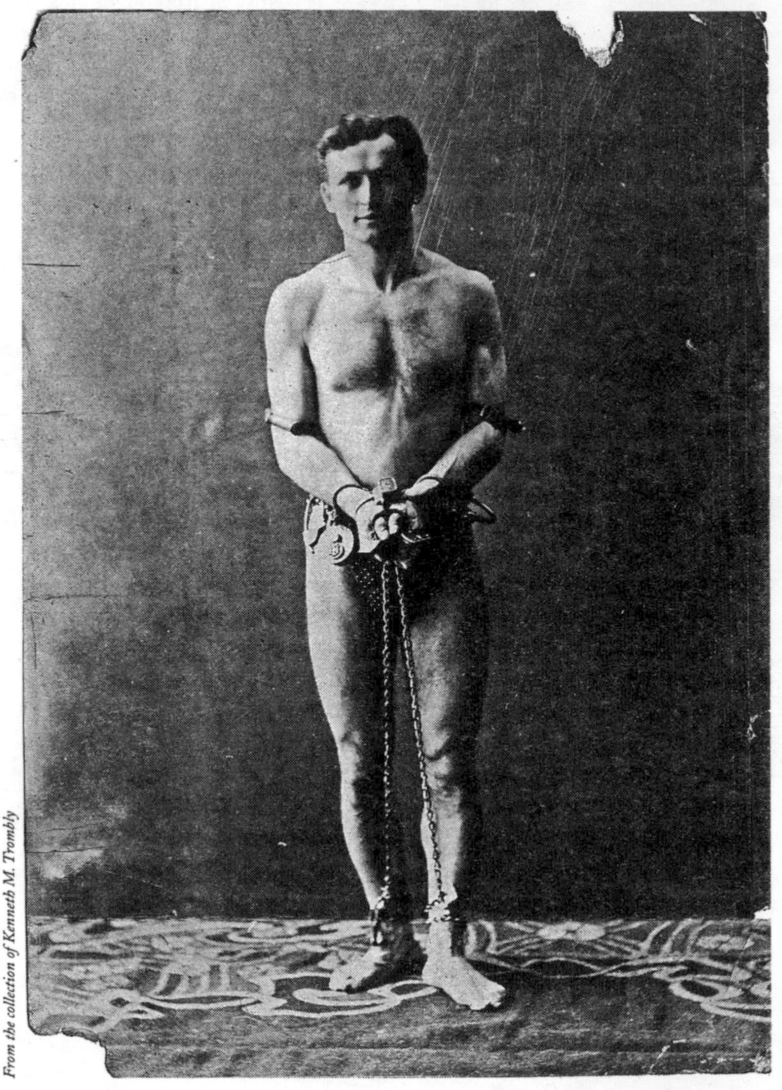

From the collection of Kenneth M. Trombly

7

Police State

HOUDINI SAT BEHIND THE DESK AT the American embassy in London, his pen poised. He entered the date, "August 9, 1900," and then proceeded to fill in the rest of the passport application for native-born Americans, which was his first lie.

> *I, Ehrich Weiss, a native and loyal citizen of the United States, hereby apply to the Embassy of the United States at London for a passport for myself, accompanied by my wife, Wilhelmina (professionally known as "Beatrice Houdini"). I am professionally known as "Harry Houdini, the King of Handcuffs." I solemnly swear that I was born at Appleton, in the State of Wisconsin, on or about the 6 day of April, 1873; that my father is a naturalized citizen of the United States; that I am domiciled in the United States, my permanent residence being at New York City, in the State of New York, where I follow the occupation of artiste; that I left the United States on the 30 day of May, 1900, and am now temporarily sojourning at 11 Keppel St., London, W.C.; that I am the bearer of Passport No. 25768, issued by State Department on the 28 day of May, 1900; that I intend to return to the United States within two years with the purpose of residing and performing the duties of citizenship therein; and that I desire the passport for the purpose of travelling.*

Underneath the oath of allegiance, Houdini signed Ehrich Weiss. Henry White of the embassy noted "(Unexpired passport surrendered.)" at the bottom of the form.

A comparison of Houdini's two passports raises some interesting questions. For one, on May 26, when he filled out his first passport application, Houdini used the proper form, the one for naturalized citizens, which he became on June 6, 1882, the same day that his father became a U.S. citizen. On that form he indicated correctly that he was born in Buda-Pest, Hungary. Both passports, however, state that he was born on April 6, 1873, which is inaccurate. Houdini's adoption of April 6 as his birthday will remain a mystery, although he explained in a letter to his brother Theo that he would celebrate on April 6 because that was the day that his mother acknowledged his birthday. The answer to the mystery may be as simple as the possibility that some parts of Hungary may have recognized the Julian calendar at the time of his birth, whereas the United States used the Gregorian calendar. The difference between his actual birth date, March 24, and his adopted one was precisely the difference between the two calendars. As to the year of his birth, he apparently thought he was born in 1873 until someone, most likely his mother, corrected him. His birth year would be corrected by the time he filled out his next passport application, but from May until August Houdini changed his occupation (from "actor" to "artiste"), grew two inches (from 5'4" to 5'6"), and changed the color of his eyes (from "brown" to "blue").

It's interesting to note that by 1910 both Houdini and Bess knew with certainty that his actual birthday was on March 24. While in Australia that year, Bess gave Houdini an engraved watch as a birthday present.

FOR HARRY
Ever Houdini
Remembering In Complete Happiness
BESS
3-24-10

Not only was his birth date correct, but Bess employed a code in the dedication as well. When you isolate the first letter of each word in the message, it spells out Harry's real name, E-H-R-I-C-H.

Somehow Mr. White, who was the first secretary at the delegation, and would go on to become, in Theodore Roosevelt's words, "the most useful man in the entire diplomatic service," allowed Houdini to surrender an unexpired passport for a naturalized citizen in exchange for a passport for a native-born citizen. According to English espionage expert Andrew Cook, this passport exchange indicates that Houdini was about to embark on a mission that entailed some risk. Presenting a native-born passport would be a safety device for Houdini. Since Germans at that time had very stringent penalties for espionage,

Houdini's original passport, which contained specific information about the date and location of his birth, would have given the German authorities a paper trail straight back to any relatives of Houdini who were still in Hungary. At that point, Hungary was part of the Austrian Reich, close allies of Germany, whose respective secret services worked hand in hand. Houdini's relatives could very well have been used as pawns to force his cooperation in the case of his arrest.

Having an asset like Houdini relaying information back from Germany would have been very valuable for a number of important people in Houdini's orbit. By 1900, the idea that Germany would be their next major adversary was current in both the United States and Great Britain. One of the proponents of this theory was Captain Charles Sigsbee, who had been the commander of the *Maine* when the battleship was blown up in Havana Harbor. Two years after that incident, Sigsbee became chief of the Office of Naval Intelligence, and it was here that he began planning measures to counter a German invasion of the United States. For years scholars attributed his concern to a paranoid delusion common to military men, but military historians in the 1970s uncovered long-suppressed evidence in German naval archives that Sigsbee was correct.

With a burgeoning population and an avid nationalistic mind-set, Germany at the turn of the century was poised to make its move on the colonial stage. As early as 1897, German naval officers began developing military scenarios where the German navy would invade U.S. waters, destroy the American navy, and occupy some part of the mainland, at either Virginia, New York City, or New England. The idea was not to overrun the country but to create an atmosphere of terror and use that as a bargaining chip to overturn the Monroe Doctrine and acquire colonies in South America.

These were not just abstract theoretical war game exercises. Germany sent some of her most important military men to the United States to spy on her intended targets. Sigsbee's concerns over Germany were echoed by soon-to-be President Theodore Roosevelt, who advocated a strong United States Navy "to interfere promptly if Germany ventures to touch a foot of American soil."

The Americans weren't the only ones to fear the kaiser and the threat of his military might. Both Inspector Melville and publisher Alfred Harmsworth were obsessed with the idea that Germany would soon be Britain's enemy. As early as 1897, Harmsworth had sent a writer to Germany to produce a sixteen-part series entitled *Under the Iron Heel* that warned of the strength of the German army and raised the real possibility that England would be defeated in a conflict with Germany. In 1900, Harmsworth wrote an editorial in his *Daily Mail* predicting war with Germany. For the next decade the *Mail* constantly played up the German threat. It was in this climate that Houdini traveled to Germany on Sep-

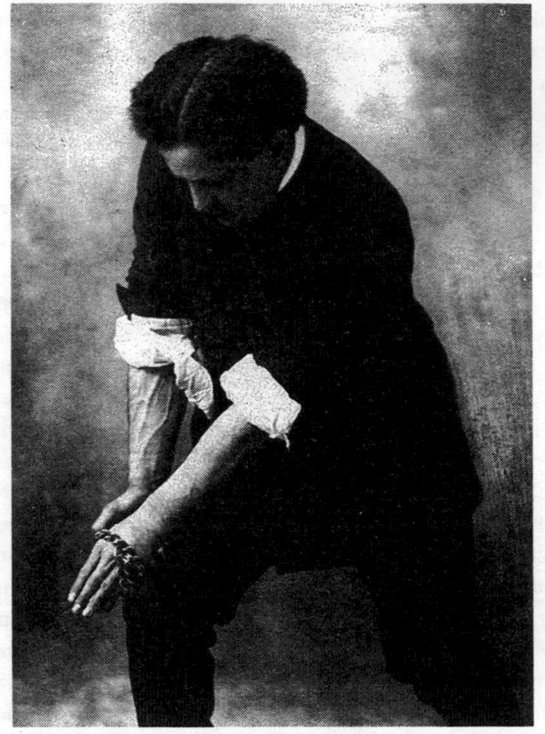

Life was not all roses for a handcuff King. *From the collection of Kenneth M. Trombly*

tember 2, 1900 and began to transmit reports back to Melville, who made note of them in his diary.

It was likely the most interesting demonstration ever undertaken in the conference room of the Berlin criminal police. It had certainly brought out all the heavyweights. There was the Berlin royal police director, Von Hullessem, and next to him, Mr. Dieterich, the high-ranking government advisor. Even Von Windheim, the president of the German police, was there. All told, three hundred criminal officers had packed the room, all to see the sensation who had been summoned down from Dresden, where he had been playing to wildly enthusiastic houses.

Houdini stripped down to his underpants. Then he was cuffed five times behind his back. Two pairs of leg irons were affixed. His mouth was bandaged, and thumbscrews were added to his burden. Then Carl Pollak, his booking agent, threw a sheet over him, and Houdini went to work. Six minutes later, the Handcuff King emerged with a radiant smile and neatly placed all the hardware on the table.

"It is not without significance for the criminal police to know what level of skill you can reach in the opening of locks of any kind without the use of any kind of tool or externally perceptible force. For the evaluation of any crime and the focus of the investigation, such a science can under certain circumstances be of great significance. Houdini's performance was very instructional," *The Dresdner Anzeiger* reported. At the end of the demonstration, Houdini received an almost unheard-of commendation from both Von Hullessem and Von Windheim.

Houdini, for his part, reported directly to Superintendent Melville, whose diary entry of September 24, 1900, is brief and to the point: *"Report received from HH."*

The newspaper accounts of Houdini's demonstrations at German police stations portray him as a police consultant rather than a mere entertainer. The truth is, he was both. Getting the endorsement of German authorities was crucial to Houdini's success. In England and America, the endorsements helped generate interest and attention. In Germany, the police could actually close your performances and fine you if you fraudulently misrepresented your act.

Back in Dresden, Houdini continued his outstanding run at the Central Theatre, smashing all box office records. The German public identified with a man who could escape from the kaiser's police force, and they were also pleased that Houdini presented his act in German, even if he butchered the grammar and syntax. The management of the theater wired the Wintergarten in Berlin, where Houdini was to appear next, seeing if they would postpone his opening there so his stay could be extended a month. The request was promptly refused, because the publicity from Houdini's escape before the Berlin police brass had whipped up the city to a fever pitch.

Houdini finally began his Berlin run on October 1, and the response was so overwhelming that the police were forced to reprimand the Wintergarten management several times for overcrowding the venue. They too wired Houdini's next stop in an effort to hold him over for another month, but this time, after four thousand marks had been dispatched off to the Viennese theater, they were able to extend his engagement.

Life was not all roses for the Handcuff King. During his Berlin run, a man walked onstage and produced another thumb cuff from his pocket. "I shuddered when I saw it," Houdini wrote. "This is a particularly devilish sort of handcuff, consisting of a small plate about three inches long by an inch wide, with two circular holes, each just large enough to admit one of the thumbs. This is slipped over the thumbs to the second flange. Then a nut at the side is turned, and circles of small steel pins, each ground to a needle point, close about the thumbs. Any movement of the hands causes these needle points to tear the flesh. Obviously if one attempts to pull his thumbs free, the flesh about the joint and the thicker upper flange will be lacerated cruelly.

"Well, having challenged the City of Berlin to produce anything it could in the way of handcuffs, I had to let the man put the thumbcuff on me. Also, I had to escape if I could. It was one of the most painful experiences of my career. The spikes penetrated to the bone, and the bleeding flesh hung in strips from my thumbs when at last I dropped the thumbcuff to the stage. Never has one of my tricks been greeted by more tumultuous applause than came to me for this demonstration, which actually was not a trick at all. And when I left the theatre, I found myself surrounded by a cheering crowd that raised me to its shoulders, and then unhitched the horses from my cab to draw me in triumph through the streets of the city."

While Houdini was thrilled at the acclaim and the adoration of the audiences, he wasn't letting his success go to his head. "I am really recognized as the biggest Trickster over here," he wrote his friend Dr. Waitt, telling him that he planned to stay in Germany "at least 6 more months, and at an excellent salary no not an excellent salary but an '*exhorbiant*' [sic] or newspaper salary." At the same time, he wrote both Waitt and his old employer Edward "Marco" Dooley, thanking them for their encouragement on the way up. "Your letter expresses more gratitude to me than I deserve for what little favor I may have done for you," Dooley wrote back, "Yet, it pleased me very much to have you express the feeling, for it is *so rare* nowadays to find anyone who appreciates kindness, and it shows, what I knew all along, that you have a good heart and it is in the right place."

It was one of the most brutal yet devious murders that the Berlin police had ever seen. Olschansky, a Frenchman, had prepared by renting out a small room on a street that was virtually devoid of other lodgers. He then wired himself one hundred marks (about $25), which were delivered by a class of German postmen called "Geld-brief," because their entire job was to deliver money that had been sent through the mail. Consequently, they often carried large sums of cash.

Olschansky's room was on the top floor. When the postman arrived that Monday morning, he found nothing unusual. The tenant was seated, enjoying his morning lunch, typically consumed at ten A.M., of bottled beer and sandwiches. The Frenchman politely offered the postman a beer, but tellingly gave him no glass. Compelled to drink straight from the bottle, the postman took a swig. Olschansky took a swing. He used a heavy board and drove the bottle halfway down the German's throat. Too stunned to put up any resistance, the postman was finished off by some fifteen blows to the head.

Olschansky's first mistake was in paying for the beer, which he had obtained on credit. When the Frenchman came to him to settle up the debt, the merchant noticed the dried bloodstains on the Frenchman's shirt cuff. His second mistake was in using the shiny gold twenty-mark piece that had just been delivered to him. When he was finally tracked down and arrested, the German police found two lock-picks among Olschansky's effects, which was how Houdini wound up in Olschansky's cell at the police presidium the next morning.

Olschansky didn't say much to Houdini. He was clever enough to know that before his trial for murder, it wouldn't redound to his credit to admit that he had been using the picks to break into locked churches to raid their collection boxes. After his execution, Houdini did manage to obtain the picks from the police and found that one of the picks enabled him to open any church door in Germany that wasn't secured with a padlock. The other key was a kind of master key for safes that utilized Bramah locks.

For a vaudeville performer, Houdini seemed to spend an inordinate amount of time and have unprecedented access at the Berlin police station. Even though his accounts suggest that his presence there was a mere coincidence, it is clear that Houdini was being utilized by the upper strata of the German police. During the same period when he interrogated Olschansky in his cell, a clever burglar went on trial. Not only did Houdini attend the trial but also, "after I had given my police performance, I was brought to him, as he had a notorious reputation as a lock picker." Houdini went on to have many interviews with him ". . . and finally he gave me the lock picker and told me how he concealed it. I handed it to the police, who allowed me to keep it." Houdini didn't reveal what information or techniques he traded to the authorities for their generous gifts and access to convicted criminals.

In his 1906 book, *The Right Way to Do Wrong*, Houdini described serving as a liaison between the IACP in the United States and the top German police brass. While in Germany, Houdini had a copy with him of *Our Rival the Rascal*, a book written by his friend Chief Inspector William B. Watts of the

Boston police force. The book contained many interesting photographs and case histories of leading criminals. Chief Watts was a member of the IACP and a crusader for international police cooperation in dealing with threats to world order from both anarchists and habitual criminals. "This book is the greatest book on the subject that I have ever seen," Houdini enthused. "I happened to have a copy with me in Berlin, when the royal police, hearing that I had the book in the country, asked me as a favor to allow them to make extracts and photograph some of the famous criminals in the book. This I allowed them to do, and in return they handed me several photos of well-known criminals to send to Chief Inspector, Wm. B. Watts."

On June 1, 1901, Watts sent Houdini a letter, thanking him for his letter "and other communications." He reminded Houdini that when the magician left the United States, "I believed you would make a success of your trip," and sent his kindest regards to his "better half." To the titles of Handcuff King, Jail-breaker, and Master of Manacles, we now must add Courier for International Police Cooperation.

Houdini's schedule seemed to be exacting a heavy toll on him. By December of 1900, despite protests from his German promoters who wanted to hold him over, he returned to England to fulfill his Alhambra contracts. After spending two months there, he returned to Germany. By the end of March, he wrote Dr. Waitt, "My nerves are all run down, and I am not well as the *perpetual* worry and excitement is beginning to tell on me." By June word of Houdini's stress had reached other friends back in the States. "I heard that you don't laugh anymore. Neither do I . . . What seems to be the matter with us?" Gus Roterberg wrote.

Regardless of his run-down nerves, Houdini kept up his grueling schedule. Since his return to Germany, he had toured Leipzig, Dusseldorf, Frankfurt, and Hamburg. On May 6, he started a three-week engagement in Essen Ruhr. Houdini was such a hit that the front doors and a side wall of the venerable Colosseum were removed to add extra seats. Despite selling standing room and even putting chairs on the stage, hundreds of people were turned away.

Essen Ruhr was important in another respect. It was the home of Krupp Works, Germany's largest munitions manufacturers, a company that turned Essen from a sleepy village to a thriving city of more than 100,000, most of them dependent on the large munitions company. Krupp was known for secrecy and very few American iron and steel industry visitors had been allowed to tour the foundry, but under the guise of assessing a challenge from the Krupp workers, Houdini was able to visit and inspect the munitions factory. In fact, the Colosseum eventually hosted a Krupp night, where Krupp workers bought out the entire theater to see Houdini come up against the finest in German technology. Initially the Krupp representatives had proposed that Houdini enter a huge cannon, the mouth of which they would heat and close with a giant press. He declined that challenge but consented to try to escape from handcuffs designed by the Krupp master machinists. It took them twenty minutes to lock the cuffs on Houdini. In thirty minutes he was free, but he paid a price.

"The cuff used was a kind of an arrangement that screwed to fit the hand," Houdini wrote Dr. Waitt. "And the Krupp man screwed it down until it touched the bone, and imigane [sic] the pain it caused me. The Krupp man has maimed my right hand so that I am unable to work, and it will be a week or so before I can have a cuff locked on me . . . I was in that dam (excuse the dam but I said worse than that) . . . I was in that cuff half of an hour and it seemed like an eternity."

Houdini had some other unusual experiences in Essen Ruhr. He met with a man named Goldschmidt, who had invented a "terrible compound" named thermite that could be utilized to burn a hole through a safe without destroying its contents. Goldschmidt's compound was a mixture of aluminum filings and iron oxide, which, when ignited, burned at the amazing temperature of three thousand degrees Celsius. Houdini noted that he was in Berlin when Goldschmidt performed his first test on a safe. He didn't explain why a stage escape artist would be at such a demonstration.

The palm garden salon was the most luxurious room in all of Budapest. It was adorned with graceful fountains, verdant palms, wonderful complex tapestries, and, of course, gilded rococo chairs and lounges. It was a setting fit for a queen. And tonight, there was one in attendance. The queen's dress had been custom-made in a small London shop. It was originally made for Queen Victoria, but she had died on January 22, 1901, and so it hung forlornly in the shop window. Until Houdini saw it. He marched into the shop and offered to buy it. At first, the owner was shocked that someone had the impudence to buy the queen's dress. When Houdini told him that the gown was for his mother, and that he planned to bring her to Europe from America and throw a gala reception for her in her old hometown, the shopkeeper relented. After what must have been severe alterations, he sold the gown to Houdini for fifty pounds with the proviso that it never be worn in the United Kingdom.

And there was Cecilia Weiss, resplendent in her finery, thrilled by her son's fanciful story of her dress's royal origin, greeting nearly everyone who had ever known either Rabbi Weiss or her back in Budapest. Houdini took the greatest

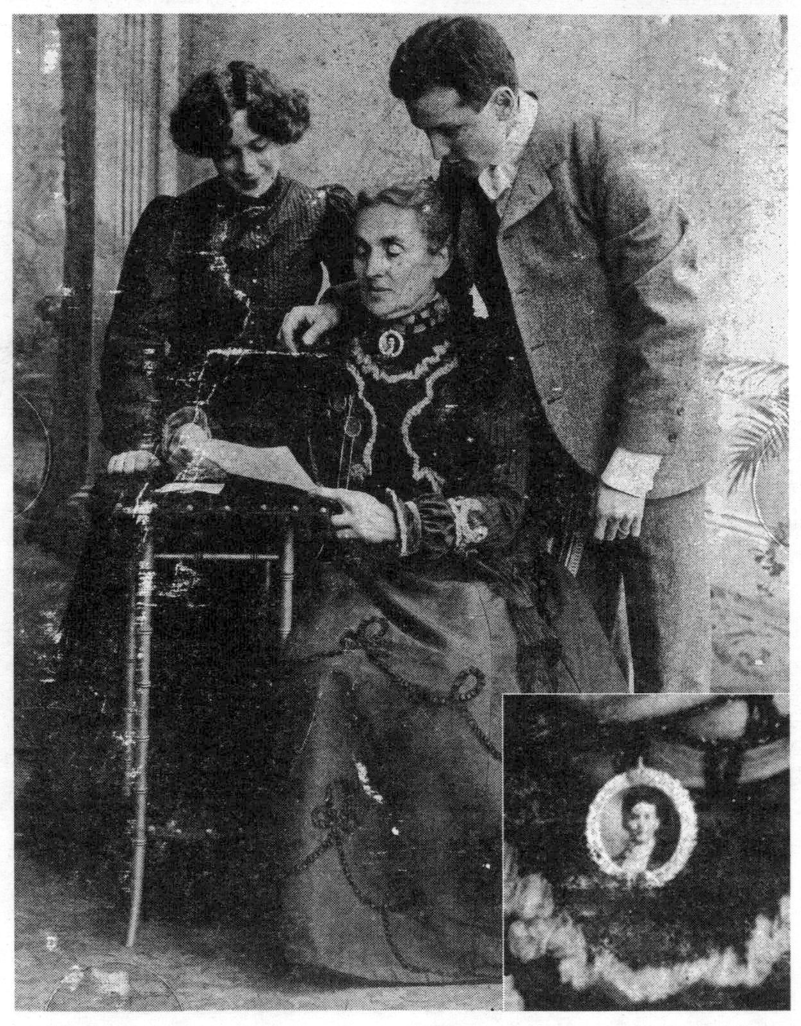

Houdini and Bess with his mother. Note Mama Weiss's pendant. *Library of Congress*

pleasure in seeing his mother's uncle Heller, the snob of the family, who had boycotted Cecilia's wedding to Mayer Samuel in protest. This would show him what the union of those two could produce. "How my heart warmed to see the various friends and relatives kneel and pay homage to my mother, every inch a queen, as she sat enthroned in her heavily carved and gilded chair," Houdini would write with glee. That night Houdini and his mother stayed up all night, recounting every detail of the party. The next day, he "escorted the Fairy Queen Mother" to her ship and her voyage home.

Houdini stayed. And why not? He was a resounding success. His mother had arrived in Germany at the end of May, just in time to see her son presented with a solid silver bowl inlaid with more than six hundred marks in silver coins in recognition of his astounding box office success. A month later, he decided to fire Martin Beck, his U.S. manager; after all, Houdini had been handling his affairs on his own since he had come to Europe. Now he took on the additional burden of acting as agent for his old friends, the acrobat Jim Bard and Alexander Weyer, the strong man. Houdini wrote Bard several times a week, giving him advice, reporting on progress getting him bookings, and generally bolstering his friend's spirits. "Dont you worry that any one can knock you now," he wrote Bard on September 15, 1901. "As you have Houdini boosting you, and today ther[e] is no better known act in Europe. I have ennimies [sic] by the score . . . but so far I am not afraid of them."

Immediately after his mother's departure, Houdini toured as the feature act of the Corty-Althoff Circus. They played Dortmund, Osnabrück, and Cologne. After taking a much needed rest in August, Houdini played Prague in September before returning to Germany to perform in Hanover. It was there that he was challenged by Count von Schwerin, the chief of police. Houdini managed to escape from police manacles at the station, but then the count had his men lace Houdini into a straitjacket. It was used to secure violent prisoners, so it had been constructed from heavy canvas reinforced with thick leather. It took Houdini one hour and twenty-nine minutes to get free, and the ordeal left him bruised and battered, with his clothes in tatters. "The pain, torture, agony, and misery of that struggle will live forever in my mind," he wrote in his diary. It must have made a big impression, for Count von Schwerin's name found its way into Melville's diary too.

Regardless of the pain, Houdini's act was an unmitigated success in every country he visited. Part of his appeal was that he tried to perform in the audience's native tongues, a tactic that he learned from Robert-Houdin's account of the Italian conjurer Bosco's endearing use of broken French. "I get through with my talk in my act better than I ever thought that I would, and it must be funny, as they laugh, as if

I were doing a monologue act," Houdini wrote Dr. Waitt. But he was also cognizant of the deeper, underlying appeal of his performance. "It does seem strange that the people over here, especially Germany, France, Saxony, and Bohemia fear the Police so much, in fact the Police are all Mighty," he wrote Waitt a month later. "I am the first man that has ever dared them, that is my success." His bravado was a bluff. He had just finished drawing up his first will.

"Your honor, I have no objections to showing the commissioners how I work my trick. But would it be possible for us to do this in a corner of the room to preserve my secrets?"

Revealing his secrets was the last thing that Houdini wanted. Reluctantly, he stood up in the courtroom on February 21 and allowed Lott, a civilian police employee of the Cologne department, to truss his body with a long chain and then fasten it with a lock. Lott then stepped back, but Houdini just stood there motionless.

The judges thought that was a reasonable request, so they followed as Houdini slowly and stiffly made his way into the far corner of the courtroom. Then, surrounding Houdini, they watched as the magician went to work. A few minutes later, the lock was open, and the chain fell to the floor.

Although this reads like a ploy by Houdini to defend himself in a case brought against him by the German authorities, in fact Houdini was the plaintiff in this bizarre case. He was suing the German police and a Cologne newspaper for slander. Back on July 25, 1901 an article had appeared under the title of "The Exposure of Houdini" in the *Rheinische Zeitung* newspaper. According to Houdini's later accounts, the article maintained that a Cologne patrolman (the lowest rank on the force) named Werner Graff was so upset at Houdini's ability to escape from Graff's lock, which had been "deadened" so that it couldn't open even with a key, that the policemen alleged that Houdini was a charlatan who misrepresented his talents and "swindled" the German public. In fact, the allegations were much more damaging than that.

According to Graff, Houdini, through another escape artist named Josephi, had heard that Graff had a handmade lock that was said to be impregnable. When Houdini got to Cologne, he wrote Graff and asked if Graff would agree to let him test it. Then Houdini visited the police department and pulled Graff aside for a private conversation. He told Graff that he intended to give a demonstration at the police department, and he wanted Graff to lock him up. Houdini would perform this test nude, and after being bound by his hands and feet, he would be carried into an empty room, where he would affect his escape. What he needed from Graff was a duplicate key, which he would hide in his anus. As a gesture of goodwill, Houdini, according to Graff, offered him twenty marks at first, but claimed that if this stunt was pulled off successfully they "both could make a lot of money."

Graff maintained that he turned Houdini down. Then, on the last night of Houdini's engagement in Cologne, he challenged Houdini onstage to escape from his lock and chain. Graff claimed Houdini told him that if he locked him so that he couldn't escape, his reputation would be ruined, since a circus clown at the Circus Sidoli had already exposed the way his Metamorphosis trunk worked. Graff insisted on the lock test, so Houdini then "fell on his knees and begged" the civilian employee Lott to give him a duplicate chain. Lott furnished a duplicate chain for twenty marks, and Houdini retired to his cabinet where he filed through the chain and removed Graff's lock. Then, leaving the sheared original chain in his cabinet, he triumphantly emerged, holding the duplicate chain and original lock. The "innocent public cried 'Bravo!'" not knowing that they were duped.

Houdini's story was different. He claimed that he had been turned down by the Cologne Police Department when he wanted to give a performance there and that the conversation with Graff never took place. In fact, it was Graff who challenged Houdini to escape from his lock, but Lott had warned him not to accept the challenge since Graff planned to switch locks and fetter him with a dead lock. The night of the performance, Bess tipped Houdini that Graff had switched the lock. Thinking quickly onstage, Houdini asked Graff to reopen the lock and make the chains a little less tight, but Graff protested that he couldn't since he had misplaced the key.

"I think I have the right to get free however I can," Houdini then proclaimed to the audience and withdrew into his cabinet, where he broke the lock. After the show, he sought out Lott and, appreciative for the tip about Graff, told him, "You're a good guy. May I give you a little something?" Then he tipped him twenty marks.

Graff's account raises two interesting questions. Would Houdini be so bold as to offer a bribe to a police official in exchange for confederacy in an escape attempt? According to Tommy Downs, the great coin manipulator whose amazing sleight of hand made it seem like he snatched gold coins out of thin air, Houdini once told him, "You don't realize how easy you get your salary. You almost catch it out of the air . . . I have to work early and late, day and night . . . If I find a lock or a jail I can't spiritualize, I must fix or arrange a way out." Downs added, "He had to fight every inch of his way."

A depiction of Houdini's trial in Germany. *Nielson Magic Poster Gallery*

Houdini had even told friends that since "our Police are not in the best of repute in Europe, especially with our American methods of Graft," his endorsements from the American police forces never impressed the European police, and eventually he "cut them out."

Granted Houdini might give a cooperative cop "a little something," the important question that emerges from this account is why didn't the German authorities press charges against Houdini in July of 1901 after a German officer went public with a bribe attempt? This is the same government that jailed Mrs. Rothe, the flower medium, for two years for misrepresenting her ability to contact the dead, and prosecuted Dr. Slade, another medium, and a woman who claimed magnetic powers. Certainly attempting to bribe a public official would generate even harsher reprisals.

The idea that Houdini was in some way being looked out for by a sympathetic official in the German government gains credence when we look at the testimony at the slander trial. In a lot of respects, the charges and countercharges boil down to one word against the other, but part of the case revolved around the attempts of Josephi, the other escape artist, to negotiate a larger bribe for Graff to remain silent after the show concluded. According to sworn testimony by both Graff and Lott, Josephi floated the idea that if Houdini would have offered three hundred or four hundred marks, the whole matter might take a different course. At that point, they claim that Josephi stated that it had cost Houdini at least one thousand marks to bribe the officers of the Berlin police to issue his certificate.

This revelation caused a sensation in the courtroom. Graff went on to disclose that after the newspaper article had appeared, Cologne Police Commissioner Riefer had interrogated Graff, Lott, and Josephi. The transcripts of this investigation had been sent to Berlin, because "in these statements the bribery of Berlin officers had been mentioned." Graff's lawyer then asked that the files be retrieved from Berlin and that the police commissioner testify. The next day Commissioner Riefer merely testified that he "had the impression that Josephi wanted to say that such certifications in general can be obtained in fraudulent ways."

There was no further mention of the bribing of Berlin police officials and no attempt at all to raise the issue of Houdini's commission of a crime. In fact, the trial devolved into another venue for Houdini to exhibit his skills. And he had certainly prepared for this all-important stage. "I knew in order to win my lawsuit I would have to open any lock that was placed before me," Houdini wrote in his own *Conjurer's Monthly* magazine. "The best practice I could obtain was to procure a position as a repair locksmith in some small shop." Houdini then apprenticed at the shop of his friend Mueller, a Berlin locksmith. "I would pass 6 to 10 hours daily, picking locks, and soon with the assistance of the four marked picks, I could open any lock." He came to court prepared too. One of the Cologne papers covering this sensational trial indicated that Houdini "had brought an entire suitcase filled with cuffs and locks and made all sorts of experiments to prove his skill."

During the proceedings, Houdini seemed to have a lot more latitude than he would have in an American court. "I . . . proved that I was a regular lawyer," he boasted in a letter to his friend Jim Bard. "I mixed the witness all up, and made them admit that they were told to lie . . . Should I win, it will be the greatest advertising that I have ever had." He also admitted that Bess wasn't holding up too well, "this worry has helped to give her a nervous spell."

On March 1, 1902 Houdini wrote Bard again to crow about the verdict. "I win my case hands down . . . [Graff] swore to a whole pack of lies, and when the other witness [Lott] came in, why I made him look like a dummy, and he gave the whole plot away." After some self-righteous indignation over his honor, Houdini admitted how he came out on top. "What really saved my cas[e], was that I showed the judge how I opened my cuffs, and that was really the best thing that I could have done."

The court found Graff guilty of slandering Houdini and ordered him to pay two hundred marks (about $40 at that time). The newspaper was fined fifty marks. Houdini himself was fined three marks for publicly insulting the officer when he cried, "This officer is a common liar" from the stage, when Graff denied he was testing Houdini with a dead lock. Graff persisted in appealing the verdict and after another drawn-out trial with twenty-five Cologne police officials testifying and Houdini bringing in witnesses from London and Vilna, Houdini once again demonstrated his ability to defeat a lock that Graff provided. This time Graff's burden increased considerably—he was forced to pay all court costs, including travel expenses and reimbursing Houdini for missed dates. Houdini's sweetest revenge came when the court ordered a public apology from the kaiser be issued to Houdini and printed in all the leading Cologne newspapers, the costs of which were borne by the patrolman. The apology would become a centerpiece in Houdini's pitch book in the years to come.

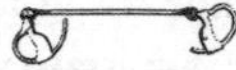

Secret Service agents Griffin and Ahearn had been on the case for weeks now, but finally they were about to hit the jackpot. Their surveillance of a Philadelphia anarchist ring had been ongoing, as per Chief Wilkie's orders, and had led them to their present location—at the bottom of a coal chute, eavesdropping on the revolutionaries, who, much to the agents' dismay, were just now talking about assassinating President McKinley. They strained to hear the details of the conversation through the bin, but just as the plotters were about to announce who had been chosen to do the actual killing, a massive load of coal was dumped on them from above, and the assassin's name was drowned out in the rumble.

During the summer of 1901, Secret Service Chief John Wilkie intensified his agency's surveillance of anarchists in the United States, after receiving disturbing reports of the growing presence of anarchist propagandists in major cities. His funds were limited and his staff was small, but after hearing his Philadelphia agents' chilling report, he immediately doubled the unofficial detail that was protecting the president, illegally diverting the money from his counterfeiting budget.

Wilkie was devastated when, after issuing warnings to President McKinley's personal secretary, the president was shot and killed by an anarchist on

September 6. The new president, Theodore Roosevelt, railed: "Anarchy is a crime against the whole human race; and all mankind should band against the anarchists." Chief Wilkie had a new mandate.

On April 3, 1902, Houdini, drained from his grueling court case and almost two years of constant touring, boarded the *Deutschland* steamer on his way home for a visit. There would be no rest for the weary, however. Once in New York, Houdini began a ten-day whirlwind visit that could only be described as manic. "I was so busy that I really did not have time to sleep," Houdini wrote his friend W. D. LeRoy. "I was home 10 days and slept one night, the rest of the time I was out, and slept in my motor car, while my brothers drove me about."

Houdini told LeRoy that he attended to a lot of business out of town too. According to his letter, he took a train to Washington, D.C., where he claimed to meet his manager, Martin Beck. The two then rode for thirty hours in a Pullman, going to Pittsburgh and back to Washington, "never sleeping except when nature called a halt. I tell you I lived 4 months in those 10 days." There's no reason to doubt Houdini's indefatigable energy in this period but there is some reason to question whether he was being candid with LeRoy. Houdini had terminated Beck as his manager in July of 1901. While they remained friendly and Houdini would seek out Beck's advice, it's odd to think that they had enough important things to discuss to warrant a thirty-hour sleepless marathon session on a private Pullman car, only to have Beck repeat the same career advice—stay in Europe until they get tired of him—that Beck had previously counseled in their correspondence.

A long-suppressed manuscript by Walter Bowen, a former private secretary to a chief of the Secret Service and its official historian, sheds light on an alternative scenario. Originally titled *The U.S. Secret Service: A Chronicle*, Bowen's book was substantially reworked by Harry Neal, a former assistant chief, and eventually published in a drastically edited form in 1960 as *The U.S. Secret Service.*

Bowen's original manuscript contained a large chapter on Wilkie that revealed, for the first time anywhere, that in 1902 (after his interview in early April with *The Washington Post*) "without publicity, the chief disappeared from Washington and was absent for four or five months traveling through Europe. He visited every capital on the continent and secured the planned cooperation of the police and national authorities in a comprehensive system of keeping track of dangerous anarchists."

Houdini, bound and manacled. *From the collection of Dr. Bruce Averbook*

That Wilkie would meet his counterpart in England, Superintendent Melville, is a foregone conclusion. That Wilkie met with Houdini before his own visit to Europe, debriefed him, and discussed the prospect of obtaining information from Russia, the epicenter of the anarchist movement, is an intriguing possibility.

Since I left America, I have been able to experiment with all of my former ideas and inventions, that I was unable to attempt in America, and do you know all the ideas are great?
—HOUDINI TO MAGICIAN FRIEND HARRY S. THOMPSON, JULY 16, 1902

Houdini somehow found time to develop his own inventions during this period. When we examine what he was actually experimenting with, we find that many of these innovations have an application in the field of espionage. He told *The New York Herald* that he invented rubber heels and cameras that work only once. *The Boston Transcript* reported that he invented "an envelope which cannot be unsealed by steam without bringing to light the word 'opened' and a wash which will remove printer's ink from paper" . . . hardly innovations of much use to magicians. In his own *Conjurer's Monthly,* he touted the use of a solution of chloride of cobalt for sending invisible messages. When heat is applied to paper that has been written on with this substance, "the letters appear in a bluish-green, which will vanish in a few moments." In the same issue, he notes that while he was in Germany he "purchased a simple method of secret writing." Houdini called it "a windowed cipher."

Besides using ciphers to transmit secret embedded messages, Houdini communicated with interested parties through the pages of magic and show business magazines. Sometimes he did it anonymously, using classified ads, but he also would convey information through his regular column in *Mahatma* magazine, the official organ of the Society of American Magicians. Under the byline Herr N. Osey, ostensibly a traveling German reporting on magicians abroad, Houdini would often write about himself in the third person and may have been tipping his collusion with the German police when he wrote, "How he ever obtained the Royal Certificates from the Berlin police is a greater mystery to me than his hand-cuff act."

Houdini also wrote a regular column under his own name for *The Dramatic Mirror*, a weekly show business trade paper published in New York. Most of his dispatches contained invaluable practical information for the professional trouper faced with touring in Europe, and he also conveyed information that would be of interest to Melville or Wilkie. On July 14, writing from Essen Ruhr, which is where the Krupp factory was located, he reports on a strange riot at a summer park where a crowd gathered to see a balloon ascension. "Despite the fact that Germany is known as a very strict 'police governed country,' strange things happen here just the same as if the police never were heard of," he prefaced his report, then went on to give a detailed, hilarious account of the systematic destruction of the park after a balloonist refused to launch his vehicle. What was interesting from a strategic point of view was Houdini's assessment of the response of the police and the bureaucratic chain of command that kept the police helpless watching the rioting until orders from Berlin were passed down the line. Also, for years Germany's experiments with the military applications of ballooning had attracted much attention in England and elsewhere, and secret agents had been sent into Germany to file detailed reports on all balloon ascents. Here was a report transmitted in a most disingenuous way, for all interested parties to see.

Houdini finished out the rest of the year dividing his time between Germany and England. Although he was making an excellent living, his success hadn't gone to his head. He could joke in letters referring to himself and Bess as "two young? people that are roaming around trying to make an honest million." His generosity continued unabated—when he won a bet from a locksmith in Vienna, he gave the money to the stagehands. Bess and Harry lived a completely unextravagant life—riding third class on the trains, sharing living expenses in Prague with his stage manager so that his room rental would be seventy-five cents a day—but he never forgot his pledge to his dying father. Responding to his friend Dr. Waitt's complaint about the rising cost of coal, Houdini wrote back, "I know all about the coal prices, as I am proud to say I have to keep my old mother, and she has explained to me WHY she must have more money." He had set her up in a nice new apartment, "the nicest little home," where he hoped to reside when he returned to the United States. It was a far cry from the days when "I had to figure out how far I could travel and how much beefsteak I could eat, so as not to interfere with other little expenses that would occur."

Meanwhile, Harry and Bess continued on their romantic, idyllic journey around Europe. Over the years, Houdini revealed very little about the intimate details of his relationship with Bess. He certainly credited his success to her,

Houdini loved children and went out of his way to entertain the sick and handicapped among them. *Library of Congress*

calling her his "lucky charm." A series of notes that he left her that expressed his affection survive. In many cases they indicate that Houdini had woken early to attend to work and didn't want to disturb Bess, so he'd gotten his own coffee or breakfast. "Honey-Baby-Pretty-Lamby, I did not want to awaken you by ordering coffee. My babykins must sleep. So I'll dine at automat. Will return about 2. All my love + more H." Affixed to some of these were sentimental love poems. Then there were the notes that simply affirmed his feeling toward her. Bess claimed that Houdini would sometimes leave six notes or letters a day for her, the sheer volume of which suggests that she somehow needed to be constantly reminded of his feelings toward her. Some of the notes suggest a man walking on eggshells. Houdini's letters to friends are full of comments on Bess's fragility, noting that she's constantly getting "sick" or having an attack of "nerves." Others commented on it too. Martin Beck closed a business letter to Houdini with "Hoping you are well and your wife is not cross, I remain, with best regards . . ."

Houdini loved children. He never missed a chance to perform at an orphanage. When he played Edinburgh, he was shocked at the number of children who were shoeless in the winter, so he bought three hundred pairs of shoes and, with the supporting acts as assistants, invited the city's poor children into the theater for a fitting. He spent countless hours entertaining his friends' children. Yet he and Bess never had children of their own. We know that there was a medical issue that prevented them from conceiving. Anecdotal family evidence points to Bess's inability to bear children. Adoption had been discussed but deferred due to the ongoing familial obligations he had inherited from his father.

In January of 1903, Houdini played the Rembrandt Theater in Amsterdam. He shared the bill with his old friend Jim Bard and a new friend, a singer and actress named Milla Barry. By February, Houdini had moved on to Germany, where he wrote Bard.

> ***My Dear Jim,***
>
> ***Never in your letters mention Barry or even her letter B. Have had some fearfuol*** [sic] ***trouble, will tell you all when you see me. Bess and I are almost squared, but she was sick. B tried her damdest to break us up, but . . .***

Unfortunately Bard's letters to Houdini on this topic have vanished, which is somewhat strange since Houdini kept a great deal of his received correspondence, especially from intimates like Jim Bard. We do have Houdini's side of the correspondence, and on March 5, he addressed the Barry issue with Bard again:

> ***My Dear Jim,***
>
> ***I had to laugh when I read your letter regarding Barry [. W]ho said that I run away with her, and how did they know that my baggage was still at the depot??? But such is life. This affair began to be a very stern affair after we left Amsterdam and*** [theater manager] ***Levin can tell you a lot of things if he desires to. But again I tell you such is life . . . I am having a hell of a time, and it will become worse . . . Keep away from Kepple*** [sic] ***Street in London, unless you want them all to know your business.***

8

Taming the Bear

"THIS IS NOT FAIR, CHIEF LEBEDOEFF. I specified that no extra locks were to be used," Houdini protested.

"Shall I inform the newspapers that you have been defeated by the carette before you have even entered it?" the chief of the Russian Secret Police inquired.

"No, I will accept the challenge," Houdini relented. "Even if the terms have been altered."

"Throw him in," Lebedoeff ordered.

The door was opened and two Russian officers picked up the handcuffed and leg-shackled nearly nude magician and deposited him in the back of the dreaded Siberian Transport Cell, which had been positioned in a corner of the courtyard of the old Butirskaya prison in Moscow. It looked impregnable, like a steel safe on wheels, as well it should, for this was the device that was used to convey Russia's most dangerous criminals to their exile and confinement in the dreaded Siberia. The cell itself was lined with zinc sheeting, a practical adornment since the carette drivers provided no bathroom breaks on the long journey east. The only light came through a small window on the door, and even that was secured with steel bars. The lock was a good three feet below the window, welded to the outside of the door.

Houdini heard the ominous sound of the massive tumblers engaging as Lebedoeff himself locked the door and added additional chains and padlocks. Then he pressed his face up against the window.

"One more thing, Mr. Houdini," the chief said. "I want to inform you that the key I used to secure the lock will not unlock it. The nearest unlocking key is

The dreaded Siberian Transport Cell. Inset: another view of the carette.
From the collection of Pavel Goldin

in the possession of a prison warder on the Siberian border, which is about a twenty-one-day journey. It would be a cold trip."

Lebedoeff laughed and moved away from the van. Now Houdini was alone. Within a minute he had released himself from the handcuffs and shackles, amazed that the Russians had used the very-easy-to-defeat British cuffs. Now all he had to do was break out of this impregnable Black Maria.

When Houdini and his new assistant, Franz Kukol, had inspected the carette the previous day, they had immediately discerned its weak point. Houdini had made a big show of examining the door lock and the distance of the lock from the small barred window but that was misdirection to divert the attention of the Russians away from Kukol, who by dropping his matchbook had a chance to get a glimpse of the underside of the carette. Sure enough, there were only plain boards beneath the body of the cell. Houdini sounded out the thickness of the zinc during his perusal of the door lock, and the escape plan was hatched. It would simply be a case of smuggling in two small tools—a miniature metal cutting tool, somewhat like a can opener, and a gigli saw, a coil of wire whose edge had been notched into saw teeth, originally used by surgeons to cut through the top of a human skull and also a perennial favorite of jailbreakers around the world. Houdini wasn't going to escape out the door; he was going to slice through the zinc, saw through the wooden slats, and escape from under the vehicle.

Smuggling in the tools was easier said than done. After the Russians made Houdini strip down to his briefs, four burly secret policemen spread-eagled him on an examining table and held him down as another agent probed his ears, his mouth, his nasal cavities, his hair, and every other available orifice for signs of concealed tools. "What a searching," he later wrote a friend. "Three secret police, or what we would call spies, searched me one after the other, and talk about getting the finger, well I received it three times, but Mr. Russian Spy found nothing." Franz Kukol, his assistant, had been forced to undergo the same examination.

The Russians were meticulous in their search of Houdini. They probed, patted, and peered into every available potential hiding space and found nothing. For all their thoroughness, they neglected to note one simple little thing—Houdini had six fingers on one of his hands. Utilizing a metal, hollow, flesh-toned false finger that contained the necessary implements to aid in escape was a favorite technique of Houdini. He would keep the false finger in one of his trouser pockets and, when first examined, would strip to the waist only. When the examination of the upper part of his body, including the mouth, hair, nose, arms, and between the fingers, was complete, he would then remove his pants, but not before putting his hand in his pocket and attaching the false finger. Now the lower body could be examined thoroughly.

Within a minute of his incarceration in the carette, Houdini had pulled off his sixth finger and was down on his knees, using the secreted tin cutter to slice a section a few feet long of the zinc floor at the corner of the carette. Then he carefully peeled back the zinc and began to saw through the underlying wood boards of the frame of the van, being careful to cut at an angle. When he had cut out a large enough section, he squeezed his way through to the ground, and reached back and pulled down the zinc flooring and replaced the sawed-off section of board. Then he ran across the yard to the relative warmth of the indoor offices.

Lebedoeff was enraged. He subjected Houdini to another grueling body inspection and ordered his assistant to undergo another one too. "They thought that [Franz] had something," Houdini wrote his friend Jim Bard. "They found his house key on him and they trued [sic] to open the door with it, but they have a swell lock on the cell and the house key is a cheap lodging house lock, so you can imagine how little it fitted." Even though Lebedoeff refused to sign a

A lithograph of Houdini's escape from the Russian carette. *Nielson Magic Poster Gallery*

certification of Houdini's escape, the news of Houdini defeating the feared secret police spread through Moscow like wildfire. Houdini's engagements in that city were extended for four months, and he drew the close attention of the royal family. "I think that I am to give a show for some grand duke or someother high muki kuck, will let you know," Houdini told Bard.

As difficult as it was getting out of the carette, it was equally difficult for Houdini, as a Jew, to get into Russia. But that story started months before. When Houdini was preparing to visit Russia, "Hebrews" were not allowed at all. While this stricture could be "overcome by simply denying your religion when you are having your passport *viséd* [sic] by the Russian consul," it didn't seem to be a prudent strategy for a performer who planned to test the police. The alternative was to "go into Russia with a license, like a dog; but no Jews are allowed to sleep in Moscow or St.

Petersburg." Later he would come to learn that Jews not only weren't allowed to perform on any stage in Moscow, they weren't even permitted to enter the city.

By contrast, the magician had official permission to appear in any city in Russia, an extraordinary set of circumstances that bespeaks the close relationship between Superintendent Melville and the Okhrana, the imperial Russian secret police. Melville had cooperated for years with the Okhrana, whose chief officer for Western Europe, Piotr Rachkovskii, was based in Paris. Houdini's bookings in Russia were made by Harry Day, a mysterious expatriate American who changed his name and met Houdini in London around the same time as Houdini's first meeting with Melville. Day would go on to book Houdini for years in Europe, branch out and own a chain of theaters, the sale of which made him a multimillionaire. He eventually became a member of Parliament and did overseas espionage for the British government.

On April 26, 1903 Houdini filed another field report with Melville. This time Melville acknowledged the importance of Houdini's transmission in his diary entry: *"Called at War Office to pass on letter from HH."*

On May 2 Houdini prepared to depart for Russia. "We leave for Moscow this evening, and hope they will not send me to Siberia," he ended his *Dramatic Mirror* column. Houdini took the courier train from Berlin and arrived at the border town of Alexandrowo, where Russian border patrolmen began to ransack Houdini's baggage. When they attempted to go through the papers that Houdini was carrying in his combination desk-trunk, Houdini balked and decided to ship the trunk and its contents back to Berlin. Then the guards came across the tools of Houdini's trade.

"As I carry a lot of burglar tools in my baggage, I had to obtain permission from the Russian Ministerium to take them into Russia, and I think they would have sent me back to Germany had it not been that I carried a permit to take in the tools," Houdini wrote. Apparently the permit worked wonders. The inspection came to an end and Houdini was allowed to proceed. But Houdini's trip into Moscow was hellish. Passengers pushed their way onto the train and were literally hanging on the walls. "I think that a butcher in America would hesitate before he would ship his cattle in one of these third-class trains. There is nothing that I have ever witnessed that has equaled it," he wrote in his first column from Russia.

"I defy the police department of the world to hold me," Houdini bellowed, gesticulating wildly. In response, a few birds shot out of a nearby tree, and a drunk stirred out of his stupor, raised his head, peered at Houdini for a second, and went right back to sleep on his bench. Undeterred, Houdini continued his walk around the isolated racetrack on the outskirts of Moscow. He was about to open in Moscow and that meant practicing his stage patter in Russian. The stage manager of the Establishment Yard, where Houdini would play, had gotten him an interpreter, but now he was trying out his Russian on an imaginary audience.

"I challenge any police official to handcuff me," he stopped and thrust his finger in the air, punctuating his defiance. "I am Houdini, the greatest of the jailbreakers and handcuff kings."

Houdini's voice was so strong and mellifluous that not only would it carry to any part of a vast theater, he could even be heard out in the lobby. So the sight of a bushy-haired, oddly dressed man screaming to himself and gesticulating majestically was bound to draw attention in a society as repressed as Russia's, especially when he was challenging the police to restrain him.

At first there were just two tall men, out on a stroll, who watched him with acute curiosity. Houdini nodded to them and continued his perambulations.

"There is nothing supernatural in what I do," he screamed, still strolling the grounds with a frenetic pace. He was so preoccupied with his address that he failed to see that there were at least three men who had begun to follow him around the racetrack. He was pleased how quickly he had picked up the language.

After another twenty minutes, Houdini called it quits. He was about to exit the racetrack, when ten uniformed men jumped out from behind some large shrubbery and tackled him to the ground.

They began to pepper him with questions, but the extent of his Russian was confined to his stage patter. Uncertain whether he was a dangerous insurrectionary or merely insane, the policemen snapped some cuffs on him and led him to a waiting police van. Houdini knew better than to try to escape these cuffs. He was taken to a police station and thrown in a cell, with six armed guards standing duty in front of it. When he missed dinner, Bess became alarmed, and with the manager's assistance, eventually located him. After an explanation, the sheepish entertainer was released.

The Russian secret service would certainly go on to assume a large role during Houdini's stay, keeping him under steady surveillance. Yet, just as in Germany, for a mere entertainer, Houdini gained unprecedented access to Russian prisons. He observed court arraignments, watched convicts being marched through the streets, and made many visits to Russian jails, later pronouncing them "some of the vilest prison pens describable" and "foul-smelling, reeking dungeons."

Houdini also showed interest in the state of the Russian army, information that was of vital concern to Melville. It's interesting that an apolitical escape artist paid such close attention to the budding Russo-Japanese conflict, expressing amazement that the "Japs were able to bring the Russian bear to his haunches." At that time, both Melville and Wilkie had few operatives in the field, relying on information gathered by private citizens and off-duty officers on vacation who traveled to countries of interest to them. Houdini's reports of such things as the strength and character of the Russian army and the army's perceptions of Japan's willingness to enter conflict, were very helpful. There was even an opportunity for Houdini to transmit this information directly to Wilkie, who, while Houdini was in Moscow, was in the midst of a two-month tour, in July and August, meeting with his secret service counterparts all across Europe.

"Aha, Mr. Houdini, I am afraid that this task will be impossible for even such a wonder-worker as you," the Grand Duke Sergius said as he looked up from the slip of paper he had just read.

"Isn't that my job, your highness," Houdini countered, "to make the impossible possible?"

Some of the other members of the royal family chuckled. They admired the brashness and the spunk of this young American. And they had been secretly pleased when he had managed to escape Mr. Lebedoeff's Black Maria. A feat like that only attested to the supernatural powers that he must possess.

"Well, what is it? The suspense is killing me," the czar said.

Sergius uncrumpled the slip of paper. Houdini had asked each of the assembled guests to write down on a slip some impossible thing they would like to have performed. The slips were collected by Houdini, placed in a hat, and then Sergius had been asked to fish one out.

"Can you ring the bells of the Kremlin?" Sergius announced. The women giggled on hearing the request.

"Well, that just might be impossible," the czar said. "Those bells haven't pealed for more than 100 years. And I don't see how even a mystic like you could effect such a thing. The bell ropes have rotted to dust by now."

"I can't promise anything. But I will certainly accept such a challenge," Houdini said and strode purposefully over to the large window that overlooked Kremlin Square. The others moved closer and gathered around him as he withdrew a handkerchief from his right pocket. Fishing some strange-looking purple powder out of his vest pocket, he sprinkled it on the handkerchief.

Outside, the snow fell slowly, blanketing the ground. Across the square, the Kremlin bell tower stood in mute testimony to the impossibility of this performance. Houdini began waving the handkerchief, forming arcs in the air in front of him.

"Powder travel through the night, your assignation before dawn's light, from Seventh Heaven to deepest Hell, do our bidding and ring the bell!" Houdini intoned, then dramatically threw one of the huge windows open. The silence was suddenly shattered by the pealing of the Kremlin bells.

The royalty was dumbfounded. Houdini smiled at Bess and was thankful that Franz, who was standing on a balcony in their hotel across the square, had been able to see their prearranged signal through the snow. As soon as Kukol saw the handkerchief waving, he aimed his air gun and fired off a volley of shots at the bells, making them ring for the first time in a century.

After that night, Houdini had become quite friendly with the Grand Duke Sergius and his wife, the duchess. They often summoned Houdini to their Palace Kleinmichel, where he never failed to astound them and their guests. On May 23, Houdini and Bess performed their Second Sight mind reading act at the palace. Dating back to the fifteenth century and newly popularized by Robert-Houdin, the Second Sight routine had been their staple. It worked on a very simple principle. Houdini had taught Bess a code that could be transmitted both by nonverbal and verbal cues. By moving his facial muscles, wiggling his ears, even changing the position of his feet, Houdini could cue information to Bess. For example, if he wanted to convey the number one, he might stand with his left foot forward of his right, for number six, he might stand with his left foot in back of his right, with his left heel raised—and other previously agreed on positions.

It was even more amazing when Bess could glean information when she was blindfolded. They did that by using a code where seemingly casual words would convey specific information, in this case a number.

Pray	*1*
Answer	*2*
Say	*3*
Now	*4*
Tell	*5*
Please	*6*
Speak	*7*
Quickly	*8*
Look	*9*
Be quick	*10*

By combining the words, repeating some, Houdini could transmit either numbers or specific letters of the alphabet to Bess, and when she would then repeat the correct answers, it would seem like a miracle. The duchess was so intrigued by Bess's ability to identify objects while blindfolded that she took Houdini aside and asked him if it would be possible to transmit this knowledge to her. Houdini took the duchess to another room and gave her a quick lesson in the Second Sight code. When they returned to the guests, the duchess announced that Houdini had imparted to her the power to receive transmitted thoughts. The other royals were amazed as Houdini roamed the room and the blindfolded duchess was able to correctly identify objects that Houdini pointed to.

On another occasion, in June, the grand duke ordered the governor of Moscow's prison to bring his most difficult handcuffs to try to defeat Houdini. Houdini was surprised when he saw that the irons were wrapped in soft leather to avoid chafing the wrists.

"Do you find Russian handcuffs very cruel, Mr. Houdini?" the duchess asked.

"In fact, I have never seen one less cruel or one more comfortable," Houdini replied.

The duchess smiled sadly. "Won't you tell this to the world, so they won't think Russians so cruel."

In some way, the duchess was most responsible for the fascination by the royal family and Czar Nicholas toward Houdini. She had taken a liking to Houdini at their first meeting and had imparted a very valuable piece of information to him. Before the end of his first performance before the royals, the duchess informed him that anyone who accepted money for their performance before the royal family was immediately relegated to a menial position. Since Houdini was more interested in prestige and maintaining an air of mystification, he took her advice and indignantly refused the grand duke's offer of a fee. On the defensive, the grand duke implored Houdini to accept gifts as a token of their esteem. Houdini deigned to accept an antique ladle that was used by Count Kleinmichel to dispense champagne, some rings, and allowed Bess to receive a fluffy white Pomeranian that they named Charlie.

In Russia, as in Germany, many people thought that Houdini effected his escapes and rapid trunk substitutions through an innate ability to dematerialize. One Moscow newspaper went further. When Houdini gave a performance in front of a special committee at the Restaurant Yar on May 1, the reporter marveled at his supernatural abilities. "Mr. Houdini, in front of the serious committee, was able to turn into a woman, then turn into a baby, then come back to his regular appearance." Possessing ability like that marked Houdini as a "wolshebnik" or miracle man. And there was no person in all of Russia more convinced that Houdini was a wolshebnik than Czar Nicholas himself.

For some years before Houdini's visit, Czar Nicholas had been disproportionately influenced by the occult and by strange religious beliefs. He believed that God spoke through the mouths of idiots, and consequently, he had collected scores of these blessed "simpletons" and installed them about the palace. One of these soothsayers was a thirty-year-old woman named Matronushka Bosoposhka (Matrona, the barefooted one). She was an itinerant mentally challenged woman who always walked around Petrograd barefoot. When the czar heard that she had the power to foretell the future, he brought her to the court, where he and the czarina would spend hours listening to her prattle on about nothing, all the while ecstatic to receive her blessings. When Matronushka lost her luster, the czar replaced her with Vastil Tkatchenko, a seventy-five-year-old soothsayer. Oftentimes, the czar's foreign policy was dictated by these outcasts.

By 1900, there was a significant faction of the royal family that had had enough of Nicholas's foolishness. This clique, led by the czar's uncle, the Grand Duke Vladimir, and his wife, the Grand Duchess Maria Pavlovna, was bitterly opposed to what they viewed as the czar's liberal tendencies and reforms. When Nicholas convened a disarmament conference in Hague in 1899, cosponsored by Queen Wilhelmina of the Netherlands, the reactionary element had had enough. Maria Pavlovna had seen an exhibition of hypnotism conducted by a man named M. Philipp. Enlisting him in their cause and paying him dearly, they introduced Philipp to the czar, who was entranced by his mystic powers and personality. Their reactionary agenda was promoted by Philipp in a series of hypnotic sessions, and the resultant actions of Nicholas in harshly suppressing a student movement and violently putting down peasant revolts were attributed to Philipp's own brand of brainwashing.

Eventually the czarina became suspicious of Philipp's sway over her husband and Okhrana agents stationed in various parts of Europe began a full-fledged investigation into Philipp, revealing that he was a Turkish ex-convict charlatan. At first the czar dismissed these allegations, but when his own personal physician ridiculed Philipp's production of the spirits of the czar's two predecessors, Philipp was exiled to Paris. This is exactly when Houdini arrived in Russia.

According to an article in *The Chicago Herald* shortly after Houdini's death, Chicago Probate Judge Henry Horner, who went on to become governor of Illinois in 1933, revealed that Houdini had informed him that he was asked to become an advisor to Czar Nicholas's court on three separate occasions. The first time was during Houdini's stay in Russia in 1903. Houdini's introduction to the royal family was made by the Okhrana through the Grand Duke Sergius, whose official title was Military Governor of Moscow. Under the patronage of Sergius, who must have known that Houdini was merely a conjurer and not a holy man, Houdini's powers so amazed the czar and his family that he was asked to replace Philipp as the czar's close confidant. Houdini rejected his entreaty, claiming that he wanted to show his art to the entire world. Two years after Houdini left Russia, his friend the grand duke was literally decapitated by two bomb-wielding left-wing revolutionaries.

Around the same time, the czarina came under the sway of an itinerant peasant faith healer named Grigori Rasputin. Rasputin's ability to heal young Prince Alexi, who suffered from hemophilia, gave him sway over the royal family and his influence in the court was considerable. Rasputin's dissolute lifestyle was chronicled in almost daily secret reports by the Okhrana, but even the secret police's chief had to marvel at Rasputin's hypnotic powers. "His influence is so great that even the old secret agents of my department fall under his sway in a few days."

Rasputin made many enemies, foremost among them Nicholas's prime minister Peter Stolypin. Stolypin presented many of these secret police reports to Nicholas, but the czar was loath to remove the man who his wife held responsible for the life of the sickly prince. In September of 1911, Stolypin was assassinated by a radical who feared that Stolypin's reforms would forestall the revolution. The opposition to Rasputin's power grew and in 1912, Houdini was contacted by the czar's court officials to come to Russia and depose the faker. Houdini considered making the trip, but never did.

Rasputin met a grisly fate on December 30, 1916 when he drank several glasses of poisoned wine and ate pastries laced with potassium cyanide, courtesy of a faction of the royal family. When the poison was not enough to kill him, he was shot by Prince Felix Yusupov, stabbed repeatedly, and finally drowned in the icy Neva River. Shortly after, Houdini was again contacted by the czar and asked to replace Rasputin. Houdini had had enough of the man who he deemed "as helpless as an infant." He was pessimistic about the ability of the royal family to enact desperately needed reforms in Russia. "Any radical change would mean that too many grand dukes would lose their jobs," Houdini quipped to the press in 1905. He was prescient. On March 15, 1917 Nicholas was forced to abdicate and on July 17, 1918 he and his family were shot by a Bolshevik firing squad and then dragged to the basement of the house they had been confined in and stabbed with bayonets.

From the collection of Dr. Bruce Averbook

9

The Challenge of the *Mirror*

HOUDINI CLOSELY EXAMINED THE MANACLES. HE didn't like what he saw.

"Ladies and gentlemen, my challenge stipulated that I could escape from regulation restraints, but I am afraid to say that these cuffs have been tampered with. The iron has been wrapped with twine, the locks have been altered, and various other expedients have been adopted to render my escape that much more difficult," Houdini said.

Most of the audience cheered sympathetically for Houdini. A few people registered their disappointment.

"Mr. Houdini, if you would care to read your own notices, you would see that I stipulated that I would bring and use my own irons. This is precisely what I've done," William Hope Hodgson, the proprietor of the Blackburn School of Physical Culture, announced dramatically. There was a smattering of cheers for the local son.

Houdini pondered the situation.

"Although Mr. Hodgson is going beyond the challenge, I am quite willing to go on with this contest provided you allow me a little extra time in which to deal with these unusual difficulties."

Houdini was roundly cheered by the 2,500 people who had packed Blackburn, England's new, beautiful Palace Theatre on October 24, 1902. He had performed two shows already that night, at seven and nine. Now it was a little after ten, and the audience was primed for the showdown. Hodgson, a twenty-four-year-old town resident who had studied judo and bodybuilding while serving in the merchant marines, had taken up Houdini's standard offer of £25 to any challenger who could cause him to fail to escape from regulation handcuffs used by the police of Europe and America.

Hodgson and his assistant, a giant hulk of a bodybuilder, began the torturous process of fettering the escape artist. First they affixed a pair of irons over one of Houdini's upper arms. They passed the chain behind his back and pulled it painfully tight and then pinioned his elbows closely to his sides. They repeated this procedure with another pair of cuffs on his other arm and padlocked both of them behind him, which had the effect of pulling Houdini's arms stiffly toward his back. Then they fastened a pair of chained cuffs to his wrists and tightened them to the point where Houdini's arms were simultaneously being pulled both backward and forward. The zeal with which the strongman assistant tackled this job led to a protest from Houdini.

"There is no stipulation in the challenge that my arms should be broken," Houdini said, to the delight of the crowd.

"His challenge clearly says that he would iron you himself," an audience member shouted out. "Where's the fair play?"

A murmur of assent rose from the audience and Hodgson was compelled to dismiss his assistant. A second pair of handcuffs was fastened to Houdini's wrists, both pairs being padlocked securely. Still the entrepreneur wasn't finished. He helped Houdini kneel down and then he passed the chain of a pair of heavy leg irons through the chains that held Houdini's arms together at the back. The leg irons were fastened to his ankles and then a second pair was added and they were both locked together. Houdini "looked for all the world as a trussed fowl" one newspaperman wrote. Hodgson and the committeemen, who had been drawn from the audience, then assisted Houdini to his cabinet. The curtains were drawn, the orchestra began to play "up-to-date musical selections," and the battle commenced.

As each minute passed, the excitement in the hall became more and more palpable. Hodgson kept a wary eye on Bess and Theo, Harry's brother, who were both anxiously awaiting the escape on the stage. After fifteen minutes, the canopy was lifted and Houdini was seen to be lying on his side, still bound. There was some concern that he had fainted, but he was able to communicate that he wished to be lifted to his knees. Hodgson refused the request, and the audience began to boo and hiss him. Theo interceded and lifted his brother to his knees. The curtain was lowered again.

Twenty minutes later, Houdini asked that the curtain be lifted.

"My arms have been quite numb and drained of blood due to the inordinate tightness of the chains," Houdini declared. "I would request that the irons be unlocked for a minute so that my circulation could be restored."

"This is a contest, not a love match," Hodgson growled. "If you are beaten, give in."

The auditorium erupted with shouts and calls. Dr. Bradley, a member of the committee, stepped into the cabinet and examined Houdini.

"Mr. Houdini's arms are quite blue and I feel that it is tantamount to cruelty to keep him chained up as he is for any longer amount of time," the doctor pronounced.

"This is a bet," Hodgson laughed derisively. "Cry quits or keep on."

Houdini raised his head. "If the audience will indulge me with some more time, I will be happy to continue this contest," Houdini said. The audience, as one, cheered.

The orchestra played for the next fifteen minutes. The curtains of the cabinet periodically fluttered from what seemed to be feverish activity inside. Just then, Houdini popped his head out of the curtain and the music stopped.

"I have freed one of my hands, and I will now take a short rest before proceeding further," he said.

Most of the audience cheered encouragingly, but a few hostile voices were raised.

"You must remember, ladies and gentlemen, I did not state the time that it would take me to get them off. These handcuffs have been plugged."

As the clock showed eleven-thirty, the huge crowd began to get a bit impatient.

"Give it up!" someone cried out.

"Keep on, Houdini. You'll do it," another countered.

A few minutes later, Houdini popped his head out of the cabinet again.

"Both of my hands are free, and it will not be long before I will be free altogether," he said.

By now, some of the audience had begun to think that Houdini had met his match. And when his brother approached the cabinet to give him a word of cheer, some of the crowd began booing. Apparently Houdini told Theo that he was thirsty, because a cool glass of water was provided him. Then he addressed the audience again from his cabinet.

"I beg you to show a little more patience. Every one of these locks has been changed, and this is making it all the more difficult to get free," Houdini pleaded.

The crowd turned on Hodgson again. Later, he would claim that he had spied a key in one of the locks, but right then a police sergeant advised him that for his own safety he should leave the premises.

The orchestra played on. At ten minutes to twelve, with no warning, the cabinet's curtain flew open and Houdini staggered out. He threw the last of his shackles to the floor of the stage as a loud shout went up. Houdini's shirt had been torn from the cuff to the shoulder. His wrists and biceps were bleeding profusely. He could barely muster the strength to stand erect. He seemed semi-conscious. The vast audience stood up and cheered for fifteen straight minutes.

Finally they stilled as Houdini raised an arm.

"Ladies and gentlemen, I have been in the handcuff business for fourteen years, but never have I been so brutally and cruelly ill-treated. I would just like to say again that the locks were plugged."

"Where's Hodgson?" someone screamed.

"Why is he not here to offer his congratulations?" another yelled out.

The huge crowd cheered wildly as Bess, his brother, and some of the committeemen helped Houdini off the stage.

The next day Houdini met with a reporter from *The Blackburn Daily Star*. Houdini again charged that the cuffs had been plugged and that pulley blocks had been added to the shackles. Then he pulled up his sleeves and showed the newspaperman his arms. They were both hideously blue and swollen, with large chunks of flesh torn out. Houdini explained that because the chains had been pulled so tight, portions of his arm had been fastened in as the fetters were locked. He had no choice but to tear out the chunks of his flesh to get free.

Two years later, on November 1, 1904 Houdini met with another reporter, this one from *The Halifax Evening Courier*. "I noticed on Houdini's arms several scars, as though some tiger had clawed him," he wrote. "He [explained that he] had simply been in Blackburn and had been put in manacles which would have made an executioner wince. The gentleman who did the trussing business had superabundant strength."

One reason why audiences identified so strongly with Houdini was that he was willing to go as far as it took to effect his escapes, scars be damned. Every handcuff, every leg iron, every chain represented his potential Waterloo. His reputation was laid on the line nightly; he could not let himself fail. It wasn't just his own honor that he was defending. Houdini had single-handedly created an entire genre of entertainment, something he called the "Challenge Handcuff and Escape Act." And right from its inception, imitators came forth and began to attempt to duplicate his methods. "Harry's success had inspired a hord[e] of imitators and most of them were terrible. Harry wasn't worrying much about the few good ones but he felt that the bad ones were going to sour the public on the whole escape business," his brother Theo wrote.

The ruthlessness with which Houdini set out to defend his domain would, at times, make the distinction between bad and good imitators superfluous. Shortly after Houdini arrived in London, he had taken out large ads in several London papers warning rival bookers that he had "fully patented" his handcuff act and would "positively prosecute any and all managers playing infringements or colorable imitations." If a manager cared to investigate further, he would have found that the ad was just a bluff. Houdini had *applied* for the patent, but his refusal to allow the government patent office to publish the specifications of his handcuff act ultimately made them classify his patent application as "Abandoned."

If Houdini had legal threats ready to counter unscrupulous managers, he was planning quite a different strategy for the imitators themselves. Houdini's friend William Robinson had called him an old fighter—"I believe you would rather scrap than eat." If there was fighting to be done, Houdini could think of no one better to bring over to Europe than his former performing partner and bigger, younger brother Theo, described by their friend Joe Hyman as a "harum-scarum, hell raisin' boy" who could "fight like a wildcat." Theo's credo was: "if you are in a fight hit the other guy first."

While Houdini was performing for the first time in Berlin, he cabled Theo in New York, "Come over. The apples are ripe." By the time that Theo had reached Berlin, Houdini had duplicated his entire escape act—right down to handcuffs, substitution trunk, and a girl assistant—and had bookings set up for his brother. Houdini had even chosen a new name for Theo. It wasn't the first time. In their childhood, Houdini had nicknamed his younger brother "Dash." When Dash joined his act, he was dubbed a Brother Houdini. He was back to Dash after Houdini replaced him with Bess. When he summoned him to Europe, at first he considered dubbing him "Hardeeni," but thinking there might be confusion with his own name, he quickly changed it to "Hardeen." "We were very quickly in strong competition with each other, and we built up the competition as a grudge fight," Hardeen remembered. "We made no secret of the fact that we were brothers but we did keep secret not only the fact that we were good friends but that Harry had set me up in business!"

Hardeen also made no secret of the fact that he was there to run interference for his brother with his other would-be rivals. On November 18, 1901, Hardeen wrote Albert Hill, who performed under the name of Hilbert, warning him that they were aware that he was "working both mine and my brother's tricks." Hilbert got the message, writing back, "Please accept my assurance that

Houdini and his bigger, younger brother Theo, who he renamed "Hardeen."
Library of Congress

I will make no pretence to originality. I may add that I desire to carefully avoid any conflict with either yourself or your brother."

Other imitators were not that lucky. Harry dispatched both his brother and another escape artist named Hangeros to bust up a rival's act. Hangeros sent Houdini back a report, noting that he would be "very sore from the kicks I got," which pained him so "I did not sleep much last night . . . They gave me a good beating, *three* (3) large lumps on my head . . . My Glasgow overcoat is ruined . . . but thats not near as bad as the punching and kicking I got." Still, Hangeros was undeterred. "I havent weakened. I'll go after any cuff faker you name any time. This is the first time I was ever beat up badly in my life—I can stand a few more."

In Germany, Houdini's imitators were even more brazen, some even using variations of his name, like Harry Rudini, Harry Blondini, or Harry Mourdini.

Houdini routinely carried "handcuff-king-defeaters"—special cuffs that he used against rival escape artists that worked but were very difficult to escape from. Kolar, an American escape artist who knew Houdini from his dime museum days in Chicago, maintained that Houdini never showed up a fellow escape man unless they "first tried to 'do' him." One of those who tried to "do" him was an eccentric handcuff man named Kleppini, who didn't have an abundance of talent but made up for that by festooning his jacket with phony medals. He even had gold letters embroidered around his collar that read, "The Champion of All Champions of Handcuff Kings."

Houdini was touring Holland in June of 1902 when a friend sent him a clipping that Kleppini, who was performing with a German circus, was advertising that not only had he escaped from Houdini's handcuffs but that the Great Houdini had been defeated by Kleppini's irons. Enraged, Houdini took a leave of absence and rushed to Essen Ruhr, where he had his hair fixed to look old and glued a fake mustache onto his lip. Then, filling up a small grip with "handcuff-king-defeaters," he traveled to Dortmund to confront Kleppini.

The disguised Handcuff King took a seat in the circus audience and waited until Kleppini began his spiel. When his rival claimed to have defeated Houdini, he leapt to his feet and screamed, "Not true."

"And how would you know this, old man?" Kleppini said.

"I am in the know," Houdini countered.

"Would you care to wager that I am right?" Kleppini asked.

With that, Houdini took a flying leap to the center ring.

"You say I am not telling the truth. Well, look!" he screamed, pulling off his mustache. "I am Houdini!"

Houdini offered five thousand marks if Kleppini would allow himself to be handcuffed. He also offered to escape from Kleppini's Chinese pillory. After a lot of back and forth haggling, the circus manager refused to back Kleppini with a five-thousand-mark deposit and Houdini returned to his seat. A large portion of the audience, disgusted by Kleppini's misrepresentations, left the arena.

The next morning the business manager of the circus visited Houdini. He proposed that Houdini and Kleppini stage a one-night duel, but Houdini refused. He did consent to testing Kleppini with a set of cuffs. After the challenge was announced, Kleppini tried to contact Houdini, but Houdini shunned his calls. Then the manager returned and asked Houdini which cuffs he would use. Houdini laid out twelve cuffs and told the manager he could choose one to his own liking. He selected a pair of French letter cuffs that opened when the correct letters were selected.

"Which word opens this cuff?" the business manager inquired innocently.

After securing a promise that he wouldn't tell Kleppini, Houdini told him that by spelling out the French word CLEFS, which meant "keys," the cuffs would open.

The manager took the cuffs, ostensibly to show them to the circus's owner.

The night of the challenge, Houdini entered the ring with his bag of cuffs. He unpacked the dozen cuffs and, as expected, Kleppini pounced on the French cuffs.

"I will open these cuffs. I challenge Houdini to lock them on me," Kleppini shouted. "I'll show him that it is us Germans who lead the world."

Houdini took the cuffs and secured them on Kleppini's wrists. Then he addressed the crowd.

"Ladies and gentlemen, you can all go home. I do not lock a cuff on a man merely to let him escape. If he tries this cuff until doomsday, he cannot open it. To prove this, though the regular closing time of the circus is 10:30, I will allow him to remain here until 2:30 A.M."

Kleppini went into his cabinet at nine P.M. He still hadn't escaped a half an hour later, when the headlining ballet feature came on. By eleven P.M. almost the entire auditorium had cleared out, but Kleppini was still sequestered. Enraged, the circus owner screamed, "Out with Kleppini," and some stagehands were ordered to topple the cabinet. Still manacled, Kleppini scurried into the dressing room as the remainder of the audience left in disgust.

Houdini wasn't finished. He walked over to the dressing room, where he stood guard over the door. At midnight, he allowed Kleppini's wife into the room. At one o'clock, Kleppini finally gave in and asked Houdini to release him, but Houdini refused unless witnesses were present. After rounding up the circus owner and a reporter, Houdini still stalled until Kleppini admitted that he knew the combination was CLEFS, but was baffled when the cuffs wouldn't open.

Houdini laughed. "You are wrong," he said. "If you want to know the word which opens the lock, it is just what you are—FRAUD."

Overnight, Houdini had changed the combination.

In July of 1902, one of Houdini's associates turned rival. Houdini had employed a machinist in Essen Ruhr named Josef Kinsky to produce a few pairs of handcuffs. When Houdini severed the business relationship, Kinsky began hounding him with a challenge to fasten him that got tremendous publicity. When Kinsky began to denounce Houdini by making speeches in public squares, the magician took up the offer.

Houdini was to put up five hundred marks, Kinsky one hundred, with the victor's take going to a fund for the town poor. An overflow audience packed an Essen hall and seemed to side with the local underdog until Kinsky, instead of attending to the fastening of Houdini, began a bizarre personal diatribe making all sorts of accusations against the escape king.

"No talking! Tying!" the crowd screamed.

Kinsky complied. For fourteen minutes he tied Houdini with a rope. "Sometimes it was disgusting to see how he tightened the rope," the local newspaper reported. "We could see with our own eyes that Kinsky tied the American as you would tie a piece of cattle."

Houdini retreated to his cabinet and emerged seventeen minutes later. He was bloodied, cut up, his hands were swollen, but he was free. The audience gave him five curtain calls. "The American had won a victory that brought sensational proof of his skills, and his quiet, considerate manner brought him the sympathy of the audience to an even higher extent."

This challenge became part of the folklore of Essen Ruhr. Poems were written about it; songs were composed. A German comedian even dressed up as Diogenes, complete with lantern, and sang an ode to Houdini. Kinsky wasn't finished with Houdini yet. He volunteered to be part of the Cologne trial, testifying for the defense of Patrolman Graff. "He offered himself as a free witness against me," Houdini wrote, "but in his excitement, he became so boisterous that the Judges ruled his entire evidence out of Order. He was asked on oath whether I defeated him fairly, and he had to acknowledge that I was his Master."

Imitators continued to plague Houdini as he returned to play the British provinces after his Russian trip. And it wasn't only onstage that they inconvenienced Houdini. On December 10, 1903 he took out a personal ad in a Huddersfield newspaper. "Will the gentleman who calls himself Houdina or Houdiana, and who in a fit of absent-mindedness walked away from Huddersfield forgetting to pay his board bill to Mrs. Scott of St. Peter's street, kindly send the lady her money. It is very impolite to disguise yourself under a name which may sound like mine, and then walk away without paying your bills. I will not be responsible for any bills made by this gentleman."

Houdini was back in the English provinces, breaking all attendance records, but it was trying, grueling work. On December 14, he was at the Palace in Blackburn, the scene of the dreaded Hodgson contest. "Back to this wretched town," he wrote in his diary. "Of all the hoodlum towns I ever worked, the gallery is certainly the worst. Had a tough job with a heel named Wilson." Houdini had been challenged onstage that night by this young man who seemed more intent on making speeches from the stage then testing the Handcuff King. "He would not let me examine his cuff, so after a lot of speech making he wanted to walk off the stage. [Then] I sneaked behind him and tore the cuffs from his grasp and snapped them on myself. Well, you ought to have heard the booing that was my share to obtain . . ." Houdini wrote. "I went into my cabinet and found out that he had deliberately cut away the whole inside of the lock and it was ten minutes ere I had both hands free. Instead of applause once again I was booed. Then I snapped them on to the rods near the footlights and it took Wilson twenty minutes to take them off himself and he had to use three kinds of instruments to do so. He was applauded and I was booed."

Perhaps it was incidents like this that made Houdini contemplate retirement. Less than a week later the theater reporter for the Blackburn *Standard and Weekly Express* wrote, "I hear that Houdini, having made his 'pile', intends shortly to retire from the stage, for the demand made on him by his performances and the brutality to which he has not infrequently to submit, are making inroads on his health."

On top of that, he was now meeting resistance from the local police departments, whose jail cells were so vital to the publicity. On December 28, Houdini noted in his diary that the police chief of Birmingham wouldn't lock him up. "Said Houdini would not get any advertisement out of him." Houdini did much better in Sheffield. The chief constable there challenged Houdini to escape from the cell that twenty-five years earlier had held Charles Peace, one of the most notorious criminals in English history. Commander Charles Scott gave Houdini a glowing letter of commendation for his escape from the triple-locked cell. Scott was a contact of Melville's and would later work closely with him to ferret out German spies in England.

Houdini continued to smash records in the towns where the police were cooperating but when he returned to London and opened at the Hippodrome on February 29, 1904, attendance had fallen off, despite having staged a special exhibition for the press at the offices of the London *Weekly Dispatch*. Houdini borrowed more than 131 pounds of antique manacles from John Tussaud's Chamber of Horrors and escaped from irons that had held prisoners at the Bastille and some of London's most famous criminals, but it didn't seem to increase his box office. "House very poorly visited. Hope business will pick up," he wrote in his diary. "Superintendent Moy again to hand. Very touching man. Touched me for five Quidlest [quid]."

Even bribes to the police weren't helping. On March 4, Houdini was refused permission to be locked up at the Bow Street police station. Three days later he wrote to the police commissioner of London for permission to break out of cells. On March 9, the police chief of old Jewry wrote back. "I am directed by the commissioner to acknowledge receipt of your letter of the 7th, and to say that he regrets being unable to grant you permission to make the attempt of effecting an escape from any police cell in the city." This was a crippling blow to the formula that was producing record box office receipts. With a jail cell escape and the attendant publicity out of the question, Houdini needed something spectacular to ensure that his star would remain on the ascendancy.

"If there are any challengers in the house, will they please step upon the stage now?" Houdini said.

A neatly dressed gentleman left his seat and walked up the steps onto the stage of London's Hippodrome.

"Will you permit me to fasten these on your wrists?" the man asked Houdini, holding out a pair of handcuffs. And what a pair they were. They were extraordinarily heavy, with a single cuff that fastened both wrists. The lock itself featured two Bramah locks: one larger-than-normal outer lock with eight sliders, and nested inside it, a normal-sized Bramah lock that contained six sliders. The key to unlock the cuff was six inches long.

Houdini examined the cuff and handed it back to the challenger.

"These are not regulation cuffs," he shrugged.

The man then motioned for the orchestra to stop playing. "On behalf of my newspaper, *The Daily Illustrated Mirror*, I have just challenged Mr. Houdini to permit me to fasten these handcuffs on his wrists. Mr. Houdini declines. In the course of my journalistic duties this week I interviewed a blacksmith at Birmingham named Nathaniel Hart who has spent five years of his life perfecting a lock, which he alleges no mortal man can pick. The handcuff I wish to fasten upon Mr. Houdini contains such a lock. The key alone took a week to make. The handcuffs are made of the finest British steel, by a British workman, and being the property of *The Daily Illustrated Mirror*, has been bought with British gold. Mr. Houdini is evidently afraid of British-made handcuffs, for he will not put on this pair."

Houdini could only repeat that the cuffs were not "regulation," and he turned his back on the journalist and proceeded to allow himself to be fettered by three other challengers who had also taken the stage. He freed himself from their cuffs in minutes.

Determined, the *Mirror* representative then asked Houdini if he could examine one pair of the cuffs he had just defeated. Houdini handed him a locked pair. The reporter walked over to the steps leading up to the stage and smashed the cuff on one of the steps. It sprang open.

"So much for 'police regulation handcuffs,'" the newsman said.

The audience roared with delight.

"Now Mr. Houdini, you claim to be the 'Handcuff King.' Everywhere I see huge posters of your feats. If you again refuse to put on these handcuffs, my contention is that you are no longer entitled to use the words 'Handcuff King.'"

The gauntlet had been thrown. Houdini turned to the audience.

"I cannot possibly accept this gentleman's challenge tonight, because I am restricted as to time. His handcuffs, he admits, have taken an artificer five years to make. I know, therefore, I can't get out of them in five minutes. There is not one lock in those handcuffs, but a half a dozen or more. I will make a match if the management here will allow me a matinee someday next week to make a trial. It will take me a long time to get out—even if I can do so."

Mr. Parker, the stage manager of the Hippodrome, was consulted and plans were finalized for the test to occur on the following Thursday, March 17. Two days after being challenged, Houdini wrote in his diary, "London in an uproar . . . All papers have an account. Press full of 'match,' *Mirror*, and Houdini." He finally had the event that would surpass any publicity he could have received from a London jailbreak.

Houdini was scheduled to perform at three P.M. on Thursday, but the four thousand spectators who jammed into the Hippodrome impassively waited through six other performers until it was Houdini's turn. At precisely three P.M., a determined-looking Houdini entered the arena and received a standing ovation. Bess was on one side of the stage, resplendent in a black Knickerbocker suit.

"I am ready to be manacled by the *Mirror* representative if he be present," Houdini said.

The reporter stepped into the arena and was greeted with a polite round of applause. The two men shook hands.

"Can I ask for a committee comprising of audience members to come onto the stage to ensure fair play for both sides?" the journalist said.

A rush of people from all parts of the auditorium descended on the ornately carpeted stage.

Then Houdini stepped forward.

"If any of my friends are present, will they please step up into the arena now to watch out after my interests?" Houdini said.

There was another procession of people leading to the stage. By now, almost one hundred people, in morning dress, some holding their top hats, had climbed onstage and were surrounding the small red-curtained cabinet.

Now it was time for the bondage. The journalist put the handcuffs on Houdini's outstretched wrists and snapped them shut. He produced the long key and turned it six times, with some difficulty, securing the lock. He nodded at Houdini, who stepped into the spotlight.

"Ladies and Gentlemen, I am now locked up in a handcuff that has taken a British mechanic five years to make. I do not know whether I am going to get out of it or not, but I can assure you I am going to do my best."

The audience cheered heartedly as Houdini withdrew into his cabinet. By now, Houdini was using a small cabinet, approximately three feet tall, so all his exertions would be from a kneeling position. The orchestra began with a waltz.

The famous *Mirror* Cuff challenge at the Hippodrome. Houdini's ghost house is visible on the left. *From the collection of Pavel Goldin*

After two and a half minutes a clicking noise was heard from the cabinet. The committee thought that Houdini was free, but there was no sign of Houdini.

Time passed by. An operatic selection succeeded the waltz. Then, twenty-two minutes into the challenge, Houdini stuck his head out of the curtain.

"He is free! He is free!" several people shouted. Their joy quickly turned to disappointment when they realized that Houdini just wanted to look at the complicated lock in strong light. Houdini retreated into his cabinet and the band played on.

Then at thirty-five minutes, Houdini emerged again. His collar was opened, and sweat poured off his face.

"My knees hurt and my legs have cramped," Houdini explained. "Please allow me to stretch them. I am not done yet."

The crowd cheered. Mr. Parker, the manager, brought Houdini a glass of water. Then the *Mirror* representative conferred with Parker. Parker nodded his

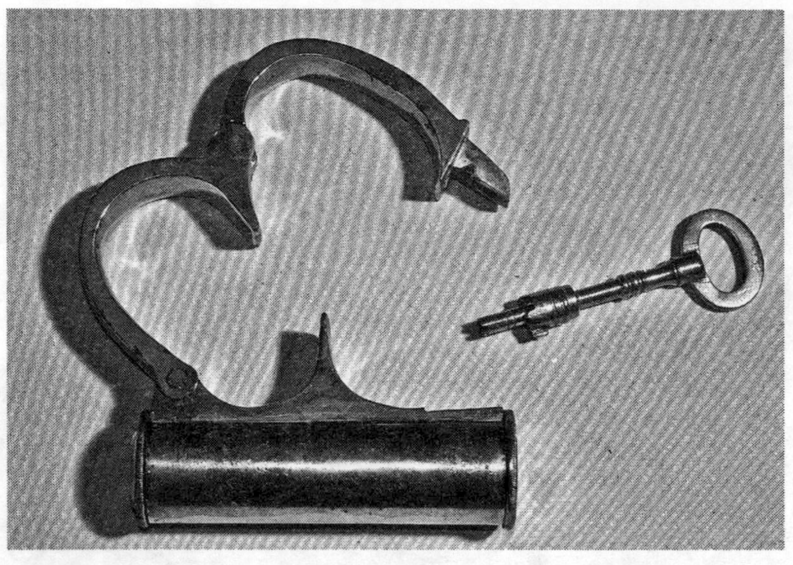

The *Mirror* Cuffs and key. *David Copperfield's International Museum and Library of the Conjuring Arts*

head and signaled to an assistant. In seconds, the assistant was back with a large cushion.

"The *Mirror* has no desire to submit Mr. Houdini to a torture test," the journalist said. "If Mr. Houdini will permit me, I shall have great pleasure in offering him the use of this cushion."

Houdini pulled the cushion into his ghost house and resumed his work, the silken walls of the cabinet quivering from his efforts.

By now, the tension became unbearable for Bess and she rushed out of the arena. Twenty minutes went by. The audience was fixated on that tiny cabinet. Suddenly Houdini came out, but the whole assemblage moaned as one when they noted that the handcuffs were still affixed.

Houdini looked like he was on the verge of collapse. He slowly advanced on his challenger.

"My coat is hurting me. Will you remove the handcuffs for a moment in order that I may take it off?" Houdini asked.

The journalist considered the request.

"I am indeed sorry to disoblige you, Mr. Houdini, but I cannot unlock these cuffs unless you admit you are defeated." The journalist seemed to think that there might have been more to Houdini's request than met the eye.

"Cut your coat off," someone from the gallery shouted.

And Houdini did precisely that. He maneuvered his fettered hands until he pulled a penknife from his waistcoat pocket. Then he opened the knife with his teeth, and with a jerking motion, threw his frock coat up over his head. Then he calmly began to cut the seams of his coat. He finished by tearing at the coat with his teeth. It finally hung from his arms by a mere shred and some of the committeemen removed the remains.

The audience yelled themselves frantic. Some screamed at the *Mirror* representative for refusing Houdini's request. Everyone was disheartened to see that Houdini had not made a dent in getting free from the restraints.

An odd audience member implored Houdini to "give it up."

"Go on, Houdini," others encouraged him.

And he did. He retreated back into his cabinet and began a last, desperate attempt to free himself. The frame of the cabinet rocked and the curtains fluttered from the exertion.

Houdini had been locked up for more than an hour. Then, just as the orchestra was finishing a stirring march, Houdini suddenly bounded out of the cabinet, holding the shiny handcuffs in one hand. He was free.

The audience roared with delight. Men pulled their hats off and waved them in the air. Hugs were exchanged. The ladies fluttered their handkerchiefs. But Houdini was not right. He half-fainted into the arms of one of the committeemen, hysterical, tears streaming down his cheeks. "Thank God! Thank God!" he murmured.

Houdini was helped backstage, but the audience still refused to disperse. They stood and cheered and exchanged handshakes for a full five minutes until he haltingly walked back out. He was immediately lifted onto the shoulders of some of the committeemen, who bore him in triumph around the auditorium. Then the crowd implored him to speak.

"I entered this ring feeling like a doomed man," Houdini said. "There were times when I thought that I could not get out of these handcuffs. But your applause gave me courage, and I determined to 'do or die.' I have never seen such handcuffs, locks within locks. I thought this was my Waterloo, after nineteen years of work. I have not slept for nights. But I will do so tonight."

He went on to praise the *Mirror* for their "gentlemanly treatment and fair play," and the *Mirror* representative, in turn, asked Houdini's permission to present him at a later date with a beautiful solid silver replica of the handcuffs. Houdini agreed. In fact, the newspaper went one better. Houdini wound up with both the original cuffs and the replicas. And therein lies the real story behind the most important challenge of Houdini's life.

The stirring story of Houdini's triumph over the *Mirror* Cuffs made every newspaper in England (and there were thirty dailies in London alone at that time). Yet Houdini's own notations about the escape in his diary are strangely low-key. On March 17, the actual day of the greatest escape in his career, Houdini wrote: "*Mirror* matinee. I defeat the *Mirror*, London, Eng. at Hippodrome. Made such a sensation the public carried me on their shoulders." The next day's entry read: "All English newspapers have wonderful accounts of me escaping out of *Mirror* handcuffs, greatest thing that any artist had in England. Extras were out and it was a case of nothing but 'Houdini at the Hippodrome.'"

It is absolutely bizarre that Houdini should describe with much greater detail an escape from a plugged handcuff at Blackburn a few months earlier than his triumph over the most deviously designed handcuff-king-breakers ever produced. Perhaps there was really nothing he could write about?

On March 20, three days after the challenge, Houdini showed up at the *Mirror* offices. "I want to make a challenge," Houdini told the editors. "You challenged me. Now I challenge the world." And he handed them a prepared statement.

A CHALLENGE TO THE WORLD

London Hippodrome, March 20, 1904
To Whom It May Concern!
Since my success in mastering the celebrated Daily Mirror *Handcuff it has come to my knowledge that certain disappointed, sceptical* [sic] *persons have made use of most unjust remarks against the result of last Thursday's contest.*

In particular, one person has had the brazen audacity to proclaim himself able to open the Mirror *Handcuff in two minutes.*

Such being the case, I hereby challenge any mortal being to open the Mirror *Handcuff in the same space of time that I did. I will allow him the full use of both hands; also any instrument or instruments, barring the actual key. The cuff must not be broken or spoilt. Should he succeed I will forfeit 100 guineas . . .*

HARRY HOUDINI

According to the *Mirror*, challengers wrote in from all over the country. On March 28, a reed-thin twenty-three-year-old "with long hair and abstracted mien" named Bruce Beaumont came onstage during Houdini's show and was presented with the cuffs. Houdini had heard that Beaumont's wrists were abnormally thin so he told the audience it would be unfair to lock the cuffs on him since he could slip out of them in an instant. Instead, Houdini locked the cuffs and then handed them to Beaumont to open. Beaumont went into a long diatribe on the ethics of challenges, prompting such booing that the orchestra was ordered to drown him out. After an animated conversation with the house manager, Beaumont tried to open the manacles, "ran his fingers through his lank hair, struck attitudes, made speeches, and eventually flung the manacles down in a temper." The stage manager reappeared and asked the audience if he should be booted off the stage. When they responded decidedly in the affirmative, Beaumont was thrown off and an army of stagehands came on to clear the stage for the "Plunging" Elephant act.

Years after Houdini's victory, suspicions were raised that there may have been some complicity in the *Mirror* challenge. Rumors were circulated in the English magic community that Houdini had really been defeated in his ghost box and he communicated via code with Bess, who then pulled the *Mirror* representative aside and tearfully implored him to give them the key to restore her husband's reputation. In this account, it was said that Bess passed the key to Houdini in the glass of water that she brought him.

It's a dramatic story, but it's dead wrong. For one, Bess didn't even offer Houdini water, the stage manager, Parker, did. And it would be hard to hide a six-inch key in a glass of water. The story also suggests that Houdini was woefully unprepared for this contest. And we now know that this was not the case. More recent theories have claimed that Houdini conspired with the locksmith, Hart, to build the cuffs and then to present them to the *Mirror* and suggest a challenge to Houdini. Proponents of this theory note that Houdini had used a Birmingham locksmith to fix some Bean Giant cuffs that he would use on imitators. We also know that Houdini had spent two weeks in Birmingham just prior to opening at the Hippodrome in London. That would have given him ample opportunity to at least examine the cuffs that "no mortal man could pick."

The problem with the Houdini-Hart conspiracy theory is that there is no solid evidence that Hart actually ever lived. Additionally, the notion that anyone had spent five years preparing this super cuff to defeat handcuff kings is implausible when the math is done. In 1899 in England there were no handcuff kings and no challenge handcuff act. Houdini was just starting to succeed in the United States. Additionally, the *Mirror* couldn't have commissioned the cuffs five years previously; at the time of the challange it had only been in existence a few months.

We have had the unprecedented opportunity to inspect both the original *Mirror* cuffs and the solid sterling replica that the *Mirror* presented to Houdini after the contest, both of which now reside in David Copperfield's wonderful

The silver replica cuffs presented to Houdini by the *Daily Mirror*.
Inset: The unique markings that proved the replica cuffs were made a year prior to the challenge. *David Copperfield's International Museum and Library of the Conjuring Arts*

collection. What struck us immediately is the fact that the cuffs are not adjustable. In fact, if they were not fitted precisely to Houdini's wrist size, there would have been no contest. Still, the cuffs revealed greater mysteries than that.

Every item made of sterling silver in England at that time had identifying marks from the London Assay office, which could date its manufacture and even signify the part of the United Kingdom, the city, and the maker who produced it. With the great help of Houdini expert Bill Liles, we analyzed the marks on the sterling replica, and an amazing fact surfaced. The replica of the cuffs, which were presented to Houdini after his triumph, was actually manufactured the year *prior* to the challenge. Since the trophy was an exact replica of the original cuffs that fit Houdini's wrists, and since *The Daily Mirror* representative intimated to the audience right after Houdini's success that "a beautiful solid silver model of the handcuffs *would* be made," it's evident that *The Daily Mirror* conspired with Houdini to create a highly dramatic and exciting challenge. In the light of this information, the initial challenge and the actual contest take on the patina of a marvelously orchestrated show.

Houdini's relationship with the *Mirror* (and in addition, *The Weekly Dispatch*, which hosted his antique-irons-busting feat weeks before the Hippodrome challenge) seemed unusually cozy. The publicity surrounding the *Mirror* Cuff challenge was played out for weeks and it created a sensation, boosting circulation at a time when the *Mirror* had just undergone a drastic repositioning due to severe circulation losses. So there was an incentive to cooperate with Houdini on a major challenge. The most telling evidence of complicity lies in the fact that both *The Weekly Dispatch* and the *Mirror* were owned by Houdini's good friend press baron Alfred Charles Harmsworth. Harmsworth had his own economic interests at heart, of course, but he also had a political agenda that relied on keeping Houdini's name prominent as the most celebrated mystifier in the world. The next stage in his relationship with Houdini would unravel six years in the future and take place half a globe away from England.

With the *Mirror* Cuff challenge, Houdini effectively scorched the earth under the feet of his handcuff imitators for all time. He was now literally, and not hyperbolically, the King of Handcuffs. That was precisely his intent. Houdini had designed an earlier prototype of the *Mirror* Cuffs that featured a single Bramah lock on handcuffs shaped like a figure eight. He slyly called them "Hungarian Cuffs" after their inventor. Unsatisfied, he developed the diabolical *Mirror* Cuffs. Thanks to his friend's newspaper, a challenge was made; he accepted it, there was tremendous publicity, and, on one night infused with drama, he defeated the world's most devious handcuffs.

Now he had his Excalibur, a sword with which to vanquish his enemies. He immediately issued "a challenge to the world." Beat this! Hardly anyone even tried. Houdini had even convinced his competitors that the *Mirror* Cuff challenge was real.

Two months later, he had moved on to expand the purview of his challenges. Back in 1902, in Essen, Germany, he had escaped from his own packing case. To drum up publicity, he offered a reward—come to my show, prove that the case was gimmicked, and you'll collect the prize money. Two years later he introduced an inspired refinement of that idea. In May of 1904, on the night before he was to receive the beautiful solid sterling replica of the *Mirror* Cuffs, Houdini accepted a challenge from a company called Howill & Son. "Having witnessed your show, and if you think you can escape out of any trunk, you are mistaken." Escaping out of a box that is so cleverly gimmicked that no one in the audience can figure out the deception and win a prize is shrewd. Escaping from a box that someone else builds and brings to the arena is heroic. For the rest of his life, Houdini would challenge the world to bring him their boxes and straitjackets and crazy cribs and mailbags and leather pouches, secure him in them, and watch as he miraculously escaped without leaving a trace. From that point on, Houdini would never be conceived of as merely the king of anything. Now he would be a Superman.

Houdini had just left the room when another guest, a colonel in the military, invited Bess to have a glass of champagne with him. For some reason, she decided to see how her husband would react to her flirting with a strange man.

Houdini had been under a lot of pressure of late. Near the end of his Hippodrome run, he had fallen ill, but somehow managed to complete his last week. He then collapsed from the strain, and on a doctor's advice, canceled his show in Newcastle. "First time I ever disappointed," he noted morosely. And now this.

Houdini returned to the party to witness Bess sipping champagne, sitting on the colonel's knee, and gazing coquettishly in his eyes, his arm around her waist. Houdini's face registered "incredulous horror," and "his knees sagged as if he had received a knockout blow." Bess had to rush to his side and help him to a taxi. He was speechless. Back home, he wept all night and brooded about the disaster for days.

Whether this was Bess's notion of retaliation for an indiscretion of Houdini's is unknown, but the whole scene was symptomatic of their day-to-day struggles. Bess's severe mood swings and regular temper tantrums are duly recorded in Houdini's diary. "Raised hell because I kidded on the phone to the operator," one despairing entry reads. He even saw fit to document a rare tenderness. "Bess has been very sweet lately; hope she keeps it up." Two weeks later, the hopes were dashed. "When I get home, she is sore, and is sore for the night."

On May 27, Houdini, Bess, and Hardeen sailed for New York, Hardeen sporting a "blue" eye and a scratched face as a result of a fight in a German club. Martin Beck, Houdini's old manager, was on the trip with them, but Houdini spurned his offer to upgrade the three of them to first class, preferring the informality of second-class cabins. In reality, Houdini would have stuck out like a sore thumb in first class. He had so little regard for his attire off the stage that once a friend who was waiting for him to arrive for a show at the stage door almost mistook him for a janitor. There was a method to his déshabille. The old clothes he wore were often garments that his mother had given to him when the family was too poor to afford a better wardrobe.

Houdini also spurned Beck's offer of bookings in the United States, since his intention was to get some rest before sailing back to England at the end of August. They arrived in New York on June 2 and Houdini stayed up all night and into the next day catching up with all his brothers. Then, over the next few weeks, he went on a whirlwind buying spree.

He paid $25,000 cash, equivalent to $2.5 million in 2005, for a four-story brownstone at 278 West 113th Street in Harlem, "the finest private house that any magician has ever had the great fortune to possess," he boasted, conveniently forgetting Robert-Houdin's manse in St. Gervais. To the Hungarian immigrant, it *was* a mansion, the physical manifestation of the fulfillment of the pledge that he had made to his father when the whole family was crammed into a walk-up tenement. In the town house, he would house his mother, his brother Leo, and his sister, Gladys, and have rooms and rooms left over for the beginnings of his soon-to-be-massive collection of magic and Spiritualism books. "Someday when I'm too old to perform, I'll spend my time writing about magic. And I won't have to search for source material. It will be here," he told his mother. He customized the bathroom with a large eight-foot mirror, before which he would practice hour after hour, and an oversize sunken tub, where he could practice his underwater endurance.

He also purchased a farm in Connecticut to use as a country retreat and spent $450 on a family plot in the Machpelah Cemetery in Cypress Hills on the Queens-Brooklyn border. Two days later, he had his father, his half brother, and his maternal grandmother disinterred and reburied in the new plot. "Saw what was left of poor father and Herman," Houdini recorded in his diary. "Nothing but skull and bones. Herman's teeth were in splendid condition."

In July, Houdini and Hardeen took a sentimental visit to Milwaukee and Appleton. They visited old neighbors and caught up with Herman's widow. In Chicago, they visited with their friend Gus Roterberg and saw their brother Nat, who was working in Chicago at that time. A note sent to Bess from Chicago suggests that Bess's absence on the trip might have been due to more tension between the two. The week apart seemed to have smoothed things over. "We will arrive Tuesday morning at 42nd Street Station & if you want to meet me, why I Think I would Kiss you in front of the audience, so as to show you that alls well." Bess took him up on the offer and met him at the station. "She looks a treat in her pale blue dress. Am certainly pleased to see her. I missed her on my trip," he confided to his diary.

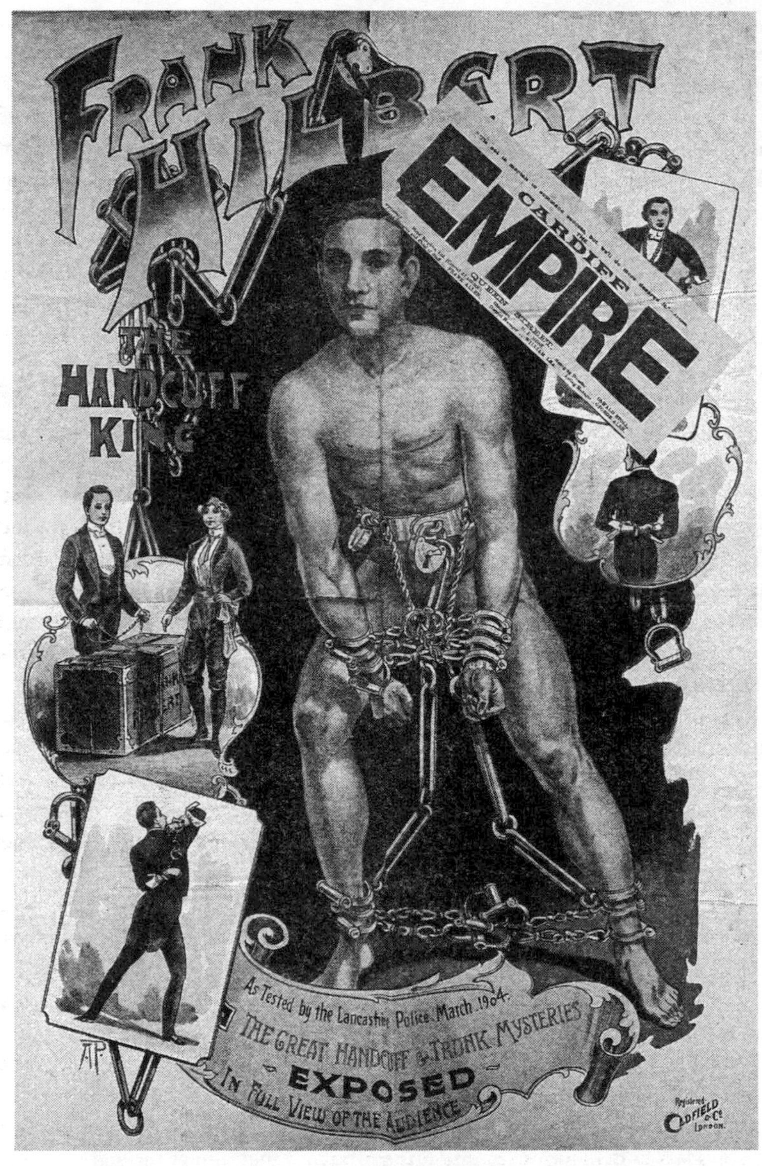

With posters like these, it's no wonder Houdini went after his imitator Hilbert.
New York Public Library

Frank Hilbert's turn at the Cardiff Empire Theater, called "The Bubble Burst," had just begun when the first cries came from the audience. Hilbert had shown how a Handcuff King could conceal instruments in various parts of his clothing and open his cuffs, when a gray-haired bespectacled old man with a beard began waving his cane in the pit.

"You're a fraud, you're a damned fraud," the man screamed with surprising vigor for someone his age.

Simultaneously, two women sitting near the rear jumped up in their seats. One of them was waving a pair of handcuffs she held aloft.

"This man does not use police regulation handcuffs. He has cuffs of his own. But I have some regulation handcuffs here and I challenge him to open them," she yelled.

The old man continued yelling, and he was soon surrounded by the theater manager and two constables. He began to swing his walking stick wildly, and it took another constable to subdue him. As they started to drag him to the side exit door, his beard fell off. It was Houdini. In the rear of the theater, the two women, who were Bess and Houdini's sister, Gladys, rushed up to the fracas.

"Ladies and Gentlemen, see how they are treating me," he began screaming. "It is not right."

"Shame, shame," some people in the audience yelled.

"Give him fair play," another suggested.

Fair play was the last thing on the manager's mind. They had been alerted by Mr. Oswald Stoll, the theater owner, that Houdini might try to disrupt Hilbert's exposé, but Houdini's disguise, which had been professionally administered by a hairdresser who Houdini hired and included a waxed modified nose, completely fooled the theater management. When they realized the old man was Houdini, they followed Stoll's orders, which were to eject him immediately.

"What shall I do, Mr. Lea?" one of the constables asked the manager.

"Throw him out," Lea said. Then Lea grabbed Houdini by the throat and tore at his collar.

"We've been waiting for you," he said, and threw Houdini into one of the constables. Houdini fell to the ground, and his knee struck one of the seats, numbing it. Then the constable kneed him in the ribs and slapped his hands over Houdini's mouth so he couldn't cry out.

Just then, Hardeen, who was also in the audience, although not in disguise, ran up and attempted to throttle Lea, but was held back by a constable.

Houdini was carried out the side door and thrown four feet down into a muddy alleyway. He screamed in pain and claimed that his leg was broken. Hardeen arrived on the scene, and his brother asked him to flag down a cab. Two of the constables pulled Houdini to his feet, and just as he began to walk away, Lea kicked him in his leg. Houdini almost fell again.

"Don't you do that again," he glared at the manager.

"Oh, that was an accident," the manager smiled.

A cab came and Hardeen and Houdini fled the scene.

Later that night, the two brothers entered the King's Theater and rushed onto the stage. Houdini's hair was disheveled and his collar still unbuttoned. He spoke in a hoarse voice.

"Ladies and Gentlemen, I must apologize for appearing like this, but I have been thrown out of the other theater," he said.

"Shame, shame," the crowd cried out.

"They have nearly broken my leg," Houdini said, and to thunderous applause, he limped off the stage.

That night Houdini opened his diary. "Went to Empire and raised a rumpus against Hilbert," he wrote. "Went disguised, was carried out. Raised hell in the streets. This helped with my business."

It was hard to fathom that he needed help in that area. Since his return to England seven months earlier, he had been smashing his own records all over the provinces. In September in Glasgow, he featured an escape from a packing case that was built onstage by a local company to ensure that the crate was not gimmicked. Thousands of people who couldn't get into the theater milled in the streets outside, stopping traffic, until they heard that Houdini had escaped in fifteen minutes.

In December, Houdini sat in a box at the Empire Theatre in London, watching his friend Chung Ling Soo perform. During the entire show, the crowd kept yelling, "Houdini!" Back in Glasgow in January of 1905, an escape from a hamper built by a local firm generated so much interest that an overflow crowd actually broke into the theater to witness the challenge. On February 18, in Rochester, playing a house on a percentage basis, Houdini netted his largest weekly salary yet—$2,150 at the then prevailing exchange rates (today, a whopping $215,000). Business like that spawned ever more imitators and even a new Handcuff King who dubbed himself "Hardini."

Going after Hilbert was personal, though. When Houdini had first returned to England in September, Harry Day had negotiated new contracts for him at much higher pay. Houdini was immediately sued by the Moss chain of theaters which claimed that they had an irrevocable option for his services.

Houdini about to be nailed into a packing case. *From the collection of Dr. Bruce Averbook*

When Houdini won the lawsuit on November 1, 1904, the owners of the Moss dynasty hired Hilbert, his old nemesis, to follow him around England, playing their theaters and doing an act exposing his escapes. By April, Houdini had had enough and he bum-rushed Hilbert's show. Houdini wasn't through with Hilbert just yet. Two months later, he received a letter from his old pal Billy Robinson. Robinson was in Manchester, where Hilbert had just closed. "I found out that the stage carpenter had made a packing case for Hilbert during his engagement. So I got quite chummy with him. A few beers and the job was done." Robinson had enclosed a detailed sketch of the packing box and just how it was gimmicked.

In June, while Houdini was performing at the Gaiety Theatre in Leith, Houdini actually rented a storefront next door to Moss's Empire Music Hall, where Hilbert was doing his Houdini exposé. He sent his assistant, Franz Kukol, and a man named Vickery, who would later be hired as an assistant, and had them pose as magicians and give a performance every half hour exposing the exposers of the handcuff act.

HOW HANDCUFF TRICKS ARE DONE

BY IMPOSTERS!

Herr Franz Kukol the CELEBRATED ILLUSIONIST OF VIENNA, and Mr Geo. Vickery the MAGICIAN OF LONDON, beg to inform the general public that they will appear at the large shop No. 23 and 25 NICOLSON STREET, next door to Moss' Empire Music Hall, where they will give performances every half hour, SHOWING HOW HANDCUFF TRICKS ARE DONE BY ALL IMPOSTERS!

These gentlemen confess they do not know how HARRY HOUDINI, who is engaged at the GAIETY THEATRE, LEITH, this week, performs his tricks. If they did they would not travel as exposers.

LIKE ALL other BOGUS HANDCUFF IMPOSTERS THEY DO NOT ALLOW ANYONE TO BRING HANDCUFFS.

NO ONE is ALLOWED ON THE STAGE. No one is allowed to examine the trunk they make use of, as THEY HAVE A TRAP IN THE TOP OF BOX, similar to other Imitators, and tear open the bottom of the bag they use!

They cannot open any Handcuff unless their own, and they must have a key to fit, just the same as all other Exposers.

THE WHOLE SWINDLE SHOWN FOR A PENNY.

NEXT DOOR TO THE EMPIRE THEATRE, EDIN.

Open from 11 a.m. to 9 p.m.

The broadside advertising an exposure of Houdini's imitators, demonstrated by two of Houdini's assistants. *From the collection of Ricky Jay*

"I'll wager that if you throw a stone in the air it will fall down and hit some one who has a handcuff key in his pocket and a 'Handcuff King' idea in his head," Houdini wrote in his *Dramatic Mirror* column in June 1905. It was the debasement of the art form that Houdini had created that was feeding his more and more frequent talk about retiring. Sure, he had conquered England and Europe, smashing all box office records, making a name for himself, earning record salaries, but it was a Pyrrhic victory. Being king of a court of would-be handcuff artists who hounded and disrespected him at every turn wasn't noble at all.

Houdini also had an acute sense of the illusionary nature and impermanence of fame. The previous December he had been walking the streets of Liverpool when he came upon a pawnshop. A large American eagle perched on top of a medal caught his eye. Inquiring inside, he found that the item had been a once-celebrated medal, worth about $3,500, that had been given to a famous minstrel singer in the 1870s. The medal bore the inscription: "Presented to Sam Hague by a few friends that know him. St. James Hall, Liverpool. May 20, 1875." While he was alive, Hague would never part with his cherished trophy, but after he had been dead a few years, his widow, in need of money, was forced to hock it. "Seeing this medal in the window brought back to my mind the medals that are pawned in New York with a well-known 'uncle' in the Bowery, who displays with pride presentation cups, loving chains and championship prizes of all sorts," Houdini wrote. "Many a time have I walked to this place and looked at the silent remembrances of past favorites, and never have I forgotten that fact that 'life is but an empty dream.'"

Houdini's last night in Leith was on July 8. He planned to sail for America on the 20th, work for six weeks that summer, then return to Europe for a final tour before he would quit show business. His fans had other ideas. On the last night of Houdini's engagement, the audience called upon him to make a speech. When he had concluded, they all stood and gave him three cheers. And later, when he appeared to make his way to the railroad station to travel to Southampton, where he would catch the *Kronprinz Wilhelm* and steam across the ocean, a waiting crowd hoisted him to their shoulders and carried him to the station on a run, the whole time singing, "And when you go, will you no come back?" In 1902, on his first trip back to the United States from England, when he spied New York Harbor in the distance he broke down and wept, morose that his father wasn't alive to see his success. Now, three years later, he wept again at this touching send-off from his fans.

From the collection of Dr. Bruce Averbook

10

Leap of Faith

"My next experiment will conclusively demonstrate that the mind is the force that moves the world," Houdini said, looking out at the seventy-odd men in the smoking room of the Boston Athletic Association. He reached into his jacket pocket and brought out a handful of sewing needles.

"I will need exactly twenty-seven volunteers for this test," Houdini said, and the men laughed. That was the last time they would laugh that evening.

"Before I perform the famous Hindoo Needle trick, I want to show you the amazing powers of the human mind. I assume that everyone is in agreement that these needles are sharp. Would anyone care to volunteer to test this truism?"

No arms were raised.

"I guess I'll have to experiment upon myself," he shrugged. Then he held one of the needles aloft and sharply thrust it through his cheek. A collective shudder went through the room.

"I would especially like my doctor friends in the audience to take note that the needle has completely pierced my cheek and yet there is no evidence of blood or trauma. It is because I have learned a technique from the Hindoos that conquers pain and allows the mind to control various bodily functions such as bleeding. Now I will need those volunteers."

A few arms were slowly raised. Houdini motioned them to the front of the room.

"I have twenty-six more needles. You will each get a needle, and you may place it anywhere you wish in my head, except for my eyes. My powers are not that great yet," Houdini said. He handed a needle to the first volunteer, who took it and punctured his other cheek. One by one, the men slowly shuffled up to the magician, obtained their pin, and thrust it into the soft flesh of Houdini's face. The cheeks were the first obvious choice but as the line progressed, men thrust their needles into Houdini's neck, forehead, ears, and lips. The last volunteers actually used Houdini's nose as a pincushion. And amazingly enough, there was not a trace of blood visible from the multiple puncture wounds.

Finally they were done. Houdini stood in front of the men in silence, his once-handsome face a grotesque mask of small steel quivers. And when he began to speak again, the effect was positively macabre, the needles quivering with each syllable uttered.

"I think it's time for dessert," he said, and he slowly began to pluck the needles out of his face, one by one, and dramatically chewed them. The audience could hear the grinding of the metal before he swallowed them. Then he swallowed a long section of thread. When he was finished, he took a drink from a glass of water that was on the lectern.

"Can I impose upon one of my doctor friends to come up and assure you that I have swallowed my metallic repast?"

An elderly medical man walked to the front and peered into Houdini's open mouth.

"I can detect no trace of the needles," he said.

"Gentlemen, a needle must be threaded. Please draw the thread," he said to the doctor.

"Where is it?" the doctor wondered.

"In my mouth," Houdini said, and he opened his mouth. The doctor peered into his mouth again and found the thread. He slowly began to draw it out of Houdini's mouth, and to everyone's utter astonishment, after every twelve inches there was one of the needles that had been stuck into Houdini's face, perfectly threaded. By the time he finished pulling the thread and the needles out of the magician's mouth, the thread was twenty-seven feet long.

Houdini bowed, but the audience was too shocked to even applaud. They had just witnessed something that they would never forget.

When Houdini returned to America in 1905, it was almost as if he had to start all over. It had been five years since he had performed in the country, and though he had gained good name recognition in places like Boston and Chicago, he was still a relatively unknown commodity in his hometown. And what's worse, he found that America, just like Europe, was teeming with his parasitic imitators.

Houdini and his brother Doctor Leopold Weiss. *From the collection of Dr. Bruce Averbook*

While still in England he had opened up a second front of his war against his rivals. In 1903, he dispatched "Doc," his brother Leopold Weiss, to Massachusetts to confront his old partner Jacob Hyman, who was then performing in Boston under the name of Houdini. Weiss brought along one of his brother's "defeater" handcuffs and an attorney named Louis Spiegel to dissuade Hyman from continuing to use the Houdini name. Their feud was short-lived, and they went on to reestablish their friendship.

One of Houdini's rivals was a man named Cunning. In May of 1905, Houdini sent another brother, William Weiss, to Hurtig & Seamon's Music Hall on 125th Street in Manhattan to confront Cunning. When members of the audience were asked to come up onstage with their challenge handcuffs, William was one of seven to respond. After all seven handcuffs were affixed to Cunning, he retreated into a steel cage, over which a curtain was lowered. He remained in the cage for an inordinately long amount of time, and the audience began to get restless.

"He's not under there. Drag him out!" the audience yelled.

Cunning finally emerged. Only one arm was free.

"I want my handcuffs back," screamed William, but Cunning ignored him and began to walk offstage. The big curtain was lowered and Houdini's brother tried to jump under it, but a stagehand blocked his way. Then he ran around the end of the curtain and got on stage, but he was thrown off the stage and deposited in the lobby by some stagehands. A portion of the audience came to his defense and began hitting the stagehands with their umbrellas, but Weiss was ultimately arrested and charged with disorderly conduct, a charge later dismissed, although he did have to spend the night in jail.

Houdini's fall 1905 season unofficially opened on September 11, when he and Hardeen sat down in their seats at the Hyde & Behman's Theater in Brooklyn and waited for Cunning to take the stage.

As soon as the ersatz handcuff king asked for volunteers from the audience with regulation cuffs, Hardeen bounded up onstage, along with five other men. Cunning allowed the other five to place their cuffs on him, but he looked at Hardeen and his "regulation" cuffs and waved him back to his seat. That was Hardeen's opening. He rushed to center stage.

"Here is a pair of handcuffs that came from the Adams Street police station that Mr. Cunning refuses to put on," Hardeen screamed, waving the cuffs in his hand. Then he reached into his pocket and pulled out a bill. "I have here a fifty-pound note on the Bank of England, which I will wager that he cannot remove these handcuffs if he puts them on."

The confrontation escalated with insults being hurled from the Cunning camp toward Hardeen and toward Cunning from Houdini, who sprang up in his seat to defend his brother. The theater manager got involved and was ready to stake Cunning in the bet, but Hardeen's stipulations got so involved and convoluted that the clock reached midnight and the theater curtain crashed down around the still-arguing participants. Hardeen was roundly jeered by the audience, and then a committee member rushed up to him and cold-cocked him with a right, sending him sprawling over a row of seats. A full-fledged riot broke out and local policemen shrewdly plucked Hardeen from the audience and dragged him out through the stage door. He was booked under the name "Theodore Frank" on charges of disorderly conduct and immediately bailed out by his brother. The next day Houdini was able to convince the judge that the entire fracas was a publicity stunt, and the charges were dropped.

Even though the local newspaper accounts differed, that month's issue of *Mahatma*, the Brooklyn-based magic magazine that had employed Houdini as its European correspondent, ran a story that claimed that Cunning had refused Hardeen's challenge and was roundly jeered by the audience. Houdini's ploy had worked.

At three P.M. on September 20, 1905, a small group of men assembled at Battery Park in downtown Manhattan. On the one hand there was Houdini, attended by his brother Hardeen. In the other corner was someone named "Jacques Boudini," allegedly Houdini's "pupil," a pale, nervous-looking young man whom Houdini had "discovered" doing a handcuff escape act in Brooklyn. He had his "manager" with him, Patrick J. Monahan. Boudini attempted to shake Houdini's hand, but Harry just stared at it coldly. Then the aggregation, trailed by a bevy of reporters, went to the nearby offices of Nathan Laufer, where each side put up $500 for a winner-take-all contest of who could be the first to escape from cuffs, chains, and leg irons after being dumped off of a tugboat into the Hudson River.

It was no contest. The two men were festooned with irons and then jumped simultaneously into the drink. After a minute and thirty seconds, Houdini's head bobbed up.

"Is Boudini up yet?" Houdini yelled to the newsmen on the tugboat.

"No," they shouted back.

Houdini lifted his arms up out of the water, displaying that his hands were free.

"The cuffs are off!" he yelled and threw them onto the tug, and then sank back out of view. A minute later, he bobbed up again.

"Boudini up yet?" he asked again. He laughed when he heard the negative and then kicked a leg in the air to signify that one of his ankles was free. Another few seconds underwater and he sprang up with the leg irons and chains in his hands.

Meanwhile, Boudini "sank and rose and gurgled and sunk again." When he was finally hauled onboard, he was still completely fettered. "Monahan got my signals mixed up," he said. "And anyway, when I saw that the other fellow was out of the handcuffs so quick I got discouraged."

The papers had a field day with their "Hou" and "Bou" comparisons, with Houdini being anointed the winner. "So Houdini proved his right to the title of Champion Mysteriarch of the World. And poor Boudini let the sad sea water trickle from his hair," *The New York World* reported. It's possible that Houdini was inspired to orchestrate this challenge after a similar stunt, where his friend Chung Ling Soo sandbagged his rival Ching Ling Foo. In that case, Soo was the imitator, trading on Foo's reputation. Here Hou seemed to create his competitor, Bou, for shortly after this stunt, Bou faded from the pages of magic history. Interestingly enough, this stunt was the first known example of Houdini releasing himself from shackles while underwater.

With his fall U.S. tour under way, Houdini returned to his tried-and-true formula of jail cell escapes to promote theater shows. And he used every police contact that he had, perhaps because one of the Keith's bookers had sent him a letter while he was still in Europe, rejecting his salary demands, because "it is absolutely impossible for us to get the co-operation of the police force in tests and experiments in connection with your work and therefore secure the valuable advertising that you are able to do in the west and in Europe." After cell escapes in Brooklyn, Detroit, Cleveland, Rochester, and Buffalo, Houdini made it to Washington, D.C., where he unleashed the heavy ammunition.

On January 1, 1906, he was handcuffed with what *The Washington Post* called an "invincible bracelet" used by the Secret Service and placed in a cell in the tenth precinct police station. That precinct housed the office of the superintendent of the Washington, D.C., force, Major Richard Sylvester, who also happened to be the current president of the International Association of Chiefs of Police, the police group with which Houdini had close ties. Sylvester did "his utmost to keep Houdini a prisoner," even refusing the escape artist a view of the padlock he was to contest. But despite a strip search, Houdini was able to break out of cell no. 3, and then break into an adjoining cell, where his clothes had been stored. He did all this in eighteen minutes.

Immediately, Warden Harris, the chief of the cathedral-like United States Jail, invited Houdini to test the efficacy of his facilities. After building up suspense for several days, Houdini, accompanied by his press agent and promoter, Whitman Osgood, and a slew of reporters, visited the massive stone citadel on January 6. With the headlines already playing before his eyes, Houdini insisted on escaping from the heavily barred cell no. 2 that had once held Charles Guiteau, President Garfield's assassin, who had been hanged at the jail in 1882. The party was then led to the south wing, where the formidable Murderer's Row consisted of seventeen cells, all brick structures with their doors sunk into the walls three feet from the outer corridor wall. The cell seemed impenetrable; when the heavily barred door was closed, an L-shaped bar moved out and then angled to the right and slipped over a steel catch, which tripped a spring that fastened the lock. The lock itself contained five tumblers. As was the case in many jails, one key would open all the doors in the corridor.

According to the newspaper accounts, on Houdini's first visit, he agreed to be immediately locked in to test the cells. He was then stripped, searched, and thrown into Guiteau's former cell, shocking a black man named Hamilton, who was currently residing there, awaiting hanging for murdering his wife. While Hamilton crouched in a corner in fear, Houdini escaped from the cell in less than two minutes.

He was just warming up. Still nude, and out of sight of the various luminaries who had withdrawn to the warden's office, Houdini ran to the next cell and opened it. Its occupant, a man named Chase, mistook Houdini for an escaping fellow prisoner. He followed the magician down the corridor to another cell door, which fell in seconds.

"What are you doing here?" Houdini asked Clarence Howlett, the present occupant.

"I'm a housebreaker," Howlett said.

"You're a bad one, or you could get out of here," Houdini replied. "Come along."

Houdini put Chase into Howlett's cell and then brought Howlett and locked him into Chase's cell. He repeated this a few times with other prisoners. Then he broke into the cell that contained his clothes, got dressed, and, precisely twenty-one minutes from being imprisoned, strolled into the warden's office.

"I let all of your prisoners out," Houdini announced to the waiting visitors and press. Two guards jumped up and rushed out into the corridor.

"But I locked them all in again," he added.

That same day Houdini received an impressive letter certifying his escape from Guiteau's cell and his release of all the other prisoners on the ground floor. "There was positively no chance for any confederacy or collusion," Warden Harris noted. The same day, Major Sylvester released his statement. "In order that defective means of restraint might be discovered in the holding of prisoners in this jurisdiction, and with a view to remedying any insecurity which might exist, Mr. Houdini, the expert man with locks, was permitted to examine a modern cell lock and attachment and then placed in an entirely different cell from the one he examined. He was searched and in a nude condition placed behind the bars and, as supposed, secured . . . In twenty-six minutes, he emerged from the cell and corridor fully attired.

"The experiment was a valuable one in that the department has been instructed as to the adoption of further security, which will protect any lock from being opened or interfered with . . .

"Mr. Houdini impressed his audience as a gentlemen and an artist who does not profess to do the impossible."

Once again, what was primarily a publicity stunt to sell tickets to Houdini's shows had been couched as a civic-minded sociological experiment to aid the police departments to improve the efficacy of their confinement abilities. Sylvester was right, Houdini wasn't professing to do the impossible. To escape from a jail cell, he would need either a key or an implement to defeat the lock. A nude search would seemingly preclude either of those possibilities, but Houdini had other tricks up his metaphorical sleeve. If the jails were using locks that employed a spring latch, they could be temporarily defeated by jamming a small wooden wedge into their socket. With the wedge in place, the lock would appear closed but in actuality would either fail to catch or catch so slightly that a good hard knock could jar it loose.

Houdini had a variety of methods to avoid detection when he brought a key or a pick into a cell. Sometimes he would hide the key in his bushy hair. When his examination commenced, Houdini would suggest to the police officers to check his hair first. Unbeknownst to them, the key, which was treated with a dab of adhesive wax, would be palmed in his hand. As soon as his hair had been examined, Houdini would run his hand through his hair in what seemed like a reflex. What he was really doing was transferring the key to its hiding place and freeing up his hand for inspection. Other times, Houdini would affix the key with adhesive tape under his instep. This was risky, though, especially if the police would ask him to lift his foot for inspection.

Houdini would often visit a jail a day or two in advance and case the place, sometimes bringing Bess along as a distraction while he would snoop. It's believed that Houdini had the ability to photographically remember the details of a unique key, so that he could make a duplicate. He would also use clay to make an impression when he didn't want to rely on his memory, a technique that was used years earlier by Wilkie's Secret Service agents when they had to duplicate keys to make surreptitious entries. Early visits to the cell would give Houdini a chance to plant tools or picks in the cell itself, sometimes in a piece of soap, hanging from an invisible thread in the toilet, or affixed under a bench with gum. If he was escaping from a particularly odious or cold jail, where sanitary conditions were lacking, Houdini might sometimes request that after a thorough search, he be allowed to put his shoes back on. What the officials didn't know was that the heels were hollowed out and swiveled open after pressing a hidden catch. This invention of Mokana, magic dealer Will Goldston's brother, was and still is a formidable subterfuge.

Perhaps the most ingenious device Houdini used to smuggle in his necessary tools were his own massive padlocks. He would convince his "captors" that the escape attempt would play better in the press if he was photographed and it was reported that he escaped from many locks and chains. Then Houdini would have affixed his own huge sturdy-looking padlocks in addition to the regulation police handcuffs and chains. What the police didn't know was that Houdini's padlocks were gimmicked; they were actually little toolboxes in the shape of large padlocks that held all of Houdini's necessary hardware. He also owned an egg-shaped container that he could open to store small tools. This could be hidden in the back of his throat and was undetectable by all but the most thorough jailers.

Barring these ploys, Houdini could also employ his hooked keys. He would solder a hook to the necessary key or pick and then station a police officer in front of his cell with his back to Houdini, so he could work without visual inspection. Before placing the officer, Houdini would fraternally slap the officer on the back, in the process affixing the key. Once inside the cell, it was child's play to reach out and obtain the key without the enabler being aware.

Then there was the last resort, used when he was convinced that the search would be grueling and comprehensive. Always the sportsman, Houdini would enter the cell and then extend his hand through the bars to shake hands with his captors and the press. The last man Houdini would shake hands with would be a friend who was wearing a finger ring with a spring clip that enabled him to palm a key or a pick. During this last emotional handshake, Houdini obtained the necessary tool.

Although the fundamentals of Houdini's escape methods have been published, the particular details are still shrouded in mystery. Much of what we now understand has come to us from Steranko, a living legend in several varied fields, including that of self-extrication. Steranko has done many of these escapes and is considered a grandmaster in the field. His writings on the subject, published in the 1960s, are still considered the reference standard.

What was notable about these Washington jailbreaks was that the reports suggest that the attempts were made without Houdini's usual procedure of examining both the locks and the cells beforehand. (There was a good reason for making those

Houdini posing prior to breaking out of the tombs in Boston. *From the collection of Roger Dreyer*

The path of Houdini's escape from Boston's tombs. *Conjuring Arts Research Center*

courtesy visits. Under the pretext of testing the lock with its key, Houdini was often able to make a wax impression of the key and duplicate it later.) Houdini's ability to not only escape from Guiteau's cell but also rearrange all the other prisoners on Murderer's Row suggests that he had either the master key or a duplicate.

In Boston in March, Houdini made a similar splash. This time it took him only sixteen minutes to break out of the dreaded tombs. Houdini made his way back to his theater and then placed a call to William H. Pierce, the astonished superintendent of prisons, who asked him to return to the jail so that the photographers could shoot him reenacting his leap over the jail fence.

"You're a great fellow," the superintendent said, and grasped Houdini's hand. "I expected that you would come here if you got out. The next time I'll take your clothes out here with me, and then you'll have to come into the office."

The acme of these staged, precisely choreographed Houdini–police chief encounters came the next time Houdini visited his old haunts in Chicago in November of 1906. "Under the personal direction, as they say in the show business, of Andy Rohan, lieutenant of detectives, Houdini, who makes a living getting out of handcuffs and locked rooms, mystified more than twenty detectives at detective headquarters last night," *The Chicago Examiner* began its story. "Houdini, who has been doing this sort of thing for six years, was secured for one performance only at detective headquarters by Lieutenant Rohan. . . . Just what good it would do a detective to learn how to break out of jail Impresario Andy did not explain."

"'You coppers and the press,'" said Andy, the manager, "'will have to stand back and give the professor room enough to swallow a paper of pins.'"

Houdini did the Needles to the delight of the crowd. Rohan wasn't through playing MC.

"'The next trick will be the big one,'" said Lieutenant Rohan, handing Houdini a cup of water.

"Louis, hand me the cuffs."

Detective Louis Bock materialized with two pairs of handcuffs and some leg irons. Houdini stripped and was shackled.

"Look at the cell carefully and attentively and also closely," Rohan said, "and see the professor has nothing concealed in the cell. Now he gets into the cell. Now I slam the door, so. Now I lock the door, so, and now I lock this padlock. Are you all right, professor?"

Houdini nodded. Rohan corralled the reporters, and they all moved back to the main room. As time passed, "Manager Rohan grew a bit restive."

"The professor will come out all right," he kept assuring himself.

The professor did it in due time, "to the visible relief of Mr. Rohan."

"Do a few more tricks for the lads," said Rohan, and Houdini obeyed to the extent of picking the locks of two other cells, taking the prisoner from one cell and placing him in another and "'vicey versey' as one of the detectives explained.

"The entertainment closed with the passing round of cigars and the showering of congratulations upon Houdini and his accomplished impresario. Anybody that could smoke one of the cigars all the way through could do a harder trick than any Houdini did yesterday," the reporter concluded.

Houdini's close relationship with Andy Rohan continued. Later correspondence revealed that Houdini would send Rohan spare parts of leg restraints, and Rohan would collect newspapers and forward them to Houdini.

Even though Houdini maintained contact with police officials and wardens, by the spring of 1912, six years later, Houdini did his last jailbreak. By then the risk to his reputation was too substantial for him to chance a mishap.

Houdini's first film sequence depicted him escaping from a jail cell.
From the collection of Dr. Bruce Averbook

Boston's love affair with Houdini remained unabated. In 1906, he played there for almost two months and continually filled the newspapers with stories recounting his exploits. Early in March he was challenged to escape from an iron-ringed wicker basket. The challengers insinuated that Houdini might have been able to pry some nails loose when he escaped from a packing crate the week before, so a wicker basket large enough to contain him was found. Before a packed house and three hundred committee members on the stage, Houdini climbed into the basket and three pairs of handcuffs were placed on his wrists. Then the cover was placed on the basket and affixed by means of several padlocks, the keyholes of which were sealed with the private seal of one of the challengers. Padlocks secured three strong iron bands. Then a network of half-inch rope and heavy chains was added. Houdini's cabinet was pulled up around the hamper and the curtain closed.

It took Houdini sixty-two minutes, but finally he threw the curtain open. He was panting, his bare arms were streaked with perspiration, and his clothes and his hair were disheveled. The audience cheered him for several minutes, and then he retired backstage, where it took him several minutes to muster up the strength to talk to *The Boston Globe* reporter. This had been the hardest of all of his tests, he assured the reporter. He couldn't wait to call his wife, who was back at the hotel because it was too much of a strain on her to witness these special, grueling tests.

Backstage, the challengers heaped praise on him. "I surrender to you," the head of the committee told him. "For years I have been planning this test for you, and I admit my defeat. I am satisfied that, unaided, except by your own strength and ingenuity, you have succeeded in accomplishing that which myself and my associates believed absolutely impossible." The reporter printed each of the challenger's words. He even printed his name, Dr. Waitt. What he didn't know was that Waitt was one of Houdini's oldest confidants.

Near the end of March, Houdini performed at a special show for 1,600 members of the Boston Athletic Association. He did card effects, the Needles and he escaped from a straitjacket in four minutes, a record for him. Earlier that afternoon, Dr. J. E. Rourke, an anatomical expert at Massachusetts General Hospital, had examined Houdini. "Houdini is the most remarkable man I ever examined.

"I have examined Sandow and most all of the physical wonders of the country. But Houdini is in a class by himself." Apparently the examination also gave Houdini a scare. "He said that my arms were too hard to be of healthy tissue," Houdini confided to a reporter. "He said that I was threatened with being muscle-bound. My success . . . lies in my agility as well as my strength. To be muscle-bound would greatly lessen my agility."

A few days later, Dr. Waitt organized a special matinee at Keith's for an invited audience of local-area doctors. Houdini astounded the doctors with both his Needles effect and by his offer to have his lips sewn up by a doctor before he escaped from handcuffs to nullify the possibility that he had hidden a key in his mouth. The offer was, of course, refused. Days later, the mystified doctors flooded Houdini with letters offering bizarre methods for the escape. "The urethra could easily be used to hide one or more small keys," one doctor suggested.

After his smashing success in Boston at Keith's, Houdini thought he could earn more if he promoted his own show and took it out on the road. Working with his friend Whitman Osgood, a newspaperman, Houdini signed up the Kita-Muras—Imperial Japanese juggling troupe, the Zancigs, who did a telepathy act, and Carver & Pollard, a comedy act. Houdini, billing himself as "The Mysteriarch, The Greatest Sensation of England and America," did a prison cell and barrel transposition and then closed the show with challenge escapes from handcuffs and leg irons. Trying to buck the established vaudeville circuits, Houdini found that his business instincts were not quite as powerful as his forearms, and after folding the show in May for the summer, he was back on the vaudeville circuit doing his own turn by the fall.

On November 26, Houdini opened a run at the Temple Theatre in Detroit. During the show, a policeman named Mark Baker challenged him to escape from a pair of handcuffs. Houdini struggled for forty-five minutes and then stormed out of his cabinet.

"These handcuffs have been tampered with," he screamed. Then he glared up at Harrison Davies, a local amateur handcuff king, who was sitting in an upper box.

"Is this your work?" Houdini said.

Davies shook his head.

"I'll get them unlocked," Houdini said grimly and retreated to his cabinet.

For the next hour, Houdini worked on the tampered cuffs, the audience breathlessly awaiting the outcome. The tension was too much for Bess, who, fearing that he had been defeated, "retired to her dressing room in tears and went into hysterics," *The Detroit Journal* reporter wrote.

Finally, Houdini emerged, the handcuffs open. The audience cheered, but Houdini was not in the mood to bask in congratulations.

"These cuffs have been tampered with. Whoever did this was certain that they would never be opened," he shouted. Then he addressed Officer Baker.

"Are these your handcuffs?"

Baker fidgeted.

"No, they were given to me by a Detroit man to put on you. Further than that, I do not care to say anything."

Houdini immediately suspected another handcuff worker, a man named Grose, who was playing opposite him at the Crystal Theatre.

All in all, it was an embarrassing, inauspicious opening. Houdini went to his hotel and brooded all night.

Standing on the Belle Isle Bridge, he gazed at the current of the river twenty-five feet below him. He had stripped down to his trousers and with the raw wind factored in, the temperature was around twenty-five degrees Fahrenheit, but even though he was shivering, he seemed impervious to it. His mind was elsewhere, focusing on the water, going over what it would feel like when he sliced into the current from that height. Right before he approached the railing,

The manacled bridge jumps were the first of Houdini's spectacular outdoor escapes.
From the collection of Dr. Bruce Averbook

he hastily scribbled a makeshift will on an envelope. He wrote: "I leave all to Bess." Then, suddenly, he was ready. *It's now or never*, he thought. He tensed his muscles. "Good-bye," he impulsively shouted and jumped off the bridge.

And the thousands of people standing on the bridge held their breath as one.

Houdini had conceived of doing a handcuffed bridge leap as far back as 1899. In July of 1901, he had been beaten to the punch when an English society illusionist named Maurice Garland dove manacled off the Wellington pier into the sea at Yarmouth. Both Houdini and Garland might have been inspired to do their spectacular leap by the example of a New York City bookie named Steve Brodie, who garnered worldwide fame in 1886 when he allegedly jumped off the Brooklyn Bridge and survived in order to win a $200 bet. His name entered the vernacular, and "pulling a Brodie" became synonymous with doing something spectacular and dangerous.

Houdini's unfortunate incident on opening night in Detroit finally prompted him to attempt his own bridge leap. "Having met with difficulty in freeing himself from a pair of handcuffs that he suspected had been tampered with while performing his stunt at the Temple Theatre Monday night, Houdini was determined to show the public that his marvelous powers of extrication have not been overrated," *The Detroit Free Press* reporter noted in his coverage of the leap. So Houdini, with entourage and newsmen in tow, had stopped off at police headquarters to borrow two new pairs of their strongest cuffs. Then they went to a police barn, where they secured 150 feet of rope. They all boarded a streetcar and made it to the bridge, which was "black with humanity."

At a few strokes past noon, Houdini jumped, the rope, which was tied to the bridge, trailing along behind him as he made his descent. He hit the water and disappeared. Two experienced oarsmen were waiting in a nearby boat in case of trouble. For a second, Houdini's head bobbed above the water, and then it disappeared. Then one hand shot up from the surface of the water. It was unencumbered. Shortly after, his head and his other hand became visible. Houdini was free and he was alive. He climbed out of the water half frozen. His left hand had cramped up and was useless. The audience cheered heartily. They had seen something new in the world of entertainment—a life-and-death public spectacle.

Houdini repeated his bridge jump on May 4, 1907. In front of about 10,000 people, including his mother (whom he was concerned about since she had not looked well lately, he wrote in his diary) and Bess, he jumped from the Weighlock Bridge in Rochester, New York, without incident—at least to Houdini. Seconds after he leaped, a drunken man, fully clothed, yelled, "Well, goodbye, Harry" and followed him off the bridge into the canal. "He was a good swimmer," Houdini noted in his diary.

On March 13, before his jump off the Seventh Street Bridge in Pittsburgh, Houdini told a reporter from *The Pittsburgh Leader* that the day before the leap he sent a cable to Hardeen, who was doing a similar act then in Europe, and the charges came to exactly $13. That same day Houdini's mail consisted of 13 letters. He switched rooms at his hotel and the new room was no. 26, divisible by 13. The letters contained 13 new challenges, the license plate of the auto that drove him to the bridge totaled up to 13, and the cinematographer who was filming the jump had exactly 1,300 feet of film in his camera.

"I feel nervous today," Houdini said. "There is a goneness in my innards that isn't pleasant." He ate an apple to settle himself down, then dove. It was exactly 1:13.

"In a minute and a half from the time I struck the water I had freed myself and was ready to rise to the surface," Houdini told the press. "Small boats were cruising about looking for me and, as luck would have it, I came rushing up at great speed just underneath one of these crafts. So rapid was my ascent that in rising I hit my head a fearful blow . . . and sank back into the water again

Sequence depicting Houdini bridge leap in Boston. *Library of Congress*

stunned and bleeding. When I struck that boat I thought of the thirteens of the day and concluded that it was up to me to battle for my life. Just when it seemed that all was over with me, I rose to the surface and willing hands dragged me to safety. It isn't any fun taking your life in your hands. Really, I'm in earnest. If a fellow wasn't married it would be a different thing, though even a single man oughtn't to be hankering for chances to risk his life."

Houdini seemed conflicted when facing these challenges. For the most part, he left his destiny in the hands of Fate. "While the manacles and shackles are being adjusted so that my limbs are powerless to move, I look down at the water flowing so far below; then I make up my mind I am going to do it," he told a reporter. "From the time I let go till the moment I strike the water everything is blank, and my ears are filled with strange songs. If the season be winter with the temperature of the water in the vicinity of freezing, the ordeal is one to be dreaded. The bitter cold of the first plunge seems to cut right into my heart, and I very often bite my lips almost through, so great is the shock."

On August 27, while preparing for a leap into the San Francisco Bay, he wrote his good friend Dr. Waitt back in Boston. "Tomorrow I will take a leap from the wharf into the Frisco Bay . . . Perhaps some day my time will come like that, but being a Fatalist, it worries me very little." After jumping into the deep, dark, and cold Mississippi River from a steamer in New Orleans, he dreaded the experience. "That's an awful river," he told a local reporter. "The worst I have ever been in . . . It's only a question of time that the man who works trained lions and tigers gets his violent passage to the other world, and it is pretty much the same with me." The reporter noted a tinge of sadness in Houdini's voice. "I'll get in the water some day, my trick will fail, and then good night!"

The stillness in the room was suddenly shattered by a muffled sound that was coming from inside the coffin. A few of the men in the front row ran up, pulled the curtain back, and rushed to the side of the casket.

"I need some more air," the muffled voice inside urged.

The men conferred, and a janitor was sent for. He had a hand drill and he perforated the coffin, a few times on each side.

"That's better," Houdini said, and the men withdrew, drawing the curtain behind them.

Earlier that day, Houdini had returned to his old haunt at the Boston Athletic Association to give the members a special treat. He was going to escape from a coffin with the lid screwed on. Now here he was, reposing in a "regulation, sound casket" that was placed upon three sawhorses so that Houdini could not get any assistance from any hidden confederates who might have rigged a trap- door below.

Still wearing his frock coat, he was handcuffed, shackled around his ankles, and lifted into his wooden enclosure. He struggled to briefly sit up, said, "Goodbye" to his audience, and then the lid was screwed into place, and the curtain was hung around the coffin.

At first, the audience watched the screen with rapt attention, especially after the new airholes had been bored into the casket. Gradually, their attention drifted from the curtain, and cheerfully confident that this test would pose no problem to the famous Houdini, they began to light up fine cigars and discuss sports, world events, and business. The time passed, and the haze of cigar smoke grew thicker, and then finally there was "the sound of a soft pad of feet as of some one landing on the floor." The curtain was suddenly whisked aside, and there stood Houdini, his frock coat disheveled, his collar and tie vanished, his shirt ripped open, and his bushy hair speckled with wood shavings. He was "panting like a stout man who has caught his car," one reporter wrote. Yet he was smiling. The cuffs and manacles were later found inside the coffin, which was still sealed. Houdini's reemergence was greeted with a hale round of "bravos" and applause, and many silk top hats were jiggled in his honor. It had taken him sixty-six and a half minutes to make his escape.

The escape had taken another toll on Houdini, at least that was what he told the reporters. "I was very tired after it was all over and the worry was as bad as the work," he said. "All the time I was in there I was thinking of death."

In private, he relished the fact that his promoter Paul Keith had managed to spirit him away from the more inquisitive committee members who wanted to examine him after the escape—to a steam room where a search would be superfluous. "Coffin affair a great big success," Houdini wrote in his diary. "Created more talk than anything I have ever done in Boston. Paul Keith sneaked me into the Turkish bath after show. That is, a committee desired to search me but we fooled them all and Paul grinned for two days."

Some of Houdini's greatest challenges were in front of Boston audiences, and this stint in early 1907 was no exception. He escaped from a giant football, a five-foot regulation hot water boiler, a crazy crib, a rolltop desk, and a glass box—a

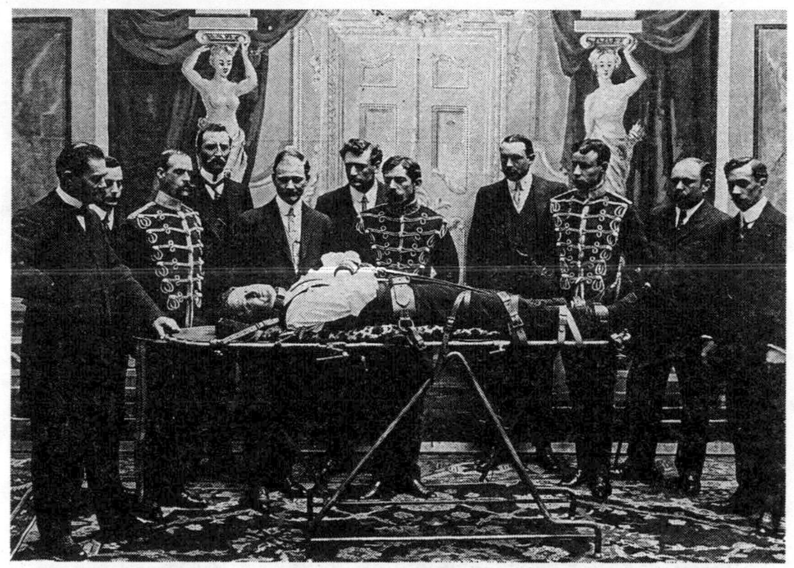

Houdini took on many varied challenges, including an escape from a "crazy crib."
From the collection of Roger Dreyer

challenge designed by his confidant Dr. Waitt. On February 4, from Providence, Houdini wrote Waitt, "How is the glass box-lets getting along?" Eleven days later, Waitt and some other challengers (a few who were friends of Houdini) stood onstage with a three-foot-long, two-foot-wide, and two-and-a-half-foot-high glass box that was held together by metal hinges and special bolts. The bolt heads inside the box were specially made to be smooth and not capable of being unscrewed. After having the box outside the theater to be examined by the audience for days, at the last minute, other bolts were substituted that had small imperceptible grooves on the inside. All Houdini had to do to escape was to smuggle in a small crescent shaped tool and unscrew the bolts from the inside. This unique bolt is a modified version of an espionage technique where similarly hollowed-out bolts are used to transmit secret messages.

From 1904 on, Houdini was the only escape artist who accepted such a wide panoply of challenges. Although many of his imitators would do handcuff and rope challenges, only a very few accepted more difficult challenges. Brindamour escaped from challenge paper bags and packing boxes; Mysto did a variation of the box challenge by getting out of a sealed coffin; and Houdini's brother Hardeen accepted challenges against Houdini's explicit wishes. Houdini struck back in a fury. He exposed Mysto onstage, called Brindamour a cross-dressing fancy dancer, and shunned his own brother until Bess was forced to make peace.

What set Houdini apart was that he managed each challenge from inception to execution, if he didn't invent them completely. The vast majority of the hundreds of challengers who confronted Houdini weren't accomplices. They were legitimate businesses that were, in effect, challenged by Houdini to challenge him. Even so, the challenger didn't have unlimited scope and control over what they could build. Houdini would happily give the details to the packing clerks and box makers. If needed, he would supply blueprints. The box was delivered to the theater a day or so before the challenge so it could be displayed to drum up business.

Sometime before the box would make its way to the stage, one of Houdini's assistants would remove a couple of long difficult screws and replace them with shorter ones. Once it was onstage, the challengers would come up, look over their box, be none the wiser, and nail the magician in, making sure to use countless nails and put them in the most difficult patterns. It didn't matter in the slightest; Houdini wasn't going out through the nailed-on top anyway.

As early as 1904, Houdini came up with the brilliant idea of "re-challenges." He would do a challenge packing case and then have the same firm re-challenge him, claiming that they knew that he had somehow tampered with the box. In 1913 in a broadside headlined HOUDINI EXPOSED!, the employees of George Scorrer, Ltd., wrote, "Dear Sir, During your last visit to Hull, you escaped from a Packing Case, but in its construction we were restricted regarding the nails and the manner of driving them home. WE ARE FAR FROM BEING SATISFIED with the result of that test, and to settle all arguments We defy you to allow us to build A STRONG PACKING CASE, of extra heavy lumber, making use of any size common flat-headed French wire nails and no restrictions placed as to the amount or manner." Sometimes these cases were even built on the stage in front of the audience. Houdini had a different method from the pre-made box challenges, but he escaped nonetheless.

In an age of virtually no mass communication, when people relied on local newspapers for their news of the world, very few theatergoers knew that this "special" challenge was something Houdini had done routinely all along his itinerary. When Houdini visited, it was imperative to go to the theater, because who knew if this would be the one night that the invincible escape artist would fail.

Houdini took all sorts of seemingly unique and unrelated challenges. He escaped from a sea monster, lit cannons, a giant football, wheels that were rotating, milk churns, diving suits, and iron boilers. Many of these he did only once and they were absolutely sensational. These one-of-a-kind challenges seemed unique, but Houdini realized that the sea monster and football escapes were more or less the same as escaping from large leather pouches or sailcloth sacks. Escaping after being chained to a lit cannon is still just a chain escape.

In some instances he refused challenges of unique escapes that didn't fall into his normal classifications. An old sea captain wanted to lock him in a diving suit with leaden boots and then throw him into thirty fathoms of water and have him escape without getting wet. The employees of an electric company proposed to blow a giant lightbulb around him and have him escape without breaking the glass. A plumber wanted to place him between two bathtubs and then spike them together. A German committee proposed handcuffing him to four horses and then have them race off in opposite directions. In San Francisco, a builder offered to build a house onstage and brick him in it. Although Houdini never accepted these challenges, they set his mind working, and he did invent a method to get out of a challenge house built around him, but he never used it.

Not content with his Boston area shows, Houdini even gave a private performance at the home of a prominent Bostonian named J. S. Fay. The magician's appearance was conceived in a discussion Fay had with Herbert Leeds, a well-to-do Bostonian who was a perennial contender for the America's Cup yacht race. Fay maintained that, as a nautical man, he could tie Houdini so securely that Houdini couldn't escape. Leeds was willing to wager that Fay couldn't. The bet was for $1,000. Leeds offered to split his winnings with Houdini and the contest was on.

On January 26, 1907, before the principals and ten close friends from their Somerset private club (who also made considerable side bets), Houdini allowed himself to be tied in Fay's living room, where a makeshift roped area, not unlike a boxing ring, had been constructed. Fay instructed Houdini to take off his coat, vest, trousers, collar, and necktie. He did not allow Houdini to remove his shoes, since he had heard of the escape artist's facility with his toes. Using stout cord, heavy silk fish line, and some twine, Fay got to work. He wound the cord so tightly around Houdini's neck that his tongue came out of his mouth from the pressure. Two of the men, both doctors, protested that Fay was choking Houdini.

"He's expanding the muscles of his neck," Fay explained. "I have to pull the rope tight enough to overcome that."

"I cannot breathe," Houdini said.

Fay shrugged and told him that the rope would expand. One of the doctors was so adamant that Houdini was being choked that Fay finally relented and loosened the cord a bit.

Then he bound his wrists so tightly that the cord was invisible from the swelled flesh. He then spent over an hour trussing Houdini. Finally, he was satisfied. Houdini then spent the next seventy-three minutes getting free, all with Fay watching him from six inches away, making sure that no hidden knife was used. Fay was a good sport, though, and he cheerfully paid off the bets. In all, a total of more than $10,000 was wagered.

"It was the hardest experience I ever had," Houdini told a Boston reporter. "He tied me so tightly that I shall have these welts on my wrists for weeks. I thought one time he was going to choke me, and I guess he would if the doctors present had not made him desist . . . Though I am physically sore, I had a good time, and I am glad if I gave a company of very entertaining gentlemen a pleasant morning."

Houdini spent most of the rest of 1907 confronting newer and stranger challenges. "Am in my usual rush. Three strange challenges. Gee but its hard to keep a[t] it all the time," he wrote Waitt. And after spending eighty minutes escaping from another boiler challenge in Toledo, he made a note to himself in his diary, "Must invent some new means of enlightening my labors. This challenge is the limit." Sometimes, Houdini would confront an astounding nine challenges a week.

Even his downtime wasn't relaxing. He was taking summers off and trying to spend time on his farm. In 1904, when he was ill and ordered to rest by his physician, he bought his farm and then spent three weeks cutting down twenty huge trees by himself. Desirous of a road leading up to the house, he singlehandedly cleared a series of boulders from the path, some weighing more than three hundred pounds.

Houdini opened his fall 1907 season with a new secret weapon against his competitors—his brother. Hardeen had been enjoying success in Europe, especially with Houdini in America for the last few years. Now the competition was heating up here, and old rivals like Cunning and new upstarts like Grose, a young Canadian, were still a threat to Harry's hegemony. Houdini realized that the same strategy that he had used in Europe would work here. At that time, Houdini was performing for the Orpheum circuit out west and Keith's in the east. The major opposition to those companies was the newly formed Klaw & Erlanger circuit. Unbeknownst to his own promoters, Houdini engaged in secret negotiations and booked Hardeen with the rival group, effectively blocking his authentic opposition from the best competing houses in the cities Houdini would play.

Houdini milked the "rivalry" for all it was worth. He brought reporters along when he boarded Hardeen's incoming ship to meet him "and learn his intentions." It was reported that the brothers had a long consultation on the dock and made peace. "I was very much alarmed, to learn that my brother was coming," Houdini told the press. "He says that he will not antagonize me, however, and will not attempt to discredit my name of 'Houdini,' though he is under contract to work in this country. We have always loved each other, and I felt very badly when I heard that he was going to fight me, but I guess the country is big enough for both of us."

Genuine bad feelings were generated when Hardeen went a little overboard in his publicity drumming. When asked by reporters about his attitude toward Houdini, he magnanimously told them that he had great admiration for him—so much so that he was willing to engage him as his assistant for a grand a week. "This got into print and it got Harry on my neck," Hardeen later recounted. "It was all right, he said, to bill myself as greater than Houdini—but this was going too far! I promised never to do that particular thing again—and good feeling was restored."

Houdini had created and stage-managed his biggest rival. He had had a hand in producing the very challenges that he would claim credit for defeating. And every night, there was the possibility of someone bringing a tampered lock to defeat him and ruin his reputation (just as he would send his brothers to his rivals' shows with similar equipment). It was no surprise that by March of 1908, Houdini would tell a reporter that he was laying up treasures "against the day when the public gets on to me."

Since 1900 Houdini had added an additional layer to this already convoluted landscape. Working as an agent for U.S. government agencies, international police associations, and special branch at Scotland Yard meant compartmentalizing a whole side of his experience that was shared on a strictly "need to know" basis. Houdini, a keeper of secrets by trade, now had a whole other secret life to protect. By 1906, there seemed to be some slippage in keeping these identities distinct and separate.

In April of that year, Houdini self-published his ninety-six-page book called *The Right Way to Do Wrong*. Billed as an "exposé of successful criminals," the book was for the most part a recounting of the successful ways con artists, bunko men, and pickpockets bilk the public, but it goes much further than simple three-card monte exposés. "It has been my good fortune to meet personally and converse with the chiefs of police and the most famous detectives in all the great cities of the world," Houdini writes in the introduction. "To these gentlemen I am indebted for many amusing and instructive incidents hitherto unknown to the world."

His idea was to sell this book at his shows, and correspondingly, a portion of the book is a pitch book of sorts, a whole chapter recounting highlights in Houdini's career. In a chapter on "Humbugs," he even gives his physician brother Leopold a plug, noting that, "Dr. L. D. Weiss, of New York, discovered that he could detect a fake mummy from an original by placing it under his X-Ray machine."

The book received good reviews, although one magic journal complained that there wasn't a chapter exposing Houdini's handcuff act, supposing that it was "The Wrong Time to Do Write." Apparently the book wasn't as favorably received by Houdini's friends in the world of law enforcement. According to *The Sphinx*, the book was banned by the police in England and Germany, and an article on rare books published in *The Providence Sunday Journal* in 1937 noted that *The Right Way to Do Wrong* was rare because "so well did it answer its title that the Government asked Houdini to withdraw it and he complied."

He didn't completely gag himself. Talking to the press was as much a part of the creation of the Houdini persona as actually appearing onstage. On March 11, 1906, a few weeks before Houdini published *The Right Way to Do Wrong*, he did a long interview with a reporter for *The Boston Sunday Herald*, where he revealed that his extensive contacts with criminals always make him a target for requests from criminals to teach them escape techniques. "But he is always on the side of law and order, and has contributed much valuable information to the secret service department of the government."

In the first decade of the twentieth century, Harlem was a fairly safe place to live. Houdini's brick town house, which had been built in 1895 and purchased by him in 1904 for $25,000, was part of a "genteel enclave" according to *The New York Times,* close to both Central Park and Morningside Park. So it was definitely an aberration when on July 24, 1906, Houdini wrote in his diary that his brother Leopold "thought he heard a burglar in my apartments. He must be mistaken. Have discovered no losses so far . . ."

It was a different story a year later. On October 25, 1907, he had returned to the town house a little after midnight. Exhausted from his rigorous schedule, he fell directly asleep but was awakened by a noise in his second-floor bedroom.

Allowing a few seconds for his eyes to get acclimated to the dark, he thought he spotted a man crouching in a corner of the room.

The last thing that the intruder expected was for his prey to jump off the bed and attack *him*. He immediately drew a razor and slashed wildly. The two men wrestled out into the hall and tumbled down a flight of stairs, locked in a deadly embrace. The noise woke Houdini's mother up, who ran into the hallway and started screaming. The two men continued their struggle in the hall, with the intruder, who had lost his razor to his victim, now getting the raw end of the blade. He had enough, and he opened a door and attempted to escape down the stairs to the basement. He wasn't quite fast enough. His coat was just a touch too long, giving his opponent a chance to grab it, and the two men tumbled down another flight of stairs.

Mrs. Weiss's screams alerted a neighbor, Dr. Reuss, and a passing policeman, Patrolman McCarty. They rushed into the house, and Mrs. Weiss led them to the basement, where she saw her son lying on the floor in a pool of blood, critically wounded. She wailed. The two men, spying an open door that led to the backyard, ran out. They saw blood on the steps and they followed the trail over a series of several fences and into a vacant lot, where they discovered the razor. The intruder had escaped.

From the collection of Roger Dreyer

11

Kill Thy Father

ON OCTOBER 26, THE DAY OF the attack in his town house, Houdini was playing an engagement at the Orpheum Theatre in Los Angeles. As great as he was, he couldn't be in two places at once. It was his brother Leopold, who closely resembled him, who was set on by the razor-wielding intruder. The police began to look for a "negro" perpetrator. In the dark, Leopold hadn't actually seen his assailant but guessed his race from his contact with the intruder's hair.

The morning after the attack, Dr. Weiss's servant, Frank Thomas, a black man who worked all day at the town house and left to sleep at his own domicile, reported for work at eight A.M. By then, the police had already cast a net of suspicion upon him, since there had been no signs of forced entry, and he was the only "negro" employed on the premises. Leopold allowed him to resume his duties, but he kept a wary eye on him all morning. His suspicions were aroused when he noticed that Thomas was keeping one hand shut, his fingers closed down over the palm. Using the pretext of handing him an object, Dr. Weiss grabbed the man's hand and peeled back his fingers. An examination revealed several strips of court plaster on his palm. Thomas was perfectly calm when he explained to his employer that he had tripped on a curbstone the previous evening on his way home and had cut his hand when he fell to the pavement.

Accepting the explanation, Leopold allowed Thomas to continue working. When a maid later found the black man's "cheap seal ring" lying in a dark corner in the lower hall, the very spot where the struggle ensued, Leopold called the police, despite Thomas's protestations of innocence. Detectives hauled the servant to the station house, Thomas still maintaining that he had nothing to do with the attack. After a grueling cross-examination by acting-captain Maher, the officer "asserted" that Thomas had made a full confession. He was locked up and, after pleading guilty at his trial, received a sentence of ten years and seven months to eleven years and seven months.

The motive was just as flimsy as the evidence. The newspaper reports vary. One suggested that Dr. Weiss had recently received a $1,000 check drawn on a Wall Street bank. When he presented the check, the bank refused to honor it, arguing that he hadn't identified himself properly. He called a friend and asked him to accompany him to the bank and vouch for him. It was "supposed" that the servant had overheard that conversation and believed that Leopold would have a thousand dollars cash in the house. Ironically enough, by the time the two men reached the bank, it had closed for the day.

The other story was similarly convoluted. This account quoted Leopold as saying that he was in a quandary whether to deposit the check in his account with the Knickerbocker Bank because of their "unsettled" conditions. He called a friend, who advised him to place the money in a safe deposit vault, which he did. He claimed that Thomas overheard his conversation and "doubtless" thought he had the cash in the house. When he saw the intruder in his room, he claimed that he was in the process of "fumbling among my papers." In a pitch-black room.

Why an employee who had access to the house would try to murder his employer rather than steal something at another more convenient time was not considered. And why a vicious would-be murderer would report for work seven hours after he had inflicted more than one hundred wounds on his employer was similarly never addressed. Judging from the description of the fierce hand-to-hand battle where the razor changed hands, a few minor cuts on one hand doesn't quite jibe with the report of a severely wounded assailant trailing blood over three backyards. With the confession in place and Thomas's long sentence, the matter ended. Amazingly, Houdini managed to keep his name out of any of the newspaper accounts of an attempted murder at his home.

Even before he had published his opus on criminality, *The Right Way to Do Wrong*, Houdini had started devoting more and more of his time to literary pursuits. "We have records for five generations that my direct fore-fathers were students and teachers of the Bible and recognized as among the leading bibliographers of their times," he would boast. Years later, he would begin to write a book that dissected the old myths and stories of the Bible, but for now, he was content to channel his literary ambitions into a new monthly magazine devoted to magic. Houdini-style magic.

Houdini always had an ambition to both organize magicians into a strong fellowship and to propagate (some might say impose) his own vision of the future of magic on his fellow performers. In 1906, he took steps to achieve both of those goals. He became a vice president of the Society of American Magicians, the strongest association of magicians in the United States. And he began to publish a thirty-two-page monthly magic periodical named *Conjurer's Monthly*.

He might not have started *Conjurer's* if he would have received more attention from *The Sphinx*, the reigning number one magic magazine in the United States. When Houdini returned from Europe in 1905, he implored *The Sphinx*'s editor, Dr. A. M. Wilson, for more coverage. Wilson replied that he would be happy to run Houdini's picture often, as long as he paid the prevailing advertising rates. This led to a long-standing bitter feud, and the creation of the new magazine.

Conjurer's Monthly was unlike any magic magazine ever published. With a staff that included most of his family, and editorial contributions from friends like Joe Hyman and Harry Day, the magazine had the feel of the monthly newsletter of a very dysfunctional family.

The first issue in September 15, 1906 set the tone. It was spotted with tacky ads for detective agencies, in-laws' restaurants, a Viennese hair and scalp specialist who claimed to have performed wonders for President Roosevelt and Mrs. McKinley, and Theodore Hardeen—"The King of all Handcuff Kings and the Mighty Potentate of all the Monarchs and Jail Breakers (bar Houdini)." Houdini's opening salutatory claimed that he didn't wish to "supplant any other paper" and that he had "no axes to grind," then in the very next paragraph he complained that every other magic magazine was in the hands of businessmen who use them as "'grafting' catalogues."

Hardeen, the "Official European Correspondent," wrote about a fistfight he had with card sharpers onboard a steamship. Houdini printed personal letters from friends like Harry Day and even an angry letter from a stranger who wrote, "I have seen you perform once, but what good are you to society?" Alongside this bizarre content was a terrific article by Houdini called "Handcuff Secrets Exposed." Besides tipping legitimate escape techniques like employing a false finger or using a split key (Houdini's own invention), the article detailed some very clever and helpful showmanship techniques. "In addressing your audience do not become bombastic or overbearing in demeanor but speak as you would to critical friends, thereby gaining their confidence and sympathy and no matter what may worry or trouble you, never let your audience detect any irritability or ill temper, but always display a bright and pleasing manner."

Conjurer's truly reflected Houdini's personality. Houdini began a feature, "Answers to Various Questions," that contained gems like "Knocker. To H--l with you. And all others like you. We shall do whatever we feel like, and no amount of advertising will make us change our plans." His book reviews displayed a similar truculence. Reviewing a book called *Mediumship* (in the monthly feature "Reading and Rubbish"), written by "A medium under control," Houdini noted that the more he read of the book, the more he was convinced the author "was under the control of the warden of an asylum" and that if the book were to be sold through the U.S. mail, "we feel sure that the Government's sleuths will be sent out after the publisher."

Old scores were settled with enemies (he called an English magic dealer who sold his handcuff secrets an "errand boy clerk"), veiled attacks were made on fellow performers ("The American Illusionist, who . . . appeared before King Edward and Queen Alexandra, cuts but a sorry figure. Like the mercenary, flat-headed, pride-inflated individual that he is, he imagined that his future standing would be rated by the present he received from his royal patron."), but Houdini's greatest wrath was reserved for his escape act imitators. Houdini relished printing police accounts of his competitors' failures to escape from jail cells and he even encouraged his readers to send in local reports of their defeats. Houdini's diatribes against his opposition were picked up by other columnists, including Leonard Hicks, a handcuff expert and mechanist who would later be mentored by Houdini. Hicks skewered a "near handcuff king" named Miller and then offered that if "Miller does not believe it in print, let him call at the hotel, and I'll tell it to him personally, where he will find me near the big chair in the lobby. He will be able to recognize me by the club and gun on my knee."

On May 24, 1921, Houdini was visiting at the offices of his lawyer, Bernard Ernst. It was six P.M. and Houdini needed a contract drawn up, but Ernst was hungry for dinner, so they agreed to go have a bite to eat and return to the office to do the legal work. Forgetting the time, Ernst led Houdini out the Liberty Street entrance of the building, which was routinely closed at six. He turned and began to walk toward the other entrance, but Houdini didn't follow. Ernst turned around and saw him huddled over the lock.

"Come on," he said a few seconds later. "It's open."

When Houdini asked Ernst what he thought of his feat, Ernst made the mistake of telling him that he would expect Houdini would be able to open a lock like that, and that he had assumed the magician was familiar with it in advance.

For the next few hours, Houdini fumed. Finally, after the contract was drawn up, Houdini couldn't restrain himself.

"You didn't seem to think very much of my opening those swinging doors. Now I want to show you that I am Houdini. Let me see your office safe," he requested.

Ernst took him to a room that contained a six-foot-high, four-foot-wide Herring-Hall-Marvin safe.

"Make sure that it's locked and leave me alone with it for sixty seconds," Houdini said.

Ernst complied. After a minute, Houdini called him in, turned the combination to the correct numbers, and opened the safe. Ernst was truly amazed. He knew that Houdini had never seen this safe before. Now he showered praise on his friend.

Houdini pulled out a letter from a large safe company that thanked him for calling attention to a defect in the locks that they used in their safes. Ernst was duly impressed. Then, in an uncharacteristic moment, Houdini pulled out a small object that he carried in a leather bag that was enclosed in a metal case dangling from his trousers on a key ring chain. Although Ernst refused to give details of this "gimmick," we now know that Houdini was showing Ernst a safe-opening micrometer. In the September 1907 issue of *Conjurer's Monthly*, Houdini revealed the existence of a version of that safe-opening micrometer, a device made from a common watch, which, when customized even "in the hands of the average person," can open any combination safe lock.

Because of the nature of deception, magic devices and espionage tools have certain elements in common, such as hiding and transmitting information and working with codes. Like Dr. Waitt's special bolts that had dual use, magicians and spies alike have used hollowed-out coins, small hollow containers that could hide tools or documents and then be secreted in various body cavities, and shoes like those invented by Mokana that have a hollow heel. Before he left the United States, never to live there again, Billy Robinson wrote a book called *Spirit Slate Writing and Kindred Phenomena*. In it, Zanzic's old running partner described a number of the devices that would seem as equally suited for espionage as for pretending to contact the dead. He detailed thirty-seven different methods for secret writing. These various methods, some using heat, some chemicals, and others light, were in great demand and interest and in fact would play an important part in spy communication during World War I. He also detailed how to read other people's letters without opening the envelopes by using alcohol to render them temporarily transparent. Another clever method for the same result involved using an embryologist's egg glass to look within opaque envelopes. Especially subtle methods to share information while being closely scrutinized were given in several variations and in detail; two were for special ways to use secret writing devices attached to hands that couldn't be seen. He even taught how to use a piece of thread to send secret Morse code directly to a medium's (or another operative's) head. A new secret at the time, which is now called black art, allowed for agents or magicians to move about without being seen, wearing a specialized form of black clothing. Robinson also described a primitive way to gimmick a fountain pen so it could shoot a cap. Years later, an acquaintance of Houdini's named Clayton Hutton, one of the major creative forces to create escape material and methods for the military, would make a deadlier version to help captured British airmen and troops escape from the Nazis during World War II.

By the March 1908 issue of *Conjurer's*, Houdini began a comprehensive series of articles on cryptography. In the stated context of promoting a secret code so "magicians can secretly correspond with one another and exchange tricks and secrets without fear of the messages being intercepted by others," Houdini published a series of techniques and a history of the art of cryptography, an art that he claimed "often . . . has been the means of giving me a friendly warning or clever hint to look out for myself."

He began by teaching the method of using what he mistakenly called a "windowed cipher" to communicate secret messages. In Germany Houdini purchased sets of pasteboards, properly known as a Cardan grille. In the example that Houdini uses, the original message would be the following: "Would like to prepare to leave my son at your house Saturday and if you wish for him to bring the late copy of the London *Times* do let me know, as I shall not refuse." When read through the pasteboard filter that covers over certain letters, the message reads, "prepare to leave your house Saturday for London do not refuse."

The next magazine installment included instructions for producing invisible ink and another cipher that employed the grouping of letters or sentences to produce a new message. In the June 1908 issue, Houdini's call for magicians to communicate via coded ciphers was echoed in a letter from an amateur magician named "Raymeen" Stone. He suggested that Houdini devote a page in each issue of the magazine that would be designated for a correspondence club of amateur magicians who could communicate to one another using one of Houdini's cipher methods.

Houdini's literary ambitions were being channeled into areas other than magazine publishing too. On October 5, 1907, while he was performing in Los Angeles, Houdini went to a local synagogue where he recited the Kaddish, the

Jewish prayer for the dead, on the fifteenth anniversary of his father's death. It might have been on his next train trip, from Los Angeles to Kansas City, when Houdini pulled out a piece of paper and modified a popular poem by Elizabeth Akers Allen called "Rock Me to Sleep." Where Allen envisioned a backward flight of time so that her now dead mother could comfort her, Houdini had turned the poem into an ode to his dead father.

In the fall of 1903, Houdini stood in front of the door of the Villa Frikell, hat in hand. He had been there all morning—to no avail. Still, he was determined not to give up. The photographer whom he had hired to snap a candid shot of the old German magician Wiljalba Frikell as he departed his home was lounging on the street corner opposite the house. There had been no sign of the conjurer, but Houdini was relentless. He had previously written the magician, requesting an interview, but he had received a curt note back, "The master is on tour." At eighty-seven, Houdini knew that was impossible. He also knew that Frikell had been a recluse for the last fifteen years, and after speaking to Kotchenbroda police the day before, he was certain that the magician was at home.

"I repeat, Herr Frikell has gone away," his wife, who was leaning out of the window above the door, told Houdini.

Houdini wouldn't take no for an answer.

"Madame, you must help me," Houdini begged for the umpteenth time. "Herr Frikell is a master of magic, and I'm sure he would be happy to lend a helping hand to one like myself, who is ready to sit at his feet and learn."

Tears began streaming down Frau Frikell's face.

"There is nothing I can do," she said.

"Please inform your esteemed husband that I am writing the first true history of magic ever, and that the debt which he owes to the literature of magic can be discharged by simply sharing with me the information that he has," Houdini pleaded.

It went on like this for hours, Houdini badgering the old woman, the old woman leaning out the window, tears running down her cheeks, insisting that her husband was away. The truth was Frikell was lying grimly on a bed on the other side of the window, listening to every word Houdini spoke.

Finally, physically exhausted, Houdini and his photographer left the house, but he didn't give up. Houdini had been compiling material since the beginning of 1902 for his projected *Encyclopedia of Magic*, an ambitious book that would contain "the biography, incidents, etc., of every magician, from the time of Moses to the present year." Frikell was desperately important to Houdini because Houdini had heard that the old magician had been the first conjurer to discard flowing draperies and cumbersome stage apparatus, a "revolution" properly attributed to Robert-Houdin.

So he continued to bombard Frikell with letters and press notices of his act. When he was in Russia, he finally received a response. Herr Frikell would be happy to receive a package containing a certain brand of Russian tea of which he was very fond. The next day the tea went out, and shortly after, Houdini received the letter he had been waiting for. Frikell would see the young magician.

Houdini immediately booked an engagement in nearby Dresden. He set a date for their meeting, Saturday, October 8, 1903. He even made arrangements for Frikell to come to Dresden a few days earlier to sit for a formal portrait with a photographer so Houdini could have an up-to-date photograph for his book. On the day of the sitting, Frikell called at the theater where Houdini was playing, but the attachés didn't even bother to inform Houdini and then refused to give Frikell the name of Houdini's hotel. After the show that night, Houdini stopped at a local café and was "much annoyed by the staring and gesticulations of an elderly couple at a distant table." He had failed to recognize Herr Frikell and his wife. They, in turn, had been too timid to approach the headliner.

Houdini arrived in Kotchenbroda well in advance of his two o'clock appointment, so he took a leisurely stroll to the Villa Frikell. Finally arriving, he rang the bell and it seemed peculiarly shrill to the magician's ears. He was so excited at the prospect of meeting this great magician, a man who had spent sixty-two years in the world of magic. A lady opened the door.

"You are being waited for," she said.

Houdini was led up to the drawing room, where the magician did await him. There was only one problem. Frikell was dead.

Apparently the strain was too much for the old man's heart. He had spent hours preparing for Houdini's visit, arranging his programs, lugging out his gold medals and his photography albums. He had donned his best wardrobe and waited for his guest, young and happy once more, his wife said.

"There we stood together, the woman who had loved the dear old wizard for years and the young magician who had been so willing to love him had he been allowed to know him," Houdini later wrote. "His face was still wet from the cologne she had thrown over him in vain hope of reviving the fading soul. On the floor lay the cloths, used so ineffectually to bathe the pulseless face and

"Two young people roaming around trying to make an honest million."
From the collection of Dr. Bruce Averbook

now laughing mockingly at one who saw himself defeated after weary months of writing and pleading for the much-desired meeting."

Houdini didn't go away empty-handed. He stayed that day and interviewed Frikell's widow, and then he returned on several other occasions and continued the interrogation. His book would be the most comprehensive book yet written on the history of magic. Somewhere along the line, the focus of the book changed. Instead of chronicling the true stories of centuries of past masters, the book became a diatribe against one magician who had, in the author's eyes, wrongfully stolen credit for the innovations of others. *The Encyclopedia of Magic* somehow morphed into *The Unmasking of Robert-Houdin*.

Since the death of his father, Houdini had gravitated to father figures. In Europe in 1902, when he had begun his research for his encyclopedia, his first stop was the grave of his idol, Robert-Houdin. Houdini made it a point during his tours in England and the continent to honor his long-dead compatriots by restoring their sometimes-forgotten overgrown graves or placing elaborate wreaths in the name of the SAM (the Society of American Magicians) on the graves of more fortunate fellow conjurers. "I stood with my hat in my hand at the tomb of Robert-Houdin, and with all the reverence and homage with which I respect his memory." After meditating over the grave for a half hour, he laid a wreath on behalf of American magicians.

On March 17, 1903, a little over a year later, Houdini tracked down an old conjurer in Muenster, Germany, named Alexander Heimburger. Houdini was thrilled to be in the company of a magician who had entertained President Polk in the White House. Alexander regaled Houdini with tales of the greats he had personally known—Robert-Houdin, Frikell, Bosco, Anderson, and Blitz. "Had he risen from a grave he could not better have commanded my attention," Houdini wrote. Intending to just visit for a few hours, he would end up staying the whole day and dining with Herr Alexander, except "I had no desire to eat, but hungrily listened to every word Herr Alexander spoke."

The only problem is Alexander was dissembling. He had never met Robert-Houdin; his only contact with the French magician was when he wrote him to see if he could obtain the German rights to publish Robert-Houdin's *Memoirs*. The French conjurer wrote back a charming letter thrilled to have heard from such an esteemed colleague but sorry that the foreign rights resided in his publisher's hands. It is not known whether Heimburger ever actually obtained the rights, but the *Memoirs* were not published in German by Heimburger.

When Houdini met with Heimburger, one of the things they discussed was Robert-Houdin's *Memoirs*, the book that changed Houdini's life. Heimburger was dismissive of Robert-Houdin's work, telling Houdini "that Houdin never wrote his book, but had it written by a Parisian journalist . . . Alexander informed me that Houdin personally told him this," Houdini wrote later. Alexander also told Houdini that his own memoirs, *Ein moderner Zauberer* (*The Modern Magician*), was "the best book ever written by a conjurer."

Houdini left Heimburger's house starstruck. "Both extending to each other the best wishes, the old master returned to his books, while I with bowed head slowly walked out into the bright sunshine, deeply thinking of the various things engraved in my memory."

The old man gently opened a scrapbook.

"I have brought you, sir, only a few of my treasures, sir, but if you will call—"

Houdini heard nothing else. He can only remember raising his hands before his eyes, "as if I had been dazzled by a sudden shower of diamonds." In the old man's trembling hands were jewels that Houdini had been pursuing for years—original program and bills of Robert-Houdin, Phillippe, Anderson, Breslaw, Pinetti, and Katterfelto, many of the great conjurers of the eighteenth and nineteenth centuries. "I felt as if the King of England stood before me, and I must do him homage," Houdini wrote.

The "King," an old stooped man named Henry Evanion, was wearing such tattered clothing that the management of Houdini's hotel was reluctant to even send him up to Houdini's room, relegating him to a chair in the lobby. Evanion had read of Houdini's interest in old magic programs and handbills, and they had arranged to meet at the hotel where Houdini was recuperating from a severe cold.

Houdini's idea of homage was to buy up Evanion's immaculate collection. He went to Evanion's home the next day, flu be damned, and spent almost twenty-four hours looking through the treasures. If it wasn't for Hardeen and the doctor tracking him down and literally dragging him back to bed, he might have stayed for days. Evanion, an ex-magician and ventriloquist, had fallen on hard times. Houdini was making more money than he could spend. So the two began a symbiotic relationship, and in exchange for Houdini's financial generosity, Evanion began to spend hours on end at the British Museum doing research for Houdini's book and other topics of interest to the young magician.

A year after they met, Houdini received word that Evanion had been hospitalized with throat cancer. After receiving additional word that he was declining rapidly, Houdini left Wigan, where he had been performing, and journeyed to London. He found Evanion unable to speak but learned that his chief anxiety was for the future of his wife and for a proper burial. Houdini came through on both counts. He immediately began sending Mrs. Evanion postal orders, and when he was notified of the old man's death on June 17, he rushed to the Evanion household and paid for the lion's share of the funeral costs. The unanticipated reward for his kindness was the "crown jewel" of Evanion's collection—an entire book filled with Robert-Houdin programs.

Between Houdini's first visit to Heimburger in 1903 and the first issue of his monthly magic magazine in the fall of 1906, Houdini tracked down and spent time with several other old father figures who, in the course of their conversations, began to belittle the contributions of Houdini's "guide and hero," Robert-Houdin. These were men who all claimed to have witnessed Robert-Houdin's performances, Henry Evanion and Sir William Clayton in England; Ernest Bach in Berlin; T. Bolin in Russia, who especially impressed Houdini with his anti-Robert-Houdin rhetoric; even Otto Maurer, who had a magical repository on the Bowery in New York. "The combined opinion of these men was that Houdin was not original, and that he was only a little above the average entertainer," Houdini wrote. So, in essence, he was an imitator.

Houdini began publishing his research on Robert-Houdin as a series of articles called "Unknown Facts Concerning Robert-Houdin" in the first issue of his *Conjurer's Monthly* in September 1906. Houdini's major indictment was his claim that Robert-Houdin stole other magicians' intellectual property and claimed the effects as his own. Throughout the series of articles, Houdini continually maintained that his mission in this book would be to restore the credit to magicians whose accomplishments had been consigned to the dustbin of magic history. "My opinion of Robert Houdin is that he had a wonderful good opinion of himself, and thought it was not such a wrong thing for him to take other people's brains and annex them as his own," he wrote in an early installment. And later, when writing about the old master Robert Heller, he was even more emphatic. "Look at the various Arts and Professions, and then at the old-time Magicians; none of them have been properly remembered! . . . A painter when he dies, leaves behind paintings, an author leaves as a monument some of his books, the music master leaves his inspirations, but how can a magician leave behind a positive proof of his genius? . . . So I contend that it is about time that someone should extol the virtues of the poor past and almost forgotten Magicians."

No one could argue with that noble pursuit. It's poignant to see Houdini battling for respect for the forgotten father figures he cultivated in his research, even more so when we see that Houdini dedicated the book to his own father, who, in his eyes, was a great scholar who never got his just recognition in this world. Houdini claimed to believe that Robert-Houdin had obscured the true history of magic. Halfway into the magazine serialization, Houdini had come up with a new name for the book. No longer *The Encyclopedia of Magic*, now it would be called *Robert-Houdin's Proper Place in the History of Magic*. And his new mission statement became: "I am actuated only by a desire to set forth before the world of magic, the true facts as ascertained by me during years of earnest investigation at home and abroad, and to do justice to those who preceded Houdin and to whom he owed a greater debt than he set forth in his autobiography." Houdini's desire to take what he saw as his rightful place in the generations of scholars that his family tree produced is palpable here.

The French magic community was justly outraged at Houdini's defilement of their national hero and immediately came to Robert-Houdin's defense and started to attack Houdini in their journals.

All that was missing was a challenge. Not for long. By the next issue of *Conjurer's*, the last to have an installment, Houdini had given up any pretense

Robert-Houdin, the great master and source of Houdini's name.
Conjuring Arts Research Center

that this fight wasn't personal. "In the Robert-Houdin articles we fairly revolutionized the history of magic," Houdini frothed. "Robert-Houdin has been uncrowned as the king of conjuring and automata, and the crown has been distributed, bit by bit, among the earlier magicians to whom it rightfully belonged. Men on two continents who once proclaimed Robert-Houdin as magic's hero now refer to him as the Prince of Pilferers," he lied.

Debate over *The Unmasking of Robert-Houdin* raged for years. The book wasn't entirely without merit. As a history of magic, Houdini did find some new, interesting information through his discovery of rare clippings, broadsides, and images that went back about one hundred years, but the book's anecdotes and analyses are riddled with errors and outright lies. The question remains—why?

Houdini was an intelligent man who understood human nature. His career attests to that. We know that it's not out of character for Houdini to lash out against his perceived enemies. He did that his entire life, taking aim and doing damage to imitators and those who might have insulted him or his family. None of those episodes even come close to his animosity toward a long-dead magician to whom he owed an enormous debt and who, unlike his imitators and enemies, couldn't defend himself. Even though he had publicly denounced his former mentor, he never once broke faith with Robert-Houdin's theories and repeatedly emulated, by his actions, his once-revered role model.

It's too simplistic to say that Houdini was brainwashed by the bitter old Alexander Heimburger, who fed him a steady diet of lies about the French magician he never met. It's charitable to suggest that this coterie of old, long-forgotten, unsuccessful magicians, who poisoned him with respect toward Robert-Houdin, stirred pity in him. Perhaps attacking the elegant French magician became a way to claim glory for them who, in Houdini's mind, might have stood in as surrogates for his own father, another revered old man who never received the recognition and acclaim that his son felt the world owed him.

One intriguing theory proposed by Ricky Jay, eminent magic historian, paraphrases Gore Vidal: For Houdini it wasn't enough to succeed; others had to fail. He felt he must discredit his mentor in order to make himself seem greater. Even so, his attack on Robert-Houdin was wrong. It also backfired. Robert-Houdin is still considered preeminent, and Houdini's twisted agenda permanently discredited him as an historian.

The controversy over *The Unmasking of Robert-Houdin* never touched Houdini the Superman. That creation remained safe and bulletproof. But cut through the chains, peel off the layers of mythology, and you'll find an uneducated boy bearing a grudge—a dark venom that permanently stained Harry Houdini the man.

ꝏ

With his immersion into historical and literary pursuits, it seemed that Houdini was finally going to make good on his longstanding desire to retire from the grueling work of being an escape artist. As soon as he put out his first issue of *Conjurer's Monthly*, his old sidekick from the Professor Marco days, Bert Kilby, wrote him and timidly asked him if Houdini would sell his act to him, since he had heard from the professor that Houdini was in New York publishing a magazine and was "going to give up the business." He added that he would never have even asked his question had he not heard that Houdini was about to retire.

Houdini had been threatening retirement, even in print. In the premiere issue of his magazine, in an article called "Tricks with Handcuffs," Houdini rationalizes that it's all right to tip some of his handcuff methods "as I claim to have the honor of having placed on the market an act or performance by which many an individual is now making a livelihood, whilst I am about to retire." On November 4, 1907, he told *The Kansas City Post* that these were his farewell dates in America. He planned to leave for Europe in May of 1908, fulfill his commitments for two years, and then "it will be to retire to private life and conduct my research in the field of magic." Ten days later, he wrote his old friend Dr. Waitt and told him he was certain he'd play Boston again before sailing for Europe but "perhaps the LAST TIME!"

By the end of 1907, the audiences seemed to be becoming inured to Houdini's myriad escapes. By now they knew that handcuffs, leg irons, straitjackets, packing cases, locked and roped trunks, glass boxes, coffins, and even giant footballs couldn't contain him. On January 6, 1908, Houdini began an engagement at the Columbia Theatre in St. Louis. The next day his mother came for a visit, and she stayed a little over a week. Perhaps it was his desire to make up for all the time lost with her, maybe it was just fatigue from the last three years on the road, and maybe it was just the audience's perception that Houdini was back with the same old material, but the box office receipts were drastically down. On January 20, two weeks into his scheduled four-week run, manager Tate called Houdini down to his office.

Tate motioned for him to have a seat. Houdini warily sat down.

"I suppose you know why I called you in," Tate said.

"No, not really," Harry lied.

"Well maybe you can't see it from your little cabinet, but there are a helluva lot of empty seats out there," Tate growled.

"Well, it has been cold . . ." Houdini started.

Tate slammed some papers down on his desk.

"It didn't stop Eva Tanguay from selling out in Chicago," he said, and bolted up from his chair and walked around his desk to where Houdini was sitting.

"I don't know how you can do it. But you better come up with something quick. You have two more weeks here, and if this keeps up, you are not worth a $5 bill to me."

Houdini just stared straight ahead. Tate's words had cut him as badly as Hodgson's brutal chaining. Perhaps he was closer to retiring than he thought. Houdini got up out of the chair.

"I hope you are mistaken, Mr. Tate," he said.

12

Death Visits the Stage

THE AUDIENCE GASPED AS THE MAGICIAN disappeared from sight into the oversize milk can, water splashing over the edge from the displacement. Time was of the essence, so his assistants rapidly affixed the metal cover. Grabbing the locks from the six audience members who were onstage surrounding the can, they rapidly locked the cover down. The cabinet was pulled out, surrounding the can, and the curtain was drawn. Now all that was left was the escape. Or else a death by drowning.

What the hell? Why isn't this moving? Is this some sick trick?

He was pounding on the inside of the can more and more frantically. The can itself was gimmicked, the neck consisting of two walls, an outer and an inner. The lid had been locked to the outer neck. So all the performer had to do was to push up on the top of the can and the whole outer neck (and locked-on lid) would telescope up and off. What he didn't know was that the can had been dropped by stagehands as it was being unloaded from the truck prior to the performance. Its side had been dented enough so that the two nested necks couldn't slide. Now he was truly locked inside a milk can filled to the brim with water.

The orchestra played and the audience waited. And waited. After two minutes, one of the assistants sensed that something was dreadfully wrong. He peered into the cabinet. The can was undisturbed. Frantic now, he overturned the cabinet and rushed to unlock the padlocks.

The committee from the audience just got in the way. They meant well, but they confused things, and now the keys to the individual locks were all mixed up. Meanwhile, the audience, realizing that something dreadfully wrong had

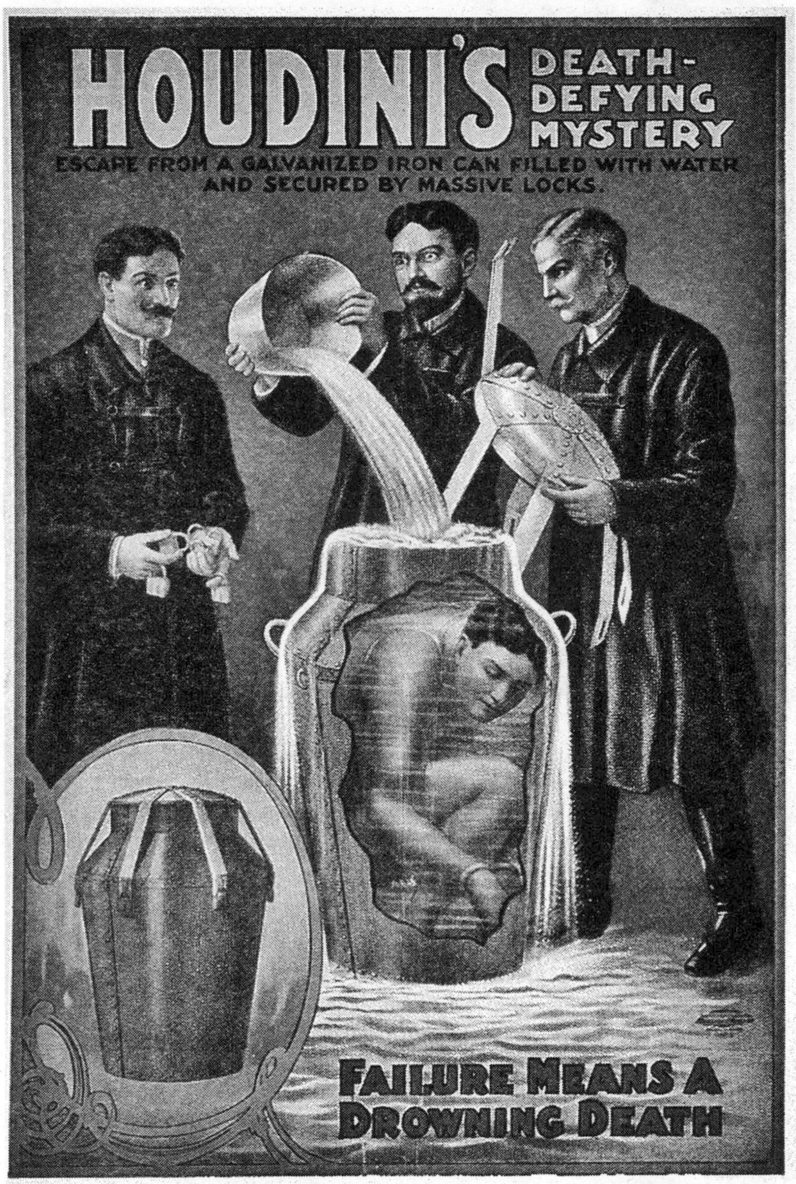

Houdini's Milk Can escape. *From the collection of Tad Ware*

happened, was in a state of frenzy. And now, to compound things, the magician's wife rushed onto the stage, hysterical.

Precious seconds ticked away as the correct combination of locks and keys was found. Finally the locks were all opened, and the assistant ripped the lid off the can. The seemingly lifeless magician was pulled out of the can and laid on the floor, the water cascading all over the stage. By then, thankfully, the theater curtain had come down, and a house doctor rushed up and began to administer artificial respiration. The escape artist was partially revived and rushed to the local hospital, where he told the doctors that in more than ten years of performing this escape, this was the first time that he had failed to free himself. It was also the last. Royden Joseph Gilbert Raison de la Genesta, who performed as simply "Genesta," died in that hospital shortly after admission. He died in 1930, performing the magic effect that had resurrected Houdini's career in 1908.

With the Milk Can escape, Houdini was able to bring to the stage the element of the real risk of death that was present in his outdoor handcuffed jumps into bodies of water. This was a crucial turning point, not only for him but also for the magical arts in general. Other than bullet catching, which despite its real bullets and real guns was still usually perceived by the audience as a "trick," real, palpable, life-and-death danger had never been presented as a dreadful consequence of a performance on the magician's stage.

Genesta's tragic death was not the only mishap incurred performing the Milk Can. Hardeen came close to death in the can. One night he fainted inside it, and his two assistants had to literally cut slits in the bottom of the container with a fire ax and then pull him out, unconscious. After a few days' rest, he was back in the can and performed the effect until he died at age sixty-nine.

Houdini might have thought that he would dissuade imitators by conceiving of such a dangerous effect, since it took him months of rigorous physical training before he would attempt the feat. Always blessed with a prodigious ability to hold his breath for prolonged lengths of time, Houdini began practicing and routinely broke the three-minute mark. On December 17, 1907, he did a trial run of the effect without adding water to the can, calling it "an escape from a galvanized liquid air can." He was trying it out both on his audience and, more important, on Bess, who had just returned from New York where she had undergone an operation. "She saw me do the can trick, thinks it is great. I offered her ten dollars if she could tell me how it was done. She failed to fathom trick. GOOD," he wrote in his diary.

Houdini's new great effect was being developed by his friend Montraville M. Wood, a brilliant inventor and past associate of Thomas Edison. Wood did an entertaining show, displaying his innovations on the Chautauqua lecture

Montraville M. Wood strikes an elegant pose. *University of Iowa*

circuit. He was a Chicago area resident, and his inventions spanned from the two-button electrical light switch to a new type of torpedo and a gyroscope that would assist pilots so they could fly at night or in windy conditions. He also touted the use of a monorail to span long distances and worked on a way to allow wallpaper to store enough light during the day that it could illuminate rooms at night. Houdini and Wood exchanged numerous letters during this early phase of development of the can, and Wood would later come up with eight different methods for Houdini to escape from the can after it had been thoroughly examined by audience members.

That Houdini's debut of the Milk Can escape is tied to St. Louis Theater manager Tate's dismissal of his drawing power is evident from his diary. The next day after he was berated, he began testing his underwater endurance. Upset that he could only hold his breath for two minutes, he began a running regimen to strengthen his lungs. Two days later, he started practicing in the actual can, finding that it took twenty-two pails of water to fill it and seven more pails to refill the water displaced when he entered the container.

Houdini before immersion. *From the collection of Roger Dreyer*

Satisfied that the effect looked "very good," Houdini debuted it on January 25, 1908. Even though he invited the St. Louis press to be present for the new escape, no one bothered to show up. They missed a great display of showmanship. Before beginning the performance, Houdini invited a committee onstage to carefully examine the airtight galvanized-iron can. Once the committee was satisfied that the can was legitimate, Houdini's assistants began filling it with pails of water, while the magician left the stage to change into a bathing suit. When he returned, he announced that "deprived of life-sustaining air," a man can only survive a short time underwater. Yet he would first demonstrate his ability to stay underwater for longer durations than most mortals by doing a one-minute test. An assistant brought out "the world's largest stop watch," to time the immersion. Houdini invited the audience to test its own ability to hold its breath, beginning the moment that his head disappeared under the water line of the can.

Houdini then stepped into the can feetfirst and slithered his way through the narrow opening into the can. Water splashed over the sides. The audience

Inside the can. *Library of Congress*

gasped, as if Houdini had already performed something wonderful. With Houdini's head still visible, his assistants refilled the tank up to the brim. Houdini waved and then submerged himself. As he disappeared from view, the entire audience began to hold its breath. The auditorium was completely silent. After thirty seconds, most of the crowd was gasping for air. At the end of a minute, one of the assistants would kick the can, a signal for Houdini to reemerge, looking none the worse for wear. The audience gave him an ovation.

Now the real work began. He crouched back down into the can and additional water was used to fill it. Then the lid of the can was quickly secured by six padlocks, and the cabinet was put in place. The orchestra broke into a popular song, and many in the audience mouthed the lyrics: "Many brave hearts lie asleep in the deep. Sailor, beware; sailor, take care."

The giant stopwatch chronicled the passing of the seconds. After it reached ninety, a worried Franz Kukol appeared carrying a fire ax. He briskly walked to the enclosure and put his ear to the cloth. His hand tensed around the ax handle. By two minutes, the tension in the theater was almost unbearable. When the watch had ticked off three minutes, there were cries of concern in the crowd. Kukol raised the ax and was about to throw the curtain open and attack the metal, when suddenly a dripping-wet Houdini threw open the curtain and basked in the sheer adulation of the crowd. In the background, the assistants drained the tank of its contents, showing the audience that the water had indeed remained inside the can.

Houdini's water can escape was so stunning that it refreshed the debate over his methods. There were even some Spiritualists maintaining that Houdini succeeded through some miraculous psychic power. He seemed willing to blur the line. If an interviewer didn't broach the subject, Houdini would often gratuitously inject the word "supernatural" for him. Of course he would also invariably deny such powers, but it's possible that he was using the word to plant the suggestion that this was indeed a possibility. Being the master showman that he was, he understood that if you mention something and then deny it, the denial is often overlooked or forgotten. When one is asked to forget something specific, it's this very thing that stands out in the mind and therefore the most difficult to forget.

When he allowed his name and image to be used in an advertisement in a Providence newspaper in 1907, the artist created an image of Houdini dematerializing and escaping in a shroud of smoke from a packing case. One might assume he would have objected and refused to let the image be printed but, to the contrary, he kept this image of himself as a supernatural being and used it for years to come in his own advertising. That same year, Boston audiences marveled at his escape from a thin, fragile paper bag. How could he make his way out leaving the bag, the cord, and the knots that sealed the neck of the bag intact? This was fundamentally different than the majority of his other escapes. It was not imprisonment; anyone could escape, but not without destroying the paper bag or envelope. Clearly keys or picks would be no help; he had another secret. In 1914, Houdini used the phrase "a feat which borders on the supernatural" in advertising another of his miraculous escapes. Later, he went so far as to

An alternative explanation for Houdini's escape. *From the collection of George and Sandy Daily*

supply various prepackaged stories that papers could run verbatim, using their own byline. More than one proclaims that "he is credited with the power of dematerialization. But he maintains a mysterious silence." From his earliest days, Houdini knew he would be dogged with questions about how he effected his escapes. In response, he created a brilliant strategy where he would deny that he had supernatural powers but suggest that he had one secret that explained everything he did. The master, of course, didn't have one secret; he had hundreds. When he claimed one thing could explain all his powers, it made him even more intriguing and mysterious.

Houdini was thrilled with the reception of his new escape. "The new Can trick is the best that I have ever invented. . . . It's a fine-looking trick, and almost defies detection," he told Waitt. Both in the United States and later in Europe, audiences were mystified by his escape, but for as long as he performed it,

Houdini could never come up with a catchy name for the effect. By May, Houdini was so desperate he advertised a reward of $25 to anyone who could suggest a proper name for "this mystery." With entries like "The Genii of the Can" and "The Ali Baba Can of Mystery," the reward money went unclaimed.

Climbing past the first story was fairly easy. The bricks were large, and he could get a good grip on the mortar between each stone. Once Houdini was twenty feet in the air, his task got a little more difficult. The balcony railing helped. He hoisted himself up to it and took a break. On the street below him, some bewildered passersby paused to peer at him, but others didn't even break their stride. While climbing up the sides of buildings using only hands and feet wasn't an everyday occurrence, there were enough "human flies" around that the average jaded New Yorker might not even notice one. That is until they fell off the building and splattered on the ground, which was the fate of Harry F. Young, "The Human Fly," who fell twenty stories from the edifice of the Hotel Martinique to his death in 1925. Then again, Houdini wasn't one to dwell on the danger. What was occupying his mind was the task at hand.

When he was about four feet from the third story, Bess stuck her head out of the window and, when she saw him, screamed. She was a bundle of nerves for the next few seconds until he had safely climbed through the window and presented her with the red roses he had carried in his teeth, roses that marked their fourteenth wedding anniversary.

It's a telling story, an exquisitely accurate representation of their relationship. Houdini the adventurous, romantic, swashbuckling daredevil. Bess the anxious, fragile worrywart. By June of 1908, they had spent fourteen years together and there was still a spark between them that could inspire such extravagant gestures. Or perhaps it speaks more to Houdini's inability to relinquish center stage. At any rate, it had not been a good year for Bess. She had been spending less time on the road with Houdini, due to a variety of illnesses, which usually got diagnosed as nervous exhaustion. Touring had taken its toll on her, and with the introduction of the water can escape, the Metamorphosis had faded from the act. Now her time was spent in making sure that Harry remembered to change his underwear.

In March, Bess was still sick. "Mrs. Has not been well of late, and she needs a rest," Houdini wrote Waitt. By the middle of April, a friend inquired whether Bess had recovered enough to be back on the road with Harry. Life on the road was never easy with Bess. She had long-standing superstitions that were abnormal even by eccentric performers' standards. If she learned that someone had whistled in a dressing room, no matter how many years had elapsed since that event, she would never enter that room, convinced that it was still under an evil spell. You could never find her wearing anything yellow. After Houdini had a hard time with an escape in Burnley, England, in 1902, Bess stormed into her dressing room and pulled off a pair of new yellow tights that she had worn for the first time. Enraged, she ripped the tights to shreds, convinced that they had hoodooed her husband.

Although Houdini seemed almost browbeaten by Bess's wild mood swings in some of his surviving notes to her, his personality certainly exacerbated some of her difficulties. At the end of 1909, Houdini's close friend Roterberg candidly wrote, "You refer to the fact that Bess is in much better health. You can always do her health good by bothering her as little as possible. Don't come in like a whirlwind and tear off a lot of talk, but take it easy when you speak to her. She is a bundle of nerves and not strong at that. Anytime that anything gets on her nerves, she does herslef [sic] a certain lot of harm. In other words be as restful as pssible [sic] while with her and you will do her a world of good. If after that you fell [sic] like going out and tearing around in your usual fashion[,] all well and good as long as she is not implicated. Seee [sic] my point?"

For the rest of the spring 1908 season, Houdini toured the United States doing his water can and straitjacket escapes and throwing in a local challenge or two to help drum up business. One of the challenges he accepted was from the Weed Tire Company, which was anxious to promote its new snow chains for auto tires. On a New York stage in April, Houdini allowed the Weed representatives to enmesh him in a series of Weed chains, looping the chains around his head, legs, and arms and then locking them together. He was then bound and chained into two steel-rimmed auto tires. Several minutes into his escape, Houdini cried for help. When Kukol drew back the curtain of Houdini's cabinet, he found that Houdini had turned blue from the tight chain that was cutting into his throat. The chains were moved down and Houdini finally released himself, but he was so drained that he couldn't deliver his customary victory speech, and he "reeled" off the stage assisted by Franz.

Houdini laid off that summer (and even induced Bess to venture into the ocean for a swim for the first time since 1894), but he certainly kept busy. He was still publishing his monthly magazine and preparing his Robert-Houdin book for publication, but he was also butting heads with the editor of the largest magic magazine and making preparations to seize the leadership of the most important magical society in the world. Houdini's vicious feud with Dr. A. M.

Snow tires were almost a match for the escape artist. *Conjuring Arts Research Center*

Wilson, the former magician-turned-minister-turned-MD, began when Wilson ran a small item by Midwestern magician Harry Helms that claimed that the Western Vaudeville Association had recently changed their policy and was now relegating all handcuff acts to their dime houses.

Seeing this as a personal attack on him, Houdini responded with a vicious editorial that compared Wilson with a "dog in a manger." In the next issue of *The Sphinx*, Wilson struck back. "Houdini is yet a young man with much to learn. I am sorry for him, for money has become his god and self-conceit has caused him to idolize himself." With the pledge to his father ringing in his ears, Houdini responded: "Houdini may be devoting all his waking hours and laboring far into the night to earn his salary, but this is because he hopes that in his old age he will have enough laid aside to support himself and those dependent upon him, without preying upon his profession and the public by perverting so-called news items into financial gain."

It only got worse. Wilson told other magicians that Houdini was calling him an "SOB" and saying that the former minister had a " little black book" crammed with the phone numbers of three hundred married women with whom he was "holding criminal relations as an adulterer and fornicator." Irate, Wilson wrote Houdini on May 20: "I cannot understand why you go about the country saying such disagreeable things about me and mine. . . . Has success intoxicated you to the extent that you believe you have the sole right to do a handcuff act or publish a paper for magicians? . . . you know, as well as I, that you could not get out of the commonest county jail, the most ordinary pair of handcuffs, or the flimsiest made dry-goods box if you were divested completely of all the keys, fakes, and other appliances that you use. . . . you can persist in your infamous attacks on my character and your slurs on *The Sphinx* so long as it pleases you so to do and I will say no more, for you are that type of Jew that has made the noble Hebrew race—God's chosen people—an execration in every country on the globe."

Wilson started working behind the scenes to poison Houdini's plan to have *Conjurer's Monthly* made the official organ of the Society of American Magicians. Houdini had already polarized some members of the SAM with his attacks on Robert-Houdin, so when Houdini did ask for the status of official organ for his magazine, "not one stood up for me" at the "stormy" meeting, he wrote in his diary. The lack of support hurt him. "You mention that certain people state that I do all my good work for the advertisements I may obtain out of it," he had written Oscar Teale, an éminence grise in the magic world, in November of 1906. "I know in my *heart of hearts* that whatever good deeds I do is simply to help along people and poor unfortunates that I may meet in my life's journey. I could tell you of the dozens of performers I have helped and of whom you have never heard a word. I have spent hundreds of dollars sending the poor stranded professional home. In fact, I was looked upon as easy prey, but all that did not stop me from helping my fellowman [sic] along, even when I knew I was getting bested. Do you know that in my hardship days I *never* borrowed a single dollar!!!!!!!!!"

Yet Houdini had a personal charisma that was undeniable and mesmerizing, and after spending some time in his company, his detractors were often charmed into becoming supporters. This happened to A. G. Waring. Thinking Houdini was a "knocker" so that he might better "blow his own horn," he met him at Teale's office in June of 1908 and came away feeling "toward him as a brother." Waring even pledged to fight behind the scenes to make Houdini's magazine the official SAM organ.

At the same "stormy" meeting of the SAM on June 6, Houdini had been elected vice president of the society. Stung by the failure to stand by his magazine and by not being mentioned by name in the SAM yearbook as the "member" who had bought the neglected cemetery plot of the great Italian conjurer Bosco and deeded it gratis to the SAM, Houdini resigned from the group on

July 6. On August 15, three days before he would sail to Europe to fulfill his old contracts, he suspended publication of his own magazine.

Houdini was planning some other changes too. Finally, after years of indecision, he followed through on his threat to give up handcuff challenges. By now handcuff kings were a dime a dozen, and Houdini had raised the bar by performing the truly life-threatening Milk Can escape, his bridge jumps, and his myriad challenges. Those would definitively separate the men from the boys in the escape world.

Houdini showed his disdain for the whole handcuff field by exposing his own methods onstage. On April 27, 1908, on the stage of Boston's Keith's Theatre, he took a pair of handcuffs that were alleged to be particularly strong and began rapping them against a chair. In less time than it takes to tell this, the newspaper reporter noted, the cuffs were open. By August, Houdini felt that he might as well be making some money off his imitators, and he decided to put the "Defiance Handcuff Act as Presented by the World-Famous Harry Houdini, King of Handcuffs" on the market. In the September issues of various magic magazines, both in the United States and in England, August Roterberg, Houdini's close friend, took out a full-page ad guaranteeing that with the "Splendid Instructions and Descriptive Matter" that came with the "outfit," "any person will be able to free himself in a few seconds from any handcuffs, leg irons, etc, furnished by strangers."

Houdini also left the country in the capable hands of one of his protégés, The Great Leonard, aka Harry Leonard, aka Leonard Hicks. Hicks had seen Houdini as a kid in Richmond, Virginia, in 1900. Six years later, Hicks was working as a desk clerk at a Chicago hotel when Houdini came in to switch hotels, because Bess hated their current accommodations. Hicks gave Houdini a beautiful room with its own bath, and in return, Houdini invited the young man to his shows. His stay was extended, and when it was finally time to leave, Houdini suggested that Hicks give show business a try. The desk clerk was speechless.

"I think you'd better," Houdini said. "You've watched too much of my work, and you're the first man not working with me who caught on. You're too dangerous to have running around loose."

Hicks moved in with the Houdinis that summer and apprenticed. He even had cards made up that read "Harry Leonard presenting the famous Houdini act by permission of Harry Houdini" and listed Houdini's Harlem address. He did handcuff escapes, the Metamorphosis, and right after Houdini left the States for Europe in August of 1908, he began doing the water can.

Houdini opened with the Circus Busch in Berlin on August 31, and the audience was littered with would-be handcuff kings who were aching for a dollop of free advertising by challenging Houdini. They went home disappointed, cuffs in tow, when Houdini debuted the water can in Europe and escaped from a straitjacket. By now, Houdini was really selling his straitjacket escape. "His contortions, while rolling about the stage, were wonderful to look upon, and this worked the spectators up to a pitch of excitement bordering on hysteria," one reporter noted.

With his new difficult escapes, Houdini may have succeeded in warding off competitors, but the day-in and day-out extreme exertion took its toll. "The act I am now doing—first the straitjacket, then the can—is the hardest on my body that I have ever attempted," he wrote that September. And that was just onstage. When he wasn't performing, he spent his time doing outdoor bridge jumps, escaping from jails, trolling for new books to add to his collection, and meeting with old magicians. As well as doing some intelligence gathering for Melville again.

The entire valley was filled with galloping horses, as far as the eye could see. And on each steed, a rider wearing a breastplate and a steel helmet, chanting in unison as his upright lance refracted the last rays of the sun. Suddenly, the galloping horses came to a halt. And from a clearing due south, a small contingent, led by a sword-waving dashing figure wearing a silver helmet that was the perch for an equally silver eagle, came to greet them. The large group, Cavalry Division A, had just completed a fifty-mile march, the longest of these military maneuvers. They were being personally greeted by German Kaiser Wilhelm II, who rode a magnificent white steed. The cavalry commander and the kaiser's retinue exchanged formal greetings, but soon the formalities had been dropped and even the kaiser could be seen eating a sandwich and drinking a good German beer, still in the saddle.

Every year in September, the kaiser convened these four-day mock war games and invited military leaders from the world over to view the splendor of the mighty German army, the world's largest, which numbered 605,000 men. The United States was represented by both Colonel John P. Wisser, who was the military attaché stationed in Berlin, and by Major General Leonard S. Wood, who came from America as the kaiser's guest. This year the "kaiser's manoeuvres" were taking place in the strategically important Alsace-Lorraine area, so there were no official French or English guests. Perhaps that was also the reason why every modern warfare appliance was on display, except for dirigible balloons. The German high command had determined that they were still in too incomplete a state of development to allow them to be seen by the eyes of the world in mock warfare.

By September 2, the kaiser was back in Berlin for the glittery annual military spectacle of the review of the guards at Tempelhof Field. In all likelihood, Houdini was in the crowd, watching the procession before working at Circus Busch that night. And back in England, William Melville, who had "retired" from Scotland Yard in November of 1903, was covertly working as a "Mr. Morgan" for a new branch of British intelligence called MO-5 (which would eventually become MI-5). More than ever convinced that Germany would be England's next great foe, he reached out to Houdini again. On September 15, he noted in his diary, *No word yet from HH.*

There was a lot for Houdini to report on. One area of particular interest was heavier-than-air flying machines. Houdini took sharp notice of German progress in this area, writing back to his inventor friend Montraville M. Wood that the country was going crazy on flying machines. In addition to that, Houdini was making contact at the highest levels of the German royal family. In early October, he visited the hunting lodge of Prince Friedrich Leopold von Preussen. Leopold was a first cousin to the kaiser and the richest prince in Germany. On October 9, Houdini gave a private performance for Leopold and his invited guests in the castle of Klein-Glienecke. According to Houdini's diary, he did card tricks, the needles, and finished with the water [milk] can effect. "They had a pair of their handcuffs at the palace, and I beat them easily." He also mesmerized the young princes when he took their silk handkerchiefs and did some magic with them. For his efforts, he received a pin and a nice letter of commendation from his old nemesis Count von Schwerin, who was by then a high-ranking military official. In November, Houdini was back in England for yet another tour.

It was pitch black, that rare type of purple darkness that induced sudden panic because there was absolutely no difference whether one's eyes were open or closed. The cramped space was too short for a person to stand erect and too narrow to sit comfortably. Inside the enclosure, the air was thin, hot, and stagnant with the odors of sweat and fear. It was frightening to imagine the vast depth this darkness could contain, but reaching out just an inch and touching a wall would instantly prompt a spine-tingling chill. Even a coffin would have been more comfortable.

Somewhere in the distance, an orchestra was playing, the music punctuated by cries and shouts of desperation, but the eight-inch-thick steel walls were lulling the outside world and its harsh noise into an amorphous amalgam—a muffled hymn. What was distinct was the rhythmic melody of short, desperate gasps of breath. Perhaps last breaths.

His hands were impervious to the darkness. As if by second nature, they skimmed the cool metal walls and zeroed in on the bulky mechanism. First the scraping sound of metal on metal, then the first welcome *click*. He listened for the specific order of sounds—a second *click*, more scraping, *click*, *click*, and then *whump*. The deep thunderous tone was like a prison door closing, but to Houdini, it was precisely the opposite.

In December of 1908, Houdini appeared at the Euston Palace of Varieties Theatre in London, a beautiful building that lived up to its name. On Friday night, December 4, he accepted a challenge from J. R. Paul, a locksmith and safe expert, who defied Houdini to escape from a safe that he would bring to the theater. Houdini accepted the challenge with the proviso that the safe be brought to the Euston earlier that day.

On the night of the challenge, Houdini was locked into the safe and then a screen was placed in front of the vault to obscure the audience's view. According to Houdini's own account, he escaped from the safe in "fourteen minutes." However, he didn't throw down the screen and triumphantly appear in front of the audience for another half an hour. One explanation is that such challenges gave Houdini both the opportunity and an alibi to conduct a mission while he was performing. We know that Melville used other magicians as operatives to do similar jobs.

This same year, Houdini stole blueprints in London. Houdini's friend Will Goldston, the London-based magic dealer, wrote a series of articles in 1935 for *The Sunday Express* called "Men Who Made Magic." In his article on Houdini, Goldston recounts an interesting anecdote. In 1908, Goldston had been feuding with John Neville Maskelyne, England's most famous magician, after Maskelyne had double-crossed the magic dealer by breaking an agreement and testifying for a German who was suing Goldston. When Houdini came to England, Goldston filled him in on the details of Maskelyne's betrayal. Since Houdini never cared much for the English magician, he sympathized with his friend. While they were in Goldston's office, a third magician came in and told them of a new illusion named the Levitated Fakir that Maskelyne was working on in complete secrecy.

"How's it done?" Houdini asked.

"I don't know," the third man said. "I'd like to."

Houdini could even escape from safes. *From the collection of John Cox*

"So would I," Goldston said.

"So you shall," Houdini smiled enigmatically.

The next morning, Houdini walked into Goldston's office and threw a large envelope on the dealer's desk.

"There you are, Will," he said. "The complete plans of Johnny's 'Fakir.'"

Goldston was astonished. He asked Houdini how on Earth he could have obtained the blueprints, especially from someone as security-conscious as Maskelyne, but Houdini just smiled "feebly" and refused to answer.

"To this day I do not know how he came into possession of these prints," Goldston wrote. "I do know, however, that he never went to bed the previous night! Whatever his methods, they were those of a master-mind."

On New Year's Day, 1909, Houdini, now the most famous vaudeville entertainer in Europe, played his three turns at the Paragon Theatre in London and then returned to his boardinghouse. "The poor old deaf landlady had a very bad meal. Went to bed after eating an apple and whatever was fit to eat left from tea," Houdini wrote in his diary. That the material trappings of success were of no interest to Houdini is obvious, but Houdini's seemingly complete lack of concern with creature comforts is still noteworthy. Later that year, his friend Roterberg would once again chide him for this. "I am always glad to hear that you are making good although you dont need the money. Because when the time comes, you won't know what to do with it. You know less about enjoying things than you should know. . . . But that is an old subject on which you and I will never agree. In occult parlance they would call you a Rajah Yogi because your pleasure lies in making the money and not in the spending of it."

Roterberg was wrong. Staying at a great hotel or traveling first-class meant nothing to Houdini, but he derived great pleasure in his various collections and when it came to them, Houdini spared no expense. In 1909, he began to direct his collecting zeal in an additional area, art, buying up paintings, etchings, and prints. In a crash course to educate himself, he began to visit museums and galleries daily. Soon he was snatching up Hogarth engravings and bidding one thousand francs for a Van Ostade painting.

Houdini's newfound passion became a source of friction between him and Bess. After they argued in a taxicab late one night, Houdini responded by leaving the house early the next day, visiting an old magician, bidding on more paintings at an auction, and buying Bess a solid silver case for her handbag to placate her. He wrote the cost of the case in cipher in his diary, which suggests that Bess routinely read his entries.

Meanwhile, he was beginning to be confronted by a new rash of imitators. In Germany, both men and women began to perform Houdini's handcuffed bridge jumps. Houdini's response was to train a female German championship diver in both the bridge jumps and the can escape, but it seems that Houdini never had to actually employ her since his original female imitator quickly faded from the scene. By 1909, imitators began replicating his water can. In America, a German woman named Minerva, who dubbed herself "the Original Woman Jailbreaker and Handcuff Queen," introduced her "newest sensation—the Death-Defying Water Escape from an Airtight Locked Barrel filled to the brim with water." She even advertised herself as "more wonderful and mystifying than Houdini." Years before, a female imitator had the gall to call herself "Miss Lincoln Houdini," with the word Houdini being triple the size of Lincoln.

Houdini was also being imitated by John Clempert, a former wrestler who had achieved some renown for his act, "The Man They Could Not Hang." Unfortunately, one night, when Clempert's noose slipped, they could. Clempert dangled from the rope unconscious for a full two minutes before his assistant realized something was amiss. Recuperating in a hospital bed, he dreamed up a new persona—the "Handcuff and Siberian Gaol Breaker." Clempert began to feature many of Houdini's escapes and even embellished the water can escape by combining it with the Metamorphosis. In his version, two cans were onstage, one full, and one empty. He went into the full one; his assistant went into the empty one. After a minute and a half, he escaped, but when he opened the filled can, it contained his assistant.

Noting that Clempert was known as "the man they could not hang," a friend of Houdini wrote, "Perhaps this is a pity, for when one man gets work on another's reputation and has the impudence to rub the fact home by exposing the methods of the originator, words are useless." Lawyers weren't. After instituting a suit, Houdini seemed to have settled the case out of court. Clempert "held up a flag of truce," Houdini wrote Goldston. "He has promised never to use my name in such a malicious manner and I believe he really means it."

Minerva and Clempert weren't exceptional cases. A French performer named Steens imitated everything Houdini did, down to his advertising. Houdini's escalation of his escapes from simply defeating handcuffs (or even jailbreaking) to cuffed bridge jumps and the water can escape had served to slightly winnow down the population of imitators. And with good reason. A man named Alburtus had attempted a straitjacket escape in the ocean at Atlantic City on a freezing day in January. The ocean was too violent so he went to the bay, dove in, and struggled to free himself. After going down twice, he finally surfaced free of his restraint. Unfortunately, he was unconscious by then and had to be saved by lifeguards moments before he would have drowned. A would-be escapologist named Menkis was fished out of the water unconscious after he dove in manacled. And in April 1909, a handcuff king named Ricardo jumped off the Luitpold Bridge in Landshut, Bavaria. He couldn't escape from his restraints and he drowned.

"I was honestly sorry to hear of Ricardos [sic] death," Houdini told *The London Umpire* on July 25, 1909. "People who attempt these feats ought to know before exactly what they are doing. I don't mind entering into competition with any man, for competition is healthy, but I do kick when they steal my act, do it badly, and then make a great shout. The fact that they are bad stealers is inclined to have an injurious effect on my show, because the people are prone to put all acts of a particular kind in the same basket."

In a fascinating footnote to the story, years later, an escape artist named Rex Palmer Gordon claimed to have been hired by Houdini to fail in his jump off the Luitpold Bridge—as Ricardo. "Joined Harry Houdini and as Rex Ricardo, jumped off the Leopold [sic] Bridge Barvia [sic]. This was done on a Friday. I was fished out unconscious. The Wife finished the week . . . HH came in on the Monday, did the job on Tuesday, with the usual success." Houdini's creativity in framing challenges, and in creating and then defeating his own competition, was brilliant.

Houdini was never rash and reckless when it came to stunts in which he faced the possibility of death, always maintaining that the only successful wizards were safety-first wizards. Still, he was performing escapes both on and off the stage that *did* carry the possibility of death, even if he *had* taken sufficient precautions to work the odds heavily in his favor. On June 17, 1908, Houdini, heavily manacled, dove off Young's Pier at Atlantic City, New Jersey, before a crowd of more than twenty thousand. He usually jumped feetfirst into waters that he was unfamiliar with, but on this day, he decided to dive, despite being warned against that by the lifeguards. He knifed through the water perfectly but then struck his head on the bottom of the ocean floor. Dazed and bleeding, he somehow managed to remove his handcuffs.

During his run at the Euston Palace of Varieties in London, he accepted a challenge from a local dairy to escape from one of their milk churns. Although it was a huge churn, Houdini was cramped inside it, and the airholes that had been drilled were insufficient. "I realized that in my efforts to escape I was exhausting the available oxygen," Houdini remembered. "It was useless to shout for help, as my cries would not be heard. . . . I rocked the churn back and forth, but could not escape. . . . Suddenly, in my thrashing, I overturned the churn, and it fell on the stage.

"The cover was held down by clamps, and as luck would have it, the churn fell so that one of the clamps struck the floor, and the blow dislodged it. The cover came loose, and I pushed it off. The air rushed in."

In 1909 alone Houdini had serious difficulties escaping from a wet sheet challenge, injured his wrists severely when he was hung from chains, and "all but choked to death" from the pressure of a leather collar when his bed slipped from position during a challenge to escape from a "crazy crib" restraint used on lunatics. And at the end of the year, Houdini had to undergo an operation to lance an infected boil on his derriere that had been worsened by the constant pressure from one of the straps on his straitjacket.

Besides the risks, Houdini was now running into resistance from local authorities, who were loath to allow him to perform some of his outdoor stunts.

Clempert the Siberian copycat. *New York Pubic Library*

Steens replicates another Houdini poster. *From the collection of George and Sandy Daily*

Early in November 1908, Houdini was set to leap from Westminster Bridge in London while both handcuffed and straitjacketed, but the chief commissioner of police refused to give permission for the attempt, fearing that the huge crowd would block traffic. Houdini was threatened with imprisonment if he went ahead without official sanction.

The following April, Houdini did just that in Paris. The newspaper report was wonderful and read:

> *The many idlers who were basking in the sunshine close to the river noticed an automobile pull up at the Morgue. A man clad in the briefest of bathing costumes descended, to the wonderment of the spectators. Two fellow-passengers gripped the scantily-clad man, secured his wrists with handcuffs and bound his arms tightly. The crowd, believing it had to do with a band of lunatics, shouted for police assistance.*
>
> *Four policemen, who had been dozing on duty at the side of Notre Dame, suddenly woke up and ran towards the wildly gesticulating crowd. In the meantime the principal lunatic, by the aid of a ladder, had climbed to the roof of the Morgue. He stood there for a moment with his enchained hands held above his head, while the four policemen below looked helplessly on: Come down, said one policeman, coaxingly. The man's reply was to plunge headlong into the river. He is gone without a doubt, was the general comment of the spectators of the incident.*
>
> *There was an immediate rush to the bank. Two working men and a policeman flung off their coats and plunged in, hoping to save the madman when he came to the surface. He appeared presently with his arms freed from the chains, and before the police could reach him was rescued by a boat which put out from the opposite bank. On reaching shore he jumped into the motor, and was driven on.*
>
> *The police, however, discovered Houdini's identity, and he is said to be prosecuted for being improperly dressed and for bathing in the Seine during prohibited hours.*

What the paper didn't report was that Houdini had hired a film crew to film the entire episode. By June, Houdini had incorporated the films into his turn and had choreographed his act to perfection. When it was time for his performance, the house lights were dimmed and two short films were shown, one of his Rochester bridge jump, the other his dive into the Seine. Then the lights came up, the curtain slowly rose, revealing a shiny zinc water can surrounded by several pails, all guarded by three imposing-looking uniformed assistants standing at attention. As the drama intensified, without even a word being spoken, Houdini strode onto the stage to a standing ovation.

After two solid weeks, the high winds had finally died down, and the mechanic, a small, stout Frenchman named Brassac, had cleared the plane to attempt a takeoff. The German army officers made their last inspection of the Voisin biplane—one of the few Voisins in the world. Reportedly, there were only a couple dozen aviators in the world at the time, so this was an excellent opportunity for the German regiment stationed at the Hufaren parade grounds in Wandsbek, a small town outside of Hamburg, to learn the rudiments of aviation, a technology that the military knew would be an essential component of future warfare.

The Voisin was an interesting-looking aircraft. It resembled a big box kite, thirty-three feet long by about six feet broad with four vertical panels, dividing the main surface into four large cells. Its wingspan was nearly thirty-three feet. The rudder was off to the rear of the plane, nested in a six-foot-square box-shaped tail, connected to the plane by four outriggers. This particular Voisin had been souped up with a state-of-the-art E.N.V. 60–80 horsepower engine, and it had a steel-shafted single aluminum eight-foot propeller that was capable of 1200 revolutions per minute. There were no ailerons on the craft since the Wright Brothers had patented those devices, so the rudder functioned both to stabilize as well as steer the aircraft.

The pilot settled in the cockpit and adjusted his goggles. His cap was worn backwards, the style of all aviators at that time. Brassac spun the propeller and the engine started. All was set. Smoothly the plane taxied for a bit on the ground and then lifted up into the air. The German soldiers cheered lustily. Suddenly, after just a few seconds in the air, the plane nose-dived and plummeted to the ground.

Brassac and some of the soldiers rushed to the wreckage. The front end of the plane had taken most of the impact, not a good omen for the pilot. Ironically enough, the rear panels that surrounded the rudder were totally intact, as were the side canvas panels, both of which were emblazoned with large letters that spelled "HOUDINI."

13

Above the Down Under

HOUDINI WALKED AWAY FROM HIS FIRST flying mishap with his dignity more injured than anything else. Although he would write in his diary, "I smashed the machine. Broke Propeller all to hell," the plane itself and, most important, the engine, had sustained little damage. A new propeller was ordered from Paris and arrived in two weeks. Houdini counted the days until he could once again attempt his first successful flight.

His interest in the nascent field of aviation had become almost an obsession. In 1903, just six years before Houdini purchased his plane, Orville Wright had achieved the first sustained, controlled flight in a heavier-than-air, powered aircraft. It took another three years until that feat was duplicated in Europe by Houdini's acquaintance Alberto Santos-Dumont, flying 722 feet in Paris. By 1908, Houdini already saw the possibility of incorporating the airplane into one of his spectacular outdoor stunts. He told a London reporter that he offered $5,000 for the use of one of the early Wright Brothers' planes. His plan was to be handcuffed and flown over London, where he would parachute from the plane, escape from the manacles on the way down, and land safely in Piccadilly Circus. The scheme was scrapped when no safe way to parachute from the aircraft could be devised.

By 1909, great strides were being made in aviation. Houdini was in London on July 25, when a Frenchman named Louis Blériot became the first man to fly across the English Channel by airplane. He had been taught to fly by Houdini's future engineer, Antonio Brassac, who also designed the monoplane that made the trip from Calais to Dover Castle in thirty-six and a half minutes. For his efforts he received a $5,000 prize, just one of many offered by Houdini's friend

Houdini over Hamburg. *From the collection of Kenneth M. Trombly*

Alfred Charles Harmsworth, who now owned and used the title Lord Northcliffe. Northcliffe's interest in aviation had grown proportionately to his wealth and power. A few weeks later, Houdini, along with a half-million other cheering spectators, attended the weeklong First International Air Meet in Reims, France. It was the social event of the year as royalty, government officials, military experts, and the crème de la crème of European society watched the daredevil fliers pilot their odd-looking flying machines.

Houdini was transfixed watching, as he would later describe it, "the aeroplanes floated about the sky like albatross soaring above some floating food." He was immediately determined to buy one but uncertain of which type. Looking down the list of events, he saw a mechanic's race listed, and deducing that they were certainly in the know, he watched carefully as Antonio Brassac piloted a plane owned by a man named Rougier to first place. That plane, a Voisin, attracted Houdini's interest. He had been set to buy a Curtiss biplane, which had won the speed race, but it didn't appear to be as safe as the Voisin. "I remembered I was but a timid bird, and I wanted to take no chances at the start," Houdini recalled.

At the same time, Houdini was designing his own aircraft. He had sent Montraville M. Wood, one of the mechanical geniuses who labored behind the scenes for Houdini, schematics for a small airplane, but Wood could not get it to work. Wood was more optimistic about a larger plane that he was testing and was grateful to get clippings and news reports about the latest in flying machine technology from Houdini in Europe.

In November, Houdini, who was playing in Hamburg, attended the opening day of Aviation Week and watched as a French mechanic named Pequet flew a Voisin airplane. While he was soaring high in the sky, flames started shooting off his plane, and seconds later, his benzine tank exploded. Pequet began to glide down to Earth, but when he was still twenty feet from the ground, he was forced to leap from his craft as the flames threatened to envelop him. He suffered minor injuries to his chest from the fall. Still, Houdini was impressed. "That machine is mine," he thought.

A few days later, it was. Houdini had located an exact replica of Pequet's biplane, perhaps even the very craft he had seen at Reims. It was built by the Voisin Brothers. Houdini paid $5,000 for it and then ponied up a bit extra to import Antonio Brassac, who was so attached to the plane that he had "sobbed like baby" on the news that it had been sold to Houdini. With Brassac on hand to assemble the machine and to instruct the fledging pilot, Houdini was poised to become the twenty-fifth man to conquer the air in a powered craft.

First, he had to find a place to fly. There were few airports then, so Houdini entered into an arrangement with the commander of the German army troops at Wandsbek, near Hamburg. In exchange for using the Hufaren parade grounds as an airfield, Houdini would instruct the German soldiers in the mysteries of flight. And for six hundred and fifty marks, Houdini could rent a shed to serve as a hangar for his Voisin.

Now all he needed was for the weather to cooperate. Brassac was bizarrely maternal toward his craft, and he was loath to have Houdini attempt to fly if there were any traces of wind. For the first few weeks, they experienced stormy German winter weather, and Houdini was forced to sit behind the wheel with the plane in the shed, familiarizing himself with the fairly simple controls. When the steering wheel was pushed forward, the plane would ascend; pulled back, it would descend. The rudder was controlled by a foot pedal. There was also a choke to the side of the steering wheel that controlled the engine.

On the first windless morning, Houdini had his accident. After the new propeller arrived and the weather cooperated, Houdini tried again. On November 26, 1909 the magician made a successful flight over the parade grounds, witnessed by fewer than fifty people. He didn't stay aloft too long, but it was long enough for photographers to record the event. Houdini duly dispatched pictures of the flight and of him in the plane, surrounded by German soldiers, to publications around the world. Three days later, he took out a $25,000 life insurance policy with the Albingia Company of Hamburg. On the back of the policy, Houdini recorded, "This is the first insurance ever taken out re accident in an aeroplane. I had to pay 10 marks (about 25 cents) every time I made a flight."

It was a sensible move. Flying was very dangerous then. On September 7, a few weeks after the Reims show, the French pilot Eugene Lefebvre crashed his Wright Model A and earned the unenviable distinction of being the first pilot of a powered aircraft to die while flying. A little over a month later, at the same airfield in France, a student pilot named Richet turned his Voisin completely over and fell sixty feet to the ground. The plane was totaled and Richet was lucky to only break a thigh and have one of his eyes gouged out.

Besides being diverting entertainment for high society, whose members flocked to the air shows to see the young daredevils take their lives in their hands, controlled, powered flight in an airship had profound implications for the future of warfare.

The emergence of smaller aircraft made the reliance on massive balloons for military applications obsolete. By 1909, a Wright Model A or a Voisin was capable of sustained flights long enough to produce aerial surveillance. A few years later, pilots were able to accurately drop explosives on targets, giving planes offensive capabilities in conflicts.

Houdini's friend Lord Northcliffe had been interested in aeronautics and aviation since 1889 and was convinced that aviation would play a major role in the next world conflict. In February of 1909, he traveled to France to see the Wright Brothers exhibit their flying machine. Appalled at England's failure to send military representatives, he wrote his friend Lord Haldane, who was Britain's secretary of state for war, decrying the fact that the British government was lagging in aviation research and development.

The correspondence continued for months; sensing a bureaucratic logjam, Northcliffe began to take his own measures to influence public opinion and force a sense of urgency on his government, the most ingenious of these being large cash incentives, through his newspapers, for completed flights. When he paid £1,000 to the French aviator Blériot for winning a contest for the first pilot to fly from France to England, it was a masterful way to further his agenda. The ensuing publicity created a storm of controversy about how vulnerable England was to an air attack from a neighboring country.

By 1916, Northcliffe had paid out over $95,000 in such prizes. (In the United States, newspapers followed his lead and also offered prize money for flights.) He also traveled extensively in Germany and France, reporting back to the war secretary on the state of aviation progress.

As 1910 approached, Northcliffe was faced with a large dilemma—how to help mold public opinion favorably to support aerial exploration and research. One way to accomplish that would be by encouraging the world's most famous daredevil to fly his own biplane with his name emblazoned on it.

Tonight was the Malwa's gala costume ball and Houdini, in his crumpled formal suit, was feeling a little bit out of place. Of course, he didn't dare disappoint Bess, who had been so excited about the event that she had spent hours working on her costume. She was dressed as a fairy queen. In fact, Harry had dutifully donned his evening clothes most every night of their journey and escorted Bess to the ballroom so she could dance. Tonight was no exception. She had been dancing up a storm most of the night with the captain of the ship, and now she had come back to their table to refill her champagne glass. The next thing Houdini knew, his wife had passed out, tumbling to the floor. He sprang to his feet, picked her up, and carried her straight out of the ballroom to bed.

Houdini downplayed the incident in his diary. "Bess fainted near me," he wrote. "I picked her up and took her to bed. First time she ever did such a thing. Think she has overexcited herself working on clothes, and she danced with the Captain, who danced only one way." Houdini may have been in denial about Bess's drinking or he may have had an eye on posterity as he penned his entries, but his notion that his wife could have overexcited herself designing her ball costume speaks volumes of the gap between them at this point in their relationship. While Bess was sewing sequins and fashioning a fairy wand, Houdini was wondering how he and his flying machine were going to get through another twenty-one days at sea until they reached Australia.

Houdini had previously vowed that he would never play Australia. "I have been all over the world except to Australia, and I'm not going there," he told a reporter in Bristol in 1904, exaggerating his globetrotting. "It's a bit too far to get back from shouldst anything happen to my mother. She is a dear, my mother is, and I've bought her two homes, one in the town and the other in the country.

A rare photo of Houdini's brain trust (l to r): Hardeen (with son), Joe Hyman, the mysterious Harry Day, the powerful Lord Northcliffe, and Dundas Slater.

From the collection of Patrick Culliton

She'll never want," he said, echoing the vow he made to his father. Yet here he was, with Bess, three assistants, and his mechanic Brassac in tow.

Houdini seemed to want people to believe that he was enduring this anguish for strictly financial reasons. "I RECEIVE FULL SALARY WHILE ON BOARD THE STEAMER," he wrote his friend Goldston, who published several magic magazines, after he had signed the contracts for Australia. "So I get paid 12 weeks for resting and 12 for working. That is the only condition I would go all that distance in and if you wish you could make use of the news, as no one knows it, I mean officially."

There was another more important agenda to Houdini's Australian trip. In their March 1910 issue, *The Player*, a New York–based show business magazine published by the White Rats, a vaudeville actors union, and edited by a friend of Houdini, reported that while the magician was in Australia he was under contract to make ten airship flights. "Houdini is the first to invade the Antipodes with a flying machine. His contract stipulates for ten flights, each to be of more than five minutes' duration, for which he will receive £20,000, or £2,000 for each flight." These figures seem large but to put them in context, in April, while Houdini was in Australia, Lord Northcliffe would pay a French pilot named Paulhan $50,000 in prize money for winning a London to Manchester air race. Aero Clubs and governmental agencies throughout the world were offering pilots premium amounts to stage flights over heavily populated areas to increase the public consciousness of the marvels of aviation. And, perhaps more insidiously, the dangers of airplanes if used for offensive military operations. At the same time that these flights were being conducted, the war department of the United States began tests of a cannon that could be used as a means of defense against possible aerial invasion.

As part of the British Commonwealth, Australia was of vital strategic importance to England. Once thought to be protected by the vast ocean around it, the advent of airplanes that could be deployed from ships made the Australians newly vulnerable to an air attack. What was particularly disquieting to the Australian intelligence community was that Japan was about to build an aviation corps and by 1911 would have four captains and twenty-four lieutenants learning flight techniques in Germany and would order two German-built floating airship construction and repairing stations.

There was an added incentive for Houdini to make the long trek to Australia. If he could successfully fly his Voisin there, he would go down in history as the first man to achieve flight on that continent. With his competitive fires stoked, Houdini threw himself into the task of preparing his aircraft. A few days before their departure, Houdini visited the Voisin factory in Paris with Brassac and noted the many improvements that had been made to the newer models. They loaded up on extra parts for both the motor and the chassis. "Hope all will be well with me and my machine," Houdini noted in his diary. He also felt compelled to record his wife's preparations for the voyage. Was there a tinge of envy in his entry? "Bess out early and shopping, buys dresses and hats, happy as a lark. Her trunks full to overflowing. She has no worries."

The next day, Houdini and Brassac traveled to the aviation grounds and watched as a female pilot flew her Voisin straight into a tree, totaling the plane. At the site, Houdini met a Belgian who was also going to Australia with his machine. Houdini noted: "Is a bit sore on me, looks on me as a rival." They returned the following day to try and taxi in the Voisin, but the weather was too foggy. On Thursday, January 6, they caught the train to Marseilles, where they would embark on their ocean voyage. Brassac was within thirty seconds of missing the train, and when he finally sprinted on board, he realized that he had forgotten a spare part of the plane's chassis that had been packed for the journey. "I gave him hell," Houdini wrote.

Antonio Brassac awoke at nearly four A.M. He was huddled underneath the wing of his cherished Voisin, which itself was perched under a huge tent on the grounds of Mr. Plumpton's paddock at Digger's Rest, a small township approximately twenty miles from Melbourne. Any minute now, Houdini's car would arrive from Melbourne, and he knew that he would be pressured into allowing the magician to try to take the big bird up. Brassac pulled a hand through his curly hair, fingered his mustache, stretched a bit, and then slowly pulled himself up. He walked over to the side of the plane where the red bandanna had been attached. Sure enough, the red flag was fluttering in the predawn wind.

"Merde!" the small Frenchman shouted, hopping around and cursing the sky with his hands outstretched. "Beaucoup de vent! Beaucoup de vent!"

It was unclear whose safety Brassac was more concerned with: Houdini's or the Voisin's.

A few minutes later, Houdini and his assistants arrived. That morning the entertainer had brought along a reporter from *The Melbourne Argus*, so when Brassac loudly informed him that this damned country of great winds had once again made it too risky to take the plane up, Houdini was forced to merely point out the features of his Voisin. Since February 24, when the plane, still in crates, had been carted out here and assembled, the predawn drive from Melbourne, where Houdini was performing to sold-out houses, had been a daily ritual that ended in disappointment. Even more disappointing were the nights when Houdini and his crew had driven out to Digger's Rest immediately after the show and had bunked down with Brassac, hoping to catch a few minutes of respite from the wind when the sun came up. It was a grueling schedule. "My eyes are getting weak, think from loss of sleep," Houdini wrote almost a month into this routine.

Oddly enough, there was another airplane right next to them in the paddock, a rebuilt Wright machine named the *Stella* owned by L. A. Adamson, the headmaster of Melbourne's Wesley College. Adamson was adamant that the glory of making the first flight in Australian history should not go to an American magician, so he hired a Brit named Ralph C. Banks to pilot his craft and ordered him up in the air at the first possible opportunity.

On March 1, Banks seized that opportunity. That morning, Houdini was just motoring up to the field when he saw that Banks was about to take off. Besides Brassac's bandanna, most pilots used the match test to determine if conditions were acceptable to fly. If the wind could blow out a lit match, you'd stay on

Houdini's aviation corps pose in Australia. *From the collection of Dr. Bruce Averbook*

the ground. Houdini lit a match. It was immediately extinguished. Houdini could only shake his head in disbelief as Banks began to taxi down the field.

The Wright machine rose to fifteen feet. "There goes the record," Houdini moaned. Brassac knew better. Banks had gone about 300 yards when the plane suddenly dove headfirst toward the ground. The entire craft was demolished with only the motor and two wheels left intact. It was a miracle that Banks wasn't killed. He escaped with a few scratches, a black eye, and a torn lip.

On the morning of March 18, Houdini got his long-awaited chance. The sun had come up and the slight breeze hardly even ruffled the leaves of the gum trees that surrounded the field. A little after eight A.M., the Voisin was taken out of its tent. Houdini warmed up by merely rolling the plane across the field a few times, without attempting to ascend. He came back to the starting point and called his mechanic over.

"Brassac, there is something wrong," Houdini said.

Brassac went to the rear box and made an adjustment to the rudder. That had explained why the plane wouldn't rise the previous day when Houdini had raised the elevating planes with the steering wheel. Brassac shooed Houdini out of the pilot's seat and hopped in. He demonstrated the effects of his subtle adjustment and then climbed down. Houdini took his seat behind the wheel.

"Un, deux, trois," Brassac counted off and then sharply twisted the propeller to start the engine. It caught and spun swiftly. Houdini disengaged the clutch and the machine began to roll. He brought his speed up to thirty-five miles per hour and after rolling fifty yards, he pushed down on the steering wheel, and the plane leaped into the air. Houdini rose to a height of about twenty-five feet and began to fly around the field.

"He's up," a few of the spectators shouted.

"I love you, I love you," Brassac shouted in the direction of the Voisin.

He had become so excited that he forgot to speak French.

Within a minute, Houdini had executed a perfect landing. He was only trying out his wings.

He immediately went back into a short roll and then quickly burst into the air. He stayed at the same altitude but remained up in the air about a minute longer. As he was easing the plane back down, he forgot to straighten out the elevating planes, which had been depressed to bring him down. Thankfully, the guard wheel at the tip of the plane made contact with the earth. The plane skidded to a stop for a few yards with its nose on the ground and its tail in the air. Houdini moved forward in his seat, getting ready to throw himself clear of the heavy propeller that was screaming behind him. At the last second, he finally straightened out the planes and the machine righted itself. Brassac and his assistants ran out and pulled up the plane.

Houdini was just starting. After a few minutes' break, he rolled out again. The plane ascended to its previous height and then headed for the big gum trees. At the last second, Houdini soared over the trees and swept gloriously up into the ether. Never descending below one hundred feet, he circled the field to the cheers of the crowd, which had been swelled by the arrival of some nearby farmers, intent on checking out the progress of the strange metallic bird. After three circuits that took about four minutes, he descended perfectly, landing within a few feet of where he took off. Houdini was the first person to fly in Australia.

Gasping with excitement and emotion, Houdini jumped out of the pilot seat and hit the ground, surrounded by well-wishers. His brow was creased with perspiration, and his hands were cold and clammy to the touch. He threw his arms up, posing for the photographers and yelled, "I can fly! I can fly!" Just then a bird landed on the wing right above Houdini's head and squawked.

Houdini laughed. "He's telling me that I can't fly worth a cuss."

Mindful of history, Houdini had the spectators sign a statement attesting to his feat. Even his rival, Ralph Banks, was pleased to shake his hand in congrat-

Digger's Rest, the site of Houdini's first flight in Australia. *From the collection of Dr. Bruce Averbook*

ulations. The magician would go on to complete fourteen more flights over the next few days at Digger's Rest, including a flight that lasted more than seven minutes and spanned six miles, but this first one was the sweetest.

There were so many people crammed onto the south side of the Queen's Bridge in Melbourne on February 17 that it looked like the structure could tip over. Thousands and thousands more lined the river wharfs on both sides of the Yarra, a good hour before the scheduled event. By one-thirty P.M., the crowd was estimated at more than twenty thousand people. With military precision, the car arrived at the appointed time. Accompanied by the manager of the opera house and Franz Kukol, Houdini, who was clad in a bright blue bathing suit, wasted no time and pushed right to the parapet of the bridge and held out his wrists for the manacling. Kukol passed a heavy chain around his neck and then over his arms, locking the ends. Placing Houdini's hands behind his back, Kukol then snapped regula-

Houdini behind the wheel of his Voisin. *From the collection of Sid Fleischman*

tion police cuffs on the magician's wrists. A committee of local men tugged a while at the irons and seemed satisfied. And then Houdini jumped.

To a chorus of cheers, he did a magnificent header off the twenty-foot-high structure, cutting into the water clean. Unfortunately, the water itself was anything but. The Yarra had such a reputation for its muddy water that Sydney residents mocked it by claiming it was the only river in the world that ran upside down. For a few seconds the crowd nervously awaited Houdini's fate. Suddenly, two figures emerged from the mucky water. The impact of Houdini's leap had dislodged a corpse from the muddy riverbed. The event so disquieted Houdini that he momentarily froze and had to be helped into the waiting police launch. When he was interviewed later, Houdini said that the river was so muddy that he had sank up to his waist in the mud on impact. When he was asked how he liked the flavor of the Yarra water, he grimaced and said it was "the least toothsome" water he had ever consumed.

When he played Sydney, Houdini replicated his feat off a high dive platform at the municipal baths. Before a huge crowd, Houdini mounted the ladder to the highest platform, thirty-one feet from the surface of the water, which was eighteen feet deep. After being chained and with his hands manacled behind his

Houdini's historic first Australian flight. *From the collection of Dr. Bruce Averbook*

back, Houdini jumped feetfirst, but the twenty-five pounds of iron tilted him forward and he struck the water face-first. He nursed a puffy eye for several days.

Before he took to the stage in Australia, Houdini made it clear in the press that though he invented the handcuff challenge act, he wasn't much interested in doing it anymore. Now he would present "mysteries" like freeing himself from a straitjacket and the Milk Can escape, which, by the way, he had also invented, even though an Australian imitator named Tommy Burns had been doing that escape and claiming it for his own. At the end of March, when he got to Sydney, he even brought Bess back onstage to perform the Metamorphosis.

In Sydney, just as in Melbourne, Houdini's theatrical shows seemed almost to take a backseat to his forays into the substratosphere. On March 29, during his show, he told the sold-out audience that he had telegraphed Digger's Rest for his plane since he wanted to fly in Sydney. On that news, the audience gave him an ovation. And he delivered. He rented a racetrack in Rosehill for £100 and announced an "Air Week," during which Houdini would fly daily, weather permitting, between nine A.M. and three P.M. Houdini had to pay Brassac a tidy sum to induce him to stay in Australia, as the mechanic was anxious to get back to the Continent and compete for the big purses that were being offered for flights.

Houdini's exhibitions in Rosehill were being monitored by George Taylor, the founder and secretary of the Aerial League of Australia. Taylor was a fascinating shadowy character who was in the forefront of promoting the military applications of both aviation and wireless technology in Australia. Trained as a builder, he worked as a cartoonist for a periodical named *Punch* in the 1890s and then segued into town planning. A pupil of Lawrence Hargrave, the Australian who had designed the box kite that had been modified into the Voisin, Taylor was the first man on the continent to fly a heavier-than-air machine, navigating a glider on December 5, 1909. Earlier that year, on April 28, he had founded the Aerial League of Australia in Sydney, a pressure group intent on promoting the military applications of aviation.

While pressing his aviation theme, Taylor also founded the Wireless Institute of Australia on March 11, 1910. Two weeks later, on March 28, while Houdini was in Australia, Taylor transmitted the first military wireless signal in Australia. His work on both aviation and wireless communication earned him a position as lieutenant in the Australian Intelligence Corps.

According to the Australian National Aviation Museum, Houdini brought his Voisin to Australia at the invitation of Taylor's newly formed aerial league, which was convinced that flights by Houdini could be of enormous help in promoting their military aviation agenda.

If Digger's Rest was the dress rehearsal, away from the prying eyes of critics, Houdini's flights at the Rosehill racetrack were a spectacle. Before cheering crowds that filled the grandstand, Houdini began a week's worth of demonstrations somewhat inauspiciously. His first trial went well, but on his second attempt to ascend, the plane just hugged the ground, mystifying Brassac. Undaunted, Houdini made a third attempt and got airborne. After some harrowing lists to the left and right, Houdini straightened out the Voisin, but his landing was so rough that he was literally thrown from his seat, landing on his hands and knees some distance from the machine. Luckily, both Houdini and the plane were intact and he made many other successful flights during that week.

Houdini's racetrack engagement was extended into May. And the publicity was exactly what Taylor and his aerial league had hoped for. "People who scoff at the idea of warfare in the air ought to have been at Rosehill race track on Sunday. Shortly after noon, when, with a roar like a thousand maniacs released, the Voisin biplane, which had been tugging at its moorings for a week in vain endeavor to break away, was released by command of the pilot, Harry Houdini," *The Daily Telegraph* reported. After a vivid description of Houdini's flight, the paper noted that "men tossed up their hats; women grew hysterical and wept for sheer excitement. A hundred men rushed toward the biplane, pulled the happy aviator from his seat, and carried him, shoulder-high, mid deafening cheers and salvos."

Houdini had been earlier lauded by *Punch* for raising the consciousness of the dangers of aviation advances. "Here is Houdini, who is an amateur, a beginner. He has taught himself to fly here amongst us, and shown us what his machine can do. He may be doing it for advertisement; he may be doing it out of mere love of adventure. The reason does not matter . . . When his great machine was circling and whirring round like a gigantic bird, the great thought was 'What of the future?' We in Australia are remote from the great world centres. We are peculiarly exposed to attack . . . We are building ships and training men . . . We are making no provision to defend ourselves against an enemy in the air. Yet the battles of the future will go to whoever is strongest in the air."

On April 29, Taylor and his aerial league honored Houdini at a special meeting at Town Hall. The crowd had been warmed up with a screening of Houdini's flights, so the magician, who had rushed over directly from his show across town, entered the hall to a standing ovation. He was presented with the trophy, a scroll in the form of a plane and a wooden plaque with a winged bas-relief globe that depicted the Australian continent.

Houdini was the perfect spokesman for the wonders of flight. "Aviation is the most wonderful thing in the world today," he told *The Brisbane Daily Mail*. "To fly in an aeroplane is an experience worth living for." Summing up his flying experiences down under in a periodical Taylor published called *Building*, Houdini wrote, "I was proud to fly here first, proud for myself and proud because I speak the same tongue as Australians, because I come from that great United States that was British born."

Houdini's mission was a great success. It put the debate about flying on the front pages of the newspapers. The next year, the Aerial League of Australia published a twenty-page booklet by Lieutenant George Taylor (Australian Intelligence Corps), titled "Wanted at Once! An Aerial Defence Fleet for Australia—A National Call to Australians." Peppered with pictures of both Taylor and Houdini flying, it again warned of the threat to Australians from a Japan that was on the brink of modernizing an air force. All this agitation worked. Australia's minister of defence, George Pearce, visited the United Kingdom in 1911, and after conferring with colleagues at Brooklands, the home of British aviation, decided to set up an aviation school in Australia under his ministry. He ordered four planes from the British government and chose two instructors to begin preparations for what would become Australia's air force.

The Aerial League appreciated Houdini's work. *From the collection of Dr. Bruce Averbook*

By 1916, the newly formed Australian Flying Corps was accomplished enough to send a complete flying unit to fight alongside the English in the Middle East. By 1917, three more squadrons were fighting with distinction in France. Its Third Squadron was engaged with the German air force the day that Manfred von Richthofen, "The Red Baron," was killed, a devastating blow to the morale of the German air corps. Even up to the last day of the war, the No. 2 squadron of the AFC was bombing the German army, which was retreating on the Western Front. "These pilots came down and fairly strafed the Hun, they bombed him and attacked him with machine guns from only fifty feet, flying amongst the tree tops; they were magnificent, they reveled in this work which was great military value to all," General Trenchard, the commander of the Royal Flying Corps, remarked. All told, 460 officers and 2,234 Australians served in the AFC during the war, and 178 were killed, a substantially smaller casualty rate than most armies. Houdini's inspiring flights over Australia had made a contribution to helping the Allies win World War I.

By 1910, Houdini had been at his game almost twenty years, and it was finally taking its toll. On his arrival in Australia, reporters were shocked to see a thirty-six-year-old whose hair was turning gray, an outward manifestation of the battering of both his body and his psyche. Perhaps it was because of the remoteness of Australia; perhaps it was with the perspective that was gained by being one of the few human beings on the planet who had soared like a real-life Icarus into the sky; maybe it was just homesickness, but Houdini seemed more vulnerable than ever when he sat down with a reporter from *The Daily Telegraph* in Sydney. It seemed like he wasn't as much answering questions as unburdening his soul.

"I want to be first. I vehemently want to be first. First in my profession . . . For that I give all the thought, all the power, that is in me. To stand at the head of my rank: it is all I ask. When I can no longer, good-bye the joy of life for me!

"So I have struggled and fought. I have done and abstained; I have tortured my body and risked my life, only for that—to have one plank on the stage where they must fall back and cry 'Master!' . . .

"You will think I am vain to tell you these things; but I am a Magyar, and Magyars are vain. American born, Magyar descended; my parents came from Austria; my father was a clergyman in Wisconsin. My name, Ehrich Weiss; my height, about 5ft. 7in.; weight, about 12 stone; 36 this month of April. Only 36, but I feel old; I have done too much in order to be, in my poor little way, Columbus.

"I am strong, as you see; strong in flesh, but my will has been stronger than my flesh. I have struggled with iron and steel, with locks and chains; I have burned, drowned, and frozen till my body has become almost insensible to pain; I have done things which rightly I could not do, because I said to myself, 'You must'; and now I am old at 36. A man is only a man, and the flesh revenges itself.

"Yet the will is its master when the will is strong enough. Do you think that these religious martyrs—the willing martyrs—those in India, say—who torture themselves by driving hooks through their flesh and swinging suspended—do you think they suffer pain? I say 'No; they do not.' I have proved it in myself. To think vehemently of a thing, of the feat, of the object of the feat, that conquers the pain—some kinds of pain. If the thought is intense enough, the pain goes—for a time. Sometimes the task set me is very hard. Not every night, but sometimes. I must fling myself down and writhe; I must strive with every piece of force I possess; I bruise and batter myself against the floor, the walls; I strain and sob and exhaust myself, and begin again, and exhaust myself again; but do I feel pain? Never. How can I feel pain? There is no place for it. All my mind is filled with a single thought—to get free! get free! And the intoxication of that freedom, that success! is sublime.

"Afterwards? Oh, afterwards. I do not say. It is the afterwards that makes me feel old at 36.

"It is good for me that I am not a tall man. Why? Because I must be quick! quick! and a tall man is always slow. It is so all through the profession: The best men are not too high. A tall man is easy-going, good-natured; a short man is sometimes good-tempered, more often not so. All the mean, cunning men that I have known—short! All the keen, eager, ambitious men—short! And for work—the tall man has too much to carry, he is too far from the ground, he cannot lose and recover balance as it is necessary, in a flash.

"Balance—and tempo—and nerve—the three things we all need in the profession. Sometimes an acrobat will lose his tempo, the time that he carries in his head for every trick; he does not know why. It is like a verse of poetry you cannot remember. What is it? What is it? You knew it yesterday; but today! and the audience is waiting. Pass!—better luck next time.

"Everyone learns to balance on the feet—but a performer such as an acrobat learns to balance in time—just as if he did it to music he carries in his head. One, two, three! and at every beat your body and limbs must be just so. Lose the tempo, and they are all astray; the trick is spoiled. Still worse when you lose nerve. Again you do not know why. You feel well in yourself, but suddenly you feel you cannot do the trick. But the audience is waiting; you drive yourself to do it—suicide! That is the way the performers of dangerous feats die. I have leaped from a bridge knowing I could not leap, knowing I would strike the water flat and be killed. But in the air my nerve came back. Almost too late, but I was able to do a little turn in the air. Only two black eyes that time!

"Some of us have superstition—yes; but I no longer. I have succeeded; my wife is la mascotte; ever since I married I have been lucky. Yet for many years I carried the Ten Commandments in a little bag, written very small. They wore out three or four years ago, and I have not troubled since.

"Of fear I do not think—or courage. In the profession it is just habit—and nerve. Take a case. You are not frightened of falling from your feet; you balance on your feet. A good acrobat learns to balance on his head just the same way. Then he will balance on his head on the top of a 20ft. pole—easier there than on the ground, because you feel it sooner when you lose balance. Dangerous of course; and very few can do it. But those who can, they do not think of the danger; they began as little boys, and have practised every day; it is habit.

Bess served tea to the flying men in Australia. *Library of Congress*

"Then one day they fall—ah! That is the test—that is the courage. Always after that they have the thought of falling; it has never really come into their heads before. To face that thought, and fight it down, and do the trick—that is courage. And to do the trick knowing that you will fall—because you must—because the audience is waiting—that is greater courage still. You feel the body shaking like a leaf, but your spirit drives it on. I was shaking so when I made my aeroplane ascent at Melbourne; why not? A mistake—and I was dead. But I looked the calmest man on the ground. . . .

"Travel helps us a lot—it is education. The agents and the managers educate. They would buy you cheap—you must sell yourself dear. When you have been bested fifty times you learn something. Three things are needed for the audience—the trick, the man, and the advertisement. Fifteen years ago, when I was 21, I was a better man than I am to-day. Youth, nerve, skill—nothing could defeat me. But I had only the trick and the man to sell, and I had trouble in getting £5 a week. Now I am well known I ask £50 a night—I sell the advertisement. Of course, behind the advertisement there are still the trick and the man;

the advertisement is no good without them. But all three together—that is success, fame, money! . . .

"So I take care of my tricks, I take care of myself, and I take care of the advertisement. The aeroplane—that was my sport, my hobby; but it brought me advertisement. It is all around the world: 'Houdini flew in Australia; yes, we know Houdini, £50 a night!' . . . The newspapers do not matter to me now as formerly; but to a beginner—very much! It is not that the good word helps greatly, but the bad word is so damaging. Many in the profession are jealous, each striving against the other; they repeat the bad word, and it may kill a really good man. So, not for myself, but for others, I would say to gentlemen of the press: Have a conscience in your criticism, and knowledge, and appreciation of the conditions. Condemn us if we deserve it, yet remember that a hasty word may go far to ruin some poor wretch. Do not kill us only for sport!"

14

The Emperor of Sympathy-Enlisters

It was past last call in the smoking room aboard the *Manuka* but that didn't stop Houdini. Bess needed another drink and that was that. He called the steward over.

"My wife would like another whiskey and soda," Houdini said.

"I'm sure she would," the steward snapped back, cheekily. "I'd like to be the skipper. But the chances of either of those things occurring are nil."

"You listen to me, young man. I'm Harry Houdini and I demand that my wife be served," he said, raising his voice.

"I hope you have your picks with you because the liquor cabinet has been locked for the night." The steward shrugged.

Houdini began to stir up such a row that, shortly, Captain Phillips walked over to the table. When he was apprised of the situation, he joked that Houdini was "evidently suffering from his liver," which sent Houdini into a rage.

"I'll have your job. How dare you treat me like an ordinary passenger? Do you know that I have been entertained by royalty all over the world? I've dined with the kaiser and the king of England. The royal family of Russia are intimates of mine. I'm not going to sit here and take this abuse," he said, and grabbing Bess, he stormed off to his cabin.

Houdini evidently felt bad about his flare-up, because he apologized to the captain before they disembarked at Vancouver on June 2, almost a month after leaving Brisbane for home. In better spirits, he challenged the local divers when they reached Suva, in the Fiji Islands. It was a tradition of the young natives to row up to the giant boat and dive for coins tossed overboard by the delighted passengers. One diver would continually surface from the sea with the coin in his mouth, as if he had caught it on its way to the bottom.

Always competitive, Houdini offered to wager that if the native's hands were tied behind his back, and Houdini's were handcuffed behind his back, and if two coins were thrown overboard, he could come up with both coins in his mouth. Houdini changed into a bathing suit and both men's hands were restrained. They stood on the side of the boat, the coins were tossed, and the men dove headfirst into the shark-infested waters.

After a minute, the native resurfaced, gasping for air. Fifteen seconds later, Houdini came up, feetfirst. When he was pulled onto the deck, with the fins of some very interested sharks circling nearby, he smiled, displaying both coins in his mouth. Both men were freed from their restraints, and Houdini gave the youth both coins. Later, he told some passengers that he simply released one of his cuffs, picked up both coins in his hand, and transferred them to his mouth. When he was asked if he was afraid of the sharks, he replied "yes and no." He had kept an eye out for them, but if he couldn't outswim them back, well, he was a fatalist. He had just wanted to demonstrate that he was as good a swimmer as any of those Fiji Islanders.

Houdini had already won three first-place prizes in sports contests onboard the ship. Seventeen days out, he won the Swinging the Monkey contest, which rewarded the passenger who could swing the longest from a rope suspended above the deck. Nobody came close to him in the Skipping Rope contest. If the handkerchief that he had tied around his ankle hadn't come loose and interfered with the rope, he would have easily surpassed his 439 consecutive jumps. And he won the politically incorrect Whistling Coon contest. To achieve victory, the man had to race across the deck to his female partner, who was holding an envelope with the name of a song in it. He would tear the envelope open, whistle the tune in her ear, and she would write the song title on the envelope. The first man back to the starting point won. Houdini not only won, "I beat Bess out of her prize," he boasted in his diary.

Houdini caused another ruckus onboard when he raged at the ship officials for awarding the first prize at the Fancy Dress Ball to a fellow passenger instead of Bess. Eschewing the fairy queen costume this trip, Bess got herself up in beautiful stage attire, but the judging committee felt that a dress that had been sewn on the voyage was more original and awarded the seamstress the prize.

Houdini did perform during one of the ship's concerts. Chief Officer Doorly had interviewed Houdini in his cabin when he was lining up the show. He placed some of the ship's "irons" on Houdini's wrists. Houdini slipped his hands under his coat and, later, returned the open cuffs to the officer. Doorly asked Houdini to do a straitjacket escape but the magician begged off, claiming it was too much of an effort. When he had first donned the jacket, it had taken him six hours to effect his escape, he told Doorly. Now he had reduced it to a minute or two, but it was still hard work. They finally compromised on some card magic.

Houdini fully expected to fly again. He was in constant communication with Montraville M. Wood, who was modifying and perfecting his own airplane with a unique gyroscopic stabilizing system. Their correspondence showed Houdini's penchant for secrecy. After being berated by Houdini for showing a fellow magician some of his letters, Wood meekly noted that the letter in question merely recorded Houdini's purchase of his Voisin and "what you thought of it." "Never have I ever spoken of getting letters from you regarding any secret work, let alone showing them," Wood promised.

Houdini's plans weren't exactly secret. At the beginning of August, Houdini attended an auction of the curios from the recently defunct Huber's Museum. He bought an Egyptian mummy for $3 and spent $6.50 for the first working electric chair. "I made my debut here years ago, at next to nothing a week. I want this chair for sweet sentiment's sake. It came while I did my first week at Huber's," Houdini said. He also told the press that he would fly in America before he went back on tour in England later that month. It doesn't appear that he attempted a flight, but he did bring the Voisin to England. And after an American named John Moisant broke a propeller on his way to a record Paris to London flight, and was stranded south of London, Houdini wired him a few days after disembarking in Liverpool. "Have 2 complete sets of alum. propellers that I use on my Voisin biplane fitted for an E.N.V. Motor also all kinds spare parts & all sizes of wires if you wish them am pleased to let you have them with my compl so that you can complete your journey."

When Moisant didn't reply, Houdini sent an indignant letter, amazed that Moisant hadn't the courtesy to respond to a letter in which "I offered you GRATIS my entire Bi-plane, Propeller, and any spare part you might have been able to make use of . . . my offer to you as from an American to an American. ought to have been at least acknowledged."

Shamed, Moisant got in touch with Houdini. They made plans to meet in September. Moisant's days as an aviator were numbered, however; he died competing for a $4,000 prize at an air meet in New Orleans in December of 1910. Houdini maintained contact with his brother Alfred, who founded an aviation school in Mineola and later supplied aircraft to the United States for the surveillance of the Mexican border.

While Houdini's interest in aviation continued, the high rate of fatalities among the pioneer pilots must have given him second thoughts about taking to the skies again. "I would advise you to leave flying aside . . . our best flyers have been killed," his friend Alex Weyer wrote him in January of 1911. "You have made a sensation, be satisfied." It was true. From 1907 to 1910, thirty-five pilots were killed in sensational crashes. The next year, another forty-one would meet their grisly fate.

Military research into aviation increased greatly. Houdini's mechanist, Montraville Wood, spent most of April in San Antonio, Texas, flying test flights with United States Army planes modified with his gyroscopic innovation, which enabled the planes to fly in windy conditions. General Allen, the signal corps leader who was the most vocal proponent of U.S. military aviation, retired and formed a private company with Wood to exploit his invention. When Wood's aero club of Illinois promoted an air meet in Chicago in August, with $100,000 in prize money, Houdini traveled to the Windy City during his summer break and hobnobbed with the elite of the aviation world, including Glenn Curtiss and Orville Wright, who mistook him for a native Australian and "wanted to know all about my country," he wrote Bess, who remained back in New York, ill. "At one time I saw twelve machines in the air. I never before saw such wonderful sights. No accidents today. Twice I grew weak in the knees at near accidents. A Curtiss flyer, Beachy, dived 3,000 feet, but, as his machine did not break, he was saved."

Houdini wrote too soon. A few days later, two pilots were killed in separate accidents. William Badger was thrown one hundred feet to the bottom of an aviation pit on the field when his propeller broke. He died hours later of a broken neck. Later, St. Croix Johnstone fell five hundred feet to his death into Lake Michigan when his Moisant monoplane malfunctioned. The day after the meet ended, Houdini participated in a benefit flying show for Johnstone's widow, who had been in the audience when her husband died. His hands and feet were shackled, and then he jumped from a plane that flew fifty feet above Lake Michigan, releasing himself under the water. The benefit raised $15,000.

Perhaps his performance revitalized Houdini's interest in flying. Even though he didn't fly again that year, he had his Voisin "remodeled" in 1912. Despite Wood's entreaties to bring it back to the States, Houdini left it in storage outside of London. In May of 1913, he authorized Donald Stevenson, a mechanist and semiprofessional magician who, along with Houdini's friend Billy Robinson, had been designing unique plywood model aircraft since 1911, to "settle" the storage account and "remove the machine."

The advertisement for his show at the Empress Theatre of Varieties in Brixton said it all. "£1000 AEROPLANE—First time on any stage," additionally promising that the airplane would be "introduced and fully demonstrated every performance." And it was. At a certain point of the show each night, the escape artist took a break from his usual rigors of handcuff escapes and introduced his newest prop—his actual airplane. He patiently explained how the machine worked and he even climbed up into the pilot's seat and took the audience through a simulated takeoff. When asked if he would attempt to fly the English Channel anytime soon, he simply smiled and said, "Find me a channel more difficult than any that has been passed, and that is what I wish to undertake." And then John Clempert performed his "Death Defying Water Escape from a Galvanized Iron Tank filled to the brim with water, locked with *two* lids and *eight padlocks*." The addition of an extra lid and two more padlocks apparently gave him the license to claim that he was the originator of the escape.

While Houdini was buying up electric chairs at auction back in the States, Clempert was already attempting to steal his latest persona—that of the dashing daredevil airman. There is no evidence that Clempert actually ever flew—in fact the clippings that Houdini pasted into the special scrapbook, devoted wholly to his imitators, read, "John Clempert Means to Fly" and report, "his education in aviation and his experience so far have been conducted in modest privacy." That didn't stop Clempert from hauling an airplane on stage, just weeks after Houdini had established a world record in Australia.

Clempert wasn't Houdini's only bane. When he returned to fulfill engagements in England in the fall of 1910, he was confronted with another dreaded female imitator, Empress, "The Female Houdini," who was doing a facsimile of his act, escaping from cuffs, straitjackets, water cans, and packing boxes.

Houdini's immediate response was to hire a new assistant, an Irishman named Jimmy Collins who was an excellent carpenter and metalworker. In December, Collins signed his formal oath, "I hereby swear by God the Almighty, not to reveal in any manner to anyone, no matter who it might be, nor even to give the smallest hint, of the secrets, instructions, plans, apparatus, constructions you have confided in me in reference to the execution of your numbers. Should I in any manner directly or indirectly act against this oath, you will have the

It was easier to do this than to get the spelling of "Needle" right. Houdini's assistants (l to r). James Vickery, unknown, Jim Collins, and Franz Kukol hold the thread. *From the collection of Kenneth M. Trombly*

right at any time to begin court action against me for perjury . . ." and began to work with Houdini on a new way to cheat death nightly that would outdo the Milk Can, which had been debased in value by his many imitators.

At first, they experimented with an escape from ice. Houdini's original conception was to don a diving suit and helmet and be lowered into a glass water tank. A chemical solution that would quickly freeze would be poured in all around his body. Once the ice was solid, the tank would be covered and the escape effected. Except it wasn't that easy to come up with such a solution. During their months of experimentation, Houdini almost came down with pneumonia, and the idea was ultimately abandoned. One can only imagine Houdini's reaction when his friend Billy Robinson wrote him in February of 1912 that he had heard that Clempert had produced "the Escape from a Block of Ice" in one of the English provinces.

By now Houdini had three full-time assistants, Franz Kukol, James Collins, and James Vickery, and he added other local helpers when the situation demanded. In England, he hired Lewis Goldstein, who was struck immediately by Houdini's dedication to his craft. "Houdini was an intense man, so completely devoted to his work that he rarely thought about anything else," Goldstein wrote.

"We were continually working and Houdini thought nothing of waking us in the middle of the night to send us scurrying off for wood to build some new gimmick, or to have us wet down the hotel's bedsheets and wrap him in them to see if he could master a new escape." According to Goldstein, Bess was the glue that kept the crew together and working harmoniously. "The pay was small, but she'd supplement our salaries by playing cards with us and intentionally losing."

Houdini showed his appreciation too. Even though he'd fire his longtime assistants in a rage (and forget about it the next day), he often, according to Collins, gave them "substantial presents and bonuses to show his appreciation." On March 2, 1913, at the Finsbury Park Empire Theatre in London, he stopped his show and called Franz Kukol center stage. He told the audience that Kukol was the best assistant he had ever had, traveling with him for ten years from Russia to Australia. He then presented Kukol with a beautiful gold pocket watch and chain inscribed with these ten-year anniversary dates.

While devising his next sensational escape, Houdini began to take more unusual and dangerous challenges. In Chatham in February 1911, he accepted one issued by four petty naval officers:

> ***We CHALLENGE you to stand in front of a loaded Government 8-cwt. Steel Gun, to which we will secure you, insert a fuse which will burn 20 minutes, and if you fail to release yourself within that time you will be blown to Kingdom Come.***
>
> ***In lashing you to the muzzle of the gun, we will place a rifle barrel between your arms behind your back, bringing your hands on your breast, where we will securely lash them. Your feet we will tie off to an iron ring which we will nail into the floor. Your body we will lash against the muzzle of the gun in such a manner that we believe it will be impossible for you to free yourself.***
>
> ***Test must take place in full view of the Public.***

A packed house watched as the sailors' conditions were executed. Houdini immediately kicked off his shoes and untied the majority of the knots in the rope with his toes. Although the local police chief had denuded the challenge of its danger by permitting the cannon to be loaded but refusing to allow the naval men to light the fuse, Houdini still escaped with ample time left.

Less than ten days after the cannon escape, Houdini received a letter from an obscure magician in Cape Town, South Africa. F. J. Peers, an escape artist, acknowledged that Houdini was the "inventor" of the Milk Can escape. If Houdini was not to tour South Africa, Peers requested permission to perform the escape there, in a can that Houdini's friend Will Goldston would produce. Moved by Peers's courtesy, he granted the magician exclusive South African rights to the effect. But, when he learned that the Great Raymond, an established fellow American magician who capitalized on the popularity of escapes, had ordered a milk can from an English dealer named Munro, Houdini fired off a letter complaining that Raymond had purchased the can knowing that it was Houdini's "original invention," and that it was patented. "I never objected to a small artiste taking any portion of my performance with which to make a living, but when any artiste with a reputation of which he might be proud, or of which he boasts, does so, I believe that it is only just and right that the said artiste should pay a royalty for any Trick that he gets or buys." Houdini noted that Raymond hadn't obtained his permission and by planning to use it in Spain, a country where Houdini hadn't patented the effect, it didn't release him from a "gentlemen's code of honor."

Raymond responded with a flip dismissal of Houdini's claims, even going as far as to say that he was surprised that Houdini should take exception to Raymond performing the effect since "the Kennington Road inventor, who sold you the trick, has sold variations of it to many artistes of lesser note, and nearly all magical dealers, and conjuring supply houses the world over, now make and catalogue the CAN." Raymond also noted that there were at least ten performers in South and Latin America performing the Milk Can escape. In one last salvo, he promised Houdini that if by chance they should be in the same city, he would "be pleased to arrange my programmes, so that they will not, in any way, conflict with yours."

Houdini was beside himself. In exasperation, he made a stunning confession in his return letter. "I don't believe that it was your intention to insult me; if you did, you are simply living up to your reputation of arrogance. You, above all others, *know that I invent my own Mysteries, my own Tricks, create my own Challenges—which you know better than my European imitators* [emphasis added].

"Whoever told you that I purchased my Trick from a Kennington Road inventor is a damned contemptible cad and liar . . . It does not interest me to know that 10 performers are working cans and barrels, it interested me to know that you have taken my Trick, without my permission, and are presenting it."

In anger, Houdini had let slip an amazing indiscretion. He had admitted, in writing, that he actually created his own challenges. A careful analysis of Houdini's challenge broadsides confirms his admission. It reveals that shipping clerks in New York and factory workers in the English provinces challenged Houdini using exactly the same language and phrasing, and raising the exact same concerns about Houdini's previous escapes. Houdini colleagues like Dr. Waitt were actively conspiring with him to create a creative challenge and then acting as part of a "neutral" committee to test the escape artist's skills. Houdini, master showman, left little to chance.

Houdini's dispute with Raymond remained unresolved and ten years later, the two men confronted each other in person and a shouting match and some fisticuffs ensued. Shortly after that, Raymond publicly apologized to Houdini before an assemblage of the Magicians Club of London that Houdini founded and presided over as president.

The procession started on the Long Wharf of Boston Harbor and continued through the winding streets to Keith's Theatre. Crowds of people followed the bizarre parade, others just stood on the sidewalk and watched in awe as Houdini's next great challenge was publicly displayed. "It" was a giant 1,600-pound sea monster that had been fished out of the ocean, a "what is it" that locals had identified as a cross between a whale and an octopus. Ten prominent Boston businessmen had challenged Houdini to be fettered with handcuffs and leg irons and escape from the hollowed-out "belly of the beast."

The scene onstage on September 26, 1911 was unbelievable. It took a dozen stagehands to carry out the "turtle-tortoise-fish or whatever it is," and turn it on its back on the center of the stage. Its abdomen had been sliced open, affixed with metal eyelets, which held a long thread of steel chain. Before the escape was attempted, Houdini was forced to sign a document that would release the owners of this monster from any liability should Houdini fail the test.

Then the steel chain was slackened, and Houdini crawled into the carcass, pausing to spray some strong perfume where his head would lie. He gave a signal, and handcuffs and leg irons were fastened to him. Then the committee went to work. Smiling through their labor, they tightened the chain, passed it around the creature's back, and secured it with locks. The cabinet was then placed around the beast and the orchestra struck up.

After fifteen minutes, the screens of the cabinet were thrown open, and there was Houdini, "grease-covered, pallid and perspiring," holding the handcuffs and leg irons aloft in triumph. On examination, the beast was as securely locked as it had been before. Houdini was not unscathed. His first words were to the stagehands, requesting them to open the windows and give him some air. Houdini had underestimated the toxicity of the arsenic solution that the taxidermist had used to preserve the sea monster, and, locked inside, he had been adversely affected by the fumes.

A few weeks later, on November 16, Houdini faced another great challenge—admitting to himself that he was sick enough to get professional attention. Perhaps Houdini himself had bought into the myth of invincibility that he projected to his adoring public. He certainly didn't take his myriad physical ailments that seriously. In fact, he wasn't really even sure where he had incurred this latest injury. Since returning to the U.S. vaudeville stage in September of that year, Houdini had put himself through a battery of more and more bizarre and strenuous challenges. At first Houdini thought that he had been injured in Buffalo in the middle of October, when a gang of longshoremen crushed one of his kidneys while tying him up in chains during a challenge. On reflection, it also could have occurred in Detroit at the end of the month, when five men stuffed him in a bag and strapped him shut using round straps that pulled so tight he felt something give. At any rate, he had been passing blood for the past two weeks, and he couldn't hide his pain and discomfort from Bess, but more important, from his mother, who was visiting him during his engagement in Pittsburgh. He had worried about his mother recently. That summer she had had such severe stomach problems that he had sent her to a hotel in the Catskills to recuperate. He certainly didn't want to contribute to his mother's unease. So, as a concession to her more than anything else, he walked through the doors of Mercy Hospital and consulted with a Dr. Wholly.

"You've ruptured a blood vessel in one of your kidneys," the doctor informed him. "This is not a trifling matter. I am going to prescribe that you return home at once and be confined to your bed for a period of at least two to three months. And I'm afraid that you must entirely abandon any strenuous stage work such as straitjacket escapes, your wet sheet challenges, basically all of your stunts that involve severe strain on your body."

Houdini laughed. "Doc, that's impossible," he said.

Dr. Wholly shot him a severe stare.

"It is my duty to inform you that by continuing your present regimen you would be committing suicide," he said soberly. "You must reconcile yourself to the fact that your strenuous days are over."

Houdini laughed again.

"How long do you give me, Doc?"

"If you continue as at present, you will be dead within a year," the doctor replied.

"You don't know me." Houdini shrugged.

The magician neglected to tell his mother or his wife about the doctor's dire warning. In fact, rather than heeding the doctor's warning, he struggled through the next three nights to finish his engagement, then canceled his Toledo dates and went back to New York. He set up shop on a couch in his library and spent the next two weeks lying there, sorting through the new additions to his growing collections. He also found time to catch up with his correspondence. "I . . . am confined to my bed with strict instructions not to move," he wrote Goldston on November 20. "So I am taking a vacation laying on the broad of my back and doing some thinking. I have cancelled a number of weeks, but I will be able to go to work as the hemmorrage [sic] has already stopped, but must give the broken blood vessel a chance to heal."

By November 30, Houdini was walking around. "I am allowed to go to work next week under the condition that I do not do any strait jackets for several months," he wrote Dr. Waitt. On December 4, Houdini opened in Columbus, Ohio. He made a concession to his condition by reintroducing handcuff escapes for the first time in years. Throwing caution to the wind, on his first few nights back, he took challenges and managed to escape from a packing case, a U.S. mailbag with an especially challenging rotary lock, and from his own milk can, which was filled with beer and then locked in another wooden box. "Think I started into work too soon. Wish I had laid off another week," he wrote in his diary. "Whilst walking down the street I slipped on the ice and fell right down flat, and I feel pretty certain that I hurt myself again."

Houdini never let the kidney properly heal. By the middle of December, he was still in severe pain, and he was writing Waitt concerned that it was "possibly going to be a permanent worry." The kidney was a source of concern for years, and Houdini took to sleeping with a pillow under his left side to protect it from pressure. What's worse, a few months later he tore a ligament in his side while escaping from a wet sheet, which compounded his daily pain and anguish.

Still, he kept right on performing. At the end of 1911, Houdini sent Dr. Wholly some photographs of him escaping from a straitjacket with the caption "Still alive and going strong." And for fifteen years, Houdini peppered the good doctor with clippings galore of his taxing and strenuous exploits, as if to rub in the message that there were some things that medical science couldn't fathom.

The last act of the vaudeville show was winding down and the audience in the Colonial Theatre in Richmond, Virginia, was looking forward to the projection of the moving pictures, when a ruckus began backstage.

"I'm being cheated. Give me my money! I demand my salary," the insistent voice wafted through the curtains. Another man tried to mollify the situation, but whoever was shouting was having none of it.

"I demand my entire salary immediately," he screamed.

Shaken, the last performer cut his act short and hurried behind the curtain. Just then, the large white sheet dropped, and the movie began. And that was when Houdini, clad in a bathrobe, stormed out onto the stage.

"I'm Houdini—Harry Houdini," he cried, shielding his eyes from the light that was projecting the images on the screen behind him.

"I want my money! These people won't give me my salary," he shouted.

Continuing his tirade, he rushed about the stage, blocking the images on the white sheet. Wary of a riot, H. B. Hearn, the theater manager, rushed out on the stage and collared Houdini. The two men struggled. Hearn began to literally drag Houdini off the stage, but the magician fought him every inch, clinging to every possible stage ornament and theater fixture to delay the inevitable. It was an amazing sight.

What wasn't amazing was that Houdini had taken his private dispute up with his audience. For as long as he had been performing, Houdini had always made it a point to relate to his audience and get them on his side. Early on, he had talked with his audiences even when he was holed up in his ghost box, escaping from his restraints. Whenever he played in a foreign country, Houdini practiced and learned at least his patter in that language, and if his attempts at communicating were unintentionally humorous, all the better, for then they were on his side.

What he said made all the difference. Houdini didn't lecture his audience, he didn't speak down to them. An astute reviewer in Sydney, Australia, had revealing insight into Houdini's psychological tactics in dealing with his audience:

> ***He is the Emperor of Sympathy-Enlisters. It is a thing which has gone far towards making him the success he is. Usually he prefaces his turn with a plaintive speech in which he refers to the kindness and fair play shown him by his Australian audiences. One gets a vague idea that other audiences used to tear him from his mysteries and kick him into insensibility. Always the gods cheer Houdini's tribute to their moderation vociferously. His gentle, trusting ways make them love him. For myself, I have not the heart of a god. I find it hard to give him my unreserved sympathy. He is too aggressive to pose as a mild genial character to the deception of persons of discrimination. F'rinstance, he suppresses opposition with the firmness of 27 Russian policemen. If an objection is raised to any phase of his***

> *performance—for instance, it may be thought that the ropes that bind him are too loose—Houdini immediately suspends his business and insists acidly on the objector's taking it over himself. Which is of course ridiculous, though the gods, being one-eyed as a result of the Mysteriarch's blandishments, cannot see it. The other night a youth* was *foolhardy enough to take over the business, whereupon the gods demanded his instant death, preferably by strangulation, and were appeased only when the interrupter was ejected, none too gently . . . A good showman is Houdini. He introduces the personal element into his turn with great effectiveness. But, as I mentioned before, it doesn't impress me one single durn.*

This critic presupposed a certain degree of cynicism in Houdini's stance toward his audience but in reality the performer did feel an emotional bond with his patrons. In London in December of 1910, British theater managers began dropping their star performers from some matinee shows to save on salaries, even though the acts were billed to appear. When the manager of the Holborn Empire tried to do that to him, Houdini acquiesced as long as the audiences were informed. The appointed day, at matinee time, Houdini noticed that he was still being billed to appear. He confronted the manager and argued that he should be allowed to do his act. He was rebuffed.

Houdini waited backstage that afternoon and just as another performer was about to take the stage, he rushed out and explained to the audience that through no fault of his own, he was not allowed to perform. He suggested that the crowd either secure the return of their money or remain in their seats until his next turn later that day. Despite the police being called in, at least half the audience remained seated until the next show. Then, when Houdini was announced, he was given a thunderous ovation. Before he proceeded, he again explained the situation in detail, even reading correspondence between him and the management.

In Richmond, Virginia, Houdini's troubles with management had been brewing all week long. At the Friday night show, in which he had been billed to escape from a navy challenge, he took to the stage and informed the crowd that the management had requested him to cancel the engagement, but he would leave it up to the audience to decide. Of course, the audience voted overwhelmingly to allow him to go ahead with his number. Houdini then spent forty-three minutes in escaping from a deep-sea diving suit in which he had been bolted, hands manacled behind his back. The next night's fracas began when manager Hearn was settling up with Houdini after his show and informed him that $400 was being withheld from his salary as a fine for his speech to the previous night's house. That led to the screaming match and Houdini's disruption of the motion picture segment of the evening's entertainment.

Even after being pulled offstage, Houdini continued to protest and refused to leave the theater. Hearn called the police, who arrested Houdini backstage for disorderly conduct. Meanwhile a huge crowd had congregated in front of the theater, blocking Tasewell Street, waiting for Houdini to exit out of the stage door. The police outfoxed them and spirited the star through a rear entrance and straight to the station house, where a fellow performer named Edward Stevens paid $50 in bail and gained his release. After his release, Houdini vowed to stay and fight the matter in court but later decided to travel to Trenton for his next engagement. "They refused to pay me my money," he told a local reporter. "I will admit that I became excited, but who wouldn't cry for $400—even make a bigger fuss than I did?"

Houdini knew there would be trouble when he spied the cop standing at the entrance to the pedestrian walkway on the Willis Avenue Bridge in Harlem.

"They're on to us," he told Hardeen, who was sitting in the backseat of the car. Behind the wheel, Houdini's publicist, Fred Rosebush, just chomped on his cigar and grimaced.

"Lemme handle this," he said and pulled the car to the side of the road. The three of them got out of the car. A few journalists were congregating at the side of the bridge. Rosebush approached the policeman, who was Sergeant Donnelly of the East 126th Street Station.

"Which one of youse is Houdini?" Sergeant Donnelly inquired.

Harry identified himself.

"Let me make myself clear. You dive off the bridge, I'm hauling you in. In fact, I'm hauling all youse in. We're wise to you."

Rosebush tried to reason with Donnelly—to no avail. So the three men rushed back to the car and drove to the Alexander Avenue Station, where Captain Post was consulted. The captain was cordial enough and seemed to feel there would be no harm done by Houdini's leap from the bridge, but he just couldn't take the responsibility of granting official sanction to the event.

Back at the bridge, Rosebush told Donnelly that the captain wouldn't help them out.

"In that case, you might as well go home, because I have no intention of allowing you to carry out this exhibition."

"How about if we jumped from a rowboat?" Rosebush suggested.

May 22, 1907 in Pittsburgh. Houdini is mid-jump. *From the collection of Dr. Bruce Averbook*

"If you try that, I'll get the harbor squad to send up a police launch and stop you."

Rosebush pulled Houdini and Hardeen aside. They conferred and agreed. Rosebush pulled the reporters aside and told them to watch the river from the bridge.

Rosebush had obviously prepared for this eventuality, because within minutes, a boat rowed by Frank Jones, bearing Rosebush and Houdini and his brother, stopped in the middle of the Harlem River, in perfect line of sight of the reporters congregated on the bridge. Just as Hardeen had affixed the leg irons to his brother, and as he was clamping the handcuffs on him, a police launch drew up alongside.

"Serves him right," Sergeant Donnelly said from the bridge.

The police on the boat began arguing with Rosebush and threatened to run the whole lot of them into the station.

"Look, we'll be finished with this in two minutes," Houdini promised. "I'll dive in, release myself, and the lads from the papers will get their stories. There's nobody else here. There's no boat traffic. If this exhibition doesn't turn out successfully, I'm the only one who stands a chance of being hurt."

Either Houdini's eloquence or Rosebush's display of gratitude finally swayed the policemen's minds. They literally turned their backs, and Houdini plunged into the river, and came up unfettered but wet. The next day, the coverage in the papers was minimal. The *Mirror* ran less than a column inch, noting that Houdini freed himself in less than a minute. The *Telegraph* coverage was downright embarrassing, spending almost the entire article on the negotiations between the police and Rosebush. When it came time to talking about Houdini's leap, all the reporter could say was, "Why prolong it? He won."

By April of 1912, Houdini had never really conquered his home city. One of his few close calls came in a New York City jail in Yorkville, where "Chief Searcher and Locker-Up" Hughey Cooney peeked through a grate and saw Houdini working at the lock with "a piece of wire." In actuality, what they thought was a piece of wire was probably a needle that had been retained in his mouth after doing his Needles effect, which was often a preamble to his jail escapes. Houdini had revealed that technique in his book *Handcuff Secrets*. To remedy his neglect in his home city, Houdini had to come up with one great stunt that could force the jaded ink-stained scribes to sit up and take notice.

The feat was scheduled for eleven A.M. on July 7. By the appointed hour, Pier 6 on the East River was "crowded to suffocation" with curious onlookers. Even the pilings of the pier were festooned with a bevy of small boys, clinging on for a good view of the proceedings. Houdini and his entourage, which numbered about fifteen, and the box were aboard a barge that was connected to the *Catherine Moran*, a well-known local tugboat. Unlike his previous attempts at bridge jumps in New York City, the newsmen came out full force to see this stunt, arriving in groups of six or more. There were at least twenty photographers present and a film crew that Houdini had hired to document the event.

Unfortunately, the police were also present, and they made it clear that they would not allow Houdini to proceed from any pier under their jurisdiction. If Houdini didn't drown himself, they were convinced that someone in the massive crowd would wind up in the drink. Undaunted, Houdini implemented Plan B. He would fill up the barge with his friends and reporters and photographers and steam out to Governor's Island, which was federal property and not subject to local police control. Houdini retreated to the bridge of the barge and, like a doorman in an exclusive club, began selecting the people who would be allowed onboard. The assembled crowd on the pier howled with disappointment as the tug began its journey.

Once in the federal waters, the preparations began. Houdini stripped down to a nice new white bathing suit and demonstrated that he had no implements on his person. The box was brought out and examined by all the newsmen present, to assure that there were no gimmicked sliding panels. Dr. Leopold Weiss, the attending physician, and Houdini's brother, informed the press that the box was precisely twenty-four inches wide, thirty-six inches high, and thirty-four inches long. At the appointed time, it would be weighted down with 180 pounds of iron. At this time, the handcuffs and leg irons were passed around for the newsmen's inspection and two reporters were enlisted to place two pairs of each on Houdini, Houdini's cinematographer capturing every minute of the preparation. Then the pine box was opened, and Houdini crouched inside it. The lid was placed on the box and nailed down, and then iron bands were also nailed to the crate. Thick rope was wound around every side of the enclosure, and the leaden weights were attached. Dr. Weiss pointed out that there were many holes punctured into the box, in order for it to sink most rapidly.

Then it was time. A platform was placed on the outside of the barge leading into the water. A small rowboat manned by a longshoreman, holding two of Houdini's assistants, was launched. The assistants held tightly to a safety rope that was tied to the box, so that it wouldn't drift away in the strong current. And then the crate was pushed into the water.

Within seconds, it was completely submerged. After about a minute, some of the newsmen began to get a bit antsy.

"This is going too far," one of the concerned scribes said.

"'E's all right," one of Houdini's assistants reassured him.

And just then, "smiling and puffing," Houdini resurfaced. He held his arms aloft in a victory salute, to show that his hands were unencumbered. Two nearby tugs tooted a salute, and the passengers on a passing Staten Island Ferry, which was jam-packed with people hoping to get a glimpse of the escape, cheered themselves hoarse. Houdini swam back to the barge. The box was retrieved and carefully inspected by the newsmen. It was intact. The escape artist was congratulated, and then the tug rushed back to Pier 6, where hundreds of people mobbed him until he was spirited away by a waiting car.

"If the public knew how much I really flirt with death in some of my stunts, I would never be accused of getting advertising free," Houdini later told a friend. It was certainly true with the underwater packing case. Even though Houdini had cleverly gimmicked the crate, there was always the danger that the box could get stuck in mud and trap him underwater. Joe Rinn, Houdini's friend who observed the escape, held his breath in suspense until he saw his friend resurface. He understood the risk his old running partner was taking.

Two years later, Houdini replicated his feat, but this time he turned it into a citywide extravaganza. He obtained permission from Police Commissioner Woods to be thrown into the water from a tugboat two hundred feet from Pier A

From the collection of Dr. Bruce Averbook

Houdini's going, going . . .

Library of Congress

. . . gone.

in Battery Park. The event was highly publicized and an hour and a half before the spectacle, four cars left Hammerstein's in the theater district in a slow cavalcade down Broadway toward the Battery. Stuffed with theater officials, newspapermen, carpenters, even Dr. Weiss with his medical satchel, they were followed by Houdini himself, clad in his swimsuit and driving a sixty-horsepower flashy racing car, with Hardeen riding shotgun. The procession was stopped twice by police and reprimanded for distributing handbills announcing the event. All along the parade route, Houdini and the other cars were cheered by passersby. When they finally arrived at the Battery, more than 100,000 people had lined the seawalls, filled up the streets, and were hanging out of the windows of the business district skyscrapers for a view of the proceedings. Additional police reserves had to be called to push the crowd back as the early-bird spectators were in danger of being pushed right over the seawall into the water.

The river was filled with boats of every description, as the McAllister lighter, with its thirty-five-person-strong official party, steamed out into the water. Earlier, an altercation had taken place when two moving picture cameramen were thrown off the ship. Houdini had protested that he didn't intend to do an act for the benefit of moving picture theaters; the place to see him was at Hammerstein's. One of the enterprising cameramen managed to get aboard a police patrol boat and got his footage.

Houdini was shackled; the box was inspected. Then its human cargo was loaded in and the lid secured. This time, one of Houdini's assistants had a stopwatch and timed the escape. If he didn't reappear in three minutes, they were instructed to fish him out. It took him a minute and forty-five seconds to make his escape, and when he resurfaced and swam a little victory lap, "the shrieks of the tugs and steamers and the applause of the multitude were deafening."

Houdini's 1912 underwater box stunt earned him his greatest publicity in New York to that date and, to capitalize on it, Houdini replicated his feat in a large tank of water that had been used for a previous act at Hammerstein's. The indoor escape from an underwater packing case was a major hit and Houdini was held over through the middle of August. During that engagement, he made an unusual request to the management—that his entire week's salary be paid in gold pieces.

"What's the idea?" William Hammerstein asked. "Don't you think regular United States currency is good enough?"

"It's not that, Mr. Hammerstein," Houdini replied. "But I have good reason for asking, and I wish you would grant my request."

Impressed by Houdini's sincerity, Hammerstein acceded.

A heavy bag laden with coins was duly dispatched to his dressing room. Houdini had two of his assistants polish up the double eagles, then took a cab up to Harlem, and went straight to his mother's room. He rushed to her and embraced her.

"Mother, do you remember the promise I made Father years ago that I would always look after you and make your days as comfortable as he made them for you? Well, Mother, I am now able to fulfill that promise. Hold out your apron," he said.

And with that, Harry poured a glittering stream of gold in his mother's apron, fulfilling the rabbi's deathbed prophecy.

Mrs. Weiss looked with astonishment at the treasure in her lap and tears welled up in her eyes. She hugged her son, and, just as he had done countless times as a child, he lay with his head on her breast. They both wept for joy.

It was the greatest thrill of Houdini's life.

15

Chinese Water Torture

"LA-DIES AND GEN-TLE-MEN," HE BEGAN IN his stentorian voice, with a crisp, staccato delivery. "In introducing my latest invention—the Wa-ter Tor-ture Cell—although there is nothing supernatural about it, I am willing to forfeit the sum of $1,000 to anyone who can prove that it is possible to obtain air inside of the Tor-ture Cell when I am locked up in it, in the reg-u-la-tion manner, after it has been filled with water."

The stark, severe-looking mahogany-and-glass box that was sitting on the stage certainly looked like it lived up to its name—the Chinese Water Torture Cell. Just the sight of the apparatus was enough to give you shivers and make you believe, as one critic noted, that you were about to witness a ritual sacrifice. And now Houdini walked briskly up to the cell, which was flanked on both sides by his assistants, who were wearing slick black rubber coats over their customary ceremonial officer's coats, making them look like unhooded executioners.

"I will first thoroughly explain the ap-paratus, and then I will invite a committee to step upon the stage to examine everything to see that things are just as I represent. The cover is made to fit into the steel frame which prevents it from being opened even if it were not locked. The steel grill acts for the double-fold purpose of con-densing the space inside of the Tor-ture Cell—which at the same time prevents my turning around even were I capable of drawing both my feet through the cover.

"In front, a plate of glass for self-protection. Should anything go wrong when I am locked up—as it's absolutely impossible to ob-tain air—one of my assistants watches through the curtains, ready in case of emergency, with an ax, to rush in, de-molish-ing the glass, allowing the water to flow out, in order to save my life. I honestly and pos-itively do not expect any accidents to happen. . . . But we all know, accidents *will* happen—and when least expected.

"The bands of steel form an im-promp-tu cage held to-gether with padlocks that enclose the same. I would like to invite eight, ten, or twelve gentlemen to kindly step up on the stage. I assure you I have no confederates, and any gentleman is perfectly welcome. A staircase at your service on this side of the stage, and now is your op-por-tunity. I thank you for your attention."

With that, Houdini gestured toward the staircase and the volunteers slowly made their way to the stage. The men circled the apparatus, inspecting every part of it. While they did this, Houdini quickly exited the stage and shortly after came back wearing a blue bathing suit underneath a robe.

"Are you quite satisfied?" Houdini asked.

One of the men suspected that the floor underneath the cell might contain a trapdoor.

"Choose any part of the stage you like and I'll have the cell removed to it," Houdini offered.

The man picked a spot, and the assistants moved it to the man's satisfaction. Then the slicker-wearing attendants began to fill up the cell with water, both from large buckets and a hose that poured a continuous stream.

Houdini took off his bathrobe.

"I am ready!" he shouted. "Begin!"

Houdini lay down flat on his back on a mat while audience members adjusted his feet in the stocks and snapped that first set of locks in place. A steel frame was then passed around his body. They then hooked a number of ropes to the steel frame, and Houdini was slowly pulled up, feetfirst, and suspended, upside down, over the top of the torture cell.

Houdini was going to go headfirst into the enclosure.

There was a dramatic pause, and Houdini drew a number of deep breaths. With two assistants, one on each side of the cell, guiding him in, the magician was slowly lowered in the cell, displacing water onto the stage as it poured over the sides of the cell.

Then things got frantic. They quickly snapped the second set of locks on the stocks that held his feet secure in place. The steel frame was crossed in front and locked, and the cabinet's curtains were drawn all around the cell.

The orchestra broke into a stirring rendition of "The Diver." The audience, as one, was holding its breath. To the side of the curtain, Franz Kukol stood with an ax, in case an accident did happen. After forty seconds that seemed like an eternity, there was a slight rustling of the curtains. The committee and the audience stared as one. And then suddenly the curtains were ripped open and

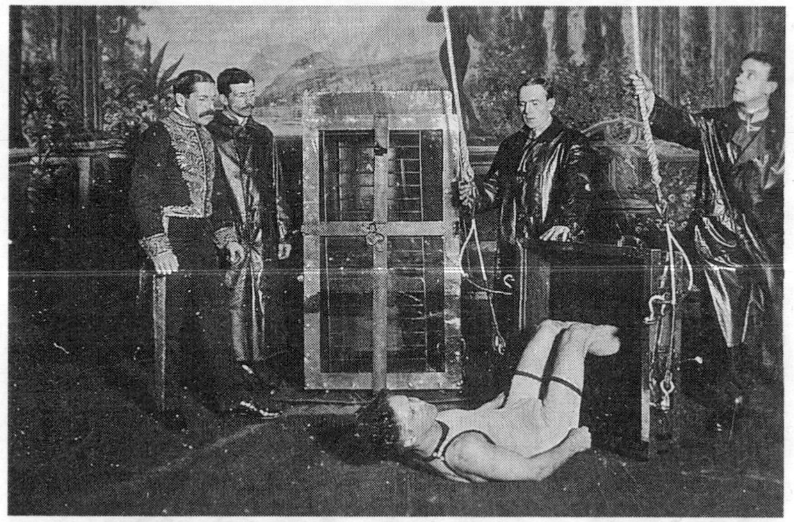

Houdini in the foot stocks before he's hoisted up and lowered into the Chinese Water Torture Cell. *From the collection of Roger Dreyer*

Houdini jubilantly bounded out of the cabinet. He was dripping wet, his eyes were bloodshot, there was even a speck of foam on his lips, but he was free.

The audience jumped to its feet and shook the walls with its applause. Quickly, the top of the cell was unlocked and removed, and Houdini scampered to the top of the tank and sat on its lip, playfully splashing his feet in the water to prove that the water hadn't been drained. The audience cheered even more lustily now as the curtain closed.

The Water Torture Cell, or Upside Down, as Houdini called it in private, was one of the greatest magic effects ever produced. Houdini first performed it in Berlin at the beginning of his fall 1912 season, but the cell itself had been in storage in London since April 29, 1911. On that day, Houdini debuted the new escape at a special matinee at the Hippodrome in Southampton, England. Legend has it that there was only one spectator in the audience since the show was unadvertised, and the price of admission had been set at one guinea—a great sum back then. What that audience member saw was a playlet in one act and two scenes entitled *Challenged* or *Houdini Upside Down*. To protect what would become Houdini's greatest theater piece, he copyrighted it as a play instead of patenting it as a magical effect.

Houdini defeats even scary monsters. *From the Granger Collection*

The Upside Down was the daring water-based escape that Collins had been working on since he joined the company. Hardeen later claimed that the cost of producing the cell was more than $20,000 back in 1911. Yet after Collins and Houdini had perfected it and it had been copyrighted, the mysteriarch waited almost a year and a half to perform it as part of his show. When he finally did, it was an immediate smash, "without doubt the greatest spectacular thing ever witnessed on the stage," Houdini wrote Goldston with his characteristic modesty. Now at last he had conceived of a death-defying stunt that his imitators couldn't duplicate. Or so he thought. Ernst Babst and Ernst Schwandtke, two German impresarios, became frequent visitors at Houdini's Circus Busch shows and several times volunteered as committee members to get a closer look at the apparatus. When Houdini moved on to Bremen to play another circus, his dressing room was broken into "to steal my act," he wrote. Sure enough, as soon as Houdini left Germany, an attractive woman named Miss Undina began performing the Upside Down, under the management of the two Germans. Houdini's lawyers obtained a quick injunction and a subsequent court ruling turned Undina right side up for good.

Perhaps to deter future female imitators (who being smaller than most men would find it easier to do the necessary contortions to escape from the Upside Down), Houdini decided to create and control his own competition once again. On November 28, he hired a woman named Wanda Timm at a rate of 150 marks per month for a one-year term. Performing under the name of Miss Trixy (which was the same name that Houdini had used for Hardeen's original assistant), Wanda and her duplicate cell made a big hit in Germany, Denmark, France, and Russia.

In January of 1913, Houdini returned to England, ready to debut his sensational new effect there. First, he fired a warning salvo in the pages of the *Strand*. "I wish to warn Managers and the Profession in General that I have invented another sensation viz. *THE WATER TORTURE CELL* which is the greatest feat that I have ever attempted in a strenuous career and hereby wish to give notice that I have *SPECIAL LICENCE FROM THE LORD CHAMBERLAIN* (granted May 2nd, 1912) as a Stage Play and I will certainly stop anyone from infringing on my rights."

Even the Water Torture Cell wasn't enough for Houdini. He continued to reprise other challenges from his strenuous career. In Hull, he escaped from a seabag, an old-time leather-and-canvas super straitjacket meant for mutineers or drunken sailors. His only condition for the escape was that no ropes should be fastened around his neck because of the danger of strangulation. It took him twenty minutes to get free. The next day a reporter interviewed Houdini and

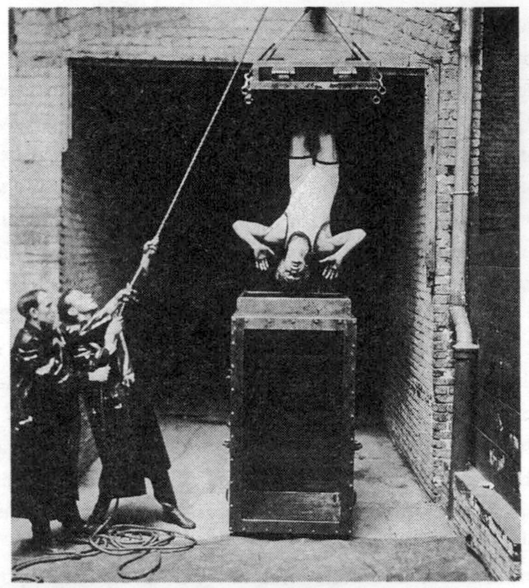

Houdini rehearsing the Upside Down. He's using the version without the inner cage.

From the collection of Dr. Bruce Averbook

suggested that his face was showing the strains of his feats. Houdini matter-of-factly replied that in the light of the amazing amount of pressure that he put on himself, he didn't expect that he would live long.

After only performing the Upside Down in England for a month, Houdini already began orchestrating "re-challenges" of it. On February 3, in Leeds, an author named S. R. Campion challenged Houdini after he had seen the magician perform the Water Torture Cell. Although he wrote Houdini that his performance of the Upside Down was "excellent," he challenged Houdini to redo the escape under the following conditions:

1. That I use my own locks which are not to be seen until the night of the performance.
2. That the iron cage be discarded.
3. That the cell be put on any part of the stage that I desire.
4. That the water be clean.
5. That I supertend [sic] the whole of the operation with the exception of your work in the cabinet.
6. That you release yourself in *four minutes*.
7. That the locks be exactly as I leave them.

None of these conditions materially affected Houdini's performance. The locks were immaterial to the escape and stipulating that they be "exactly as I leave them" makes Houdini's job easier. Houdini himself would later discard the iron cage, since the horizontal bars gave people the idea that he could climb up out of the cell using the bars as leverage. Houdini always offered to move the cell to any part of the stage. The water being clean only enhanced the effect on the audience. Campion's supervision was immaterial. Giving Houdini four minutes to complete the task was more misdirection. Houdini would usually escape within a minute from the cell. With Campion's stipulated time frame, Houdini would actually have three more minutes to increase the tension in the audience before leaping out from behind the curtain.

It had taken numerous letters and then seventeen telegrams, but finally Clayton Hutton found himself sitting in the office of Major J. H. Russell, an intelligence officer of the British War Department. With the threat of a second war with Germany looming larger every day, Hutton figured that his experience during

World War I as a pilot in the Royal Flying Corps would make him a useful asset. In addition to that, he had spent four years as a protégé of Lord Northcliffe, whose patriotism could never be questioned. Hutton's experience as a journalist and later as a publicist for the motion picture industry could be valuable for the Intelligence Division. Or so he thought. Apparently, Major Russell didn't share his enthusiasm. It seemed that the major had deigned to see the crackpot, who had continually sent him missives, in an attempt to end his annoying communications once and for all. Until Hutton happened to mention that twenty-five years earlier, as a young man, he had tried to outwit Houdini at the Birmingham Empire.

Russell immediately perked up at the sound of the conjurer's name.

"I've got a copy of the original challenge in my wallet. I remember how—"

"Let me see it," Major Russell broke in surprisingly.

Hutton fished the tattered paper out of his wallet that contained the challenge. Back in April 1913, Hutton had been working at his uncle's timber mill in Saltley, England. A big magic fan, he attended Houdini's show and was so impressed that he went backstage afterward to meet him. Houdini had announced that he would give £100 to anyone who could produce a wooden box from which he couldn't escape, so Hutton offered to take him up on the challenge using his uncle's carpenter. Convinced that Houdini's packing cases were gimmicked, Hutton suggested that they build the box on the stage, in full view of the audience. Houdini agreed, with the stipulation that he be allowed to visit the mill and converse with the carpenter who would construct the box onstage.

With his uncle in the dark, Hutton invited Houdini to come to the timber yard at lunchtime. On the appointed day, a hansom cab drew up and out stepped Houdini, resplendent in a fur-lined coat and "gaudy carpet slippers" and "smoking a fat cigar." He pulled Ted Withers, the master carpenter, to the side and engaged him in a long chat. Then, to Hutton's astonishment, Houdini began pacing off the front wall of the mill. The next day, Hutton arrived at work to see a bright yellow poster covering the front wall, advertising Houdini's show.

The night of the challenge, Hutton and three of his colleagues brought the pieces of the box onstage and Withers assembled it. Then Houdini was handcuffed, put in a sealed sack, and laid inside the box. The carpenter then nailed the lid shut and the crate was roped. The orchestra played some loud martial music and fifteen minutes later, Houdini emerged from his tent, bathed in perspiration, dangling the handcuffs from one hand.

It wasn't until 1920 that Houdini confessed to Hutton that he had paid Withers £3 to affix only two nails into the end of the crate where his feet would rest. Then he simply pushed the end panel out with his feet, shimmied out of the box, and, using a small hammer and some proper nails that were concealed in the post of his ghost box, he then hammered the panel back on, under the cover of a Sousa march.

Major Russell was enthralled with this story, interrupting Hutton's narrative many times to ask penetrating questions. When Hutton finished his account, Russell abruptly pushed aside some paperwork, stood up, and signaled Hutton to follow as he walked down a long corridor.

"You may be the very man we want," he said. "We're looking for a showman with an interest in escapology. You appear to fit the bill."

Hutton was then introduced to a Major Crockatt, who bade him repeat his Houdini stories and quizzed him on the psychology of escapes. Within minutes, Hutton had been enlisted to work for MI-9, a division of military intelligence that was charged with developing gadgets that would help troops, especially airmen, who found themselves behind enemy lines or captured to escape and make their way back to England. Houdini had been the first escapologist who had tutored English intelligence in escape and lock-picking techniques. Now Hutton, a protégé of both Houdini and Lord Northcliffe, began to design unique escape aids. He created a tool set inside a cricket bat, hid Gigli saws in shoelaces, created cigarette holders that were actually high-powered telescopes, and silk maps of Europe so thin that they could be secreted inside playing cards and gramophone records. He even magnetized every safety razor in Great Britain so they could be used as impromptu compasses. Even from the grave, Houdini had helped alter the course of world history.

Mama Weiss felt so proud. She was sitting in the backseat of a luxurious Lenox automobile, being chauffeured from the Catskill Mountains back to New York City by two of her sons. Her son the doctor was driving. His practice was booming, his client list top-rate. It's not everyone who could afford a Lenox. Now if only he would settle down and find himself a nice woman. And what needed to be said about her other son, the entertainer? He was the most famous magician in the world. Magician? He was the most famous entertainer, a real star of the highest magnitude. Still she worried about him all the time. Every time he came back to visit, he looked that much older. How could he possibly take care of himself, with all that traveling? At least he had a devoted woman at his side. If it weren't for Bess, she was sure that he wouldn't stop to eat a decent meal or even change his clothes, with all the running around after books and strange magic things, not to mention the jumping off bridges. Ah, if it makes him happy.

She leaned back and closed her eyes. Bess, sitting next to her, took her hand and cradled it. On her other side, Gladys, her daughter, was trying to sleep. She often thought about that terrible accident, the boiling water overturning and splashing Gladys's face, mostly blinding her. She also wondered why God would have allowed something like that to happen to such a good person. Then her thoughts turned to her oldest son, William, the one that they had just left upstate. He had been diagnosed with tuberculosis. It was such a horrible word. Then she remembered how Leopold assured her that there were medical advances every day.

What Cecilia didn't want to think about was her own health. Seventy-two now, she had had chronic stomach trouble for the last few years, bad enough that she would cry out in pain to her son the doctor. The Catskills helped, being in the fresh mountain air, but now they were on their way back to Harlem and, in a few days, Harry was leaving again for Europe. She felt like she hardly ever saw him. If he wasn't far off someplace in Europe, he was touring in the States. Now he was going to play for the King of Sweden. Her pride took away some of the sting of regret to see him go. He had been home barely more than a month. And for the first two weeks he was playing at Hammerstein's. He needed more of a rest than that.

She looked out the window of the car. In the distance, she saw the bright lights of New York. And then she made up her mind that they would go to the cemetery tomorrow. Visiting with her husband would help clear her mind and make her strong.

Whenever Harry was about to sail away, his mother insisted that he go to the cemetery to get his father's blessing before leaving. So the next day, July 6, Houdini rented a car and drove his mother, brother Nat, and brother Dash to the cemetery. When they got out there, Houdini suddenly had a compulsion to lie down on his father's plot so that he could say that he lay down there before Mother did, but Dash talked him out of the strange notion. Cecilia came to the cemetery often to get her late husband's blessings and she was very proud of the immense plot that her son had bought for the family.

On the way home, Harry made a detour and stopped at a tea company that was a creditor of his brother Bill's. Houdini told them that he would make good on his brother's debt. His proud mother gave him a kiss. "*Nu, wirdst du mehr gluck haben* (Well, now you'll have more luck)," she promised him.

On sailing day, July 8, Houdini awoke early. His mother was still in bed, weakened from the way that she had lain on the couch downstairs the previous

The Weiss siblings (l to r): Nat, William, Harry, Dash, Leopold, Gladys.
From the collection of Dr. Bruce Averbook

night. Houdini thought that this was a sign that his mother was getting smarter and resting more. He didn't want to acknowledge that she was getting weaker all the time. He hired another car and took his mother, his brother Bill, and Bess's mother to Hoboken to see them off. Houdini was the last person to board the steamship; he kept boarding and then running back on the gangplank to kiss his mother good-bye. She was worried that the boat would sail without him and told him to get back on board, but he kept coming back to embrace and kiss her again.

While he held her in his arms, she looked at him peculiarly.

"Ehrich, perhaps I won't be here when you return," she said.

She had expressed that morbid sentiment at his other departures and he tried to cheer her up, but he felt depressed himself because the "servant girl" who took care of his mother had just quit.

Finally he kissed her one more time.

Houdini's last view of his beloved mother. *From the collection of Dr. Bruce Averbook*

"Get along, in God's name," she shooed him away.

"Look, ladies and gentlemen," he appealed to the crowd on the pier. "My mother is pushing me away from her."

"No, that's not so," she said, embarrassed.

He finally boarded and the gangplank was rolled away. As he stood on the deck, waving to his mother and mother-in-law and his brother, Cecilia asked him to bring her back a pair of warm, woolen house slippers. "Don't forget, size six," she said. Houdini and Bess started throwing long streamers to the folks back on the pier. Houdini's aim was impeccable, and Cecilia grabbed a few of the streamers he threw.

As the ship steamed away, Bess and he yelled, "Mama, hold them, Mama." And Mama Weiss held the streamers until the force of her son's sailing away split the paper in two.

Houdini landed in Hamburg on July 16 and took the midnight train to Copenhagen, arriving at ten in the morning. His assistants met them at the station. Houdini deposited Bess in their hotel room and then he and Franz headed for the theater. On their way Kukol gave Houdini a cable that had come before he arrived.

He performed at the Cirkus Beketow that night, before two members of the Danish royal family. Afterward he was feted at a press reception. During a lull, he remembered the cable, read it, and collapsed to the floor, unconscious.

Library of Congress

16

Forgive

"My dear little mother. Poor mama," he sobbed after coming to. The cable that he had neglected earlier contained the message that his mother had died. Moved by his grief, the reporters and dignitaries left the room.

Too weak to even walk, Houdini was helped to the hotel by Bess and his assistants. He seemed to be in a trance, and Bess found him incapable of thought or action. Back in his room, he was helped to bed, where he lay in abject agony. A Danish doctor was called and, after an examination, he told Bess that the shock of Houdini's mother's death had precipitated an attack of chronic kidney disease. He ordered immediate hospitalization, but Houdini mustered up enough strength to reject that idea. In lieu of that, the doctor recommended a long rest cure.

Bess and the Danish physician went outside to consult, leaving Houdini alone with Jim Collins, one of his trusted assistants. As soon as they departed, Collins locked the door and walked back over to the bed. He bent over his shattered boss.

"Mr. Houdini, can't you do anything for your mother?" he asked.

The question seemed to jar Houdini from his stupor.

"What do you mean, Jim?"

"You know what I mean," Collins said. "Can't you do anything for her?"

An uneasy silence fell between them.

"Do I understand you, Jim, that you think I really possess some power whereby I could help my mother?" Houdini finally said.

"Yes."

Houdini sighed.

"No. No, Jim, this is the will of the Almighty, and God's will be done. There is nothing that can be done."

Collins slowly sat down next to the bed.

"Maybe I could go back to America for you," he suggested.

"No," Houdini said. "We'll all go back on the next steamer."

That Houdini's own assistant believed that he possessed superhuman powers is telling, but it was really only a residue of the myth that Houdini had been creating for almost twenty years. Despite his denials, Spiritualists were convinced that Houdini was able to dematerialize and pass his etheric body through solid substances like packing cases and water cans, rematerializing once free of the constraints. Others posited that Houdini weaved his magic by hypnotizing the entire audience. In any rate, many were in agreement that Houdini possessed some potent powers. "You could have founded a religion on the strength of what you were doing," one friend wrote him, a religion that presumably would encompass resurrection of the flesh.

Houdini immediately canceled his engagement, even though in Denmark breach of contract was a criminal offense. Herr Beketow took sympathy on his grief-stricken star, and Houdini later repaid him by taking out a large boxed ad in the circus's program, thanking him for his display of sensitivity. Now arrangements for the return trip had to be made. When it was ascertained that the party would have to wait until the twenty-third for the return trip of the ironically named steamer, *Kronprinzessin Cecilie*, Houdini immediately cabled Hardeen and ordered him to delay the funeral. Houdini's desire to see his mother one last time took precedence over Jewish law that mandated immediate burial. Apparently the other children of the rabbi acceded to Houdini's unorthodox request.

Still in obvious distress, Houdini was accompanied by the Danish specialist as far as Germany, where a local doctor took over. In Bremen, the dutiful son remembered his mother's last wishes and purchased a pair of woolen slippers, size six. The weeklong return trip gave Houdini ample time to imagine the circumstances of his mother's death over and over again in his mind. Houdini most likely got the true details of her demise when his brother Leopold met him on the revenue cutter. He would have learned that Cecilia had accompanied Hardeen to his Asbury Park engagement on July 14. That day, Hardeen jumped off a fishing pier while manacled and chained. In the evening, he did challenge handcuff releases, and then escaped from a straitjacket and the Milk Can. Later that night, back at the Imperial Hotel, Cecilia suffered a severe stroke. A local doctor pronounced her condition serious. Theo called his sister, Gladys, and she arrived the next morning. By then, Cecilia was on the critical list.

Nonetheless, Hardeen continued his performances. After Wednesday's show, he went directly to his mother's bedside. She tried to tell him something about Houdini, but the stroke had impaired her speech. She fell into a fitful sleep. Shortly after midnight, she died.

As soon as Houdini entered his house, he went straight to the parlor where his mother's corpse had been laid out for burial. "She looked so dainty and restful, only a small spot on Her cheek, and the Face which haunted me with love all my Life is still and quiet, and when She does not answer me I know that God is taking Her to His Bosom and giving Her the peace which she denied herself on this earth," he wrote in his diary. "And tomorrow Mother will be laid alongside of Her best friend, one for whom she mourned ever since he obeyed the mighty command. . . . And I know if there is a Meeting Place, Both are Happy in this event, which leaves all us children miserable, unhappy, and mindfull [sic] of sorrow."

Harry brought a steamer chair from his mother's room and placed it by her side. He would not move from that chair until the next day. At some point he placed the new slippers inside the coffin.

It was a dismal day, and it perfectly mirrored Houdini's mood. Once again, he set out for the cemetery. Wearing a black suit, a black bow tie, and a black hat, he strolled distractedly among the rows of graves, noting each marker. Just the week before he admitted to his diary that he was "feeling a bit better," but quickly he qualified that with, "but July 17 is always in my mind."

Even here in Monte Carlo, thousands of miles from where Cecilia lay at peace, Houdini could find solace only among the dead. He had tried to reenter the land of the living in September, when he left New York after almost daily visits to the cemetery and traveled to Germany to fulfill his contracts, but it was hard work. On September 16, 1913 Houdini opened in Nuremberg, performing the Needles and the Water Torture Cell. "Act works beautifully," he wrote in his diary. And then "had a terrible spell after show on account of my darling Mother." Even before his opening, Houdini had spent days getting his mother's letters typed up in good German so that he could bind them in book form and carry them with

Mr. and Mrs. Houdini in Monte Carlo. *From the collection of Dr. Bruce Averbook*

him. It was a poignant exercise. "Many a bitter tear I am shedding. In the entire lot of letters, which I have saved since 1900, each is a love story, a prayer to God to protect her children, a plea that we should be good human beings."

Two days later, the German authorities tried to maintain that Houdini was not a good human being and hauled him into court for presenting a professional performance without obtaining police permission when he jumped manacled into the Dutzend Lake twice in one day. He was fined fifty marks for bathing in the water, fifty marks for not obtaining prior allowance for the performance, and an additional twenty marks for walking on the grass. Houdini naturally appealed the case, and the local police became laughingstocks in the press when it was revealed that they had attempted to prevent the jump into the lake on the day *after* it had occurred. It was also wryly noted that while city authorities had warned Houdini against carrying out his publicity stunt, the city's municipal streetcar administration had placed additional cars in service to transport the thousands of citizens who flocked to see a performance that was verboten.

His troubles in Germany didn't even rate a mention in a letter to Hardeen. Writing on black-bordered mourning stationery, he confessed, "I am working in a sort of a mechanical way and feel so lonely that I dont know what to do properly, but am hoping that eventually I will have my burning tears run dry, but know my Heart will ALWAYS ACHE FOR OUR DARLING MOTHER. Dash, I knew that I loved Mother, but that my very Existence seems to have expired with HER, is simply writing my innermost thoughts. I trust that The Almighty will allow Our Darling Mothers Prayers to sheild [sic] us, and that She from Heaven will look cown [sic] on us and guide our footsteps on the Rightous [sic] path. With all my efforts, I try and still my longing as I Know positively that Mother would not like the way she Passing Away has effected [sic] me, but what can I do, All HER LIFE was spent in making Motherly Sainted Love to us, and I am simply weeping at our Loss. My brain works naturally, and I try and scheme ahead as in the Past but I seem to have lost all ambition. . . . Must try to cheer up and be a man. . . . Bess seems to be sick to me, but perhaps she is anxious about my welfare, for I must worry her."

By November he was still miserable. Now playing in Paris, although Houdini did great business thrilling audiences with the Needles effect and the Upside Down, he was "very melancholy" and only met one challenge the whole month. Still obsessed with Cecilia's death, he wrote to Hardeen near the end of the month. "Dash its [sic] TOUGH, and I can't seem to get *over it*. . . . Time heals all Wounds, but a long time will have to pass before it will heal the terrible blow which MOTHER tried to save me from knowing." This cryptic reference remains a mystery to this day.

Houdini canceled his December Paris dates and took Bess to Monte Carlo to divert himself with the casinos. He won two thousand francs but soon got bored with the gaming tables. What seemed to pique his interest was the special graveyard that contained the bodies of people who had committed suicide after losing their life's fortunes. Houdini made several visits to this bleak landscape. It's unlikely that he himself was contemplating such a grisly fate but if he was, the visits seemed to disabuse him of that notion. "A terrible feeling pervades the first time one sees the graves, and thinks of the human beings who finish their lives in this manner." More sociologist than potential suicide, Houdini made some acute observations about the phenomenon in his diary. He noted that there were more suicides in winter than in summer; that the casino workers would stuff money into the bare pockets of recently discovered suicides to suggest other motives than financial; and that the casino now offered to pay for shipping bodies back to their hometowns to "keep things quiet." A grave of a man and woman who committed suicide together particularly fascinated him.

> *My mother has been the* **one great love and adoration of my life.** ***I have loved others, but it has seemed to me always that beneath and above any other affection was my love for my beautiful mother.***

Houdini scholars have always emphasized Houdini's seemingly over-the-top devotion to his mother. In the context of his time, Houdini's sentiments don't seem excessive. Houdini didn't pen the mother tribute above; Clyde Fitch, the most popular playwright in America in the early 1900s, wrote it. "A mother is a mother still/ The holiest thing alive," the poet Coleridge observed, and Houdini quoted that in a letter to Bess seeking to differentiate his love for her and Cecilia. "My Dear Girl, whereas I say you are mine, my mother claims me as her son. So the two loves do not conflict. . . . Indeed I love you as I shall never again love any woman, but the love for a mother is a love that only a true mother ought to possess, for she loved me before I was born, loved me as I was born and naturally will love me until one or the other passes away into the great Beyond, not passing away but simply let us say 'gone on ahead.'"

Though he didn't follow the Jewish religion to the letter, as witnessed by his postponement of his mother's interment, Houdini did believe in an afterlife—one where the deceased might even be able to intercede with God on behalf of those still living. In 1916, Houdini was interviewed by a Cincinnati journalist who came across a picture of an austere-looking, gray-haired, bearded man in his dressing room. "That's my father," Houdini told him. "I think [he] has given me my success. When he died he asked me to pray for him every night. He would watch over me and assure my success. . . . I have followed his request."

Cecilia had urged Houdini to visit the cemetery before departing on his journeys to get his father's blessing. Whether the dead could actually communicate with the living was an issue that always fascinated Houdini. Throughout his life, he had made pacts with many of his friends, creating a unique, secret code for each one. Whoever pierced the veil of death first would then attempt to relay the code from beyond the grave. Years later, Bess suggested that Houdini and his mother had made such a code before her death and that the operative word was "Forgive." According to Bess, Houdini's youngest and oldest brothers had been estranged. Although Leopold, the youngest, had been Houdini's favorite sibling, the magician sided with his older brother. Bess claimed that the family tragedy was enough to have contributed to Cecilia's death. "In his heart he wanted to forgive his brother, but pity kept him silent," she said. "Only that word, 'Forgive,' from his dead mother, could have brought about the reconciliation for which he longed."

Houdini loved children and animals. *Library of Congress*

After his mother's death, Houdini would often wake in the middle of the night and say out loud, "Mama, are you here?" When he didn't get a response, he would morosely fall back down to bed and sigh with disappointment. On Christmas Day, 1913, Houdini, now in London, sent Hardeen a revelatory letter. "Just a Christmas letter on this day, which finds me with a heavy heart and a soul of pain. But must drop you a letter as I am alone and hope you have had a happy time in the midst of your family and trust the future will brighten up and may the Almighty permit you to bring up your children so that you may be proud of them. I pray that they will respect, honor, and obey their parents. Can't wish you anything better, for as our Angel Mother used to say, '*Kinder machen die altern stolz und Meiner Kinden sind meiner ganzer leben*' [Children make their parents proud and my children are my whole life.] Tis true God has seen fit not to Bless Bess and myself with children even though Ma prayed for it, but perhaps tis best so after all. I am very unhappy Dash at the present time of my life." Houdini's mother's death had two profound effects on him. It crystallized a deep sense of guilt that he felt in leaving her frequently for such long stretches. That sense was memorialized in a short story he wrote about a strong man who neglects his pledge to his father to care for his mother and leaves her alone when he's seduced away from her by men who tempt him with a sweet-tasting drink (money and success). Her death also released him from his oath. He had honored it to the letter and now he was beholden only to himself and his legacy.

Houdini may very well have felt that he had gained the world but lost his soul. His mother (and his entire family) had suffered no want, but at what price? Houdini's rootless, nomadic existence may have been romantic when he and Bess were two young people traversing the globe, trying to make an honest million, but as he neared forty, the death of his mother seemed to have prompted a reassessment of what was really valuable to him.

Houdini opened his show by proving to the audience that he had coins that were so obedient, they would mysteriously travel through the air faster than the eye could discern and arrange themselves inside an empty crystal cash box that was suspended by two ribbons over the stage. First, he opened the box and let the audience see that there were no coins inside. To demonstrate that conclusively, he hooked the box onto the two ribbons and then dramatically swung the box. There was no sound of coins rattling to be heard.

Then the mysteriarch strode across the stage. He turned back toward the box, which was still describing an arc across the stage. He picked up a handful of coins and, one by one, made a tossing motion in the direction of the box. The coins seemed to magically vanish into thin air, and then, one by one, they mysteriously began to rattle inside the swinging box. When they were all released, the magician walked back to the box, stopped its motion, opened the lid, and removed the same coins.

The Crystal Cash Box was an old effect that had been created by the great French magician Robert-Houdin. What was startling about its presentation this night was that the magician who was producing the coins in the small crystal box was much more likely to be escaping out of a giant crystal box. Houdini, the world-famous self-liberator, had transformed himself into Houdini, the self-described Supreme Ruler of Mystery.

It wouldn't be fair to suggest that his mother's death had impacted Houdini's shift in magic aesthetics, as if performing illusions on stage was some form of comfort food for a bereaved soul. Houdini had been planning to mount an all-magic show for a year before her death, and he had been quietly buying up new and old apparatus from magicians and dealers in England and France, including the Palingenesia from the show of Dr. Lynn, the illusion that entranced him as a child in Milwaukee. If anything, his mother's death had postponed his efforts in that direction. Back in November of 1913, Houdini wrote Goldston, whose wife, Leah Laurie, had sold him an expanding die effect created by the stunningly brilliant French magician Bautier De Kolta. "Re the big show, if I can get my mind on work, it may take place, but I am afraid the material I have on hand is not quite what I would like. Since July 17th I have not had my mind to myself. . . . Can't even start in to think of a program and am simply trying to occupy my mind."

By his birthday the following year, his mind had settled enough to have conceptualized his Grand Magical Revue. He tried it out first in the English provinces in April and later in June, alternating it during a week's engagement with his usual turn of Needles and the Water Torture Cell escape. The show opened with the Robert-Houdin Crystal Cash Box, a interesting choice considering he had attacked the French magician so unmercifully in his *Unmasking* book. One critic suggested that Houdini buying a replica of a Robert-Houdin illusion was akin to "a primitive hunter gorging on his slain wolf to ingest its power." Good-Bye Winter and Hello Summer were two effects that Houdini had purchased from the English magician Charles Morritt. In Winter Houdini vanished a "living, breathing human being in mid-air." During Summer, a beautiful "Fairy Queen Gardener" was produced from a pyramid-shaped box.

A more startling production occurred during the presentation of De Kolta's Marvelous Cube. A small valise was brought onstage, and Houdini told the audience that it contained a young lady. He reached into the case and pulled out a black die, eight inches square. The die was placed on top of a low table and when Houdini stepped back, it began to mysteriously swell. By the time the motion had ceased, the die had grown to a cubic yard, and when Houdini lifted the now giant cube off the table, a young lady appeared, sitting cross-legged.

Houdini closed the show with his Metamorphosis, putting Bess into service for the first time since Sydney, Australia. "Bess working as though she had never retired," he wrote in his diary. A few weeks later, after another presentation of the Magical Revue, he wrote, "Best show I ever presented. Bess works magnificently." According to Houdini the critics agreed with his assessment of the revue. "Said by all the great English critics to be the best mystery show ever presented," he annotated an ad for the show in one of his scrapbooks. Unfortunately, the theater managers (and, presumably, some of the audiences) didn't agree. They preferred the ex–Handcuff King and present Self-Liberator. Undaunted, Houdini packed up his illusions and put them into storage. "If the English want escapes, they can have them," he told Goldston. "But I'm determined to give a good magical show before I die."

He began plotting that show almost immediately. With no more responsibilities to his mother, Houdini felt free to mount a world tour. He would return to the United States for his Hammerstein engagements that summer, but by January 1915 he planned to travel back to the continent, perform across Europe, return to Russia, and then take the Trans-Siberian Railroad into Japan. There his party would tour the interior of Japan and China using a specially designed huge car that could be opened to six times its own length and seat five hundred people around its stage. The idea of barnstorming around the countryside in a special van that could be opened at will to accommodate a large audience was not new. In fact, Houdini first learned of the idea back in New York as a boy when he read *The Memoirs of Robert-Houdin*.

When Houdini had added the amazing galvanized milk can to his show in 1908, he brought the real risk of death to the stage. It worked as high drama, even if it was his prop, his invention. By 1911, he turned his own can into a challenge vessel by inviting local dairies and breweries to fill the can with their liquid.

In early 1914, after he had been performing his Water Torture Cell, another death-defying effect of his own invention, Houdini took the challenge concept to a new and unprecedented level when he escaped from a barrel that had been built by a man in Bradford, England. Houdini had escaped from empty barrels before, but this one was different. It was filled with water. He had two minutes to figure his way out or die a drowning death.

What the audience didn't know was that the challenge had been prearranged on a cold January evening when Houdini paid a visit to the home of a fellow escape artist named Carleete. Needing something special to pack the house, he was shown a barrel that Carleete had been using as a prop in his own show. Without even trying it out, Houdini negotiated a sum for its use and had Carleete come to the theater and challenge him under his real name, Howes. The escape went over wonderfully, and Houdini returned the barrel the next day, but a new challenge had been born. Over the next few years, Houdini repeated this barrel or cask escape, sometimes letting local brewers fill it with their beer.

Houdini kept pushing the envelope with his challenges. In 1917, he challenged the Atlantic City police department to chain and cuff him before he jumped off a pier into the Atlantic Ocean. When Houdini and his brother did most of their manacled leaps into bodies of water, they used special handcuffs called "bridge jumpers." Hardeen later quipped that keeping the cuffs on until he hit the water was the hardest part of the bridge jumps. Unless Houdini had friends in the Atlantic City police department who used gaffed cuffs, his 1917 jump was singularly risky.

The next year, he took the death-defying challenge one step further. On April 18, 1918, Houdini was challenged by the expert packers of the American Chicle Co. Claiming that they didn't "trust" the box that Houdini was using to do his underwater packing case escape at the Hippodrome, they challenged him to allow them to pack him into a "special extra-heavy export case" that had been drilled full of holes, secure it with screws, nails and iron bands, and then throw him into the huge pool at the theater. Needless to say, Houdini lived.

All of these years of challenges created the cumulative effect that became the myth of the superman. Houdini could get out of anything, he could defeat any defi thrown at him. He was more than a man, he was a superman. Every member of his audience both rooted for him and basked in his reflected glory. He was greater than us but, in the end, he was one of us.

By 1914, Houdini was as famous as any man on the planet. That June, when he played the Nottingham Empire, after his second show, he could have dined with any local celebrity, aristocrat, or business mogul of his choice. Instead, he hired a car and traveled forty grueling miles to Sheffield. He was going to see a teenager who still lived with his mother.

After they dined, Randolph Douglas led his mother and Houdini to the attic of the small house. Once there, Randolph asked Houdini to strap him into a straitjacket. Thinking he was going to see the young man emulate his hero, Houdini played along. What Douglas did next would change the course of magic's history. He had his mother tie his feet with a long rope and had her thread it through a block and tackle hung from the wall of the A-frame. With Houdini's assistance, the two of them pulled and pulled until Randolph had been hoisted off the attic floor and was suspended from the roof. And then, hanging upside side, Douglas escaped from the straitjacket in front of his audience of two.

Houdini went forty miles out of his way that night because the world of magic is a strict meritocracy. Money, prestige, titles, pretensions count for nothing in the face of raw talent. Unlike the Masons, a secret handshake doesn't open doors in this world, but the perfect mastery of a difficult sleight commands immediate respect. The world of magic is made up of all strata of society: doctors, lawyers, professors, firemen, garbagemen, accountants, janitors, prison guards, intelligence officers, and the lowest-level government employees. Once gathered behind closed doors, the job descriptions, net worths, and titles disappear. Nothing can be faked in a world where a premium is placed on the execution of perfect deception.

The evening's concert entertainment, a joint benefit for the German Sailors Home and the Magicians Club of London, had begun with some Puccini. As the passengers settled back into the comfortable, plush chairs in the Grand Salon of the S. S. *Imperator*, the Ritz Carlton Orchestra played some selections from *La Bohème* and then Madame A. Cortesao joined them and sang a magnificent aria from *Madame Butterfly*. Now it was time for Houdini.

He began his presentation with some simple close-up magic, producing and then changing the colors of silk handkerchiefs, even turning water into wine. While he was doing some card flourishes, he noticed that the walrus-mustachioed bespectacled man who was sitting next to Victor Herbert, the famous composer, was watching him like a hawk. Houdini was convinced that the man had seen through all his misdirection, and it would be extremely difficult to baffle him. Until the slates.

"La-dies and gen-tle-men. I am sure that many among you have had experiences with mediums who have been able to facilitate the answering of your personal questions by departed spirits, these answers being mysteriously produced on slates. As we all know, mediums do their work in the darkened séance room, but tonight, for the first time anywhere, I propose to conduct a spiritualistic slate test in the full glare of the light."

The crowd buzzed with excitement. Houdini picked up some sheets of blank paper, some envelopes, and a few pencils and began to walk among the audience, distributing them seemingly at random.

"If you will be so kind as to write upon the blank paper a question that you would like the spirit world to answer . . . then fold the paper and seal it in the envelope provided so there is no chance whatsoever of my seeing the particular query," Houdini said.

When he reached the table where Herbert and his bespectacled friend, Theodore Roosevelt, sat, Houdini gave the astute card observer a blank piece of paper. As the man began to write his question, holding the piece of paper in the palm of his hand, Houdini walked back to the table carrying an *Atlas of the World*, a book that was part of the ship's library and had been sitting on a nearby table.

"Pardon me, Colonel," Houdini said, handing him the *Atlas*. "Use this as a support."

Houdini winked at Victor Herbert.

"Turn around. Don't let him see it," Herbert counseled his friend. "He'll discern what you write from the movements of the pencil."

The Colonel followed his advice, turned his back, wrote his question on the blank piece of paper, then he turned back around and handed the book to Houdini.

"Fold that paper so that no one can read what you have written," Houdini said, and then walked back and replaced the book on the other table.

"Now place that paper in the envelope and seal it please," Houdini said as he walked around the audience and collected the other envelopes in a hat. Returning to his own table, Houdini put down the hat and picked up two slates. He walked back to the Colonel's table.

"I am sure that there will be no objection if we use the Colonel's question," Houdini said. The audience murmured agreement.

"Now you have written down a question that you would like the spirits to answer, is that correct?"

"Yes, sir," the Colonel said.

"And you have sealed that question in the provided envelope, and no one other than yourself knows the aforementioned question, is that correct?"

"That is correct," the Colonel agreed.

Houdini showed him the slates—which were basically small two-sided chalkboards in a wooden frame.

"Can you confirm to the audience that there is absolutely nothing written on these slates?" Houdini asked.

The Colonel nodded as Houdini showed him each side of the two slates.

"They are blank," the Colonel affirmed.

"Now if you will be so kind as to place your envelope between the two slates," Houdini opened the slates and, after the envelope was placed between them, he sandwiched the paper.

"Can you please tell the audience what your question was?" Houdini asked.

"Where was I last Christmas?" the Colonel said.

Houdini opened the slates and held them up for the audience to see. On one slate was a detailed map, in colored chalk, of Brazil with the River of Doubt in the Amazon highlighted. The other slate contained the message: "Near the Andes" and it was signed by W. T. Stead, a Spiritualist journalist who had drowned when the *Titanic* sank.

Now you see them, now you don't. Houdini retouches out fellow passengers on the *Imperator* and leaves Teddy Roosevelt in the picture. *Library of Congress and the collection of Kevin Connolly*

The audience screamed in astonishment, and the Colonel jumped up, waving his arms and laughed uproariously until tears began streaming down his cheeks.

"By George, that proves it!" Colonel Theodore Roosevelt, the ex-president of the United States shouted. And the passengers applauded Houdini even more vigorously.

The next morning, Houdini and Roosevelt took their usual constitutional around the upper deck of the steamship. Roosevelt stopped halfway around the deck and put his arm around Houdini. He looked him straight in the eye.

"Houdini, tell me the truth. Man to man. Was that genuine Spiritualism or legerdemain last night?"

Houdini was amazed that this brilliant statesman, who would go down in American history as one of its most colorful characters, was undecided whether the effect was genuine or not.

"No, Colonel," Houdini shook his head. "It was hokus pokus."

Houdini didn't have the heart to tell Roosevelt exactly how he performed that miracle. It wasn't until years later, when "this craze of Spiritualism" started "running through the world," that Houdini, seemingly as a public service, revealed his methods.

It was a brilliantly executed effect, showing both Houdini's opportunistic genius and his marvelous flair for showmanship. It also revealed that Houdini was well versed in the techniques of spies. He began to plan for the effect before he had even boarded the ship that would take him and Bess home to New York for his summer 1914 run at Hammerstein's. When he went to the Hamburg-American Steamship Company offices to pick up his tickets, the clerk tipped him off that Teddy Roosevelt was going to be a fellow passenger. Knowing that he was scheduled to perform, he began to think of an effect that could fool Roosevelt. The ex-president had been in London after making a long trip to South America, and Roosevelt's story of his trip in the Amazon was about to be published by *The London Telegraph*, so Houdini immediately took a taxi to the *Telegraph* offices and procured inside information, including detailed maps of Roosevelt's explorations, from his friends in the newsroom.

Houdini then conceived the idea of presenting the information in the context of a Spiritualist séance, so he prepared the two slates with the map and the actual signature of Stead, which he traced from an original letter from the Spiritualist in his collection. Once on the ship, Houdini met Roosevelt, and the two men began an early morning walking regimen. One morning, Houdini steered the conversation to Spiritualism, and then arranged for a ship officer to interrupt the two men to remind Houdini of his upcoming performance. The magician asked Roosevelt what he would like to see Houdini do; of course, the Colonel suggested a séance.

On the night of the show, Houdini had already loaded the hat that was to contain the passengers' questions with envelopes that all posed the same question: "Where was T. R. last Christmas?" Houdini claimed that he planned to palm the legitimate questions and pick one of his loaded slips, but he didn't even have to do that. Houdini was able to discern Roosevelt's question without ever opening the envelope it was sealed in because on the morning of the show, Houdini went into the Grand Salon and picked two books off one of the tables. He took them to his stateroom, where, with the aid of a razor blade, he lifted back the cloth of each of the book's front and back covers, then inserted a piece of paper and then a carbon on top of the paper. Leaving a small string on the edge, he then pasted all four covers down. When this procedure was done, he returned the books to the salon. When the gimmicked book would be used as a support to write out the question, the pressure from the pencil would make a carbon impression on the loaded paper, revealing the query.

Houdini's thoughtful gesture of giving Roosevelt a book to lean on ensured that the magician would obtain his question. Houdini himself was amazed when, as he was returning the book to the table after Roosevelt had used it, he pulled the string, peeked underneath the cover, and found that Roosevelt had asked, "Where was I last Christmas?" obviating the need to use his own loaded questions. Houdini's séance was the talk of the ship and an account of his "hokus pokus" was relayed by the *Imperator*'s radio operator to Newfoundland, where it was then dispatched to New York. Before the ship even docked, the story made all the New York papers. The success of the fund-raiser was another matter. After collecting 707 marks, half of which went to the German Sailors Home, Houdini was able to present the Magic Club treasurer Stanley Collins with a check for a little over £17. "You see the passengers are returning home and are broke," Houdini explained.

They may have been broke but they were certainly glad to be returning home since the world was teetering on the verge of catastrophe. The *Imperator* set sail from Hamburg on June 17, stopped in Southampton, England, to pick up more passengers, and arrived in New York on June 25. Three days later, the assassination of Archduke Franz Ferdinand, the heir to the Austro-Hungarian throne, threw Europe into chaos. By August 4, Germany, Russia, France, and Great Britain were all at war. This would be the last trip the *Imperator* would make until the war ended.

Houdini had foreknowledge that the present war was brewing and "just managed" to get out of Germany in time. Roosevelt's fortuitous departure from London suggests that the ex-president might have been advised to get back to the States before the conflict began. There were other intriguing characters on board the *Imperator* for that last ride home, including Robert Goelet, who besides being one of America's wealthiest men and a member in high standing of New York society was also a captain in the military intelligence section in Washington.

That a U.S. spy would be traveling aboard the Hamburg-American lines was no shock, considering that the German-owned line was actually a front for the Imperial German Navy since the 1890s. By 1908, the Hamburg-American Line officials were routinely encouraging their employees to transmit sensitive intelligence on the Royal Navy. In addition, the offices of the HAL in New York City became the hub for German spies who were operating in the United States for years before she entered the war.

Mike Caveney's Egyptian Hall Museum

17

Fighting Our Way to the Grave

THE LAST THING THAT THE AUDIENCE expected to see was bricklayers. But there they were onstage, with their dowels and mortar and bricks. As the orchestra played, they worked at a frenzied pace and constructed, brick by brick, a solid impenetrable wall that bisected the two seamless rugs that had been previously placed crosswise on the floor of the stage.

"I would now like to invite any doubting members of the audience to come up and examine the wall to assure themselves that there is no trickery involved," Houdini said. The spectators who took him up on the offer were allowed to peruse the cloth and even hit the wall with supplied hammers. When they were convinced of the impenetrability of the bricks, Houdini told them to form a semicircle facing the edge of the wall that pointed away from the audience.

Now Houdini, the man who no jail could hold, was going to demonstrate in front of a live audience that walls couldn't stop him either. The mysteriarch stood solemnly next to the structure. He certainly couldn't go around the wall; either the audience or the committee onstage would catch that. It was nine feet tall, so he couldn't scale it without being detected. The seamless carpet prevented him from going under it. So he had only one option: to walk through it.

Two six-foot-tall screens were brought onstage. One was placed around Houdini, the other was set up on the other side of the wall. Houdini held his hands up over the enclosure. "Here I am," he shouted. His hands dropped. "Now I'm going." Suddenly, a plank that had been placed on top of the screen on the other side of the wall was knocked to the floor. "Now I'm here!" Houdini said, and he stepped out from behind the screen on the other side of the wall. He had walked through a solid, hand-built brick wall.

"Houdini . . . gave the most remarkable performance that has ever been witnessed in American vaudeville," a *Billboard* magazine critic gushed. "He walks through a solid brick wall without disturbing a brick. The audience sat spellbound for fully two minutes after this feat was accomplished. They were too dumbfounded to applaud." When his turn was over, Houdini received four curtain calls.

With war raging in Europe, Houdini had put his magical bus tour idea on hold and introduced a new effect that bridged his twin identities of escape artist and master magician. The effect was not his own invention. Houdini had licensed the American rights from a British magician named Sidney Josolyne. Whether they were his to sell is still in dispute. Josolyne called his version Walking Through a Steel Plate. Just as the name implied, the magician would miraculously pass through a steel wall and materialize on the other side. Of course, dubious audiences might think that the wall was gimmicked, and the magician, after being shielded from sight on one side of the wall, would simply pass through a secret panel in the structure and get to the other side. Houdini quelled those notions with his brilliant staging.

That Houdini's feats often completely astonished his audiences to the point of incredulity was evidenced by a disclaimer that Houdini was forced to issue as he continued to tour America with his Water Torture Cell. "There are people who have seen my act . . . who are inclined to be skeptical. They think the feat is a misrepresentation. They imagine that it is all an optical illusion just performed to deceive the eye," Houdini wrote. "It is not a sham. . . . Since my youth I have studied mechanics. . . . The water torture cell was constructed by myself. . . . It took two full years. Another year was required to give me sufficient courage to attempt same. And can you blame me? Imagine yourself jammed head foremost in a cell filled with water, with your hands and feet unable to move and your shoulders tightly lodged in this imprisonment. . . . I believe it is the climax of all my studies and labors. Never will I be able to construct anything that will be more dangerous or difficult for me to do. Having flown a biplane and taught myself to become an expert aviator, I am in a position to state that flying is child's play in comparison."

In December 1914, while playing in Washington, D.C., Houdini was summoned to the White House for a private audience with President Woodrow Wilson, and the visit had a profound impact on the magician. "I hold the memory of my visit to President Wilson as an honor that is sacred," he told reporters. "I have appeared before the rulers of nearly every civilized nation and the potentates of many uncivilized races, but I have never met so gracious a ruler, so human a man, as the President of my native land." As Houdini was leaving, Wilson, who was then under pressure from all sides with respect to the war, bade him farewell. "Sir, I envy you your ability of escaping out of tight places," he told Houdini. "Sometimes I wish I were able to do the same."

Energized by his visit with the chief executive, Houdini began to apply some of his mechanical ingenuity toward inventions that could have practical applications and not merely serve as vehicles of entertainment. By the end of the month, headlines proclaimed "Houdini to Aid U.S. Government." Couched as a "Christmas gift to the nation," Houdini revealed that he was at work perfecting a diving suit that could be easily shed to enable disabled deep-sea divers to escape death by drowning. As soon as the invention was perfected, he planned to donate the apparatus to the U.S. government. "For some time I have been wondering how I could devote to the public good some of the ingenuity, which I have utilized in making my own way in the world," Houdini told the reporter. "All the things by which I have managed to fool the public for many years have been done for the purely selfish motives of building up my own reputation, and I feel that it is only right that what brain and gifts I have should benefit humanity in some other way than merely entertaining the people."

Houdini had been spurred to develop his improved suit when a friend of his in Melbourne, Australia, drowned while deep-sea diving. Eerily, the two men had had plans to meet for dinner that night. His friend's death hit Houdini hard and he "formed a strong impression" that the friend had attempted to communicate with him, urging him to invent a safer suit.

This was not just empty rhetoric from a master publicist. A few years later, Houdini took out patents in both the United States and England on an improved diving suit that allowed the user to shed it in forty-five seconds by pulling a lever, which disconnected the top of the suit from the bottom. True to his word, Houdini did donate his invention to the U.S. Navy.

All his touring and inventive tinkering couldn't get his mind off the death of his mother. As soon as he realized that the war had thwarted his chances to tour with his magical bus through Europe, Houdini had packed up all his belongings and moved out of his Harlem brownstone and moved in with Hardeen and his family in Flatbush. "The Home is a Home no longer for me and must be disposed of," he wrote his friend and confidant Dr. Waitt. The following spring, Houdini took five months off, except for his usual July dates at Hammerstein's and in Atlantic City. On July 5, 1915, he wrote friend A. G. Waring, "I have worked hard and faithfully, and never knew what it was to shirk work, until one morning I awoke and found that my Mother had departed—and since then I 'loaf' in my work."

"I have not recovered from my Mothers Loss, and July 8 was the (1913) last time I saw and [held] Her in my arms kissing Her a genuine Goodbye, and about the 17 of each month the feeling comes back to me, and I get melancoly [sic] moods," he admitted to his old partner Jacob Hyman. On the second anniversary of her death, Houdini, Theo, and Leopold drove to Asbury Park and stayed in the room "in which My Darling Mother went to Sleep for Evermore."

"Now I need three more gentlemen on this stage and there is a man here tonight who doesn't know I am aware of his presence but I would be highly honored if this one man, who is the equal to three, would come up. I refer to Mr. Jess Willard, our champion," Houdini bellowed from the stage of Los Angeles's Orpheum Theatre on November 30, 1915.

Momentarily stunned, the audience of more than two thousand responded with tumultuous applause, cheers, and shrieks. Jess Willard was the recently crowned heavyweight champion of the world. Dubbed another "Great White Hope" by racist boxing aficionados who despaired at having the crown reside with Jack Johnson, a flamboyant black man, Willard had knocked Johnson out in twenty-six rounds in over one-hundred-degree heat in Havana the previous April. A six-foot-seven, 265-pound giant, Willard was such a hard hitter that in 1913 a fighter named "Bull" Young died after their bout. His victory over Johnson had made him an instant celebrity, and he capitalized on his newfound status by making personal appearances with Buffalo Bill's Wild West Show and even doing a vaudeville turn at Hammerstein's in New York. He was exactly the type of celebrity Houdini would have loved to befriend.

Yet Willard, who was sitting with his trainers, seemed to sink into his seat after Houdini's request.

"I assure you, Mr. Willard, that everyone here would like to have you as one of the committee and to prove it to you, we will leave it to the audience. Those who are in favor of having Mr. Willard on the stage, please signify by applauding."

The audience gave him a resounding, lengthy ovation.

"Aw, g'wan wid your act. I paid for my seat here," Willard groused at Houdini.

"But, Mr. Willard. I—" Houdini seemed at a loss for words.

"Give me the same wages you pay those other fellows and I'll come down," Willard said.

The audience fell silent.

"All right," Houdini said brightly. "I accept your challenge. I'll pay you what I pay these seven men. Come on down—I pay these men nothing. Don't crawfish. Kindly step right downstairs and come on stage."

Another huge cheer. Willard half rose and in his distinctive guttural voice yelled, "Go on wid the show, you faker, you four-flusher. Everyone knows you're a four-flusher."

Several people hissed the champion. Emboldened, Houdini walked right down to the footlights near Willard and, "white with rage," threw his best haymaker.

"Look here, you. I don't care how big you are or who you are. I paid you a compliment when I asked you to be one of the committee. You have the right to refuse, but you have no right to slur my reputation. Now that you have thrown down the gauntlet, I have the right to answer, and let me tell you one thing, and don't forget this, that *I will still be Harry Houdini and a gentleman when you are no longer the heavyweight champion of the world.*"

The reaction of the crowd was captured vividly by Houdini in a beautifully descriptive letter to his sister. "I have roamed all over the world, I have raised Cain in thousands of theatres, I have tried through many a sleepless night to invent schemes to make an audience appreciate some worthy effort of mine, but nothing like this howling mob of refined ladies and gentlemen ever crossed my vision of success. . . . My reply to Mr. Jess Willard just set those twenty-three hundred human beings stark, raving mad. Instead of a place of entertainment, it was a seething, roaring furnace. For ten to fifteen minutes I had to stand perfectly still until the audience became exhausted in their tirades against Willard.

"All this time he shook his great fists at me and offered me a thousand dollars to come up to him, as he wished to annihilate me. But he could not make himself heard above the din of the hydra-throated monster he had aroused by insulting their compliments, and there he sat, swearing and blaspheming, until the head usher warned him that if he did not cease he must leave. Willard finally departed, crestfallen and defeated."

The controversy raged for days, front-page headlines screaming, "Champion Driven from Theater by Hoots and Calls," "Houdini Makes Monkey out of Jess Willard," "Sneaks out of Town as Indignant Fans Roast His Conduct." Willard did, in fact, leave town, failing to make a scheduled appearance as a wrestling referee the next day. Commentators claimed that the entire sport of boxing had been given a black eye by the "Pottawatomie Giant."

Houdini even used the occasion to publicly declare his patriotism. A month after Willard won his crown, Germany had torpedoed the *Lusitania*, a passenger steamship, killing 128 Americans in the process. Rallying around (some might say wrapping himself in) the flag, Houdini told the *Los Angeles Record*, "I am an American and am more proud of that fact than anything else. That's why it cut me so to realize that Jess Willard, whom I regarded as OUR champion, would act as he did. I have performed for kings, emperors, czars and princes in Europe, but I value one little audience with Pres. Wilson more than I do all the honors that they heaped upon me. The day that our president sent for me was the one which I shall always treasure in my memory as the happiest in my life, for I love my country and respect its president more than the greatest princes of the earth. So that's what hurt me when Jess Willard . . . failed to live up to our ideals in public. An American is always a gentleman, in my opinion."

The Willard bout was like a tonic to the man who had seemed a shadow of himself after his mother's death. "[Willard] was not only hissed out of the theatre, but Houdini struck him a blow that knocked him out of the theatre, knocked him down and out of the hearts of hundreds of thousands of his admirers," the magician wrote his sister. "Honest, Gladys, I have received at least a million dollars' advertising space from this fray . . . You will smile to know that I am greeted on the streets as, 'Hello, Champion.'"

Whether this was a courageous act of defiance or a cunning way of bullying a not-so-bright prizefighter into a David vs. Goliath no-win situation, Houdini seemed to be afraid of only one person in that theater, and she didn't stand six feet seven inches tall. "Bess was in the wings," he reported to his sister, "her face flaming red. I felt sure she was going to give me the dickens, and just think of it—there I was hurling defiance at the greatest fighter of the human race, and when I beheld my beloved little helpmate I actually was afraid. But she was with me. In fact in all my fights when she thinks I am right she is alongside, helping me load the machine guns. So when I noted that Bess was not angry with me, I did not give a rap about what Willard thought of me."

Houdini trumpeted his victory over Willard to all his friends, even sending clippings to his latest confidant and correspondent Quincy Kilby, who was keeping a Houdini scrapbook. His only regret was that his new friend, Jack London, the novelist, wasn't at the theater that night. "As you will have noticed from the papers I am the Newspaper Champion Heavy of the World????? What a scene you could have written had you been present and witnessed the battle," he wrote London. He was only half joking—London was an amateur boxer and an avid fan; as a celebrity journalist he covered the Johnson-Jeffries fight in 1910.

Houdini and Bess had met Jack London and his wife, Charmian, a week earlier in Oakland. London and Houdini struck up a fast friendship and found that they had both been self-educated and had suffered privation before gaining

The Houdinis meet the Londons. It was love at first sight. *From the collection of Roger Dreyer*

wealth and fame. London was the literary equivalent of Houdini—a courageous, adventurous thrill-seeker who channeled his wide-ranging experiences into best-selling novels like *The Sea Wolf* and *The Call of the Wild.* There were differences too. London had been a longtime socialist and a strong advocate of women's liberation. He had divorced his first wife after a torrid affair with Charmian Kittredge, who was five years his senior. Charmian shared his love of adventure and the outdoors, and her liberated stance toward their marriage included open sexual experimentation.

Befriending a world-famous author certainly fed into Houdini's own vision of himself as a literary man. Houdini made fast friends with London. The author and his wife had come to back-to-back shows, and Houdini dined solo with them the first night and with Bess on the second. Then the next day, Thanksgiving, he asked them to a holiday dinner in his hotel room, inviting Hardeen, who was appearing at a rival theater, to witness his new celebrity friendship. Houdini then had to leave for Los Angeles and his date with heavyweight destiny, but the couples made plans to get together again soon.

"Charming Houdini," Charmian London noted in her diary. "Shall never forget him."

He had stopped into the Trav Daniel Sporting Goods store to pick up a pair of white Spaulding track shorts. "They're pretty good for underwear," he told the awe-stricken young clerk, who, after screwing up his courage, gushed to the magician that he had loved his show the previous night at the nearby Majestic Theater. Never one to shun a compliment, Houdini struck up a conversation. And when the kid told Houdini that his older brother was a trick motorcycle rider, Houdini left the sporting goods store with more than just a pair of shorts—he had the concept for a new stunt that he would pull off the next morning.

The clerk's brother was Ormer Locklear, a twenty-five-year-old mechanic who had a fascination with cars, motorcycles, and airplanes. Houdini met him and instantly thought that Locklear had the requisite charisma and good looks to win over any crowd. So he proposed that Locklear drag him, hog-tied, behind his motorcycle down Fort Worth's Main Street. While careening down the street, Houdini would make his escape. At first, Locklear was reluctant to participate in what seemed to be a recipe for disaster, but Houdini assured him that he would minimize all danger. "A good stuntman always knows what his limits are."

Besides its being the busiest thoroughfare, Houdini chose Main Street because it was the only "paved" street in Fort Worth, the "paving" merely being a series of wooden stumps that had been inserted into the dirt to protect horses' hooves. The next day, Houdini donned thick, quilted overalls and protected his head with a hood. He asked some volunteers to tie his hands behind his back and then, as he lay down on the street, a rope that was attached to Locklear's motorcycle was tied around his ankles. With a large crowd lining both sides of the street, one of the locals shot a starting pistol and Locklear revved his cycle and took off, hauling his human cargo. Apprehensive about really gunning his engine, Locklear started off slow and gradually increased his speed. Within seconds, Houdini had freed his hands and untied the rope attached to the cycle.

Houdini had chosen a very interesting time to make his first tour of Texas. On May 15, 1915, President Wilson had directed the Secretary of the Treasury to order the Secret Service to investigate an ongoing operation by German secret agents in the United States aimed at sabotaging the munitions industry, which was selling its armaments to the Allied cause. What they found was shocking. The German government had smuggled more than $150 million in cash (the equivalent of about $13 billion today) into the United States to finance sabotage, propaganda, and a conspiracy to get the United States embroiled in a diversionary war with Mexico by seeding Pancho Villa's bandit rebellion against the U.S.-backed government of General Carranza. To make sense of all this intrigue, a new form of intelligence gathering and surveillance was needed. To that end, it was decided that the army's First Aero Squadron, stationed at Fort Sam Houston in San Antonio, would be deployed in aerial surveillance missions.

Beginning at the end of January 1916, Houdini spent a week in San Antonio, playing the Majestic Theater. Since January 1910, Fort Sam Houston in Texas had been the site of the aero division of the U.S. Army. That sounds grandiose because until April 1911, the army had only one plane and one pilot, Benjamin Foulois. The situation was so bad that a few months before, when the War Department wished to test the efficacy of using airplanes in war by attacking ground troops with dummy bombs, six aviators who were participating in a local aerial tournament in San Antonio were enlisted to fly their machines and bombard the detachment of troops from Fort Sam Houston.

In April, things began to change. Houdini's mechanist, Montraville Wood, spent most of April at Fort Sam Houston, flying the army's Curtiss two-seater, sometimes alone and sometimes with a Lieutenant Beck, experimenting with his gyroscope, which could give the plane added stability in adverse wind conditions. Wood's mechanical improvements were incorporated in additional planes that the army purchased.

In July 1911, pilot Foulois was transferred to the Signal Corps in Washington and fell under the command of General Allen, who would go on to become the president of Wood's airplane company. In December 1913, Foulois was assigned to the Signal Corps Aviation School in San Diego, where, the following year, he organized and assumed command of the First Aero Squadron. In the fall of 1915, Foulois's squadron was moved by rail to Fort Sill, Oklahoma, then flew for the first time as a unit to Fort Sam Houston, where they were based when Houdini came to Texas.

We know that Houdini entertained soldiers from Fort Sam Houston onstage on February 4 when they challenged him to escape from a seven-foot plank. There is anecdotal evidence that suggests that Houdini may have actually even flown during his stay in San Antonio. In a Providence newspaper, Houdini is credited as being "one of the heroes of the Panama-California exposition in 1915, a wizard of the first order and last but not least an aviator of the United States Army." Around the same time, while he was performing in Boston, Houdini told the noted Boston reporter Ira Mitchell Chappelle, "I'm an American, though first, last, and all the time. I'm an aviator, and in case there's war, will surely be a member of the aviation corps."

It was high noon and Pennsylvania Avenue between Thirteenth and Fifteenth Streets was crammed with people taking up every available inch of space on the sidewalk. The more adventurous had shinned up light poles or hung out of the windows from the neighboring buildings. "Human beings don't like to see other human beings lose their lives, but they do love to be on the spot when it happens," an astute observer of human nature once said. Well, on April 20, 1916, he was proven correct. The police estimated that 100,000 people had shoved, pushed, elbowed, and wedged their way in front of the Munsey Building in downtown Washington, D.C., then spilled down the street for blocks and blocks. They also said it was the single largest assemblage of people in that city's history outside of a presidential inauguration.

Captain Peck of the Washington police department stood on the makeshift platform in front of the building as the man was escorted by the police through the frenzied crowd. The rope, a sturdy thick variant, had been tested and retested to make sure that it would hold the man's weight. Finally, about twenty minutes past noon, the rope was securely affixed to the man by the authorities.

And then the public hanging began.

Houdini, who had just been securely fastened into a straitjacket by two attendants from an area mental hospital, was hoisted by his legs one hundred feet into the air, parallel with the fourth story of the massive office building. For a few seconds he was completely still. Then, as the crowd gasped, he began to jerk frantically from side to side, the veins in his face standing out like great purple cords. It seemed that his arms had some play now; he was able to jerk them from side to side. The crowd cheered. Now he had managed to work his arms slowly and painfully over his head. A huge cheer reverberated through the

While Houdini is strapped into his straitjacket, more than a few curious onlookers gather.
From the collection of Dr. Bruce Averbook

human canyon. One by one, he opened the straps, managing to unfasten them through the heavy canvas with his extremely strong fingers. With each strap liberated, the crowd roared anew. Now he was completely free of the restraint, and he held it mockingly in the air for a few seconds before he released it and it fluttered in the wind to the street below. The audience yelled as one, and Houdini crossed his arms on his chest and pulled himself halfway up, saluting the crowd with an upside-down bow.

Houdini's outdoor upside-down straitjacket escape was one of the greatest publicity stunts ever devised, appealing to both the finest and the basest instincts of his audience simultaneously. It was the pinnacle of his stunts, primarily because it was the only outdoor stunt he ever did where the escape was in full view of the audience. Much of what he did onstage was hidden from view; the bridge or pier jumps used the water to mask the action. The suspended straitjacket was perfect from start to finish, and Houdini dangling in the air above thousands and thousands of astonished spectators became the magician's iconic image—an image that was inspired by a visit to a young man's attic in Sheffield, England.

Even dangling upside down in a straitjacket, Houdini knew to pose for the camera.

From the collection of Dr. Bruce Averbook

One of the most spectacular outdoor stunts in history. *From the collection of George and Sandy Daily*

Houdini did it first in September of 1915 in Kansas City, where five thousand people watched as he was hoisted twenty feet in the air and then shed his restraint. By the middle of 1916 the crowds had swelled ten or twenty fold and the height had increased to as high as two hundred feet. For the most part, Houdini retained his early formula for a successful publicity stunt—he did the escape hanging from the building that housed the local newspaper, guaranteeing front-page coverage, and he performed it exactly at noon, ensuring himself a street filled with lunchtime spectators.

Of course, he would have to come to the site a day earlier to "inspect" the building and the harness and speak with the local authorities who would do the strapping of the jacket, spurring a newspaper article that would promote the actual event the next day. In San Antonio, he met the two police officials who were charged with securing his straitjacket and hoisting him up.

"String me up just as high as you can. If I drop I want to be sure it's going to be the finish. I'd rather have a lilly [sic] in my hand than go through life crippled and a burden to others," Houdini told them, within earshot of the eager reporter who scribbled down each word. After all, human beings don't like to see other human beings die, but . . .

As dangerous as it looked, the upside-down straitjacket escape was somewhat safer than his manacled bridge leaps or escapes from submerged crates, even when he started affixing an additional safety rope after a stray wind blew him into the side of a building and cut him badly. But when you're dangling one hundred feet in the air by your feet, twisting and jerking to free yourself, anything can happen. In Oakland, California, *after* he had freed himself and thrown the jacket to the adoring crowd, when he gave the signal to be lowered, he didn't budge. During his gyrations, he had entangled the ropes. He was forced to hang upside down for a full eight minutes until a ladder, held secure by six men, was extended off the roof and a window cleaner shinned down it and untangled the ropes.

By April 19, 1916, the day before his massive outdoor stunt in the nation's capital, Houdini's weariness seemed to be catching up with him. "I've about reached the limit, it seems to me," he told the *Washington Times* reporter. "For the last thirty years . . . I've been getting out of all sorts of things human ingenuity has devised to confine a human being. Up to date there hasn't been anything made that confined my activities to any alarming extent. But some day some chap is going to make one. And I'm going to quit with a clean record before he comes along. I've about made up my mind that this is the last stunt I'll perform. Hereafter I intend to work entirely with my brain. See these gray hairs? They mean something. I'm not as young as I was. I've had to work hard to keep ahead of the procession. I'll still be entertaining the public for many years to come. But I intend to do it along lines not quite so spectacular. As an escapist extraordinary I feel that I'm about through."

Two days after Houdini's huge stunt, President Wilson, who was continuing to try to steer the United States on a course of neutrality despite Germany's ever-more-blatant submarine attacks on unarmed American merchant ships, snuck away from the White House with his new bride to see Houdini escape from his Water Torture Cell. The next afternoon, Houdini paid a visit to the Senate visitors' gallery. While presiding over the session, Vice President Thomas Marshall spotted Houdini and waved to him. Other senators stopped their business and followed suit.

A page was dispatched to Houdini and delivered a note, inviting him to the vice president's chamber. When Houdini complied, the senators called a recess and crowded into the vice president's chambers. "It was the proudest day of my life," Houdini would later say.

Buoyed by the honor accorded him by the president and the Senate, Houdini went back home and came face-to-face with his own mortality. He had spent part of his forty-second birthday at the grave of his parents. Now, three weeks later, he ran into old Mrs. Leffler, his landlady when he and his father first moved to New York. "I nearly cried, as she was a pal of my Dad and Mrs. L is the only one left of the Old Guard," he wrote in his diary. Two weeks later, on Mother's Day, he sent flowers to all the "Mothers graves" he knew, and then visited Mrs. Leffler and hand-delivered her a bouquet. The following week, after seeing his dentist, he took a sentimental trip to the East Sixty-ninth Street apartment where his dad died. He stood there in silent meditation for half an hour, replaying his father's final exit from the building. "It grieves me more now than it did then," he wrote in his diary. He remembered comforting his mother that day, asking her not to weep. "If you had 28 years of heaven, you'd weep too," she responded. As a tribute to his parents, Houdini commissioned his friend Oscar Teale to design an extravagant exedra that used many tons of Vermont granite. After years of restoring the graves of magicians he had never known, it was time to honor his parents' final resting place.

Wearied by the constant touring and the years of abusive challenge escapes, Houdini came up with a get-rich-quick scheme, "which if it only materializes half way decent, will bring in lots of money to my celler [sic]," he wrote a friend. With the film business beginning to make major inroads into competing entertainment forms, Houdini was approached to bankroll a German aniline dye expert named Gustav Dietz who invented a new process for developing film stock that was allegedly cheaper and better than the methods that were currently in use. Houdini seeded the company to the tune of $4,900 in September and then approached friends and raised $100,000 in capital. August Roterberg, one candid friend who didn't invest, was wary of Houdini's business acumen. "You are old enough to know that there is a vast difference between inventing a successful developer and developing the developer, or in other words handle it along commercial lines and make it pay. I hope that you won't fall down on the latter part."

Houdini's relentless publicity seeking and his innate understanding of what was believable combined to push his name into the language. As early as 1899 the word *Houdini* began to be used synonymously with escape. Newspapers referred to escaped criminals as Houdinis or as "doing a Houdini." By 1917, the guardians of the language noticed that cartoonists, lexicographers, preachers, the *Literary Digest,* and even a U.S. congressman were using Houdini's name as a comparison for other people's activities in elusion. Houdini didn't completely understand the power of his own name then, and he petitioned a popular publisher to have "houdinize" added to their dictionary. He was successful, but ironically, he didn't understand that as a verb, "houdinize" was meaningless, since the word *Houdini* had already become a noun and adjective.

The end of 1916 was marked with family tragedies in the Houdini household. His brother Nat was in the process of an ugly divorce with his wife, Sadie, which might have prompted Houdini to remind Bess of his feelings toward her. "Your Love bestowed upon me is Duly Appreciated though at times I may be apparently thoughtless, my mind is compelled to carry so many things, but my heart only one on earth and that is you," he wrote. Contrast that with his feeling toward his relatives that he expressed in a letter to Kilby, thanking him for a thoughtful Christmas present. "Your gift is far and away more welcome than you have an idea. You see I send out dozens of checks to folks in need, and all I ever get from my relatives, those that are left write saying 'You have everything you want I dont know what to buy you.' Mrs. H makes something for me to put on the dresser, but [as] it is made by 'herself' that counts a good deal. My Sainted Mother, would send cookies and a few pair of silk socks to all parts of the world, and honestly since MOTHER has passed away Christmas (and I am the son of a Rabbi) seems somewhat empty."

After a bittersweet Christmas, Houdini spent a forlorn New Year's Eve alone in Philadelphia as Bess stayed home to deal with an unknown family tragedy. His New Year Day's letter was revelatory: "Keep up your courage, sweetheart, and bear your loss like the brave little soldier that you are, for we are all more or less an army fighting our way to our own graves, but let us do so stout of heart, smile and cheer our less fortunate brethren who are also in the trenches of life and who are not as well equipped with mates as you and I are, nor with the world's goods."

The new year found Houdini's name in papers across the globe for a compassionate gesture toward one of the world's greatest actresses. Sarah Bernhardt, who was on a tour of the American stage, had been honored the previous December by a group of American actors who presented her with a bronze statuette depicting her in one of her most famous roles. Unfortunately, she was also presented with a bill for the cost of the sculpture by the artist's wife. Indignant, Bernhardt returned the figurine along with the bill.

Houdini had long been a fan of the French actress, often writing up her exploits in his *Dramatic Mirror* columns, and he had been especially moved by her strident advocacy for the human rights of Jews in Russia. Anxious to avoid an embarrassing scene for American actors abroad, Houdini immediately dispatched a $350 check to the sculptor's wife, took possession of the statuette, and offered to personally present the gift anew to Madame Bernhardt. The resulting

Houdini, Bess, his assistants, and his parrot pose in front of the Christmas tree. Houdini's parrot was trained to squawk, "Hip, hip, hoorah, Houdini's home!"
From the collection of Dr. Bruce Averbook

publicity kept Houdini's clipping service working overtime—more than 3,500 articles were generated. Ironically enough, Bernhardt relished the publicity but left Houdini in possession of the statuette. The two-foot-tall sculpture eventually found a home in the living room of Houdini's friend Quincy Kilby, who was pleased when Houdini then sent him both his telegram to Bernhardt and the canceled check for the purchase of the piece. "[This] completes the story," Kilby crowed. "It shall be preserved in the archives."

In February, both Bernhardt and Houdini found themselves playing Boston at the same time. She invited him to visit her at her hotel, where Houdini entranced her with more than a half hour of close-up magic. The next day, she rode in a car with the magician and watched him free himself from a straitjacket while being suspended sixty feet in the air. The previous year had been rough for the French actress; ten years after a serious injury, her right leg was finally amputated and she was continuing her stage career with the assistance of a wooden leg.

The Houdinis meet the Grand Dame Sarah Bernhardt. *From the collection of Dr. Bruce Averbook*

On the way back to the hotel, the Divine Sarah suddenly embraced Houdini.

"Houdini, you are a wonderful human being," she purred. "You must possess some extraordinary power to perform such marvels. Won't you use it to restore my limb for me?"

Houdini was shocked when he realized that she was dead serious.

"Good heavens, Madame, certainly not," Houdini sputtered. "You know my powers are limited and you are actually asking me to do the impossible."

"Yes," she said, leaning closer to him. "But you *do* the impossible."

"Are you jesting?"

"Mais non, Houdini, j'ai jamais été plus sérieux dans ma vie."

Houdini's eyes welled with tears.

"Madame, you exaggerate my ability," he said.

Houdini would often brag that without the aid of any memory devices, he was able to recount the exact date of the birth of the Roman Emperor Caracalla. He could even tell you the day of the month in 1593 when dissenting clergymen were hanged in Scotland. He most likely also knew the exact day that Napoleon abdicated; the day Robert Peary reached the North Pole; and maybe even the day that Stilicho stymied the Visigoths in the Battle of Pollentia.

Of course, the correct answer to all of these is April 6, Houdini's adopted birth date (except for Caracalla, who unbeknownst to Houdini was actually born on April 4). On April 6, 1917, Houdini celebrated his forty-third birthday and had a new milestone to add to his list. The day before, his brother Leopold had scandalized the family by marrying Sadie Weiss, who until March 26 had been legally married to his brother Nat. Reeling from a family secret that had finally gone public, Houdini woke up to a birthday present from his friend the commander in chief. On that day, President Wilson declared war on Germany. In one fell swoop, Houdini's midlife crisis had been solved. Escapologist, illusionist, collector, businessman, author, philanthropist—all his myriad identities suddenly paled in comparison with his new vision of himself: Houdini the Patriot.

From the collection of Dr. Bruce Averbook

18

Death by Misadventure

THE PROCESSION HAD THE AIR OF a funeral, even though the intended victim was still very much alive. A long line of Boxer warriors, the fanatical Chinese cult that believed they were magically impervious to foreigners' bullets, slowly made their way to the site of the execution, banging gongs, mournfully beating on drums, and chanting. Two of the Boxers, who had tied red sashes over their shiny brass plate armor, were carrying what looked to be very primitive rifles for 1918. At a time when most armies had gone to automatic weaponry, these Boxer marksmen had old twelve-gauge single-barreled muzzle-loading rifles with a small ramrod tube nestled under each barrel. Each time the rifle was to be fired, the rod was pulled out of its tube and used to ram the charge into the barrel. Apparently these sharpshooters didn't plan on having to reload.

Suddenly the line of soldiers parted and a garish ebony-and-gold palanquin was carried in. It was set down on the ground and one of the warriors opened the door. A tall Asian man stepped out, wearing an ornamental headdress that culminated in a spike and a long studded, quilted robe. It would have been easy to mistake this man for the regiment leader—he had that air of charisma and inscrutability, even though he hadn't said a word. But he wasn't the leader. He wasn't even a Boxer. In fact, he was the one who had been condemned to death.

With the victim off to one side, the two gunmen lined up opposite him. They were joined by two British soldiers, only one of whom was in uniform. The Chinese gunmen handed the Brits their rifles for inspection. Amused at first by the antiquity of the arms, the Englishmen carefully peered into the barrels, pulled out the ramrods, and fingered the triggers. When they were satisfied that the rifles were in working order, another warrior then presented them with a large wooden box that was filled with bullets. The men were instructed to each select a bullet. The ammunition was large and round, resembling lethal lead marbles. Each soldier held his chosen bullet up in the air and then a small Chinese woman carrying a small metal cup walked up to them and signaled for them to drop the bullets inside.

Then the man who seemed to be in charge of the proceedings sprinkled some gunpowder from a tin onto a small tray.

"Real gunpowder? Is it real?" he asked.

One of the soldiers bent over and smelled the gunpowder.

Then the Boxer touched a lit match to the powder. It exploded into a plume of white smoke, and the unmistakable smell of spent gunpowder suffused the air.

"Yes, real powder," the Boxer chuckled.

He poured a measure of gunpowder into each of the rifle's barrels. An assistant then stuffed the cotton wadding in and another pulled out the ramrod from its sheath and inserted it into the barrel. All this was done under the supervision of the British soldiers. Now all that was necessary was for the ammunition to be loaded and the percussive caps put in place. Yet throughout all of this preparation, the intended victim seemed strangely impassive, as if he had been through this before.

Suee Seen had taken the cup that contained the bullets and walked out into the audience to find two other volunteers to mark them. When each one had a distinctive mark on it, she would return to the stage of the Wood Green Empire Theatre in north London and give the bullets to the two British soldiers, who would note the marks and then load the rifles.

With the rifles finally ready, the funeral drumming started up again and the two British soldiers were escorted to the side of the stage so they could watch the denouement of the effect.

"Ladies and gentlemen, silence please," Frank Kametaro, the chief assistant, said. He pointed at two men in the audience. "Two bullets! You have seen to it that the bullets were marked." Then he nodded toward the British soldiers. "And you have seen the guns loaded. Now silence, and watch closely. Everyone watch."

On cue, the two riflemen took fourteen steps toward stage left, while Chung Ling Soo, the Marvelous Chinese Conjuror, backed slowly to his spot on the far right of the stage. All that stood between him and certain death was a small porcelain plate, which had been handed to him by an assistant.

All was ready. The drumming abruptly ceased as the riflemen took up their positions. Kametaro, who was between the victim and his executioners but well behind the line of fire, drew his sword and held it poised over his head. He looked at Soo for the signal.

The magician lowered his head, took a deep breath, and then slowly raised the plate until it was shielding his chest. He would not merely deflect the bullets with the fragile little piece of porcelain, he would stop them in midair and, with a graceful twist of his wrists, delicately balance them on the plate, so that they could be inspected and found to be the same marked ammunition that had been loaded into the rifles.

It took complete concentration. So with his porcelain shield held aloft, Soo repositioned his feet. The audience was so still that they could actually hear him draw another long, deep breath. Then suddenly, a man in the front row stood up and shouted something. Nobody could discern what he had said and Soo waited until the man sat down again, and then he shifted his weight on his feet, repositioned the plate, and took another deep breath. Then he quickly nodded to Kametaro.

The assistant's saber sliced through the air and, almost simultaneously, two loud explosions echoed throughout the theater. A second later, the porcelain shield fell to the floor and shattered on the stage.

"Oh, my God," Soo said, and staggered backward, toward backstage. Frank Moody, the stage manager, saw a crimson ribbon of blood illuminated in the spotlight. He rushed onstage and cradled Soo as the magician slowly slumped to the stage.

By now the crowd had sensed that something had gone horribly wrong. The few smatterings of premature applause had morphed into screams.

"My God, ring down the curtain, something has happened!" Soo gasped.

Just as the curtain came down, which effectively shielded the audience from this horrific scene, Soo's wife, the diminutive Suee Seen, rushed to her husband's side.

"Dot, fetch a doctor quick," the magician said.

Sergeant Spain, the policeman on duty, rushed to the fallen magician's side. Soo was drifting in and out of consciousness.

A few stagehands worked feverishly to stop the bleeding. One of them ripped down part of the border from the stage scenery and wrapped it around the wounded man to keep him warm.

"I cannot stand it, I cannot stand it," he mumbled.

"Oh Will, whatever have you done?" Dot said.

The few people witnessing this tragedy backstage were among the first to learn Soo's secret. Actually, any attentive audience member could have been tipped off too. For as soon as that errant bullet entered his chest, pierced his heart, grazed his liver, and exited his back before shattering a mirror near manager Moody's desk, the Asian magician who spoke not a word of English suddenly became fluent in his distress. Shortly the whole world would know that the man inside those

The mysterious Chung Ling Soo was in actuality the equally mysterious Billy Robinson.

From the collection of Dr. Bruce Averbook

Inset from the collection of Todd Karr

ceremonial robes and beneath the greasepaint was not the Mysterious Chinese Conjuror Chung Ling Soo but actually William E. Robinson, the equally mysterious American mechanist who had disappeared eighteen years before. While the life was slowly ebbing from his friend who lay on an English stage, Houdini was halfway around the globe, saving the lives of young Americans.

"The reason people drown on a sinking vessel is because they lose all sense of direction," the instructor said. Houdini looked out at the fresh faces of the young recruits and, for a fleeting second, reflected on what it was like when he was their age. Life seemed so much simpler then, he thought, and for another fleeting second he envied their ability to be in a position to make the ultimate sacrifice—to give their lives for their country. He would do everything in his power to make sure that eventuality would never transpire.

For their part, the Sammies, the appreciative name that the French gave the American soldiers, felt a mixture of apprehension and awe. In weeks, they would be crossing the ocean to fight in France alongside their counterparts in the English and French armed services. Basic training had been rigorous, but who could believe that it would have included a course on how to escape from a sinking torpedoed vessel given in a small room on the promenade floor of the enormous Hippodrome theater by none other than Harry Houdini? They all wondered if they would be able to get his autograph at the end of the session.

"The first rule when you find yourself underwater is: do not succumb to panic. I can't stress that enough," Houdini lectured. "Stay calm. Use your eyes. If visibility is clouded, slowly allow your body to rise up in the water until your hands come in contact with a deck, side, or the floor of the craft."

Houdini picked up a length of rope. "Now, I want to teach you the basic principles of extrication from entanglements of all kinds—whether from ropes, broken pipes, beams, or wreckages. Can I have a volunteer, please?"

Every arm in the room immediately shot up.

When Houdini got through tying up the young soldier, he looked like a trussed turkey.

"Now, I have restrained this young man in the same manner that I would use if I were to tie a medium to prevent him from being able to produce any physical manifestations in a séance room. I would venture to say that he's not going anywhere."

The Sammies all laughed.

"The odds are that your captors will not go to such lengths," Houdini lectured. "They might simply tie your hands behind your backs, but even such a simple restraint would be effective if you don't perform a subtle maneuver, which I shall show you, that will allow you to obtain some slack in the rope, and ultimately to free yourself from the bondage."

Houdini walked over to the table and picked up a pair of handcuffs.

"If your captors are particularly well equipped, they might have a pair of these German handcuffs as standard issue, in which case, your escape from their restraints would be harder, but not impossible," Houdini said. "After I show you

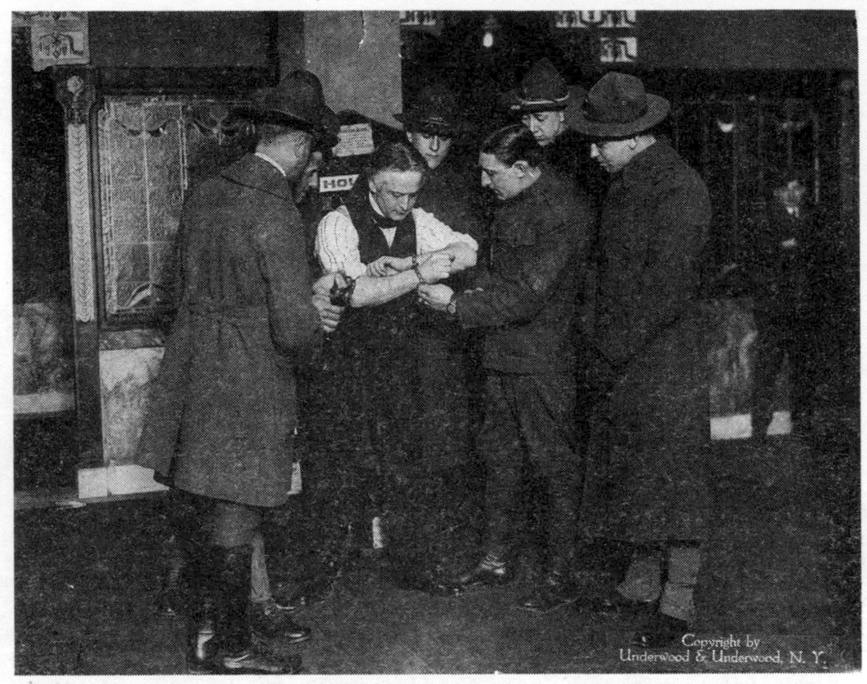

Houdini does his bit training doughboys to escape from German handcuffs.
From the collection of Kenneth M. Trombly

the rope escape, we will learn a few simple, effective techniques of defeating these German irons. And then . . ."

He strolled over to the other side of the room, where a large iron cage had been set up.

"This is a prison cage that has been fitted with typical German locks. As you see, this particular one can accommodate up to three prisoners in the field, but there are variations that go twenty-two feet long and can haul a dozen or more men, each securely chained to the other. As a measure of last resort, I will teach you a method to defeat the lock on the cage, so you can free yourself under cover of night. Any questions so far?"

Houdini looked out at his audience. They seemed intimidated by the master magician.

"I think our friend here has a question," Houdini said, glancing at the soldier that he had tied up so expertly. "But he can't raise his hand."

Houdini learned of his old friend Billy Robinson's death when he received a cable from Joe Hyman, who for a short time had been one of the Brothers Houdini. It read: "Soo Robinson Killed Doing Bullet Trick." The next day, March 26, 1918, Hyman sent a letter that contained some intriguing details. Hyman was currently sharing a bill with a woman named Annie Rooney, who had been on the bill at the Wood Green Empire the night Robinson died. According to Rooney, Soo had some "trouble" with one of his assistants; the argument escalated into "an open row" that ill-fated night and, between the two shows, Robinson "had it out with his chap." Early the next morning, Robinson died. "It is known for a fact that the rifle that was used for the trick had been tampered with," Hyman reported to Houdini. "This was discovered after the bullet had passed clean through poor Rob's body." After a short inquest, Robinson's demise was deemed "death by misadventure."

Houdini's response to his good friend's death was fascinating. On April 5, he wrote his friend and father figure Harry Kellar, the freshly retired master illusionist, now noncritically called "dean" of American magicians, that "it seems as if there were something peculkar [sic] about the whole [Robinson] affair." Then two weeks later, Houdini announced that he would do the Bullet Catch at a joint benefit for the SAM hospital fund and the Showman's League of America on April 21, at the Hippodrome. Whether Houdini was merely exploiting the tragedy to get press (which he received) or whether, as was reported in *M-U-M*, the official organ of the SAM, he was "dissuaded by management of Hippodrome from taking up this dangerous feat," he ultimately didn't perform the effect that night.

When news filtered out to Kellar in California that Houdini was even considering doing the Bullet Catch, the magician fired off a warning salvo to Houdini on May 1:

> ***Now, my dear boy, this is advice from the heart.*** DON'T TRY THE D—N Bullet Catching trick ***no matter how sure you may feel of its success. There is*** always ***the biggest kind of risk that some dog will "job" you. And we can't afford to lose Houdini. You have enough good stuff to maintain your position at the head of the profession. And you owe it to your friends and your family to cut out all stuff that entails risk of your life. Please, Harry, listen to your old friend Kellar who loves you as his own son and don't do it.***

Kellar's view on the risk involved in Houdini doing the Bullet Catch is telling. He isn't worried about the gun malfunctioning. For him, doing the Bullet Catch would expose Houdini to some "dog" who was out to physically assault, or even murder, him.

When the United States declared war against Germany on his birthday in 1917, Houdini immediately went into action. For most of 1916, while on his vaudeville tour, Houdini, at his own expense, had been recruiting local magic clubs to join the SAM in an effort to revitalize what he felt was a moribund organization. Working with Oscar Teale, an eccentric old ex-magician and Spiritualist exposer, another in a succession of father figures in Houdini's life, Houdini persuaded groups in Buffalo, Detroit, Pittsburgh, and Kansas City to come aboard. Now, a day after war was declared, Houdini introduced a resolution at the Society of American Magicians' meeting that was unanimously passed that "its members collectively and individually do hereby tender their loyalty to the President of the United States of America and express a desire to render such service to the country as may be within their province." Teale dispatched the resolution via letter to President Wilson.

Houdini led the war efforts of magicians by example. On June 2, Houdini was nominated for president of the SAM and elected unanimously without opposition. Taking control of the house organ, *M-U-M*, Houdini began filling the pages with news of the SAM members' contributions to the war cause, and even reproduced an article from *The New York Times* that described how the U.S. government was actively seeking magicians and mystifiers to aid in the wartime effort.

Fellow magicians took up Houdini's call. Archie Engel, a Washington, D.C., magician, became a secret agent for the Treasury Department during the war. Dr. Maximillian Toch, a chemist and New York City SAM member, was put in charge of the military's camouflage division and, working with other magicians, he developed the battleship gray formula used by the U.S. Navy. Toch's chemical expertise was also used in devising ways to transmit secret messages. Eventually, a camouflage section of the Regular U.S. Army Engineers was formed and the SAM members from all over the country enlisted in it and shared their expertise for the war effort. An amateur magician named Dr. Charles Mendelsohn, who was an expert cryptographer, was put in charge of deciphering German codes for the U.S. Military Intelligence Division. Even before we entered the war, the Department of Justice hired a magician named Wilbur Weber to do counterintelligence on German spies who were operating in the Northwest. He used his magic tour as a cover for his spying activities.

Heavyweight champion Jack Dempsey about to deliver a right to Houdini's jaw as boxer Benny Leonard holds back the escape king, all in the name of entertaining the troops.
From the collection of Roger Dreyer

Houdini seemed energized by the prospect of serving his country. "I register tomorrow for enlisting. *Hurrah*, now I am one of the boys," he wrote Goldston back in London. "When I see your flag flutter it makes my old heart flutter, but when I see them flutter together, your and our flag, well, there is too much to be said." Canceling his entire fall vaudeville season, Houdini began to devote his full time to entertaining troops and raising money for the war effort. In June, the National Vaudeville Association staged a benefit featuring the greatest aggregation of stars ever assembled, including Sophie Tucker, Eva Tanguay, Eddie Foy, and Jim Corbett. Houdini made a side wager that he would register the greatest hit of the evening and he won his gamble when he made his entrance into the Hippodrome accompanied by a company of U.S. Marines. The ovation was enormous and then Houdini enlisted some army officers to strap him into a straitjacket. He made his escape in one minute, twenty-three seconds, a new record for him.

In July he embarked on a series of fund-raising benefits for the Red Cross, and then dashed from camp to camp entertaining the troops. And when Secretary of the Treasury William McAdoo began to finance the U.S. war effort by issuing "Liberty Bonds," Houdini became one of his most determined fundraisers, in one case by literally selling the shirt off his back. During a Hippodrome appearance, a man in the audience offered to buy $1,000 in bonds if the magician could get out of his shirt in thirty seconds. By the time the audience counted six, Houdini was waving his torn shirt above his head. "I'll buy another $1,000 bond if you will give me that shirt," the audience member screamed, and went home with his prize. Within a year, Houdini had sold a million dollars' worth of bonds. By some accounts, by war's end the total reached two million dollars' worth.

When Houdini performed at military camps, he made sure to include his "Money for Nothing" routine, where he seemingly materialized a succession of $5 gold pieces out of thin air. Each coin produced was presented to a boy heading overseas. In this manner, over time, Houdini personally gave away more than $7,000 (which today would be about $250,000). This same year, he also contributed money to build a hospital ward that he dedicated to his mother.

The closest Houdini got to waging war was on the propaganda front. He gave numerous interviews recounting how he had forced the kaiser into a public apology when he was touring Germany. He even used the German manacles that he escaped from before the German court in his lectures to U.S. soldiers. In another article, he wrote that he had been an "advocate of war" with Germany dating back to his first European tour. In his official bios, he excised all mention of his early flights in Germany, attributing them instead to Australia. In private, he fretted that the German soldiers he had taught to fly might kill American boys, so he destroyed all the photographic evidence of those lessons that he could. To underscore his fervent patriotism, Houdini went out of his way to tell people that he was born in Appleton, Wisconsin, even often gratuitously adding that "fact," along with his invented birth date, to his signature.

Houdini's desire to help the war cause and his long-standing commitment to honoring his elders in the world of magic coalesced on November 11, when Houdini orchestrated a Carnival of Magic extravaganza to benefit the families of the Americans who had been killed when the *Antilles*, a transport ship that was on its way back to the United States after bringing soldiers to France, had been torpedoed by a German sub. Organizing "the biggest magical feat recorded in the history of magic," he persuaded Dean Harry Kellar to come out of retirement one last time and perform.

After Kellar finished his routine, he informed the audience that since he would never again appear onstage, he wished to present Houdini with all of the apparatus he had used that night. But then Houdini one-upped Kellar. Refusing to allow the dean to walk off the stage in his final exit, he signaled for four

Houdini with the great past master and dean of magicians Harry Kellar.
Library of Congress

magicians, who carried out a large, decorated chair. Kellar was forced to sit in the sedan chair as twenty-four magicians escorted by twenty-four "fair women" walked on the stage with military procession, accompanied by a like number of stage assistants, each carrying a large basket of flowers. As they bombarded Kellar with the flowers, the 125-piece Hippodrome band broke into a stirring version of "Auld Lang Syne," as the sold-out audience stood up and serenaded the magician. Kellar, "weeping like a child," was finally carried off the stage by his magician honor guard, bathed in another shower of flowers.

With the new year, Houdini transformed his war work from entertaining to educating. In February, he wrote Secretary of War Newton Baker and offered to conduct classes in extrication from ropes, handcuffs, and even shipwrecks. He began his classes during intermissions of *Cheer Up*, a patriotic show that Houdini joined at the Hippodrome. A room was set up and officers could telephone in and make appointments to bring their regiments in for the instructions. According to *Billboard* magazine, the theater was "daily besieged by hosts of boys in khaki."

By June of 1918, a mere fourteen months after war was declared, Houdini had sacrificed more than $50,000 between lost salary and his own out-of-pocket expenditures in his ongoing war efforts. In a letter to R. H. Burnside, the manager of the Hippodrome, he recounted his efforts that helped "buy ambulances" and raised funds for the Liberty Bond campaign. "My heart is in this work, for it is not a question of 'Will we win' or 'Will we lose.' *We must win*, and that is all there is to it."

"La-dies and gen-tle-men. Perhaps you have al-rea-dy heard of the fame and ac-comp-lish-ments of my very spesh-ul guest," Houdini intoned. "Allow me to in-tro-duce Jen-nie, the daughter of Barnum's Jumbo, who is the world's first known vanishing el-e-phant!"

The first inkling that something special was about to happen came when a dozen or so Hippodrome stagehands, dressed in circus livery, wheeled a huge cabinet that had been painted to resemble a circus cage out onto the enormous stage. They placed the cabinet about fifteen feet from the rear backdrop and nearly forty feet from the apron of the stage. One end of the trailer had a circular window, covered by curtains. On a command from Houdini, the men pulled the curtains back, revealing a series of bars running across the window from top to bottom, adding to the cagelike effect of the enclosure. At the other end of the box was a set of double doors, each with a half-circled curtained window. The men opened the doors and pulled a ramp into place at the opening.

Thanks to the enormous backstage area at the Hippodrome, Jennie was able to rush out onstage in a full trot, led by her trainer. The giant pachyderm, which was almost eight feet tall and scaled in at more than five tons, looked ominous as she circled Houdini a few times, her head swiveling from side to side in time with her thunderous short steps. When she finally came to a stop next to the magician, she positively dwarfed him, but her ferocity seemed somewhat muted by Houdini's touch of placing a baby-blue ribbon around her neck and an oversize fake wristwatch attached to her left hind leg.

"As you can see, Jen-nie is dressed up like a bride," Houdini quipped. "Though she weighs over ten thousand pounds, she is gentle as a kit-ten. To demonstrate her tran-quil nature, Jennie will now give me a kiss."

On cue, the elephant sidled up to Houdini, lifted her huge trunk, and leaned her face down to the magician's. Houdini rewarded her with a handful of block sugar.

Houdini bonds with Jennie before he makes her disappear. *From the collection of Kenneth M. Trombly*

"I think that Jen-nie may be the single lar-gest con-trib-u-ting factor to the sugar shortage," Houdini joked. "Per-haps there will be more sugar for us after she dis-appears."

"Now Jen-nie, say good-bye to the aud-ience," he commanded, and Jennie waved her head and trunk on cue. As the orchestra broke into a march, the trainer led her up the ramp into the trailer. The stagehands immediately closed the back doors and pulled both the back and front curtains shut. Since the trailer had been positioned sideways, they then took up positions at each end of the enclosure and, with the aid of a block and tackle, slowly moved the huge box a quarter turn so that the circus "cage" front windows faced the center of the audience.

Houdini signaled for the music to stop.

"Although she is a very large beast, she will literally vanish in the space of a few seconds, so I want you to watch very closely," Houdini warned.

A drumroll commenced. Houdini clapped his hands and the stagehands rushed to either end of the enclosure and pulled aside the curtains on each end.

"As you can plain-ly see, the a-ni-mal is com-plete-ly gone!" Houdini intoned.

And he was right. The stagehands, some of whom were dressed as circus clowns, peered through the box and under it. And the audience members who sat in the center sections could look straight through the box and see the Hippodrome's brightly lit backdrop. The elephant had disappeared.

There are magicians and magic historians who claim that Houdini, while a brilliant escape artist, was at best a mediocre magician. An escape artist, by definition, is a magician. Escapes are just another branch on the tree of magic; they are not a tree unto themselves. They are a form of magic in that they have not only an effect but also a secret method. His escapes notwithstanding, Houdini was still brilliant as a magician even if some said he wasn't graceful like Howard Thurston, or that he lacked the urbanity of Charles Carter. But Harry Kellar, dean of magicians, said, "He is a grand man when you know him and he stands head and shoulders above all other magicians of our time." Houdini mystified other magicians too. "I hear Carter has been in to see me half a dozen times and as yet hasn't properly doped out the elephant illusion," Houdini boasted to Kellar. Even today there is no consensus as to how he managed to do it.

If some magicians thought the Vanishing Elephant wasn't good magic, the press and the public certainly did. The spectacle received rave reviews. "So Mr. Houdini puts his title of premier escape artist behind him and becomes The Master Magician," Sime Silverman wrote in *Variety*. William Hilliar, in his magic column for *Billboard* magazine, waxed poetically: "Houdini's prodigious presentation of perfect prestidigitation at the New York Hippodrome, where twice daily he causes a huge elephant to vanish in thin air in about ten seconds, has amazed New York. . . . When a magician can become the big feature of the Hippodrome Show of Wonders, and he is billed like a circus, the art is certainly on the boom. What are you going to do next, Harry?"

What was next would have to wait. Originally booked for two weeks, Houdini's elephant mystery drew so many people to the *Cheer Up* revue, which had been running for a month before he even joined the show, that his run was extended to an amazing nineteen weeks, the longest engagement in one theater in Houdini's career. That Houdini would present what he called the largest illusion in magic history at the Hippodrome was quite fitting. With a seating capacity of more than five thousand and a stage that could comfortably contain an entire circus, re-creations of warring armies, water ballets, diving horses, and a five-hundred-person chorus, it was the largest and grandest theater in New York. It's a testament to Houdini's genius as a magician that he was able to hold a capacity crowd spellbound as he performed not only the largest illusion, with the aid of Jennie, but one of the smallest, his Needles.

To Houdini's mind, his success in presenting the largest illusion in magic history was revitalizing the entire art. All aspects of magic interested him. He made voluminous notes on every field. Although only considered a top card expert in his own mind, he did associate with the crème de la crème, occasionally even hosting the likes of Henry Gavin, aka Arthur Finley, still considered by many to be the most skilled card expert of all time. "Magic is now the vogue," he wrote Kellar. "My efforts are bringing it back into style. . . . The public are commencing to like magic, and actually demand same. Good. Twill make it good for Thurston and all other illusionists."

Emboldened by his triumph as a grand illusionist, Houdini dreamed of opening his own magic theater, inspired by the Parisian theater of Robert-Houdin of sixty years earlier. He found a small theater near Times Square that held three hundred, and Houdini hoped to entirely remodel it to look like an Egyptian temple, similar to Maskelyne & Cooke's Egyptian Hall in London. He hoped to employ in his new "Temple of Mysteries" state-of-the-art electronics such as "talking machines" that could be set in motion by the weight of a patron as he stepped on certain spots on the floor. Houdini claimed to have the backing of a few prominent Broadway producers, including Oscar Hammerstein and Charles Dillingham, who created the *Cheer Up* show, but in the end, the moneymen were too savvy to try to finance such an ambitious project as the war raged.

That wasn't the only disappointment Houdini was facing as 1918 began. His business venture, the Film Development Corporation, was hemorrhaging money, and Houdini was trying to stem the flow with large cash infusions from his savings. Between Houdini's outlays and his sacrifices for the war effort, he was facing a cash crisis for the first time since his sideshow days. It was so bad that he was forced to curtail additions to his growing library. Commenting on a theater collection that had just gone up for sale, Houdini told Kilby that "if I had been flush would have spent a great deal more."

On top of all this, his personal life seemed to be in turmoil too. After four years of living with Hardeen and his family, things had reached a breaking point. It's uncertain why Houdini and Bess couldn't tolerate Brooklyn any longer but after a period of unpleasantness, they decided to move back to the old brownstone in Harlem in the middle of a harsh cold spell in February. It took four twenty-foot vans to cart Houdini's books alone. Once they were back in the house, the great cold wrought havoc on the plumbing. On top of that, a coal shortage had forced Houdini to burn fifteen-year-old shutters and Venetian blinds that had been stored in the basement.

Even before he moved back to the house "I bot [sic] for my Beloved Mother," Houdini was still grieving her death. "I am fighting hard not to feel melancholy for it is five years since My Sweet Mother went to Sleep, and I am still as worried as I was then."

There were other, darker, unspoken problems Houdini was confronting. "Been having a hard time with my private affairs," he informed Kilby. "It's been a bit cloudy of late for all of us," he wrote Teale.

They met in a small café in Greenwich Village. She had gotten there first and had just taken her white fur coat off, revealing her smart white serge dress, when he arrived. He paused before the table and devoured her with his eyes. Then he gallantly took her hand, kissed it, and sat down opposite her.

"You were trembling all over when I touched your hand," Houdini said.

The woman in white blushed.

"I hardly slept last night after our phone conversation," she admitted. Houdini smiled.

"You know, when I first came in here, I didn't recognize you. You look just like a young girl," Houdini said.

"My charming magic man. You haven't changed at all," she said.

"Did you get my letter? Actually, the letter within a letter. I addressed it to the woman in white," Houdini asked.

"No. It never came. Did you have the right address?"

"Never mind. I'll just have to re-create it for you in person," Houdini said.

"That would be lovely," she sighed.

A waiter came over. The woman in white ordered a glass of champagne, and Houdini settled for a soda water.

"Would you like to see a menu?" the waiter asked.

"I don't think so," she said.

"You don't seem human to me," Houdini said, staring into her eyes. "I wonder if you have to eat."

"You're so sweet," she said. "So tell me what was in the letter."

"I wrote that now I know how kings have given up their kingdoms for a woman," Houdini said, delicately stroking her hand. "You are gorgeous. You are wonderful."

A pause.

"I love you," he said.

The woman in white trembled all over.

According to Harold Kellock, who wrote Houdini's official biography based on Bess's recollections, after many years of marriage, Houdini used "many a deft little artifice to foster the romantic element."

"Mrs. Houdini, you are a modern woman of liberal ideas," he would say. "You will not be angry if I keep a date this evening. I expect to meet the most beautiful lady in the world at such and such a corner at 6:30. I shall be home very late."

Bess would pick up the cue and dress herself in her most stunning outfits and make the rendezvous. Houdini would gallantly escort her into a waiting car and they would repair to a jazz club where Houdini would have made arrangements for a private dining room. Bess would order champagne and Harry would drink water. The waiters would fall for the "illicit and non-connubial atmosphere" of these assignations. According to Kellock, that old vaudeville gag—"'Who was that lady I seen you with last night?' 'That wasn't no lady, that was my wife'—might have been written seriously about these romantic escapades of Houdini."

This rendezvous was not part of a fantasy role-playing scenario. The declarations of love and the trembling hands and the hearts a-fluttering were as real as real could be. The woman in white *was* a lady, and she *wasn't* his wife. She was Charmian London.

From the collection of Roger Dreyer

19

Art Imitates Life

WHEN HE HEARD THE NEWS THAT his friend Jack London had died in November of 1916, Houdini immediately dispatched a telegram to his widow Charmian. "Papers here report Jack's death please let us know if this shocking information is founded on facts." He signed it "your sincere friends Harry and Bessie Houdini." London was only forty years old but he had been ill for years and, though his death was certified as due to uremic poisoning, there was speculation that he might have deliberately overdosed on the morphine he was using to control his pain. Though separated geographically, the two couples had become fast friends. When Charmian confirmed Jack's death, Houdini immediately wrote his friend Kilby, who had been compiling a huge Houdini scrapbook, to tell him the news. "Did I ever send you snap shot of us both?" Houdini asked, with his eye on posterity.

The following October, Charmian found herself in New York overseeing the final details of the publication of her latest book. She saw Houdini perform and after the show, the two met. Within two hours of their meeting, Charmian sat down and wrote the conjurer a letter. Noting that Houdini seemed almost "shocked" to see her looking "so well and blooming," Charmian took a defiant stance. "I *refuse* to be beaten! I am going to put in whatever years life still hold for me as profitably in the pursuit of happiness as I possibly can. You have lost and suffered. Am I not right in my attitude?" Informing him that she would relocate for a while in New York, she hinted at future meetings. "Someday, at exactly the right time and place, I shall tell you more about this past year and the other remarkable experience I have had that I've really carved out for myself. This is your letter. Please destroy it (but don't forget it.) C. L." There were no salutations to her friend Bessie.

On January 17, 1918, Charmian received tickets from Houdini to see his wonderful elephant vanish at the Hippodrome. They met backstage after and began to keep in closer touch by phone. A week later, a "declaration" that Houdini made to her over the phone "rather shakes me up," she wrote in her diary. Two weeks after that she was referring to him as "Magic Lover." Other than cryptic references in letters to Houdini's friends ("Been having a hard time with my private affairs"), all we have is Charmian London's account of their affair as recorded in her diary. (The Houdini connection was discovered a decade ago by brilliant Houdini biographer Kenneth Silverman.) Some of the passages are even written in a stenographic code, the only decipherable entry being "278," Houdini's address in Harlem. What we can comprehend paints a picture of a passionate, romantic whirlwind. There's swooning, trembling, experiences that stir to the depths. Charmian can barely sleep, "too swept still." For his part, Houdini's declarations continued: "I'm mad about you." "I give *all* of myself to you." And the ultimate accolade: "I would have told her—my mother—about you."

The liaison continued through April, when she made plans to return to her home in California. She took a side trip to Boston first, and when she returned to New York, their telephone conversations seemed inadequate. "Am I never going to see you again?" Houdini pouted. As her date of departure loomed imminent, his despair grew. "Poor, sad, lonely thing," she wrote. "He is *very* alone, & worse than he had feared." With Charmian back in California, Houdini could only write to tell her how much he missed her and take some solace in the "magic of memory." It had been a confusing few months for the master magician, and there had been quite a few changes in his life, some of which were speaking to Houdini's fundamental conception of himself.

"A plot with international ramifications was revealed to the police late yesterday afternoon to waylay and assassinate Houdini, the magician appearing in Cleveland this week," reporter John De Koven of *The Cleveland Leader* revealed on December 23, 1916. "The actor, according to the information which was transmitted to police headquarters by a mysterious telephone call, is to be lured to the E.9th St. pier, where he will be set upon by thugs, knocked over the head, bound with leather strips and flung through the ice off the end of the pier. . . . The person who telephoned the warning yesterday is believed to be a woman, the voice, according to the police, being feminine with a noticeably foreign accent. It implicated John Royal, manager of the Hippodrome, as one of those in the conspiracy and indicated that he would be active in persuading Houdini to go to the pier. The time set for the attempt, according to the telephone message, is at noon today."

De Koven could go no further without revealing to his readers that Houdini was in on the plot. In fact, he had been traveling around the world filming scenes such as these for a projected motion picture in which he would star. What was brilliant about this ploy was that Houdini was framing the filming of his picture as a stunt, inviting the audience to assemble, watch, and then, hopefully, flock to see more of him at the Hippodrome.

Houdini had made a short motion picture in Paris in 1901, but he saw the potential for a career in the movies as early as 1912. In November, his friend Billy Robinson had written him that Houdini's old friend who used to manage the Coliseum in Glasgow was now running a cinema where they were clearing more than the equivalent of $1,250 a week showing films all day. "He said it was the only game nowadays. And he is right," Robinson noted. Houdini agreed. In June of 1913, he approached E. F. Albee, one of his old managers, who still ran vaudeville houses on the Keith's circuit. Sounding him out on doing movies, Albee was adamantly against the move. "Your value in vaudeville would be very much lessened on account of your name being advertised as extensively as it would be in motion picture houses," he told Houdini.

In February of 1915, Houdini had meetings with representatives from Universal Film in connection with a filmic adaptation of Jules Verne's *20,000 Leagues Under the Sea*. The role was tailor-made for Houdini's aquatic abilities but negotiations broke down. "I am afraid that I want too much money," he wrote Kilby. "For your judgement is right the Managers will object, and if I do not get a big sum close to Fifty Thousand I cannot afford to take a chance at this time of my life. Perhaps in a few years when I can't get work??? I may take less. I hope not."

Though Houdini continued to hire a crew and film some of his celebrated stunts, his real involvement with the motion picture business began in 1917 when he reached an agreement to star in a movie for the Williamson Brothers, the creative duo who had contracted with Universal for the Jules Verne movie. J. Ernest Williamson and his brother George had pioneered the development of undersea photography, adapting a deep-sea tube that had been invented by their father, who was a sea captain.

"Expect to leave for the Bahaman Islands, within eight weeks, to be featured in the sensational film and am receiving the biggest money every paid for a single picture," Houdini bragged to Harry Kellar on March 31, 1917. Six days later, the United States entered the war.

Houdini's teaming up with the Williamson Brothers to make a submarine film was headline news the following week. Cognizant of the world situation, Houdini tried to spin his new movie career as patriotic service. "I want to call attention to the fact that I am a true American citizen," he told the newspapers, "and that I am convinced the Williamson inventions can be utilized in our country's defense should Uncle Sam find himself embarrassed by enemy submarine boats. My patriotism received quite an impetus as I pondered this, and it is gratifying to be associated with such a business-like organization—one that will make sacrifices for the country's good if necessary." He also informed the newspapers that he would escape from the Williamson tube without breaking the two-inch glass, while it was underwater, without allowing any water to enter the vessel. The photographic evidence would then be incorporated into the film, which was tentatively called *Houdini and the Miracle*.

"I am doing this because I wish to leave behind a legacy to posterity to prove irrefutably that I was actually within the chain wrapped packing cases, steel boilers, nailed-up coffins and other unusual containers in which I have been manacled and thrown overboard times without number," Houdini told the press. "Through the aid of the Williamsons' devices for submarine photography, I will be able to release myself in full view of the camera. There can be no doubt whatsoever henceforth as to the authenticity of my performance."

Houdini had been tracking the smugglers for days now with no luck. So when he stumbled onto an old warehouse that was being used as a dormitory and staging area for the gang that he had been reconnoitering, he devised an incredible plan to destroy it. He removed all the supporting pilings of the three-story building, leaving only those that were absolutely necessary to keep the building standing. Then he covered the roof with dirt and stones so it bore an incredible resemblance to the surrounding area. When the signal was given and the last supports destroyed, the building would implode three stories and the roof would blend right in so no one could tell that any alteration in the landscape had been made.

While preparing the building for destruction, Houdini noted that there were subterranean passageways that led right from the warehouse to the docks, where the submarine base was located. This made him alter his plans slightly. Now he would rig the building so that it would set on fire when the phone would ring, and the fire would not only implode the building but also distract any onlookers so they wouldn't see their mad dash to the submarine base. Houdini wasn't alone on this mission. He had a young man named Jimmy and a girl named June, both of whom he had rescued from the smuggling group. Houdini felt an extra responsibility toward June. She was the daughter of his friend, the chief of the Secret Service.

They were all on the third floor when they heard stirring downstairs. That meant that one of the smuggling crews was back. Now Houdini had to figure out a way for them to escape without being detected. They did a quick survey of the room and noticed all the windows were nailed shut. Jimmy was about to smash a window to get away when Houdini restrained him. Grabbing a large section of flypaper that was hanging from a distant wall, Houdini placed it on the window. Using the edge of June's diamond ring, Houdini cut a large circle out of the glass and carefully removed it, soundlessly, since the glass had adhered to the flypaper.

Houdini disappeared into one of the third-floor bedrooms and came back with a handful of bed sheets. He made a ladder of the sheets, threw it out the window, and slowly lowered Jimmy and June out on the side of the warehouse that faced away from the busy street. They were all to rendezvous on the dock, but first, he had to prepare the firebug. He spread paper and straw all over the floor and then set up a row of candles, all connected by a shoelace. He tied the other end of the shoelace to the bell of the telephone. When the hammer would ring, which it would as soon as he called, it would tug on the string, pull the candles over, and start a blaze that would soon cause the structurally weakened building to implode. He had just lit the very last candle when three men rushed into the room and overpowered him.

The smugglers forced Houdini into a chair and, with strong rope, lashed him to it.

They hadn't left the room for thirty seconds when the phone rang. It was the gang's leader, checking on the warehouse. Nobody was there to answer and within seconds, the candles were toppled and an inferno began to rage all around Houdini. With no time to spare, he frantically squirmed in his chair, using any available slack to loosen his bonds. The flames were lapping at his feet when he finally broke free of the restraints and literally dove through the window. He caught himself on the outer ledge of the window and quickly kicked his shoes off. Using his big toes as pincers, he held onto the cables that held up the roof coping and made his way from window to window. Just as he jumped the final six feet to freedom, there was a loud blast and the warehouse seemed to vanish. He didn't have time to admire his landscaping because he was already on his way to the docks.

It's been said that all writing is autobiographical. The above rendering of Houdini's treatment for a film that he never made supports this idea. Houdini biographer Bernard Meyer said, "It was not only as a highly imaginative and versatile performer but also as a storyteller and maker of motion pictures that Houdini left a legacy rich in clues concerning the secrets of his mind and heart. These stories and films of which he was the author, or at least the co-author, are for the most part obvious self-portraits which, while not qualifying as great art, often provide a revealing and often surprising glimpse into the darker corners of his character, apparently unsuspected and unexplored by some of his biographers." Meyer's theory anticipated the new evidence of Houdini's espionage work. In many of Houdini's films, he plays characters who are Secret Service or Justice Department agents. When he wrote these films, he was partially writing about himself. Doing so wasn't unique; the great novelist W. Somerset Maugham also worked as a secret agent for the U.S. government during the Great War, and he too memorialized his contribution in his novel *Ashenden: or the British Agent.*

When it was time for Houdini to make his first movie, he presented the Williamson Brothers with the above scenario for a film that he tentatively called *The Marvelous Adventures of Houdini: The Justly Celebrated Elusive American*—and indeed Houdini's cast of characters was very telling. Harry Houdini was described as "Harry Houdini, as known to the public," implying a hidden covert side that remained unknown. The leading lady was named Beulah, "the personification of refinement," at ease in the highest social circles in London and Germany, a world traveler whose heart would beat rapidly when she saw Houdini cheat death, but who was existential enough to know to live in the present. Was Beulah's character based on the cosmopolitan Charmian London?

Houdini's character interacts with someone named Siddons, "the Chief of the Secret Government Police," he wrote in his description. "Such a man as would be selected by the brain force of a great nation, to have complete control of the Secret Service, in fact a prototype of Flynn—suave, polished, a gentlemen [sic], and silent as the Sphinx." William James Flynn had worked for the Secret Service in New York since 1897, except for a two-year interlude from 1910 to 1911 when he stayed in the city to weed out corruption in the NYPD's Detective Bureau. Rejoining the Secret Service in 1911, he succeeded Wilkie as chief in 1912 and ran the bureau out of his New York office. He resigned in 1917, the same year that Houdini wrote this scenario. Flynn would later produce a film that exposed fraudulent spirit mediums at the same time that Houdini would wage his own crusade against them.

By July of 1917, three months after signing a contract, Houdini was still hashing out the script with the Williamsons. Both the war in Europe and a war between the Williamsons derailed the project. Desperately trying to salvage his film, Houdini entered into an arrangement with a company called Westart to film the opening scenes of his scenario, a manacled jump into the sea off the pier at Atlantic City. Though Westart would in a few years produce a series of low-budget Westerns, this one-day shoot appears to be all that became of *The Marvelous Adventures of Houdini*.

Houdini's movie career began in earnest when he met a Californian movie producer named B. A. Rolfe. Houdini again pushed his own script but Rolfe convinced him that his first outing should be a fifteen-part serial, where each weekly installment left Houdini's fate up in the air. Arthur Reeve and Charles Logue, the writing team behind the successful *Perils of Pauline* serial, were hired, but from the beginning, Houdini's input was crucial. "Houdini has an inborn gift, and, with it all, is one of the deepest students I have met," Reeve told a reporter. "Everything he does is figured out from a logical beginning [and] is the result of years of work and study."

Working together, the three men blended elements of Houdini's script into *The Master Mystery*. Instead of playing himself, Houdini would play the part of Quentin Locke, an undercover agent for the Justice Department. Ostensibly working as a chemist, Locke was infiltrating a company named International Patents, Inc. that had been set up by powerful industrialists to purchase innovative inventions solely to keep them off the market. In Houdini's first onscreen scene, he was covertly listening in to the wiretapped conversation of the owner of the company.

There were enemies galore, including an evil hypnotist, a Chinese Tong leader, a strangulation expert from Madagascar, and, for the first time in movie history, a robot in the form of a larger-than-life tin automaton. The serial featured a romance between Locke and the daughter of one of the evil industrialists who has a change of heart and tries to repent before he is stricken down with Madagascar Madness, thanks to an infusion of gas from his still-evil partner. The plot paled in the face of the showcasing of Houdini's amazing skills. He finally got to use his diving suit escape but in addition, he burst out of straitjackets, handcuffs, and jails. He defied death by escaping from an electric chair, an oncoming elevator that threatened to crush him, and corrosive acid that threatened to consume him while he was lying bound on the floor. In one spectacular escape while he was hung from his thumbs, he used his legs to get his captor in a scissors hold and then choked him. Kicking off his shoes, he used his toes to find a key in the man's pocket, which he then inserted in the door directly opposite him, unlocked the door, and turned the knob with his feet. With the door ajar, he then walked up it with his feet and tumbled into a backward arch, loosening his restraints with his toes and freeing himself!

Filming in Yonkers during the summer and fall of 1918, Houdini literally threw himself into his work. By the end of shooting, he had suffered seven black eyes and

The screen's first robot threatens Houdini. *From the collection of Ricky Jay*

broken his left wrist when he fell off a swinging chandelier during one fight sequence, but he was thrilled with the final product. "I have *seen* all the Serials, and believe that the Houdini Serial is the greatest ever screened," he wrote Kellar, with typical modesty. "If it goes over, think I shall make the Silent Drama my next venture." It did more than "go over." On its opening weekend in New York, thousands were turned away from the theaters. In Boston, five thousand people milled outside, unable to get in. In one day in New England, Houdini set a record-making fifteen personal appearances to promote the film.

Now Houdini was faced with a dilemma. He had been working on a big new illusion, Buried Alive. When Kilby wrote to ask him about his progress, Houdini was uncertain. "The Movie Fans are 'clambering' for another Houdini serial, and as that is much easier than my Self created hazardous work, I may step that way." In February of 1919, two months later, Houdini's return to film seemed certain. "With the finish of the Houdini serial, our income will *cease*," he wrote Kellar. "——and then???"

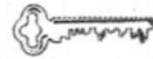

The two planes were flying over Beverly Hills and heading for the ocean. Director Irwin Willat was in the third plane, along with the cameraman. They were filming the climatic scene of Houdini's first full-length movie, *The Grim Game*,

French poster for *The Master Mystery*. *Library of Congress*

when, unexpectedly, tragedy struck. "I thought . . . my end had come," Houdini told the press. "I was 3,000 feet up in an aeroplane, circling over another machine. The plan was for me to drop from my 'plane into the cockpit of the other by means of a rope. I was dangling from the rope-end ready for the leap. Suddenly a strong wind turned the lower plane upwards, the two machines crashed together—nearly amputating my limbs—the propellers locked in a deadly embrace, and we were spun round and round and round. . . . But, by a miracle, the 'planes were righted into a half-glide, and, though they were smashed into splinters by their terrific impact, I managed to escape unhurt."

Willat was quick thinking enough to keep the cameras rolling during the crash and descent, and the resultant footage was among the most spectacular in the then-short history of cinema. Stills of the two planes locked in their "deadly embrace" were struck and prominently featured in the advertising campaign along with a typical Houdini challenge: "$1000 REWARD TO ANY PERSON PROVING that the above picture is not a genuine photograph of an aeroplane collision during the filming of an aerial battle in the clouds." Of course, the reward was never paid out because the collision had happened. There was a bit more deception in Houdini's recollections of the crash. When the planes came down, not only had Houdini been safe on the ground the entire time but he wasn't even in the scene. His part in the aerial action had been played by a stunt double.

The Grim Game was the first of a two-picture deal that Houdini signed with producer Jesse Lasky a few months after *The Master Mystery* had been released, and like its predecessor, *The Grim Game* was another showcase of Houdini's marvelous escapes and stunts. He does an upside-down straitjacket escape, frees himself from a bear trap, and, in an incredible sequence, rolls under a passing car, catches the transmission bar, and hangs on for dear life, hitching a ride so he can come to the aid of the heroine.

The reviews were raves. "Houdini has stepped to the front as a film star," *The New York Herald* opined. "Houdini is honestly a star. . . ." *The New York American* agreed. "There is more excitement in one reel of *The Grim Game* than in any five reels of celluloid I have ever watched," T. E. Oliphant of *The New York Mail* wrote.

Houdini was excited at the prospect of doing features. "I am drifting away from vaudeville, and with the exception of my European dates have no plans re a return," he told Kilby. Where he was drifting to was Hollywood, where the temperate climate and the chance to rub elbows with other movie stars were appealing to him. He became friendly with stars like Charlie Chaplin and Fatty Arbuckle and spent time on the Lasky set with a young sultry star named Gloria Swanson. She sent him an autographed photo ("To Mr. Houdini, Please show me some of your tricks. Most sincerely, Gloria Swanson") that he kept in one of his scrapbooks.

Houdini was also thrilled to spend time with Harry Kellar, who lived only a few miles from the studio. He and Bess also frequently socialized with his old partner Jacob Hyman, who was married to an actress and was practicing medicine. Although still down-to-earth for the most part, Houdini began to show some signs of a Hollywood temperament. One night he was a guest at a "bohemian" dinner given by a prominent westerner who loved to be surrounded by an artistic crowd. Someone introduced Houdini to the company as "having been supplied by Mr. M——." Houdini immediately bristled, "I was not supplied by anyone. I am too great an artist to be 'supplied' by anyone. I am here as a guest." After a modicum of mollification, Houdini did consent to perform the Needles.

With two films under his belt, Houdini was learning his new craft. Although some modern self-styled acting critics have tried to fault Houdini's acting, he never seemed out of place on the big screen. He generally got favorable notices, even for his acting ability, and by the time he was shooting *The Grim Game*, he had taken his craft seriously. "Picture actors and stage actors are entirely different," he wrote from Hollywood. "And though the spoken stage may ridicule pictures, never the less picture must be intelligently *portraied* [sic] and is an art in itself. The

ABOVE: Houdini shooting *The Grim Game*.
Library of Congress

RIGHT: Of course, it was a real accident, but Houdini wasn't anywhere near it at the time.
From the collection of Roger Dreyer

TOP: Two of the most famous entertainers of all time, Charlie Chaplin and Houdini.
From the collection of Roger Dreyer

BOTTOM: Harry gets cozy with a young Gloria Swanson.
From the collection of Dr. Bruce Averbook

smallest movie star can make the biggest spoken stage star look like a nickel before the camera, especially if they do not know the angle of the lens."

The genesis of the idea that Houdini was stiff and wooden as an actor may be Harold Kellock's Bess-endorsed biography, in which it is claimed that Houdini's "puritanical soul" shrank from love scenes with his gorgeous young costars. One director allegedly even asked Bess to leave the set because "whenever we get him to the point of kissing the girl, he spoils the shot by glancing anxiously at you." That might be true from the point of view of Houdini trying to avoid a browbeating from a jealous wife, but there is ample footage of Houdini with his co-stars, some even just lounging between shots, that shows a relaxed, flirtatious, and even frisky Houdini. Contemporary reviews bear this out: "As a screen actor Houdini also wins laurels, playing his scenes with the heroine in a manner which reflects great credit to him," a *New York Telegraph* reviewer noted.

Houdini's films were widely distributed internationally, especially the serial, and the star began receiving fan mail from all around the planet. The letters from men usually were pleas for Houdini to share the secrets of his magic, while females were more apt to ask for autographed photos. One Japanese girl wrote that after seeing *The Master Mystery*, she "was charmed by your excellent art with a lovely face." Another American female fan harkened back to his escape days to compose her ode:

I wish that I was Mr. Keith And in my house you'd play
For you my maiden heart does seethe, And has since that first day
When I sat in my seat and gasped, While you the hand-cuffs wrecked—
I'd rather have my arms tightly clasped About your swarthy neck.

I'd like to be put in a box With you, all clasped about
With seven different kinds of locks—I bet you'd not get out!
Your powerful, sturdy, graceful pose; Your shirt sleeves white turned up;
Your curly hair; your handsome nose; With you I'd like to sup. . . .

I'd like to be put in that bag, And then put in the trunk
Where you so closely follow, O 't would make my feelings drunk.
My consciousness would leave me, I would not think of harm
If in that bag and trunk with you, My waist within your arm.

I'd keep the people waiting, Expectantly, for days,
While in the trunk with you I sat, My feelings in a maze;
My head upon your shoulder, My cheek against your tan.
O! Harry H. Houdini, You are the only *man.*

The Houdinis' twenty-fifth wedding anniversary gala. *From the collection of Dr. Bruce Averbook*

With temptation all around him in Hollywood, and Charmian London on her ranch forty miles north, Houdini decided to make a very public show of his affection toward Bess on the twenty-fifth anniversary of their wedding on June 22, 1919. At first he put the word out that he was planning to renew their vows. Houdini even asked his friend Kellar to give away the bride. Whether they had actually ever been legally married at all remains an open question, and eventually the affair morphed into a celebratory dinner in the main ballroom of the Hotel Alexandria, Los Angeles's crown jewel and the location of choice for the burgeoning film industry. In front of two hundred guests, all seated at one very long table, Harry and Bess entered the room as the band played "The Wedding March." Bess was overcome with emotion, and Harry had to sprint to the bar and bring her back a bracing glass of wine.

Houdini spared no expense for the gala event. The long table was covered with orchids, roses, and sweet peas. Two brilliantly lit fountains sprayed fragrant rose water into the air. A tiny bouquet of orange blossoms was set next to each guest's name card. And what an A-list gathering it was. Will Rogers, Fatty Arbuckle, and other stars from Lasky's studio were there, along with many behind-the-scenes power brokers.

Back at their hotel room, Houdini presented Bess with some magnificent diamonds in a silver setting—"Wear this dear heart. It is my gift to my bride with all the love that is possible to give." He also gave her two more love notes. The first, addressed to "My Soulmate Wife" and written while Bess and their niece Julia were "busy at the mirror making up," seemed a candid declaration of love. "We have starved and starred together. We have had our little tiffs, but your sunny smile and my good sense (?) always robbed them of bitterness. I love you, love you, dearest, and I know you love me." He signed it "Yours to the end of life and ever after. EHRICH (Harry Houdini)." At two A.M., Houdini added an addendum. "How wonderful you were! The most beautiful and wonderful of all. You will only surpass yourself, my Dearest, when you will be my Golden Bride. If the years pass as quickly as these twenty-five have done, we ought to begin at once to prepare to celebrate our golden wedding together."

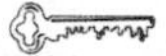

The gale winds were buffeting the small launch, and now the worst happened: The waves had knocked out the steering gear, making it impossible to steer the small craft in the raging sea off Catalina Island. When the engine sputtered dead, the boat started dragging anchor and it rounded the reef blowing a distress signal. The boat was near the jagged rocks and no one dared risk their lives to save the four souls who seemed minutes away from a horrific fate.

Except for Houdini. As soon as he heard the distress signal, he rushed down to Buttershell Beach, seized a line, threw it around his waist, and plunged into the surf. Someone threw him a circular life preserver and, using it to shield his head from the battering waves, he tried to swim out to the launch. He managed to get within twenty-five feet of the vessel when the seething giant waves, as if angry at his defiance, shook and flung him back against the rocky shore, but he wasn't finished yet. He jumped back in the water and had almost made it to the boat when a baby tidal wave engulfed him and hurled him sixty feet right back into the rocks. Fortunately, he had had the presence of mind to put the life preserver around his neck, shielding his face, but now he found himself crushed

Houdini does card magic for Fatty Arbuckle despite having a cast on his wrist.
From the collection of Dr. Bruce Averbook

against the rocks, holding on for dear life, threatened with being caught in the great undertow and swept back out to sea and a watery grave.

If this had been a serial, the episode would have ended right here. Houdini *was* on Catalina Island in November of 1919, filming his second Lansky picture, *Terror Island*, but what was happening now was scripted only by Mother Nature. The launch, the *Catalina Flyer*, belonged to the production and had been carrying some of the film crew, who were on their way to set up the next shot. Houdini's instincts were noble and heroic, and he actually did risk his life to save the men, but life didn't imitate art in this case. Battered and bleeding from several cuts, Houdini weakened in the water and two deep-sea divers had to swim out and rescue the rescuer from the violent surf. With the star back on terra firma, a motorboat was sent out for the disabled launch. After a harrowing battle with the ocean, which was by then being filmed by the production's cameraman, the men and the launch were finally rescued.

Terror Island itself gave Houdini another chance to show off his underwater prowess and an opportunity to get close to his stunning costar Lila Lee, who, according to the comedian/film star Georgie Jessel, claimed to have a romantic fling with Houdini. Perhaps Houdini was thinking of more than just the weather when, back in frigid New York in December for a stopover on his way to London, he wrote Kellar and told him he missed "sunny California."

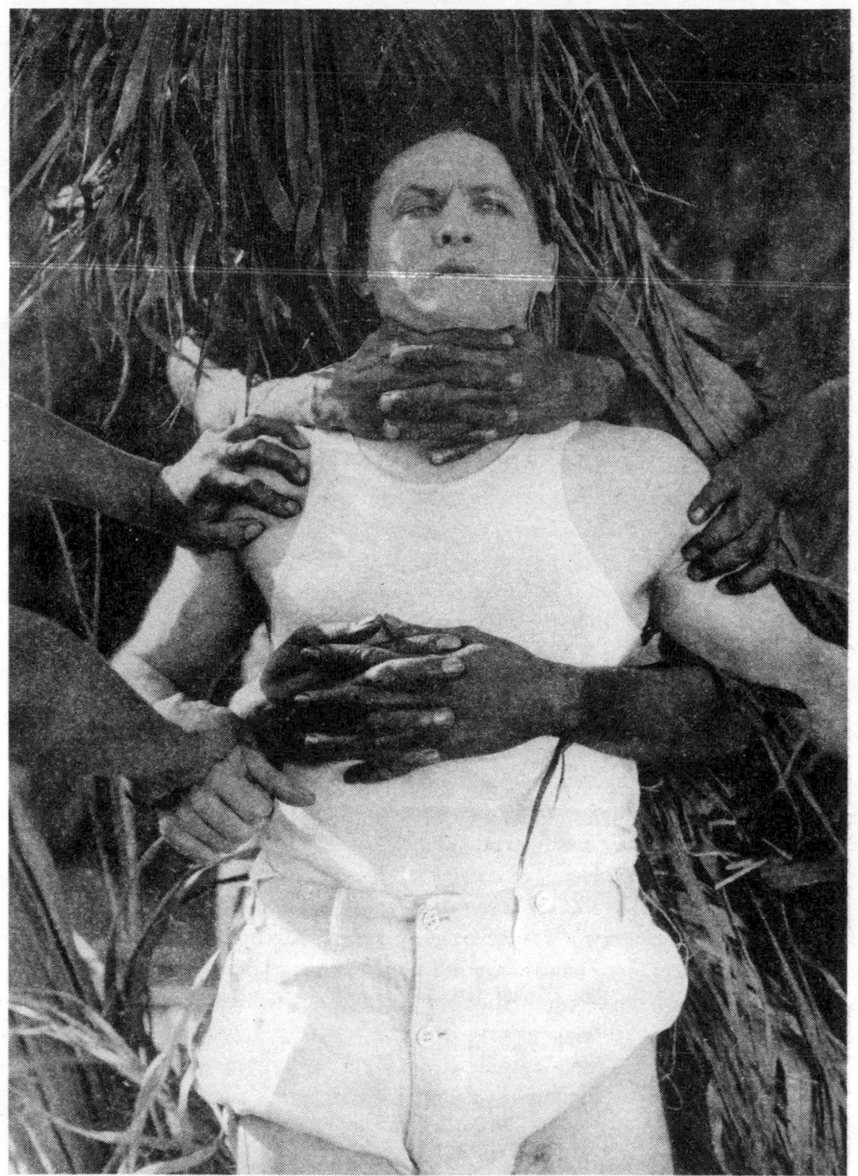

They didn't call it *Terror Island* for nothing. *From the collection of Roger Dreyer*

Collins and Vickery were not pleased. They knew something was wrong when Houdini made an awkward move inside the Water Torture Cell and seemed to flinch. Within seconds, he was standing outside of the structure.

"Nearly cracked my neck," Houdini fumed, massaging his injury.

Luckily for everyone, this was literally a dry run; they had been reluctant to fill the cell with water for fear of breaking the glass. Houdini was trying out a new torture cell preparatory for his return to the vaudeville stage in London, where old contracts that had been disrupted by the war were finally about to be fulfilled.

One week into his performances, during his first show of the night, the glass broke in the cell, forcing Houdini to use a reserve pane in the second show. About a week later, Houdini injured his right ankle doing the stunt. It must have been painful, for the usually stoic escape artist saw a doctor named Parsons, who examined his ankle, did a general checkup, and proclaimed that Houdini was in "danger of death." After a series of treatments that included a regimen of electrical "baking," the ankle responded and Houdini informed the managers he could complete his tour. The doctor didn't fare quite as well. Within two weeks, Parsons was dead. While Houdini noted the irony of the doctor's death, Parsons' warning must have had some impact on the conjurer. A few months later, Houdini sat for a bust of himself to be placed on his grave after his death.

Accounts of Houdini's show on that tour suggest that he was treading creative water. His half-hour turn was filled with one or two short effects, the Upside Down water cell escape, and a long monologue peppered with anecdotes from his movie career. In Nottingham, the newspaper's reviewer actually apologized to his readers for writing advance promotion for the show once he had actually seen it. "Why on earth should Houdini imagine that any audience would be entertained by hearing a long and uncalled-for account of what he has been doing during the past six years . . . people go to a Vaudeville house to see a performance . . . not to hear a diatribe on the personal pronoun worked around 'the story of my life, sir.'"

The cynical English critic didn't understand but the people did. Houdini broke all records that tour, and earned the highest salaries of his career, pulling down $3,750 a week. "Blame it all on the fact I have been successfully in the movies," he crowed to Kilby. "*The Master Mystery* has been showing over a year . . . so the people think they know me personally. Have to make speeches every night. It's wonderful to think that after all my hard work, I can draw the Public without killing myself."

With his mind still in Hollywood, Houdini hired a film crew and shot exteriors in England and France for a film about counterfeiting that he tentatively titled *The Dupe*. He found that the cameras were attracting gawkers that were ruining the filming. In what might be one of the first uses of concealed cameras, he was able to achieve natural-looking cameos from the unsuspecting extras. His heart was elsewhere too. In April, he sent Charmian London what she deemed a "sweet" letter, and when he returned to New York in July, she received two more "love-notes" from her Magic Man.

Once again flush from his film work and his record-breaking English dates, Houdini had added to his theater collection, and back in New York, he hired a full-time librarian to organize his entire library. On the advice of Robert Gould Shaw, the great drama collector, Houdini hired an eccentric seventy-four-year-old drama aficionado named Alfred Becks, who had spent ten years in charge of Shaw's collection that resided at the library at Harvard University. Becks immediately moved into the Harlem brownstone.

With Becks's unnecessary encouragement, Houdini added enormously to his library, running afoul of Bess in the process. For years, Bess had felt in competition with Houdini's various collections, seeing them as a mistress vying for her husband's attention. It got to the point where Becks would literally creep up the front steps, stash the new acquisitions in the vestibule, then sneak down and ring the basement bell for admittance. Passing Bess's muster by appearing empty-handed, Becks would go upstairs, quietly open the front door, retrieve his cache, and spirit the books up to the library.

Too poor to amass a drama collection himself, Becks had his heart set on buying a set of drama books that were coming up at auction, which he thought he could obtain at a reasonable price. His mistake was to tell Houdini of the potential score. On the day of the auction, Houdini sent an emissary to bid on them under an assumed name. Becks returned to the house crestfallen and Houdini, ashamed, hid the books in the basement. When his faithful librarian died in 1925, Houdini, overcome with remorse and grief, sent three floral arrangements under three different names to make it appear that Becks had not been forgotten by his friends. After the funeral, Houdini returned to his home and wept over his loss. Suddenly he remembered his hidden stash. "Now I suppose I can get those books out of the cellar." He brightened and dashed down, retrieved the package, dusted them off, and gave the books a prominent spot on his shelves. When this was done, he returned to his easy chair, groaned, "Poor old Becks!" and began to sob.

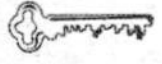

The audience had chuckled inappropriately at spots but when the primitive savages of *Terror Island*, to appease their god, stuffed the heroine into a small regulation office safe and threw it over a precipice into the ocean, only to have Houdini emerge from his submarine underwater at the exact spot where the safe landed so he could fiddle with the dial, open the safe, and rescue its human contents, it was enough to make the crowd laugh outright, which is not good when your film is a melodrama. Houdini's third film received poor reviews but it was the script and not Houdini's acting that was singled out for criticism. *Variety* savaged the writers and directors for "an almost incredible incompetency in providing a vehicle for Houdini which might prove less exasperating." Even Houdini, who rated the film as "excellent" in his diary, was forced to admit that he didn't "like the way it is cut. They have omitted important details." His solution was to start his own motion picture company, where he would write, produce, and star in his own films with no outside interference.

Houdini's recent experience with his Film Development Company might have given him pause before rushing into this new business venture. Since early 1918, he had been infusing cash into the company to keep it afloat. As the months progressed, Houdini forced his creative partner, Dietz, to give back stock and cut back on his salary. With his brother Hardeen now working full-time at the plant, Houdini painted a rosy enough picture to entice a fellow magician stockholder named Arnold DeBiere to advance more money into the corporation. Even Harry Kellar, in California, added to his FDC portfolio. Houdini's optimism was misplaced. By April of 1918, he was writing Kellar that "Dietz is the smoothest liar I ever met" and later that month, he fired Dietz summarily. "I am afraid that I shall have to THROW Dietz out of the factory. Getting too [incompetent], shiftless and he is always working and not accomplishing anything," Houdini wrote Kellar. "He will ruin us. We [turned] out more work since he left than when he was with us, and the real improvements of the machine belong to your friend Houdini. . . . I have become quite an expert re the factory and handle it as if 'twere a handcuff. . . . So it is time that I took charge myself and either go one way or the other."

It was going south. Perhaps anticipating bankruptcy, Houdini transferred the title of his house to Beatrice's name on July 23. A few weeks later, Houdini's former friend DeBiere tried to engineer a hostile takeover, forcing Houdini to beg Kellar to allow him to vote his shares, giving Houdini a clear majority and total control. By the end of November, Houdini was entertaining thoughts of selling the business outright or affiliating with another factory, with more than $65,000 of his own cash invested to that point. There was a prospect of a sale in February of 1919 but the Chicagoan who was looking for an East Coast plant apparently didn't like what he saw, so Houdini was forced to infuse cash into the business all through 1919. On top of that, in April he made another investment, buying up a majority ownership of Martinka's, the venerable old magic business in New York. Within a year, he had bailed out, apparently able to keep seeding only one failing business at a time.

By the end of October 1920, even Houdini's unflagging optimism in his FDC seemed dissipated. Kellar had reached the end of his own rope and had sent a representative to Houdini to handle the sale of his stock. "I informed him of our financial difficulties, and as a matter of fact, have just loaned the F.D.C. another 3,000 dollars," Houdini wrote Kellar. "Hardeen has pawned his bank books so that we could get [film] stock to keep the factory open. It certainly has been an awful drain on my finances, let alone the terrible worry. Am not doing anything as yet, but trying to interest capital in a Houdini Mystery Corporation. If only I had invested my money in production, we would at least have some pictures to 'peddle.' My associates in the *Master Mystery* cleared, according to their books, 70,000 dollars, which they squandered on salaries and overhead expenses. I have over 100,000 dollars invested in the F.D.C. but have never received a penny from same. This does not include the many weary months I spent in and around the place trying to make a success of what an ordinary man in the business would have known was a failure. My education is certainly costing me a high price." Kellar seemed to have taken pity on his friend. Less than two weeks later, he instructed his representative to sell all of his stock to Houdini's sister, Gladys, for the princely sum of $1.

Houdini's attempt to "interest capital" for his movie production company fared little better. "Been somewhat unfortunate in my choice of associates for the Mystery Picture Co.," he wrote Kilby in October. Four months later, that had presumably changed. In association with a principal in the Boston Orpheum Theatre and a Boston banker named H. V. Greene, Houdini finally settled on a name and incorporated the Houdini Picture Corporation, capitalizing it to the tune of $500,000. "I am investing $25,000 of my own money and let us hope I shall have better luck than we have had with the F.D.C.," he wrote Kellar. Houdini's confidence must have been shaken, though, when Greene's Boston-based finance company shortly faced multiple lawsuits from irate investors for misrepresentations.

By October of 1921, seven months after incorporating, Houdini had wrapped two full-length feature films. For once, he had complete creative control, coming up with the storylines, hiring a screenwriter or writing the script himself, choosing a director who worked under his supervision, and orchestrating the distribution and promotion. What he chose to put on the screen was fascinating. *The Man From Beyond*, self-described on the invitation to the premiere as "the weirdest and most sensational love story ever told on the screen" certainly lived up to the first part of its billing. Houdini played Howard Hillary, a shipmate who had been frozen in an Arctic wreck for more than one hundred years until he was revived by explorers. Back in civilization, he is brought to the home of Professor Strange, one of the brothers of the explorers, where he witnesses the nuptials of Felice, the professor's daughter. Convinced that Felice is actually his own lost love, and still unaware that he had been in suspended animation for more than a hundred years, Hillary disrupts the ceremony and tries to claim Felice for his own. Committed to a mental hospital, he has no trouble escaping from a wet sheet bondage, and he spends the rest of the movie battling evil scientists and convincing Felice that she harbors the soul of his own long-lost love.

With one film in the can, Houdini immediately started in on his next project. A handwritten page filled with "M.P. Ideas" (motion pictures) survives from that time. A catalog of small bits that he would incorporate into the films, it reads like a litany of escape, or spy, work:

> POISONING—tip of pen, or flap of envelope.
> CONCEAL revolver in valise to murder person opening it . . .
> COAT GAG—pin message on waiters coat, or chalk mark to give signal to confederate, as waiter turns around . . .
> CUTTING out eyes of painting to see in other room . . .
> TAPPING telephone—3 times with key, as signal to confed[erate].

Houdini had three scripts under consideration. One, *The Mystery of the Jewel*, was another film about reincarnation based in ancient Egypt. *Yar, the Primeval Man* chronicled the adventures of a caveman. Houdini finally chose the third, *Haldane of the Secret Service*. (Viscount Haldane, i.e., Richard Burton Haldane, Lord Northcliffe's friend and the Secretary of State for War in the Liberal government during Edwardian Britain, had chaired the subcommittee in 1909 that recommended the creation of a British Secret Service.) Houdini played Heath Haldane Jr., the secret agent son of a U.S. Secret Service agent who had been murdered on the job by an international counterfeiting ring. He's drawn into investigating the ring when he comes to the aid of a young woman who's being attacked near Washington Square Park. His investigations lead him to a warehouse on the Hudson River, the distribution center for the fake currency. Detected by the bad guys, he's overpowered, roped up, and thrown into the Hudson. Freeing himself from his bonds, he swims to a transatlantic steamer headed for London, where he has a clandestine meeting on Westminster Bridge with agents from Scotland Yard. His investigation

Nita Naldi vamps it up in *The Man From Beyond*. *From the collection of Roger Dreyer*

takes him to Paris and then to the gang's lair, an old monastery in a rural village, where masquerading monks capture him and bind him to the spokes of a huge waterwheel. After a surprise ending that reveals the true identity of Dr. Yu, the "mysterious Chinaman" in charge of the operation, Houdini wins the day, captures the bad guys, and proposes to the heroine, who had gotten caught up with the gang inadvertently.

"I know it will displease you to hear this but I have just discounted between $8,000 and $10,000 worth of notes for the Film Developing Corporation," Houdini wrote Kellar in October of 1921. "Poor Dash is not well . . . He works very hard giving all his time to the laboratory. It will be a Godsend for all of us if we get away from it in a legitimate manner. The only good of the whole thing is that it was the cause of my going into pictures. Let us hope that I have not made a serious mistake. My two pictures are finished. Now I must put them on the market and will see how good they are."

Marketing the movies was essential. Since he was an inexperienced producer, the films went way over budget and Houdini was forced to take a nine-week vaudeville engagement, his first in two years, to offset their costs. On the eve of his first production's premiere, Houdini used every bit of his P. T. Barnum-esque marketing skills to promote his movies.

As he had aged and sought respectability, he had disavowed some of his earlier publicity stunts, like sending seven bowler-hatted men to a Paris corner where, on cue, they would doff their chapeaus and reveal that each bald head had a letter painted on it that collectively spelled H-O-U-D-I-N-I. With his financial health on the line, Houdini threw all caution to the wind. He printed up an elaborate press kit for *The Man From Beyond* that contained reviews and even suggestions for the local cinema owners on how to exploit the movie. One tactic was to create a rubber boot with a rubber stamp built into the sole that would stamp the word "Houdini" with each step. He suggested that the booted promo man be sent out early in the morning so the rush-hour crowds could see the freshly imprinted message.

Another ploy was to dress an actor up in the clothes of a hundred years prior and have him placarded as "The Man From Beyond." "This must be done in a very dignified way," Houdini warned. Another idea was to invite as many centenarians as the local promoters could find to the theater as guests and promote the old folks' reunion heavily.

Taking no chance on failing to make a huge opening splash, Houdini debuted the film at the Times Square Theater in New York in April of 1922, and trotted out one of Powers's elephants to reprise his Vanishing Elephant illusion. A few weeks later, when the film opened wide, he sent out three separate touring troupes to play on the same bill as the movie. With all the hoopla, the film didn't draw very well. The critics were kind but noted that the film had a schizophrenic quality about it; as a melodrama it was adequate, with one rescue scene from the rapids leading to Niagara Falls absolutely top notch. The problem was that the film was reaching for literary and spiritual import too. "The trouble is that the resumption of high literary meaning in the rest of the story is all bosh. So the net effect is pretty unsatisfactory. Serial melodrama and screen uplift won't mix," the *Variety* critic opined.

Houdini's moguldom came to an abrupt end with the release in November of 1923 of *Haldane of the Secret Service*. He came up with another great promotional campaign, including thousands of doorknob tags that read, "This lock is not HOUDINI-proof. He could pick it as easily as you pick a daisy. See the Master-Man of Mystery HOUDINI in *Haldane of the Secret Service*. A picture that will thrill you to your marrows." Despite the promotion, the reviews were brutal and the audiences were sparse. Even *Variety* was forced to note, "Perhaps the renown of Houdini is fading, or more probably the Broadway managers were wise to how bad a film this one is. . . . There is only one [escape], and that is a poorly staged affair showing the star free himself from a giant water mill . . . instead of going in for his specialty Houdini waltzes around in a tuxedo and dress suit."

A little picnic on the movie set. They obviously weren't serving Harry's favorite repast.
From the collection of Dr. Bruce Averbook

Haldane was the death knell of the Houdini Picture Corporation. Succeeding productions were shelved and the company dissolved. In retrospect, Houdini's involvement in movies, financially speaking, was a nightmare. He had to sue the Williamson Brothers twice, once to recoup a $2,500 promissory note for money he had advanced them, the second time for back salary from a movie that never got made. He wound up in litigation over his fifty percent share of the profits for the hugely successful *Master Mystery*. When he branched out on his own and took charge of the productions, his quirky sensibility and attempt to run away from the elements that made him successful onstage doomed their success. The only positives from Houdini's involvement in motion pictures were that it spread his fame worldwide and greatly increased his vaudeville salary, ironically at a time when he had no real interest in performing again.

"I believe magicians are much much too honest to succeed away from our own business *and this is not a jest*," he wrote his friend Goldston. "We are so busy with illusionary material that the businessman in a legal way out-trades us." Now, nearly fifty, and with his best days as an escape artist behind him, he had squandered a fortune and suffered his greatest failure yet. It was time for a metamorphosis.

From the collection of Ricky Jay

20

Saul Among the Prophets

ATLANTIC CITY, NEW JERSEY—JUNE 18, 1922.

The curtains were drawn, fluttering from time to time with the gentle caress of the sea breeze. There was a writing pad on the table in the living room of the suite, along with two ordinary pencils. The medium was sitting in front of the pad. To her side sat her husband, Sir Arthur Conan Doyle, the world's most famous mystery writer, the man who created Sherlock Holmes. He bowed his head.

"Almighty, we are grateful to you for this new revelation, this breaking down of the walls between two worlds. We thirst for another undeniable message from beyond, another call of hope and guidance to the human race at this, the time of its greatest affliction. Can we receive another sign from our friends from beyond?" Doyle recited.

He reached out and gently touched his wife's hands, as if he were transferring power to her. Taken by their sincerity, Houdini closed his eyes and meditated on religious thoughts, so he could help as much as possible.

Lady Doyle suddenly seized a pencil and began to strike the table with her hand.

"This is the most energetic the forces have ever come," she said.

She seemed to almost resist the agency that was making her hand quiver as she poised the pencil over the pad, but then she seemed to relent and the pencil began to move, as if on its own.

"Do you believe in God?" Lady Doyle asked. It was a cautionary question, to ensure that an evil spirit had not taken control of her.

Houdini desperately sought to contact his dead mother (pictured with Houdini). Lady Doyle facilitated it. *From the collection of Kenneth M. Trombly*

As if in answer, her hand beat the table three times, which was an affirmative response.

"Then I will make the sign of the cross," she said, and she drew a cross on the top of the pad.

Sir Arthur soothed her as she began to write, as if he was admonishing the spirit to be gentle with her.

The pad began to fill up with frenzied scribbling, page after page.

"Who is standing alongside of Houdini?" Sir Arthur inquired. "Is it Houdini's mother?"

The medium struck the table three times. She continued to frantically fill up page after page, with Conan Doyle tearing off the pages, one by one, and passing them to Houdini.

He began reading.

"Oh, my darling, thank God, thank God, at last I'm through—I've tried, oh so often—now I am happy. Why, of course, I want to talk to my boy—my own beloved boy—Friends, thank you, with all my heart for this. You have answered the cry of my heart—and of his—God bless him—a thousand fold, for all his life for me—never had a mother such a son—tell him not to grieve, soon he'll get all the evidence he is anxious for—Yes, we know—tell him, I want him to try to write in his own home. It will be far better so.

"I will work with him—he is so, so dear to me—I am preparing so sweet a home for him which one day in God's good time he will come to—it is one of my great joys preparing it for our future—I am so happy in this life—it is so full and joyous—my only shadow has been that my beloved one hasn't known how often I have been with him all the while, all the while—here away from my heart's darling—combining my work thus in this life of mine.

"It is so different over here, so much larger and bigger and more beautiful—so lofty—all sweetness around one—nothing that hurts and we see our beloved ones on earth—that is such a joy and comfort to us—Tell him I love him more than ever—the years only increase it—and his goodness fills my soul with gladness and thankfulness. Oh, just this, it is me. I want him only to know that—that—I have bridged the gulf—That is what I wanted, oh so much—Now I can rest in peace."

Houdini leaned back in his chair and took a deep breath.

Sir Arthur looked at Houdini. "Why don't you ask her a question? Some test so that you will be certain that this really is your dear mother."

"I don't know if the spirit will answer direct questions," Lady Doyle cautioned.

"Ask her if she can read your mind," Sir Arthur suggested.

Houdini didn't even have the time to get that question out of his mouth, when Lady Doyle grabbed the pad and began to write furiously.

"I always read my beloved son's mind—his dear mind—there is so much I want to say to him—but—I am almost overwhelmed by this joy of talking to him once more—it is almost too much to get through—the joy of it—thank you, thank you, thank you, friend, with all my heart for what you have done for me this day—God bless you, too, Sir Arthur, for what you are doing for us—for us over here—who so need to get in touch with our beloved ones on the earth plane—

"If only the world knew this great truth—how different—life would be for men and women—Go on, let nothing stop you—great will be your reward hereafter—Good-bye—I brought you, Sir Arthur, and my darling son together—I felt you were the one man who might help us to pierce the veil—and I was right—Bless him, bless him, bless him, I say from the depths of my soul—he fills my heart and later we shall be together—oh, so happy—a happiness awaits him that he has never dreamed of—tell him I am with him—just tell him that I'll soon make him know how close I am all the while—his eyes will soon be opened—Good-bye again—God's blessing on you all—"

It had taken nine years but Houdini's mother had finally contacted him.

An ex-physician and a current magician among the spirits, Sir Arthur Conan Doyle meets Houdini. *Conjuring Arts Research Center*

That the creator of the world's most rational and analytic materialist, Sherlock Holmes, would embrace a religion that viewed itself as the antidote to that moribund philosophy would seem odd, but Conan Doyle's conversion came after years and years of spiritual inquiry.

Arthur Conan Doyle was born in Scotland on May 22, 1859 to Charles and Mary Doyle, both religious Catholics. His father was a visionary artist who early in Arthur's life descended into alcoholism and mental illness and was repeatedly institutionalized. Growing up in poverty, Arthur became extremely close to his mother, who sent him to Jesuit schools. Doyle rebelled against the strict teachings of the Church, but he sought alternative outlets for his spirituality, even while studying medicine. In 1880, he attended his first Spiritualist lecture, while his father was undergoing his horrific descent into madness. The next year he graduated medical school and set up a small practice. Business was slow so he began to write short stories. He delved into esoteric spiritual practices like mesmerism and Theosophy, and began experiments in telepathy. His successes opened him up to the possibility of psychic phenomena, and in 1887, the same year that his first Sherlock Holmes story was published, he attended a séance of an elderly male medium. He was so impressed that he wrote a letter to a Spiritualist magazine proclaiming that the séance "showed me at last that it was absolutely certain that intelligence could exist apart from the body."

By 1889, Conan Doyle was convinced of the basic indestructibility of the human soul. By then he was writing full-time and his Holmes stories were beginning to catch on, a pleasant development since he now had a wife and son to support. As his success grew, he began to branch out—writing sprawling historical novels and answering a call to wanderlust. He was like an English Teddy Roosevelt, large, raw-boned, walrus-mustached, roaming the world in ill-fitting clothing, soaking in experience. He accompanied Lord Kitchener on his Egyptian campaign and traveled to South Africa for a firsthand glimpse of the Boer War. It was his book on that war and his defense of English foreign policy that led to his knighthood in 1902.

By then, Doyle was one of the most celebrated authors in the world. He had killed off his fictional detective Holmes, and then revived him when an old friend named Fletcher Robinson told him of the legend of a phantom hound that haunted the man who killed the dog and his wife. To the delight of the literate world, Holmes returned in the book *The Hound of the Baskervilles*, originally planned as a collaboration between the two men. In 1906, Doyle's wife died after a long bout of tuberculosis. A year later he married Jean Leckie, who he had fallen in love with ten years earlier, supposedly maintaining a secret, platonic relationship with her as his wife's health slowly deteriorated.

It was through his second wife, Jean, that Doyle finally embraced Spiritualism as a religion. The ranks of Spiritualism began to swell as grieving families sought to come to terms with the loss of their soldier sons in World War I. Doyle saw the devastation firsthand, visiting the French and Italian fronts. Back at home, Jean's friend Lily Loder-Symonds moved in with the family. Lily was an avid Spiritualist and a devotee of automatic writing. In autumn of 1916, she produced a series of messages from her dead brothers. Skeptical of automatic writing, Conan Doyle quizzed her about a conversation he had years earlier with Jean's dead brother Malcolm. When she accurately recalled the conversation, Doyle was convinced.

Now Doyle saw the war as a spiritual conflict between forces beyond comprehension using the competing armies as mere pawns. The war had wreaked havoc on the Doyle-Leckie families, ten members dead from combat or disease. Doyle lost his brother, his son Kingsley, two brothers-in-law, and many nephews. "Where were they? What had become of those splendid young lives? They were no longer here. Were they anywhere?" Doyle would ask in a later lecture on Spiritualism. "The question was [by] far the most pressing in the world. It filled my mind." He began to connect the rappings and table thumping of Spiritualist séances with attempts by dead spirits to communicate. "I understood at last that these foolish phenomena were really not so foolish, but had a purpose. They were signals."

On September 7, 1919, the signals bore full fruit. Doyle and his wife attended a séance given by Evan Powell, an amateur medium. They went to Powell's hotel room, accompanied by a few friends. The medium insisted he be searched and then tied to a wooden chair by Doyle. A megaphone with luminous paint was placed beside him. The room was darkened. Suddenly a deep, strong voice issued from the void. It was the voice of an Indian spirit, Black Hawk, Powell's spirit control. He told them that "Leely" wanted to speak with "the Lady of the Wigwam." It was Jean's by then departed friend Lily.

Thrilled with the séance, the Doyles returned the next night. "Then came what to me was the supreme moment of my spiritual experience," Doyle would write. "Almost too sacred for full description."

In the darkness, a voice called out.

"Jean, it is I."

Lady Doyle felt a hand on her head and she cried out.

"It is Kingsley."

Doyle heard the word "*Father.*"

"Dear boy, is that you," he whispered.

"*Forgive me!*" the voice said.

Then a large, strong hand rested on his head and he felt a kiss just above his brow.

"Tell me dear, are you happy?" Doyle asked.

There was silence and Doyle feared that he was gone.

"*Yes,*" the voice finally answered. "*I am so happy.*"

That was the turning point in Doyle's life. "Therefore my wife and I determined that we would, so far as possible, devote the rest of our lives to trying to make people understand that this subject is not to be laughed at, but that it is really the most important thing in the world," Doyle wrote, obsessed with spreading the gospel of Spiritualism. With this monomania came the intolerance of the true believer. "He carried it to extreme lengths showing impatience with anyone who expressed the slightest doubt," an acquaintance noted.

"With all modesty I am inclined to ask, is there any man on this globe who is doing as much psychic research as I?" Doyle would later ask. "I have clasped materialized hands . . . I have listened to prophecies which were quickly fulfilled. I have seen the 'dead' glimmer up upon a photographic plate which no hand but mine had touched . . . I have seen spirits walk round the room in fair light and join in the talk of the company. I have heard singing beyond earthly power . . . If a man could see, hear, and feel all this, and yet remain unconvinced of unseen intelligent forces around him, he would have good cause to doubt his own sanity. Why should he heed the chatter of irresponsible journalists, or the head-shaking of inexperienced men of science, when he has himself had so many proofs? They are babies in this matter, and should be sitting at his feet."

Doyle began to recruit an army of believers. What better way to aid in this crusade than by spreading his gospel and converting other prominent men? Now Doyle received another important communication. It wasn't from a departed spirit, though; it was from the very corporeal Master Mystifier, Harry Houdini.

"Have you read that some of the folks like Conan Doyle . . . are dabbling in Spiritualism again?" Houdini wrote Kellar at the very beginning of 1918. With his move into film and his hoped-for retirement from the stage, Houdini was planning to write more books, and one of his first projects was a tome about Spiritualism. Houdini had maintained interest in the subject since his own days as a phony medium before the turn of the century. He had even been approached by a prestigious lecture bureau at the end of 1919 to take the negative side of the subject and debate a prominent Spiritualist like Conan Doyle or Sir Oliver Lodge, a British scientist who had converted to Spiritualism after getting in touch with his dead son, Raymond. Houdini turned the offer down mainly because he was about to travel to England for six months to make up bookings that had been postponed by the war.

Once in England, he settled into his typical routine. "Am very busy," he wrote to a friend. "Taking a few shots for a proposed new picture, appearing at Trade showings, writing a book against Spiritualism, and doing my Show as usual." At this stage, Houdini was researching his book and it seemed to be hard going. Although Houdini was thought by a leading British psychic researcher to have powers of dematerialization after he had served as a committeeman during one of Houdini's Milk Can escapes, most mediums were wary of sitting for him.

Houdini's attitude toward communication between the dead and the living was complex. There had been strange circumstances in his own life that he had been unable to explain. In Berlin once, he had been handcuffed and roped and locked in a cabinet so securely that he thought that he wouldn't be able to escape. Bess, on hearing his groans, realized that he was in deep trouble and began to pray for assistance from Rabbi Mayer Samuel, who, before his death, had promised the young boy that if he ever ran into any difficulty, he would return to aid him. Within seconds, Houdini had solved the mystery of the cuffs and had escaped. Years later, while en route to a performance in Europe, Houdini saw a fleeting vision of his mother. The next day he was informed that she had died.

"I too would have parted gladly with a large share of my earthly possessions for the solace of one word from my loved departed—just one word that I was sure had been genuinely bestowed by them," he wrote. "In this frame of mind I began a new line of psychical research in all seriousness and from that time to the present I have never entered a séance room except with an open mind devoutly anxious to learn if intercommunication is within the range of possibilities." So it was both as researcher and seeker that Houdini sought out mediums during his stay in England. Who could be a better character reference for him than Sir Arthur Conan Doyle?

Soon after arriving in England, Houdini dispatched a copy of his book *The Unmasking of Robert-Houdin* to Doyle. On March 15, 1920 Doyle wrote and thanked him for the book and asked him a question about the Davenport Brothers, the American performers who were thought to have been aided in escaping their secure rope ties by cooperative spirits. "Some of our people think that you have yourself some psychic power, but I feel it is art and practise," Doyle commented. Within two months, Doyle would change his mind.

Houdini was tactful in his correspondence with Doyle. When the author pressed him on whether the Davenports had real occult power or were just tricksters, Houdini responded diplomatically, "I am afraid that I cannot say that all their work was accomplished by the spirits. . . . You will note that I am still a sceptic [sic], but a seeker after the Truth. I am willing to believe, if I can find a Medium who, as you suggest, will not resort to 'manipulation' when the Power does not 'arrive.'"

Now the floodgates were open. Doyle suggested two or three honest mediums, singling out Mrs. Annie Brittain as the best. "In a series of 72 clients whom I sent her, she got through 60 times, 5 failures and the rest half and half," he wrote. On April 25, accompanied by Bess and their niece Julia, they sat with Mrs. Brittain. Houdini's diary entry reflects his disappointment. "Mrs. Brittain not convincing. Simply kept talking in general. 'Saw' things she heard about. One spirit was to bring me flowers on the stage. All this is ridiculous stuff."

Two weeks earlier, Houdini had finally met the Doyles. He went alone as Bess "was not able" to make the trip. Houdini lunched at their house and was regaled with tales that would make a materialist cringe. "Sir Arthur told me he had spoken six times to his son," he wrote in his diary. "No possible chance for trickery." A few days later he wrote Kellar. "[Doyle] saw my performance Friday Night. He was so much impressed, that there is little wonder in him believing in Spiritualism so implicitly."

By the end of May, Doyle was convinced that Houdini was masking his true occult powers. The magician was playing in Bristol and had accepted and won a challenge to escape from a packing box built onstage. "I heard of your remarkable feat in Bristol. My dear chap, why go around the world seeking a demonstration of the occult when you are giving one all the time?" Doyle wrote him.

With his search for a genuine medium stalled, Houdini turned his attention to spirit photography, a phenomenon where depictions of spirits were unintentionally captured in the course of taking regular photographs. Houdini wrote Doyle asking to see some photos taken by a psychic researcher named Crawford but Doyle didn't have the photos on hand. "They are too precious to have lying around. . . . But I have something far more precious—two photos, one of a goblin, the other of four fairies in a Yorkshire wood. A fake! you will say. No, sir, I think not. However, all inquiry will be made. These I am not allowed to send. The fairies are about eight inches high. In one there is a single goblin dancing. In the other four beautiful, luminous creatures. Yes, it is a revelation."

The Doyles and the Houdinis cavort in Denver. *From the collection of Dr. Bruce Averbook*

Houdini was too polite to comment on the fairy pictures. Doyle stuck to his guns and eventually published a book touting the photos as real and revelatory. Years later, the teenager who took the photos of her nine-year-old niece cavorting with the fairies would admit that the pictures were faked. If Doyle had done better research, he would have determined that the fairies had been cut out of one of the most popular children's books of 1915, a book that contained one of his own stories.

Houdini was disappointed by his experiences with mediums in England. "I went to 100 spiritualistic Séances trying to discover something *new*—it is the same old routine," he wrote Robert Gould Shaw, the theater collector. "Booth & Jefferson believed in it—I have an open mind, but am still to be converted." A

One of the fairy photographs that fooled Doyle. *Conjuring Arts Research Center*

year later, by the summer of 1921, Houdini was asking the newspapermen to keep his name out of any stories that involved exposing fake mediums. He needed access to the world of Spiritualism to research his new book. At the same time, he was being drawn into the controversy by both the media and the rabid anti-Spiritualist faction among his closest friends. It was all a result of his latest book, *Miracle Mongers and Their Methods.*

The book's subtitle said it all: *A Complete Exposé of the Modus Operandi of Fire Eaters, Heat Resisters, Venomous Reptile Defiers, Sword Swallowers, Human Ostriches, Strong Men, Etc.* Houdini had drawn on his sideshow and circus background and written a fascinating book revealing the secrets of these eccentric entertainers. The book was so good that the reviewers urged him to next set his sights on exposing phony mediums, who were beginning to be seen as a scourge on society. "If Houdini doesn't do it, someone else will, sooner or later, but it should be Houdini," the *Variety* reviewer argued. "He would have the moral support of every clean periodical in the country." *The New York Times* was so impressed with Houdini's "merciless exposure of miracle-mongers who claim to be endowed with mysterious powers" that they nominated him for membership in the Seybert Commission, a prestigious academic group that studied mediums, if they ever resumed their investigations.

In addition to the press, Houdini was being pressured to go full tilt against phony mediums by his close associates. His secretary in the SAM was Oscar Teale, a venerable magic theorist who had done an act exposing the tricks of phony mediums years earlier. Houdini was also consulting regularly with W. S. Davis, a New York City printer whose knowledge of the tricks in the séance room came firsthand; he was a reformed medium.

Although pressured by the Spiritualist opposition, Houdini still kept an open mind about the possibility of communicating with the dead. Having been unable to see some of the leading mediums in Great Britain, he sent his old friend and fellow magician DeVega to investigate mediums and report back their results. "I believe you could not be easily fooled," he noted and offered to pay all expenses. A month later, DeVega obviously came through because Houdini wrote back: "Glad to get the confessions of the mdeiums [sic]. What I want particularly is Spirit Photos and their methods. I will willing[ly] pay all your expenses, to any sceance [sic] you may go to, nomatter [sic] what it is write it down in detail and send it along." DeVega came through on that count as well, making a visit to the famous Crewe circle and sending back a full report. Houdini was grateful. "The detailed data you have 'red-inked' was especially interesting. Do you think you could dope out some way to duplicate this stuff, if you had the paraphernalia?"

Houdini kept up his correspondence with Doyle, and Sir Arthur, convinced of his friend's supernatural power, was only too pleased to stay in touch. It would be a boon to the movement if Doyle could get Houdini to come out of the psychic closet and embrace Spiritualism. He would get his chance to facilitate that when they met again face-to-face in April of 1922 when Doyle came to proselytize in the land of the free.

It was only natural that with Sir Arthur in his home, Houdini would try a little experiment. The two men, along with Houdini's lawyer and confidant, Bernard Ernst, were in Houdini's library—a misnomer since Houdini's entire house was filled with books and memorabilia—when the master magician produced what looked like a typical slate, eighteen inches long and fifteen inches high. Holes had been bored through the top two corners of the slate and long wires had been looped through the holes. A hook had been attached to the ends of the wires. Next to the slate, Houdini had brought out four small cork balls, an inkwell filled with white ink, and a tablespoon.

The slate was presented to Sir Arthur for his inspection. Bemused, he saw that it was a normal slate.

"Would you be so kind as to suspend the slate anywhere in the room by means of the hooks that are attached to the wires?" Houdini asked. "I want the slate to be able to swing freely in space. This is being done to eliminate whatsoever the possibility of any electrical connection to the slate itself."

Sir Arthur and Ernst walked around the room and chose a spot. They hooked one of the wires over the edge of a picture frame, the other onto a large book on one of the bookshelves. Now the slate was free to swing in space. Satisfied, Houdini cleaned the slate.

Holding out the saucer that contained the four cork balls, Houdini asked Doyle to examine them.

"You will see that these are ordinary cork balls. In fact, you may select any one you like, then cut it in two with your pocketknife, verifying the fact that these are unprepared solid cork balls," Houdini said.

Doyle chose a ball and cut it in half with surgical precision. Then Houdini had Doyle select another ball and, using the spoon, dip it into the inkwell and stir it, until the white ink had thoroughly permeated the cork. The ball was then left in the inkwell, allowing it to soak up as much ink as possible. Houdini then made Doyle a present of the other two balls.

"Have you a piece of paper in your pocket upon which you can write anything?" Houdini asked Doyle.

Not only did Doyle have paper but he had a pencil too. He was a writer, after all.

"Sir Arthur, I want you to go out of the house, walk anywhere you like, as far as you like in any direction; then write a question or sentence on that piece of paper; put it back in your pocket and return to the house," Houdini said.

Doyle complied. He left the town house and walked for three blocks before he stopped, took out the paper, placed it in his palm, and scribbled the words "*Mene, mene, tekel, upharsin*," a biblical quote. Then he folded up the paper, put it back in his pocket, and returned to the library.

"Now I want you to stir the cork ball once more, thoroughly saturating it in the ink and by means of the spoon, hold it up against the slate," Houdini commanded.

When Sir Arthur complied, a strange thing happened. The cork ball stuck to the slate, as if it had a mind of its own. Then it suddenly began to roll across the clean slate, leaving a white trail of ink as it moved. The ink slowly formed the letter "M," then an "e," and an "n," and before a thoroughly mystified Doyle, his phrase was mysteriously written out on the slate board. When the last word was completed, the ball suddenly dropped to the floor.

Conan Doyle was stunned. Houdini asked him to take the paper out of his pocket and verify that this was the phrase he had written. Of course, it was.

"Sir Arthur, I have devoted a lot of time and thought to this illusion; I have been working on it, on and off, all winter. I won't tell you how it was done, but I can assure you it was pure trickery," Houdini lectured. "I did it by perfectly normal means. I devised it to show you what can be done along those lines. Now, I beg of you, Sir Arthur, do not jump to the conclusion that certain things you see are necessarily 'supernatural,' or the work of 'spirits,' just because you cannot explain them. This is as marvelous a demonstration as you have ever witnessed, given you under test conditions, and I can assure you that it was accomplished by trickery and by nothing else. Do, therefore, be careful in the future, in endorsing phenomena just because you cannot explain them. I have given you this test to impress upon you the necessity of caution, and I sincerely hope that you will profit by it."

Sir Arthur just smiled. *So Houdini's still being cagy about his power,* he thought. *Is not this yet another demonstration of his psychic ability?*

Houdini's experiment was a gentle caution to Sir Arthur on his 1922 visit to the United States that there were greater things in this world than his devotion to spiritualistic doctrine.

Doyle had run into trouble before he had even disembarked from his steamship in New York. Attacked by a headline-hungry press, he was pressed to give his views on heaven. When he theorized that in the spirit world whiskey and cigars were available to those inhabiting their etheric bodies, the cynical reporters front-paged these statements, even making up new heavenly delights. "Doyle says they play golf in heaven" one headline screamed.

After lecturing in New York, Doyle took his road show to Boston, Washington, D.C., and Philadelphia. Back in New York in early May, he and Lady Doyle visited Houdini at his home. Conan Doyle was anxious to see Houdini's Spiritualism library and seemed disappointed that so many of the books were antagonistic toward the subject. Claiming that the pro-Spiritualism books were scattered about the house, Houdini promised to devote an entire floor to the subject. He also tried to demonstrate to Doyle that certain séance room manifestations could easily be faked by showing him how "spirit hands" could be molded using a rubber glove and hot paraffin. Doyle was much more impressed by Houdini's feat in the taxi ride back downtown. The master magician performed the simple little effect of seeming to slide the end of his thumb off and then reattaching it. Apparently, Houdini was convincing. Writing about the visit, Doyle told him, "I think what interested me most was the little 'trick' which you showed us in the cab. You certainly have very wonderful powers, whether inborn or acquired."

Two weeks later, Houdini invited Doyle to attend the annual Society of American Magicians' banquet. Since becoming president of the SAM, Houdini had made it a practice to invite distinguished guests from the upper echelons of business, politics, and journalism in an attempt to elevate the status of his profession, and at the same time, bask in the reflected glory of his prominent guests. By 1923, even President Harding was sending in regrets for not being able to attend.

For Doyle's "special benefit" Houdini had arranged after- dinner entertainment where prominent magicians would reproduce séance room effects. The magician undoubtedly saw this as part of Doyle's ongoing education, but the mystery writer recoiled at what he perceived as an affront to his religion. "I fear that the bogus spiritual phenomena must prevent me from attending the banquet, which you have so graciously proffered. I look upon this subject as sacred, and I think that God's gift to man has been intercepted and delayed by the constant pretence that all phenomena are really tricks, which I know they are not," Doyle wrote Houdini. Houdini immediately backtracked and promised Doyle that "There will be nothing performed or said which will offend anyone."

It was a gala evening. After the first course had been served, every guest received a silk, gold-trimmed Houdini mascot doll. It had taken Bess three solid months to dress each doll individually. After dinner was completed, Doyle addressed the assemblage. He began by confessing that he had a friendly feeling for conjurers because they helped to destroy the great enemy of real Spiritualists, the crooked mediums. "On the other hand when a conjurer does occasionally attack spiritualism as a whole, he deals in a subject which he does not understand," Doyle maintained. Suddenly, he announced that he would show a motion picture that featured extinct animals. He described the pictures as "psychic" and "preternatural" but not "occult" or "supernatural." He also claimed that the pictures would speak for themselves and that he would answer no questions regarding them, either for the guests or the press. With a straight face, Doyle had the lights dimmed and the screen filled with startlingly detailed images of very realistic-looking dinosaurs "clawing and biting, and fondling in the primaeval slime."

The next day's newspapers were filled with accounts of Doyle's "hoax" at the magicians' dinner. "Whether these pictures were intended by the famous author and champion of spiritism as a joke on the magicians or as a genuine picture like his photographs of fairies was not revealed," *The New York Times* reported. "The audience was left strictly to its own conclusions, whether the sober-faced Englishman was making merry with them or was lifting the veil from mysteries penetrated only by those of his school who know the secret of filming elves and ectoplasm and other things unknown to most minds."

Doyle admitted in a letter to Houdini the next day that his presentation was merely to provide "a little mystification to those who have so often and so successfully mystified others." What he didn't admit was that it was really a sneak preview of the film version of his novel *The Lost World*. If some modern-day anthropologists are correct, this would have been the second hoax that Sir Arthur perpetrated involving this book. Ten years earlier, a gravel pit near the village of Piltdown yielded an amazing discovery: the remains of an early human fossil that could be considered to be the missing link between apes and homo erectus. It took forty years from this discovery for academics to realize that the so-called Piltdown man, the pride of British science, was a clever fake, a composite of a human skull and the jaw of a female orangutan. There were other bones, teeth, and antlers from extinct mammals found at the site. In 1983, a researcher named John Winslow theorized that the perpetrator of the Piltdown Hoax was none other than Conan Doyle. Doyle had access to all the exotic bones on his many forays overseas, he lived in the vicinity of the find, he described the area in his novel *The Lost World*, and, tellingly, he had a motive—to embarrass the materialists in the scientific community in England then. One of their most prominent members, Edwin Ray Lankester, the director of the British Museum of Natural History, was an avid anti-Spiritualist who had exposed the self-styled Dr. Henry Slade, the leading medium of his day. Richard Milner, an anthropologist at the American Museum of Natural History, concurs that Conan Doyle had the strongest motive to mount the hoax and suggests that Doyle didn't reveal his authorship because with the outbreak of World War I, Doyle desired to be an advisor to the government. A hoaxer would have much less credibility.

Flying high from his successful showing at the SAM meeting, Doyle set his evangelical sights on Houdini. On June 9, he invited Houdini and Bess to join him. "Why not come down—both of you? The children would teach you to swim! and the change would do you good," Doyle enthused.

Houdini gladly accepted the invitation, suggesting they come down for the weekend of June 17. Doyle seemed pleased. "There will be a few Spiritualistic friends from Brooklyn (barristers) but you won't clash," Doyle informed Houdini, after he had already accepted Doyle's invitation.

On Saturday, at four-thirty in the afternoon, Houdini met Doyle and his two boys in the swimming pool of the Hotel Ambassador. Houdini taught the boys how to dive and float. Sir Arthur marveled at Houdini's feat of holding his breath underwater. Later, Lady Doyle joined them as Houdini and Doyle sat on some deck chairs, looked out at the blue Atlantic Ocean, and talked Spiritualism. Doyle told Houdini about a wonderful spirit photographer named Mrs. Ada Deane who had been producing amazing results. Houdini held his tongue, knowing that the Magic Circle in London had trapped the medium red-handed with marked plates, but he was amazed to hear that Doyle had raised $125,000 on his lecture tour, the money all earmarked for the Spiritualist cause.

During their conversation, Doyle's children ran up and told Houdini that they had no fear of death, since the spirit survives physical extinction. The group, sans Bess, all repaired to a swimming meet that evening where Houdini forced an antsy Conan Doyle to stay to the end lest he disappoint the young boys vying for prizes.

On Sunday, Houdini and Bess were sunning themselves on the deck chairs when a small boy led Conan Doyle to them.

"Houdini, if agreeable, Lady Doyle will give you a special séance, as she has a feeling that she might have a message come through. At any rate, she is willing to try," Doyle said.

Then he turned to Bess.

"We would like to be alone. Two people of the same mind, either positive or negative, could interfere with Lady Doyle getting any writing from the spirits that controlled her. You do not mind if we make the experiment without you?" he said.

"Certainly not, go right ahead, Sir Arthur; I will leave Houdini in your charge," Bess said.

Sir Arthur marched Houdini to their suite, and Lady Doyle proceeded to deliver the fateful message from Houdini's mother.

After the séance was over and the letter from Houdini's mother had been read, Conan Doyle advised Houdini to follow his mother's advice and practice automatic writing when he went home.

Houdini picked up one of the pencils.

"Is there any particular way in which I must hold this pencil when I want to write, or does it write automatically?" Houdini asked.

Then he poised the pencil over the pad and wrote down the word "Powell."

Sir Arthur was thunderstruck. He jumped up in the air when he read that word. "The Spirits have directed you in writing the name of my dear fighting partner in Spiritualism, Dr. Ellis Powell, who has just died in England. I am the person he is most likely to signal to, and here is his name coming through your hands. Truly Saul is among the Prophets. You are a medium!" Doyle rejoiced.

According to Doyle, Houdini, who had looked "grimmer and paler" as he read the letter from his mother, was genuinely moved at the end of the séance and when he tried to do automatic writing, a strange look came over him.

"Then he looked up at me and I was amazed, for I saw in his eyes that look, impossible to imitate, which comes to the medium who is under influence," Doyle wrote. "The eyes look at you, and yet you feel that they are not focused upon you."

Houdini explained to Doyle that he had been thinking of his good friend Frederick Eugene Powell, a magician who was about to go out on the road with one of Houdini's touring companies to promote his film *The Man From Beyond*.

Now Doyle was more convinced of Houdini's mediumship than ever. And more intent on persuading him to go public as a Spiritualist.

The day after the Atlantic City séance, Doyle wrote Houdini and urged him to go on the lecture circuit and talk about his experiences with Spiritualism. "I can see you sometime, as your true experiences accumulate, giving a wonderful lecture, *Phenomenal Spiritualism—True and False* in which, after giving an account of your adventures with fakes, you will also give an account of those which bear inspection. It would be a very great draw. Fake photos and true ones. I could fit you up with a few of the latter," Doyle wrote.

Then he dropped a bombshell. "I may say that your mother again came back with words of passionate love through Mrs. M[etcalfe] of Brooklyn last night. She said, 'My son has now told his wife that he is mentally convinced of the truth of this revelation, but he does not see his way and it is dark in front of him. He is now seated in his room thinking it over.'"

Doyle was relentless. The next day he sent Houdini another letter refusing to accept Houdini's Powell explanation, since at the Metcalfe sitting on Sunday night, Doyle's Powell had come back and told him that he was sorry that he had to speak so abruptly at Houdini's sitting. "It confirms me in the belief that it *was* Powell. However, you will no doubt test your powers further."

Back in New York the following Tuesday, Houdini ran into Doyle and, recounting the séance, told him, "I have been walking on air ever since." They also had a long talk about Houdini's "powers." Houdini described an inner voice that gave him advice during the execution of some of his dangerous bridge jumps. "He stands above some awful place from which he will spring," Doyle later wrote. "He has to wait patiently—sometimes for many minutes—until something within him tells him that the time is ripe for his effort. This, he says, is universal among all men who do such stunts. 'If you don't wait for that moment you have about as much chance as a celluloid dog in Hell.' He was tempted once to trust himself instead of his unseen guides, and then he nearly broke his neck. 'You stand there,' he said, 'swallowing the yellow stuff that every man has in him. Then at last you hear the voice, and you jump.' It may be the subconscious self which assures itself that all is well. It may be spiritual."

During the Doyles' stay in New York, their friendship blossomed. The Doyles went to a screening of *The Man From Beyond,* and Conan Doyle delighted in the last scene of the movie. The hero and the heroine are united, reading a passage from Doyle's *The Vital Message*. "The very best sensational picture I have ever seen," Doyle accommodated Houdini by giving the papers a capsule review. "It holds one breathless . . . one of the really great contributions to the screen."

He did another favor for Houdini before he left for home, giving him a letter of introduction to Miss Besinnet, the celebrated medium who Doyle had made a detour during his tour to sit with. "I have gone far in giving you that letter to Miss B., for you have the reputation, among Spiritualists, of being a bitterly prejudiced enemy, who would make trouble if it were possible," Doyle wrote Houdini. "I know that this is not so, and I give you this pass as a sign that I know it. She is safe in your hands."

On the eve of the Doyles' departure back to England, Houdini invited them to celebrate his twenty-eighth wedding anniversary at the theater. Houdini, called up from the audience, did his Needles effect and literally stopped the show. The next day, the magician accompanied the Doyle family to the ship to see them off.

Back home, the two men kept up their correspondence, trading medium stories. By August, Houdini began to lecture on Spiritualism, but not before he invited W. S. Davis to preview and critique his talk. Davis seemed disappointed and wrote Houdini that he was handling the subject too cautiously. "I must do it," Houdini wrote back, "otherwise they will not allow me at the seances."

A little more than four months after the Doyles had received the fateful message from Houdini's mother, Houdini destroyed his relationship with Sir Arthur. He didn't set out to do it, and he certainly didn't comprehend that the ramifications of an article he wrote would forever change his life. In fact, he wasn't even writing about his friend Doyle.

In October, the New York General Assembly of Spiritualists, taking a tack from Houdini and Rinn, offered a reward of $5,000 to any person who could produce by "trickery, fraud, or deception" eight specific manifestations of spirit power. Houdini answered the challenge in his article entitled "Spirit Compacts Unfilled." It was a throwaway sentence in that article that enraged Doyle. "My mind is open. I am perfectly willing to believe, but in the twenty-five years of my investigation and the hundreds of séances which I have attended, I have never seen or heard anything that could convince me that there is a possibility of communication with the loved ones who have gone beyond."

That one sentence made Lady Doyle mad. Doyle was asked to comment by the newspaper but he decided to write Houdini instead. "I felt rather sore about it. You have all the right in the world to hold your own opinion, but when you say that you have had no evidence of survival, you say what I cannot reconcile with what I saw with my own eyes. I know, by many examples, the purity of my wife's mediumship, and I saw what you got and what the effect was upon you at the time," Doyle wrote. "I have done my best to give you truth."

Writing years later, Doyle was still furious recalling the affront to his wife's mediumship but he played loose with the facts, claiming that Houdini had asked for the séance. "The method in which Houdini tried to explain away, minimize and contort our attempt at consolation, *which was given entirely at his own ur-*

gent request and against my wife's desire, has left a deplorable shadow in my mind which made some alteration in my feelings for him." [emphasis added]

Houdini immediately replied to Doyle's letter. "You write that you are very sore. I trust that it is not with me, because you, having been truthful and manly all your life, naturally must admire the same traits in other human beings." After explaining why he would have thought of his friend Powell, he got to the heart of the matter. "I know you treat this as a religion but personally I cannot do so, for up to the present time I have never seen or heard anything that could convert me."

Houdini was being coy. Before he had walked back with Doyle to the séance, Bess had employed their old second sight code and, using subtle language and gestures, had already tipped Houdini off that Lady Doyle had been pumping her for information on Houdini's relationship with his mother the night before the séance. He still went into the séance with an open mind, but when he saw Lady Doyle draw the sign of the cross and then have his mother unleash a torrent of sappy words in perfect English, without even mentioning that that day happened to be her birthday, Houdini was crestfallen.

Too polite to overtly abuse his friends, Houdini took his umbrage out on Doyle in a sly way. When asked to begin his mediumship by practicing his own automatic writing, Houdini made a big show of grabbing the pencil. Doyle had mistaken Houdini's penetrating Master Mystifier's glare for the otherworldly gaze of the mystic. In Houdini's later written account he admitted that using Powell's name was a "deliberate mystification" on his part. "Or let us say a kindlier word regarding my thoughts and call it 'coincidence.'" It seems evident that Houdini knew of Doyle's friend's death and had used the name to turn the tables on Doyle and thoroughly mystify the man who was intent on converting him. Houdini couldn't resist the little bit of perverse pleasure he enjoyed from letting Doyle believe what he had done was real, even though he fully knew it would further strengthen Doyle's irrational convictions.

Doyle had invited Houdini to another séance that day, one that was being conducted with his Brooklyn friends. Again, Houdini wasn't impressed.

"I noticed that, at a séance, Sir Arthur would ask a question and then change his mind and ask another one. Eventually, when he would get an answer to a question, he had evidently forgotten that he had asked that specific one, and, on receiving a reply to same, would naturally think that he had never spoken on the subject before," Houdini wrote in his day book. "All during the séance he was willing to believe. It was not a case of being deceived, but merely a case of religious mania."

Houdini's *New York Sun* article must have been embarrassing to Doyle for other reasons besides the perceived affront to his wife. Apparently Doyle had been spreading the word in England that Houdini had seen the spiritualistic light. A few weeks after Houdini's response to Doyle, he received a letter from E. J. Dingwall, who was a researcher for the Society for Psychical Research in England. "Dear Houdini—Is there any truth in the story of Doyle that you got an evidential message from your mother through Lady Doyle? Also that you have become an automatic writer?"

Dingwall's letter had a chilling effect. Houdini had been walking a fine line with Doyle, not being fully candid in the hopes that he could continue to use Doyle's credibility to gain access to the mediums for his research. Now this tactic was blowing up in his face. Houdini had been working his entire life toward a singular goal—respectability. Houdini knew that with his conversion, Doyle would have snagged the ultimate trophy for his cause. "Sir Arthur Conan Doyle has repeatedly told the Spiritualists that I eventually will see the light and will embrace Spiritualism," he wrote later. Apparently, Doyle was claiming that eventuality had come to pass.

On December 19, 1922, Houdini swore out a deposition and had it notarized. It began:

THE TRUTH REGARDING SPIRITUAL SÉANCE GIVEN TO HOUDINI BY LADY DOYLE

> ***Fully realizing the danger of statements made by investigators of psychic phenomena, and knowing full well my reputation earned, after more than thirty years experience in the realm of mystery, I can truthfully say that I have never seen a mystery, and I have never visited a séance, which I could not fully explain; and I want to go on record regarding the séance given to me by Lady Doyle in the presence of Sir Arthur Conan Doyle, at Atlantic City, June 17, 1922.***

Houdini went on to document that he never felt his mother's presence in the slightest, she couldn't speak or write English, and he wrote the name "Powell" of his own volition. He ended the statement with "I put this on record so that, in case of my death, no one will claim that the spirit of Sir Arthur Conan Doyle's friend Ellis Powell guided my hand."

As far as we know, at that point, no Spiritualists had threatened the mystifier's life. One of them had prophesied his death, however. Doyle had saved face after the Atlantic City séance fiasco by claiming that Houdini was too nervous at the séance to admit that it had been genuine, but the Doyles also believed there was another reason that Houdini denied the authenticity of Lady

Doyle's message from Mrs. Weiss. It seems that the medium had received an additional message from the spirits in Atlantic City, and this message indicated that Houdini would die very soon.

They gathered around the table again, the same as the night before and the night before that. Lady Doyle had her pad and pencil at the ready. Conan Doyle soothed her and held her hand and the communication started flowing. But on this night there was a major breakthrough. Tonight, Sir Arthur was going to be in direct communication with his own spirit guide, a guide who would control him, literally, for the rest of his life. Conan Doyle's mother made the introduction, but first she had to thank Sir Arthur for making plans to lay flowers on her grave.

I am so happy, my beloved son. We all know and love you for the thought. But not while you are so busy, dear one. I can't bear you to tire your dear self.

"What about the undeveloped spirit?" Conan Doyle asked. During the last séance, an undeveloped spirit had come to them for advice.

Your guide says you did him untold good. He has progressed far. He is almost here. His mother guards and helps him onwards and up. Your guide is such a high soul! He loves you beyond words. You are often with him at night. He helps and instructs you over here. The name is Pheneas. He is a very, very high soul, sent especially to work through you on the earth plane. He died thousands of years ago in the East, near Arabia. He was a leader among men. He wants me to say, dear one, that there is much work before you.

"In this world?" Conan Doyle asked.

Why, of course, my darling, it is here on this grey earth that you are needed. Your guide is here. He places his arm round you and kisses your brow and blesses you, and blesses you both. It gives us such joy over here to see the love light always round you in your own dear home. It is our earth centre. We are happy in that sweet atmosphere. Bless and keep you all, my dears. Your guide is here.

"I am proud to have such a guide," Conan Doyle said.

And then, for the first time, his guide spoke directly to him.

Pheneas speaking. We are brothers. Your wife is invaluable to us. We use her a great deal.

"Do I work on right lines?" Conan Doyle fretted.

You are right. Go on as you are doing. You are doing far more than you have any idea of. It is far-reaching, the effect of it.

"What is this sign which we hear of?" Conan Doyle asked.

It is this way. God has ordained that a great light shall shine into the souls of men through a great external force which is slowly penetrating through into the earth's sphere. It is something which the most ignorant must see and believe. It will come very soon. The world will be staggered. It is the only thing which can arouse the lethargy of the human race. Such a shock! It is like Sodom and Gomorrah.

"It is destructive, then?" Conan Doyle worried.

Not entirely so.

"Will it be here?" he asked.

Yes, it will be here and everywhere. It must *be. The world of men will not wake otherwise. And this truth has got to be as a great cloud of knowledge settling down all over the world. All the shams and ceremonies must be swept away for ever, and only this sweeping power can do that.*

This has been a happy evening for me. I have often wanted to come to you, for you see you are so much to me, and it hurt that I meant nothing to you. Now we are close. It will be easier for me to work through you in consequence.

Then, for the first time, Lady Doyle spoke up.

"Have I done wrong by being angry with the persecutors of the Cause?" she asked.

Quite right, my dear soul, Pheneas assured her. *We, too, are furious, so how can we blame you for being so? But they too will know the truth very soon. It will be the biggest thing that has ever happened in the earth's history. But great blessings will follow. All the shadows will flee away.*

"Is it like Atlantis?" Doyle asked.

Yes, very much. Only much bigger—more sweeping and different.

"But how would any cataclysm convert folk to Spiritualism?" he astutely asked.

By what everyone will see for themselves at that supreme time. Another time I will tell you more—much more. There will be no preparation.

"Shall we go to America?" Doyle asked.

It is God's will. It is ordained.

"The children too?" he said.

Yes, emphatically. Yes. You are all needed, each in your own way doing work for the cause.

Pheneas's first message was of a total upheaval of the world order. The enemies of the cause would be meeting their end in a cataclysm similar to those that befell the heathens at Sodom and Gomorrah. With Lady Doyle enjoying more prestige thanks to Pheneas's commendations, she began to assert herself on the Doyles' second American adventure. Shortly after arriving in New York, she went to a Westinghouse studio on the top of the Ritz-Carlton Hotel and broadcast a wireless message extolling Spiritualism to 500,000 people. Doyle was impressed. "The stars were above, the lights of the huge city below, and as I listened to those great truths ringing out in her beautifully modulated voice it was more like an angel message than anything I could imagine." A few weeks later, that angel voice turned strident. With Doyle lecturing in Pittsburgh, Lady Doyle, back in New York, publicly rebuked Mayor Hylan when he made some unflattering comments about "that man Doyle" and his Spiritualist beliefs. Then she wrote a long newspaper article that was headlined "Mansions in the Sky Like Our Earthly Home Says Lady Doyle."

On the second lecture tour, which covered the Western states that Doyle had neglected on his first go-round, pretenses were dropped and battle lines were drawn between him and Houdini. Instead of feting Doyle, the SAM, which Houdini completely controlled, offered to reproduce any of the most puzzling phenomena that Spiritualism had to offer. "Conan Doyle has seen fit to call magicians tricksters. . . . Sir Arthur has not shown himself a competent judge," the SAM officer and brilliant magician Servais LeRoy told the press.

Relations with Houdini were deteriorating rapidly. When Lord Carnarvon, an explorer who led an expedition to the tomb of King Tut in Egypt, died under mysterious circumstances, Doyle was quoted around the world theorizing that an evil spirit may have been responsible. "I think it is possible that some occult influence caused his death," Doyle said. "There are many legends about the powers of the old Egyptians, and I know I wouldn't care to go fooling about their tombs and mummies. There are many malevolent spirits."

Houdini jumped into the controversy. He agreed with authorities that the death was due to blood poisoning from an insect bite and asked Doyle why no other Egyptologists had befallen a similar fate. Despite the controversy, Doyle still harbored hopes of converting Houdini to the cause and referred him to mediums who might sway him. "I have found the mediums very averse to sitting with you, and they all regard you as one who has insulted them, but I do my best to clear away that impression," Doyle wrote Houdini on April 30. There was one medium who would never sit with Houdini again, and she was Lady Doyle. "Pray remember us all to your wife," Doyle ended that letter. "Mine is, I am afraid, rather angry with you."

Even though their relationship was deteriorating, Houdini still tried to engage Doyle in reasonable discussion about spiritualistic phenomena. While lecturing on Spiritualism in Los Angeles in April, he investigated a spirit photograph that had been taken at the funeral of a medium named Mary Fairfield McVickers. Convinced that the ghostly apparitions were a product of the irregular surface of the wall, Houdini hired a photographer, went back to the church, and attempted to replicate the original photo, taking ten exposures. When his own photos were developed, Houdini was shocked to find a weirdly shaped luminous streak in the second negative. Convinced that there was no normal explanation for the strange streak of light, Houdini sent a copy of the photo to Doyle in New York. Blinded by his anger, Sir Arthur missed his opportunity to restart the conversion of Houdini and deemed Houdini's photo absurd. Undeterred by Doyle's negative response, Houdini still urged his audiences to attend Sir Arthur's upcoming lectures.

In May, Houdini and Doyle found themselves in Denver at the same time. Even though the Doyles attended Houdini's show and Bess sat through Doyle's lecture, relations were strained, especially after *The Denver Express* ran a huge headline: "DOYLE IN DENVER DEFIES HOUDINI AND OFFERS TO BRING DEAD BACK AGAIN." The article quoted Doyle as challenging Houdini to a $5,000 bet to attend a sitting where he would bring his own mother back in physical form. Doyle rushed up to Houdini in the lobby of the hotel where they both were staying to apologize profusely for the story, claiming he had been misquoted. Houdini told Doyle that the papers misquote people all the time and he wouldn't hold it against him, but then he went to the paper's offices, where the editors told him that Doyle positively was not misquoted.

Later that month, the tables were turned. Doyle was enraged when Houdini was quoted in *The Oakland Tribune* to the effect that Doyle had been fooled by two mediums who had been discredited. Doyle counterattacked in the pages of the paper and then wrote Houdini and asked him to send him a written denial of making his original charges. "Our relations are certainly curious and are likely to become more so, for so long as you attack what I *know* from experience to be true, I have no alternative but to attack you in return. How long a private friendship can survive such an ordeal I do not know—but at least I did not create the situation."

The final straw occurred a few days later, when Houdini participated in a séance that exposed a leading American medium. Houdini's explanatory letter went unanswered and, as far as we know, there was no further correspondence between the two for the next seven months.

After not corresponding with Doyle for months, Houdini wrote him in December, presumably asking Doyle for some favor. The Spiritualist's response was curt. "I was surprised and sorry to get your letter. . . . You can't bitterly and of-

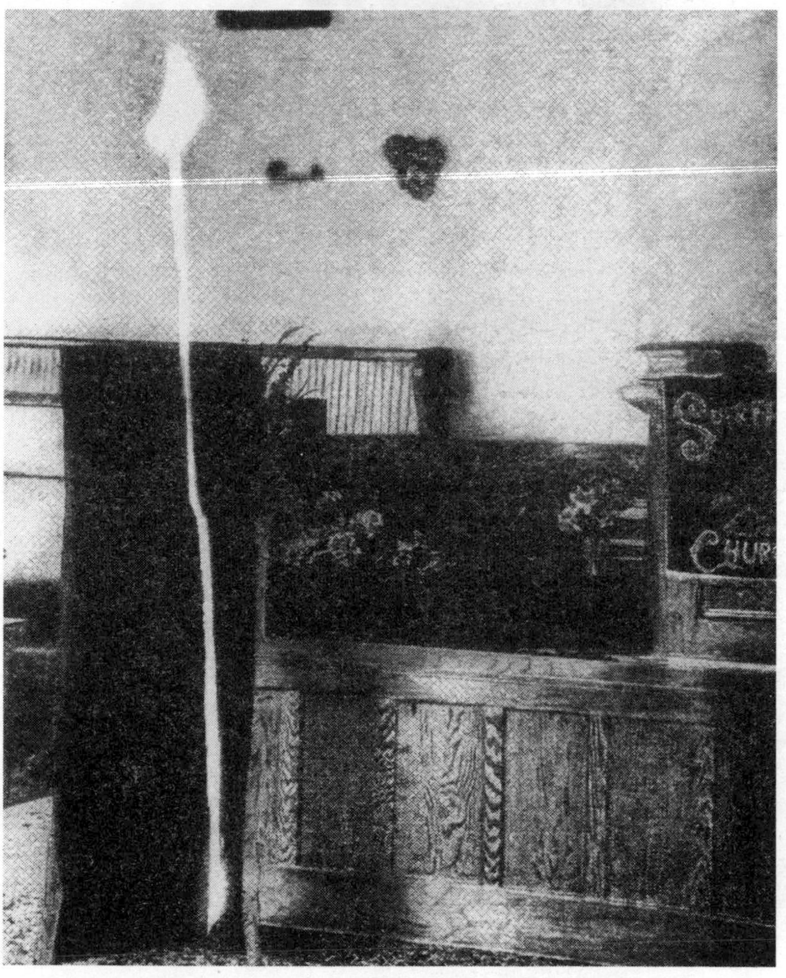

The spirit photograph that Houdini couldn't explain. *FATE magazine*

A spirit photograph Houdini could explain. *From the collection of George and Sandy Daily*

fensively—often also untruly—attack a subject and yet expect courtesies from those who honour that subject. It is not reasonable. I very much resent some of your Press comments and statements."

Two months later, the charade was repeated. Houdini wrote Doyle asking for permission to use some of his writings in his book on Spiritualism. Doyle shot back a letter on February 26, 1924. "You probably want these extracts in order to twist them in some way against me or my cause, but what I say I say and I do not alter. All the world can quote.

"What you quote, however, about your own frame of mind is obviously a back-number. . . . I read an interview you gave some American paper the other

Another spirit photo, Houdini style. *From the collection of George and Sandy Daily*

day, in which you said my wife gave you nothing striking when she wrote for you. When you met us, three days after the writing, in New York, you said 'I have been walking on air ever since.' I wonder how you reconcile your various utterances!

"I observe that, in your letter, you put down my starting my world-mission 'in a crisis of emotion.' I started in 1916. My son died in 1918. My only emotion was impersonal and the reflection of a world in agony. Our regards to Mrs. Houdini."

Those were Doyle's last words directed at Houdini, at least in private. When Houdini sent him a note on May 5 offering to send him a copy of his book *A Magician Among the Spirits*, Doyle didn't even deign to reply.

From the collection of George and Sandy Daily

21

Little Sister Will Do Exactly As Big Brother Says

THE SIX FRIENDS WERE SEATED AROUND the table, bathed in the faint red glow from the specially prepared lightbulb, red light being the color of choice for those in the other world. Everyone was so solemn that Mina, the lady of the house, who was younger than the others present, began to laugh out loud.

"This is a serious matter," Dr. Crandon, her husband, rebuked her. He had recently attended a lecture on Spiritualism by the famed English physicist Sir Oliver Lodge, who recommended some books for him to read. Deciding to model his own experimentation after the standard family circles in the Spiritualist literature, he had a séance table built to the same specifications of psychic researchers. Then, on May 27, 1923, he invited his friends Dr. Edison Brown and his wife, Frederick Adler, and Alex Cross to a room on the fourth floor of his Boston town house at 10 Lime Street for an exploratory séance.

They completed the psychic circle by linking hands over the table. At first, there was a slight motion under them, but then the whole table began to slide to one side, rise up on two legs, and crash back down to the floor. Something or someone was trying to get their attention.

Crandon, determined to identify the medium, sent each person out of the room, one at a time. The only time that the table remained stable was when Mina

Mina Crandon, the artist soon to be known as Margery.
From the collection of Libbet Crandon de Malamud

was gone. She returned to a sitting ovation. The circle now had its medium. The world would soon know her as Margery.

By the second séance, Crandon was intent on communicating with the spirits who made their presence known by tilting the table and rapping upon it. He devised a simple code—one rap for "no," two for "don't know," three for "yes," etc.—and the spirits began to answer questions.

Crandon still wasn't satisfied. The third sitting was on June 9, this one held at the home of Dr. Brown. Even on Brown's regular table, in red light, the phenomena became more refined. Now a tin plate, which rested on a shelf above the table, slowly moved off the shelf and spilled onto the floor while the table remained motionless. After the plate was then placed on the table, at the request of the sitters, it moved without being touched. Crandon needed more.

"Our means of communication with your world is clumsy," Crandon addressed the unseen spirits. "It would be much more efficient if you were to utilize the medium's own vocal cords to convey your messages."

The import of this was apparent to Margery. For the spirits to talk through her she would likely have to go into a trance and if that were the case, she would miss out on all the fun of the séances.

"I will do nothing of the sort," Margery declared.

Crandon shot her a stare that could kill.

"Little sister will do exactly as big brother says," the good doctor said, with surgical precision.

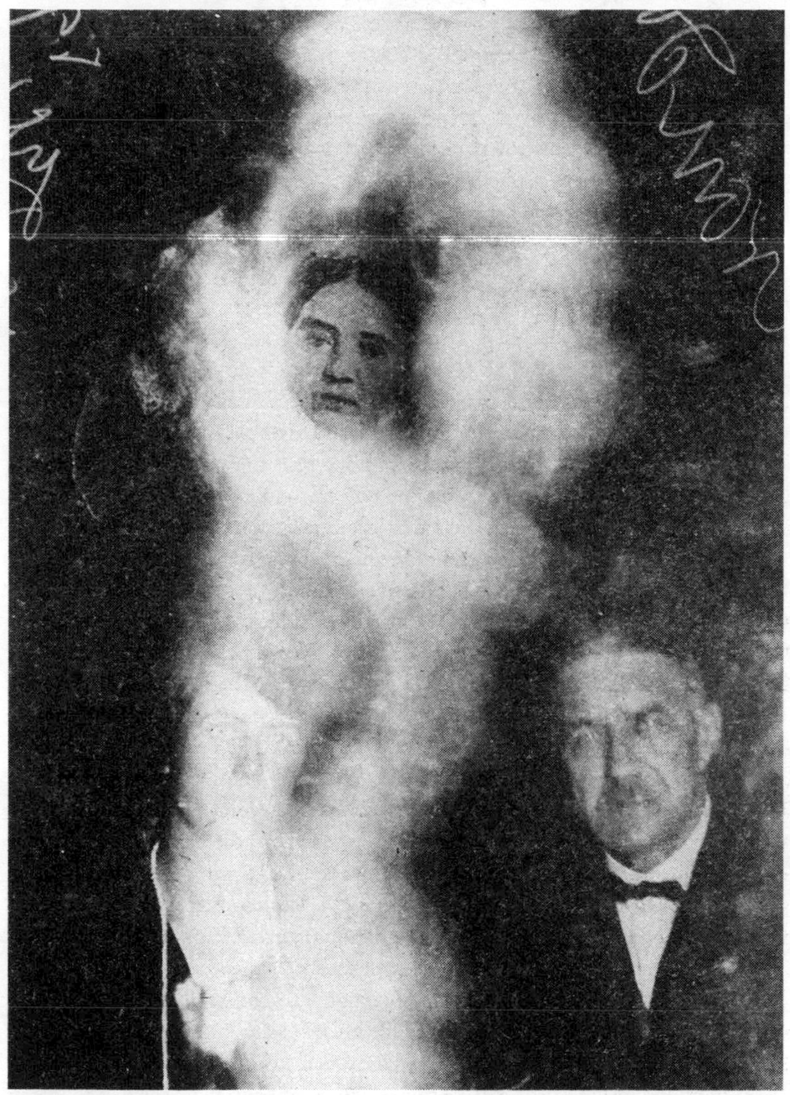

Dr. Crandon poses stoically as a spirit obscures his wife in the photo.

From the collection of Libbet Crandon de Malamud

The table rapped three times, indicating the spirits agreed with Crandon.

The group rejoined hands over the table and concentrated. Several minutes later, the attention of the others was drawn to Margery. She began touching the sides of her face in a most peculiar way, as if she were trying on new skin. Then she sighed deeply, closed her eyes, and began swaying back and forth in her chair.

Suddenly, a loud, brash, masculine voice was heard to emanate from her lips.

"I said *I could put this through!"*

It was Walter, her beloved big brother, who had been dead for twelve years.

The Crandons were a decidedly odd couple. She was young, just thirty-three, vivacious, charming, and quite attractive. A blue-eyed, blond Canadian farm girl, Margery had migrated to the Boston area to live with a sister and to escape the fundamentalist bleakness of her father. Her joy was compounded when her favorite sibling, her brother Walter, divorced his wife and moved in with his two sisters. Shortly after, Margery married Earl Rand, a grocer. Less than a year later, Walter, who worked as a locomotive fireman, was crushed to death when his train derailed on the Provincetown line. Two years later, Margery gave birth to a son.

Sometime in 1917, Margery had been hospitalized, most likely for appendicitis, and she was operated on by Dr. Le Roi Goddard Crandon. Crandon was a Boston Brahmin who could trace his lineage to one of the original twenty-three *Mayflower* passengers. His father was the president of the Boston Ethical Society. Le Roi graduated from Harvard Medical School and then eleven years later received a master's in philosophy from Harvard. He was one of the most prominent surgeons in the Boston area, earning the nickname "Button Hole Crandon" for his innovative technique of doing appendectomies through the belly button to avoid unseemly scars. It was this procedure that resulted in a scandal that nearly cost him his job when he operated on a woman who was reporting appendicitis-like symptoms but in actuality was suffering from another undiagnosed ailment. The blow to his reputation led him to other outlets to feed his bloated ego. He immediately joined the Boston Yacht Club and bought a yacht. Within a year, he had a new trophy wife too, marrying Margery shortly after she divorced her grocer husband. The new couple continued to purchase their groceries from Margery's ex.

Crandon was a peculiar man. Arrogant, dour, antisocial, he seemed to live in his own world. Margery, almost twenty years his junior, was his third wife. He had honeymooned each bride at the exact same resort in the Bahamas. An atheist, he was morbidly preoccupied with his own death; perhaps this was his intellectual

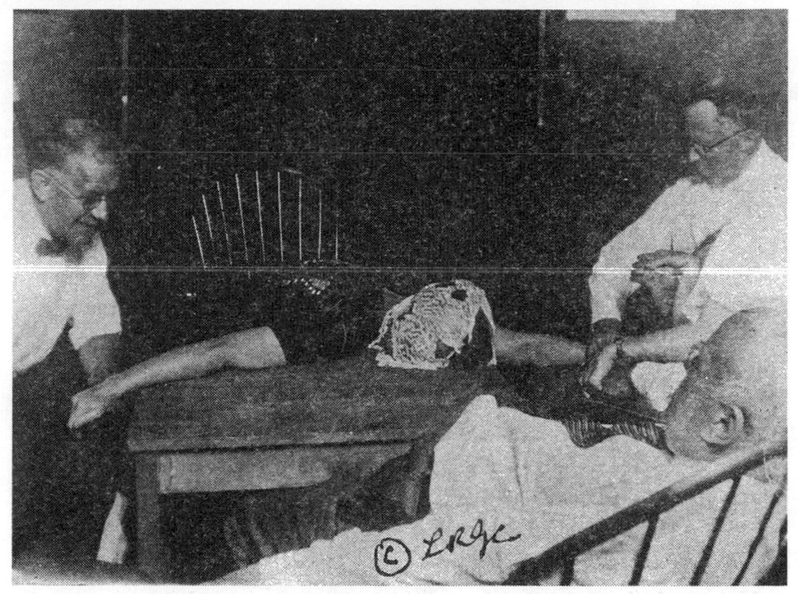

Margery collapses under the weight of her ectoplasm.
From the collection of Libbet Crandon de Malamud

attraction to the Spiritualist notion that death was not the end. Now with a medium in his own household, they held nightly séances that eventually expanded beyond the intimate circle of friends and became a sought-after destination in Boston society. In this way, Crandon could enjoy the company of a prestigious expanded social circle with Margery acting as both hostess and mystic.

Less than a month into Margery's mediumship, Crandon fired off a letter to "Dr." Arthur Conan Doyle, who was in the United States for his second Spiritualist lecture tour. He reported Walter's communications through his sister and asked for advice. He also invited Doyle to sit with them in Boston. Doyle responded from a train in Canada, warning that a medium might be placed at risk going into a trance in a large circle where "undesirable elements" might be attracted. "It is different where all are religious Spiritualists. There you have a guardian control."

Crandon immediately responded. "My little circle have now become all religious spiritualists and I feel that we have a guardian control in the brother of the Psychic. . . . Repeatedly putting the question of danger to the Psychic up to Walter he replies, 'Do you think I would let anything happen to her?'"

A relationship was quickly formed, then cemented in December of that year, when Crandon and his wife sailed to London, where she gave a number of séances before various psychic groups and then sat at Conan Doyle's London apartment. Sitting in a makeshift cabinet consisting of a three-way screen covered by a rug, in the dark, Walter manifested at once, tilted, and then levitated the table. Crandon then turned on a regular white lightbulb and the table continued to levitate. All hands were visible on the tabletop, and Margery's feet were controlled in a unique way—they were nestled in Sir Arthur's lap. Back in the dark, Walter whistled, shook the cabinet so violently that the rug flopped down over Margery's head, and made a dried flower from the shelf materialize on the floor. Perhaps it was the flower production, perhaps it was the unique foot control, but Doyle remembered Crandon's "charming" wife fondly, and spread the word of her mediumship. It was through Doyle's recommendation that Margery became a candidate for the prize that had been offered by *Scientific American* magazine, which sought out a medium who could "produce a visible psychic manifestation" to the full satisfaction of their panel of judges, one of whom happened to be Harry Houdini.

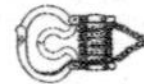

"You will be doing the human race a favor when you get your Spiritistic book on the market," W. S. Davis wrote Houdini. "And the sooner the better. A man like yourself is needed at this time, to correct general misconception and to expose ignorance and superstition." By May of 1924, the zealous Davis got his wish. Houdini's *A Magician Among the Spirits* was an eminently readable social history of Spiritualism and the mediums and entertainers associated with that movement. There were chapters on key personalities ranging from the Fox sisters to D. D. Home to Palladino and Dr. Slade, the celebrated slate writer. Houdini exposed the secrets of slate writing and spirit photography. In a chilling section, he chronicled the many deaths associated with the movement, including a family who according to a witness was "cranky on spiritualism" and "no fewer than four of them agreed to take poison!" They were not alone. In Providence, Rhode Island, a fourteen-year-old rapping medium named Almira Bezely tapped out a message that her infant brother would die. Almira helped the prediction along by purchasing arsenic and administering it to her sibling. Years later, in the same town, a Ruth McCaw was sentenced to twelve years in prison for poisoning her stepson, Leon, who somehow managed to survive. Oddly, she wasn't tried for the death of her stepdaughter, Elsie, who was handicapped and eventually succumbed to the poison. McCaw confessed to trying to kill Leon and noted that the spirits had prompted her actions.

Despite Houdini's assertions that he approached the subject with an open mind, his book was immediately attacked by the Spiritualists as a one-sided diatribe. Critics correctly pointed out that there were many factual errors in the book, but Houdini chalked those up to his editors at Harper and Brothers who cut 100,000 words from the manuscript. In a letter to the author Upton Sinclair, who was sympathetic to Spiritualism and other psychic phenomena, Houdini explained his urgency to get the book to market. "The publishing of my book had been so long drawn out that I had a slight premonition that perhaps I would not live to see the book in print if I waited much longer, so I allowed them to rush it, against my judgment, and made some of the very important mistakes, they did not think worthy of correction."

Sir Arthur Conan Doyle had been spending most every night in his home circle, where Pheneas had now begun to speak directly through Lady Doyle. According to the ancient spirit guide, 1925 was the year of doom. *"In September the earth will be shaken from the sky. There will be great loss of life. It will be terrific. All humanity will be shaken to the core. Shams will then fall away. God will come into his own. After that comes the deluge. England will not suffer as badly as the rest of the world. . . . It is not like Atlantis. It is not indiscriminate. Our plans are made. . . . no one will suffer that should be spared. God is love. Remember that. It will be like a great sieve passing through all that is worthless, retaining only the fruit."*

Around this time, Pheneas directed Doyle to keep a record of these messages, and to eventually publish them in book form. *"Every sect is done for. The people know too much,"* Pheneas said. *"They have failed in the past and people will turn to those who have been in direct spirit communication. The medium knows this. She senses it. Her powers will develop greatly. She will be, as it were, a small bridge between two enormous countries. . . . Take all this down. We are most anxious to have a record as it will be invaluable. It is this script that the whole world, not England alone, will cling to in its great extremity."*

"Is it the Second Coming?" Doyle wondered.

"Yes," said Pheneas. *"It is the Second Coming, even as prophesied."*

At the beginning of July, one of Walter's most impressive manifestations was the ringing of a bell box in the séance room, while the medium was under strict control. A box had been devised, and modified over the months, that contained a bell assembly and a battery. Two eight-inch-square boards had been hinged together along one edge of each. Small metal plates had been attached to various points of their inside surfaces and a spiral spring was permanently affixed, keeping them apart. The boards were wired to the battery so that when enough pressure was put on them for the plates to make contact with each other, the bell rang. To mitigate any chance of a stray human hand producing the contact in the dark, the upper contact board was covered with a plaque that had been coated with luminous paint.

On July 13, the bell box was on the floor to Margery's left. Her hands and feet were controlled by those sitting on either side of her. In spite of this, Walter rang the bell at will and on request, even giving combinations of long and short rings. One of the sitters then asked to see Walter's finger when it pressed down on the box. In response, there emerged from under Margery's chair a dollop of strange-looking light that was in the shape and size of a forefinger. It slowly moved across to the box. When it arrived there, the bell rang. Now everyone wanted to see this new phenomenon.

"*Never mind the circle,*" Walter said. "*Everybody get up and stand around and look at it.*"

They all complied, breaking control, of course, but what they saw astounded them. Again the strange finger-shaped light seemed to float across and depress the box, causing the bell to ring.

Two nights later, the séance room became a three-ring circus. Walter made the bell ring, he talked and whistled through a megaphone, shook a tambourine, and brought Laura Crandon's long-dead dog back, who barked obediently. On top of this, a strange psychic light spotlighted the tambourine. Margery's laughter permeated the room. Stunningly, all of this phenomena was happening simultaneously.

WOMAN ASTOUNDS PSYCHIC EXPERTS. BOSTON PROFESSIONAL MAN'S WIFE MAY WIN $2,500 PRIZE FOR MEDIUM, SAYS J. MALCOLM BIRD. NOT THE LEAST HINT OF FRAUD. SPIRIT CONTROL SCATTERS ROSES—SOMETIMES CARESSES WITH NON-MATERIAL FLOWERS. HER DEMONSTRATIONS ARE INFINITELY CONVINCING.

The New York Times headline screamed. Three days later, the *Times* carried a follow-up story: "Margery, the Boston Medium, Passes All Psychic Tests. Scientists Find No Trickery in a Score of Seances. Versatile Spook Puzzles Investigators by Variety of His Demonstrations."

The world was welcoming Margery and Walter with open arms, thanks to J. Malcolm Bird's glowing articles in *Scientific American*. Now the stage was set for a visit from Houdini. He had previously exposed two frauds who had applied for the committee's prize money. George Valiantine was able to produce lights and have spirit trumpets prance around the dark room, at one point bopping Houdini in the head. But the manifestations weren't considered evidential, considering that an electrical connection had been rigged to the medium's chair that showed that all the phenomenon coincided with the times that the medium surreptitiously left his chair.

When a young Italian named Nino Pecoraro had almost convinced the committee of his psychic powers, Houdini had to rush to New York from Little Rock, Arkansas. Despite being tied up with rope, Pecoraro, with the assistance of Eusapia Palladino, who while she lived had been a medium and was now acting as his spirit control, was able to ring bells and jangle tambourines. Houdini took one look at the 180-foot length of rope that had been used and realized that Pecoraro was really an escape artist who knew how to use slack to get out of the rope ties. When Houdini had finished tying him with a series of short ropes, a process that took the Master Mystifier an hour and a half, all Palladino could do was curse Houdini and complain that her young friend was uncomfortable. J. Malcolm Bird, the secretary of the *Scientific American* committee, had to restrain Houdini from arguing with the dead medium.

Those were different cases, though. Margery wasn't a professional medium and she had actually stated that she would refuse to accept any prize money. Her husband was a prominent Boston surgeon. These weren't the fraudulent mediums that Houdini was used to debunking. He vowed to go into the séances with an open mind. If he determined Margery to be a fraud, he'd expose her in a second, but if she really had the power to channel the dead, he promised to scream that news from the rooftops.

Still, Crandon was wary of Houdini and saw the sitting with the *Scientific American* committee as a potential skirmish. On June 6, he had written Sir Arthur: "We continue to sit with the *Scientific American* Committee every night. Every night I insist on their living up to their agreement and giving me signed copies of their notes. . . . if they ever make any announcements not consistent with these notes you can readily see I have the material to crucify them.

Margery gives Houdini her best "come hither" look as J. Malcolm Bird (above) and *Scientific American* publisher O. D. Munn look on. *From the collection of Dr. Bruce Averbook*

We are not wasting any time in compliments or politeness. It is war to the finish and they know I shall not hesitate to treat them surgically if necessary."

"It is not [Houdini's] 'clever lying' but his acrid psychic atmosphere which stops phenomena," Doyle responded. "I wonder if Walter can rise above it."

Walter fired the first salvo in the war. During his séance on July 11, attended by committee members Dr. Daniel Comstock, Hereward Carrington, and the magician Fred Keating, Walter manifested lights, rang the bell box, and then caused Margery's breast to glow sporadically. He also took time to compose and sing a little ditty about Houdini: "*Harry Houdini, he sure is a Sheeny, A man with a crook in his shoe. Says he 'As to Walter, I'll lead him to slaughter.' 'But,' says Walter, 'Perhaps I'll get you!'*"

July 23, 1924

Dear Sir Arthur,

Tonight Houdini and Mr. Munn, owner of the* Scientific American, *sit with us for the first time and will be here several days. I think Psyche* [Margery] *is somewhat stirred up over it internally because of Houdini's general nastiness. She is vomiting merrilly* [sic] *this morning. However, some of her worst days have given the best sittings.

L. R. G. Crandon, M.D.

That night Margery and Walter both got their first glimpses of Houdini. He came to 10 Lime Street accompanied by magazine owner O. D. Munn, and they convened in the fourth-floor room where the Crandons held their nightly séances. Just down the hall, Margery's twelve-year-old son had been locked into his bedroom, to nullify any accusation that he was a confederate of his mother. The circle that night consisted of Margery, her husband, a man named Conant, who was the lab assistant for the committeeman Comstock, who was absent, Munn, Houdini, and Bird. Carrington had left town to avoid sitting in the same room with Houdini.

Margery sat down in her makeshift cabinet, really just a three-fold screen. As usual, Dr. Crandon sat at his wife's right, controlling her right leg and hand. Houdini was given the position of honor at her left. Bird lurked outside the circle, making sure Crandon's control over his wife was never broken by circling the fingers of Margery and Crandon with one of his hands. To test Walter, the bell box and a megaphone were in the room. The lights were dimmed.

Soon the sound of whistling filled the room. Then there was whispering. Walter had arrived.

"Very interesting conversation you two men had on the train," Walter addressed Houdini and Munn. *"I was there. I can always be where my interests lie."*

After a few minutes, Houdini felt something touch him on the inside of his right leg.

"That's me," Walter said gleefully. He repeated this a few times more.

Walter then requested an intermission, asking that the contact bell box be brought out of the medium's cabinet and placed in front of Houdini. This was done but nothing happened.

"I need the illuminated plaque. Bird, go fetch it and bring it back and put it on the contact board," Walter ordered.

Bird left his post, but couldn't find the plaque.

"Control," Walter yelled, before Bird had a chance to get back to the circle. Everyone held hands again, making sure the medium's hands were accounted for.

"I've got the megaphone in the air," Walter said. *"Houdini, where should I throw it?"*

"Towards me," Houdini said.

Seconds later, the megaphone crashed at Houdini's feet.

"Bird, take your place in the doorway," Walter commanded, and before Bird could even get there, Margery's cabinet was thrown violently on its back.

A third intermission was taken, and a red light was turned on to rearrange the cabinet.

The illuminated plaque was brought in and put over the contact board. During the last part of the sitting, the plaque was seen to oscillate and move slowly back and forth and then finally, the contact box rang, once long and several times with short peals.

Walter had produced.

After the séance, committee secretary Bird drove Houdini and Munn to the hotel where they were staying. Bird, as usual, was lodging with the Crandons. The secretary parked his car in front of the building and the three men held a quick postmortem. Of course, Houdini took the floor first.

"Well, gentlemen, I've got her," Houdini said confidentially. "All fraud—every bit of it. One more sitting and I will be ready to expose everything. But one thing puzzles me—I don't see how she did that megaphone trick."

Bird suggested some hypotheses that the committee had come up with, including the idea that the megaphone was on her shoulder.

"It couldn't have been there," Houdini said, adding that he had explored that possibility during the séance. Suddenly a look of relief crossed his face.

"The megaphone was on her head. That's the slickest ruse I ever heard of," Houdini marveled.

His reasoning was simple. When Bird had left the room that freed up Margery's right hand and foot, leaving her husband as the sole control, which was no control at all. Using her right hand, she tilted the corner of the cabinet enough to place her foot under it. She then quickly picked up the megaphone with her free right hand, and placed it on her head, as if it were a dunce cap. Throwing the cabinet over was easy with her foot under one corner. Then Walter immediately asked for control and Margery gave Houdini her right foot. With the megaphone already loaded on her head, she had no need for her hands being free; a simple tilt of the head in the desired direction would achieve her purposes.

What Houdini didn't tell them yet was just how he had figured out that it was she and not Walter who had rung the bell. He had done some advance research and determined that Crandon always sat to Margery's right. Since the séance was being played to him, he anticipated being on Margery's left, and he had worn a tight "silk rubber" bandage around his right leg below the knee all day, making that part of his leg swollen and tender. The slightest flexing of Margery's muscles or any movement of her ankles would immediately be discernible to him in his sensitive state.

That night's sitting held at committeeman Comstock's apartment was anticlimactic. Houdini was able to detect almost every time she made a move. She also used Walter to gain advantage to perform her maneuvers. At one point, Walter bellowed for everyone in the room to move back from the table so he could summon up additional energy. In reality, Margery moved back too, and was then able to bend her head and push the table up and over. Houdini caught her using this tactic twice. He had worked out a code with Munn, so that after a prearranged signal, they would break control and Houdini would have an opportunity to grope around the table in the dark. Twice her head ran into his hand. That was enough for him.

"Will I denounce and expose her now?" Houdini whispered.

"You had better wait a while," Munn cautioned.

When it came time to ring the bell box, Walter literally hit a snag. The box was placed between Houdini's feet and Margery tried to employ the same tactics as the night before, but she couldn't move her foot far enough to apply the necessary pressure.

"You have garters on, haven't you," she finally said to Houdini.

"Yes," he said.

"Well, the buckle hurts me," Margery complained.

When he reached down to undo the garter, Houdini found that Margery's stocking had been caught up in the garter, immobilizing her leg so that she couldn't reach the bell box.

"You, Munn and Houdini, think you're pretty smart, don't you?" Walter said. *"Straighten up there!"*

When the séance was over, Houdini had Munn call the Committee into a room. Houdini explained Margery's tactics. Rather than expose her right then and there, the committee decided to go back to New York, where Houdini would file a general report for the entire group. Mrs. Crandon was not to be informed that Houdini had detected her in fraud. Houdini was still pushing for rapid exposure, citing that other mediums had been.

"We will do it differently this time," Bird said.

Houdini and Munn took a night train back to New York, and Bird rushed back to 10 Lime Street, to tell the Crandons everything that just had transpired in the secret meeting.

"I know something about Houdini that might interest you, but it's a little embarrassing and I never even told my wife about it," the Philadelphia patent attorney told his friend, who was a Houdini collector. It was sometime in the 1970s and the two were at a magic convention. "But I am telling it to you now, because she's dead and gone and I'll be going pretty soon anyway."

He proceeded to relate that years earlier he had been invited to one of Margery's séances at her home in Boston. As an out-of-town visitor, he was accorded the prime spot of controlling Margery's left hand.

"As soon as the lights went out, in the dark, Margery took my hand and put it between her legs. She was naked under her robe. She tried to make me masturbate her but I was embarrassed and I pulled back," he recalled, still sheepish all these years after the incident. "She pulled me in again and finally I just pulled my hand away and froze. I was very embarrassed."

There is a long, rich, lurid history of sex in the séance room, especially between mediums and the men who investigated them. Sir William Crookes, the eminent British chemist who had discovered the element thallium, had sponsored a beautiful young medium named Florence Cook who materialized a female spirit called Katie King. King was supposedly the daughter of the famous pirate John King, whom other mediums materialized, yet she looked suspiciously like a young Victorian lady who pinned a handkerchief over her head, someone like Florence. Crookes's insistence that the materializations were real made more sense when later psychic researchers revealed that the two were lovers, using the cover of the darkness of the séance room for their assignations.

Materialization séances were often just fronts for prostitution rings both in England and in America. Joseph Rinn, Houdini's ghost-busting friend, reported that in the late 1880s there were more than a hundred mediums in New York City who advertised in the personal columns of newspapers, many of them actually madams who ran prostitution rings. As late as 1979, the sociologist Dr. Elisabeth Kubler-Ross had clients have sex with "materialized spirits" as part of a therapeutic regimen for people with morbid fears of death.

The most notorious medium who used her sexual charms to seduce her scientific investigators was Eusapia Palladino, the same woman who was channeled by Nino Pecoraro when Houdini tied him into submission. Palladino had no qualms about sleeping with her sitters; among them were the eminent criminologist Lombroso and the Nobel Prize–winning French physiologist Charles Richet. After being discredited, Palladino's career was revived in 1909 when Hereward Carrington, acting as her manager, brought her to the United States. Whenever she would be caught cheating during séances, Carrington chalked it up to laziness and her stubborn Italian temperament. Once prodded to produce, he claimed she came through with flying colors.

Besides actual sexual activity, there was often an element of voyeurism in the séance room. Eva C (Carriere), a medium who had originally used her real name, Marthe Beraud, until she was exposed, claimed to be able to produce large quantities of a strange, otherworldly substance called ectoplasm, which was thought to be produced by the bioenergy of the spirits. She was investigated extensively by the highly regarded German physician Freiherr von Schrenck-Notzing, who would watch as Eva's sponsor (and mistress) Mademoiselle Bisson would, during the course of the pre-séance examination, introduce her finger into Eva's vagina to ensure that no "ectoplasm" had been loaded there beforehand to fool the investigators. The whole procedure was so enjoyable for Eva that she often stripped nude at the *end* of a séance and demanded another full-on gynecological exam.

It wasn't surprising that there would be an air of sexuality suffusing the Margery séances, especially when, prior to the sittings, Dr. Crandon would proudly display nude photographs of Margery during the throes of her mediumship duties. Margery was perhaps the most beautiful medium since Florence Cook. According to Thomas Tietze, her biographer, "She was a slim and pretty woman whose roundness of limb and pertness of attitude men found 'too attractive for her own good.' She dressed well and the fashions of the twenties were good to her. Photographs show clear, frank eyes and an expression both saucy and penetrating."

Besides her physical attributes, Margery also had the useful ability to make people think that their relationship with her was unique, creating a network of secret allies, who might then be induced to drop control of her hand at a crucial moment during a séance. Malcolm Bird was captivated by her, a likely outcome even though he had already been warned by committee member Dr. Walter Franklin Prince that if he wanted to be taken seriously as a psychic researcher he had to "avoid falling in love with the medium." Bird attributed her interpersonal skills to her remarkable ability as a "drawer out." "She possesses an insatiable curiosity, and that one of the ways in which she most effectively feeds it is by just that devise [sic] of shrewdly guessing that something is so and then drawing out the persons that would know about it if it were. And her shrewdness as a guesser is approached only by her skill as a drawer out," he wrote years later.

Bird had moved in with the Crandons during the earlier months of the investigation, a dubious practice for a supposedly impartial observer. In fact, Crandon's heretofore unseen correspondence reveals that Bird was actively conspiring with them in stage-managing the séances and achieving a positive vote from the majority of the committee. It's likely that Bird would have loved to have slept with Margery but anecdotal reports suggest that she found him repulsive. Apparently, at that point, she had reserved her amorous affections for Hereward Carrington, the champion of Palladino and a voting member of the *Scientific American* committee.

Margery's relationship with Dr. Crandon had always been rocky and volatile. When Carrington moved into their spare room on Lime Street, the stage was set for a torrid tryst. Margery was open about her affection for the English researcher. One night before a sitting, she approached Carrington in the parlor and, in front of Crandon and the other sitters, embraced him and asked, "Wouldn't you like to kiss me?"

"What was I to do," Carrington would later write. "She was there in my arms . . ."

According to a later investigator who got close to Margery, she told him that she had an affair with Carrington that was so intense that Carrington asked her to sell the Lime Street house, which was in her name, and elope with him to Egypt. Bird confirmed that Margery and Crandon had been on bad terms during this period, with Crandon acting decently toward her only after she produced a good séance. Bird also confirmed Margery's account of an affair with Carrington but he added an interesting addendum—Carrington had borrowed a considerable sum of money from Crandon that he was unable to repay.

Judges sleeping with contestants in a contest that they are to judge was not a unique phenomenon, albeit a good strategy from Margery's point of view. Carrington owing money to Crandon casts even more doubts on his ability to vote impartially, but what's critical to this story is Carrington's background. He was not only a psychic investigator but he was a skilled and knowledgeable magician too, who had written Houdini, thanking him for advising him before his entry into American vaudeville. Carrington also brought a friend of his into the Crandon circle, a man who spent a lot of time in and out of Lime Street in 1924. His name was F. Serrano Keating, also known as Fred Keating, and he too was an accomplished magician.

In the middle of all this, Houdini filed his will. He left Bess his dramatic library and all his personal effects. Hardeen, who had given up his own career to run the ill-fated FDC, would receive Houdini's magical apparatus, which was to "be burnt and destroyed upon [Hardeen's] death." Houdini's library on Spiritualism and the occult was earmarked for the American Society for Psychical Research, his magic library to the Library of Congress. He made provisions for his assistants Vickery, Kukol, and Collins of $500 each, and pledged $1,000 to the SAM. The rest of the estate was set up in a trust to be divided equally among his siblings, with one proviso. "It is my express desire, intention and direction that no part either of the principal or income of my estate shall ever directly or indirectly go to SADIE GLANTZ WEISS, the divorced wife of my brother NATHAN JOSEPH WEISS and the present wife of my brother, DR. LEOPOLD DAVID WEISS." This was a curious clause. We know that Houdini had traveled with Leopold as late as 1920 when they visited England. Sometime after their return something happened. One author who had access to Leopold's files theorized that, in retrospect, Houdini may have blamed Leopold and Sadie's unseemly liaison for the premature death of their mother. As if to punctuate the will, Houdini and his good friend Loney Haskell went to the Elks Club to deposit a letter specifying his funeral arrangements.

Before Houdini filed his séance reports, he literally made Munn stop the presses and remove another pro-Margery article in the September issue. Then, for safekeeping, he kept a copy of the original article. Houdini was anxious to get a majority vote to discredit Margery immediately, but the other members of the committee, all academics, wanted more sittings. Houdini was shocked. Couldn't they see she was a fraud using tricks that went back to the Davenports?

Houdini family portrait before things shattered when Sadie (third from left, standing) divorced Nat (fifth from left standing), and married debonair bachelor Dr. Leopold (far right).

From the collection of Dr. Bruce Averbook

Crandon meanwhile came up with a new idea: solus sittings, one-on-one séances with just an investigator and Margery (and Walter, of course) present. Writing Doyle, he felt using solus sittings the "sitters can be converted as fast as they sit." There was a danger in them, though. "The only negative that Houdini can get will be 'no phenomena.' There is a danger, as you can readily see, that he might insert his toe into the contact machine when he sits alone with Psyche and thus prevent a ring. She has been instructed, therefore, by the rest of the committee that if Houdini's leg breaks connection with her she is to cry out at once 'Houdini has broken his control.' Furthermore, if the bell does not ring, Walter instructs friendly members of the committee, after a reasonable time, to come in quietly and seize the box for their examination before Houdini has a chance to withdraw whatever he may put in to prevent contact ringing.

"It is such a pity in a big thing like this, that we have to plan to catch a crook!"

The committee requested that the final sittings take place in New York, but that was scrapped when Dr. Crandon stated that he didn't have time to come to New York and that he categorically refused to allow Margery to sit without him present. So everyone agreed to trek back up to Boston. This time they would bring

Joseph DeWyckoff, Margery's multimillionaire supporter.
From the DeWyckoff family collection of Carolyn Withstandley

along a "comfortable restraint" for the medium, one which would prevent her from moving her hands and feet and, as Houdini charged, cause the phenomena.

With the sittings scheduled for the end of August, it was time for Crandon to bring in his big guns. One of Margery's most avid supporters was a wealthy steel mogul named Joseph DeWyckoff. DeWyckoff had a very interesting and checkered past. Born in Poland, educated in Russia and London, he came to America and practiced law but soon ran afoul of it himself. He was jailed in Boston for embezzlement, then a few years later fled Chicago after absconding with more than $3,000 from the law firm. He wound up in Havana, where, in 1898 he was recruited by John Wilkie, the Secret Service chief, as a co-optee and was involved in spying for the United States during the Spanish-American War. Perhaps as a reward, he was given the contract to salvage the Battleship *Maine* in the Havana harbor.

By the 1920s, he had formed his own steel company and had amassed a tremendous fortune traveling to Europe to do business while exploiting his contacts in Russia. On one trip to London, he sold ten million dollars' worth of war munitions to the Russian government. He was also an avid Spiritualist. On

August 14, DeWyckoff and his wife, Minerva, visited Lime Street and sat with Margery. During this séance, Walter invented a new form of control. With DeWyckoff controlling Margery and his wife controlling Doctor Crandon, Walter was able to not only ring the contact bell but tap out messages in Morse code, as well as bang on a tambourine and whistle through a megaphone at the same time. DeWyckoff left Boston for a fishing trip in Maine but, convinced of the importance of the impending Houdini showdown, cabled Crandon from Bangor: "OWING PRAXIMITY [sic] OF COMMITTEES FINAL TESTS AND IMPORTANCE OF PREVIOUSLY TRYING APPARATUS IN FRIENDLY CIRCLE HAVE DECIDED FOREGO FISHING TRIPS RETURN BOSTON ARRIVING THERE TUESDAY PM STOP SHALL BE HAPPY TO ASSIST ACCORDINGLY IF AGREEABLE STOP KINDEST REMEMBRANCES TO MARGERY AND YOURSELF AND BROTHER WALTER IN WHICH MADAME JOINS ME DR WYCKOFF"

Crandon had one more trick up his sleeve. Alarmed by reports that Houdini had constructed a large wooden box that would effectively prevent Margery from craning her neck and stretching out her legs to produce phenomena, he planned a counterattack. On August 18, a week before the showdown, he wrote Sir Arthur. "We frankly feared that with 'Marjory' in a mechanical control, in the dark, Houdini could only win by a *blank* [a sitting that produced no results] and hence he would by trickery insure a *blank*. Walter solved it by announcing he would give them nothing hereafter except by red light phenomena! If he is able to do this, and I have no doubt he can, no control, other than the eye will be necessary."

It would be a major breakthrough if Walter could produce his phenomenon with red light on in the room. The mediumship would come out of the dark, control could be visually checked, and there would be no need for anything as crude as Houdini's big wooden box.

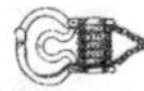

While the Crandons were preparing for the invasion from New York, Sir Arthur was getting more details from Pheneas about the impending catastrophe, and about the spirit's love for the medium.

"I am full of love and joy," Pheneas spoke. *"I love our talks. I was with the Medium this morning. I had a message. I am in close touch with the Medium all the time."*

"Do you alone influence the Medium?" Doyle wondered.

"Sometimes it is her own guide," Pheneas explained. *"Would you like more about the catastrophe, as you call it?"*

"Yes, indeed," Doyle said.

Pheneas then went into another horrific prophecy of the accounting to come. Continents submerged, earthquakes in north England, tidal waves in the south of France, a huge storm in the north of Italy.

"I hope I shall be strong enough," Doyle worried.

Pheneas reassured him.

"Will the dear medium be at my right hand?" he asked.

"Of course she will," Pheneas said soothingly. *"You must see it, friend, from her point of view. She does not think herself so essential, and therefore she has fears. She will be close to your side, as she has been in the past, in the fight for the spreading of this great knowledge and comfort. She will come into her own with you and with her dear ones."*

During the next séance, at their country home in New Forest, Pheneas provided more details of the impending doom, at the same time conveying how close he felt to the Doyle circle.

"God bless you! I love being with you. Is it not nice round the fire? I am one of the family in the home circle. I will guard over you in this house as long as you sojourn in it. That is a word the medium never uses. Her tongue could hardly say it. She is very tired to-night."

"You do her good," Sir Arthur enthused.

"We love her," Pheneas spoke. *"We have chosen her for this work."*

From the collection of Roger Dreyer

22

Margery's Box

When Collins and Houdini finished setting up their wooden enclosure in committeeman Comstock's room at the Charlesgate Hotel, it looked more like a crate for an old-fashioned slant-top desk than a device to restrain a human medium, except for the holes bored out to allow Margery's head and arms to protrude from the box. Houdini had been extremely secretive about his "fraud-preventer," refusing to allow Bird to drive the device up to Boston, especially since Bird was leaving a few days prior to the August 25 séance. Once in Boston, Houdini refused to be seen at his hotel and when he met an associate at the Back Bay railroad station, he dragged him to a telephone booth where he held his conversation with the door closed, explaining to reporters that he was being "watched" and "shadowed" by "hostile interests."

Apparently Margery hadn't yet learned to perform her effects under red light, so the séance would be conducted in the dark again. When Crandon arrived and saw the wooden cage that Houdini had devised, he objected to it vociferously and demanded that Margery have a dry run in the box with members of her friendly circle. This was granted and at 9:15 a group of sympathizers, who included Crandon's sister Laura and Joe DeWyckoff, sat with Margery for a half hour. *"Leave everything to me and be of good cheer,"* Walter assured them. At 9:45, the committee was ushered into the séance room and Margery's friends exited. Crandon also demanded a change in the order of the circle. Instead of Munn controlling Houdini's left hand, he asked that Comstock be assigned that job. Houdini later complained that Comstock did such a good job of it that he was unable to break free to paw around in the dark to detect implements.

Houdini in Margery's box. *Library of Congress*

The séance began. Eight minutes into the sitting, the bell box, which was on a table in front of the cabinet, rang and there was a corresponding loud noise. Houdini reported that the front of the crate had been forced open and the two thin brass strips that held the box together had been bent. He immediately accused Margery, a strong woman, of lifting the lid with her shoulders, stretching out her head, and pressing down on the bell box. Crandon suggested that Walter had broken the cabinet and the two men got into a shouting match. At 10:13 Walter called for a recess and asked for his friendly circle to return.

The friends of Walter met in the room for twenty-two minutes, Walter whistling "with his best cockiness."

At 10:35, the committee returned. Bird, who had not been at the first sitting, tried to have a seat but he was excluded from the room by the rest of the committee. Margery's circle was allowed to remain in the back of the room.

After eight unproductive minutes, Walter piped in.

"Houdini, have you got the mark in just right? You think you're smart, don't you? How much are they paying you to stop these phenomena?"

"This is *costing* me," Houdini replied. "$2,500 a week to be here."

"Where did you turn down a $2,500 *contract in August?"*

"In Buffalo," Houdini said.

"Where were those contracts?" Walter asked. *"You didn't have a job for this week."*

"What do you mean by this, Walter? This talk isn't psychic research," Comstock intervened, trying to be the voice of sanity while addressing a spirit.

"Comstock, take the box out in the white light and examine it, and you will see what I mean," Walter said.

Comstock complied and returned to the room to report that a small rubber eraser from a pencil had been jammed between the two boards where they make contact. It wasn't impossible to actually ring the bell, but it was about four times harder to make the connection, which shouldn't affect a strong incorporeal spirit but would be a calamity for a person who was straining to push the board with her forehead. Since the contact box hadn't been examined before the second committee sitting, suspicion for the plant would point to the "friendly" circle, who had just been in the room at Walter's request. After the eraser incident, the séance was ended.

The committee and others had convened in another room for some post-séance chitchat when Houdini suddenly realized that Margery and Crandon were missing. He found them back in the séance room, surrounding the box, talking in hushed tones. Unaware of his presence, he watched as they measured the gap in which her neck was secured. The size of the aperture had been an issue earlier in the night, but when he spoke to them about it later, they claimed that it was fine.

Before the next night's sitting, Dr. Crandon insisted on inserting into the record a statement from Margery that there was "no precedent in psychic research where a medium has been so enclosed," maintaining that "such a closed cage gives little or no regard for the theory and experience of the psychic structure." By now, Margery's camp was theorizing that the medium herself was responsible for ringing the bell box, under Walter's bidding, through the agency of a pseudopod that extended from between her legs and, acting as a lever, actually produced the manifestations. Obviously, the box would block this "psychic structure." Why Walter, who had previously ravaged furniture and overturned cabinets and whacked people on the head, couldn't himself press down on the box and make the bell ring was never addressed. Before the séance began, Bird again tried to attend, a row ensued, and the secretary resigned on the spot from the committee because of accusations of misbehavior, betrayal of committee, and collusion with Margery, charges that had been leveled by both Prince and Houdini.

With these administrative details out of the way, Margery entered the room and climbed into her cabinet-box. For this sitting, Houdini would control her left hand and Prince her right. Houdini later recalled that as he carefully watched her face, he "could tell by the way she pulled down on her neck that she was 'reaching' for something." Convinced that she had concealed something, he repeatedly told Prince not to let go of her right hand until the séance was over.

At 9:14 the séance began. Nine minutes later, Walter arrived.

"*Houdini you are very clever, indeed, but it won't work,*" Walter said. "*I suppose it was an accident those things were left in the cabinet?*"

"What was left in the cabinet?" Houdini asked.

"*What did you do that for, Houdini?*" Walter raged. "*You God damned son of a bitch. You cad you. There's a ruler in this cabinet, you unspeakable cad. The idea of your putting up a plant like that on a girl. You won't live forever Houdini, you've got to die. I put a curse on you now that will follow you every day for the rest of your short life. Now you get the hell out of here and don't you ever come back or I won't!*"

Dr. Comstock intervened. "Walter, if you will reflect for a minute you will see that this box has been in the room where there are tools and workmen and it is indeed possible that someone may have left or locked a ruler in it."

"*That is possible,*" Walter admitted. "*I apologize to Houdini. You may cut all the nasty words out of the record, but leave all the rest.*"

Houdini asked that the entire abusive remark remain part of the record.

That ended any chance for any phenomena. Collins was called in and he swore on his mother's life that the ruler wasn't his. The séance dragged on for another two and a half hours, but with the medium in the box, which was locked this night, the bell box remained silent.

"*A great chance I have to do anything with all you and myself in this state of mind,*" Walter bellyached. "*I admit I lost my temper,*" he said toward the end of the night. And then he said, "*Goodbye.*"

What was most significant about this sitting was that the Crandon camp, who had control over the signed séance minutes, immediately falsified the record to make it appear that Houdini had been caught planting the ruler and was remorseful for his actions in the séance room.

In Crandon's version of the séance, which was immediately published in Spiritualist periodicals around the world, and later in both Bird's and Crandon's books, when the lights were turned up after Walter's tirade against Houdini, the magician had buried his face in his hands and was almost weeping.

"Oh, this is terrible. My dear sainted mother *was* married to my father! This is terrible. I don't know anything about any ruler. Why should I do a thing like that?"

In another Crandon version, Houdini was reputed to have said, "I'm not myself. I don't feel well."

According to Bird's book, Houdini was reacting to the original significance of the term "son of a bitch"—namely that he was a bastard. It's interesting that this allegation was made by the Margery camp. At that time, there had been rumors circulating in the magic community that Houdini and Hardeen were half brothers. For this story to be dredged up suggests that some insider might have been feeding Crandon information to use against Houdini. At any rate, the Crandons certainly knew how to push Houdini's buttons; any slur against his mother would be considered more than fighting words.

Who planted the ruler became a raging debate between the two camps. In 1959, a Houdini biography by William Lindsay Gresham claimed that years after the fact, Houdini's assistant Collins admitted that Houdini had secreted the ruler into the cabinet. The source of the story was the magician Fred Keating. It was not until our perusal of the files in Margery's great-granddaughter's possession that we uncovered the close relationship between Keating and the medium.

The ruler imbroglio raises a more interesting issue that goes to the heart of both Margery's and Lady Doyle's disparate mediumships. To gain insight into their skills, we need look no further than the ventriloquist. At the beginning of an exhibition of ventriloquism, our logical side immediately sees a clearly and unmistakably lifeless figure. Nonetheless, a few minutes into a soundly constructed ventriloquism routine, our emotional side suspends disbelief, short-circuiting our critical and analytical capacities. Now the figure comes alive, sometimes to the bizarre extent that the ventriloquist's figure has been attacked for something *it* has said.

By now, Margery had morphed from a trance medium into a direct or independent voice medium. Proximity to her was now the condition on which the spirit world, in the form of Walter, depended, but his voice was not hers, it emanated from outside her physical form. She was not possessed by him, he just needed her nearby. Over time, Margery's stamina improved and Walter became capable of all sorts of phenomena. She may have been one of the most versatile mediums in the history of spirit contact.

As a medium, Margery was a descendant of Eurycles of Greece, the most famous of the pre-Delphic oracles, who had a "demon" voice that emanated from his chest and made oracular predictions. The twentieth-century incarnation of the oracles was decidedly less appealing, and more akin to a carnival sideshow. Walter just performed stunts, like a trick dog. On the rare occasion it was given, his advice was inferior.

If we agree that Margery and the other mediums who have been caught are one hundred percent pure frauds, then we must examine their voices. Margery had an advantage in that it was even easier for the audience members at her séances to suspend their disbelief since her performance took place under pitch-black conditions. There was no way to scrutinize her lips. During the progression of her mediumship, Crandon cronies built scientific-looking machines that were meant to control her breath, proving that Walter's voice was truly independent. The machines were impressive-looking but bogus—a piece of gum secreted in her mouth could short-circuit the entire control.

Margery and Crandon demonstrated that they had a diabolical understanding of the psychology of magic. They knew that her séance was a performance. More than once Margery and Crandon disagreed and Walter sided with Crandon. This brilliant device has the effect of undermining the sitter's natural intuition. We all innately know that sane people don't argue with themselves. We are smoothly lulled into accepting Walter as real.

Occasionally clues are unintentionally left, as in the case of Walter complaining of sabotage. On the first occasion Walter demanded that the bell box be removed to the light and examined, something was wrong. Perhaps this was a setup by the Crandons to implicate Houdini; perhaps Houdini did try to rig the switch. It can't be known. During the next day's séance, Margery made a tactical blunder. As soon as the lights went out, Walter screamed bloody murder, accusing Houdini of planting the ruler in the box. For eighty years the power of the ventriloquist's suspension has clouded this story. Biographers have both accused Houdini and acquitted him with no proof, only anecdotal evidence. If we allow only our rational brain to look at the situation, we can cut through the fog. In the séance room that night, Margery entered the box in the light, her arms were pushed through the side holes, and the top was closed around her neck. She never had use of her hands in the box; they were being vigilantly held by Houdini and Dr. Prince. Yet as soon the lights were out, Walter appeared and accused Houdini of planting a ruler. If we realize that Walter doesn't exist, we must ask ourselves: How does Margery know that a ruler is under her cushion?

It's a folding carpenter's ruler, something that would, by using her toes, feel like a nondescript rectangular object. In the dark, nestled under the pillow, there was no way that she could have known what it was if she hadn't brought it in or known in advance it would be in the box.

Margery knew there was no Walter, just as Lady Doyle knew there was no Pheneas.

Six months before his arrival, Conan Doyle had written and commented on a controversial English medium named William Hope, the head of the "Crewe Circle" that Houdini had dispatched DeVega to spy on. "Hope is a perfectly genuine medium . . . but he is a fanatic, and in my opinion would do anything his 'guides' had ordered him to do." Suddenly Conan Doyle had his own spirit guide, who came to him through his wife's hand, and he began doing everything his guide commanded.

Doyle's earlier advocacy of the fairy photographs had been a stunning blow to his credibility. Some critics suggested that he was more like Dr. Watson than Sherlock Holmes. With his reputation in jeopardy, Lady Doyle shrewdly realized that Sir Arthur, incredulous and stubborn, literally needed a control. Another miscue like endorsing patently faked photographs of children's book fairies and goblins illustrations could turn him into a laughingstock and ruin his reputation. One way to prevent that and to prevent him from being exploited by devious mediums would be to channel the vast majority of his communications with the spirit world in the home circle. That goal was accomplished when she developed her talent for automatic writing. It was reinforced when she introduced Sir Arthur's guide, Pheneas. It's no coincidence that the first words out of Pheneas's mouth were *"We are brothers"* and *"Your wife is invaluable to us."* Coincidence, like Houdini said, is a kindlier word. Deliberate mystification is more accurate.

The next afternoon, Munn, Prince, Houdini, and Margery had lunch together at a restaurant in a Boston suburb. Houdini was scheduled to play a vaudeville engagement in Boston in a few weeks, and Margery was fearful that he would denounce her as a fraud from the stage.

"If you misrepresent me from the stage at Keith's some of my friends will come up and give you a good beating," Margery said.

This was no idle threat. Margery devotee Joe DeWyckoff had a history of violence, once stalking and smashing his walking stick over the head of a man who had offended him and then continuing to rain punches on the man's face before they were separated.

"I am not going to misrepresent you," Houdini replied. "They are not coming on the stage and I am not going to get a beating."

"Then it is your wits against mine," she said, and gave Houdini a "furtive" look. "How would it look for my twelve year old son to grow up and read that his mother was a fraud?"

"Then don't be a fraud," Houdini suggested.

That night, a new control box was tried. It was Comstock's invention and it was for solus sittings. Both the medium and the observer, sitting opposite each other, would put their feet into the contraption, which covered half of their shins. A board was then locked in place, making any foot movement impossible. The committee sat for an hour, waiting for something to happen, to no avail. Margery was running out of time to make her case before these men.

"Houdini, I wish you would go into a trance state," Margery said.

Then the dour Dr. Crandon spoke up. "Some day, Houdini, you will see the light and if it were to occur this evening, I would gladly give ten thousand dollars to charity."

"It may happen," Houdini shrugged. "But I doubt it."

"Yes sir, if you were converted this evening I would willingly give $10,000 to some charity."

Houdini wasn't converted, Walter couldn't come through, and the séance ended a few minutes later.

The next night, Walter was feeling his oats in the séance room. Before his friendly circle, he was hailed for forever discrediting Houdini as a psychic researcher. The official record reflects that Walter "had quite a lot to say about Houdini and the jolts Walter might give him every day, reminding him of the curse he had hurled at him. He said that if Houdini said anything false on the stage, Walter would finish him."

On the same day that Margery was threatening to have Houdini beaten up, Conan Doyle was composing another letter to Crandon. They had been exchanging almost daily letters by now. Doyle thanked Crandon for the successive séance reports and then turned to Houdini. "Something will happen to that man H. You mark my words. Better to get between the metals when an express is due, than block the way of the spirit. I could give many examples. Did you ever hear of the death of Podmore!" Frank Podmore was an English writer who wrote many books on Spiritualism, none quite rabid enough for Sir Arthur's taste. He drowned in August of 1910, with some people speculating that his death was a suicide.

With the failure of Margery to produce at these crucial sittings, the Crandon camp went into damage control mode. The good doctor wrote letters to the leading Spiritualists around the world, trumpeting Houdini's total "exposure" by Walter. When Carrington heard the séance reports he was aghast at Houdini's cagelike restraint but overjoyed at Walter's attack. "I would have given a lot to have been present at that sitting when H. wept!" he wrote Crandon.

The Crandon camp began to think that Houdini had somehow tricked the cabinet-box. After getting carbons of the sittings, DeWyckoff wrote Crandon with a suggestion. "All circumstances, from every angle, point to Houdini's guilt and there is not a doubt in my mind but that *he is guilty* in both instances—viz. 'planting' the rubber and the ruler! . . . I feel deeply for you and Mrs. Crandon and for the cause of 'Truth' and it is a pity that Walter had seen fit to mitigate or withdraw the *curse*. 'Truth' was *shrieking* when Walter used the only forcible language accessible and applicable to a cad like Houdini under the circumstances. . . . We must all now use our best judgment—individually and collectively as to what to do in the immediate future . . . It occurs to me that of moment we ought to try and ascertain who actually constructed the box for Houdini and let me interview him or 'reach' him."

Crandon responded and assured DeWyckoff that the curse on Houdini was still in place. "We are quite content, even jubilant, over the issue, so don't feel sorry for us. Walter did not mitigate or withdraw his curse. He only withdrew the individual words which might not be published, and distinctly said that all the rest was to remain." Then he invited DeWyckoff to Boston to discuss strategy.

Houdini's box was also on Doyle's mind. He called it a mystery, but he had some advice on how to get to the bottom of it—they should 'reach' Dr. Comstock's assistant. "If Conant would quarrel with Houdini or if he were amenable to persuasion of any sort we should get at the facts," he urged Crandon. What sort of persuasion, he left to the good doctor's imagination.

On September 5, Pheneas decided to comment on the situation in Boston.

"There is a great deal going on in America at present. . . . The evil forces are very strong, but the forces of light are stronger. Truth always prevails. Houdini is going rapidly to his Waterloo. He is exposed. Great will be his downfall before he

descends into the darkness of oblivion. He has caused a terrible fate. . . . Prince will not be far behind him. They will be centres of evil, like a whirlpool with its eddies, dashing humans to destruction."

This was even before Doyle had received word from Crandon that Walter had claimed to expose Houdini. A few days later, Doyle asked for more information about the Crandons.

Lady Doyle threw up her hand.

"Houdini is doomed, doomed!" Pheneas almost shouted. *"A terrible future awaits him. He has done untold harm. It will not be long first. His fate is at hand. He, and all who uphold him, will be, as it were, chained together and cast into the sea. Your friends the Crandons will even in this world reap the reward of their brave work. . . . In the fearful crisis which is soon to come, America in her sore need will find that she has here a sure and well tested bridge to that spirit world. . . . They will play a great part in the crisis and it is then that they will fully come into their own."*

Doyle wrote Crandon and reported Pheneas's conversation. As if to underscore it, on September 11, Lady Doyle wrote directly to Margery. "My husband's fine guide told us that all that you have done is going to have very great results in the future. . . . When the . . . upheaval comes to the world and America is stricken, as she will be . . . you will be a great centre . . . and they will flock to you as a bridge of knowledge & hope & comfort . . . We were also told that Houdini is *doomed* & that he will soon go down to the black regions which his work against Spiritualism will bring him as his punishment."

This exchange of information among the mediums is significant. Sir Arthur believes what he's told. Lady Doyle and Margery, however, are the women behind the curtains. Lady Doyle is writing to Margery in code. They can't be overt because it's always possible to have a letter intercepted. Lady Doyle's message could be decoded as "You have doomed Houdini on your side, I have done likewise. Between the two of us, the word will get out and this bastard who is standing in our way will get exactly what's coming to him."

Houdini seemed circumspect during his September engagement in Boston. He confided in Prince that he was beginning to believe that Crandon was actively "aiding and abetting" his wife in the séance room but whenever the press asked him about the recent sittings, he declined comment. He even spurned an invitation to meet Margery when she phoned him during his Keith's stay. The only thing new about his half-hour vaudeville turn was his thinning hair and the extra few pounds in his midriff. The motion picture that warmed up the audience was taken eighteen years earlier when he dove into the Seine and escaped the gendarmes. Then he did his Needle Mystery, brought Bess out of retirement once again for the Metamorphosis, and closed by escaping from a straitjacket.

Houdini's reluctance to comment on the Margery case seemed strategic. A few months later, he had self-published a pink pamphlet called "Houdini Exposes the Tricks Used by the Boston Medium 'Margery' to Win the $2500 Prize Offered by the *Scientific American*." In the pamphlet, which was chock-full of photos and line drawings of the séances, Houdini opened up. "I charge Mrs. Crandon with practicing her feats daily like a professional conjurer. Also that because of her training as a secretary, her long experience as a professional musician, and her athletic build she is not simple and guileless but a shrewd, cunning woman, resourceful in the extreme, and taking advantage of every opportunity to produce a 'manifestation.'"

When Prohibition came, the loss of business caused Frank Brophy to close down his Hotel Princeton in Princeton-by-the-Sea, a picturesque seaside town about thirty miles south of San Francisco. Ironically enough, the tiny town boasted three piers in 1924, and they were in constant use to bring in the bootleg booze that was flowing up from Los Angeles. This process wasn't as easy as it sounds with the California Prohibition director taking a proactive stance against this kind of smuggling, but even the bootleggers wouldn't think that the authorities would send a swimmer into the frigid nighttime October waters to reconnoiter their "rumrunners" and report back. What human could possibly withstand that cold water for that long and not get hypothermia?

As if he didn't have enough to do battling the Margery crowd and crisscrossing the country lecturing on the evils of phony mediums, Houdini was now back working for the government. In the February 17, 1967 edition of the *Oakland Tribune*, two longtime Bay Area residents were interviewed and they reminisced about their star-studded past. Hattie Mooser, along with her sister Minnie, had run a famous restaurant during Prohibition that all the visiting entertainers frequented. Their brothers George and Leon managed many famous magicians and were some of the men who encouraged Houdini when he was just starting out. According to Hattie, Houdini was visiting the restaurant one night when he pulled her out, hailed a cab, and directed the driver to cruise down to the waterfront so Houdini could point out where he had done some missions for the government. "Not many people knew it but Houdini helped the Coast Guard round up a ring of rum runners. They often asked him to assist an investigation because he was such a good swimmer and had trained himself to withstand cold. He would swim out to a suspected rum runner's boat, look around, and report back to the authorities."

This information was confirmed by an escape artist and Houdini buff who befriended the Moosers in the sixties. Both of the sisters told him that Houdini had worked for the Secret Service and had drawn on those experiences for his movie *Haldane of the Secret Service*. According to the women, Houdini's skills as an illusionist who worked with equipment that contained hidden compartments was valuable to the government in assessing how the rumrunners were bringing their contraband onshore. Houdini's interest in smuggling went back to his early days in Europe when he filed reports back via his *Dramatic Mirror* column. On January 8, 1904, writing from Scotland, he reported that a New York gang was smuggling jewels to the United States from Germany and France in tin boxes stuffed into the cadavers of Americans who had died in those countries.

Houdini may have had another connection to the rum-running gangs that he was surveilling for the government. Many California millionaires, some of them in the budding movie business, were the financial angels for a bootlegging ring that smuggled rum over the Mexican border using not only coast-hugging ships but airplanes too.

Hattie often alluded to having an affair with Houdini. Even at ninety, in the small apartment she shared with her sister in Westlake, she kept a life-size autographed photo of him on her wall. "Houdini is mine!" she told the reporter. She might have cryptically revealed her liaison when she told another reporter that she and Bess watched as Houdini dangled headfirst nine stories above the ground on March 27, 1923, doing a straitjacket escape in front of the *Tribune* building. "Bess took my hand and her nails dug into my palm," Hattie remembered. "It surprised me and I asked her what on earth was wrong. 'It's such a little bit of a thing, you've seen him do much more dangerous things,' I told her. Bess held my hand tightly and said, 'Yes, he has many tricks but he only has one heart.'"

That 1924 San Francisco visit must have been quite complicated. Bess was traveling with Houdini on this leg of his lecture tour, and besides Hattie Mooser, Charmian London lived nearby. Houdini had kept in touch with her since their affair in 1918 and, according to Charmian's diary, she never could get "Magic Man" out of her consciousness. With Houdini in town, she found it impossible. Not immediately hearing from him, she decided to buy her own ticket to his show. That same day, she had lunch with a friend at the Mooser sisters' restaurant, where Hattie regaled her with stories of Houdini's early years. The next day she saw "Magics" [Harry and Bess] and when asked to meet them later she declined, "& feel like a fool!" Halloween was a particularly hard day. "Dream of Magic a lot . . . Poor night—Too intense from Magic. Calls up early. I am asleep. Calls up 12:30—will call up again in an hour to see where we'll meet for an hour. Meet planned and I wait alone in apt., & finally sorrowfully leave." Apparently that was the last she heard from Houdini. A week later she wrote, "Complete silence from Magic. Wonder if wire raised ructions."

"Houdini Hits Conan Doyle—Magician Says Englishman's Occult Teachings Are Menace to Sanity and Health," trumpeted the Los Angeles headlines on the morning of October 29, 1924. After months of lecturing, and his contretemps with the Crandon crew, Houdini started to take the gloves off in public. "Doyle thinks he is a Messiah who has come to save mankind by instructing them in the mysteries of occultism," Houdini told the reporter, as if he had read Pheneas's mind. "But instead of that he is misleading the public and his teachings are a menace to sanity and health."

Houdini's lectures were having other more concrete effects too. After he left the Los Angeles area, police raided a group named the National Independent Spiritualist Association and indicted its president, vice president, and eight other officers on charges of conspiracy and fraud. One of the officials was charged with luring many of his five hundred female clients to his office, where he enticed them to pose nude. The undercover investigation was aided by a L.A. reporter who had been in close contact with Houdini the whole time.

Houdini's efforts were beginning to draw the notice of Spiritualists besides the Margery camp. On December 9, 1,500 Chicago area Spiritualists met to protest Houdini's attacks on their religion. Calling him an ignorant "itinerant paid magician," Reverend C. Burgess ridiculed Houdini's attacks on such distinguished men as Doyle, Lodge, and Barrett and claimed that the magician belonged in an insane asylum.

Back in Boston, Doyle was assuming a larger and larger role in the Margery damage control efforts. Crandon seemed ready to defer to Doyle's advice on almost every issue, including who would get to sit with Margery. When Eric Dingwall, an investigator from the British Society of Psychical Research, attempted to get sessions with Margery, Doyle reminded him that he was the gatekeeper to the medium. Angry at Dingwall for his part in exposing one of Doyle's favorite mediums, he foolishly wrote Dingwall, "I have been desired to cable Mr Crandon how far they would be wise in acceding to your request to sit with 'Margery.' I cannot answer this until I have some assurance that the injustice done to Hope will be removed. How can I possibly recommend you to a second medium when the first has been so ill-used? Mr. de Brath seemed to think yesterday that there was some chance of a revision of the Hope case. Should I have your assurance to that effect I would regulate my reply to Mr Crandon in accordance."

Doyle's strategy backfired. Dingwall, irate, immediately sent Crandon a copy of "the extraordinary letter" from Doyle "in which he tries to make a bargain with me upon the case of Mr. Hope." He also forwarded Doyle's letter to the council of his organization. Chagrined, Crandon had no choice but to allow Dingwall to come to sit with Margery.

Meanwhile Margery was forced to deny the charge, published in Houdini's pamphlet, that she had threatened Houdini with a good beating. "Can you imagine any lady making any such threat?" she asked innocently. "Did you ever hear anything so absurd? And Houdini is as strong as a horse, too," she chuckled.

By the end of December, Margery had more denying to do. Banner headlines across the country proclaimed, "Houdini Gets Death Threat—'Evil Spirits' Put Curse on Him." The articles went on to report that Houdini had been condemned to death by "evil spirits" for impugning the validity and honesty of Margery's mediumship. Houdini publicly scoffed at the threats, telling the papers that "this Boston group can't even give me a pimple by sticking hat pins through my photograph and, what's more, they can't get in touch with the dead by retiring into fake trances in fake medium cabinets."

Once again, Margery was in denial mode. "Magician Conjured Story That 'Evil Spirits' Were Loosed to Kill Him in Year for His Own Amusement, Mrs. Crandon Claims," the papers reported. "All talk by Houdini that spirits are plotting his death within a year is not only false but absurd," Margery said. "Why, I never heard of 'Black Magic.' I regard his statement as a joke." But confirmation of the curse came from an unlikely source. Earl Rand, Margery's ex-husband and current grocer, confirmed that his mother-in-law had attended a séance at the Crandons' in October where Walter appeared and announced that he gave Houdini *"but one year more to live."*

In November, the SA committee issued a preliminary report that was inconclusive; Prince, Comstock, and McDougall remained swing votes, and desired more time to study the mediumship. In October, Prince had a one-on-one sitting with Margery. After Walter rang the bell box, Prince speculated that Margery might have had an apparatus concealed beneath her gown. She immediately stripped it off, leaving herself nude, and gave it to him for examination. Whether this was done under red light was not recorded.

By December, Houdini's strident anti-Margery statements had rankled the rest of the committee. Dr. William McDougall, the Harvard professor of psychology, had been out of town for the Houdini sittings but on his return he lambasted the magician in the press. "I understand that he came with his beliefs already fixed and was unable to admit any possibility of there being a new force," he said. "The only thing which I personally hold against him is his attempt to make it appear that the committee was on the point of awarding the prize to the Crandons until he stepped in and saved it from itself. This I strongly resent, as it makes him seem to have a monopoly of intelligence and of caution. I do not require Houdini to teach me something about which I probably know more than he does."

That was all Houdini needed to read. Now he had two foes in Boston.

Wearing a fedora and a heavy wool overcoat to ward off the winter weather, Houdini stood in front of Boston's City Hall and fanned $10,000 (about $400,000 today) in bonds in his hand. The eager photographers snapped away. Although Mayor Curley had found himself "unavailable," City Collector William McMorrow was at the magician's side as Houdini literally put his money where his mouth was.

"I agree to forfeit the sum of $5,000 to any charity selected by Mayor Curley if I do not detect, expose or have explained any mystery or manifestation performed three times in my presence and in the presence of the committee of newspapermen, clergymen and magicians," Houdini announced. "This is especially aimed at Mrs. L. R. G. Crandon. . . . I have already challenged her and offered to forfeit the same amount of money if I am unable to duplicate or have duplicated every last one of her manifestations.

"Now I have another $5,000 in my hands here which I will put up as bond for my challenge to Professor McDougall of Harvard University. According to his statements, he does not need me to teach him anything about mystery and psychic phenomena. He has made serious charges against me with respect to the Margery mediumship. I will wager him a sum equal to his year's salary that his

Houdini holding bonds worth $400,000 in today's money. He'd offered half of it to Harvard professor William McDougall if he would escape from a packing crate thrown into the Charles River. *Library of Congress*

knowledge of psychology will be useless to him if he lets me nail him into a heavily weighted packing case and throw him into the Charles River, a condition from which I have escaped repeatedly all over the world. I assure you that Professor McDougall's friendship with Margery and all her spirit controls will not get him out of the box before he drowns."

"Wouldn't it be difficult to collect on that bet?" one of the newspaperman asked.

"Yes," Houdini smiled. "I guess I'd have to make the wager with the professor's estate."

Houdini strode out onto the stage, to the cheers of the packed auditorium. His firm steps resounded on the wooden boards of the stage, as he smiled and acknowledged the applause with several short bows. Then he turned serious and walked directly to the footlights at the edge of the stage.

"Ladies and Gentlemen. Before starting I would like to impress on your minds, if I may, please, that I positively am not here to attack any religion. Everyone has the right to worship in his own way as long as it does not conflict with the laws of the country or the laws of humanity. I am not a skeptic. I am perfectly willing to believe, my mind is wide open. For over thirty-five years, day in and day out, night in and night out, I have been seeking the truth. No one in the world has a greater right to want to believe than I. My parents are on the other side, and if there is anyone who worshipped their father and mother it is your humble servant," Houdini intoned, standing on the lip of the stage of Boston's Symphony Hall.

More than a hundred clergymen, press people, and magicians flanked the center of the stage as an extended committee. Even Mayor Curley and his children were in attendance. Margery, who had been invited, was not.

"And so that you may properly weigh the religious, I am called a charlatan, a mountebank, a vaudevillian, and an itinerant magician. I am proud of those names. It has taken me years to get to my position. And so that you may rightfully weigh my words—and I am not telling you this in a boastful manner—I honestly came from a family of scholars. I possess two wonderful libraries, one the fourth largest dramatic library in the world. I only tell you this because when they shout the words 'itinerant magician' I want you to come to my home in New York and look at my library. I am only telling you this in self-defense, because when I get to the Margery affair and tell you that two of the committee, one who calls himself Dr. Carrington, and who paid $75 for that title—" Houdini was interrupted by appreciative laughter.

"—he is good. And the other, who is a prize student—he is—I think he has won a second prize for some essay, J. Malcolm Bird—when I get down to the Margery séances I will give you my opinion of them, and then I am going to prove what I say. Therefore, despite the fact that they call me the itinerant magician I am very proud of it. It is an honest name. It is not purchased and not stolen."

Houdini's years of experience and his charm and charisma had completely won the audience over when he finished his introduction. Now he went on to give his own anecdotal history of the fraudulent Spiritualism. He talked about his early years as a spiritualistic medium, which gave him the knowledge to expose other frauds who might fool eminent men like Lodge or Doyle. "I am not denouncing spiritualism, ladies and gentlemen, I am showing up the frauds. I

Houdini exposing Spiritualists' tricks onstage. *Library of Congress*

cannot show up an honest medium. But trot her out," he said, to much laughter and applause.

He talked about his aborted séance with Lady Doyle, irate that Sir Arthur had assumed that his mother was illiterate and had been able to come through in English because she had studied it in the spirit world. "My sainted mother, God rest her soul, having been educated on the Continent and in a convent, read, wrote and spoke five languages but not one word of English!"

Now Houdini dimmed the lights and showed slides of famous mediums, dating back to the Fox sisters. When that was done, he invited a member of the committee onto the stage and demonstrated how fraudulent mediums did their slate writing trick. The beauty of his demonstration was that his volunteer was made to put a hood over his head, replicating the conditions of the séance room, while the entire audience got to see how the phony medium performed the effect. The methods exposed were captivating and highly entertaining. It was marvelous theater. Through the course of the evening, the audience interrupted him forty-three times with laughter and applause.

Then it was time for his well-advertised Margery exposure, but first he wanted to perform a little miracle. He took two pairs of slates and showed them to the audience, all four sides perfectly clean and empty. Then he bound two slates together and did the same for the second set.

"I want you to watch me very carefully, ladies and gentlemen, because if things are right, this will be a very extraordinary experiment—if things are right."

He walked over to a committeeman and asked him to hold the slates over his head so the entire audience could see that he wasn't a confederate.

Then he picked up a standard dictionary and asked another man to drop a card that he provided him into any part of the book he desired. Since it was a very thick book, Houdini told the audience that it would be impossible for any human being to give him the correct numbers of the pages that the card had been inserted between. So he had to call upon the "best known spirit in the world" to give him a sign of his presence.

"Spirit, I command you to read the first and last words and the numbers on the two pages," Houdini intoned.

"Where is the gentleman who selected the pages? What number is that please?"

The man told Houdini the pages were 116 and 117 and that the first words on those pages were "crowfoot" and "ice."

"I have called upon the best known spirit in the world today to give us a sign. And when I say the best known spirit, it must be the one that is known best to all present. And so there can be no mistake, that I have not shoved anything between there, watch it please, because when it is all over they will say 'Well, I saw him insert something. You are a confederate.' A string? Nothing."

Houdini opened up the first pair of slates. The numbers "116" and "117" were marked on it, along with the words "crowfoot" and "ice."

And then he opened up the second set of slates, reminding the audience that he had asked the well-known spirit to show them a sign. There were two photographs between the slate and Houdini held them up for the audience to see. The first was a photo of a young Walter Stinson, Margery's brother and spirit guide. The second had been autographed. It read, *"My last photograph. Love to all, Walter."* It was a photo of Walter taken minutes after he was crushed to death between the engines on the night of his fatal accident. Houdini's ire toward the Crandons had reached ghastly proportions.

The year of the forewarned great catastrophe, 1925, began with Conan Doyle and Houdini at each other's throats again. On January 26, Doyle's defense of Margery was published in *The Boston Herald*. The editors waxed sonorously that Sir Arthur was using the very methods of deduction made famous by Sherlock Holmes to make sense of all the phenomena produced by Margery. Noting that he was writing this essay on Christmas Day, he felt that it was an appropriate time to fight for truth and to help restore the honor of a "most estimable" lady such as Mrs. Crandon. There were no bombshells in the piece, only an indictment of Houdini as an egomaniacal, discredited researcher who had been bribed to sabotage Margery's victory by planting a rubber eraser and a ruler during the séances. Houdini's master plan was foiled at each turn by Walter, who protected his "*kid*" sister both by warning that Houdini would *"slip a die into the contact box"* two days before it even happened, and by calling him out for planting a ruler so she could use it to reach the bell box and make it ring.

Houdini immediately threatened to sue Sir Arthur unless a retraction was forthcoming, although he admitted that he didn't really take the attacks too personally since some of Sir Arthur's "sharpness" might have been a reaction to Houdini's belief that Lady Doyle was not a valid medium. There was one other mitigating possibility too, Houdini related. Conan Doyle was a "bit senile" and therefore easily "bamboozled," but he still felt that Doyle was a menace to mankind.

While he was sparring with the Spiritualists, his own investigations into the mysteries of life after death continued. Repeated exposure to fraudulent mediums hadn't made him lose hope of contact with the dead. His brother Bill had been fighting tuberculosis for years and had been living at a sanitarium in Saranac Lake, New York. During a heavy snowstorm, Houdini drove up to the mountains and stood on Bill's front porch and performed some new effects for him. As Bill's condition worsened, Houdini had a phone installed at his bed and instructed the nurse to ring him when the end was imminent. Shortly after the New Year, the call came and with the nurse holding the receiver to his brother's ear, Houdini shouted, "Remember our compact. After you die, communicate with me." A minute later, Bill was gone. Houdini holed himself up in a room on the top floor of his house and waited for twenty-four hours, going without food or drink, for the message that never came.

Back in Boston, Margery was sequestered too. Just a few short months ago, Margery was a *nom de séance* in a report by Bird on a promising new medium, but with the unbelievable exposure from the Houdini sittings and the challenges, Mrs. Crandon found herself a Spiritualist superstar. She was quickly deluged with mail, asking for séances. Her failure to show up for Houdini's challenge and his exposure of her methods necessitated some new stunts in the séance room. She began trying them in October, relying less on physical manifestations and more on mental manifestations, but her sittings with Prince were less than revelatory for him. By the end of December, though, she received a very interesting letter from a Charles K. Tripp. "I have read, with a great deal of interest, the articles in the paper in reference to your controversy with Harry Houdini. I have known Houdini for some twenty-five years. I was once expelled from Keith's Theatre through the stage door because I volunteered to act as one of the committee that he had asked for, to come upon the stage. I brought suit against Keith's for assault and this was settled out of court to avoid publicity. I was a manufacturer of mechanical apparatus from 1890 until 1898 and had manufactured apparatus for nearly all the best magicians in the country at that time. If I can be of any assistance to you in showing up Mr. Houdini as being one of the greatest fakers in the century I will be glad to do so."

Dr. Crandon responded to his letter the day he received it.

What Tripp didn't tell the Crandons was that he had been a Houdini imitator. In 1906, Tripp did jail cell and handcuff escapes and, according to Harry Kellar, was one of the most able magic innovators around. The fact that Carrington and Keating were her confidants and that according to *The Boston Herald*, Houdini's rival and Spiritualist sympathizer Howard Thurston was "a friend of Dr. Crandon's," as well as Conan Doyle's, suggests that Margery was getting tutored by some serious magical minds. In the next few years, Walter would perform standard card tricks and even do a version of the linking rings using wooden rings of differing grains.

Margery's mediumship took on new dimensions when Eric Dingwall arrived in the summer of 1924. According to Margery herself, when Dingwall arrived, "the first thing he told me was to take off my clothes." His admonition was hardly needed. Mrs. Crandon would often sit in the nude, and routinely wouldn't wear anything more than a kimono with nothing underneath. It was reported that she would sometimes sprinkle luminous powder on her breasts, creating a nice effect when the kimono slipped off her shoulders.

During Dingwall's sittings, Margery began to produce strange-looking ectoplasm that oozed out of a slit in her dressing gown and seemed to originate in her vagina. It was Walter's idea to demonstrate the materialization of this ectoplasm, so while Walter laughed merrily and Margery snored in a trance, Doctor Crandon held a red light to her groin area while Dingwall observed what looked like a flaccid hand protruding from her vagina. Margery later boasted of giving Dingwall sittings where she was completely nude. Years later, Professor McDougall would charge Dingwall with having had improper relations with the medium.

To counteract Houdini's damaging anti-Margery lectures, Crandon rented a hall in Boston and announced that on January 31, Margery would rebut Houdini's exposure by performing a public séance, duplicating the phenomena she had produced for the committee. Apparently she got cold feet and, at the last minute, Dingwall substituted for her with a boring lecture on her mediumship.

With battles raging on several fronts, Houdini's life seemed more frantic than ever. On January 19 he wrote Kilby three times in one day. In his first letter, he praised Kilby for determining who had brought Dingwall into the Margery picture. He also complained about his fellow committeemen. "Just to show you how matters stand, although I am still a member of the committee in good standing, in speaking to Dr. Prince yesterday he informed me that Margery had a new routine of manifestations, but he refused to tell me what they were. Can you beat this? And here I am giving them all the secrets that I possess, and they will not help me." In his next letter, he asked Kilby to spy on the Margery camp. "If it is at all possible, I would like to get a report on what Margery will do at the séance on the 31st. I am told that she has changed her entire program since my expose," he said in one letter. He also told him that despite Munn's denials, he had in his possession page proofs of the September issue of *Scientific American* with Bird's suppressed article on Margery.

The third letter of the day was chilling. "I have just received warning letters of what Margery and the Spiritualists are going to do to me. Well, time will tell. *I know I am right,* and I will stick to my guns until I know that there is no hypocrisy in these manifestations, and then I will shout the truth from the house tops. Regarding Margery, I would very much like to get a report of what takes place at her séance on the 31st. If possible, can you engage a stenographer to go there and get a report? I will pay all expenses. Nothing surprises me about Margery. A woman who will drag her dead brother from the grave and exploit him before the public as a means of gaining social prominence, would do anything."

Houdini was not being an alarmist in taking these threats seriously. Spiritualists had dealt ruthlessly with their antagonists for years. In 1904, his good friend and partner in exposing Spiritualists, Joe Rinn, was forced to carry a gun for protection after several attempts on his life by phony mediums who had lost clients because of Rinn's scrutiny. Mediums like Minnie Williams had thugs on her staff who routinely beat up anyone who tried to stem her cash flow. Madame Diss Debar, who had a long history of Spiritualist scams, was thought to have poisoned an art dealer named Samuel Loewenherz, after she received forty paintings from his gallery. After delivering the artwork, Diss Debar gave him some wine and cake. He then returned to his office, where he fell asleep. A few days later, he was found there comatose and he subsequently died in the hospital. Unfortunately an autopsy was never taken, so there was no proof linking her with the crime, although the administrator of Loewenherz's estate did swear out a warrant for her arrest.

Houdini himself had warned Rinn in his dealings with the Spiritualist crowd. "All materializing séances are fakes," he told Rinn back in 1895. "You can get legal evidence to convict [medium] Rogers any time at his séances, but don't try to do it alone. Those mediums are bad actors and would think nothing of putting you in the hospital or worse." Sometimes the mediums employed the "spirits" to do their bidding. When a heckler would try to interrupt his séance, one medium insisted that a committee should bind him with rope to a chair and place the heckler in the cabinet with him. Under the cover of darkness, the medium would release his ties, beat the heckler with a blackjack, all the time singing a loud hymn, and then throw him out of the cabinet and fasten his bonds again. When the lights were turned on and the medium was seen fastened, the audience believed that the spirits had meted out justice to the troublemaker.

Houdini had too long a history in the exposé game not to take these threats seriously. So on February 13, he sent his brother Hardeen a letter, along with a copy of the page proofs of the September issue of *Scientific American*. "I want you to save this in case anything should happen to me as evidence that the press was stopped and these pages thrown out." He then gave Dash a background into Munn's dealings with Bird and the rest of the committee. "Put these records away and I will mail things from time to time, to be filed for future evidence. Do not leave these photostatic copies out of your hands please."

February was the cruelest month for Margery and Walter. On the twelfth of that month, the *Scientific American* committee finally reached its verdict on her mediumship. By a vote of four to one, the men rejected her claim to the prize. Houdini was the only member who claimed that she was a fraud. The three academics merely argued that she failed to convince them that she produced her phenomena by supernormal means; what predisposed them toward her credibility was that she was a private, noncommercial medium who "had no history of association with magicians, mediums and jugglers who might teach her the art of mystification." So much for the thoroughness of their investigation. Later that month, McDougall, who had finally glimpsed the ectoplasm that issued from Margery's nether regions, claimed that it looked a lot like the lung tissue from an animal.

Crandon immediately put his spin on the failure. "We dismissed them on January 20," he told the press. "The effort today of the *Scientific American* psychic committee to save its face in the presence of the almost unprecedented psychic power of Margery has only two defects. It is three weeks too late and it is dishonest. We have done the dismissing, not they." He also expressed relief that now Margery could travel to England, where the study of her supernatural powers could continue "unhampered by a handcuff king and his allies."

For his part Houdini was elated. "Houdini Sees Plot to Spirit Margery Away," a New York headline read. "The implication that she cannot properly be investigated in this country is ridiculous. It strikes me she is just trying to get away from Houdini," he said. Not so fast. Margery's plans became more nebulous when Walter put his ectoplasmic hand down. Although the medium desired to travel to London, her dead older brother had so far failed to give her assurances that the London fogs would agree with him. He did seem like his usual feisty self, though, on February 21, when during a séance at Lime Street, he composed a spontaneous song to the tune of "It Ain't Gonna Rain No More":

Oh Houdini won't talk no more, no more
He ain't goin' talk no more.
What in the hell will the newspapers do,
When Houdini won't talk no more?

Houdini won't write no more, no more,
Houdini won't write no more.
He writ so much that his arm got sore,
Houdini won't write no more.

Crandon had a different way of expressing his defiance. On February 28, he wrote Sir William Barrett and claimed that McDougall's final judgment on the case must have been "dictated" by the powers-that-be at Harvard who felt that no self-respecting university would have anything to do with psychic research. "We have only just begun to fight," Crandon bellowed. "And we shall keep it up till their skins or ours are nailed on the wall."

23

My Own Secret Service

WALTER LIPPMANN, THE CHIEF EDITORIAL WRITER of *The New York World*, leaned into the circle of men in the corner of the room and whispered, "I'm thinking of Lord Curzon in the Foreign Office."

Hardeen repeated his statement for accuracy, wrote it down on a slip of paper, and handed it to Lippmann. Now it was Bernard Baruch's turn. The Wall Street multimillionaire and wartime chairman of the War Industries Board stared at Hardeen.

"Don't give up the ship," he said succinctly. Hardeen repeated the phrase and wrote it down for him.

The other men looked to Dr. Edward Kempf, an eminent psychiatrist.

"I'm thinking of Buffalo Bill's monument in Wyoming that was designed by Mrs. Harry Payne Whitney," Dr. Kempf whispered. Hardeen repeated the procedure. Now they were ready.

This was the most prestigious committee that Houdini had ever assembled. Along with these three men, there was Ralph Pulitzer, the publisher of *The New York World*, whose father had established the prize for outstanding journalism that was named after him, and Arthur Train, a novelist who specialized in themes that bore on criminality. A blue-ribbon panel of New York's power elite, for sure, but they weren't assembled on the stage of the Hippodrome. They were congregated together in the parlor of Houdini's home in Harlem to witness the magician give a demonstration of thought transference.

In January 1925, Gilbert Murray, a professor and a member of the British Society for Psychical Research, reported that he was able to successfully read thoughts that had been announced aloud by his friend the Earl of Balfour, even though Murray had left the room and was thirty-five feet away at the time. Murray's ongoing experiments had delighted Sir Arthur Conan Doyle, who as far back as 1923 had written to Houdini claiming that this demonstrated the proof of telepathy. When Pulitzer got Murray's latest report, he decided that the tests proved supernormal power. Houdini didn't jump to the same conclusion and offered to replicate Murray's experiment. "My only desire is to show that Professor Murray did not perform a supernatural feat," Houdini told the press. "I would not expose any man who claimed he was doing a trick, but I feel that a claim of the supernatural is wrong and has driven people insane." Houdini didn't just plan on duplicating Murray's experiment; he was, of course, planning on going it one better. Instead of just leaving the room when the committee decided on a thought, Houdini would have himself escorted to the third floor of his house, stripped naked, and locked into a box.

That was the finale. The experiment began when the men and women of the committee gathered together in the parlor. Hardeen, Houdini's brother, would play the role of the Earl of Balfour. Bess, to avoid suspicion, was banished from the room. Then Houdini walked up the stairs to a room on the third floor and closed the door. A member of the committee stood guard outside the door.

After the three committeemen documented their thoughts, Houdini was brought back down into the room.

Lippmann's phrase gave him trouble. He was unable to receive Lord Curzon's name. Then he turned to Baruch. He wasn't getting anything at first, then he lowered his head and concentrated deeply.

"I'm visualizing a huge body that's heaving and swaying," he said. "In fact, you're thinking of an enormous body of water, and I can see a lot of shipwrecks."

The committee decided that was a hit.

Now it was Kempf's turn.

"I see a large plain. A great herd of black oxen. They appear to be stampeding. I see a man who is very hungry," Houdini said dramatically. "He's seated on a racing horse. He's chasing these oxen—no, they are not oxen, they are buffaloes. They have their heads down, and they are going like a whirlwind. He is shooting at them—no, I am wrong. I see a great many people who are hungry. They are thinking of food. This man is supplying them with food. But you are not thinking of this man. This man has long hair and piercing eyes. You are not thinking of the man, though, but of the monument. It is Buffalo Bill. You are thinking of his monument in Wyoming and the sculptor—is that right?"

Dr. Kempf was flabbergasted. "That's amazing," he said. "I had said nothing of Buffalo Bill's activities but I did visualize him killing buffalo and feeding hungry railroad workers. That is absolutely astounding."

Now for the ultimate challenge. Houdini marched back upstairs accompanied by Pulitzer and Lippmann. He stripped off his clothes and was placed into a box that had been carefully examined by the newsmen. The publisher demanded that the box be taken off the floor, so Houdini suggested it be put upon a desk. Pulitzer demurred and they finally compromised by placing the box on top of a bench. The two men then stood guard over it.

Downstairs, the rest of the committee decided on one thought: Mrs. John Barrymore's portrait by the Spanish painter Ignacio Zuloaga. Houdini, who had paused to throw a large blanket over his shoulders, was brought downstairs.

"I see Shakespeare, his home at Stratford-on-Avon," he began. "There are large audiences. No, wait, it's not England, it's America. I know why I thought England, it's an American theatrical family who came from England. You're thinking of the Barrymore family, possibly Jack."

He missed the gender and he didn't pick up the painting, but Houdini's high percentage of hits had shocked his committee. He refused to tell them his secret, other than that it was done by perfectly normal means. What the distinguished guests didn't know was that they were at that moment reposing in a house that had been surreptitiously wired from cellar to roof.

Houdini's house had been customized to enable him to astonish his visitors. It began with the front door, which didn't open conventionally; when you turned the doorknob, the door would swing open from what should have been the hinged side. Once again, Houdini was paying silent homage to Robert-Houdin, who had loaded his house with wonderful little inventions. In Houdini's home, there were secret panels and hidden passageways. One of those secret panels was in the library, where Houdini had fooled Doyle with his Mene Tekel effect. Houdini (or Ernst) had forced Doyle into putting the blackboard into a corner that covered a secret panel behind some of the books on the shelf. A hidden assistant then opened the panel, removed the books, and stuck a long rod with a magnet on its end. The cork ball Houdini had subtly forced Doyle to choose had a magnetic center so it could be controlled from the rod on the other side of the blackboard. All the hidden assistant had to do was trace out the phrase backward and it would magically appear on the front of the board.

Crucial to Houdini's method was his ability to hear the conversations of guests who were reposing in the parlor. That room had been completely wired so that every little whisper could be picked up by a series of hidden Dictaphones and transmitted to an operator concealed in the basement. Whatever was said could either be noted down or retransmitted to other parts of the house through an elaborate labyrinth of hidden wires that sometimes even terminated in induction coils under the carpet. For Houdini, on the top floor, to hear these transmissions, he only had to wear an electric belt that established an invisible connection via electromagnetic induction with the loops of wire under the carpet. The belt was composed of many turns of the wire and terminated in a miniature telephone receiver that could be hidden in his hand, the wires running down his sleeve to the belt. For this last test, when Houdini had voluntarily removed his clothing, he relied on a concealed coil that was built into the box. It was a real-life replication of the opening scene of Houdini's *The Master Mystery*, where, as a secret agent, he eavesdropped on his corrupt boss via a hidden Dictaphone.

Louis C. Kraus, a nephew of Houdini's who worked for the Treasury Department, which oversaw the Secret Service, had originally wired the house. He may have gotten the idea from Feri Felix Weiss, who worked for the Treasury Department. Weiss was involved in investigating German espionage during World War I, and his article about the use of Dictaphone systems for spying was cut out and pasted by Houdini into one of his scrapbooks. By the time of Houdini's thought transference experiment in February 1925, the entire surveillance system had been rewired and made more sophisticated by a brilliant, mysterious young magician named Amedeo Vacca. Vacca had established himself as a magician in Chicago when he ran into Houdini at Gus Roterberg's magic shop in 1921. Impressed by his talent, Houdini wrote down his address and told Vacca that if ever came to New York, his services might be wanted. Two years later, Vacca showed up and Houdini immediately put him on the payroll. He wasn't just another assistant, though. For the next three years, Vacca became the lynchpin for a side of Houdini's life that was so secret, it was kept from even Bess and his brother Hardeen.

The young magician was sworn to absolute secrecy. No one was ever to know of the relationship between the two men. They never spoke to each other in public or even showed the slightest sign of recognition when they were in the same room. When Vacca was at any of Houdini's public appearances, he seemed to be just another spectator, but in reality he was there as an undercover operative. Before Houdini would come to a town to play an engagement, Vacca would make a preliminary visit, examine the facility closely, and install highly secret apparatuses. When they had to meet, Houdini came up with a novel solution. He bought a barbershop two blocks from his Harlem house and sent Vacca to night school for a crash course on the barbering trade. Under the cover of getting a trim, Houdini could plot strategy with Vacca.

"Now I have placed myself, my entire life and salvation, in your hands," Houdini told Vacca. It wasn't hyperbole. Houdini was about to begin what would seem to the press as a one-man crusade against phony mediums. He was about to risk his entire reputation, which to him was his life, in this pursuit. In reality, he would be supported by a whole combat division—what he later called "my own secret service"—that consisted of a brilliant mechanist in Vacca, beautiful young female showgirls/undercover agents, private detectives, an eccentric medium/escape artist/poison resister, and even his own niece. The Margery exposure had been just the opening skirmish. Now Houdini was going to war.

Florence B. Rush arrived at Henry Brooks's house promptly at eleven A.M. Sunday morning. Mr. Brooks was still in the middle of a healing session, so Mrs. Brooks showed her to a seat in the makeshift waiting room of their two-story house. Florence told her that she was very interested in mediumistic work and that she wanted to start her own church. She also related that she was a widow, even at her young age, but that her husband had left her quite well off. The two women chatted amiably until Mr. Brooks finally came into the room.

Brooks was nearly sixty, at least a decade older than his redheaded wife. He was wearing a torn gray sweater and his personal hygiene was on a par with his wardrobe. He smiled at Florence and revealed less than a complete set of teeth. Before meeting his new client, he pulled his wife out of the room and into the kitchen for a short conference. A few minutes later he returned and took a seat next to Florence.

"Let me tell you a little bit about myself," he began. "I've been doing spiritualistic work for thirty years now. I am what you call a trance medium. Now some people who come to me for treatments might say I was fresh, but that's because they don't understand how magnetic I am and what power comes from the spirits through these hands."

He held up his hands for Florence to examine.

Without any further ado, Brooks leaned back in his chair. He started breathing heavily, then his head suddenly relaxed and he began to snore. Suddenly his body convulsed a few times.

"Good morning," he said to the spirits.

"Do you see my husband?" Florence asked.

"Yes, he is right near you," he answered. "He loves you so."

"Is he sorry for what he's done?" she asked.

"Yes, and he asks your forgiveness," he said. "And there is a little girl right near him. She has beautiful curls. She's about five years old. Your little girl."

Florence leaned in to hear him better.

"Your little girl says, 'Mother, I love you so,' but she's not with your husband. She died sooner than him, didn't she?"

Florence nodded.

"I see someone who speaks a foreign tongue. It sounds to me like Arabic."

"Yes, that was my grandmother," Florence said.

He told her that her grandmother was bringing her little girl to her.

"Your husband tells me to tell you to go into this work—you'll be quite successful," he said. "How many children have you?"

"Two," Florence said.

"I was just coming to that," he said. "You have a beautiful body, but you should not repress your passions. You have a choked feeling in your chest. I can cure that for you for I have healing power. You have to be purified before you can go into this work, you know."

"Can you ask my husband where I could find someone to assist me in starting my church? I do have all this money that he left me, and I'm anxious to invest it," she said.

Suddenly it seemed like the spirits themselves were speaking through Brooks.

"*Ask the Medium after you get through, and he will tell you. The Medium is very good, he can give you a charter for your church. The Medium can cure you physically, and you have to be purified before you can do this work.*"

Then the words stopped. Brooks began to breathe heavy and snored and shuddered and suddenly he started rubbing his eyes. He was out of the trance.

"What did I say?" he asked her.

She repeated everything the spirits told her.

"Yes, that can be done," he said. "I get the vibration that you would be very successful as a public worker and do good work."

Then he got up and walked into an adjoining room. It was supposed to be a bedroom, but it was devoid of all furniture except for a trunk piled up with papers and a gallon jug filled with a red fluid that was probably wine. He closed the door and after two minutes returned to the room with a framed charter for the First Church of the Divine Light.

"Now this charter cannot be granted to you until you do some spiritual work," he told her. "And before anything can be granted you still have to be purified. Can you come back tomorrow night?"

"Can I be purified right now?" Florence asked. "I really want to start having séances by Wednesday night."

Brooks acted reluctant but then he agreed.

"All right, I will purify you now, but have you any corsets on?" he asked. "The steel will interfere in the purification process."

Florence shook her head. Brooks stared lasciviously at her.

"All right, now fix your dress as I will have to see more of your body and touch your skin. I must get close to the body."

He put his hands on her neck.

"Can you remove your hat and your wrap?" he asked.

Florence complied. Then she adjusted her underwear, lowering her brassiere so he could see part of her chest.

Brooks began to make several mystic passes over her head, then made the sign of the cross over her face. He ran his hands up and down her spine over her dress and then slowly rubbed the small of her back.

"Lord, please help me to show this new worker the light. Please allow me to remove this congestion so that she may be cured and purified."

During the prayer, Brooks was touching her all over her body, and then he inserted two fingers inside her dress and touched her left breast. He squeezed it. Florence didn't resist. He then took his other hand and placed it right on her other breast and squeezed hard, breathing heavily and gasping the whole time. He then made several more crosses over her whole body, running his hands over her thighs and down to her ankles and then returning them to her thighs.

"Dear God, bring this worker closer to me," he prayed and drew her toward him.

Florence held herself rigid. Brooks tried to pull her to him several more times, but she resisted.

"What do you see?" he asked.

"I see beautiful children who look like little fairies dancing around," she said. "Now I see a draped figure beckoning me to him."

Florence got up from the chair and Brooks came up off his knees.

"I feel much better," she said. "You are very magnetic."

"We have to try this again as you still have that congestion of the chest," he said. Florence gave him a ten-dollar bill and he gave her $8 back. She tipped him an extra dollar. She got her ordination papers and paid him an additional five dollars for that. She made sure to get a receipt. He insisted that she undergo some more healing before her first séance and she promised to come back later that night, after she had tended to her children.

Then the new Reverend Florence B. Rush, who was sometimes known as Rev. F. Raud, but whose real name was Rose Mackenberg, left the house and headed straight back to the hotel where Houdini was anxiously awaiting.

On February 7, 1925, *The New York Herald Tribune* made Houdini the subject of their editorial page, titled "Showman and Scientist." They wrote: "Those of us belonging to that portion of humanity which does not subscribe to belief in the existence of spooks should be grateful to Houdini, the handcuff king. . . . But the thing that Houdini is fighting is too big for one man. The dragon with which he is engaged dwells in the slough of human ignorance. That is a swamp that is not to be drained and reclaimed for many centuries; yet the extent of the task does not lessen the obligation of this and coming generations to keep working at the job. In the meantime Houdini has invaded the morass and annoyed the monster that feeds there.

"There are in New York, as there are in every other city in the United States, spirit mediums who make a fat living out of the mental insufficiencies of a part of the people. It is, usually, that part which is unattached to a church and lacks the philosophy to find comfort in the thought of a short, conscious existence. That there are such people may serve as a reminder that Jew and Gentile in their churches have for centuries been fighting this battle that Houdini, the son of a rabbi, now wages in his shrewd, dogged manner. This sort of spirit medium is a type of ghoul that seeks profit from the dead outside of graveyards. The victim is the bereaved person whom the affliction of death has caught unprepared by religion or philosophy.

"The claims of 'Margery' that she is able to receive at will the spirit of her dead brother are the latest example of the more pretentious medium who seeks scientific indorsement [sic]. The fact that her husband, Dr. L. R. G. Crandon, has some connection with Harvard University gave her séances an extra touch of distinction. In exposing the falseness of 'Margery's' claims Houdini has shown himself far more than a handcuff king. He is a good citizen and a convenient neighbor."

Houdini instinctively knew that his battle against fraud was too big for one man, and he began collecting recruits almost from the beginning. Back in May 1924, he wrote the famous Washington, D.C.-based journalist Betty Ross and enlisted her to make an undercover visit to a D.C.-based spirit photographer named Dr. W. M. Keeler. "Please make careful notes of everything that takes place and what is said, immediately," he counseled the journalist. Houdini was also acutely aware of how valuable newspapermen were to him in general. In the early twenties, he and Joe Rinn would visit the New York newshounds at their favorite watering hole, Andy Horn's bar, on Park Row near the Brooklyn Bridge.

Houdini catching his breath while in Paris. *From the collection of Dr. Bruce Averbook*

Although Houdini and Rinn weren't drinkers, they would buy the rounds and gain either information or cooperation as needed.

The idea of creating a network to assist him in his Spiritualist investigations was a natural to a man who had been cooperating with the espionage services of the United States and Britain. His adversaries, the fraudulent mediums, had organized themselves into a tight-knit network that routinely shared information. They did this through what was called the *Blue Book*, a book that contained the names, occupations, addresses, family trees, and other minutiae about potential local marks, information that could disarm them and lead them to believe that the psychic they were consulting had real power.

According to Bernard Ernst, Houdini's lawyer and confidant, during the course of his investigation into fraudulent mediums, Houdini accumulated a vast "secret archives" into which he had "filed away, details and information, which he had unearthed, regarding the personal life-histories of practically everyone connected with the subjects—and this, not only regarding mediums, but investigators and others as well!"

In these files, the records of these individuals went back at least to the day of their birth. "There are things in those files about me which I could swear no one but God knew!" a prominent magician whose identity Ernst was loath to reveal had said. According to the lawyer, the quantity of these files was "appalling," filling huge packing cases that were stored in the basement of his town house. "He spared himself neither time, money nor effort in order to secure this material," Ernst wrote. "He must have spent thousands of dollars in acquiring it, and he employed a regular net-work of spies to conduct his investigations. Probably no other living man would have either the means or the inclination to prosecute this inquiry as he did, nor would he have had the interest and the specialized knowledge to do so. All this rendered him the formidable antagonist . . . that he was."

In 1925, he began to put together this network in earnest. Houdini shrewdly realized that using women, especially women posing as widows, was the best strategy to weed out corrupt mediums. Houdini hired Rose Mackenberg, who ultimately became his chief investigator. In two years, she attended hundreds of séances and filed detailed field reports that described the premises, the audience, and the medium. She was ordained six separate times as a full-fledged spiritualistic reverend with the right to perform marriages, baptize infants, and bury the dead. It took her as little as twenty minutes and five dollars to obtain her certification. Because Rose became the subject of the amorous advances of so many trance mediums like Brooks, Houdini suggested she carry a gun for protection. She refused but, according to some reports, Houdini packed a derringer wherever he went.

In addition to Mackenberg, who would travel to a city ten days in advance of Houdini posing variously as a widow, a jealous wife, a factory worker, or a neurotic schoolteacher, Houdini employed female operatives who worked for him on an ad hoc basis when he came to a town. He used the services of a showgirl named Alberta Chapman who, along with a friend, infiltrated séances in Chicago. Houdini would drive with the girls until they were a block away from their destinations, and they would get out of the car and walk the rest of the way. Chapman was instructed to remember such minutiae as the number of doors and windows in the séance rooms, and what pictures hung on the walls. Sometimes it would take three trips to make a complete accounting. According to Alberta, if she ran into fortune-tellers who really believed in their hearts that they were doing good, she was to jettison the investigation. The ones who were "leading" her on became prime targets. When she left a house, she was to put a chalk mark on the side of the house or by the steps to commemorate her visit. She was laying the groundwork for future court cases.

Along with the women, who included Houdini's niece Julia Sawyer, a few men worked as secret operatives. Clifford Eddy Jr., a magazine writer who was collaborating with Houdini on a few literary projects, filed many field reports. Houdini even reached out to college students to pose as medium bait. Barkann Rosinoff, an undergraduate at the University of Pennsylvania, learned so much from Houdini's exposés that he was asked to demonstrate them for his fellow students at the college. He later became a magician and a member of the SAM.

Although not a formal member of the investigative team, an Ohio eccentric named Robert H. Gysel provided Houdini with invaluable inside information for his investigations. Gysel first came to Houdini's attention when he wrote the magician a letter while he was publishing *Conjurer's Monthly* in January of 1907, inquiring about the handcuff acts that magic dealers were selling. They forged a friendship, especially when Houdini realized that he and Gysel shared such diverse interests as escapes, poison resistance, cryptography, and scaling buildings without equipment.

By the 1920s, Gysel had been a practicing medium and had learned almost every trick in the séance room, including materializing dead wives for well-to-do bankers. In Michigan, he swindled a wealthy old lady out of $1,000. That night he stayed at a cheap hotel and, for the second time in his life, opened up a Bible that was on the dresser. The first words he saw were: "as ye sow, so shall ye reap."

"Goodnight I said, I quit reading and it made me think, well whoever wrote that line knew what he was talking about. I quit."

Gysel's knowledge was invaluable to Houdini, as was the extensive list of mediums that he generated. Using the name Joseph R. Johnson, he infiltrated

Houdini's niece Julia Sawyer (left) infiltrated séances when she wasn't performing onstage.

From the collection of Dr. Bruce Averbook

the inner circles of the summer camps where fraudulent mediums fleeced their credulous marks, who were derisively called "shut-eyes." At one point, he was one of the chief suppliers of magic effects to mediums who became too wise to buy their phosphorescent paint and other séance room supplies from conventional magic dealers.

By 1924, Gysel was busting up the work of other fraudulent mediums. He threw sneezing powder into the room at a séance by the Reverend Nina Challen. In the confusion, he caught her speaking through a spirit trumpet. When Houdini was unable to sit with Ada Besinnet, one of Doyle's favorite mediums, Gysel threw a brick into the séance room. He was so disruptive to the orderly business of Midwest mediums that the secretary of the Indiana Spiritualist Association wrote a friend that she'd like to "put poison" in his coffee. Gysel's expertise was invaluable during Houdini's investigation of Margery.

Mrs. Cecil Cook, the pastor of the W. T. Snead Memorial Center, was sitting in the middle of the basement room of the town house on West Eighty-eighth Street in Manhattan, and her audience, thirty-five in all, surrounded her in a circle. To her left, on a table, was a pan of water that contained two small tin trumpets.

After her attractive young assistant had circulated around the room and collected the $1 "donation," Mrs. Cook began her lecture.

"I am a trumpet medium," Cook began. "Through a power given me by the Lord, I am able to converse with dead spirits who manifest themselves through these trumpets."

She talked about the spirits for a few more minutes and then they dimmed the lights. The assemblage sang a hymn and shortly after, the first spirit came through. It was a Mr. Sten.

An old black woman in the audience perked up.

"Ask him about my operation," she said.

"*No, you don't have to take it,*" Mr. Sten replied.

"I have already been operated on once," the woman said.

"*You don't need it,*" Mr. Sten decided.

More spirits came and went. Some of the women were so moved after conversing with their dead husbands and children that they broke down in hysterical sobs.

A visitor named Mrs. Michaels spoke up next. "I've had some problems with my throat. What should I do?"

"*Why, you have tuberculosis,*" a spirit answered.

Mr. Sten suddenly interrupted. "*We have another spirit here. It is a young man named Alfred.*"

The old man sitting near Mrs. Michaels seemed startled.

"What did he say?" he asked his young attendant.

"Alfred," she repeated.

"Alfred?"

"Yes, your son."

"Your son, Alfred," Mrs. Cook spoke up.

"Is that Alfred, my son?" the old man said.

"*Is that you, Dad?*" Alfred said, speaking louder for the old man's benefit.

"Yes, yes, my son," the old man said.

"*Dad, you have had a very, very hard time but it is all over and I will take care of you and brighten up everything for you and make things comfortable,*" Alfred promised.

As Alfred was talking, the old man had gotten down on his knees and, aided by touching the knees of the people around him, was crawling toward the medium in the center of the circle, carrying a large electric flashlight. Just as he got within a few feet of Cook, the flashlight struck a pan of water, spilling some of its contents.

"What was that?" the medium suddenly said.

The old man quickly retreated back to his seat.

Mrs. Cook then turned toward Mrs. Michaels.

"Your brother Frank is calling you," she said, but when she got no response, she said, "No, it is your father."

"Ask Frank if I should go west," Mrs. Michaels said.

"*No, you need not make the journey,*" Frank told her. "*Drink plenty of milk and stay out in the fresh air.*"

Just then, the old man stood up and turned on his electric flashlight, shining it right at the medium's face. The women in the audience shrieked at the sight of the light, especially when it revealed that the medium was holding the trumpet up to her own mouth. Cook froze. Then she screamed so loudly that passersby on the street ran in to offer help. It was too late.

Mrs. Michaels leaped to her feet and turned on the overhead electric lights.

"You have the trumpet in your mouth," the old man shouted. "I thought the spirits were speaking."

Mrs. Cook threw her tin megaphone to the floor and then pitched over to one side, chair and all.

"You killed the medium!" one of Cook's admirers screamed at the old man and Mrs. Michaels as she rushed to her side.

"I'm killed! I'm killed!" Mrs. Cook shrieked, lying on her side with her eyes closed.

One of Mrs. Cook's male aides started advancing on the old man, who suddenly threw down his cane, jettisoned his thick eyeglasses, and pulled off his white wig.

"I am Houdini!" he shouted.

Now several of Cook's followers lunged at the magician but a large man intervened.

"I am Detective Joseph Greene and this is Policewoman Elizabeth Michaels. Nobody make a move."

All hell broke loose. Mrs. Cook, who had been helped to a chair by some of her followers, suddenly revived herself.

"You rascal," she shouted at Houdini.

"Rascal? You are getting money under religious disguise," Houdini shouted. "You spoke through the trumpet and these police officers are witnesses."

"I did not!" Cook said indignantly.

"You're a liar! She didn't have the trumpet," her assistant screamed.

Houdini just smiled, picked up his hat and cane, and walked briskly out of the room. Mrs. Cook and her assistant, Miss Benson, were taken to the station and charged with obtaining money under false pretenses and fortune-telling. Several of her followers accompanied her to the station and were dismayed when the police refused to allow her to post bail.

Houdini replicated this scene all around the country, following up the leads his investigators uncovered. In Cleveland, accompanied by a newspaper reporter and in disguise, Houdini smeared medium George Renner's trumpet with lampblack during the séance and shone his flashlight when he sensed the trumpets had been touched. In the light, Renner's face and hands were smeared with the black substance. Renner was found guilty.

Houdini even struck at the heart of his enemies' camps. For six years, he had been on the trail of a fraudulent spirit slate writer named Pierre Keeler. In 1925, he sent his very attractive niece Julia Sawyer up to Lily Dale in upstate New York, where Keeler was one of the featured mediums in residence. For three dollars, Julia got messages from a dead sister who never existed and from the spirits of two of her still-very-much-alive relatives. After the reading, she mentioned to Keeler that her wealthy uncle Bill was waiting for her at the railway station. Keeler accompanied her and after exchanging greetings, Uncle Bill, who was sitting in a wheelchair accompanied by a male nurse, whipped off his long white beard and revealed himself to be Houdini.

"I've got you Keeler," Houdini shouted. He reintroduced his "nurse," who was a New York reporter.

"Houdini, let me down easy," Keeler begged. "We're both in the same line."

If he was being shut out of séance rooms, Houdini enticed the mediums into his theater. At the beginning of his run in every town, Houdini would post a public notice. In Hartford, he ran the following: "HOUDINI CHALLENGES LOCAL MEDIUMS!—WARNING TO ALL ORGANIZATIONS OF SPIRITUALISTS—Instead of abusing me you ought to thank me for calling attention to your subordinates; if they are not giving charters on the level, STOP IT! I am not fighting the religion of Spiritualism, but there are a number of mediums in town, who claim they are more than human and have the power to communicate with the dead. I hereby challenge the following mediums who have taken money from my operator to come to PARSONS' THEATRE TO-NIGHT and take some more of my money." He then listed the mediums' names and addresses.

Some mediums even took the bait. In Indianapolis, Reverend Charles Gunsolas came onstage to answer Houdini's allegations. When he denied the account of Rose Mackenberg, a large number of detectives from the National Detective Agency as well as Houdini's private operatives stood in their seats in all parts of the theater and recited from their notarized accounts of their séances with Gunsolas. In Pittsburgh, Reverend Alice Dooley actually took up Houdini's challenge to have the spirits answer three of his questions that were placed before her in sealed envelopes. The answers were nonsensical and when Houdini exposed her as a fraud, a woman follower stood up in the balcony and precipitated a near riot by her hysterical ranting. Houdini had to promise to meet with the local mediums and test them under more favorable conditions.

Houdini's crusade drew unprecedented coverage. If he were in a city for a weeklong run, he would be the subject of front-page headlines every day of the run. Committed Spiritualists filled the papers with letters denouncing him as a charlatan and an Antichrist. Of course, all the attention was good for business, not only for Houdini. After the crusader denounced John Slater in Pittsburgh, the famous medium came to town and, riding Houdini's coattails, sold out Carnegie Music Hall.

Houdini was genuinely baffled at the reaction of the Spiritualists. "They are holding indignation meetings all over America against my exposé, but as long as they are not willing to give a demonstration before what I would call a qualified committee, I will stick to my guns!" he wrote to Harry Price, the English psychic researcher. "You know I am not a skeptic."

In fact, he was still looking for the one medium who could exhibit genuine powers. During Mrs. Cecil Cook's trial in New York, Houdini was asked by her attorney if he believed that everybody who practices or professes communications with the dead are fakers.

"No, sir, under no circumstances," he responded.

On a hot day in July 1925, Houdini and his secretary, Oscar Teale stormed into the offices of the Francis P. Houdina Company, a radio equipment firm, which was located on upper Broadway in Manhattan, not far from his house. According to Houdini's account, he was there to complain about some merchandise that was being charged to him, which he hadn't ordered or received. When he saw a tag on a packing case that was addressed to "Houdini," he tore it off and refused to return it to one of the employees.

George Young, one of the proprietors, had a different version of the story. He claimed that Houdini and his "father" had come to his office to complain that the company was using his name, spelled slightly different, to exploit their remote-control automobile enterprise. When he and a few of his workers tried to explain to Houdini that Francis Houdina was an inventor "of fifteen years standing," Houdini refused to listen.

Then all hell broke loose. "I had to protect myself," Houdini wrote to his pal Tommy Downs the following week. "You know the 'gorillas' here get a man on the floor and kick him insensible, cripple him and send him to the hospital. Two of the men started towards me and two were behind. Picked up a chair with such good results that they unlocked the door in a hurry and threw it wide open. You see they locked the door on me before they advanced, so that I should not get away. Teale was thrown up against the wall, staggering. Had no idea I was smashing up chandeliers. All I thought was to save myself. They have a charge of 'disorderly conduct' against me which is only a smoke screen to hide their real intentions."

The Houdina incident was not the first time that Houdini had seemed to have irrationally lost his temper in the last year. On his last trip to Los Angeles, he discovered that the theater manager where he was to perform had placed photos of two of his supporting acts in the newspapers and omitted his. "Lost my temper," he wrote in his diary. "I raised hell foolishly in Prazza office. All wrong on my part, *but I could not help it*. . . . I was so sore I had a headache all that afternoon."

When Houdini wound up his tour in mid-June 1925, his lawyer and intimate Bernard Ernst, noting that Houdini looked drained, persuaded Bess to take a summer rental in Glen Head, Long Island. At first, Houdini thought that it might be a place where he could do "some writing and thinking," but a cavalcade of invited relatives kept the house crowded all summer. "I have a four hour job of commuting every day, which upsets my 'equilibrium' as well as my business affairs," he wrote to a friend just a week into the rental. As it turned out, Houdini spent only about ten nights in Long Island the whole summer.

The affairs he was tending to might not only have been business-related. According to gossip circulating in the magic world, Houdini had been smitten with a stunning redhead named Daisy White, who worked behind the counter of the old Martinka's magic shop after Frank Ducrot, a friend of Houdini's, had purchased the business. A voluptuous vixen with "mocking green eyes," Daisy would enthrall her clientele by doing card effects, all the time bending over the counter and using her considerable cleavage as misdirection. Journalist Maurice Zolotow once quipped, "Houdini loved only two women, his mother and Daisy White."

Houdini's niece Marie Hinson Blood disclosed that Houdini would often "walk along the river in the early . . . evening" planning his next show and rejuvenating his "psyche." On one occasion, Bess had prepared his favorite dinner, Hungarian chicken, spaetzle, and custard bread pudding, then she and their little niece waited and waited but Houdini never showed up. The next day, Bess would explain to the young girl that Houdini "forgot about the dinner as he was walking and thinking and never thought about time." Invariably, a huge bunch of red roses would arrive the next day in an attempt to make amends. On August 2, Houdini, who was in a hotel in Boston, wrote Bess a strange note: "Honey Lamb Sweetheart It is 8 A.M. No one pay any attention to me you are not with me. So even though you do get a 'tantrum' and give me hell, I'd rather have you with me."

Houdini wrote to Kilby that he spent the summer "getting ready for my forthcoming season and battle with the spiritualists." He added, "They are sure panning H--- out of me, but consider it a compliment." He began to lecture about the tricks of phony mediums to 150 detectives and rookies in the New York Police Academy, but he still seemed obsessed with one medium back in Boston. Planning to publish an addendum to his Margery pamphlet, Houdini desperately needed to find out her latest moves in the séance room. He enlisted Kilby to do some investigations on Crandon's cronies and asked W. S. Griscom, a crack *Boston Herald* reporter, to keep him posted on the goings-on at Lime Street, giving Griscom his private phone number and telling him to call him "any night after midnight."

Houdini also used an undercover medium named George to investigate mediums, including Margery. The only correspondence from him to Houdini that survives is a rambling five-page letter that shows what serious business this had become. Tailed around New York, followed onto trains by private detectives, George pleaded with Houdini, noting that he had been providing him with valuable information. "Let me remind you I have *always* been on the level with you and others. If I were not on the level I would never have written so much about workers in my own handwriting and on my typewriter and in other ways mentioned certain things to you about workers. For one in my position to double-cross you, to betray you in *any* way would be tantamount to 'business' suicide. I know full well what you could do to me if I double-crossed you. It would be a comparatively easy matter for you to make all kinds of trouble for me by publishing what I wrote for you, you could also make trouble with the police even though my work is clean and on the level, and I never take money from poor people, or young girls, but give them good advice free, and lie to them and say the spirit says not to take the money."

In May, Houdini played Boston. While he was performing at Keith's, Dr. Crandon dispatched a rich businessman friend named Carl Dennett to report back on the show, which included a demonstration of Houdini's exposure of Margery. Dennett was vocal in defending Margery during the Q&A period and Houdini invited him back to his dressing room for further discussion. Dennett wrote Crandon that Houdini was "very anxious to find out who I was and arranged to have men follow me when I left his dressing-room but we were able to throw them off the trail, so that he could not learn my identity." The Crandon spy was wrong. A few days later, Houdini sent Dennett a scathing letter complaining about how the businessman had been misrepresenting their encounter all over Boston.

The *Herald*'s Griscom became an invaluable ally to Houdini. As a top local reporter, he was welcomed into the séance room and given a seat of honor next to Margery. Walter took an immediate liking to him and said that he wanted him to come back the next week whether the Crandons wanted him to or not. *"If you don't come, I won't,"* Walter pouted. Griscom's letters to Houdini are filled with good insights into her new manifestations and juicy gossip about her investigators. When the Crandons asked Griscom about Houdini, the reporter said that he liked him a lot and felt him sincere in his attitude to psychic research. "Well, I like and respect Houdini's attitude much more than most of the others," Margery said. "At least he's not afraid to say where he stands, which is more than most of the others will do."

Crandon and Walter didn't share Margery's opinion of Houdini. At the next séance Griscom attended, Crandon brought up the magician. "Houdini's exploded," he blustered. "He's done for." Walter immediately agreed. *"Yes, it's all over with Houdini, that faker; why, he tried to plant the kid. But he didn't get away with it, did he?"*

Ultimately Griscom told Houdini that the deeper he investigated, the more blatant the fraud became to him. "You . . . have to admit that they are damn clever magicians. You should get them in your show," he wrote. Houdini agreed that they were clever. "I believe she has improved and must work like a professional at the present time," he wrote back. To his mind, Dingwall "certainly must have given her a liberal education" in preparing for a "master séance."

While Houdini worked behind the scenes to penetrate the Crandon camp, Dr. Crandon employed several attack dogs to go after Houdini. J. Malcolm Bird began a cross-country lecture tour to publicize his book on the Margery mediumship and at every stop he lambasted Houdini for attacking Margery for mercenary reasons. Mark Richardson, a noted bacteriologist and an early advocate of Margery's cause, wrote countless letters to the other committee members, decrying that they never disassociated themselves from a rogue like Houdini. "I think we have Houdini on the run," a friend of Margery named Nola wrote the editor of *The Banner of Life,* a Spiritualist publication that continually blasted the magician. "From what I hear about town he is a nervous wreck. Says this is his last appearance in vaudeville and perhaps in Boston. Amen!"

Upholding the banner of the Spiritualist movement was making Margery even more of a nervous wreck. As early as April 1925, Dr. Crandon's sister wrote a confidential letter to J. Malcolm Bird. "My family doesn't know I am writing. Mrs. C[randon] is reaching her limit nervously—& the goose who lays the golden eggs is going to be killed unless there is some let up somewhere. She is threatening not to sit at all for any of you anymore . . . The doctor doesn't realize the nervous strain of having so many people there all the time. She is frightfully nervous."

On top of the constant strain to produce for a nightly coterie of important people, Doyle was sending messages to Boston that when the calamity came Crandon and Margery "will be the centre of American hopes." Doyle had often warned Crandon not to overtax the medium but Crandon flogged Margery relentlessly. After he brought Dingwall in for séances to counteract the negative *Scientific American* report, he immediately pushed her into sitting for a new group of Harvard students and professors after Dingwall failed to give her mediumship unmitigated praise.

By the time that Houdini played Boston in May, his spy network was already uncovering some damaging information on the Crandons. There had been allegations that Margery had slept with Carrington and had made advances on almost all of the male researchers, even the gray eminence Dr. Prince. According to Grant Code, one of the new Harvard researchers, who was also alleged to have slept with the medium, Houdini had actual photographic evidence of Margery's sexual dalliances. That was nothing, however, compared with the information his private secret service obtained about Dr. Crandon.

August 4, 1925

Dear Sir Arthur:

Here is a little problem for Sherlock Holmes: about December first I had Mr. DeWyckoffe bring over a boy from a London home for possible adoption. December 21 I sent him back as unfit. January first came Dingwall. January 19th McDougall told Dingwall not to believe the teleplasm that it was probably something "surgically manipulated". Four of the Harvard observers expressed an opinion in writing that the hand seen was something made or produced by me. In April 1925, our Secret Service Department at Washington received a letter saying that I had first and last sixteen boys in my house for ostensible adoption, and that they had all disappeared and advised the Department to look us up. Last week I had a telephone from the Boston manager of the White Star Line saying that an M.P. had sent a long questionnaire to the White Star Line at London concerning the going and alleged return of the English boy. It is quite apparent that there is an enemy here either Houdini or McDougall. It seems possible that there is an enemy in England (either McDougall or Dingwall). I will try to get the name of the M.P. In the meantime, ask Sherlock Holmes to think it over.

On August 10, 1921, according to a Boston newspaper clipping, Dr. Crandon's *sons*, ages ten and eight, were rescued from a raft at Winthrop. John Crandon, Margery's son, was the younger boy on that raft. The older boy was an English adoptee who was so unhappy at the Crandon household that he was trying to make his escape, bringing John with him. Two years later, when Margery began her mediumship, there was no trace of that boy in the household.

Beginning in early 1924, the good doctor reached out to his friends in the English Spiritualist world to be on the lookout for suitable boys to adopt. In June, Crandon told Doyle that he dispatched his sister Laura to England to "bring back to me a small boy whom we discovered there in December, whom we are going to adopt" by the name of Horace Newton. Crandon wasn't through, however. "We are in a state of mind to adopt still another at the same moment if he could be found: a boy six to nine years old, free from tuberculosis, syphilis, alcohol or insanity in the immediate parents. It occurs to me that it is possible that you or Lady Doyle may know of just such a boy whom we could get for adoption." Similar letters were sent to other friends.

Meanwhile, there were snags with the Horace Newton adoption. Horace was then residing at the National Children's Home and Orphanage, because his parents were dead. His sister was balking at allowing the adoption because of Dr. Crandon's demand that Horace be cut off from all communication with his family back home once the adoption went through. When Crandon backed off that demand, Iris, Horace's sister, gave her consent. Crandon dispatched Joe DeWyckoff, one of "the faithful circle," to pick up the boy and bring him back. "I want the boy brought in legally, of course, but for details in this matter I shall have to put the decision up to you, just as if you were doing it for yourself." Crandon's next letter to DeWyckoff amplified his agenda. "It occurs to me that if you get up against it legally in this matter your relations with the Financial Department of the Republican National Committee ought to be able to help. . . . We shall call the boy, if he comes, Edward Winslow Crandon. Perhaps you can get him in the way of responding to that. Tell him tactfully that it will be much pleasanter for him living in our house to have the same name as we have."

DeWyckoff tried to use his connections in Washington, making certain to keep the Crandons' name out of the talks. He didn't have much luck, so his new strategy was to bring Horace in as a visitor and at the end of the expiration of his visa, take him to Montreal and reenter using the quota law. Apparently, Horace came here on a visiting visa. He didn't last long at 10 Lime Street. At the end of December, Margery brought him aboard the S.S. *Doric* and shipped him back to England. According to Crandon's friend, the doctor of the ship, Horace/Edward Winslow had "quite a successful trip" being "very popular with everybody."

Crandon's letter to Doyle seven months later was the first time that the doctor acknowledged that he was being investigated in connection with a potential multiple missing persons case. He was absolutely right that Houdini had a hand in the matter. What Crandon didn't know was that Houdini had enlisted his newspaper friends at *The Boston Herald* to do some investigations of their own. On June 12, A. J. Gordon, Griscom's colleague, wrote Houdini. "The U.S. inspectors have been up to see me regarding the boys. Have you heard anything more from England on the matter. As soon as you do for[ward] the information to me, so that I may transmit it to thos[e] working on the story with me."

Twelve days later Griscom wrote Houdini, telling him: "Gordon wants me to ask you . . . what you are doing to find out about that boy in New Jersey. This . . . particularly interests us." At one time, the body of a "homeless" boy had been found on the fringes of the vast estate that Margery inner circle member Joseph DeWyckoff maintained in Ramsey, New Jersey.

Doyle responded to Crandon's letter to Sherlock Holmes by asking him to find out the name of the British M.P. so Doyle could make inquiries. "I seem to see the hand of the Roman Catholic Church and not of a private individual, but perhaps Watson speaks not Holmes," he wrote. Four months earlier, he had written Crandon suggesting that the same Vatican hand had enlisted Houdini through his Catholic wife.

Strangely, many of the letters to Doyle regarding the investigation into the boys have been expunged from Crandon's files, an anomaly for a man who seemed to keep every last newspaper clipping about Margery's mediumship. We do have Doyle's side of the correspondence, and it reveals that Doyle was continuously asking Crandon for more information. On August 22, Doyle found out the name of the M.P. and was beseeching Crandon: "I am not clear how many boys have gone across. You will let me have the facts. . . ." On September 1, he wrote Crandon again with some background information on the British politician spearheading the probe. "I want all the information you can give me about the boys and I will then be in a position to tackle him [the M.P.] if the occasion should arise."

Doyle did take up Crandon's defense to the M.P. In his first letter to the politician he wrote, "I am sure that you would not wish to act as the unconscious agent of any personal enemy, so I should be extremely obliged if you would permit me to tell [Crandon] how the matter arose." After more correspondence, the M.P. was put in direct contact with Crandon. Crandon wrote him explaining that he had adopted Horace Newton, "an attractive boy, an orphan in an institution" but the boy "did not seem to fit in our household" and was sent back. "In return for this information . . . I beg you to tell me who was interested to find out these facts. Your communication I will give you my word to keep private and personal. For my good faith, I beg to refer you to Mr. George E. O'Dell, through whom I was introduced not long ago to Mr. Ramsey MacDonald." MacDonald was the former prime minister of England and then current head of the Labour Party to which this M.P. belonged.

While waiting for the answer, Crandon wrote Sherlock Holmes again. He deduced that a British M.P. would "only pay attention to a request from a Britisher." So that narrowed down his suspects to McDougall, Dingwall, and possibly Maskelyne, the British magician who was a chum of Houdini. At that point, Crandon concluded it was McDougall. Crandon was no Sherlock Holmes. The British M.P. wrote him back informing him that it would be "a breach of confidence were I to disclose the names of those who called my attention to the original circumstances." That M.P. was none other than Mr. Harry Day, one of Houdini's closest friends for more than twenty years.

If he didn't have enough trouble, now Crandon saw the entire credibility of Margery's mediumship in deadly peril when the Harvard investigators issued their report at the end of October. What the doctor didn't know was that Houdini spy and *Herald* reporter Griscom was instrumental in forcing the Harvard people into their condemnation with his behind-the-scenes tactics. When he learned that one researcher's account of the sittings was about to be published in *Atlantic* magazine, he convinced Crandon to show him the official reports of the Harvard committee's séances, giving Crandon a chance for damage control before the magazine article hit the stands. Griscom told Houdini that his purpose was twofold: one, to get a scoop for his newspaper, and, two, to create such "a stink" that the scientists on the committee would have to "talk in self-defense." Griscom spent two days at Lime Street, poring over the records, and having many interesting talks with the medium.

Griscom's plan worked to a tee. His newspaper account stated that the Harvard preliminary report, which the reporter played up as a final report and which was signed by the junior researchers, stated that the investigators, while discounting supernormal phenomena, all agreed that the Crandons acted in good faith. When the bigwig Harvard professors on the committee heard that, they immediately issued a statement accusing the Crandons of fraud, a statement that was signed by three of the four men who issued the original nonfraud summary.

While perusing Crandon's official séance reports, Griscom stumbled upon an interesting entry. In the séance of June 30, one of the Harvard investigators saw Margery draw three objects from the region of her vulva. One was not described. One was shaped like a flat hand or a glove. The third resembled a baby's hand.

Griscom's letter to Houdini on the eve of Halloween was jubilant. "This is really all a great triumph for you. 'Margery' said to me the other day, 'Just think how Houdini will shout. He will say that he discovered in one sitting what it took the Harvard crowd eight sittings to find out.'" (Margery was wrong.

Houdini wrote his friends that it took the Harvard investigators six months to accomplish what he did in one night.)

"I answered that of course you would, and also you would be able to say you discovered the methods she used, too. As a matter of fact, Houdini, I am convinced, and so is Gordon and absolutely all of the Harvard crowd, that Dr. Crandon himself has a double personality in all this business. In other words, he is a sincere believer and at the same time overlooks or participates in the trickery. As the Harvard people say, he has amnesia, is cuckoo, nuts or what have you.

"I also believe that 'Margery' might take a chance and confess if Crandon did not firmly believe. She knows it would end all their relations and she doesn't dare do it. She and I had a private conference the other afternoon and I advised her to admit it was all a hoax. She smiled broadly and asked how she could when it wasn't true. Then she said, with a grin, 'Aren't people damn fools. Such damn fools. The investigators most of all. I should like to write a book about investigators. Do you know, some of them say they hear voices and all that sort of stuff.'

"I agreed and she went on, 'I respect Houdini more than any of the bunch. He has both feet on the ground all the time.' That was somewhat significant. It was significant in another way, too, because 'Walter' had said exactly that about me in a sitting a week earlier. Funny how 'Walter' and 'Margery' use the same phrases and think so exactly alike.

"Although she had never actually confessed, when we are alone it is tacitly admitted between us that the mediumship is all trickery. I think she respects me on exactly the same grounds that she does you, because we weren't taken in by her. But not Crandon. He is a fanatic on the subject, and can't be argued with. He is now trying to get the Massachusetts Institute of Technology to start a new investigation. He wouldn't do that if he wasn't crazy."

Dorothy Young was a seventeen-year-old tourist in New York City when she answered an ad in *Variety* for a "girl dancer for Broadway show and tour of the United States." She jettisoned her parents and went to the Longacre Theatre, where she was the last to audition. She did a Charleston and she was hired on the spot. At the time, Dorothy had no idea who Houdini was, but he told her that he had been famous for years and this was his dream—the chance to star in his own Broadway show. She signed a contract, went with Bess to choose materials for her costume, and then ran into her parents, who absolutely forbade her to go. Houdini then set up a meeting with her minister father and her mother.

He promised to look after Dorothy as if she were his own daughter, so she was allowed on the tour.

On the train to the first show, Houdini called her into his private car, sat her down, and talked to her all about his life. He even did some magic for her. After a while, it was time for dinner and the two of them joined the others in the dining car. "I remember the expression on Mrs. H's face when he came back from talking to me. I didn't like the expression," Dorothy said. "So when we were having dinner, as young as I was, I made up my mind, 'Mrs. H will be my friend, not Houdini.'"

She described their year touring as the most wonderful year in her life. In contrast to many people in the magic community who, without ever having met Houdini, dismissed him as an arrogant egomaniac, Dorothy thought that he was "so kind, so thoughtful." She never saw him turn down a person who needed money, telling her, "I'll never forget what it is to be without money." They also shared a belief in the "hereafter," Dorothy remembered. Houdini told her that he was trying to contact his mother. "I know it's impossible," he said, "but if there's any way at all, I will do it."

According to Dorothy, even though Houdini adored Bess, she thought it was "strange" that she never saw any tenderness expressed between the two of them. Houdini was all business, working all day with Collins on the show, having a communal dinner with Bess, his nieces, and Dorothy, and then going back to work on the business end of the show with Mr. Smith, his tour manager. That left the days open and Bess and Dorothy became running partners. Bess was a "funny duck," a real "free spirit," who shocked Dorothy when she gave her an introductory course in sex education. Every day they'd go out shopping, one time even buying matching fur coats, and then they'd lunch together and just laugh at "anything." One time they came back from their day's excursion with chameleons on leashes.

When they were playing in Buffalo, Bess and Dorothy rented a car and went to Niagara Falls. On the Canadian side of the border, on a whim, Bess decided to buy a bottle of liquor and smuggle it into the United States, which by then had been dry for three years. They succeeded. That night at dinner someone mentioned their brush with the law. It was "the only time I remember Houdini really getting angry," Dorothy told us. "His eyes snapped and he said, 'Do you realize the adverse publicity we would have had if they had found that liquor?'"

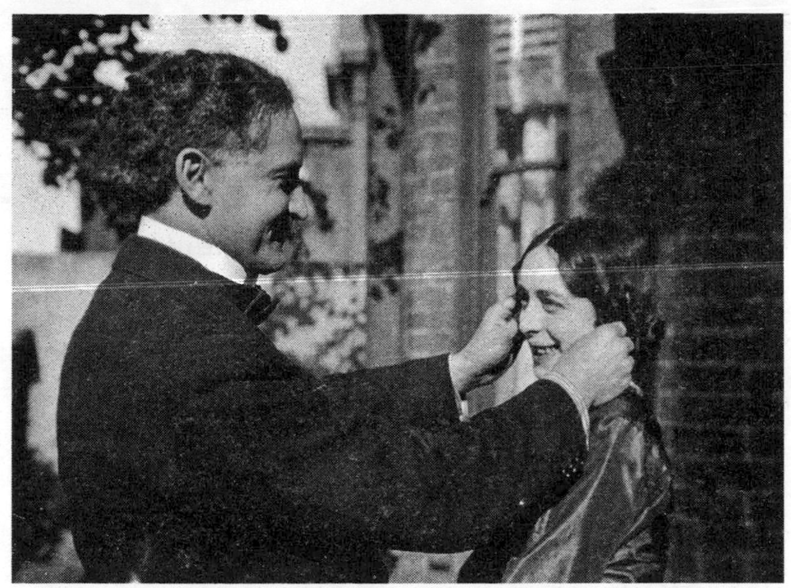

According to Dorothy Young, affectionate displays like this were less frequent later in the Houdinis' marriage. *From the collection of Dr. Bruce Averbook*

Houdini was only a few minutes into his exposé of fraudulent mediums—the third act in his one-man *Houdini* revue—when he was interrupted by a local Worcester, Massachusetts, man.

"You don't know what you're talking about," Armstrong LeVeyne, the husband of a local medium, shouted.

"Then come up here and tell the audience," Houdini suggested. LeVeyne ambled up to the stage.

"History repeats itself," he began. "Christ was persecuted and now we Spiritualists are being persecuted. Some day, as in the case of Christ, the people will see the light!"

"But Christ never robbed people of $2, did he?" demanded Houdini.

"Your tricks are frauds," shouted LeVeyne. "You are duping the public exactly as you claim Spiritualists are."

"I studied years to do what I'm doing," Houdini countered. "The people know I am deceiving them. I give them optical illusions for entertainment, part of which is derived from their efforts to discover how I do it. I challenge you to duplicate my feat with the locked water tank or any other of my tricks."

LeVeyne refused. The audience hissed him.

"Letty LeVeyne was my mother. She was a famous Australian vaudeville star—the greatest woman who ever lived. I loved my mother. I love my wife. I am here today to protect my wife. My wife is a member of the National Spiritualist Alliance, and she is backed by it. She is backed by law. She is backed by the people, and she is backed by the White House. She will give a demonstration at any time of her psychic ability, an endowment given her by the Deity."

"All right, let her perform here," Houdini countered. "The public is here, eager to see her perform."

"This is not the place. We need a church," LeVeyne shouted. "How can this be considered a church even for a few minutes when so many women appear on stage half-dressed?"

For a moment it looked like Houdini was going to jump across the stage and attack LeVeyne. The audience broke out into derisive boos and hissing. Then Houdini called Bess and her niece Julia Sawyer from out of the wings.

"Folks, this is my wife, Mrs. Houdini, to whom I have been married thirty-one years. And this is Miss Sawyer, my niece. Have you anything to say against their characters?"

"No. They're all right," someone in the audience shouted. "It's LeVeyne who's all wrong."

That was too much for Mrs. LeVeyne. She stood up from her seat.

"But what do you know about them?" she screamed.

The audience ignored her as Houdini held up his hands.

"Now I want you to hear the testimony of Reverend F. Raud."

Houdini pointed toward a woman in a side box who had just stood up. She was dressed all in black and wearing a long black veil that completely covered her face.

"This is one of my investigators. She goes by the name of Frances Raud, but we call her F. Raud for short. F-R-A-U-D. She is disguising herself tonight because we have had reports that there are a number of photographers who are in attendance tonight with the explicit purpose of taking her photograph. At present, she is unknown to the mediums so she can continue her investigations."

Houdini turned to the LeVeynes.

"I am greater than you are. I own a church. See, here are my certificates and my charter," he said, pulling out some papers from a folder on a table next to him onstage. "They prove that I own a church. And Miss Raud is its pastor. So Reverend Fraud, please tell the audience your experience with Mrs. LeVeyne."

When children were too ill to come to his show, Houdini brought it to them.
Library of Congress

"This woman told me that my dead husband and dead child were together in the spirit world and were endeavoring to communicate with me," Mackenberg said. "I asked her how she got these messages and she told me that her spirit guides had given them to her. I thanked her and offered her a dollar but she said her price for a reading was two dollars, which I paid her. I have never been married, nor had any children."

"I never saw this woman," Mrs. LeVeyne screamed from her seat.

"Now you said in the papers you were coming here to accept my challenge," Houdini told Mrs. LeVeyne. "Will you keep your promise?"

"The law says religion must not be commercialized," she answered.

"Just collect the two dollars," someone in the audience shouted.

Rose Mackenberg resumed her speech, but when she mentioned that she had purchased the charter to Houdini's church from Hubert O'Malley, one of the area's leading spiritualistic mediums, the theater became a bedlam.

"Get him, make him prove something," people shouted. It took a full five minutes to restore order.

Then LeVeyne jumped to his feet.

"Our Spiritualist Church will hold an indignation meeting next Sunday," he shouted.

"I drove out the fakes in California and I intend to drive them out of Massachusetts," Houdini boasted.

The audience cheered.

"You are not a God yet!" LeVeyne shouted over the din.

"No, but I know a great deal about mediums," Houdini replied.

"I'll protect my wife—" LeVeyne began.

"And I'm protecting the public," Houdini finished.

The audience cheered lustily.

It was like that every night of his run in Worcester in December 1925. The Spiritualist segment that closed the show had evolved into a surrealistic town meeting where mediums and Houdini shouted each other down. It hadn't hurt the box office. Houdini was selling every seat he could, except for the matinees, when he made sure there were blocks of free tickets distributed to the city's crippled children or orphans.

24

I . . . Am a Fake

"WHAT IS YOUR FULL NAME?" THE gentleman from Michigan inquired.

"My name is Harry Houdini."

"What is your business?"

"I am an author; I am a psychic investigator for the scientific magazines of the world; and then I am a mysterious entertainer."

He had created a great legend and became the most famous entertainer alive. Now he was transforming himself into a public advocate. This should have been the acme of Houdini's career, one of his proudest moments. He was sitting behind a table in the caucus room of the House office building in Washington, D.C., giving expert testimony with respect to proposed legislation that would ban people from "pretending to tell fortunes for reward or compensation" or "pretending to unite the separated." He wasn't just testifying, though; he was actually instrumental in getting the bill drafted, working closely with his old friend Sol Bloom, who had gone from organizer of the Midway Plaisance at the Chicago World's Fair to music industry mogul to U.S. congressman. This was the culmination of Houdini's crusade against fraudulent mediums, his own stage in the nation's capital where our esteemed legislators could join with him in dealing with this menace to public order. Instead, it had devolved into a three-ring circus.

The hearing room was packed with a motley group of Spiritualists, mediums, clairvoyants, gypsies, and astrologers. They filled up every chair and squatted in the aisles, peppering Houdini with a constant barrage of verbal abuse, ethnic slurs, and threats. The entire four-day hearings in February and May 1926 were an exercise in the theater of the absurd. Houdini gave demonstrations of slate writing and spirit trumpet manifestations to the congressmen. Senator Fletcher's wife testified and claimed that in thirty-five years of psychic research she had never encountered a phony medium. Houdini flashed $10,000 in U.S. currency as a challenge to any medium to tell him what his father had nicknamed him, then Madame Marcia jumped up and screamed, "That money belongs to me! I predicted the election of President Harding and his death."

A Spiritualist named Charles William Myers took the witness stand and, referring to Houdini and Bloom, declaimed, "In the beginning . . . 2,000 years ago, Judas betrayed Christ. He was a Jew, and I want to say that this bill is being put through by two—well, you can use your opinion."

Reverend H. P. Strack, the secretary of the National Spiritualists Association of America, speaking of Houdini, was shocked that anyone would heed the words of "a pronounced atheist and infidel."

After being insulted by witness after witness from the Spiritualist camp, Houdini requested to make a statement.

"My religion and my belief in the Almighty has been assailed. . . . I have always believed and I will always believe. I am a Mason, and you must believe in God to be a Mason. My character has been assailed. I would like to have as a witness here Mrs. Houdini."

To the laughter of the crowd, Bess stepped forward.

"One of the witnesses said I was a brute and that I was vile and I was crazy. . . . I will have been married, on June 22, 32 years to this girl. . . . There are no medals and no ribbons on me, but when a girl will stick to a man for 32 years as she did and when she will starve with me and work with me through thick and thin, it is a pretty good recommendation. Outside of my great mother, Mrs. Houdini has been my greatest friend. Have I shown traces of being crazy, unless it was about you?"

The audience laughed.

"No," Bess testified.

"Am I brutal to you, or vile?"

"No."

"Am I a good boy?"

"Yes."

"Thank you, Mrs. Houdini," he said dramatically. The hearing room filled with applause.

One of the few substantive moments of the hearings came when Rose Mackenberg was called to testify about her encounters with Mrs. Jane Coates and Madame Grace Marcia, two of Washington's most notorious mediums. The congressmen actually allowed the two corpulent ladies, who had been sitting in

Houdini poses with two famous mediums and a bevy of Congressmen before all hell breaks loose at the fortune-telling bill hearings in Washington, D.C. *From the collection of Roger Dreyer*

the front row, to stand on either side of Houdini's chief investigator. According to *The Chicago Daily Tribune* reporter, if looks could kill, their looks "would have seriously injured, if not destroyed the existence of Miss Rose Mackenberg."

Mackenberg began to recount her experiences of the previous day at the two mediums' houses, Houdini prompting her as if he were a prosecuting attorney. Rose had just testified that Mrs. Coates had told her that "most of the senators did consult astrologers," when the medium inched a little closer to the investigator.

"I insist that Mrs. Coates keep away from the witness," Houdini said. "What did she tell you about the White House and séances being there?"

"I object!" Coates screamed. "You are talking about me. Mr. Chairman, I demand the right to answer this."

The gallery erupted into cheers.

"You will have an opportunity to be heard," Congressman McLeod said.

"I suggest we finish with Madame Marcia first," Congressman Houston said, trying to keep some logical thread to the testimony.

"I am ill and I have something to say," Coates insisted.

"Madam Marcia told me her charge and I asked her if she would not accept less than $10. She said $10 or nothing; in fact, $15 for a written horoscope and $10 for the other. She said a number of Senators were coming to her for readings; in fact, almost all the people in the White House believed in spiritualism, and that she was very much chagrined to think that I was trying to reduce her fee from what she asked," Mackenberg testified.

Bedlam broke out. Mediums were shrieking, Spiritualists had jumped to their feet, arguing with the smaller number of Houdini partisans.

Representative Hammer, a gentleman from North Carolina, looked perturbed as he banged his gavel and pleaded for order. The crowd finally quieted down.

"While I was at Madam Coates's place she said Houdini was up against a stone wall. She said, 'Why try to fight spiritualism, when most of the Senators are interested in the subject? I have a number of Senators who visit me here, and I know for a fact that there have been spiritual séances held at the White House with President Coolidge and his family, which proves that intercommunication with the dead is established.' Then she mentioned the name of Senator Capper, saying his wife had died recently, and that he attended spiritualistic séances. She also mentioned Senator Watson, Senator Dill, and Senator Fletcher, whose wife is a medium. . . ."

With each name, the clamor increased.

"Liar!" "Faker!" "Traducer!" the audience shouted.

Finally, there was too much commotion for Mackenberg to continue. The two mediums looked like they wanted to pounce on the undercover operative and began to advance menacingly toward her. Representative Hammer made them sit down.

Meanwhile, John Ferguson, a fishmonger from Dayton, Ohio, advanced on Houdini, who had earlier made disparaging remarks about his medium wife.

"I'll break your nose," he threatened, and was about to throw a punch just as Representative Hammer threw himself between the two men.

"Gentlemen, *if* you are gentlemen, must act as gentlemen," Hammer said.

On the verge of tears, Hammer then called in the police, who finally restored order.

Yet on the last day of the hearings, Hammer engaged Houdini in a bizarre line of questioning.

"The original Houdini was a Hindu, was he not?" the congressman asked.

"No," Houdini replied.

"You are Houdini the second?"

"No."

"You are the original Houdini?"

"No, the original Houdini was a French clock maker."

"I thought he lived in Allahabab," Hammer said.

"Are you joking?"

"No, I am in earnest. . . . You said the other day that you were president of the Magicians Association of America."

"Society of American Magicians," Houdini corrected him.

"Is it a secret organization?"

"No, only regarding our exploits."

"Have you branches in foreign countries? In Russia?"

"Not in Russia," Houdini said.

"Have you ever been in British India?"

"Never in my life, no sir."

"Were both of your parents Hebrews?"

"Yes, sir . . ."

"Is your father living?"

"No, sir. Has this anything to do with this bill?"

"No, but—"

"I know that you are asking spiritualistic questions and I want to let you know that I know it," Houdini flared.

"No, I have been told that your people came from British India. That is all I was trying to find out. It is contended here that you are a medium and do not know it. These people really believe that you have divine power and that you won't admit it. That is the reason I am asking you these questions."

"Pardon me," Houdini said.

"Have you ever been to Allahabab?"

"No, sir."

"You have read the *Arabian Nights* stories?"

"Yes, sir."

"But you have never been there?"

"No, sir."

"Where were you in 1925?"

"In America."

"You were not out of America that year?"

"Yes, sir."

"Did you do any work in Alaska at any time?"

"No, sir."

"Did you ever know a man by the name of Hugh Weir, on *Collier's* magazine?"

"Never heard the name before," Houdini said.

"Did you ever know a man by the name of D'Alory Fechett, a celebrated Frenchman in Paris?" Hammer asked.

"Not that I know of."

"Is William J. Burns a member of your association?"

Suddenly a significant question. Burns was a former Secret Service operative and Bureau of Investigation chief who had formed one of the largest private detective agencies under his name. Houdini had used his agency for his spiritualistic investigations. Burns was also, ironically, a friend of Conan Doyle's.

"He may—" Houdini began but was interrupted by his niece Julia Sawyer, who was there to testify about her undercover operations against mediums.

"No," she said flatly.

"She knows every member of the organization," Houdini added.

"Have you any relation and has your association anything to do with the movie association and theatre association of America?" Hammer asked. "These questions I am asking you were not inspired by any Spiritualists."

"You did not get those out of the air," Houdini fumed. "Why are you asking me those peculiar, irrelevant questions? They haven't anything to do with the bill and are not the kind of questions that a man in your position would ask. They were given to you by some rabid medium and I am surprised that you should ask me same. You did not make them up yourself. You did not get them out of your head."

"That is all right as to where I got them, but I did not get them from any spiritualist, and I did not get them from any divine power either, because I do not claim that God makes revelations to me. . . . Did you have anything to do with numerology? Do you know anything about it? The figure 3, you know, as numerology says, represents a serpent."

"I do not believe in that truck—in numerology."

"You do not believe in that any more than you do in astrology or fortune-telling or soothsaying?"

"All in the same junk basket," Houdini said.

"There is none of that in any of your performances? It is all really tricks and sleight of hand?"

"Yes, sir."

"I am very much obliged to you," Hammer concluded.

At the close of the last day of hearings, Madame Marcia approached Houdini in the corridors of the House of Representatives.

"You're a smart man, Mr. Houdini," she began. "But perhaps I can tell you something you don't know."

"What's that, Madame Marcia?" he asked genially.

"When November comes around, you won't be here."

"How's that?" He grinned.

"You'll be dead," she said.

Mackenberg didn't escape the ire of the Spiritualists either. During her testimony, Jane Coates suggested that she saw right through the "widow" who came for a reading. "You are doing a work that is killing you," she told Mackenberg at their sitting. "In your heart you are sick of the whole dirty job and if you don't stop it, you will not live 18 months."

Rose Mackenberg's startling testimony of séances in the White House and Spiritualism in the Senate rocked Washington. The White House didn't deign to comment but "friends of the Coolidges" assured the press corps that "neither the president or Mrs. Coolidge is interested in spiritualism." The following day's *Washington Post* headlined "Houdini Expreses Regret to Coolidge—Leaves Letter Deploring Yarn About 'Seances Held at White House.'" It was a misleading headline; it reported that Houdini personally hand-delivered a letter to Coolidge at his executive offices that expressed regret that the president's name had been dragged into the hearings. In actuality, the article accurately noted that Houdini's letter contained Rose Mackenberg's affidavit of her conversations with the mediums. Houdini himself was quoted, "Believe me, it was no desire of mine to embarrass the President, but I have spent a large portion of my time and fortune in this fight against fraudulent mediums and I am accustomed to accept the facts without garnishment, no matter how unpleasant they may be." In other words, he couldn't sugarcoat the fact that mediums had penetrated into the upper echelons of the Washington political scene.

Can it be a mere coincidence that the senator who controlled the Senate side of the committee responsible for the fortune-telling bill, Senator Capper, was named by Mackenberg as a devotee of séances and that to this day the Senate hearings on that bill have never been published by the Government Printing Office? According to contemporary newspaper reports, the Senate hearings were just as raucous and contentious as the House ones. In August, Houdini wrote a friend to report that his bill "has not reached Congress as yet and I do not know what will happen to it, unless the Senators are interested, and I think that they are. I think they were more interested in my manifestations than they were in the mediums. I was sorry to see that, as I really am sincere about the law." With Mackenberg naming names of prominent senators connected with the Spiritualist movement, it's not a surprise that the bill died in committee.

Houdini had begun his campaign against mediums in the nation's capital by pleading with President Coolidge back in January of 1926 to throw his "vast influence" with the campaign to abolish the "criminal practices" of spirit mediums, but after his own investigation he was convinced that the president and his wife were believers and that he could prove his case. They certainly fit the profile, having recently lost a son. After the hearings, Houdini wrote his friend the journalist Walter Lippmann, who had been the special assistant to the secretary of war during World War I. "Sorry to tell you that I have heard on rather good authority that they do hold séances in the White House and am looking for further proof regarding same. This is, of course, in strict confidence."

Houdini's campaign against fraudulent mediums was costing him more than $40,000 a year out of pocket, "rather a large sum for private individual to lay out for this subject," he wrote Harry Price. How could he *not* wage this war, though?

"I believe the work I am doing is the greatest humanitarian achievement of my life," he told a reporter. "I have spent many hours on the stage and public rostrum but now I am helping to alleviate the years of worry that is driving many to the brink of insanity by their inordinate desire to communicate with the dead." Thinking ahead to retirement, he had Bess look for property on their last trip to Los Angeles. His plan was to finally build a bus that could be converted to a small stage, seating almost two hundred. Then he would "tour California taking his fight against spooks and their accomplices to the smaller towns."

The banner year of his crusade was 1926. In January, in New York, he exposed the Reverend John Hill, who manifested Rose Mackenberg's dead "husband," who wept and knelt before her. Houdini was particularly proud of this catch; Hill was the "self-claimed private medium to the Vanderbilts, Harrimans, Honeywells, Huntingtons and other prominent New York families," he boasted. In February, he canceled one of his own lectures to attend a mass meeting of Spiritualists in Philadelphia who came to hear Malcolm Bird lecture on the Margery case.

Houdini, still seething from the implication in Bird's book that he was a bastard, leaped onto the platform and launched a shrill attack on Bird. "You liar,

Houdini offering the $10,000.00 prize in print. *From the collection of Roger Dreyer*

you contemptible liar," he shrieked at the cowering journalist. "You lied in your book when you said my father was not married to my mother. Ladies and Gentlemen, in his book he said Houdini had his hands soiled and said that is his trouble, that my father was—now, do I look like a man like that. If a man would have said that to me I would clean the floor up with him, and so would any other man who loved and respected his mother."

Houdini's campaign peaked in Chicago during an incredible eight-week stay at the Princess Theatre. Adding Ruth Mason and Lillian Stuart to his team of spies, Houdini unmasked more than eighty local mediums, some in spectacular fashion. The Spiritualists struck back. In addition to threatening his life, they inundated him with frivolous slander suits. Before he left town, he won a victory in the first case. His greatest victory, though, was the surprise visit to his dressing room from a stocky, matronly woman named Annie Benninghofen. Before she married, she had been known as Anna Clark, the "mother medium," the woman responsible for mentoring Cecil Cook, the trumpet medium who Houdini had unmasked in New York. Benninghofen had been so moved by Houdini's civic campaign and her own remorse that she offered to do anything to help him to stamp out the menace.

"I really believed in Spiritualism all the time I was practicing it," she told Houdini. "But I thought I was justified in helping the spirits out. They couldn't float a trumpet around the room, I did it for them. They couldn't speak, so I spoke for them. I thought I was justified in trickery because through trickery I could get more converts to what I thought was a good and beautiful religion." Benninghofen's public refutation of Spiritualism prompted death threats from her one-time brethren.

Houdini's show was in three acts now, a veritable greatest hits extravaganza. The first act featured his production of silks from a fishbowl and the original Dr. Lynn dismemberment illusion he had been entranced by as a child in the Midwest. The second act was highlighted by his now-famous Water Torture Cell escape. The Spiritualist debunking was the third and final act. By now Houdini had refined the portion of his show that dealt with Spiritualism to an entertaining romp through a gallery of rogues and their underhanded methods. "I have all reason to believe that this is the most important part of the evening's entertainment and long after you have forgotten everything that has gone before I feel certain you will not forget some of the things said and done in the next thirty or forty-five minutes," he began.

Reminding the audience of his $10,000 challenge to any medium, he reveled in the lawsuits and threatened to expose "every last one" of Chicago's three hundred mediums. Then he gloated about Margery. "I caught Margery, the medium in Boston, the most wonderful medium that ever medied . . . Bird wrote voluminous articles about her . . . I detected her the first night and exposed her and called her a fraud, but [the professors] had been examining her for one year, and a year later they apologized to me. . . . They admitted they were wrong. They were gentlemen. When I walked into the séance room and saw that beautiful blonde, her applesauce meant nothing to me. I have been through apple orchards. And they call that a religion?"

With each new assault, the spiritualists countered back with lawsuits and indignation meetings. Houdini became the focal point of all their opposition, not only in America but also across the globe. Just a few months earlier, a delegate to the International Spiritualist Congress in Paris had moved for strong action to protect psychic workers because "at the instigation of a certain magician, some of our best mediums, principally in Boston, have been prevented from holding séances." A British resolution to protect the seers from charges of fraud and insanity was adopted enthusiastically.

They also countered with vicious letters attacking Houdini. "I get letters from ardent believers in spiritualism, who prophesy I am going to meet a violent death soon as a fitting punishment for my nefarious work," he told a magazine writer.

The first leg of Houdini's 1926 tour ended in May, giving him almost four months away from the stage. "Am going to lay off . . . and do nothing but investigate and look into these fraudulent medium affairs," he wrote a friend. He also found time for other, related projects. In August, he exposed a different kind of mystic. Hereward Carrington, his nemesis on the Margery committee, was promoting a young "Egyptian" fakir named Rahman Bey, who claimed that he possessed supernormal powers that were able to help him achieve marvelous feats like arresting his pulse, piercing his cheeks with needles without bleeding, and cheating death by having himself buried alive in an airtight coffin. While the young mystic performed the feats, Carrington provided an ongoing commentary on the young man's mastery of yogic power and "cataleptic trance."

What was particularly galling to Houdini was that he had already exposed these so-called miraculous feats in the pages of his book *Miracle Mongers and Their Methods*. After going with Rinn to see Bey perform, Houdini issued a challenge. "I guarantee to remain in any coffin that the fakir does for the same length of time he does, without going into any cataleptic trance." His job got a little tougher when Bey duplicated his own burial stunt in the Dalton swimming pool, where he stayed submerged for a full hour. On August 5, before a prestigious invitation-only audience, Houdini entered the pool area of the Shelton Hotel. He submitted to a quick exam by a physician, who pronounced him fit but who worried that he could only survive in a sealed box of that dimension for three to four minutes.

Houdini immersed in a coffin in the pool of the Shelton Hotel. *Library of Congress*

"If I die, it will be the will of God and my own foolishness," he told the assemblage. "I am going to prove that the copybook maxims are wrong when they say that a man can live but three minutes without air—and I shall not pretend to be in a cataleptic state either." Stripped down to trunks, he stepped into a specially built, but not gimmicked, galvanized iron casket that was lowered into the pool. Despite some additional weights that had been added, eight swimmers had to stand on top of the casket to keep it submerged. Even still, one lost his balance and the coffin shot up out of the pool. It was quickly resubmerged.

Houdini managed to stay in the coffin for more than an hour and a half. Despite a three-week-long vigorous workout regimen that burnished him into top shape for a fifty-two-year-old, Houdini emerged exhausted, irritable, and with grossly abnormal vital signs. According to one eyewitness he looked "deathly white." Once at home, he wrote the details of his experiment for a physiologist with the U.S. Bureau of Mines, cognizant that his experience might help trapped miners. He still had a metallic taste in his mouth and felt weak, but disregarding his mother-in-law's pleas to get some rest, went off to the YMCA, where he spent an hour playing handball and sprinting on the indoor track.

On his summer break Houdini turned his energies to his library and his literary output. He weekended at his lawyer Bernard Ernst's Sea Cliff, Long Island, summer home and carried a trunkful of scraps and notes for various book projects involving magic, imploring Ernst for his assistance. One of these might have been his autobiography, sections of which had been completed and are unfortunately lost. He even began work on a novella, tentatively titled *Lucille*, which featured the ultimate villain—a man who possessed an insider's knowledge of magic. He had begun collaborating with the horror writer H. P. Lovecraft on a number of magazine stories and with Oscar Teale on a book on the effects produced at spiritualistic séances. Ultimately, the lion's share of his attention was focused on a monumental history of superstition that spanned from biblical days to the present. Despite exhaustive research that included consultations with scholars of all "creeds," he worried that his efforts would go unrewarded. "I am very busy working on a book that I think is of the greatest importance—the only unfortunate part is that I have not a college grade nor possess degrees, and therefore it may not be taken as serious as I would like it to be," he wrote Davis. To help polish his rough edges, he planned to attend Columbia University and take English courses, a project perhaps partially motivated by the editors of *Who's Who*, who overrode his own capsule description of "occupation" from "actor, inventor and author," substituting "magician" instead.

Houdini formed yet another corporation, Houdini Attractions, Inc. Its mandate was to buy, lease, produce, exhibit, or publish "literary, dramatic and magical works and productions, including the magical entertainment heretofore given by Harry Houdini." Ever more intellectually ambitious, he made plans to start an accredited university of magic and, with Dr. Wilson of *The Sphinx*, drew up a proposed curriculum. Houdini had the singular capacity to hold grudges for years and then forgive and forge a close relationship with his former enemies. After fighting viciously with Dr. Wilson for many years, the two had reconciled and Houdini immediately began to venerate him as a father figure. Long-standing disputes with Dr. James W. Elliot, champion card manipulator, and Dr. Saram Ellison, founder of the SAM, ended in a similar fashion, only we had to take Houdini's word on their rapprochement since by then, both men were dead.

Houdini mainly stayed home that summer of 1926, organizing and poring over his cherished books. The volumes engulfed the entire house, from basement to attic. "You know, I actually live in a library," he told one woman who

"I actually live in a library," Houdini wrote. This was just his desk.
From the collection of George and Sandy Daily

wrote him to ask about a fine point in the history of Spiritualism. One day in July, his friend the magician Charles Carter, who was touring, visited him in Harlem. On his train ride back to his home in San Francisco, Carter sat down and wrote Houdini thanking him for the experience.

"Perfectly amazed at the profundity of erudition you are the justly proud possessor of, both in the tomes and manuscripts of your library, and that which is stored away in your massive brain," Carter wrote. "How I should like to spend days browsing about through the great labyrinth of historical and other data which encompasses you. I am afraid though that too many tears are dried by the dust of some of those valuable, and at the same time sorrowful records.

"It seemed too that these have saddened you for behind your wholesome laugh there is irony and a wee bit of the weariness that comes with thought. But be consoled as I am for some things always remain the same such as our eternal lament, our tears and the evenings weariness—the immeasuraby [sic] crushing weariness!"

On August 20, Houdini left the following note for Bess in his safe deposit box at the Lincoln Safe Deposit Co. on Forty-second Street, opposite Grand Central Terminal:

AUGUST 20, 26

Darling Wife & Loved one

In case you feel so disposed destroy all of these negatives. I am not important or interesting enough for the world in general & so it is just as well you destroy them unless you yourself either have a book written or write it yourself for pastime—but otherwise destroy all film. Burn them

Your devoted husband
Houdini

I bequeath all these negatives to my beloved wife Beatrice Houdini and the **only** ***one who has actually helped me in my work.***

Houdini

"Are you still in pain, Harry?" Gertrude Hills asked, worried. She felt responsible in some way for his injury that summer. After all, he was performing at the benefit at her suggestion, and she had no idea that in his attempt to free himself from the straitjacket he would injure himself so.

"I still don't feel myself," Houdini admitted. "I just can't seem to shake this ptomaine poisoning."

"This might be very serious. Suppose you should die from it?" Gertrude worried.

"No man should regret dying because of a good act," Houdini said. "In fact, it's a privilege."

His attitude was no surprise to her. Four years before, he had even foretold his own death to her. And the last time they met, he went into his wishes for his funeral in elaborate detail. "I will not raise a finger to detain myself one moment from joining my mother," he told her. She knew he meant it too.

He hadn't always been that open, though; it took a while for them to get past his innate shyness, especially when it came to matters of the soul. Now, after all these years, the door was open wide. He had found in her someone who had suffered spiritually as much as he had, she thought.

The tea had steeped by then and she filled two cups. When she came back in the room, Houdini was poring over one of her new books about reincarnation.

"You know, sometimes I wonder if I truly am a reincarnation of a great old magician," Houdini mused. "Magic never did seem a mystery to me."

"I don't know if you were a magician, but I know you're an old soul, Harry," she said.

He put the book down and returned to his chair. The tea was bracing.

"How could Doyle and Lodge delude themselves so?" He shook his head. "They're far too intelligent to be dupes of that movement. How can you call it 'religion' when you get men and women in a room together feeling each other's hands and bodies?"

"The difference between you and them is evident, Harry," Gertrude said softly. "They are afraid of dying."

Harry nodded. "Do you know that Doyle actually thinks you smoke cigars and drink wine in the hereafter?" he marveled. "Can he not see the ineffable majesty of the Almighty? How can one not stand in awe of Him? Instead of being driven to his knees, he's visualizing playing cricket!"

Houdini caught himself. He was starting to sound like his father, the rabbi.

Gertrude smiled. "Why do you think they maintain that they need mediums?" she asked.

"Because they cannot face themselves," Harry shot back. "Is the power of the Almighty so trivial that all he can produce is a tipped table and the ringing of a bell? Would the God that created the most breathtaking mountain ranges and spectacular waterfalls stoop to manifest something as vile and base as ectoplasm?"

They sat and sipped their tea in silence. When Houdini snuck a peek at his pocket watch she knew it was time for him to go. He was about to start his tour and she knew she wouldn't see him for a while, but when he paused at her door and she looked into his gray eyes speckled with yellow, she instantly knew that this was the last time they would ever see each other. He knew it too and, overcome, he rushed out.

When he was gone, she could only hope that if he could break through the veil and communicate with her, it wouldn't be merely to send back a message. She hoped that he might grace her with a reply, one that hadn't been made before he left her that last time.

The medium now sat in a wooden Windsor chair in a glass cabinet. Underneath her kimono, her undergarments were held to the skin by surgeon's adhesive tape. Her wrists and ankles were fastened with No. 2 picture wire to eyebolts in the floor of the cabinet. The wire itself was made immobile by surgeon's tape. Her hair had been cut short to preclude the possibility of hiding objects in it. To prevent any forward movement of her head, her neck was now immobilized by a locked leather collar that was fastened by a horizontal rope leading to an eyebolt in the back of the cabinet.

Despite all this control, it took Dr. J. B. Rhine and his wife, Dr. Louisa Rhine, one sitting on July 1, 1926 to see right through Margery. Rhine may have looked like a country bumpkin but he was an astute observer and he was infuriated that he had transferred from the University of West Virginia to move to the Boston area so he could study what he thought was a most promising case of mediumship. Besides figuring out every one of seven of Margery's manifestations, he was irate at the behavior of the other sitters. "It is evidently of very great advantage to a medium, especially if fraudulent, to be personally attractive; it aids in the 'fly-catching business.' Our report would be incomplete without mention of the fact that this 'business' reached the point of actual kissing and embracing at our sitting, in the case of one of the medium's more ardent admirers. Could this man be expected to detect trickery in her?" We don't know whether Rhine was referring to Malcolm Bird or Joseph DeWyckoff.

Besides exposures, Crandon found himself in other trouble. "He is being sued for $40,000 for operating on a woman for cancer, when she was simply pregnant, and destroying the foetus," Dr. Prince wrote another psychic researcher. "A highly incredible story which persists is that a boy who was in his family some weeks mysteriously disappeared. He claims that the boy is now in his home in England, but still official letters of inquiry and demand are received from that country. This is no mere rumor, for I was shown some of the original letters. I asked why the authorities in England did not look for the boy where he was said to be. M[argery] said that it was, she supposed, because they didn't want to. Doctor C[randon], she tells me, was threatened with arrest by the immigration authorities at one time. The matter has been going on for more than a year. It is very mysterious."

Crandon responded by giving lectures, accusing Houdini of preventing Walter's manifestations in the séance room. To counteract the negative Harvard report, he commissioned a 109-page book entitled *Margery, Harvard, Veritas*, financed by Joseph DeWyckoff, and sent a copy to nearly every major library and university around the world. Bird began "doing his damnest" to ruin Houdini, trying to get information about the magician's family.

Pheneas had been upset lately at Doyle. His constant fishing for information and news about the coming catastrophe had prompted Pheneas to start calling him "*Whale.*" And his impulsive behavior had caused Pheneas to chastise him. *"Do not act on your own too much,"* Pheneas told him. *"We are three, the Bridge, you and I. When you get loose on your own we are like a cart where one trace is loose and one is fastened."*

In the summer of 1926, William Elliott Hammond, a Spiritualist missionary lecturer, published a pamphlet entitled "Houdini Unmasked." After attempting to counter Houdini's charges that a belief in Spiritualism often led to insanity, depravity, or violence, Hammond quoted one of Houdini's speeches: "Tell the people all I am trying to do is to save them from being tricked and to *Persuade them to leave spiritualism alone and take up with some genuine religion.*" Irate, Hammond struck back. "We should like to inform our professional enemies, including Houdini, that the strength of Spiritualism and its numbers are unknown—it should be so. Now that we are being attacked openly we shall focus our numbers, if for no other reason than that of defense. Our enemies seem to say, 'Be ready, gods, with all your thunderbolts; dash (them) to pieces. . . .' The Crusaders and Houdini will live to learn that we Spiritualists are in this contest, struggle, war or fight . . . and we intend to stay in it until the end. We will go down if we must, but we shall do so with our colors flying!! . . . We say to our professional enemies, 'let slip the dogs of war' and give battle. You shall find the leaders of Spiritualism inspired by the words of Roosevelt—Aggressive fighting for the Right is the noblest sport the world affords. . . . *Victory is ours for the fighting!*"

The threats had been ratcheted up another notch.

Margery posing proudly with the cup Doyle sent her. *From the collection of Dr. Bruce Averbook*

On September 1, Houdini wrote Bess another of his little notes, while his manager was counting up the "monies." He signed it: "Love and kisses and lots of them as always your husband until and after the curtain rings down on our lives, e'er to the crack of Doom." He signed it "Harry Houdini (Ehrich)."

One Saturday afternoon in September the phone rang at Fulton Oursler's house.

"Hello, Oursler. Listen, I'm leaving on tour in a little while. Probably I'm talking to you for the last time."

It was another manic call from Houdini. For the last four months, the magician had been exhibiting suspiciously uncharacteristic behavior, including aggressive confrontations and severe mood swings. Oursler, who was the top editor at *Liberty* magazine, and who under the nom de plume of Samri Frickell had been active in exposing fraudulent mediums, had been inundated by calls like this one during that time. They would come at all hours of the day or night, but as a night owl, Oursler dreaded the seven A.M. calls the most. During these conversations, Houdini had seemed unusually quarrelsome. "In his voice there was a feminine, almost hysterical note of rebellion as if his hands were beating against an immutable destiny," Oursler wrote later.

"What is it?" the editor asked.

"You know my detective system?"

Oursler was well aware of Houdini's secret service. He knew that Houdini had undercover operatives deep in almost every major Spiritualist circle and church.

"They are going to kill me," Houdini asserted.

"Who?" Oursler wondered.

"Fraudulent spirit mediums. Don't laugh. Every night they are holding séances and praying for my death."

Oursler remembered that Walter, Margery's spirit control, had put a curse on Houdini's life. When he raised the issue, Houdini admitted that these curses and predictions weighed on his mind.

"But that's not all I wanted to tell you," the magician continued. "They are beginning to take notice of you too. The fake mediums are circulating your picture and your biography all over the United States."

"How do you know that?" Oursler asked.

"I have a copy of the data they are sending out about you. When I return from my tour, I'll show it to you. Meanwhile, keep to yourself what you know," Houdini said, and hung up.

The Houdini Show began its fall tour on September 7 at the Majestic Theatre in Boston. By now another set of professors who were working under the auspices of the American Society for Psychical Research was testing Margery. Near the end of Houdini's first week, two members of the new committee visited him backstage. Houdini told them that he would be delighted to duplicate Margery's new manifestations for the new committee, using the same apparatus, but he was shocked that Crandon would permit him to visit Lime Street again. Around that time, Houdini received a call from Amadeo Vacca, one of his undercover agents, who warned him that Margery had a new effect in her repertoire that was designed to thwart Houdini's replication of her phenomenon. After a series of curt communications (some by registered mail) between Houdini and Crandon, each side blamed the other for backing out of the confrontation. It was clear from the correspondence that Crandon had believed Houdini would not be able to duplicate Margery's feat while tied in the glass cabinet, and this was his final attempt to destroy Houdini's reputation. Crandon had falsely claimed in his last letter that after Houdini had an in-depth two-hour conversation with the researchers and learned "the detailed rigidity of the Margery control, [he] discreetly and wisely declined to come."

Houdini was greeted in Boston by even more lawsuits from Spiritualists. Now he had more than one million dollars in actions hanging over his head. He was taking these suits so seriously that before he left on tour, he sold his complete show, outfits, illusions, paraphernalia, and wardrobes to Bess for the sum of $1. So when he began the last part of the show, his spiritualistic exposés, he pointed out a court stenographer who was sitting in the orchestra pit, taking down his entire speech in shorthand. Houdini then introduced a local judge who told the audience that he had vetted the legal statement read by Houdini. When two spotters for the management alerted Houdini that there were two people in the audience taking down every word for the opposition, Houdini magnanimously offered them transcripts of his official notes and proceeded with the exposé.

Houdini slowly climbed into the glass-fronted brass coffin. It fastened shut, and the coffin was gently lowered into a huge glass-fronted vault. Then the sand came, a full ton of it, slowly obscuring the coffin and its occupant. One small misstep and Houdini would be suffocated onstage under a mini-mountain's worth of sand.

Within two minutes, Houdini was free. The escape, called the Mystery of the Sphinx, was the magician's first new escape in years, but he had been working on it for ten years, going back to those experiments in the moist Santa Ana soil where he had to literally claw his way to the surface to survive, where a lesser man would have succumbed. Even at age fifty-two he was coming up with new ever-more death-defying escapes. He debuted the effect in Worcester,

Massachusetts, and it went over well. Because of the intense preparation necessary, Houdini decided to hold it for venues where he would be playing at least two-week stands.

In Providence, the next stop of the tour, Houdini and Bess went to dinner with H. P. Lovecraft and Clifford Eddy Jr. Both men were working on a book for Houdini called *The Cancer of Superstition* but Eddy was also an undercover operative for Houdini, filing many field reports on his visits to fraudulent mediums. Houdini had been expecting to hear from a man named C. R. Sharp, who apparently had some valuable "spiritualistic papers," relating to an exposé of a medium, that he was to deliver to the magician. Sharp never showed, however. Shortly after meeting with Eddy and Lovecraft, Bess was stricken with a nonspecific form of poisoning, probably from food. Houdini immediately summoned Sophie Rosenblatt, a nurse who had worked for the family previously; but by Friday, October 7, Bess's condition had deteriorated so badly that Houdini stayed up all night comforting her. She improved a little the next day, which was the last day of the run, so Houdini arranged for her and Sophie to leave straight for Albany, the next tour stop, while he took a late night train to New York, where he had meetings scheduled for Sunday.

Houdini conferred with "some of his associates" even while on the midnight train to New York. His Sunday meeting with his lawyer was to review the millions of dollars' worth of lawsuits from the Spiritualists. At six P.M. sharp, Houdini arrived at Ernst's, but the family was still at their weekend retreat. Sleepless for more than sixty hours, Houdini dozed off on the living room sofa for twenty minutes, until the Ernsts returned home. When the meeting concluded, he checked in with Rosenblatt in Albany and decided to postpone his train back.

At some point after midnight, Houdini called his friend Joe Dunninger, the mentalist.

"Joe, I just got in town today and have to hurry right out again," Houdini said. "I want to move some stuff from the house. Can you come up with the car?"

Despite heavy rain, Dunninger got in his car. By the time he reached 113th Street, Houdini was waiting at the doorway of the house. He was wearing some ragged old clothes and a weather-beaten straw hat. There was a Holmes security officer there to make sure the alarm didn't go off. Houdini had some bales of papers and magazines stacked up, and the Holmes employee helped load them into the car. Houdini tipped the man fifty cents.

Hungry, the two men stopped for something to eat. When they returned to the car, Houdini told Dunninger to drive through the park, but when they reached the Central Park West exit at Seventy-second Street, Houdini grabbed his friend's arm.

Years after his experiment in the California soil, Houdini finally performed his Buried Alive effect. *From the collection of George and Sandy Daily*

"Go back, Joe!" he said in a hollow, tragic voice.

"Go back where?"

"Go back to the house, Joe."

"Why—did you forget something?"

"Don't ask questions, Joe. Just turn around and go back."

Dunninger complied. When they arrived the rain was even more intense, but Houdini got out of the car, took off his hat, and just stood in the downpour, looking up at the dark house. He returned to the car but said nothing. When they approached the exit of the park again, Dunninger noticed that Houdini's shoulders were shaking and he was crying.

After a few seconds Houdini looked up.

"I've seen my house for the last time, Joe. I'll never see my house again."

Just as Houdini was hoisted into the air prior to his immersion in the upside-down water tank, he gasped and his face twisted in pain. In agony, he was released from the stocks, and a call went out to see if there was a doctor in attendance. An Albany bone specialist named Dr. Hannock examined Houdini in the wings and determined that the magician had probably suffered a fracture.

"You will have to go to the hospital at once," he ordered.

Houdini just waved his hand toward the audience and told him he couldn't disappoint them. Hopping back out onstage, he did his Needles effect on one leg and finished the rest of the program. Appreciative of his valor and courage, nearly the entire audience waited to cheer Houdini at the stage door after the show. Houdini went straight to the hospital, where doctors confirmed he had indeed fractured his left ankle and advised him to stay off his feet for a week. He stayed up all night and devised a brace that would permit him to perform the next day.

When Fulton Oursler read about his friend's injury, he immediately dispatched a telegram to the theater. The next day, October 13, Oursler received a strange letter from a medium named Alice A. Wood, who for years had been Dr. Prince's secretary:

> *Three years ago, [the spirit of] Doctor Hyslop said to J. Malcolm Bird of the Psychical Research Society: "The waters are black for Houdini" and he predicted that disaster would befall him while performing before an audience in a theatre. Doctor Hyslop now says that the injury is more serious than has been reported and that Houdini's days as a magician are over.*

Oursler contemplated enclosing that message in a second letter he was sending Houdini but decided it would be in bad taste to forward that communication to someone who was trying to recover from an injury. Meanwhile, Oursler got a response from Houdini. It said, "Thanks for your wire. I have 'only' an interior fracture of the ankle. . . ."

By five P.M. on Tuesday, October 19, the ballroom at the McGill University student union in Montreal was packed with the largest crowd in the university's history. Every available inch was taken, and some undergraduates had even climbed up a ladder to get a better view. Professor Tait was the first to ascend the slightly elevated platform, followed by Houdini, Julia Sawyer, and Rose Mackenberg. After a short introduction from Tait, Houdini limped to the center of the platform. His face was pale and drawn; dark shadows played under his tired eyes. *Was this the same man who had filled half the world with awe and admiration?* some of the students wondered.

As soon as he began to speak, those questions were dispelled.

Houdini began with a short dissertation on magic. He told the students that his feats depended on iron nerve, dexterity, and perfect coordination, but they were all done by natural means. People lacked the true ability to see, he lectured; if they could only educate their eyes, they could readily see through almost every one of his so-called miracles.

To be an escape artist, he explained, you need to condition yourself to reject all fear. Our imagination magnifies, if not causes, our pain. If you condition yourself to reject the fear and the pain, you could achieve what seemed to be miraculous feats. To prove his point, he did something he'd done hundreds of times before: He sanitized a needle and stuck it through his cheek. No blood oozed out.

Then he got onto the topic of his lecture: spiritualistic frauds. He lauded those who followed Spiritualism as a religion, but he had only contempt for the "religious racketeers" who preyed on the most vulnerable people. The industry exploited the ignorant, and the credulous had grown to colossal proportions—these frauds were profiting to the tune of millions of dollars every year. "There [are] three kinds of mediums," he declared. "Those who are honestly deluded, those who are psychotics, and those who are criminals."

He excoriated Margery and Lady Doyle to such a degree that the next day's *Montreal Gazette* headline read: "Houdini Assails 'Slickest' Medium—Reiterates Charges Against 'Marjorie' of Boston as Fake—Tilts at Lady Doyle."

According to him, he was the only person in the world to whom Lady Doyle had ever given a séance. "She produced for me twenty-three pages of classical English in a message from my mother . . . who [could not speak a word of English] . . . Don't you ever believe that any medium can take a message for your Mother when she has passed to eternal rest."

He pledged to continue his battle even though mediums the world over loathed him "with a deadly hatred." He ended his lecture with a simple declaration. "If I were to die tomorrow, the Spiritualists would declare an International holiday!"

When the lecture broke up, Houdini was surrounded by a circle of admirers in the billiard room downstairs on his way out of the building. According to eyewitness accounts, Houdini was only too happy to prove his mastery over pain and his ability to withstand hard blows "without personal injury" by challenging anyone to deliver a punch to his stomach. Houdini's public display of his abdominal prowess was a new development in the mystifier's arsenal, but as far back as 1918, in an interview with a female magazine writer, Houdini bragged that he was extremely proud of his washboard stomach, "an endowment . . . of an ancestral cleanliness." According to the showgirl/spy Alberta Chapman, by 1925, Houdini did informal demonstrations of his ability to withstand punches. On this occasion at McGill, a nineteen-year-old ex-football player named Gerald Pickelman took up Houdini's challenge to hit him with all his might. The magician withstood the blow and left the building. After performing at the Princess Theatre that night, he rushed to a Montreal radio station to do a live interview about his campaign against fraudulent mediums.

On Wednesday night, Houdini unleashed his attacks on the local Montreal mediums. After enduring some heckling from Spiritualist sympathizers in the audience, he introduced Sawyer and Mackenberg, who gave detailed accounts of their séances in town. Then, switching gears, Houdini began naming some prominent Montreal residents who were in the audience. As if he were a seer, he recounted intimate details of their private lives. After their amazement died down, he explained that his same spies had passed on all that information to him, employing the same methods that crooked mediums use to fleece unsuspecting victims.

The next day, a Montrealer named James P. Clarke dispatched a letter to Conan Doyle. Clarke had been in the audience the previous night and had taken exception to Houdini's exposé. During the Q&A period, when Houdini was asked how prominent men like Doyle thought it worthwhile to study psychic phenomena, Clarke reported that Houdini had gone off on a tirade against the celebrated author. "His reply was grossly insolent, insofar that he spoke of you as being just a 'writer of detective stories' and eaten up with but one subject.

Furthermore he said you were no different from the ordinary man—intellectually that you were not a scientist—and acted like a 'big school boy' at a conference in New York. He also stated you would believe anything—and the contemptuous manner in which he passed this remark was exceedingly unfair.

"And now I come to the most important part. As a final retort he said he wished you were there in front of him. He would 'tear you to ribbons.' Obviously he was taking advantage of the distance between London and Montreal. As these remarks were passed publicly, before a large crowd, I think it only right you should know of them. I was shouted down when I indignantly objected—he had the crowd with him."

On Thursday, October 21, Pheneas came to the Doyle circle.

"*All is going admirably. All is according to schedule,*" he said. "*Those who have misled others and stood in the way of God's light they shall be removed.*"

"But there will be the terror which they suffer," Doyle worried.

"*No, there will be no time for terror,*" Pheneas spoke. "*It will all be very sudden. You remember years ago how I warned you not to go abroad. You would not be here to-night if you had not taken my warning. I have kept pictures of what would have happened to you. I will show them when you come over. The evil forces had plotted your destruction.*"

"I am greatly obliged to you," Sir Arthur said.

"*It was not so much for your sake as for the sake of the world that we saved you,*" Pheneas responded.

Sam Smiley, along with his friend Jacques Price, waited anxiously outside the Princess Theatre on Friday morning. Smiley had hung on every word during Houdini's lecture at his school, all the while sketching the magician. When his fraternity brothers brought the drawing backstage after one of Houdini's shows, the magician was delighted to autograph it and told them to invite the artist to come to his dressing room on Friday so that he could render another portrait for his own personal collection.

At about ten minutes before eleven, Houdini, Bess, Julia Sawyer, and Sophie Rosenblatt emerged out of a car in front of the theater. Some passersby who were examining the outdoor display of locks, chains, and manacles congregated around Houdini. Sophie reminded him to eat something, but Houdini brushed her off. He told her that if he was hungry he could always get something to eat, and then, ever the showman, he miraculously produced a hot dog from the coat lapel of one of his admirers.

When Smiley reminded him who he was, Houdini seemed delighted that he had come and ushered the two students to his small, dank dressing room. The magician offered the boys a seat and then, after taking off his coat, opening his collar, and rolling up his shirtsleeves, he lay down on a couch on the opposite side of the room. Apologizing for reclining on the couch, Houdini told the boys that he had to get rest because of his accident in Albany. His ankle was still bothering him but he had willed himself to conceal his limp during all his shows. This was no exaggeration; he would later write to two friends telling one that the injury had rendered him "a semi-invalid" and complaining to the other that "the broken bone in my foot is causing a lot of worry." He propped himself up on a few pillows and wondered if it would be all right if he read some of his correspondence before he posed.

Smiley's first impression of the magician was confirmed in these close quarters. "His sallow complexion, his tightly drawn skin, the dark shadows encircling his tired-looking deep-set eyes, the muscles about the temples and at the side of the mouth twitching nervously—here was a picture of a man who was a little weary and much in need of a long, carefree vacation. His mouth and eyes were tense and firm; they revealed the overwhelming desire and the tremendous will to fight fatigue and illness with the mind."

As Smiley began to draw, the showman regaled the boys with a biographical sketch. He talked of adopting the name Houdini—"The name . . . was like magic . . . It stuck." He talked about his movie career and told them that he would not return to that arena—the returns were too meager. When the conversation turned to his secrets, Houdini demurred, but told them that in a year or two he would write a book revealing those secrets and hold off publication for many more years. When talking about the feats of the Indian fakirs he even demonstrated how he could, by dint of will, make it appear that his heart had stopped beating and his breathing had ceased.

After a while, there was a knock at the door, and Julia ushered in a tall man wearing a long blue gabardine coat that seemed ill-fitting. He was carrying four books under his arm, and Houdini introduced him to the others as J. Gordon Whitehead. Whitehead had come by to return a book he had borrowed from the magician a few days before. It turned out that although Whitehead was clearly older than the other boys, approximately twenty-eight, he was also a theology student at McGill. "His face was ruddy, his hair very thin on top; his frame was powerful though loosely knit, and his neck was inordinately long. He spoke softly with an exaggerated Oxford accent," Smiley remembered.

As soon as Whitehead entered the room, he dominated the conversation, peppering Houdini with countless queries, enough to annoy Smiley since Houdini kept turning his head to answer the man. Smiley was intrigued by what Houdini had to say.

"It seems that Houdini had been a detective for many years and had aided in unraveling so many mysteries and had read so many detective stories, that he boasted of being able to piece together any detective story, unknown to him of course, by hearing three or four paragraphs from different sections of such story," Smiley wrote.

At that point, Whitehead, who conveniently had a mystery book with him, tried the experiment. After reading just three or four excerpts, Houdini was successful in relating the outlines of the plot. Was Whitehead a confederate in a preplanned exhibition to astound Smiley and Price? Again, we will never know. The episode was punctuated with one of Houdini's favorite sayings—"Think of the trouble I might have caused if I had used my talents for ill."

Then Whitehead changed course dramatically. He began to interrogate Houdini about the Bible. "What is your opinion of the miracles mentioned in the Bible?" he asked.

Houdini suddenly drew back. "I prefer not to discuss or to comment on matters of this nature," he said. "I would make one observation, however—what would succeeding generations have said of Houdini's feats had he performed them in Biblical times? Would they have been referred to as 'miracles'?"

Whitehead seemed taken aback at this statement. He immediately turned the subject to Houdini's physical prowess.

"Is it true, Mr. Houdini, that you can resist the hardest blows struck to the abdomen?" Whitehead asked out of the clear blue.

To Smiley, Houdini didn't seem to be very proud of his abdominal musculature. He ignored Whitehead and said, "My forearm and back muscles are like iron! Feel them."

The three complied and were duly impressed, but Whitehead was unrelenting, steering the conversation back to Houdini's abdomen.

"Is it true that your stomach muscles can stand very hard blows?"

"My forearm and back muscles are extremely strong. They're like iron," Houdini repeated.

Whitehead wouldn't be put off. "Would you mind if I delivered a few blows to your abdomen, Mr. Houdini?" he asked.

"Whether it was a matter of professional pride or whether Houdini felt that it would hurt his prestige to refuse—I do not pretend to know. Before I knew it Houdini had accepted this challenge and then and there he lay supine, but apparently not quite ready to receive Whitehead's blows. Hovering over his outstretched form, Whitehead, with elbow bent, suddenly struck four or five terribly forcible, deliberate, well-directed blows to Houdini's abdomen," Smiley wrote.

Smiley froze with shock but Price leaped to his feet and pulled Whitehead off Houdini.

"Are you mad?" he shouted at the man with indignation.

Houdini had seemed to wince with each succeeding blow. Finally, he made an arresting gesture with one hand and, looking at Whitehead, a wry smile played across his face. "That will do," he mumbled.

The atmosphere in the small room became charged with tension. Smiley felt that Whitehead didn't at all seem repentant about his attack. He and Price felt so uncomfortable that the artist finished the portrait and packed to leave. Houdini seemed pleased with the drawing and asked Smiley to sign and date it.

"You made me look a little tired in this picture," the mystifier said. "The truth is I don't feel so well."

Then the three visitors said their farewells and departed.

The first indication that something was wrong came at dinner that night. Houdini was continually rubbing his stomach, which alarmed the nurse. He admitted to her that he was in pain. He seemed to suffer through Friday evening's performance and, according to Rosenblatt, "complained continually" about his pain.

He must have tried to maintain some stoic front because that night, according to Bess, Houdini threw a champagne party in his room and invited Julia and Sophie. Later that night, about two A.M., Bess, who appears to have been rooming with her nurse, got a call from Houdini. Besides the pain, he was now experiencing horrific cramps. Bess massaged his stomach.

The next morning, Bess found a note from Houdini.

"Champagne coquette. I'll be at the theatre about noon." He signed it, "HH Fall Guy."

With so little sleep, Houdini dozed in his dressing room before the Saturday matinee, and, according to Rosenblatt, nearly fell asleep during his performance. Later that afternoon, he complained of awful pains in his stomach, "just where I got the blows," he told the nurse. She gave him a Sedlitz powder for his indigestion. During the evening's performance he was so weak and in so much pain that he was unable to raise his left foot to step into a cabinet used during a vanishing illusion. Collins had to assist him both then and at a few other points during the performance.

After Saturday's evening show, the troupe prepared to take an overnight train to Detroit, where they were scheduled to open their run on Sunday night. Houdini sat in an armchair in the lobby of his hotel, the Prince of Wales, reading a newspaper and waiting for the others. There was a door in the back of the lobby that led to a bar called the Pig and Whistle. As Houdini sat and read the paper, three young men entered the lobby from the bar and walked up to the magician. One of them, who according to eyewitnesses appeared burly like a football player, without any warning, delivered a crushing blow, right through the newspaper, to Houdini's stomach.

He doubled over in pain.

"You shouldn't have done that," he said to the stranger, and then slowly stood up and walked out of the lobby.

The opening night sold-out crowd at the Garrick Theater in Detroit was getting antsy. Houdini's show was scheduled to start at eight-thirty, but after a short announcement that there was a delay due to the late arrival of personnel and equipment from Toronto, it was almost nine and there was still no sign of the mystifier. Suddenly, the familiar strains of "Pomp and Circumstance" echoed through the theater and Houdini walked onstage.

"We have just made a thousand-mile journey from Montreal, and we are tired," he exaggerated, as he began to perform magic. From the beginning, the audience sensed something was wrong. He covered a bare table with a large cloth, but he was so clumsy in uncovering the table that the audience was able to see how a bowl filled with water and a goldfish had appeared. When it came time to unfurl a long silk streamer from the bowl, Collins had to step in and pull it out for him. Houdini tried to maintain a good front, though. When he began to do a card effect, a heckler from the balcony threw his own deck of cards onto the stage and asked the magician to use them instead of his own. At first, Houdini frowned at the interruption, but then he gingerly bent down, retrieved the cards, and used them for his effect, to the delight of the audience. Clearly something was wrong, though. Several times during the show, he touched his side and whispered to people in the wings.

As he walked through the curtains at the end of the first act, he collapsed and had to be carried to his dressing room. His temperature was 104 degrees, but somehow he willed himself to go back out onstage. A doctor had examined him before the show and had urged him to go to the hospital immediately, but Houdini had refused. "They're here to see Houdini," he spoke of the sold-out house. "I won't disappoint them." Somehow, he made it through the Spiritualist portion of the show, challenging local Detroit mediums, but he was speaking faster than ever, and his sentences sometimes trailed off. When the last question had been taken from the audience, Houdini looked down at the footlights, said good-bye to the audience, and slowly walked backward, bowing at each step. When he made it through the curtain, he collapsed.

He was rushed to his dressing room, where he lay down. The outer corridor was filled with well-wishers but only F. L. Black, a collector friend of his, was allowed inside. Black talked to him for a few minutes and went away with the impression that he was "suffering intensely." Even still, Houdini found time to type a reply to his friend Fulton Oursler's letter, telling him that while he was in the Midwest he hoped to find time to go to Toledo to have a séance with the medium Ada Besinnet.

An ambulance was waiting outside the theater but Houdini stubbornly insisted on taking a cab to his hotel room. At the hotel, Bess became hysterical and insisted they call the house doctor. A young physician named Daniel Cohn, who was substituting for the vacationing Hotel Statler doctor, saw Houdini. He was so concerned that he called a staff surgeon at Grace Hospital, Dr. Charles Kennedy, who arrived at the hotel around three A.M. Kennedy concurred on immediate hospitalization but Houdini balked. Finally they called his New York physician, Dr. William Stone, who got on the phone with the magician and ordered him to the hospital.

Houdini was admitted to Grace Hospital at about four A.M. Monday morning. They sought a private room for him since he was so famous, but there were none available. "Well, if there is nothing but a double room, that will do for me," Houdini said. Dr. Cohn took his new patient's case history. When he asked his occupation, Houdini answered, "Author. And magician." From the start of his stay, he was a model patient. Every time an attendant or nurse would do the most trivial thing for him, like mopping his brow or giving him a sip of water, he would look them in the eye, smile, and thank them.

For reasons unknown to this day, Houdini wasn't operated on until Monday afternoon. He requested to walk into the operating room and was upset when the request was denied, but as the two young, burly stretcher orderlies wheeled him in, Houdini put up his mitts and joked, "Say, I can still lick the two of you." Houdini also had one other strange request right before surgery. He called Dr. Kennedy to his bedside and, pointing at Bess, said, "Please keep that woman out of my room all the time, because she is the most peculiar woman I have ever known in my life." This request was complied with, and Bess was kept away for days.

Dr. Kennedy made an exploratory incision right down the middle of Houdini's abdomen. From the previous night's examination and interview with Houdini, Kennedy suspected that the blows Houdini received in Montreal had ruptured his intestine or caused a clotting of the large blood vessels to the intestine. Appendicitis was never seriously considered because he was told the blows had been struck on the left side of his abdomen and that was where Houdini reported his pain.

According to one newspaper, right after the exploratory incision, "pus overflowed from Houdini's abdomen and spilled onto the floor of the operating room." Kennedy was shocked to see that Houdini's appendix was "a great long affair which started in the right lower pelvis where it normally should, extended across the midline and lay in his left pelvis, exactly where the blow had been struck." He concluded that Houdini's appendix had ruptured, allowing deadly poison to seep into his system. He removed the gangrenous mass that had been Houdini's appendix and closed him up.

Immediately after the surgery, a medical bulletin was issued to the waiting reporters. It noted that Houdini had been operated on for acute appendicitis and that the physicians "expressed grave concern regarding his chances of recovery. Delay in applying for medical attention may hurt his chances of recovery, they indicated." Privately, they gave him twelve hours to live. At ten P.M., another bulletin was issued stating that his condition remained unchanged, he was still under the effects of ether, and that a team of physicians remained at his bedside.

One of that team was the young Dr. Cohn. Thrilled that he had such a famous patient although he was just out of medical school, he spent night and day at Houdini's bedside. As the magician's condition seemed to stabilize, Dr. Cohn listened with rapt attention as Houdini, in halting sentences, reminisced about his childhood in Appleton. One night, Houdini suddenly turned to Dr. Cohn.

"I have a yen for Farmer's Chop Suey," he said.

Since Houdini had no appetite during his hospital stay, the request was probably made out of sheer nostalgia for his childhood. Farmer's Chop Suey was a popular dish in Jewish homes—a medley of raw vegetables slathered in rich sour cream. The dutiful doctor walked across the street to a nearby delicatessen and brought back two portions.

"If I die, don't be surprised if phony spiritualists declare a national holiday," Houdini mused, between bites.

On Tuesday a post-operative specialist named Dr. George LeFevre was brought to Detroit from Montreal, where he been attending a conference. LeFevre was a homeopathist who had devised an experimental serum to combat the poisons circulating through Houdini's G.I. tract. LeFevre seemed pleased with Houdini's condition after the serum was administered. He noted that the magician's temperature had dropped to 99.4 and his pulse was 100. Collins telegraphed the news back to coworkers in New York. "HAS IMPROVED WONDERFULLY DOCTORS PLEASED WITH RESULTS BUT STILL VERY GRAVE BETTER SIGNS DAILY SATURDAY DECIDES THE TURN WILL KEEP YOU INFORMED HOPE BAGGAGE AND ANIMALS STORED OK HUNDREDS OF WIRES DAILY FLOWERS AND LETTERS COLLINS."

On Friday, October 29, Houdini's condition worsened. Peritonitis had developed and the poison had spread to his intestines and paralyzed them. A second operation was ordered. "Mr. Houdini has reacted to the second operation much better than we expected he would," the medical bulletin read. "His condition is very grave, but hope for his recovery has not been entirely abandoned. His temperature is 103, pulse 130 and respiration 40."

Houdini remained conscious and cognizant. On Saturday, he composed a letter to a friend. "Box offices here are S.R.O. which certainly makes me smug and quite happy. Except that I feel none too well at the moment, but suppose that I will get over this waviness in no time."

His surgeon, Dr. Kennedy, remained at his bedside and the two had many interesting discussions about magic, Spiritualism, and related philosophical fields. At one point, Houdini turned to the doctor. "Doctor, you know I always wanted to be a surgeon, but I never could. I have always regretted it."

Kennedy was taken aback. "Why, Mr. Houdini, that is one of the most amazing statements I have ever heard. Here you are, the greatest magician and the greatest entertainer of your age. You make countless thousands of people happy. You have an unlimited income and you are admired and respected by everybody, while I am just an ordinary dub of a surgeon trying to struggle through life."

Houdini looked at Kennedy and smiled. "Perhaps those things are true, doctor, but the difference between me and you is that you actually *do* things for people. I, in almost every respect, am a fake."

Early Sunday afternoon, a group of ashen-faced doctors hovered over the bed in room 401. Houdini was surrounded by his brothers Hardeen and Nat. Leopold had known enough not to come. Ehrie looked up at his kid brother Dash. "I guess I'm all through fighting," he said with resignation. Bess, who had been admitted to the hospital herself a few days earlier, was finally brought into the room, accompanied by Harry's sister, Gladys. When she saw her husband's condition, she screamed.

"Harry! Harry!" she sobbed.

There was a tube inserted in one side of Houdini's mouth. A doctor was listening through a stethoscope, monitoring his heartbeat. Tears were streaming down the faces of the doctors and the nurse.

Houdini's eyes, those amazing penetrating organs, seemed to stare vacantly off into space. He struggled to say something, but then his eyes fluttered shut.

"He's gone," the doctor said.

Bess burst out laughing and they carried her back to her room.

It was 1:26 P.M., Halloween, and the Spiritualists were finally able to declare their national holiday.

From the collection of Dr. Bruce Averbook

25

An Eye for an Eye

THE SPIRITUALIST CELEBRATION HAD ACTUALLY ALREADY begun. On the day before Houdini died, Joseph DeWyckoff, the wealthy member of Margery's inner circle, sat down and put his pen to paper. He wrote an extraordinary letter to his friend Crandon:

Dear Roy:

Excepting an occasional inclination due perhaps to hereditary strains, the Masonic principle of an "eye for an eye" seldom finds response in my mental make-up when I, personally, suffer from unkind acts of men. But—when my dear and good friends are wantonly and systematically injured by a campaign of persistent calumny and base and despicable lies—I must confess that the teachings of Jesus of Nazareth become a dead letter to me and I crave to pull "a tooth for a tooth" if not the entire dentistry of the offender in one clip!

For some days—a cad who has grossly injured my dearest friends and made Truth shriek again and again has been groping for the "fourth dimension" in Detroit—

I may be sinning, I ask forgiveness of the supreme intelligence, but I calmly await the result of this groping and I need not tell you what other thoughts are possessing me—A verse by Heine keeps ringing in my cranium which may be apropos:

"Keinen Kadish wird man sagen [No Kaddish will be said,]

Keine Messe wird man singen" [No mass will be sung.]

Permit me to say that "Kadish" is the name of the Jewish prayer—recited for the Dead and you know that "Messe" stands for Catholic "Mass." When the immortal Heine thus sang he had reference to a jew-renegade.

With much love to you and Mina.
Yours sincerely,
Cheerio!
Joe

According to the certificate of death no. 14840 filed on November 20, 1926 with the State of Michigan Department of Health, the actor and lecturer Harry Houdini died of diffuse streptococcic peritonitis that was occasioned by a "ruptured appendicitis." The "traumatic appendicitis" was thought to have been caused by a blow struck by a student of McGill University in Montreal during a playful sparring session in Houdini's dressing room. It's curious that all of Houdini's doctors swore out affidavits saying that the root cause of his death was "traumatic appendicitis," a condition that has never existed. These doctors must have known this fact. Because of the sparring-trauma-rupturing-neglect-death scenario, there was no consideration of other theories like foul play and, consequently, there was no autopsy. The only dissent seemed to be raised by New York publisher Bernarr Macfadden, who sent an open letter to the superintendent of Grace Hospital demanding to know what Houdini was fed during his hospital stay and what exactly was in Dr. LeFevre's "mysterious" new serum. No answers were forthcoming from the medical community.

The next questions were raised by the underwriters of Houdini's various life insurance policies. Because of a double indemnity clause, Houdini's estate was seeking to collect twice the face value of the policies due to the accident. After an investigation, H. J. J. McKeon, the Montreal manager of New York Life Assurance Co., claimed that the report of Houdini being struck after his lecture at McGill was without foundation and that according to an interview with Abby Wright, the manager of the Montreal theater where Houdini performed, the magician was a "sick man" upon his arrival, bringing with him a nurse who had accompanied him to the McGill lecture and was overheard to say, "I must get him out of here at once," at its conclusion. The insurance company salvo was immediately answered by Bernard Ernst and Houdini's other attorneys, who obtained affidavits from the entire touring troupe affirming Houdini's health prior to the punches and from Smiley, Price, and Whitehead, who described the dressing room incident. The specter of foul play had still not surfaced.

On Halloween night, the circle formed at 10 Lime Street and Walter soon whistled, signaling his arrival. He said that Houdini would have a long period of "acclimatization" and that the magician would be very confused and resistant to the idea of his death.

"*I am not sure but that I shall have something to do with Houdini and his admission,*" Walter crowed.

That same day, Margery had issued a statement to the press about Houdini's death. "We are sorry to hear of the passing of Houdini. He was a virile personality of great determination and undoubted physical courage. We have entertained him and our personal relations with him in this house always had been pleasant. At other times and places we have had our differences."

That evening, Margery, hounded by newsmen, denied "emphatically" that "she had ever said a curse was upon Houdini or that he would die within a year." Newsmen weren't the only ones asking that question. Dr. Robin Tillyard, an Australian entomologist who had pledged his "admiration, devotion and love, eternally" to Dr. Crandon and Margery, wrote Crandon in December: "Do send me some details about Houdini's sudden death! I have heard that Walter had said that he would 'get' Houdini. Is that true? If so, he might have influenced that young man, who, so I heard, punched Houdini in the abdomen. Also you will remember that Walter sent McD[ougall] a message through me (I never delivered it, of course) that he 'would meet him again *soon, over here.*' If he can deal with Houdini, he can probably manage McD. as well."

Crandon was quick to answer Tillyard. "It is true that a McGill student is alleged to have punched Houdini in the abdomen at Houdini's request but that he did it unexpectedly and probably caused a minute leak in his sigmoid flexure which caused peritonitis and death. Walter never said he would 'get' Houdini, but 71 times in our records he has said in the last 13 months 'Give Houdini my love, tell him I will see him soon.' I think that is what you heard him say, but it was addressed to Houdini and not to McDougall. Walter hates nobody and he was in no way a causal relation. He may see causes converging before we do. That is all."

How Crandon can claim with such authority that Whitehead punched Houdini at the magician's request is mystifying, especially since Whitehead would be the only one who took that position in the depositions for the insurance companies, but those wouldn't take place until three months after Crandon wrote his letter to Tillyard.

Of course, Sir Arthur was asked to comment on Houdini's death. "His death is a great shock and a deep mystery to me," the noted author said. "He was a teetotaler, did not smoke, and was one of the cleanest living men I have ever known. I greatly admired him, and cannot understand how the end came for one so youthful. We were great friends."

Except for the description of Houdini's lifestyle, the entire comment is an unmitigated lie. Pheneas had predicted Houdini's death for a year, dooming the magician for standing in the way of the great movement of which Doyle was the chief earthly representative. Since Houdini's rebuff of Lady Doyle's mediumship, the two had been great enemies, not friends.

If one were to suspect Houdini a victim of foul play, then the section of organized crime that was composed of fraudulent spirit mediums must be considered likely suspects. Consoling lonely and bereft people was big business and Houdini's campaign and its attendant intense publicity made inroads in raising public consciousness about this ruthless con. That the Spiritualist opposition would use violence against exposers is well documented. Both Rinn and Houdini took the threats against their lives seriously enough for them to arm themselves.

The Spiritualist underworld's modus operandi in cases like this was often poisoning. Both Houdini and Bess suffered from some form of nonspecific poisoning previous to Houdini's death. Bess's illness lingered and she was admitted to the hospital while Houdini was dying. According to Bess, the doctors considered her illness "so much more dangerous than his, at that time, and the doctors feared for my life." Even though Houdini took the Spiritualists' death threats seriously, there was much less emphasis put on security back in the 1920s. In Houdini's last programs, he asked his audiences to relate stories of getting robbed by fraudulent mediums and he listed his home address for the responses. If someone were hell-bent on poisoning Houdini, it wouldn't have been very difficult.

That the fraudulent mediums didn't take kindly to a disruption of their cash flow was also evidenced years after Houdini died. In 1976, M. Lamar Keene wrote a book called *The Psychic Mafia*. The book's title reflected perfectly its thesis, and it was written by a former fraudulent medium. Keene revealed that he had sat in on meetings where various means of "expediting the demise of certain elderly folk who were sure to leave a lot of money to the spiritualist cause were discussed." During that discussion one female medium claimed to be an expert on the administration of untraceable poisons. Keene's break with the mediums and his subsequent exposure prompted two separate attempts on his life. In the first, before the book was published, an assassin shot at him while he was strolling on the lawn of his Tampa home. He threw himself to the ground, and the bullet narrowly missed him, lodging in the wall. In 1979, he wasn't as lucky. Strolling in Miami, he was gunned down by a hit man in a passing car and his femoral artery was severed. He was saved by the quick ministrations of the EMS. Detectives on the Miami police force told psychic researcher William Rauscher that the incident was an "attempted homicide" and that the gunman was probably a hired assassin deployed by the psychic mafia, which had warned Keene that if his book exposed names he would be killed.

After Houdini's death, Max Malini, the sleight-of-hand magician who played on the same bill in New York with Houdini thirty-eight years earlier, had an interesting comment about his old friend. "He made a mistake in bucking up against educated men like Sir Oliver Lodge and Conan Doyle. Those men are not fakers. They believe in what they are doing. Harry thought they were like the bunco spiritualists he showed up so easily."

If the phony mediums loathed Houdini for jeopardizing their incomes, Doyle and the true believers despised him for standing in the way of the New Revelation. Doyle had more of an impetus to dislike him; in his eyes, Houdini was possessed of spiritual powers himself, yet his public stance was anti-medium. Despite his public utterances, Doyle made no bones about his dislike for Houdini to his personal acquaintances. As early as November 1, 1924, Doyle, writing to Crandon about the SA investigation, predicted that both Prince and Houdini "will get his deserts very exactly meted out . . . I think there is a general pay-day coming soon that we can await it with equanimity."

In a letter to Fulton Oursler, Doyle was even more forthcoming about Houdini's fate. "His death was most certainly decreed from the other side," he wrote. Part of his reasoning was that Houdini was hiding his real psychic powers under the guise of conjuring. "The spirit world might well be incensed against him if he was himself using psychic powers at the very time when he was attacking them."

Given that Doyle felt that the spirit world "decreed" Houdini's death, is there any reason to suggest that Doyle, like Annie Benninghofen and others like her, was capable of helping the spirits along in their desires? According to his contemporary psychic researchers, Doyle was a man who would brook no opposition to his ideas. "He was not a man who was accustomed to being told he was wrong," Eric Dingwall observed. Nor was he above fudging with facts to support his spiritualistic theses. Walter Franklin Prince noted, "The mistakes of Houdini very frequently do not help his argument—that is, if he had got the facts straight they would have served his type of propaganda just as much, while Sir Arthur's blunders nearly always work to the favor of his argument."

Doyle was also not above using threats to force his will. In a dispute with Harry Price over Price's exposure of one of his favorite mediums, Sir Arthur threatened to have Price evicted from his laboratory and suggested that if Price persisted in spewing "sewage" about phony Spiritualists, he would meet the same fate as Houdini.

It's hard to extrapolate from these predispositions and suggest Doyle played an active role in enacting Pheneas's death sentence on Houdini, but that's not to say that Doyle's circle's condemnation of Houdini and the forecasting of his doom for standing in the way of their movement wasn't read as a code by other Spiritualists. What gave all this an added sense of urgency was that Doyle and his intimates knew that time was running out. The great crisis of the world was at hand; they were in the end times.

On January 5, 1927, Dr. L. R. G. Crandon was one of the keynote speakers at the Thirty-second Annual Convention of the Massachusetts State Association of Spiritualists. Sharing the bill with him was William Elliott Hammond, the author of "Houdini Unmasked." With Houdini out of the picture, Crandon and Margery had begun a national tour to promote the spiritualistic doctrine and fulfill Pheneas's wishes for them to be the leaders of the U.S. movement.

The files of Walter Franklin Prince contained an astute analysis of Dr. Crandon. "[He] is a man who has never learned to play. He takes everything seriously.

Mrs. Crandon, on the other hand, is extremely fun loving. Dr. Crandon took up Spiritualism as a violent hobby and Mrs. Crandon played it for all it was worth. He is able to pose as a martyr to science, likening himself to Galileo. A half million uncritical Spiritualists in the country regard Margery as a sort of Messiah. In this way Dr. Crandon receives a balm for his prestige in certain quarters, which he feels entitled to because of his surgical skill. Another interesting point is that Dr. Crandon's upbringing has been violently anti-supernaturalistic and this whole business seems a reaction against this. He claims that Walter has entirely removed the fear of death for him. This fear was evidently of a rather morbid sort, judging by certain books in his library."

There's an especially poignant letter in the Margery archives that was written by Margery's biological son to Dr. Crandon's biological daughter, who the doctor had disowned after he divorced her mother. "Dr. Crandon . . . was a supreme egotist," John Crandon wrote. "He could tolerate no one who opposed him in any way." He paints a picture of a man who, because of his "pathological egoism" had to "be a big wheel," suggesting that was the reason for the tremendous investment in Margery's mediumship. Concomitant to all this, Crandon had control issues, to which John attested. "I never did *one thing* against Dr. Crandon's wishes!" he told his stepsister. "In spite of the fact that I had no particular desire for medicine, I went into medicine for his sake." He also wrote: "I owe everything I have to your father."

It was alleged among Crandon's enemies in Boston psychic circles that the doctor had threatened an investigator who had the temerity to touch some of the ectoplasm that Margery produced. He was quoted as saying, "If he had carried out his test, he would never have left the house alive." Young John Crandon is the source of another disquieting story about his stepfather. According to his recollections, Dr. Crandon and Sir Arthur Conan Doyle made a late-night trip to a hospital morgue to lift fingerprints off a cadaver to assist Margery in her production of fingerprints during her séances.

In 1932, Eleanor Hoffman, Dr. Prince's secretary, cultivated a friendship with Margery and began filing confidential reports to Dr. Prince. Some of their conversations pertained to the Houdini-inspired investigation by the Secret Service and the British M.P. Harry Day into the disappearance of young boys in the Crandon household. Margery's statements affirm that there was at least one additional boy other than Horace Newton who came over from England. According to her account, this boy's parents were still alive, although poor, and Crandon's sister Laura took the boy from a home and brought him to Boston. They kept him all summer and wanted to adopt him, but according to Margery, the family would not allow the adoption so they returned him to England. Before he was allegedly returned, Margery said that "the poor little fellow had adenoids and had to be circumcised," so Crandon performed the operation at home. After the operation, "the little fellow sat up in bed and looked at himself and said, 'I aren't pretty anymore,' and John told him that was all right, he looked like that too."

When the little boy left, according to Margery, "people wrote asking his whereabouts, and the prime minister of England cabled to ask where he was and demanded a cable reply. Why people even said Dr. Crandon committed illegal operations on little children and murdered them," she told Hoffman. Doyle seemed worried, too. In an undated letter during Day's investigation, he wrote Crandon, "Concerning that blessed boy—was he lost on the way back? This answer reached me today. I have to know the details of the affair in case I have to meet any question."

On the same day that Margery related the circumcision story, she opened a closet door to put away some fingerprints Walter had produced and showed Hoffman a "whole rack of pictures of little children—most of them really lovely." When Hoffman commented on the pictures, Margery told her: "Those are Dr. Crandon's caesareans—aren't they sweet? All caesareans." As far as we know, Crandon was a surgeon who was not noted for delivering babies, naturally or by Caesarean. There were much more than one hundred pictures of young children in Crandon's closet.

When Houdini received the blows to his stomach in Montreal, the prime minister of Canada was Mackenzie King, a closeted Spiritualist who used to hold séances to commune with his dead mother and dog. King's secret interest in the spirit world was only revealed to a shocked Canadian public in 1950, two years after he had finally left office.

A similar revelation might have transpired in the White House. Houdini had been intent on proving that his assertions about séances in the Coolidge family were correct. In 1929, in a letter to British psychic researcher Harry Price, Crandon informed him that a Theron Pierce, "a man long interested and active in psychical research," had been formally delegated by the ASPR, which Crandon controlled by then, to represent that society during Margery's London experiments. "You may further recognize him as a host . . . to the President and Mrs. Coolidge last summer for three months. Mr. Pierce's estate was the summer White House."

The Pierce family obtained their vast wealth through oil interests. Was Pierce close to Joseph DeWyckoff, another Spiritualist multimillionaire? Did their influence extend up to the White House?

The man who viciously assaulted Houdini in his dressing room remained a stranger to history until Montreal journalist Don Bell began a twenty-year journey to ascertain his identity. Bell's groundbreaking book only added fuel to the notion of a conspiracy against the master magician. Joscelyn Gordon Whitehead was the son of a pool hall owner in Kelowna, British Columbia, a small town with a rough reputation. Although he wrote that he graduated from Kelowna High School on his McGill student card, Bell could find no record of Whitehead's attendance there. What he heard from close associates of Whitehead was a different story. According to them, Whitehead's father was a British consul in either Hong Kong or Singapore, and Joscelyn was believed to have had a proper English education before enrolling at McGill.

Bell discovered that after Houdini's death, Whitehead became a virtual recluse, living in a dank apartment that was stacked from floor to ceiling with old newspapers. The only human interaction he seemed to have had was with various women who were interested in spiritual pursuits. One of these women happened to be Lady Marler, a wealthy heiress and the wife of Sir Herbert Marler, a long- time ally of the Canadian prime minister and a one-time ambassador to the United States. Lady Marler was said to be extremely close to the devout Spiritualist prime minister. How she got to be close to Whitehead was never determined.

A close examination of the depositions given by Whitehead, Price, and Smiley reveals some interesting facts. When Whitehead appeared at Houdini's dressing room that fateful day, he had already had a prior relationship with the magician. He had come to return a book he had borrowed and Houdini was well enough acquainted with him to introduce him to the other two students. According to Whitehead's deposition, he had several encounters with Houdini that week. In one, Whitehead claimed that the two had spoken about longevity and that Houdini had given him an advance copy of the November *Scientific American*. A perusal of the table of contents revealed that there was an article about longevity in that issue written by Houdini's old friend A. A. Hopkins.

What's curious about Whitehead's account is that he claimed that he called upon Houdini in his room at the Mount Royal Hotel. Bell learned that Houdini's troupe had been staying at the Prince of Wales Hotel that was adjacent to the Princess Theatre. In Houdini's archives, there are several notes in Houdini's handwriting, even one to Bess, written on Mount Royal stationery. Was Houdini maintaining a separate hotel room in a different hotel? Why would he do that?

We know that Houdini had double agents who had ties to the Spiritualist community. Could Houdini's interactions with Whitehead have been an attempt to create another such agent? If Houdini was taking the threats on his life seriously, as we know he was, it would be prudent for him to maintain a separate hotel room away from the others in his group. Whitehead stated in his deposition that he had called on Houdini at the Mount Royal twice, one time leaving his card. They had obviously met before the punching incident on Friday, and in fact, Whitehead claims that they met twice after the incident. The later visits may have been intended to make light of his vicious attack on Houdini. What's certain is that Whitehead's line of interrogation in Houdini's dressing room that fateful Friday is eerily reminiscent of Spiritualists who sought to engage people in discussions of the Bible to promulgate their claim that Jesus and His disciples were spiritualistic mediums who performed miracles.

Whitehead's insistence on talking about the miracles of the Bible seemed to catch Houdini off guard. When he refused comment and suggested that he would have been considered a miracle worker in biblical days, Whitehead seemed disturbed by his answer. The assault took place just seconds later. According to Whitehead, Houdini invited the punches, but we know from the other two eyewitnesses that it wasn't the case. Was the wry smile that crossed Houdini's face after the pummeling a realization that the Spiritualists had gotten to him? Was the attack the fulfillment of Margery's threat to have her friends beat him up? Was the bizarre assault in the lobby of the Prince of Wales hotel part of a Spiritualist plot?

There were hundreds of people at Grand Central Station on November 2, awaiting the train that would bring Harry Houdini back to New York for the last time. As his coffin was borne through the station, people wept openly and bared their heads. Two days later, more than 2,500 people jammed into the Elks Club in New York for the funeral. A far larger number of people thronged the streets outside, almost closing it off to traffic. All of Houdini's siblings, including Leo, attended. Bess, wearing a veil and a black silk dress, was accompanied by Sophie Rosenblatt and collapsed when the coffin lid was permanently affixed. Rabbi Bernard Drachman eulogized Houdini, claiming: "He possessed a

Mourners line up before Houdini's coffin. *From the collection of John Cox*

wondrous power which he never understood and which he never revealed to anyone in life." Rabbi B. A. Tintner added: "He was exceptional, a unique personality, and besides that, he was one of the noblest and sweetest of men."

After the ceremony, as the last strains of Chopin's Funeral March faded, a procession of twenty-five cars tied up traffic as it made its way through the Manhattan streets and over the Queensborough Bridge. When they reached the gravesite at Machpelah cemetery in Queens, Bess collapsed again.

Newspapers around the country had extensive coverage, and the tributes to Houdini were plentiful. *The New York World* wrote, "Starting out as a magician, he developed so much that by the end of his career he had fairly earned the title of scientist." *The New York Times* lauded him as "a man of wide reading, a collector both of books and of art." *The New York Sun* lamented: "His death removes a great artist and a useful scientist, and he was both without impairment of the qualities of heart and soul that endeared him to his fellows of the stage and his unnumbered admirers in front of the footlights." *The New York Daily News* headline seemed to sum up the outpouring of grief: "Wanted: More Houdinis."

Heartfelt tributes came from all quarters. "Houdini was the greatest showman of our time by far," the great humorist Will Rogers wrote. "I played with Harry at Keith's Philadelphia over eighteen years ago for the first time. I was roping at my pony on the stage and was billed to close the show. . . . Harry was just ahead with his handcuff tricks. It was late when he went on. He held that audience for one hour and a quarter. Not a soul moved. He would come out of his cabinet every fifteen or twenty minutes, perspiring and kinder size up that crowd to see just about how they were standing it. Now, mind you, when he is in that cabinet there is not a thing going on. A whole Theatre full are just waiting. Now he had that something that no one can define that is generally just passed off under the heading of showmanship. But it was in reality, Sense, Shrewdness, Judgment, unmatched ability, Intuition, Personality, and an uncanny knowledge of people."

"Harry Houdini was a picturesque figure," his friend Charles Carter wrote in *The Billboard*. "He was much maligned and generally misunderstood. His life was unselfish and devoted always to the betterment of those he loved and those less fortunate. His deeds of charity were manifold. Indigent showfolk by the score he has relieved and made prosperous. So unostentatious was he in such acts that only his closest friends were cognizant of them. He made the long, long fight. He fought for a principle; this principle was the kernel of magic, its respectability. He fought everywhere—on the stage, in the press, in the home, on the floor of the U.S. Senate, in the church and, lastly, in the little back room of Martinka's or wherever the meeting room of the Society of American Magicians happened to be. He stood as the greatest figure of usefulness to, and representative of, the conjurer in his generation. He was an institution, and we, the exponents of modern magic, owe his memory a debt that we can never pay. His name alone lent dignity to magic."

At a memorial service a few days after the funeral, the movie star Eddie Cantor, in the midst of eulogizing his friend, broke down and had to be helped off the stage.

In Houdini's will there was a provision for Hardeen to inherit Houdini's props. It was meant to be a loan, not a bequest, for Houdini also stipulated that upon Hardeen's death, the material was to be destroyed. Hardeen immediately resumed his career. He was booked to open January 10, 1927 at the Ritz Theater in Elizabeth, New Jersey. On that same day, William Matthews, the Ritz's manager, revealed that threats against the life of Hardeen had been received and asked for

Fellow magician Charles Carter (center) wrote an eloquent eulogy for Houdini.
From the collection of Sid Fleischman

police protection for the performer. According to Matthews, Hardeen's life had been threatened because "he fell heir to certain of Houdini's secrets." It seems more likely that Matthews was referring to Houdini's investigative files on the Spiritualists rather than his production of silks from a globe.

Six months later, Scotland Yard detectives began investigating a break-in at the home of Colonel Harry Day. Day was concerned about the slashing of a painting that was given to him by Houdini in 1909. It had been inscribed "To Harry Day from his sincere pal, Harry Houdini." Day told the press that he "could not imagine a motive for the vandalism." Was the slashing of the Houdini gift a random act of vandalism or a symbolic message to Day? Or were the intruders looking for something hidden in the slashed painting?

A British newspaper clipping of the incident was sent to Crandon by the psychic researcher Eric Dingwall, who was still angling for sittings with Margery. "This is the man whom Houdini got to ask about your kid. You are revenged!" Dingwall wrote. Although it was hardly news to Crandon, the clipping and the note wound up in Crandon's scrapbook.

Also in the scrapbook was a copy of the letter that Crandon sent Doyle on July 6, two weeks after the Day break-in.

Dear Sir Arthur:

Did you notice June 22 that the apartment of Harry Day, M.P., was robbed and destroyed by Vandals? If we were superstitious, *we might be inclined to say that old John G. Nemesis were on the job. Consequent but not because of unfair treatment of Margery, the following events should be noted:*

1. Dr. Walter Franklin Prince loses his job at the American S.P.R.
2. Dr. Comstock has mysteriously shutup.
3. McDougall was "promoted" from Harvard.
4. Code has left Harvard.
5. Foster Damon has left Harvard.
6. Marshall has left Harvard.
7. Hillyer has left Harvard.
8. Houdini is dead.
9. Dingwall has left the S.P.R.
10. Harry Day, M.P., is a victim of Vandals.

We hope you and Lady Doyle are thinking well of a possible visit to us. It would mark a new peak in metapsychics. A book by you fully describing all the phenomena at Lime Street as observed by you yourself, ending up with the finger-prints, would do as much towards turning the world over as any one thing you could do. Our love to you all.

As ever,
L. R. G. Crandon, M.D.

On August 15, 1927, Hardeen, who had just returned home from a western tour, went to the Snider Avenue police station to report that his Brooklyn home had been broken into while he was on the road. A friend of Hardeen, who had been forwarding his mail, saw that the pantry door had been forced open and two panes in the door from the pantry to the kitchen had been cut away. While jewels, linens, other valuables, and $15,000 in Liberty bonds were undisturbed, the "thieves" had taken apart several pieces of Houdini's apparatus, looking for something. The crime was never solved.

Sometime later, in the presence of Joe Hyman, Houdini's old friend, Hardeen destroyed all of Houdini's personal files by burning them in the basement furnace of his home. According to Hyman, Hardeen "incidentally almost burnt his residence down doing so."

Hereward Carrington, who had been loaned a vital piece of evidence (Walter's thumbprint) and was once the sole supporter of Margery on the *Scientific American* committee, had become convinced by August 1932 that she was a fraud. When he returned to his apartment after a day trip to Philadelphia, he was amazed to see that someone had entered his residence by forcing open a window. Writing to the owner of the thumbprint, he had an idea about who had engineered the break-in: "I spoke to several people about this incident, at the time, and was warned that certain people would stop at nothing in their attempts to obtain evidence, or destroy existing evidence. I was warned quite frankly that I was in a way dealing with the 'underworld,' and advised to act accordingly."

Carrington was convinced that he had just had a visit from John G. Nemesis.

"I do not believe [Bess] will ever fully recover," Frank Black wrote Kilby after Houdini died. "He was more to her than the average husband." After the funeral, she began her recuperation with a trip to Atlantic City. Then she went back to the brownstone and began boxing up her husband's books and going through his effects. One box that she opened was filled with love letters to Houdini, including some torrid letters from Daisy White. When Bess raged at Daisy, the counter girl told her that the letters were just a put-on and somehow managed to mollify the widow. The other authors weren't as lucky. Bess made appointments for them to visit her and when they arrived, all at the same time, the maid informed them that Mrs. Houdini was too ill to receive them and to send each one home with their love letters in a neat bundle.

Having disposed of her flesh-and-blood rivals, Bess wasted no time in banishing Houdini's other true love—his numerous collections, with which she had been forced to share her home. It took Bess a few months to arrange her husband's books, some of which were going to the Library of Congress. She sold the drama collection and gave away several of Houdini's effects to his close friends. Then she sold the house at a loss and bought a smaller house, where she lived with her

After Houdini died, Bess did a massive housecleaning but kept all the trophies.
From the collection of Dr. Bruce Averbook

mother, niece, and sister. According to the magician William Frazee, before the move "she called in a junk man and he took several wagon loads of things away. if Houdini knew it he would turn over in his grave. Boxes of Hancuffs and thousands of keyes, faked mail bag locks, keys from cell locks from all over the world etc. *Sic Transit Gloria Mundi.*" The very stuff of Houdini's soul, his locks, manacles, and keys, were now just junk to be disposed of in the back of a junkman's wagon. To Houdini, they were just as precious to him as trophies, and they didn't even earn the dignity of winding up in a pawnshop window on the Bowery.

Houdini had made many arrangements with friends, giving each one a unique code so they could communicate from beyond the grave with him. By one count, he had made more than twenty compacts, each one unique. On December 2, 1917, he visited his friend W. J. Hilliar in his office at *Billboard* magazine and dropped a copy of *Roget's Thesaurus* on his desk. Hilliar opened the book and found a penciled inscription on the inside. He began to thank Houdini for the gift, but his visitor cut him off.

"Hilliar, there is *our* code," Houdini whispered. "But never breathe it to a living soul. If I go first and you get a message from me which includes these words you will know it is genuine."

Hilliar used the book over the years, always noting the inscription on the front page, but when he picked it up three weeks after the magician's death, he was stunned to see that while Houdini's signature was still prominent, the code words had faded out. Hilliar consulted handwriting experts, who told him that penciled words should never fade away. A minute examination revealed that the indentations of the pencil still existed and Hilliar carefully traced them over. He was shocked to learn that overnight, the code had once more faded from the page.

Houdini seemed to be manifesting himself in other unusual circumstances too. When he had posed for the marble bust that eventually would adorn his grave, he had had three clay copies made. He kept one and gave one to Harry Day and one to Joe Hyman. Ten days after Houdini's death, Joe's fell to the floor and shattered. A few days later, the exact same thing happened to Day's version.

Strange things had happened even before Houdini died. Robert Gysel, who was one of Houdini's Spiritualism investigators, wrote Fulton Oursler to report such an occurrence. "Something happened to me in my room on Sunday night, October 24, 1926, 10:58. Houdini had given me a picture of himself which I had framed and hung on the wall At the above time and date, the picture fell to the ground, breaking the glass. I now know that Houdini will die. Maybe there is something in these psychic phenomena after all."

In November, Sir Arthur began a correspondence with Bess, after he had a report that Houdini had come back to a medium. Unfortunately Bess's response never surfaced but it may have been similar to what she told *The New York Times* when asked for comment about a message from Houdini that was received from an Attleboro, Massachusetts, medium. Houdini's communication was largely garbled but a few phrases were decipherable. "Tussle with death was agony" was one, along with "God is truth, God is love, God is without peer" and "See some of my friends and tell them Houdini still lives."

"Houdini was an unusually intelligent and brilliant man," Bess told the *Times*. "All these messages without exception have been silly . . . I alone have the key to any messages which might be received, a quotation which Houdini used in his work, and which would enable me to recognize anything which really came through."

It wasn't as if Bess wasn't trying. She told *The N.Y. Evening Journal* that every day on the hour of his death she sat in front of his picture and waited for a sign. "Before he died he promised to come back to me then if he could. . . . As I sit before his picture, I feel he is guiding me and telling me what to do. But if only he could speak!"

Bess had at least one person who agreed with her that all of the Houdini messages to date had been "false and ridiculous." Dr. L. R. G. Crandon, now identified as a lecturer on psychic matters, scoffed at the notion that Houdini could be back. "If we know anything at all, we do know that people cannot communicate with us until they have been in the sleep for four or five years. We learned that from Walter." That explained why Margery had made no attempt to communicate with Houdini, the doctor added.

By December, Doyle was exchanging weekly letters with Bess. After both sides regretted the estrangement that grew between Houdini and Doyle, the two began a debate over whether Houdini truly had psychic powers. The closest Bess got to agreeing was to entertain the notion that if he did have psychic power he might not have known it. Meanwhile, Bess let Doyle know that she was hopeful contact would still be made. "Surely, our beloved God will let him bring me the message for which I wait, and not the silly messages I get from the various people who claim they hear from him. Please believe me when I say that I have taken an oath to tell the world when I do hear from him—also if a message directly to you, with our code comes through. The hour his soul went to his Maker (Sunday at 1:26 P.M., October 31, 1926) and every Sunday at the same hour, I spend with him, alone, in prayer."

With the New Year, the intensity of the Doyle-Bess correspondence grew. Doyle sent Bess the letter he had received from Clarke in Montreal reporting that Houdini threatened to tear him "to ribbons." On the defensive, Bess claimed that Houdini would never have said such a thing and that he in fact had said that he would tear any Spiritualist books to ribbons. By now, Doyle was sending Bess to New York mediums he knew and enclosing letters of introduction for her. One or two minor "communications" had impressed Bess and she had reported them to Sir Arthur. "I am most thankful that you have got so far," he wrote her back on March 8. "Thank you for your bravery & frankness in admitting the facts. You have now earned the fulfilment. It *may* have been a test of you."

Bess was now offering $10,000 to any medium who could put her in touch with her beloved husband. She began to be inundated with letters from every crank in the country. As the first anniversary of Houdini's death loomed, Bess began to fall apart. On October 10, she attended a debate at Carnegie Hall between Arthur Ford, who spoke for the Spiritualist view, and Howard Thurston, who represented the magic community. It was a strange encounter. Ford denounced Thurston for claiming that most spiritualistic phenomena could be reproduced by using an instrument the size of a watch and bet him $10,000 that he couldn't. He referred to Lady Doyle as one of the world's best trance mediums and claimed that "all spiritualistic phenomena stand or fall with Margery." When Thurston spoke, he backtracked and claimed that he had seen mediums do things that he could never explain.

A week later, the unveiling of Houdini's gravestone found Bess near collapse. At the service, Houdini's lawyer Bernard Ernst read Bess a letter from Conan Doyle. "I should like to send a message of good will upon the occasion of the unveiling of your husband's monument. All differences must be suspended at such a time. He was a great master of his profession and, in some ways, the most remarkable man I have ever known."

Doyle wrote her again and sent some clippings. A month later, Bess responded, explaining that she had been "very ill" since the unveiling. In December, out of the blue, Bess announced that she was going to do a vaudeville turn, and freeze a man in a cake of ice, an effect that Houdini had been working on years earlier in England. She called a press conference in a vacant store in Manhattan where Waka Tanka, a Sioux Indian mystery man wearing a rubber suit, was lowered into a metal container and a ton and a half of ice was frozen around him. Once the ice had formed, a hole was chopped in the front to expose his face. Bess told the assembled press that along with the ice stunt, she planned to escape from either handcuffs or a straitjacket. A month later, Bess and the Indian performed another demonstration of the man in ice, and she was overcome by fumes from the carbon dioxide used to produce the ice. According to the papers, she was taken to a doctor while "the Indian looked for a hot fire." Bess's show never made the circuit.

She had one admirer, though. "I wish you every possible success with your new act," Conan Doyle wrote her on February 12, 1928. "May all go well." Then he responded to Bess's report that Houdini may have been responsible for a mirror breaking in her house. "I think the mirror incident shows every sign of being a message. After all such things don't happen elsewhere. No mirror has ever broken in this house. Why should yours do so? And it is just the sort of energetic thing one could expect from him if for some reason he could not get his message. Supposing our view of the future is true is it not possible that the Powers that be might for a time forbid him to use those gifts which he was foremost in his life in denying. But you will get your test—I feel convinced of that."

From the collection of Dr. Bruce Averbook

26

There Is No Death

JUST AFTER NOON ON JANUARY 8, 1929, REVEREND Arthur Ford and his followers arrived at Bess Houdini's home on Payton Avenue. She had taken a nasty fall a few days earlier and she was lying on her French sofa, her head wrapped in a bandage, covered with a blanket. Ford arranged some chairs around her in a semicircle and then lowered the blinds to shut out the sunlight. Accompanying the medium were members of his circle. There were Francis Fast, a wealthy businessman with whom he shared an apartment; John Stafford, an associate editor at *Scientific American*; his wife, Dorothy; and another lady named Helen Morris. Besides them, there were two reporters present, Harry Zander of the United Press and Rea Jaure, the women's editor of *The New York Evening Graphic*. Bess's press agent, Charles Williams, and her old dear friend Minnie Chester were also in attendance.

Ford was there to deliver a coded message from Houdini from the other side.

For almost a year now, the medium had been receiving messages from both Houdini's mother and from Houdini himself. On February 8 of the previous year, in a trance, David Fletcher, Ford's control, had brought Mrs. Weiss to the circle. She had one word to transmit—*forgive*. A letter had been dispatched to Bess from Ford's First Spiritualist Church in Manhattan, informing her of the breakthrough.

Bess wrote back, impressed. "It was indeed the message for which he always secretly hoped . . . this is the first message which I have received which has an appearance of truth."

After spending months in England and Europe, Arthur Ford returned to New York and resumed his sittings. From October 9 to January 5, both Mrs. Weiss and

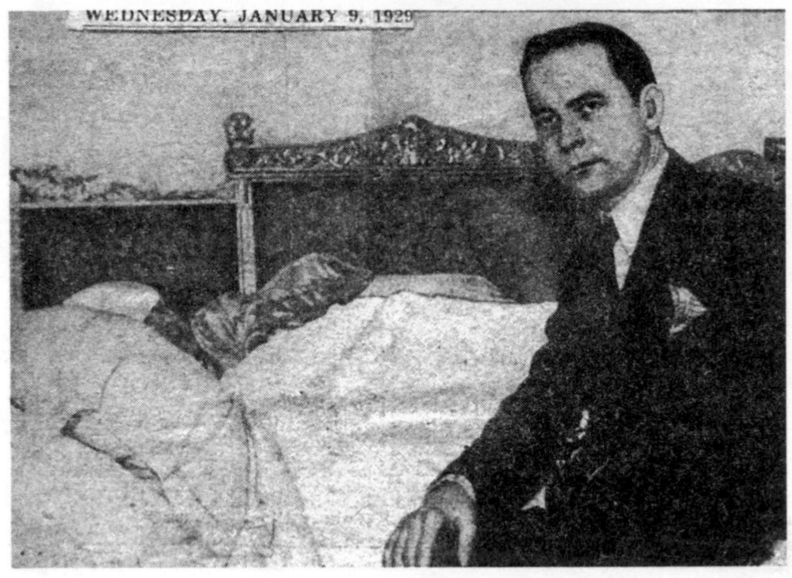
WEDNESDAY, JANUARY 9, 1929

The Reverend Arthur Ford poses next to a bandaged and sedated Bess right after channeling Houdini's spirit. *From the collection of Patrick Culliton*

Houdini visited his circle and gave them a ten-word code, which they were to bring to Bess. When she heard the code, she was to complete the pre-arranged message with Houdini. Getting this through was of vital importance to Houdini.

"*I came to impress you that this is of great importance—greater than you have ever dreamed,*" Houdini said through Ford's voice. "*I desire to bring this message before the world. It will make your names, coupled with mine, appear in headlines in all the papers of America and Europe, in the statement that Houdini has proved to the world that survival after death is a fact.*"

Houdini's code, as delivered by Houdini through Fletcher, was: *Rosabelle—answer—tell—pray—answer—look—tell—answer—answer—tell.* "Houdini says the code is known only to him and his wife, and that no one on earth but those two know it," Fletcher told the group. "He says that she must make it public. It must come from her; you are nothing more than agents. He says that when this comes through there will be a veritable storm, that many will seek to destroy her and she will be accused of everything that is not good, but she is honest enough to keep the pact which they repeated over and over before his death."

Now, armed with the message, they were at Bess's house for the conclusion of the process. Ford sat down in a chair and covered his eyes with a Liberty silk blindfold. He relaxed and went into a trance. When his body quivered, it was a signal that Fletcher had come through.

"This man is coming now," Fletcher said. "The same one who came the other night. Houdini is here and wishes his wife as faithful in death as in life to receive his message. He tells me to say, 'Hello, Bess, sweetheart,' and he wants to repeat the message and finish it for you. The code, he says, is the one you used to use in one of your secret mind-reading acts."

He repeated the ten words to Bess.

"He wants you to tell him whether they are right or not," Fletcher said.

"Yes, they are," Bess said.

"He smiles and says, 'Thank you.' Now I can go on. He tells you to take off your wedding ring and tell them what *Rosabelle* means."

Bess pulled her left hand from under the blanket and slowly took the ring off her finger. Holding it before her, she began to sing in a weak voice:

Rosabelle, sweet Rosabelle, I love you more than I can tell;
O'er me you cast a spell, I love you! My Rosabelle!"

Bess wiped a tear from her eye.

"He says, 'I thank you, darling. The first time I heard you sing that was in our first show together years ago,'" Fletcher relayed.

Bess nodded assent.

"Then there is something that he wants to tell me that no one but his wife knows. He smiles now and shows me a picture and draws the curtain so, or in this manner," Fletcher said.

Bess picked up the cue. "*Je tire le rideau comme ça*," she said. It was the French phrase that Houdini had taught her when she drew the curtain while performing the Metamorphosis in France.

"And now the nine words besides *Rosabelle* spell a word in our code," Fletcher relayed Houdini's message. Houdini explained how in their code *answer* stood for the letter *B*, *tell* the letter *E*, *pray, answer* the letter *L*, *look* the letter *I*, and *answer, answer* represented *V*. When the code was translated, it spelled out the word *believe*.

"The message I want to send back to my wife is '*Rosabelle, believe*,'" Fletcher relayed. "Is that right?"

"Yes, yes. That is the message. Harry—Harry!" Bess said, stifling tears.

"He says 'Tell the whole world that Harry Houdini still lives and will prove it a thousand times and more.' He is pretty excited. He says 'I was perfectly honest and sincere though I resorted to tricks, for the simple reason that I did not believe it true, and no more than was justifiable. I am now sincere in sending this through in my desire to undo. Tell all those who lost faith because of my mistake to lay hold again of hope, and to live with the knowledge that life is continuous. There is no death. That is my message to the world, through my wife and through this instrument.'"

Bess lay back on the couch, almost delirious.

Houdini had broken through.

Houdini Breaks Chains of Death, Talks From Grave in Secret Code
Harry Houdini's Message Arrives!
Houdini Speaks From Grave to Aid Spiritism

The news made headlines around the world the next day, fueled by moving accounts of the séance written by the two journalists present. Spiritualists around the world celebrated their greatest holiday yet.

Interviewed by reporters, Bess stood by the séance and made plans to go to the safe deposit box to retrieve the code. "My friends will call me mad, I know. I have received advice and warnings from many who are near to me not to go on with this. But it is what Harry asked me to do. He ordered me to do it. It was the arrangement we had before he passed on." To reinforce her convictions, she issued a statement: "Regardless of any statements made to the contrary, I wish to declare that the message, in its entirety, and in the agreed upon sequence, given to me by Arthur Ford, is the correct message prearranged between Mr. Houdini and myself. Beatrice Houdini."

The very next day the entire enterprise was smeared with not a taint but a large, messy stain of conspiracy. In a remarkable turnaround, the reporter who had written the previous day's article, Rea Jaure, revealed that the entire séance and the transmission of Houdini's secret code had been choreographed step by step by Ford and Bess. Under an even bigger headline, "Houdini Message a Big Hoax!" Jaure admitted that her initial article had been written the day before the actual séance, because Bess had taken her through a line-by-line rehearsal of the transmission. According to Jaure, Bess had invited her to many wild booze-fueled parties thrown by "temperamental people" in the weeks before the séance and had introduced the reporter to her escort, a young, attractive man named David Fletcher. Visiting Mrs. Houdini the day before the séance, Bess showed her the letter that contained the code that had been dropped off by Fast and Stafford. Jaure then borrowed the letter and rushed to her office to have a photostatic copy made. When she returned to Bess's house at six P.M. she asked Bess what would transpire at the séance.

"I shall lie on the living room couch. When Mr. Ford enters . . . I will be introduced to him and say, "I don't suppose you remember me. I came with others once a long time ago to Carnegie Hall, where you were denouncing Houdini from the platform."

"'Yes,' Ford will say. 'I was told afterwards that you were Mrs. Houdini. This is not a good way for us to meet again. Come, let us sit and see if I can convince you that I am at least sincere.' Ford will appear to go in a slumber and directly say, 'Hello, Bess, the guide will be David Fletcher.' He will say 'Houdini is here and wishes his wife as faithful in death as in life to receive his message.'"

Bess then continued her narrative about the séance. According to Jaure's second article, it unfolded exactly as Bess had told her it would, except that the widow had forgotten to say, "Harry—Harry" until she was prompted by her friend Minnie.

The day after the séance, Jaure called Ford, who was ecstatic over the publicity the séance had generated. She wanted to meet him to discuss it and he told her he had to attend a lecture in New Jersey that night but that if eleven P.M. was not too late, he would stop by her house then. Jaure said she was working but that if they could agree on a time, she would leave work and meet him at her apartment. They set the assignation for 11:15 P.M.

Jaure got home by eleven, accompanied by William Plummer, her managing editor, and Edward Churchill, another reporter. The two men hid in the kitchenette. Arthur Ford arrived right on time. Sitting in the living room, Rea began by asking Ford if he remembered the "peculiar" party where they had met. "You went with Bess and I first met you as Mr. David," she said.

"Yes, indeed," the medium said. "Wasn't it funny? Bess and I had a great time among those temperamental people, didn't we?"

Then Jaure lowered the hammer. She told Ford that she had written her story twenty-four hours before the séance and showed him her original notes with the code written out by Bess. Ford's face turned white.

"But you must play ball," he pleaded. "Really. I would be glad to make financial compensation."

"Reporters never take money," she replied.

"Then I'll give you tips on big stories. I have some very prominent people who call upon me," he said.

"I get all the tips for stories that I want." Jaure shrugged.

After Houdini's death, Bess associated with some "temperamental" types.

From the collection of Dr. Bruce Averbook

"Then I will give you friendship—undying friendship."

"The first thing you know David, you will be proposing."

They both laughed.

"I understand that you and Mrs. Houdini are going on a free-lance lecture tour," the reporter said.

"Well, I'm going to—I'm always making lecture tours," he said.

"Who is financing this one?" Jaure asked.

"Why I am. Mrs. Houdini supplied the message and code, and I am supplying the finances."

"Then you did not get the message from Houdini?"

Ford smiled. "You know, Rea, I could never have done that!"

Ford tried to get Jaure to admit that the *Graphic* couldn't reverse their story after the first had already been in print, but the reporter told him that the story was just getting interesting.

"Is there anything—anything at all I can do to make them forget it? Anything I can do for you, Rea? You just play ball and I will give you a nice big story tomorrow." Ford seemed desperate.

"But I am out to get a story to-night." She smiled, thinking of the concealed men and their Dictaphone. Jaure made sure to walk the Reverend Ford out so that the doorman could see him again and be able to make a positive identification if need be.

Jaure's second story exposing the hoax opened up the floodgates. Now Houdini's friend the mentalist Dunninger jumped into the controversy. First he told the press that Houdini had told him shortly before he died that he would never contact anyone through a medium. Then Dunninger produced a new witness, a fish peddler named Joseph Bantino, who met with the press at Mrs. Houdini's house to clear Bess's name of complicity in the plot.

"You guys get me straight. I ain't after no dough, see?" he told the assembled reporters. "If you guys think that, I'm gonna jam right now. I just ain't gonna let nobody kick a lady when she's down."

Bantino, who had been brought to Bess's place by Dunninger, told the newsmen that he was going out with a girl who knew Daisy White, who happened to live in the same building as Bantino. According to the fishmonger, Ford got the message from Daisy White, who had learned it from Houdini long before he had turned incorporeal.

Bess seemed bewildered by this revelation and she indignantly denied that Daisy White "had had her husband's confidence." Now all hell broke loose. People started shouting, Minnie Chester denounced Bantino, and Dunninger looked pained.

"They've dragged my name through the dirt enough," Bess wailed, holding her bandaged head.

"Am I trying to help you or not?" Dunninger protested.

"You'd die for me. You'd die for me," Bess sobbed, "releasing her head long enough to press one hand to her chest and extend the other dramatically toward the mentalist."

Minnie's fight with Bantino escalated. When Bess started crying hysterically, everyone left the house. *The New York Telegram* reporter reached Daisy White, who was at Arthur Ford's apartment, and she admitted "slightly" knowing Bantino, and denied everything else.

Ford, meanwhile, began issuing broadsides accusing Jaure of concocting the hoax story because he wouldn't "play ball" with her in her attempt to persuade Bess to publish her correspondence with the former editor of *The New York World,* who was in Sing Sing serving a life sentence for murdering his wife. The whole sordid affair had devolved into a "he said, she said" circus. What nobody realized at that time was that there had been a much bigger conspiracy to put Houdini's message over—a conspiracy that stretched its way up to Boston and then across the ocean to the London home of one of the most famous writers in the world.

The question of whether or not Houdini was deliberately killed may never be fully resolved. There is no doubt that the death of the world's greatest magician benefited the Spiritualist movement and only their movement. Crandon may have had the greatest motive to get rid of Houdini in the first place, but once Houdini was gone, it was Doyle who immediately understood the implication of his death and went to work. Once the Spiritualists make contact with Houdini and he becomes their de facto spokesman from the other side, they have won. Houdini's legacy, his reputation, the respectability that he was yearning for his whole life, the status that he, even on his deathbed, thought he never achieved—all that could be hijacked in one fell swoop.

Dunninger was very clear about how to go about this. "There is one primary rule in the fakery of spirit mediumship. That is to concentrate upon persons who have suffered a bereavement." When Houdini died, who had suffered a greater bereavement than Bess? Who would be a more convincing conduit for Houdini's message than the grieving widow who loved him so much?

Within two weeks of Houdini's death, Doyle had written Bess. If he couldn't convert her husband, he would go to work, with all his silky eloquence, on, as he called her to Crandon, "the widow." Frustrated by the delays on January 8, he sent Crandon a directive. "I wonder whether it would not be possible for Walter to get us something really evidential about Houdini. If he made inquiry I think he would find that the period of coma is very much less than he has thought . . . I am in quite intimate touch with Mrs. H who is a splendid loyal little woman. She seems quite to accept our point of view but is very keen on getting some evidence which she can give to the world."

Doyle knew just the man who could get that evidence. The Reverend Arthur Ford.

Arthur Ford grew up in Fort Pierce, Florida, in a Southern Baptist family. His first inkling of his psychic power came in the army in World War I when he would hear the names of his fellow soldiers and days later, read the same names on the casualty lists. In 1924, he became a full-fledged trance medium, controlled by "David Fletcher," a pseudonym for one of his childhood friends who had died back in Florida. Ford was extraordinarily ambitious and before he turned thirty, he headed his own Spiritualist church in New York.

"When I first met Arthur Ford, I could hardly believe that this was indeed the already-celebrated medium," Conan Doyle would later write. "He is a young, clean-shaven, fresh-faced man, carefully dressed, with all the appearance, and indeed the habits, of a man of the world, who thoroughly enjoys the things of this life. He is gentle, sympathetic, and likely to be popular with the ladies. His manner is silky. His voice is low. He is a man who would be popular in any company, however cosmopolitan, and who would be quite at home in the gayest circles." In short, he was the man for Doyle's job, which was to get the Houdini message through and validate the Spiritualist agenda, and, at the same time, hijack Houdini's legacy.

Houdini would not be the first Spiritualist adversary who Doyle brought back seeking penance. In 1927, Doyle's skeptical friend the writer and publisher Jerome K. Jerome died. Soon afterward a medium friend of Doyle's brought back a message: "Tell him from me that I know now that he was right and I was wrong. . . . Make it clear to him that I am not dead." Doyle immediately trumpeted the message to the world. Similar sentiments had been brought back, through Lady Doyle, from Sir Arthur's mother.

Ford quickly became Doyle's protégé. "We *must* put the séance on a business footing," Doyle wrote Ford. "It is your job as writing is mine. You must let me send you such a cheque as is suitable." Plans were made for Ford to proselytize around Europe. In short time, *The Psychic News* was referring to Ford as Sir Arthur's successor, "the psychic apostle of this age." But first he had business in New York.

After staying in London for six months, Ford returned to the United States. In the fall he wound up in Boston and met with the Crandons. As Ford was the first to admit, the state of Spiritualism in the United States was quite sorry, as Houdini's crusade had made serious inroads into combating spiritualistic influence. Perhaps as the opening salvo on the Spiritualist side, the bizarre Carnegie Hall "debate" between Howard Thurston and Ford was staged. Ford went on the attack; Thurston conceded all his points. It's instructive to realize that Thurston was a friend of both Doyle and Crandon and a Spiritualist sympathizer. This event was also where Ford met Bess.

Ford's first ploy was to target Daisy White, Houdini's alleged mistress. Soon, Daisy had full-out converted to Spiritualism, joined Ford's church, and was lecturing on Spiritualism and magic.

On February 8, in trance, Fletcher brought Houdini's mother through and received the *forgive* message. That night, Francis Fast, using what he called Bentley's code, sent Doyle a cable in cypher informing him of the night's activities. Doyle immediately wrote Crandon. "I had a mysterious cable from N York in cypher. It seemed to mean that our people had discovered the Houdini cypher and that the widow admits it. I await particulars."

Doyle got his particulars in days. Ford sent him clippings from the newspapers and Fast fired off a letter. "The news itself, I felt was of such importance that I cabled the gist of it to you. . . . The message translated read: HAVE RECEIVED THROUGH ARTHUR FORD—OUR CIRCLE—HOUDINI CODE WIDOW ADMITS TRUTH PUBLICLY TODAY PLEASE ADVISE HORACE LEAF." (Leaf was an English medium and friend of Ford's.) Fast gave Doyle some fascinating details of the aftermath. "The frank and honest manner in which Mrs. Houdini accepted the whole thing was quite a revelation. First the publicity was of her own volition and she wrote Arthur Ford in her own hand a letter almost of gratitude. . . . I learned privately, last evening, from one who is friendly to Mrs. H. that when she received it, the strength and veracity of the message stirred her to tears, and now she awaits eagerly with reason to hope that the way may be made clear for the message from her husband."

Ford would make her wait. In March he returned to England for three months, and then, with Doyle's blessing, toured Sweden, Denmark, and Germany. By the time that Houdini's mother began to transmit Houdini's code to Fletcher in October, Ford already had the entire code. Daisy White would admit that she was close to Ford and knew the code itself, but the actual content of the message could only have come from Bess. It's not hard to imagine that Bess would do anything for Ford because by the time of the séance at her home, she had been hopelessly in love with the charming, effete medium for well over a year.

"Dine at Village Grove—home early no drink or weed."

—BESS HOUDINI DIARY ENTRY, OCTOBER 19, 1927

Bess had been drinking heavily on the last tour, even before Houdini's death. A year later, as the October 19 and other entries show, she was making an effort to curtail her input of drink and drugs, including marijuana. It was a losing battle. Meeting Arthur Ford didn't help. Ford himself was a raging, and sometimes very public, alcoholic. One clever way he dealt with the problem of other people knowing about his habit was to have his "spirit control" Fletcher threaten to never come to another séance unless Ford stopped drinking. This is as silly and as brilliant as Margery and Walter arguing over a manifestation.

By the time of the confirmation Houdini séance at her house in January 1929, Bess was literally on her last legs. On New Year's Eve, she had attended an all-night party with Arthur Ford. Too drunk to stand, she fell and struck the back of her head on the floor, rendering her unconscious. When she came to, she was taken home and confined to bed. She was on heavy painkillers to induce sleep.

On January 4, the day before the final Ford sitting where Houdini's code came through in its entirety, Bernard Ernst, Houdini's longtime lawyer and confidant, was summoned to Bess's house. It was late at night and when he got there, Bess was unconscious after a suicide attempt. She had written him a letter early that day, which was handed to Ernst as soon as he arrived. In it, Bess told him about the many debts she had incurred, and the fact that she had to pawn her jewelry to pay them off. And she told him she had done a terrible thing. "I'm so ill—I want to go to Harry—he always shielded me from pain. There are some things I want you to attend to after I go. I am very weary. I thank you dear Mr. Ernst, you were a true friend to Houdini and his unhappy wife."

This wouldn't have been Bess's first suicide attempt. She had made other previous attempts to take her life. Three nights later, Bess called Ernst to her home. She told him exactly what was going to happen at the next night's séance with Ford. When Ernst accused her of giving Ford the code, she didn't deny it, she just said she had no recollection of it. She told him that the code was in the safe deposit box of the Houdini Estate at Manufacturers Safe Deposit Company. When the lawyer informed her that he had inventoried what was in the box and that there was no sealed code from Houdini, Bess neglected to tell him that she had placed the code in the box in November, using, it was later discovered, an envelope that had been manufactured *after* Houdini had died. She also lied in telling Ernst that she hadn't seen or communicated with Ford for several years, when in fact she was dating him for over a year and exchanging letters with him when he was in England.

Bess told another version of how Ford got the code to a mutual friend of theirs named Jay Abbott. According to him, Bess said that she was washing her hands one day and her wedding band fell off. Ford quickly retrieved it. Engraved inside the ring, Bess maintained, were the words to "Rosabelle, sweet Rosabelle." How the rest of the words of the code came through went unexplained.

At best, Bess was a dupe, at worst, an architect and coconspirator in pretending to bring Houdini back from the grave. This begs the question, Why? Was it just that she wanted coverage in the press? No, she wanted once and for all to claim her rightful place. She needed Houdini to come back to *her*, not to Milla Barry, or to Charmian London, or to Daisy White. Not to Leopold or to Dash. She needed him to come back to her, just as he had after his indiscretions. But her ruse didn't work. She fooled no one.

After the séance, Bess fell into a deep depression. She derived no joy from having heard from her loved one. On January 27, she wrote Ernst. "I am so ill that when anyone speaks to me I want to scream, and if I anyone who knows me I'm almost as bad . . . the case against me about the message looks bad. Don't you see I'm mixed up in a sordid affair? I cannot talk yet. This is why I tried to do what I did January 4 . . . Having my friends believe me of deliberately betraying Houdini hurts—and it really hurts me sorely."

In the meantime, Ernst had confirmed from multiple sources, including Daisy White, that Ford had made many purchases of gauze, phosphorescent paint, and mediumistic effects from magic dealers. He had also consulted some magicians in an attempt to learn tricks. Ernst also learned from Bess that she had attended many wild parties with Ford, including some which were held at a "speakeasy" alleged to have been run by Daisy White. It was rumored that both Bess and Daisy ran the "speakeasy," which was also a brothel. At any rate, Daisy White's petite fingerprints were also all over the transmission of the code to the leader of her church, and when some of Houdini's friends threatened to expose Daisy White's involvement, she threatened to go public with her sexual relationship with Houdini and she had "one or more witnesses" ready to vouch for her story.

Increasingly despondent, drugged, drunk, and delirious, Bess was admitted to the West Hill Sanitarium in the Bronx. She spent over a month there. "Spiritualism was a forbidden subject" there, she told Ernst. She was being deprogrammed and dried out.

Sir Arthur's response to the Houdini message backfiring was classic Doyle. He wrote a twelve-page article where he once again flogged Houdini for framing Margery, excoriated him for snubbing Lady Doyle's message, and gave a glorious account of Ford's transmission of the message. And in the end, he waxed poetic. "If these loving hands can meet through the veil, then ours also can do so. . . . Is that a sad or an irreligious thought? . . . As Houdini is today, you and I will be to-morrow. Is it then a message to be slurred over or obscured, that Death does *not* disconnect us or break our natural feelings, and that an all-wise Providence is giving this much-needed knowledge to a generation which has had much to endure? In this case a deliberate test was proposed. If it had not been fulfilled it would have been counted a strong argument against survival. But it was fulfilled. Surely it cannot be dismissed as if it never occurred." After the Ford-Bess scandal broke, Conan Doyle made two corrections to his final draft. He added "apparently" after the "But" in the next to last sentence. And then he tacked on two sentences at the end: "It is true that in the last resort we are dependent upon the veracity and honesty of Mrs. Houdini. But I, for one, am not cynical enough to question it."

Perhaps Doyle qualified his essay after receiving two long handwritten letters from Bernard Ernst that detailed much of the sordid information presented above. Ernst was careful to point out that he had handwritten the letters so that even his own secretary wouldn't see the sad details of Bess's descent into madness and despair. He then asked that Doyle keep the letters in confidence. Doyle's response to that was also true to form. He immediately wrote his friend Dr. Crandon. "Now about this Houdini test. There is a dangerous snag there and Walter must not run up against it. . . . Houdini's lawyer tells me that Mrs. Houdini has taken to drink, drugs, and the Lord knows what, and is thoroughly unreliable. He says there never was a letter in the strong box containing a code. . . ." Crandon immediately typed the letter up and forwarded it to two members of his own circle.

Library of Congress

Epilogue

HARRY HOUDINI WAS DEAD BUT HOUDINI the myth was young and vital. Ehrich Weiss had been born into poverty and cast into the world with an inadequate education and a great burden. This flawed mortal struggled, schemed, and persevered, transforming himself into America's first international sensation by creating the idea that he could beat any possible restraint. This idea was so powerful that he broke into the language and became mythic, a popular legend, an embodiment of Nietzsche's Übermensch, a superman who would submit to no human authority. We all enjoy a level of pride in being human that comes in his reflected glory.

Inspired by Sarah Bernhardt's advocacy for the Russian Jews, the superman morphed into a superhero. Using his unprecedented fame like a fire hose, he cleaned the streets of the ruthless frauds who were preying upon the bereaved, the most vulnerable among us. He had transformed himself again, now into a public defender.

Yet he didn't believe his own myth. He told his wife that the greater world wasn't interested in his story and, on his deathbed, he confessed to a stunned doctor that he was a fake. The great irony is that while we can see his successes so clearly in hindsight, Houdini couldn't see them in the moment. He was the most popular entertainer of his age. No one has yet filled his shoes as a magician. Fifty years after his death his name was added to the Oxford English Dictionary, and it's being used every day.

Houdini has become truly immortal.

The last years of his life were not kind to Sir Arthur Conan Doyle. His finances were drained by the losses of a psychic bookstore that he opened in the shadows of Westminster Abbey. On his evangelical trip to South Africa in 1929, he presented a slide show during his lectures that featured several interesting examples of spirit photography. In Nairobi, after showing one slide where the spirit looked truly lifelike, a man named Spencer Palmer got up in the audience and announced that he was in fact the spirit, and the photo had been an obvious hoax taken by his brother at a "ghost hunting" party in England. As soon as Doyle returned to London, he tried to shore up the veracity of the photo by writing an article about it, claiming that the negative of the photo had been sent to him by a F. R. Melton. To bolster his claim, he sent the negative to a Nairobi newspaper, *The East African Standard*, and issued a $1,000 challenge to Palmer if he could prove that it wasn't the original negative of the photo. Palmer had inadvertently destroyed the negative, but an analysis of Doyle's photo showed it to be a negative derived from a print of the photo. In fact, Palmer's print was a more complete representation of the scene. When Palmer accepted Doyle's challenge and the expert testimony had labeled Sir Arthur's negative a fraud, Doyle sent a letter to the newspaper claiming that his source, Mr. Melton, "has made a sudden and mysterious disappearance from his residence and suicide is feared."

Doyle was having trouble within the Spiritualist movement too. A controversy over a book review that criticized one of Doyle's Spiritualist friends as being too lax in his control of mediums caused Sir Arthur to submit his resignation to the SPR, a group of which he had been a member for thirty-six years. On top of this, he was having problems with Pheneas. Doyle had been expecting the end of the world for several years now and was frustrated by Pheneas's laxity when it came to timetables. If he pressed Pheneas on this issue, his spirit control would mock him as a *"whale,"* always hungry for information. In October of 1929, though sick, Doyle set out on a tour of Scandinavia, against Pheneas's wishes. While he was there, Pheneas came and chastised him for *"breaking his traces,"* telling him *"you must work with me and not get out of hand."*

The trip took a lot out of Doyle, and by the end of 1929, he was suffering from a severe case of angina pectoris. Drained and weary, Doyle began to have doubts about his eschatology. Writing in March of 1930 to a medium friend who also was receiving messages about the imminent end of the world, he noted, "There has been some sort of lull in the last year, as if the powers that be felt that they had said enough and that now we had only to wait. I have moments of doubt when I wonder if we have not been victims of some extraordinary prank played upon the human race from the other side. I have literally broken my heart in the attempt to give our spiritual knowledge to the world and to give them something living, instead of the dead and dusty stuff which is served out to them in the name of religion. But they tell me that I shall be rejuvenated if I keep quiet for a few months and at the end of that time I shall be ready to do the work which they ordain."

Less than four months later, on July 7, 1930, propped up in a chair overlooking his beloved Sussex countryside, Sir Arthur died at the age of seventy-one, surrounded by his family. His last words were to his wife. "You are wonderful," he said.

On October 26, during a sitting in the same house, the spirit of Conan Doyle returned. After the séance, Lady Doyle pronounced that she and her children were "perfectly satisfied" that they had spoken with Sir Arthur and she was so delighted that she scheduled another séance for the following week. The medium was Arthur Ford.

Doyle's spirit also made many appearances to Margery. At the end of her mediumship, she had developed a knack for automatic writing and she was able to channel the spirits of Doyle and William Butler Yeats and their old friend Robin Tillyard, the bug hunter. Doyle told her that he would produce some writings that she could publish under the title *Sherlock Holmes in Heaven*. "*You carry my mantle onward*," he encouraged her.

By then Dr. Crandon had already passed on. He died two days after Christmas in 1939, after a long illness as a result of tumbling down a flight of stairs. His relationship with Margery had been rocky for years, but in 1935, after Walter's purported fingerprints had been finally proved beyond doubt to be identical to the fingerprints of Margery's dentist and her mediumship was irrevocably tainted, Crandon seemed to have lost interest in her. By then the constant stress to produce had turned Margery into a hopeless alcoholic. The vibrant young woman who had marched for suffragette rights and peace before Dr. Crandon had stage-managed her into the world's most famous medium had turned into a dowdy, overweight middle-aged woman who had lost her considerable allure to the opposite sex.

She had paid a price to be Margery. For years she had been dogged by rumors that Crandon had surgically altered her vaginal opening to allow for the production of bigger apports in the séance room. Bird's confession didn't help her cause. In 1930 he wrote a confidential report to the ASPR admitting that Margery had nervously approached him before one of the Houdini sittings and pleaded with him that if no phenomena occurred he should ring the bell box or "produce something else that might pass as activity by Walter."

Margery's misery came to a head in 1932 when, supposedly under the influence of an evil spirit, she left the séance room, climbed onto the roof at 10 Lime Street, and seemed poised to dive off it. Only the recitation of the Lord's Prayer by one of her sitters brought her back to her senses.

After Crandon died, Margery began an affair with William Button, the president of the ASPR. She moved in with him in his New York apartment and shuttled back and forth between New York City and Crandon's Massachusetts farm. The stress of the last few years seemed to have taken their toll on Walter too. For months in 1940 he had been promising to materialize the loving cup that Doyle had sent Margery years earlier at the farm. Séance after séance, he came up with excuses for not producing it. Finally on March 19, 1940, the last recorded séance we have, Walter "gave us very encouraging statements that we will soon begin to have important phenomena."

By the middle of 1941 Margery was gravely ill. She moved back to 10 Lime Street to await the end. A few days before she died, Nandor Fodor, a psychic researcher, sat at her bedside, pad in hand, and suggested that it might be best if she came clean about her whole mediumship. He would take down her confession and document her secret methods.

Margery mumbled something indiscernible.

"Can you repeat that?" Fodor asked, pen at the ready.

"Sure," said Margery. "I said, you can go to hell. All you 'psychic researchers' can go to hell."

She laughed.

"Why don't you guess?"

She laughed again.

"You'll all be guessing . . . for the rest of your lives."

A few years after Houdini's death, Bess visited Houdini's former showgirl Dorothy Young in Palm Beach. Dorothy was struck by how old Bess seemed and how she had let her hair go completely gray. She was wearing a white dress, with a white cape. "The lady in white," Bess joked. Dorothy was struck by something else. Bess was now a prime target for young gigolos, and had shown up on the arm of one who happened to be friends with Dorothy's husband. Other seducers may have sought her out at a tea room that Bess ran for a short time on West Forty-ninth Street. It had a magic theme but among the things that vanished was her investment. Between the failed business and the young pretty men, things became so bad that, according to Dorothy, Hardeen had to step in and take control of what was left of the insurance proceeds so Bess would have some portion of her nest egg remaining.

In his own way, Arthur Ford had been one of those who played Bess, only he had been after Houdini's reputation, not his money. In 1930, while visiting Rye Playland in Westchester, Bess ran into a man named Edward Saint. His real name was Charles David Myers and he was a longtime carnie man who, performing as "The International Smileless Man," would offer audience members $1,000 if they could get him to crack a smile. What the audience didn't know was that due to a nerve paralysis of certain of his facial muscles, it was impossible for him to smile at all. Whatever he called himself, he was a godsend to Bess. He controlled her alcoholism, managed her career, and put a lot of energy into keeping Houdini's legacy alive.

One of the events that kept Houdini's flame burning was the tenth anniversary Houdini séance. Saint convened an interesting circle that included the president of the Southern Californian SAM, the editor of the magic magazine *Genii*, Dr. Jack Hyman, Houdini's first partner, the president of the L.A. Association of Spiritualist Churches, and, perhaps in a sly tip to Houdini's covert career, a representative of the U.S. Naval Intelligence service. The séance took place on the roof of the Knickerbocker Hotel, near the famous intersection of Hollywood and Vine, in Los Angeles. Three hundred invited guests filled the temporary bleachers that were set up, and a live radio transmission brought the event to millions across the country.

During his introductory remarks, Saint revealed an interesting fact. "He had safes and vaults in his home, and vaults in banks that his lawyers had access to; but one secret, now made public for the first time, is the fact that Houdini had one safety deposit vault in a bank or trust company in the East under some familiar name other than Houdini, and of which the secret location rested only in Houdini's brain," Saint said. "In this vault was kept highly secret papers, and into which was always placed a certain glass case of jeweled medals and a diamond question mark pin with a rare pearl drop, a gift from Harry Kellar to Houdini. . . . Many things were left untold because of the unexpected death of Houdini in Detroit. There is a law, a time limit. Madame Houdini has year-by-

The lady in white. *From the collection of Dr. Bruce Averbook*

year awaited word that the Federal Government had located or opened this box, long overdue. Perhaps the vault was rented and paid years in advance. However, this secret vault has never been located to this day. No medium or psychic has ever brought forth information from Houdini or the spirit world touching on or leading to its discovery. So, if any circle tonight in any city or town in the world believes they are contacting Houdini, let them identify themselves by bringing forth this information regarding the secret vault."

Unfortunately, no one did and Houdini failed to manifest himself in L.A.

At the end of the séance, Saint turned to Bess. "Mrs. Houdini, the zero hour has passed. The ten years are up. Have you reached a decision?"

"Yes," Bess said sadly. "Houdini did not come through. My last hope is gone. I do not believe that Houdini can come back to me—or to anyone. After faithfully following through the 10-year Houdini compact, using every type medium and séance, it is now my personal and positive belief that spirit communication in any form—is not impossible. I do not believe that ghosts or spirits exist. The Houdini Shrine has burned for ten years. I now, reverently—turn out the light. It is finished. Good Night, Harry!"

And with that, she slowly switched off the red lightbulb that had illuminated a photo of Houdini.

Over the years, Bess was continually asked about the Houdini messages that had come through Arthur Ford. "There was a time when I wanted intensely to hear from Harry," Bess told the press. "I was ill, both physically and mentally, and such was my eagerness that spiritualists were able to prey upon my mind and make me believe that they had really heard from him." To friends, she was a bit more coy. Speaking of Ford, she said, "But he was such a *handsome* young man."

When Ed Saint died in 1942 at the age of fifty-one, Bess was devastated. "After Ed's death, I just collapsed," Bess wrote Hardeen. "The big Palooka left me with files and files of junk—he took every picture that Harry ever had taken and had hundreds of copies made—hundreds of busts—even photostats of his letters—now who the devil wants all that . . . Poor Dear Ed—he spent every cent he could get to have something made of Houdini—even went to Washington to have some H.H. copyrighted games . . . and although I never got angry with Ed whilst he lived—I'm sore at him now for leaving me this mess."

Bess wound up at a nursing home, where she laid down the law the very first day. "The nurse came to my room with a wheelchair—what I told her to do with it is still spoken of in the nurse's quarters," she related in the same letter. "You have no idea how I miss Ed. He did everything for me—ill as he was he

Even after Houdini had died, Hardeen kept himself in his shadow. *Library of Congress*

would tend to me like a baby—now I'm alone—miserable but hope to be strong enough by spring to come to N.Y."

Bess tried to come home, but she died en route on February 11, 1943. The name of the stop where her body was removed from the train was Needles, California.

Hardeen continued to play the vaudeville circuits, basically doing Houdini's act, except for the Upside Down. He couldn't fit into the small cell. He played for five years on Broadway in *Hellzapoppin,* a Broadway revue staged by Olsen and Johnson. During World War II, he performed for the troops, just as his brother had done decades earlier. He was planning on writing a book about Houdini and had started on it when he went into Doctor's Hospital for an operation. He never came out. He died on June 12, 1945 at the age of sixty-nine. The newspapers reported that now Houdini's secrets would finally be buried with him.

There were a lot of questions that remain unanswered about Harry Houdini, the man. You could start with why he changed his birth date to April 6 when he knew the real date. What made him turn on Robert-Houdin with such ferocity? Was he ever really married to Bess? How extensive was his spying for Melville? Did he truly believe that his brother Leopold's dalliance with another brother's wife contributed to his mother's death?

If you were in New York in the early 1960s, you could have potentially gotten the answers to those questions—right up until October 6 of 1962, in fact. On that evening, a slightly eccentric old man with bushy white hair, who somewhat resembled Einstein, left his tiny studio apartment IC and took the elevator to the top floor. He climbed a set of stairs and opened the door onto the roof. Most days he would feel his way around the clotheslines and go right to his wooden chair and sit and look out on the Hudson River. He didn't see much because when he had turned seventy, his eyesight had failed him. He was eighty-three now. Twenty-two years ago he had been a multimillionaire with a huge Connecticut estate and a wife with expensive tastes. But the marriage ended bitterly and his wealth was lost in the stock market crash. And now he was alone, living in a studio apartment in Inwood.

On that night, he didn't stop to sit. He walked over to the 215th Street side of the building, climbed up onto the ledge, and jumped off. This was no magic stunt. He fell six stories, careening right past seven-year-old Gary Schmidt's bedroom window, and he hit the pavement with a sickening thud. And with that, Dr. Leopold Weiss exited this world, and the remaining secrets of Harry Houdini departed with him.

Houdini—forever on tour. *Library of Congress*

Acknowledgments

This book would not have been possible without the incredibly generous support of the magic community. From David Copperfield to Ricky Jay to David Blaine to John McLaughlin, every single person in the world of magic overwhelmingly embraced our project (with the singular exception of the owner of a Midwest magic club for collectors) and we are humbled by their response.

If you're ever in a room with Michael Weber, beware. He can read your mind. At once one of the most talented and creative magicians alive, Weber was instrumental in the conception of this project, spending hours with us brainstorming, and helped a great deal along the way. Without his input, there would have been no book.

As an illustrator/designer/writer, Steranko has cut a fierce path through the pop-culture universe, but magic has never been far from his creative heart. His daredevil stunts inspired the comic book superheroes Mister Miracle and The Escapist, in addition to the protagonist of *The Amazing Adventures of Kavalier & Clay*. He not only allowed us to tap his memorabilia and letters collection but also his knowledge and experience regarding Houdini's methods and mentality, generating a level of understanding that otherwise would not have been possible.

Ricky Jay is the reigning godfather in the world of magic history. It's exceptionally difficult to find a subject that he doesn't know cold or one in which he hasn't done original research. He promptly responded to every one of our frantic phone calls and worried e-mails; his replies were always infused with his own acute insight and arcane knowledge.

David Copperfield is the most successful magician who has ever lived. His International Museum and Library of the Conjuring Arts has more Houdini apparatus and personal effects than nearly all the other collections combined. If Houdini were to come back from the grave he could go to Mr. Copperfield's museum and resume his show. We thank him for allowing us unlimited and unprecedented access to this unbelievable collection. Chris Kenner, one of the world's finest sleight-of-hand men, spent many days helping us uncover all sorts of wonderful new details about Houdini. He is Mr. Copperfield's right hand and he knows his collection like the back of it.

A big thank you to David Blaine—a great friend and inspiration to us both. We think Houdini would be proud to pass his mantle on to him. He was happy to make his one-of-a-kind Houdini memorabilia available to us for our research.

The magic world is full of people who know all about Houdini. Some know a little and some a lot. We believe that Patrick Culliton might be the most knowledgeable of them all. Patrick was eager to reply to every e-mail that was peppered with strange questions and he took the time to send us thousands upon thousands of pages from his great Houdini files. He is also the only Houdini scholar to have ever played the role of Franz Kukol in a movie.

Jim Steinmeyer is one of the great minds and historians in magic. We were lucky to have access to both his collection and his astute counsel.

Little did we know that when we met Anna Thurlow at Sid Radner's annual Houdini séance, she would provide one of the major keys to unlocking some of Houdini's mysteries. The charming great-granddaughter of the celebrated medium Margery invited us to her house, plied us with food and drink, and then unveiled what would become one of the centerpieces of our research—the Libbet Crandon de Malamud Collection. Anna's mother, Libbet, was an academic who had faithfully preserved every last scrap of paper in Dr. L. R. G. Crandon's archive of Margery material. She had wanted to incorporate this information into a work about Margery before her untimely demise. We hope that this book will, in some small way, fulfill that wish.

Andrew Cook is one of the world's leading experts on British espionage. Not only did he give us access to his personal collection but he also acted as a sounding board for our theories.

John McLaughlin took time from his unimaginably busy schedule to read our manuscript and write the preface. We're also grateful to him for helping us check for material in the MI-5 archives.

Bill Liles is one of the world's leading experts on Houdini. He helped us immeasurably in delving into the minutiae of Houdini's history and methods. His insights were inspiring.

John Gaughan is one of the great geniuses of our time. He can build, rebuild, or restore anything. As magic historians we are truly lucky to have him among us. His knowledge of Houdini is vast, and, specifically, his comprehension of the mysteries of Houdini's Water Torture Cell is perfect. He restored it once and then, when it mysteriously burned, he built it again. Only John could have done this next-to-impossible feat. Thank you, John, for your help with this project and allowing us access to your archives.

When we tracked down Thomas Tietze, he was expanding his wonderful 1973 book on Margery. He made his files available to us, and he was thrilled to talk about Margery for hours on end. His enthusiasm was absolutely contagious.

We had a hunch when we started this project that we would uncover previously unknown Houdini collectors. Dr. Bruce Averbook is one of those people. He made his awe-inspiring Houdini collection available to us and went to great trouble to provide us with many rare and unique photos.

George and Sandy Daily own and maintain an enormous collection of Houdiniana. We thank them for their generosity in sharing it with us and allowing us to use so many of the great images from their collection. George has gone above and beyond on so many occasions and selflessly helped us countless times.

Roger Dreyer, the CEO of Fantasma Magic, is one of the great Houdini collectors. We're grateful for his generosity in providing us with both images and printed material for the book.

Many of the great images throughout the book have come from Kenneth M. Trombly's excellent collection. After a hard day's research at the Library of Congress, Kenneth entertained us in his home and we talked Houdini over wonderful burritos from Chipotle.

We are indebted to Kevin Connolly, a great Houdini collector, who went out of his way to answer each of our frantic phone calls for images by scanning items from his personal archives.

Mike Caveney, the curator of Egyptian Hall Museum, one of the great magic collections in the world, went to great lengths to address our questions and to make his material available.

On our way to do research in Appleton, Wisconsin, Houdini's hometown, we ran into Tom and Renee Boldt. The Boldts have one of the largest private collections of Houdini letters and personal papers in existence. They were extremely hospitable and generous. Special thanks for the great photo of Houdini's father.

Nestled in a large apartment in New York is another great Houdini collection. We thank Maurine Christopher, a gracious southern belle, for generously allowing us unfettered access to the enormous archives built by her late, great magician husband, Milbourne.

Sidney Radner helped us all along the way. He invited us to his Houdini séance and then entertained us in the Massachusetts home that he shares with his lovely wife, Helen. He has so much Houdini material that he couldn't even find all of it.

The groundbreaking research into the men who delivered those fateful blows to Houdini's midsection was done by the late Don Bell, a Montreal journalist and bohemian bon vivant. Two of Don's children, Daniel and Valerie Bell, welcomed us to their city and helped us schlep boxes and boxes of their father's archives to a local copy center. We wish Don was still around to see the fruits of his earlier labor.

We were privileged to meet the only surviving member of Houdini's troupe. Dorothy Young invited us to her New Jersey seaside home and regaled us with tales of working with the Master Mystifier. Her appreciation and devotion to the man and not the myth was revelatory and enlightening to us.

French film producer Christian Fechner is one of the greatest magic scholars of our time. His collection is one of the best in the world and he has graciously shared it with us and others many times.

Volker Huber is one of the preeminent magic historians and collectors in the world. We are indebted to him for unearthing many interesting documents relating to Houdini's birth.

Magic Christian is Vienna's most prominent magician and historian. We're grateful to him for finding obscure Houdini clippings from old Austrian papers.

In addition to the above, many other people contributed in some fashion during the creation of this project. Some opened their archives, some gave their counsel, and some answered our never-ending stream of questions. We are grateful for the assistance of Jim Alfredson, Dr. Michael Baden, Eric Baker, Steve Baker, Siri Baruc, Gordon Bean, David Ben, Norman Bigelow, Thomas Boghardt, Vanni Bossi, Gordon Bruce, Dr. Peter Bruno, Cliff Callahan, Christopher Cannon, John Cannon, Mark Cannon, Mario Carrandi, Dr. Gar Chan, Diane Coulson of *Fate* magazine, John Cox, Pat Croce, Frank and Barbara Cuiffo, Edwin Dawes, Trevor Dawson, Simon Dardick of Vehicule Press, Anthony DePalma, Mark De Souza, Diego Domingo, Jason Draper, Michael Edwards, Bob Farmer, Tim Felix, Jules Fisher, Sid Fleischman, the late Jack Flosso, Stephen Forrester, Steve Forte, Kiva Renee Foster, Gary Frank, Phyllis Galde of *Fate* magazine, Gary Garland, John Gaughan, Dr. Louis Goldfrank, Chris Gower, Gabriel Grayson, Lennart Green, Andy Gregit, Jim Hagy, Mick Hanzlik, George Hardeen, Paul Harris, Richard Hatch, Mrs. Ron Hilgert, Ed Hill, John Hinson, Jim and Carolyn Hougan, Derek Hughes, Gary Hunt, David Jacobson, Penn Jillette, Roy Johnson, David Kahn, Todd Karr, Ken Klosterman, Peter Lamont, Peter Lane, Dean Richard Lariviere, Brian Lead, Robert Legault, Tina Lennert, Jim Lesar, the late Robert and Elaine Lund, Stuart Lutz, Bill Malone, the late Jay Marshall, Eric Martin, Dr. Gene Matsuura, Max Maven, Pierre Mayer, John McCulloch, Bill McIlhany,

David McNaught, Janet Merrill, Austin Metze, Richard Milner, Stephen Minch, Mark Mitton, Gale Molovinsky, Arthur Moses, Andrew Muir, Norm and Lupe Nielson, Mrs. George O'Toole, Stanley Palm, Diana Parikian, Mark Pilkington, Fred Pitella, James Randi, Rev. William Rauscher, the late Bob Read, Charles and Regina Reynolds, Bernard Rosenthal, David Roth, George Schindler, Gary and Margot Schmidt, Mark Setteducati, Kenneth Silverman, David Singmaster, Christy Smith, Stephen Sparks, Richard Spence, Manny Sperling, Denise Stineman, Juan Tamariz, Fred A. Thomas, Philip Varricchio, Byron Walker, Tad Ware, Christoph Wasshuber, Bill Weber, David Williamson, Carolyn Withstandley, Roger Woods, Tim Wright, Harry Zarrow, Herb Zarrow, Phyllis Zarrow, and Josh "Chunk" Stern, Vicky Maude Derf, Pfc. Kate Rush.

We have spent the last two years visiting institutional collections all over the world. We are indebted to the following people for their assistance in gaining access to rich Houdini material: Clark Evans, Margaret Keickhefer, Mark Dimunation, and, especially, Joan Higbee at the Library of Congress, Helen Adair, Richard Workman, Pat Fox, Leslie DeLassus and Rick Watson at the Harry Ransom Humanities Research Center at the University of Texas at Austin, Matthew Carpenter and Kim Louagie of the Houdini Historical Center at the Outagamie Historical Society, Betty Falsey, and Tom Ford of the Harvard University Houghton Library, Matthew Skidmore of the Harry Price Collection at the University of London's Library, Nick Scheetz and Heidi Rubenstein at the Georgetown University Library, Wayne DeCesare at the National Archives Research Administration, Mike Sampson and George Rogers of the United States Secret Service, Nelda Webb and David Strader at the Duke University Rare Book, Manuscript and Special Collections Library, Dorothy Lickteig of the Anderson County Historical Society, Kristin Nute and Elena Tsvetkova from Blitz Research, Jamie Andrews of the British Library, Alan McCormick of Scotland Yard, Patrick Baird of the Birmingham Local Studies and History service, Professor Ellen Belcher of the John Jay College Special Collections, Rosemary Cullen of the John Hay Library at Brown University, Lynda Hammes of the Council on Foreign Relations, Sue Hodson and Gayle Richardson at the Huntington Library, Jennifer King at the George Washington University Library, Jennifer Lee of Columbia University, Ros Westwood of the Buxton Museum, Jozsef Berkes and Dorottya Szabo of the National Archives of Hungary, Ed Chichirichi of the Historical Society of Delaware, David Hibbert of the Magic Circle Library, Mike Keely of the Social Sciences Library, Manchester, Jim Klodzen of the American Museum of Magic, Anders Liljegren of the Archives for UFO Research, Louise Martzinek of the New York Public Library, Vern Morrison of the Cleveland State University Library, Christopher Morrison at the State Department, Susan Perkins of the Herkimer County Historical Society, Tuja van den Berg of the Theater Institutt Nederland, the American Museum of Natural History Research Library, Sotheby's Auction House, Museum of the City of New York, the American Jewish Historical Society, Princetown University, the Montreal Public Library, the Bentley Historical Library at the University of Michigan, Brooklyn Public Library, Chicago City Archives, the Family History Center of Brooklyn, New York, Kathryn J. Hodson and Jacque L. Roethler of the Redpath Chautauqua Bureau Collection, University of Iowa Libraries, Iowa City, Iowa; Judah Magnes Center in Berkeley, California, the Milwaukee County Historical Society, the New York City Municipal Archives, New York University, Bobst Library, the Philadelphia City Archives, U.C. Irvine ASAP Information Services.

We were lucky to have such a wonderful team working with us, all of whom made vital contributions to the book. Steve Cuiffo, who is becoming very well known in New York as one of its finest young actors, is also one of its finest magicians. A gifted sleight-of-hand artist, Steve has proven to be a gifted researcher as well. He quickly mastered the myriad and complex new tools of the digital age and has been an enormous asset to our team. He diligently combed through millions of pages of records looking for our needles in the binary haystack. Whatever the job was, Steve would do it. He traveled with us around the globe and made numerous important contacts and discoveries. Without Steve this would have been a different book.

Our quirky "girl on the street" was Sarah Galvin, a 4.0 NYU grad who quickly proved to us that she could find anything anywhere. For the first several months she never even came into the office. She would text message or phone in for her assignments and then go about her mysterious sleuthing and later deliver the fruits of her research. She was so thorough at her work that she once found a critical heretofore-undiscovered article from a Detroit newspaper and then uncovered an important detail that had been published in the morning edition had been redacted in the afternoon edition. Sarah found documents that were never intended to be found. She also enlivened our in-house electronic forum with her witty and off-color posts.

Xenia Viray, Carrie Schulz, Dr. Lori Pieper, Sara Butler-Dockery, Kennlynne Rini, Jennifer Butler, Gary Au, Janie Brookshire-Kipp, and Maria Yakovenko, all of the Conjuring Arts Research Center, went above and beyond the call of duty. Jill Matheson and Carrie Schulz handled all of our transcribing duties. Pavel Goldin not only found photos we couldn't but he also magically transformed some unusable photographs using his genius computer skills and made them sparkle with new life.

Alexander (www.askalexander.org) saved our lives on a daily basis. Without this amazing research tool, we couldn't have written this book. For many years building something like Alexander had been a fantasy but with the collection of the Conjuring Arts Research Center and the diligent scanning of Sara Butler-Dockery, it became closer to reality. But when Gary Au wrangled the computer genius Mike Friedman, the dream was realized. Mike built the search engine in record time and then diligently kept improving it. It's been many a late night that Mike received a frantic e-mail asking him to do some minor fix, and Mike always came through.

It was a pleasure to work with such consummate professionals at Atria Books. Working under severe time constraints so that the book could be published on the eightieth anniversary of Houdini's death, everyone went the extra mile to ensure a smooth delivery. In an age when some publishing houses have become monolithic paper factories, it was refreshing to work with a core group of people who really care about the end result. Judith Curr, our publisher, was always supportive of our ideas and, on the few occasions that we disagreed, our interchange was enlightening and the end result was invariably an improvement. Greer Hendricks and Hannah Morrill encouraged us every step of the way and helped us meet every deadline (almost). Vivian Gomez assembled a crack team of copy editors and proofreaders. Linda Dingler and Suet Chong shepherded the book through the production process with dexterity. A very special thank you goes out to Peter Guzzardi, who under incredible time constraints worked around the clock in North Carolina and masterfully honed a massive draft into the final manuscript.

We are indebted to our agent David Vigliano for finding this book a home at Atria Books. David's associates Elisa Petrini, Michael Harriot, Kirsten Neuhaus, Celeste Fine, and Kirby Kim were diligent in representing our interests.

We sent an early draft of the book to the following people and we are very appreciative for the time and effort they took to read it and send us their comments: Bruce Averbook, Jack Bramson, Patrick Culliton, George Daily, Richard Hatch, Paul Harris, Robin Harvey, Ricky Jay, John McLaughlin, Arthur Moses, Marianne Santo, Michael Simmons, Jim Steranko, Kenneth M. Trombly, Madeline Zero, and Harry Zimmerman.

Each of us has personal debts to repay incurred during this book.

William Kalush would like to thank:

My late father, Edward T. Kalush, who regaled me with stories about Houdini vanishing an elephant. My sister, Trudy Kalush, followed his lead, giving me gifts of handcuffs and my first and only straitjacket. My mother, Jean

Kalush, and my aunt Flossie Finningsdorf facilitated my strange preoccupation by driving me to my first job (nonpaying) at Sorcerer's Apprentice magic shop, where Brian DiPietro, Carl Jarboe, and Chuck King liberally augmented my education. Along the way I've become indebted to many great men, many of whom helped with this book. Some, like the late Carl Mainfort, taught me sleight of hand. Others, like the late Robert Lund, taught me to love the history of the art, and the late Jay Marshall taught me to love the people who made that history. Once the Houdini project started, I've relied on friends for all types of support, without which I couldn't have done this work. Thanks to Lindsay Smith for all her support and help. Thanks as well to my friends Melissa Fazio, Catherine Hickland, and Mark Silverstein, who've helped me retain a modicum of sanity. A special thank you to Marianne Santo, who has helped me in some fashion on every day of this project. And also to the little monster Munito, always the center of attention and always a welcome distraction.

Larry Sloman would like to thank:

David Blaine, who introduced me to both the world of magic and my coauthor on this wonderful journey to the heart of Harry. Kinky Friedman, who took time out from his Texas gubernatorial race to help facilitate our Texas research. Bob Dylan, Nick Cave, and Antony and the Johnsons, who provided the soundtrack to the writing of the book. Leonard Cohen for encouraging me to do this project, then cautioned, "Please don't talk bad about Houdini—he loved his mother." Jaromir Jagr and his teammates, who made a noble run for the Cup. Louie and Sal DiPalo of DiPalo's, who fueled the furnace with their incredible Italian cuisine, along with J.D., who sent us wonderful pizza from Totonno's. Jeff Lieberman, who put our Shallow Entertainment ventures on hold. John Alpert, who drove me to our hockey games and listened to more Houdini stories than he wanted to. Rick Rubin, who provided an air of mystery. Anthony Kiedis for the midday tea and diversion during the writing process. George Barkin, who checked in on me for a pulse periodically. Rachel Tadeo for brightening a grueling period by giving birth to a beautiful baby boy. Jade Bush for her understanding and for lowering the ring tones of her cell phone. And finally, special heartfelt thanks to my wife, Christy Smith-Sloman, and our dog, Lucy, who welcomed back the stranger who reentered their lives after the book was finally completed.

Index

Page numbers in *italics* refer to illustrations.